ODE

TO

KIRIHITO

PART TWO

OSAMU TEZUKA

VERTICAL.

TRANSLATION—CAMELLIA NIEH
PRODUCTION—HIROKO MIZUNO
SHINOBU SATO

PUBLISHED BY VERTICAL, INC., NEW YORK.

ORIGINALLY SERIALIZED IN JAPANESE AS *KIRIHITO SANKA*
IN *BIGGU KOMIKKU*, SHOGAKUKAN, 1970-71.

ISBN 978-1-934287-98-9

MANUFACTURED IN THE UNITED STATES OF AMERICA

SECOND EDITION

THIS IS A WORK OF FICTION.
THE ARTWORK OF THE ORIGINAL HAS BEEN PRODUCED AS A MIRROR-IMAGE
IN ORDER TO CONFORM WITH THE ENGLISH LANGUAGE.

VERTICAL, INC.
1185 AVENUE OF THE AMERICAS 32ND FLOOR
NEW YORK, NY 10036
WWW.VERTICAL-INC.COM

CONTENTS

ODE TO KIRIHITO

(CONTINUED)

CHAPTER 12

NECROSIS

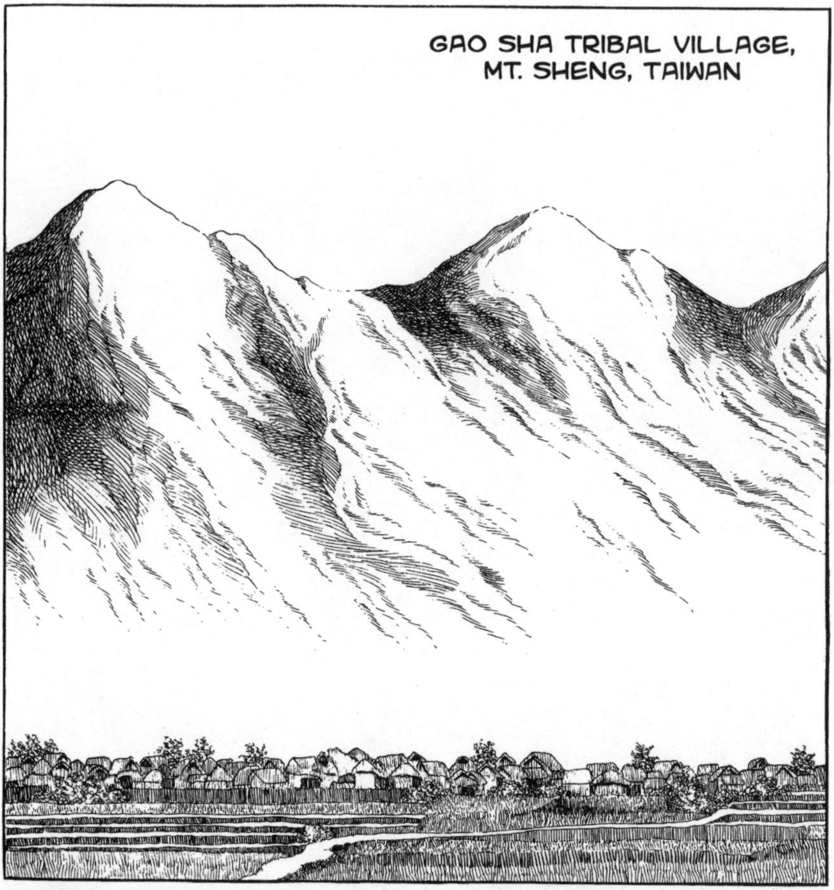
GAO SHA TRIBAL VILLAGE,
MT. SHENG, TAIWAN

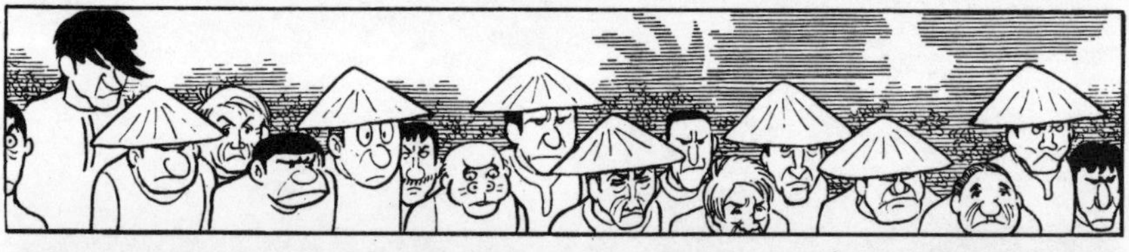

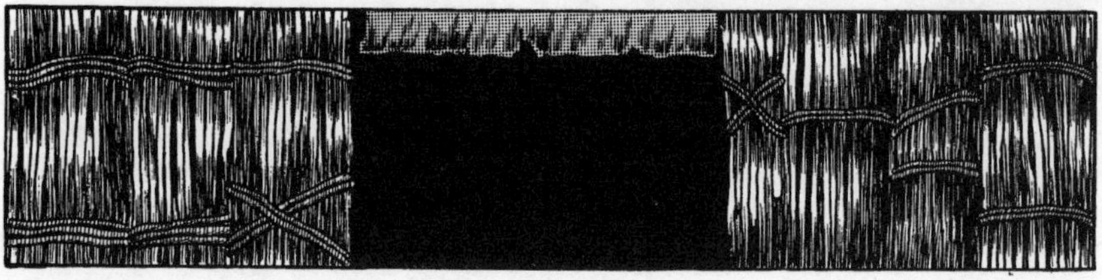

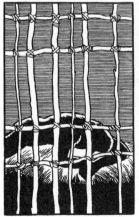

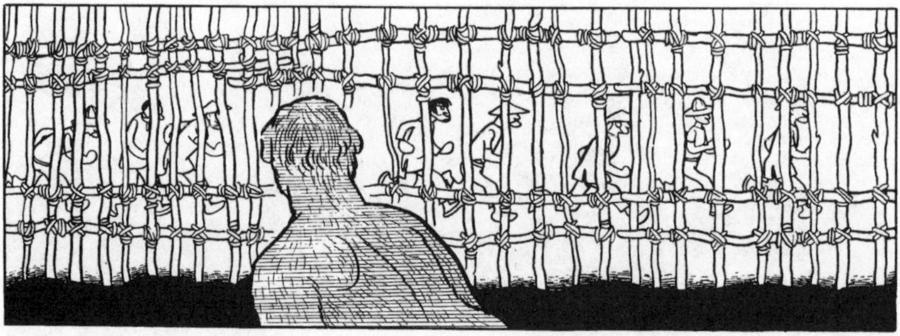

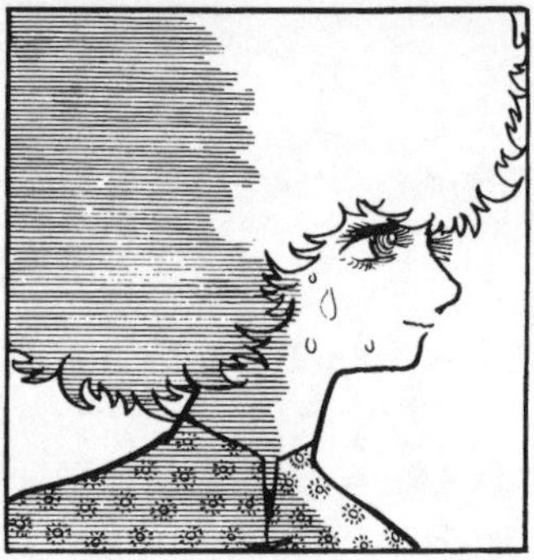

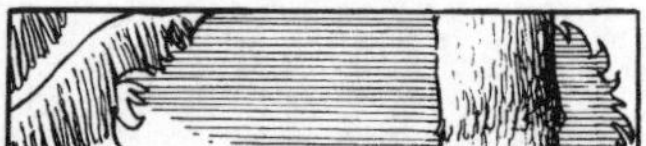

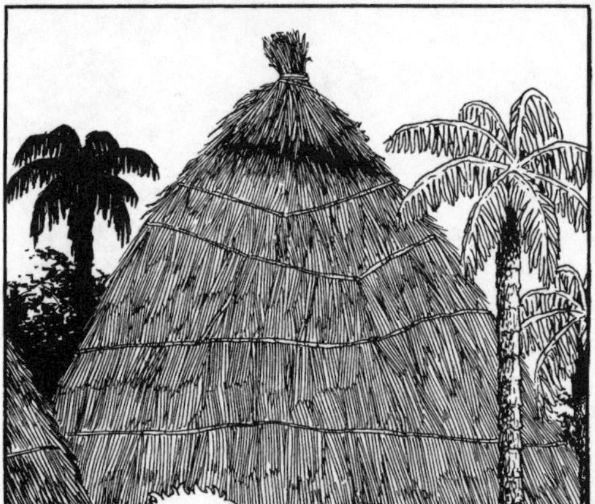

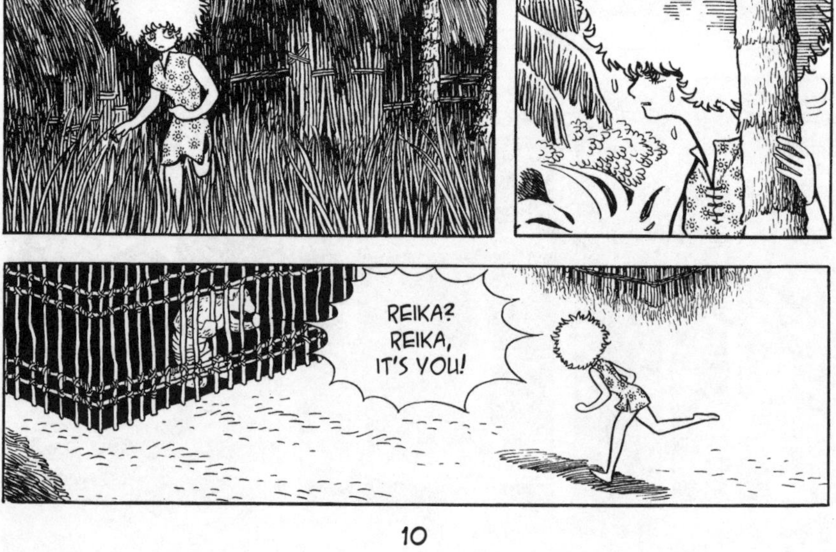
REIKA? REIKA, IT'S YOU!

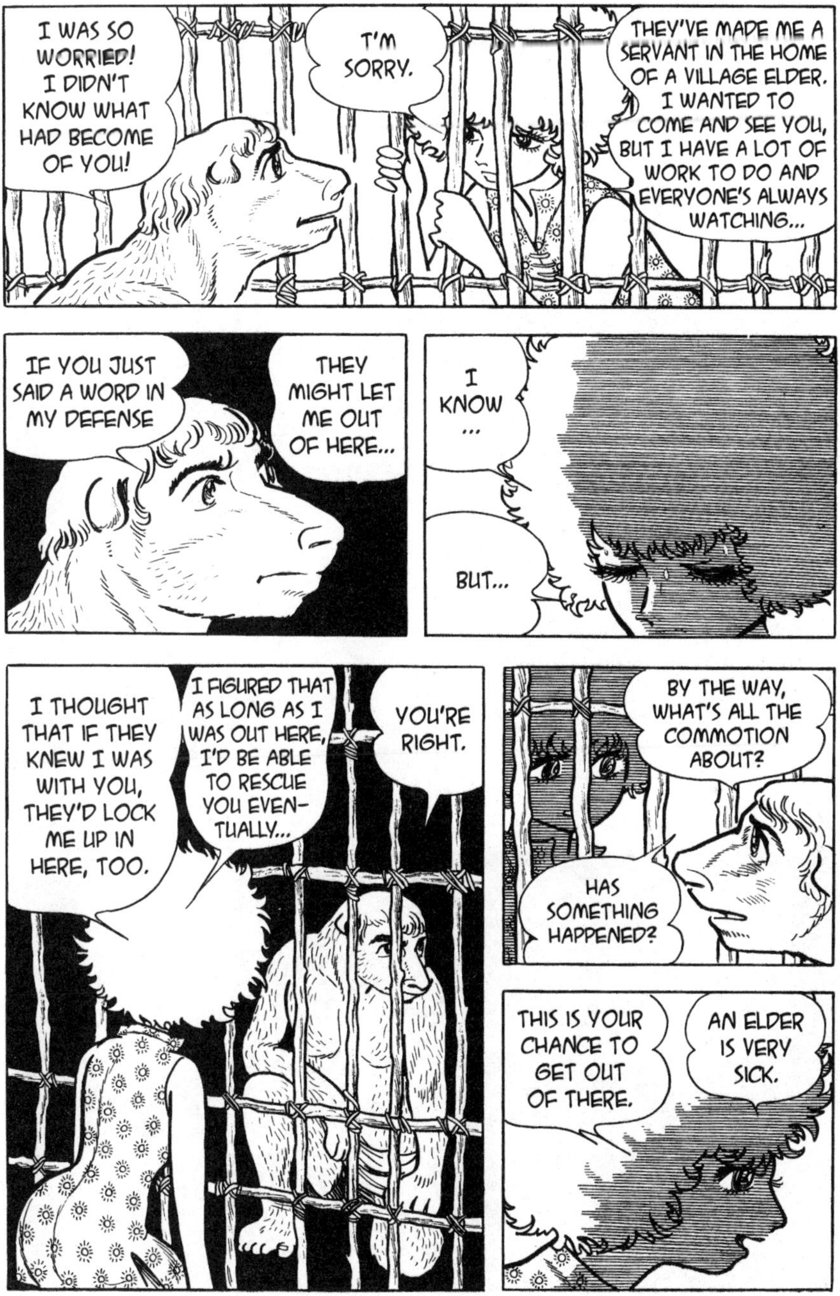
I WAS SO WORRIED! I DIDN'T KNOW WHAT HAD BECOME OF YOU!
I'M SORRY.
THEY'VE MADE ME A SERVANT IN THE HOME OF A VILLAGE ELDER. I WANTED TO COME AND SEE YOU, BUT I HAVE A LOT OF WORK TO DO AND EVERYONE'S ALWAYS WATCHING...
IF YOU JUST SAID A WORD IN MY DEFENSE
THEY MIGHT LET ME OUT OF HERE...
I KNOW...
BUT...
I THOUGHT THAT IF THEY KNEW I WAS WITH YOU, THEY'D LOCK ME UP IN HERE, TOO.
I FIGURED THAT AS LONG AS I WAS OUT HERE, I'D BE ABLE TO RESCUE YOU EVEN-TUALLY...
YOU'RE RIGHT.
BY THE WAY, WHAT'S ALL THE COMMOTION ABOUT?
HAS SOMETHING HAPPENED?
AN ELDER IS VERY SICK.
THIS IS YOUR CHANCE TO GET OUT OF THERE.

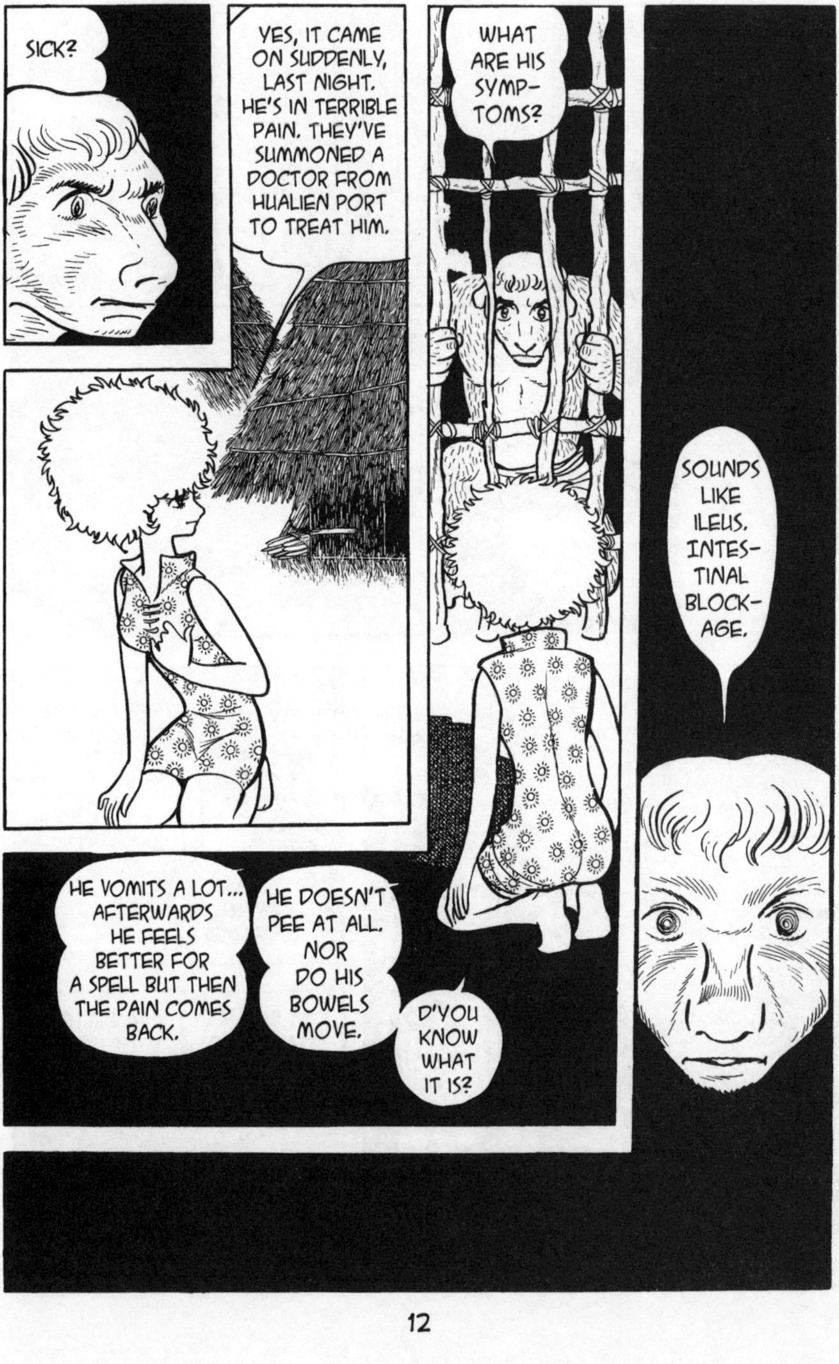
SICK?
YES, IT CAME ON SUDDENLY, LAST NIGHT. HE'S IN TERRIBLE PAIN. THEY'VE SUMMONED A DOCTOR FROM HUALIEN PORT TO TREAT HIM.
WHAT ARE HIS SYMP-TOMS?
HE VOMITS A LOT... AFTERWARDS HE FEELS BETTER FOR A SPELL BUT THEN THE PAIN COMES BACK.
HE DOESN'T PEE AT ALL. NOR DO HIS BOWELS MOVE.
D'YOU KNOW WHAT IT IS?
SOUNDS LIKE ILEUS. INTES-TINAL BLOCK-AGE.

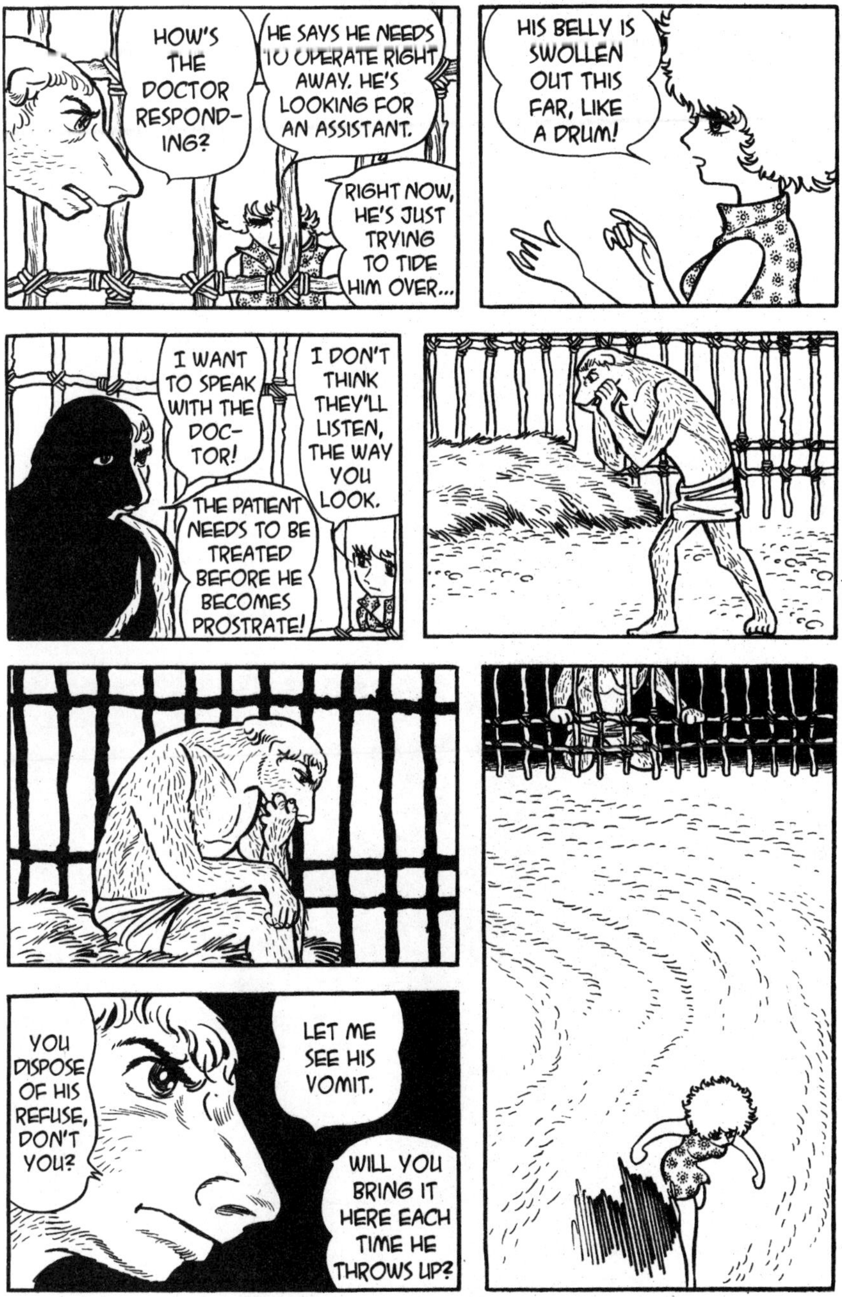
HOW'S THE DOCTOR RESPONDING?
HE SAYS HE NEEDS TO OPERATE RIGHT AWAY. HE'S LOOKING FOR AN ASSISTANT.
RIGHT NOW, HE'S JUST TRYING TO TIDE HIM OVER...
HIS BELLY IS SWOLLEN OUT THIS FAR, LIKE A DRUM!
I WANT TO SPEAK WITH THE DOCTOR!
I DON'T THINK THEY'LL LISTEN, THE WAY YOU LOOK.
THE PATIENT NEEDS TO BE TREATED BEFORE HE BECOMES PROSTRATE!
YOU DISPOSE OF HIS REFUSE, DON'T YOU?
LET ME SEE HIS VOMIT.
WILL YOU BRING IT HERE EACH TIME HE THROWS UP?

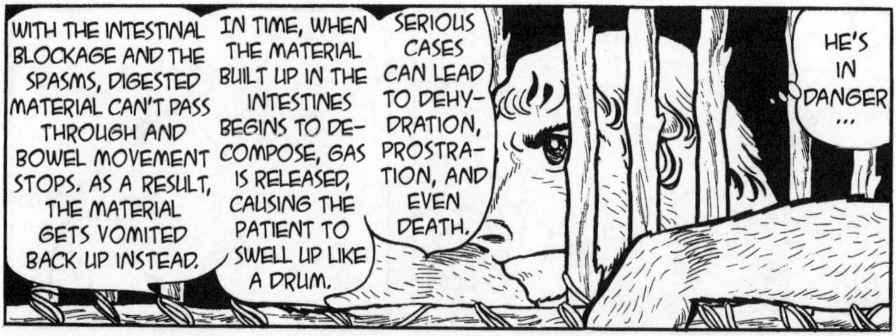
WITH THE INTESTINAL BLOCKAGE AND THE SPASMS, DIGESTED MATERIAL CAN'T PASS THROUGH AND BOWEL MOVEMENT STOPS. AS A RESULT, THE MATERIAL GETS VOMITED BACK UP INSTEAD.
IN TIME, WHEN THE MATERIAL BUILT UP IN THE INTESTINES BEGINS TO DE-COMPOSE, GAS IS RELEASED, CAUSING THE PATIENT TO SWELL UP LIKE A DRUM.
SERIOUS CASES CAN LEAD TO DEHY-DRATION, PROSTRA-TION, AND EVEN DEATH.
HE'S IN DANGER ...

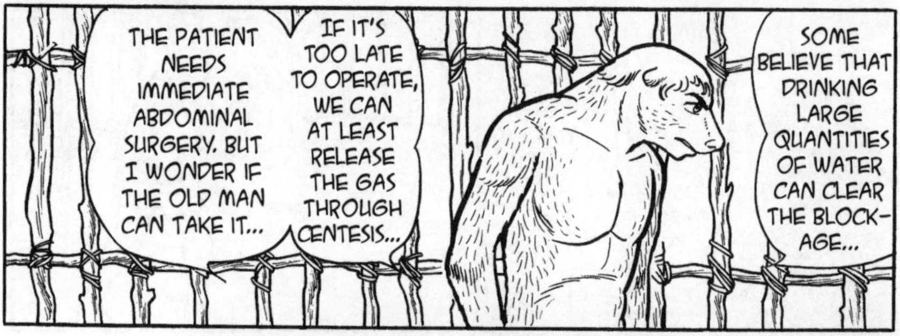
THE PATIENT NEEDS IMMEDIATE ABDOMINAL SURGERY. BUT I WONDER IF THE OLD MAN CAN TAKE IT...
IF IT'S TOO LATE TO OPERATE, WE CAN AT LEAST RELEASE THE GAS THROUGH CENTESIS...
SOME BELIEVE THAT DRINKING LARGE QUANTITIES OF WATER CAN CLEAR THE BLOCK-AGE...

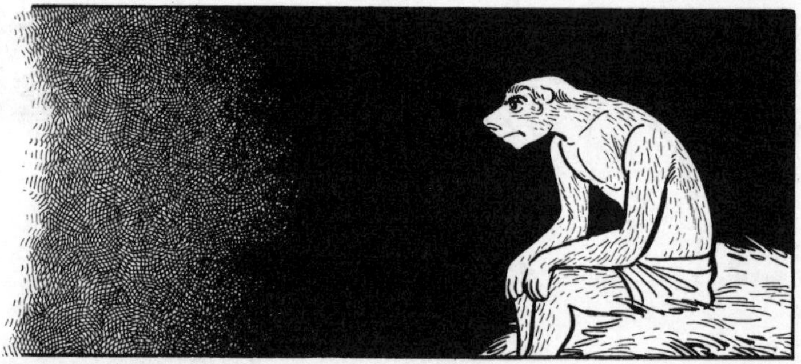

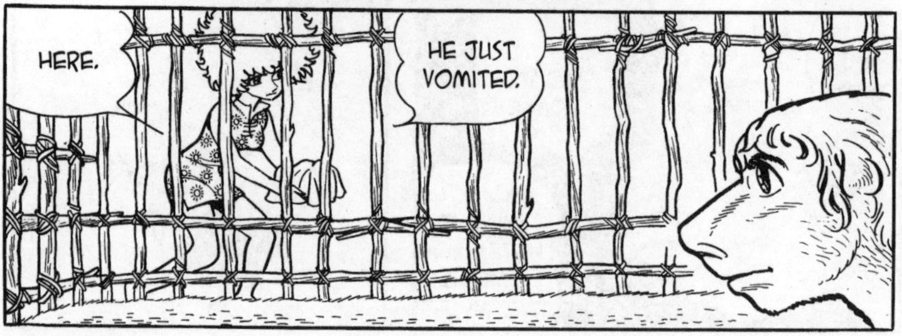
HERE.
HE JUST VOMITED.

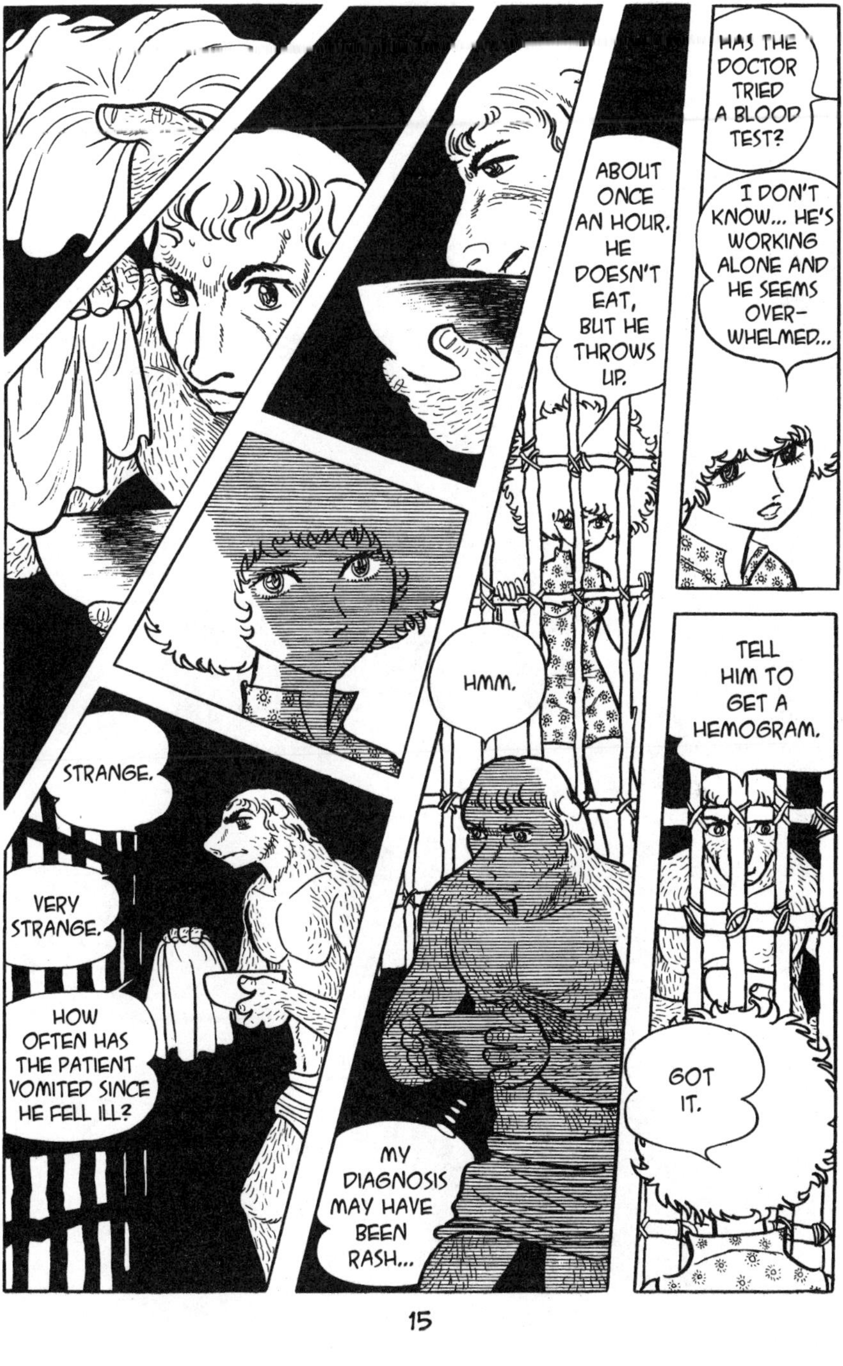
STRANGE.
VERY STRANGE.
HOW OFTEN HAS THE PATIENT VOMITED SINCE HE FELL ILL?
ABOUT ONCE AN HOUR. HE DOESN'T EAT, BUT HE THROWS UP.
HMM.
MY DIAGNOSIS MAY HAVE BEEN RASH...
HAS THE DOCTOR TRIED A BLOOD TEST?
I DON'T KNOW... HE'S WORKING ALONE AND HE SEEMS OVER-WHELMED...
TELL HIM TO GET A HEMOGRAM.
GOT IT.

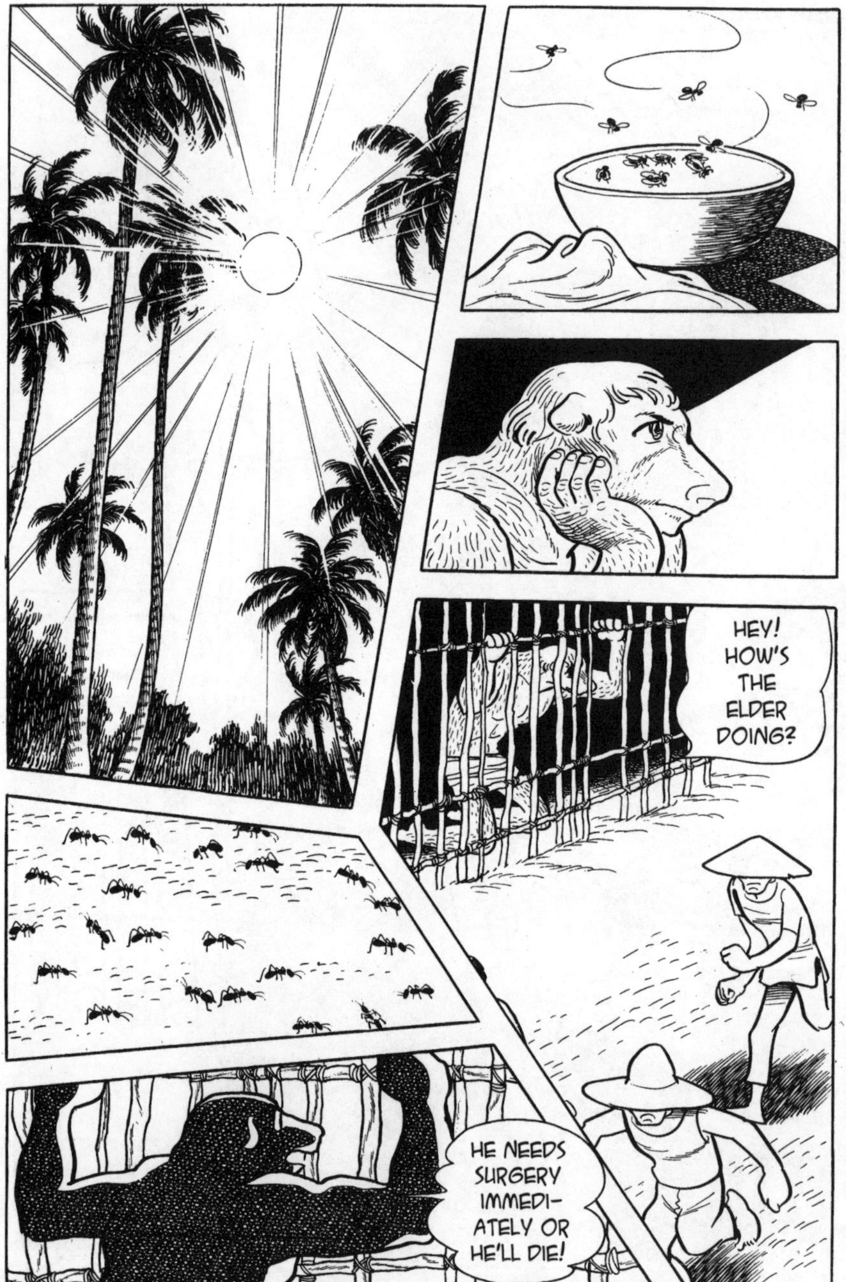
HEY! HOW'S THE ELDER DOING?
HE NEEDS SURGERY IMMEDI-ATELY OR HE'LL DIE!

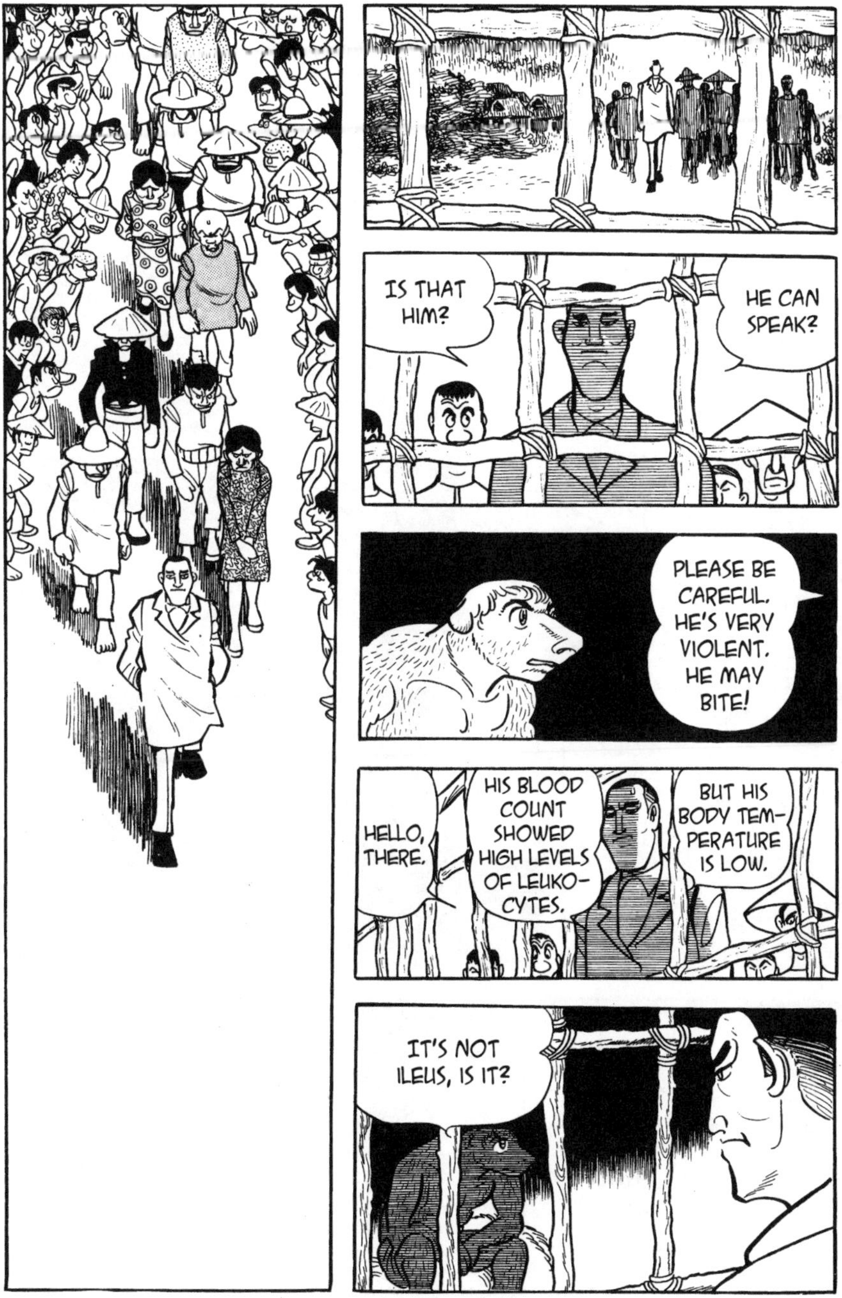
IS THAT HIM?
HE CAN SPEAK?
PLEASE BE CAREFUL. HE'S VERY VIOLENT. HE MAY BITE!
HELLO, THERE.
HIS BLOOD COUNT SHOWED HIGH LEVELS OF LEUKO-CYTES.
BUT HIS BODY TEM-PERATURE IS LOW.
IT'S NOT ILEUS, IS IT?

WHO ARE YOU?

THE FOLKS HERE SAY YOU'RE A DOG-MAN.

WITH ILEUS, THE VOMIT BEGINS TO SMELL LIKE FECES AFTER A WHILE, WHEN THE PATIENT HAS NOTHING ELSE LEFT TO VOMIT

AND BEGINS TO HEAVE UP THE CONTENTS OF THE COLON, WHICH CONTAIN INDOLE AND SCATOLE...

I KNOW. BUT IT'S ONLY BEEN A DAY SINCE THE PAINS BEGAN...

THEN HOW DO YOU EXPLAIN THE RISE IN LEUKOCYTES?

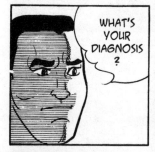

WHAT'S YOUR DIAGNOSIS?

PANCREATIC NECROSIS!

...

HMM, ACUTE PANCREATITIS...

ARE YOU A DOCTOR?

THIS IS A SURPRISE!

THERE'S NO TIME FOR THAT NOW. IF WE DON'T OPERATE IMMEDIATELY, THE PATIENT MAY BECOME PROSTRATE...

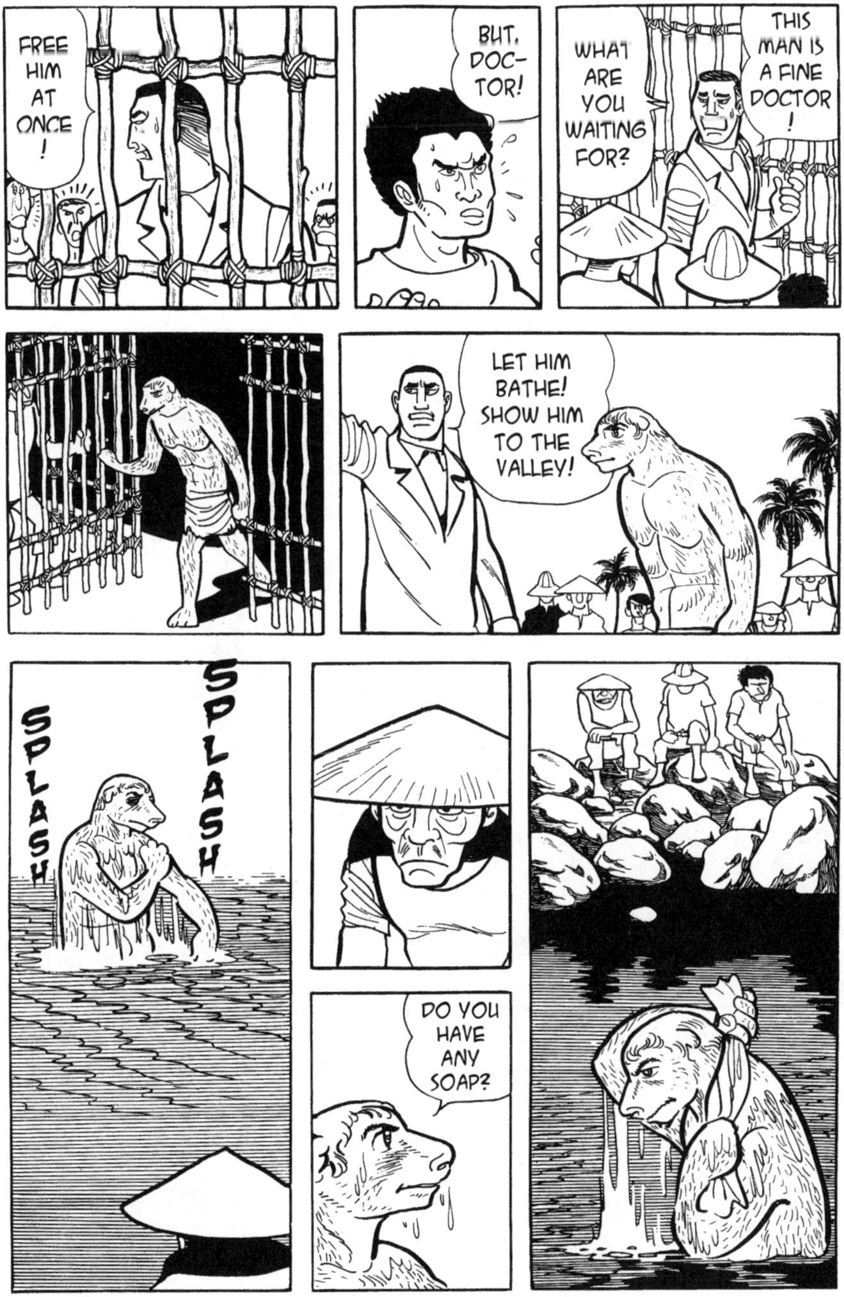
FREE HIM AT ONCE!
BUT, DOCTOR!
WHAT ARE YOU WAITING FOR?
THIS MAN IS A FINE DOCTOR!
LET HIM BATHE! SHOW HIM TO THE VALLEY!
SPLASH
SPLASH
DO YOU HAVE ANY SOAP?

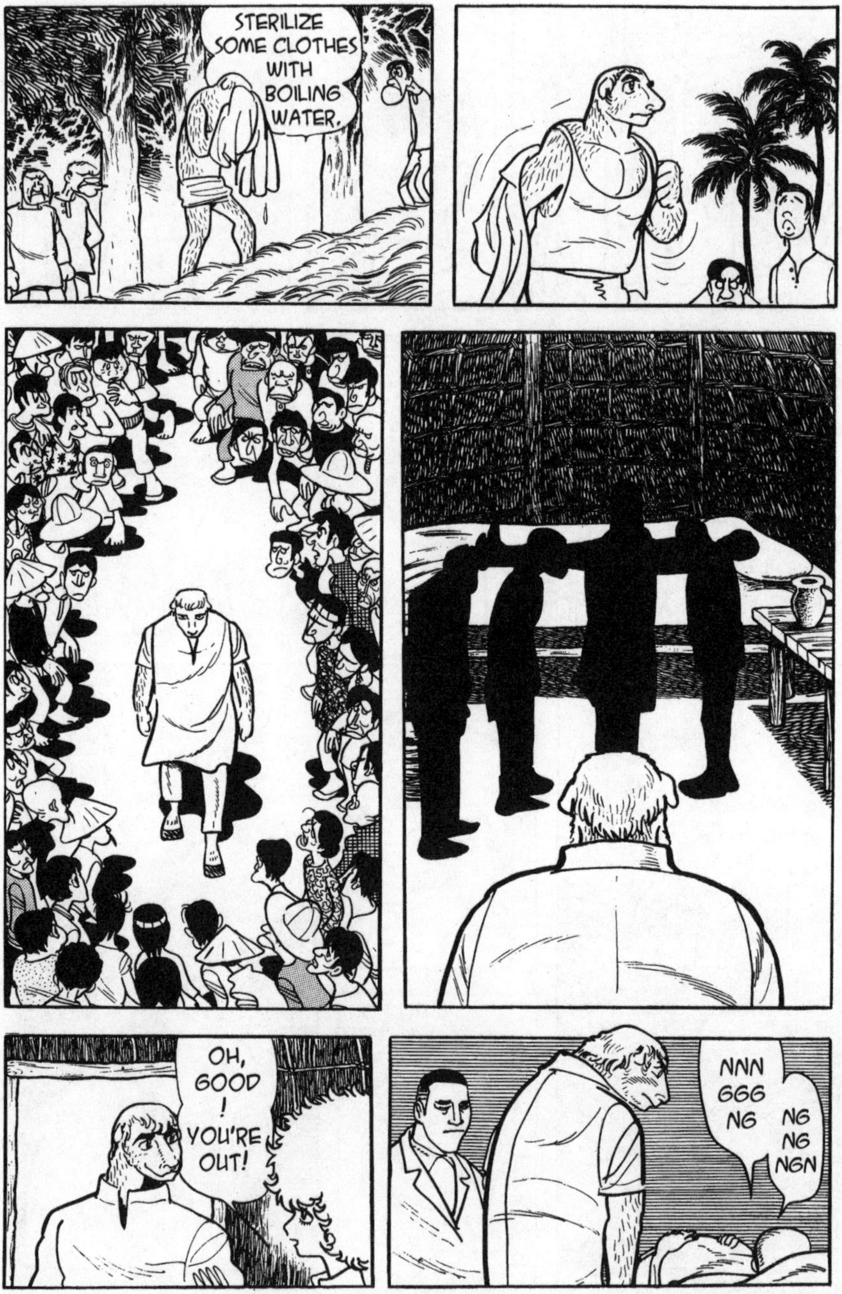
STERILIZE SOME CLOTHES WITH BOILING WATER.
OH, GOOD! YOU'RE OUT!
NNN GGG NG
NG NG NGN

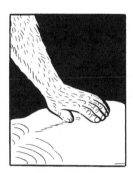

NG—
NG—
NG

NGN—
NNN

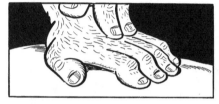

OPEN
WIDE.

IF YOU DON'T MIND
MY ASKING... HAVE
YOU EVER TREATED
PANCREATITIS
BEFORE?

I'M AFRAID I
HAVEN'T. I'VE ONLY
BEEN PRACTICING
4 YEARS...

WHAT
ABOUT
PANCREATIC
CANCER?

AFRAID
NOT.

I KNEW IT
WASN'T
CANCER
SINCE THERE
WAS NO
CACHEXIA...

THE PAINS
WOULDN'T
HAVE
STARTED
SO SUD-
DENLY,
EITHER.

21

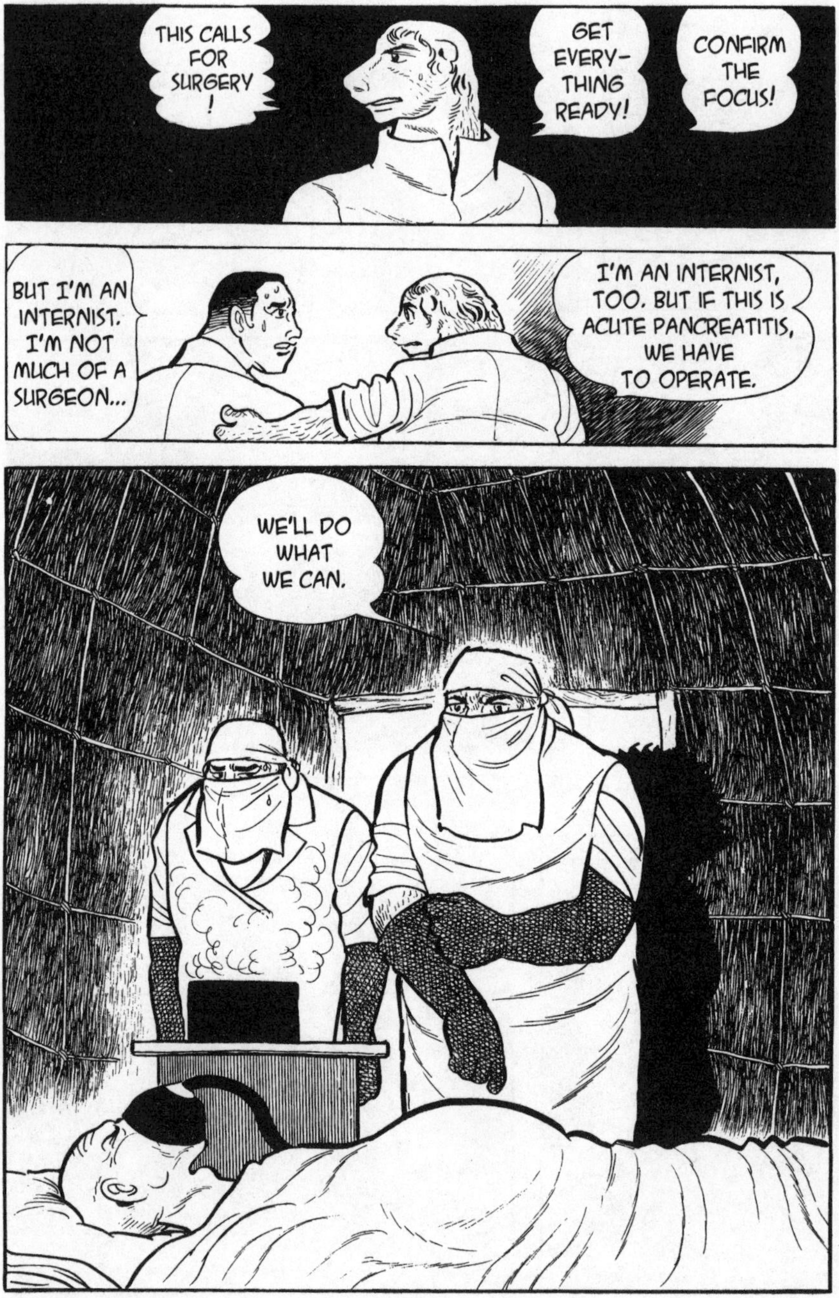
THIS CALLS FOR SURGERY !
GET EVERY-THING READY!
CONFIRM THE FOCUS!
BUT I'M AN INTERNIST. I'M NOT MUCH OF A SURGEON...
I'M AN INTERNIST, TOO. BUT IF THIS IS ACUTE PANCREATITIS, WE HAVE TO OPERATE.
WE'LL DO WHAT WE CAN.

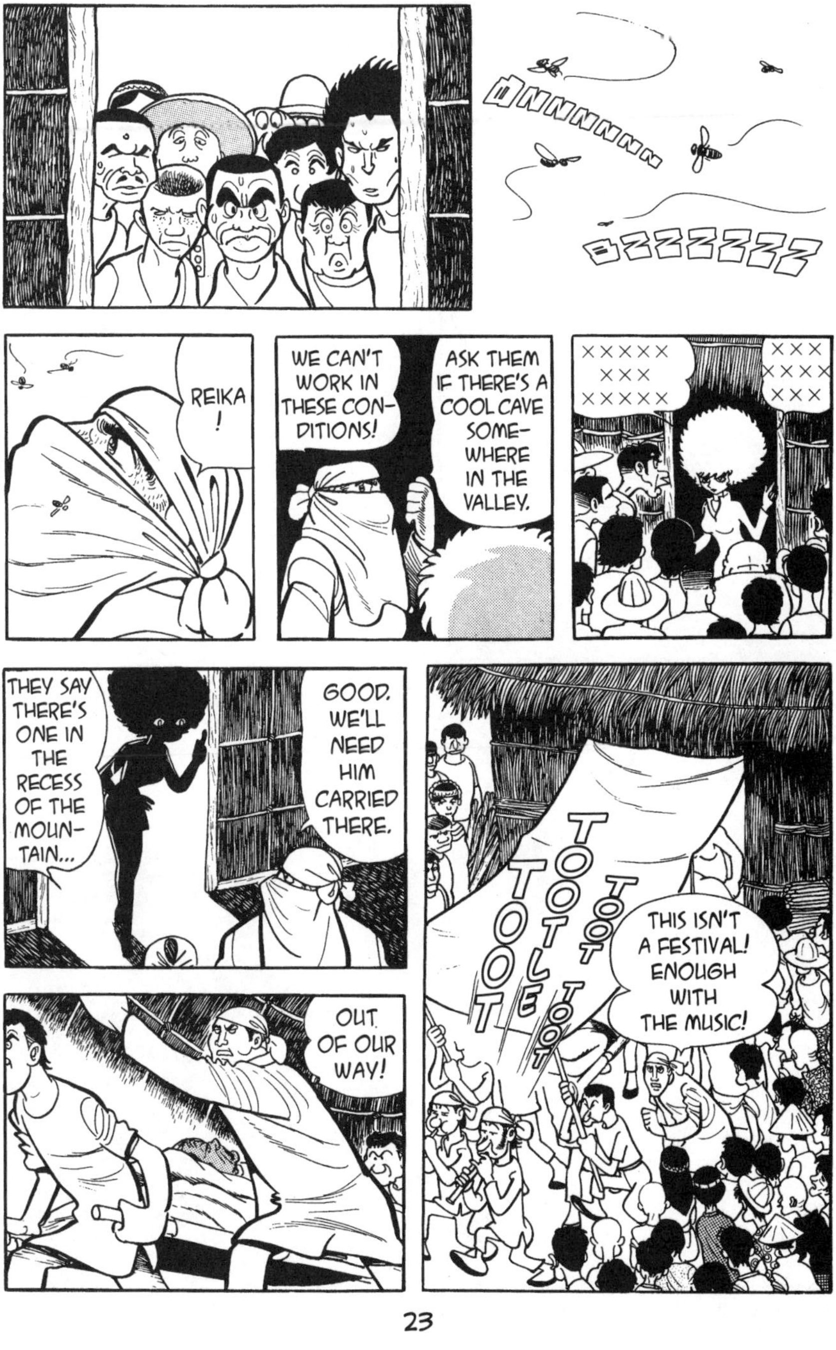
BNNNNNNNN
BZZZZZZZ
REIKA!
WE CAN'T WORK IN THESE CONDITIONS!
ASK THEM IF THERE'S A COOL CAVE SOMEWHERE IN THE VALLEY.
×××××
×××
×××××
×××
××××
×××
THEY SAY THERE'S ONE IN THE RECESS OF THE MOUNTAIN...
GOOD. WE'LL NEED HIM CARRIED THERE.
OUT OF OUR WAY!
TOOOT
TOOTLE
TOOT TOOT
THIS ISN'T A FESTIVAL! ENOUGH WITH THE MUSIC!

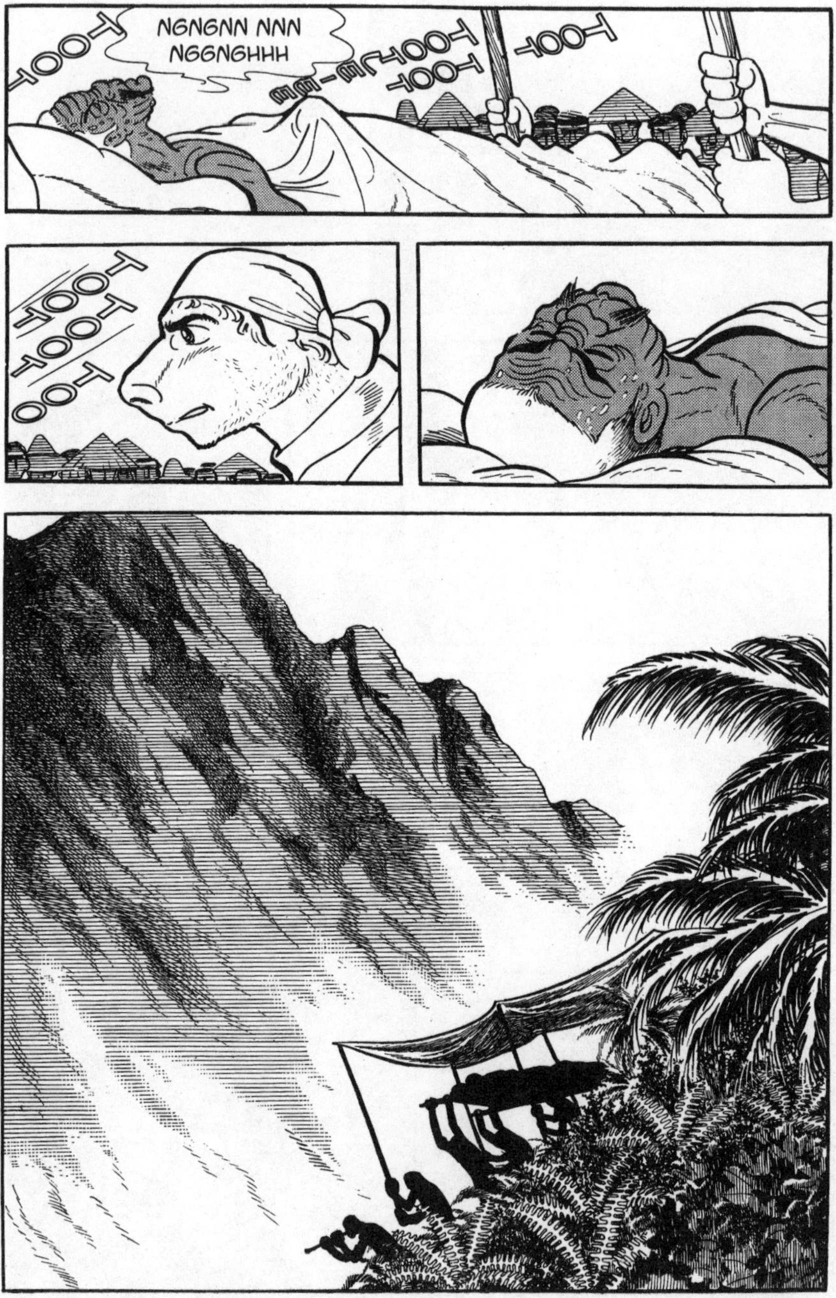
TOOT
NGNGNN NNN NGGNGHHH
TOOTLE-EE
TOOT
TOOT
TOOT TOOT TOOT TOOT

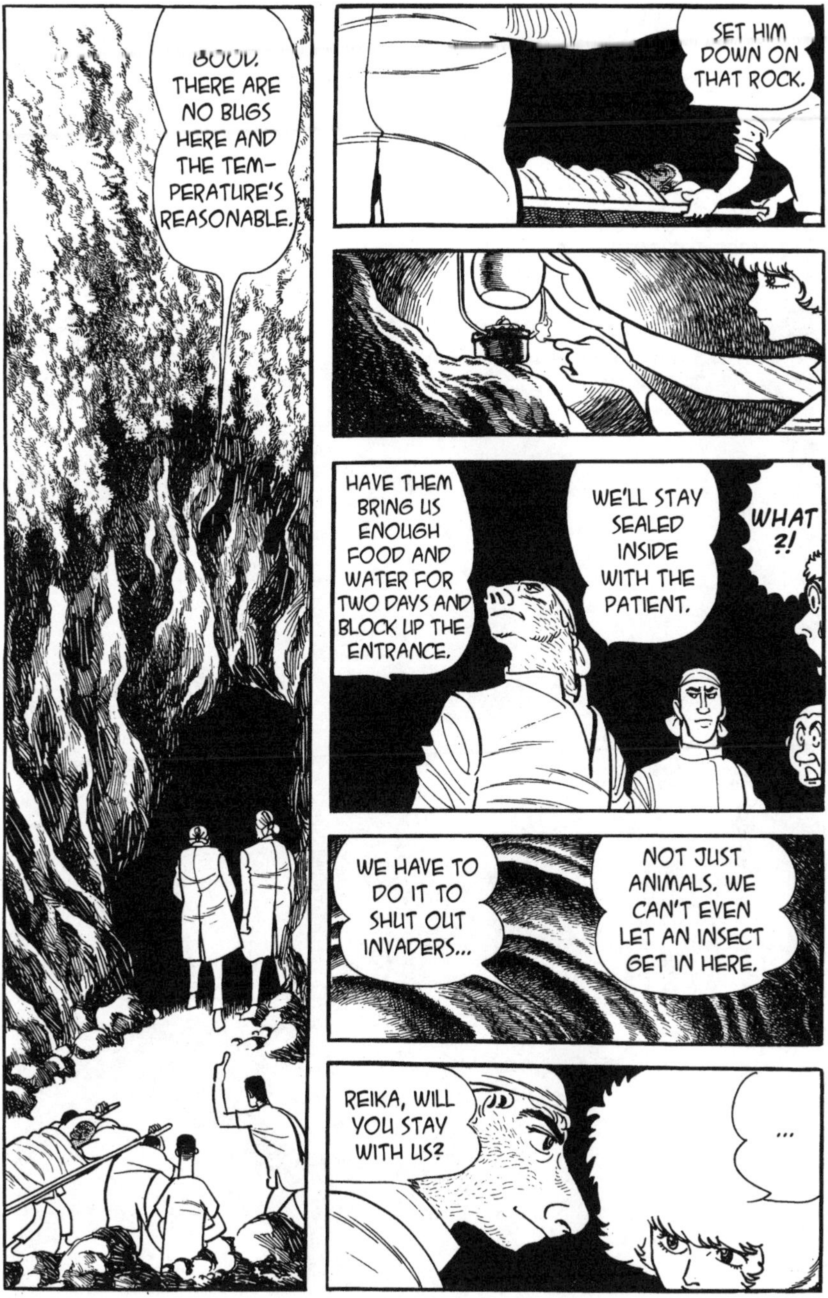
GOOD. THERE ARE NO BUGS HERE AND THE TEM-PERATURE'S REASONABLE.
SET HIM DOWN ON THAT ROCK.
HAVE THEM BRING US ENOUGH FOOD AND WATER FOR TWO DAYS AND BLOCK UP THE ENTRANCE.
WE'LL STAY SEALED INSIDE WITH THE PATIENT.
WHAT?!
WE HAVE TO DO IT TO SHUT OUT INVADERS...
NOT JUST ANIMALS. WE CAN'T EVEN LET AN INSECT GET IN HERE.
REIKA, WILL YOU STAY WITH US?
...

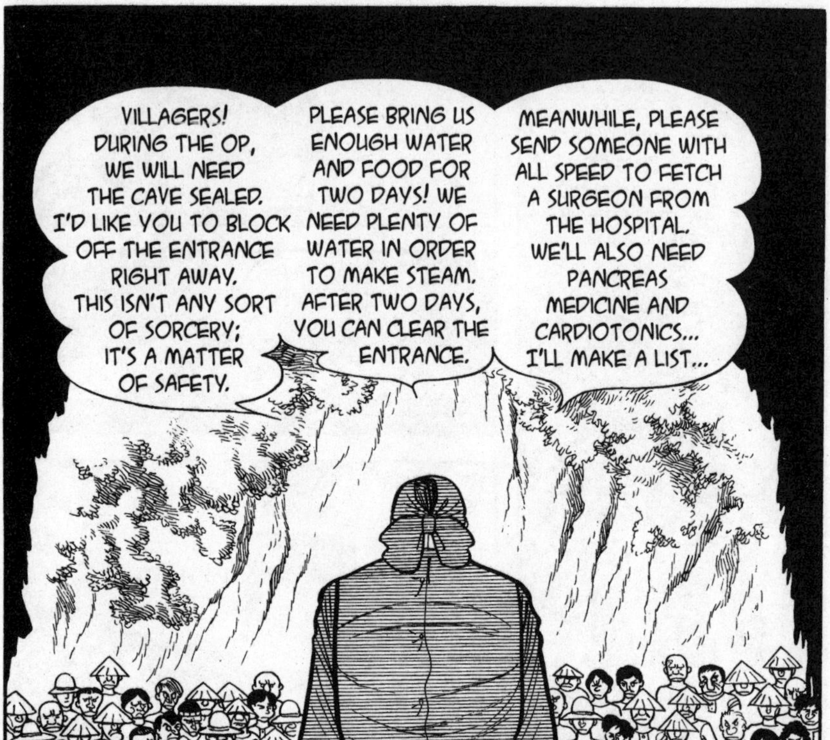
VILLAGERS! DURING THE OP, WE WILL NEED THE CAVE SEALED. I'D LIKE YOU TO BLOCK OFF THE ENTRANCE RIGHT AWAY. THIS ISN'T ANY SORT OF SORCERY; IT'S A MATTER OF SAFETY.
PLEASE BRING US ENOUGH WATER AND FOOD FOR TWO DAYS! WE NEED PLENTY OF WATER IN ORDER TO MAKE STEAM. AFTER TWO DAYS, YOU CAN CLEAR THE ENTRANCE.
MEANWHILE, PLEASE SEND SOMEONE WITH ALL SPEED TO FETCH A SURGEON FROM THE HOSPITAL. WE'LL ALSO NEED PANCREAS MEDICINE AND CARDIOTONICS... I'LL MAKE A LIST...
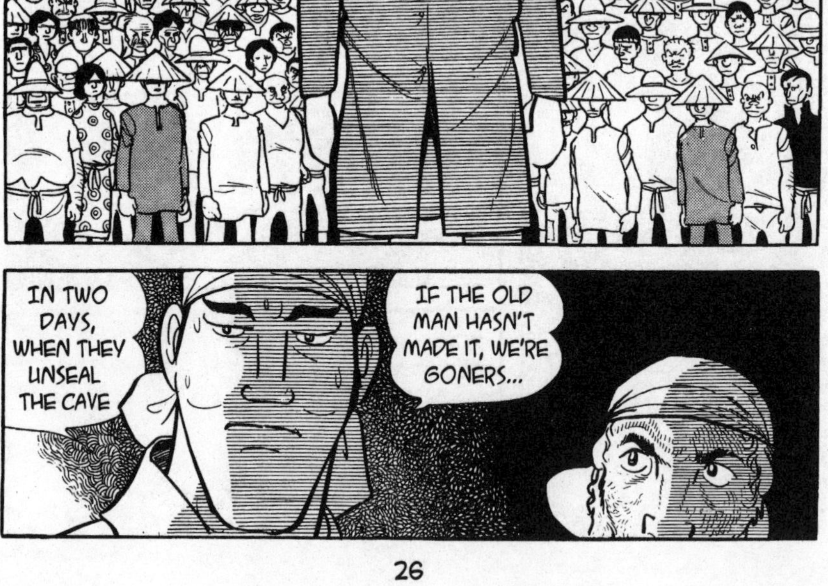
IN TWO DAYS, WHEN THEY UNSEAL THE CAVE
IF THE OLD MAN HASN'T MADE IT, WE'RE GONERS...

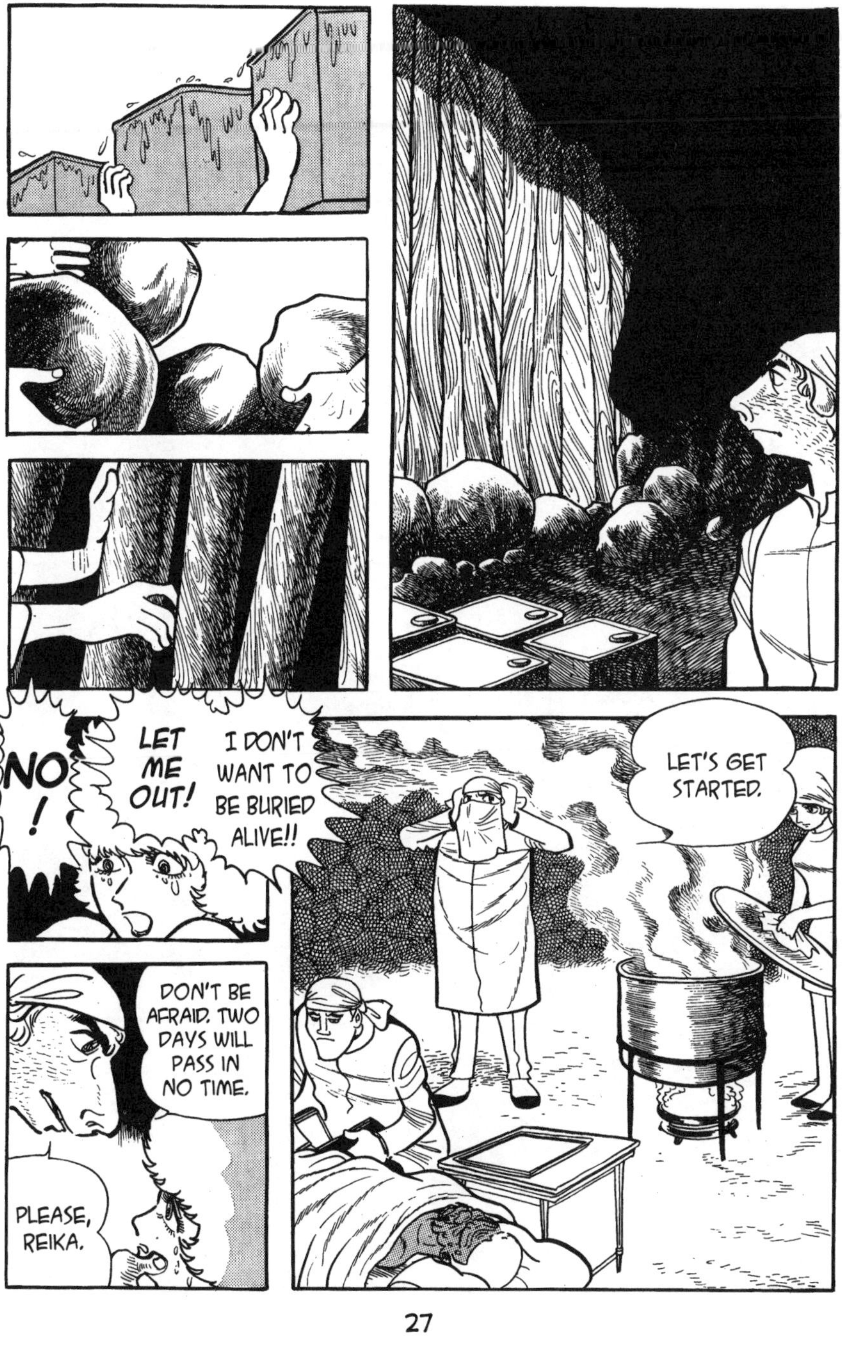
NO!
LET ME OUT!
I DON'T WANT TO BE BURIED ALIVE!!
DON'T BE AFRAID. TWO DAYS WILL PASS IN NO TIME.
PLEASE, REIKA.
LET'S GET STARTED.

ROLL HIM ONTO HIS SIDE.

NOW BEND HIS BACK AS MUCH AS POSSIBLE ...

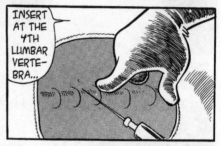

INSERT AT THE 4TH LUMBAR VERTE-BRA...

CAN YOU DO IT WITH THOSE HANDS ?

UU-UU-UUN-GGH

CATH-ETER.

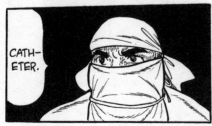

28

INJECT XYLO-CAINE.

PHEW!

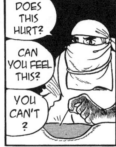

DOES THIS HURT?

CAN YOU FEEL THIS?

YOU CAN'T?

THE ANES-THETIC IS WORKING.

I DON'T KNOW IF I CAN DO THIS! WE HAVE NO EQUIPMENT, AND I HAVE NO EXPERTISE OR EXPERIENCE! AND THE PATIENT IS AN OLD MAN, NO LESS! THE ODDS ARE ALL STACKED AGAINST US!

BUT IF WE DON'T OPER-ATE, DO YOU THINK HE'LL LAST EVEN A DAY? IF YOU WEIGH THAT AGAINST THE RISK, I'D RATHER GAMBLE ON THE SURGERY.

I'LL OPERATE...

YOU HANDLE THE BLEEDING, LIGATURE, AND SU-TURING.

ALL RIGHT.

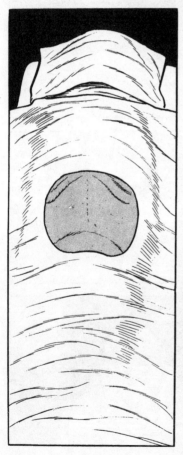

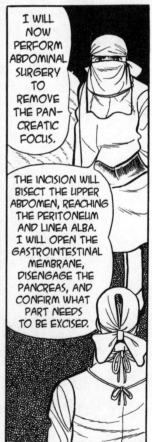

I WILL NOW PERFORM ABDOMINAL SURGERY TO REMOVE THE PANCREATIC FOCUS.

THE INCISION WILL BISECT THE UPPER ABDOMEN, REACHING THE PERITONEUM AND LINEA ALBA. I WILL OPEN THE GASTROINTESTINAL MEMBRANE, DISENGAGE THE PANCREAS, AND CONFIRM WHAT PART NEEDS TO BE EXCISED.

REIKA
SCAL PEL.
SWAB THE BLOOD !

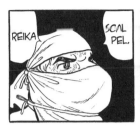

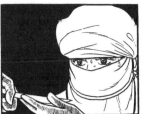

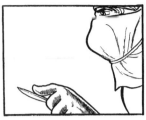

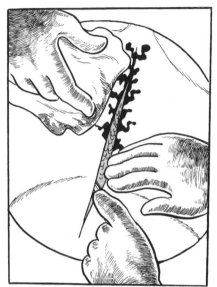

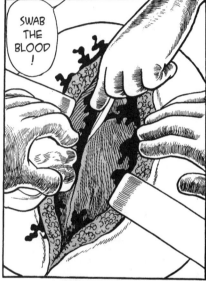

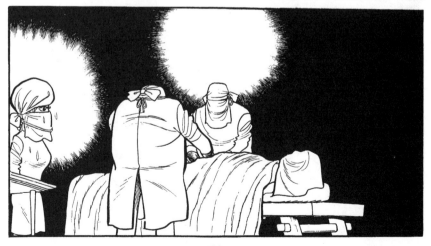

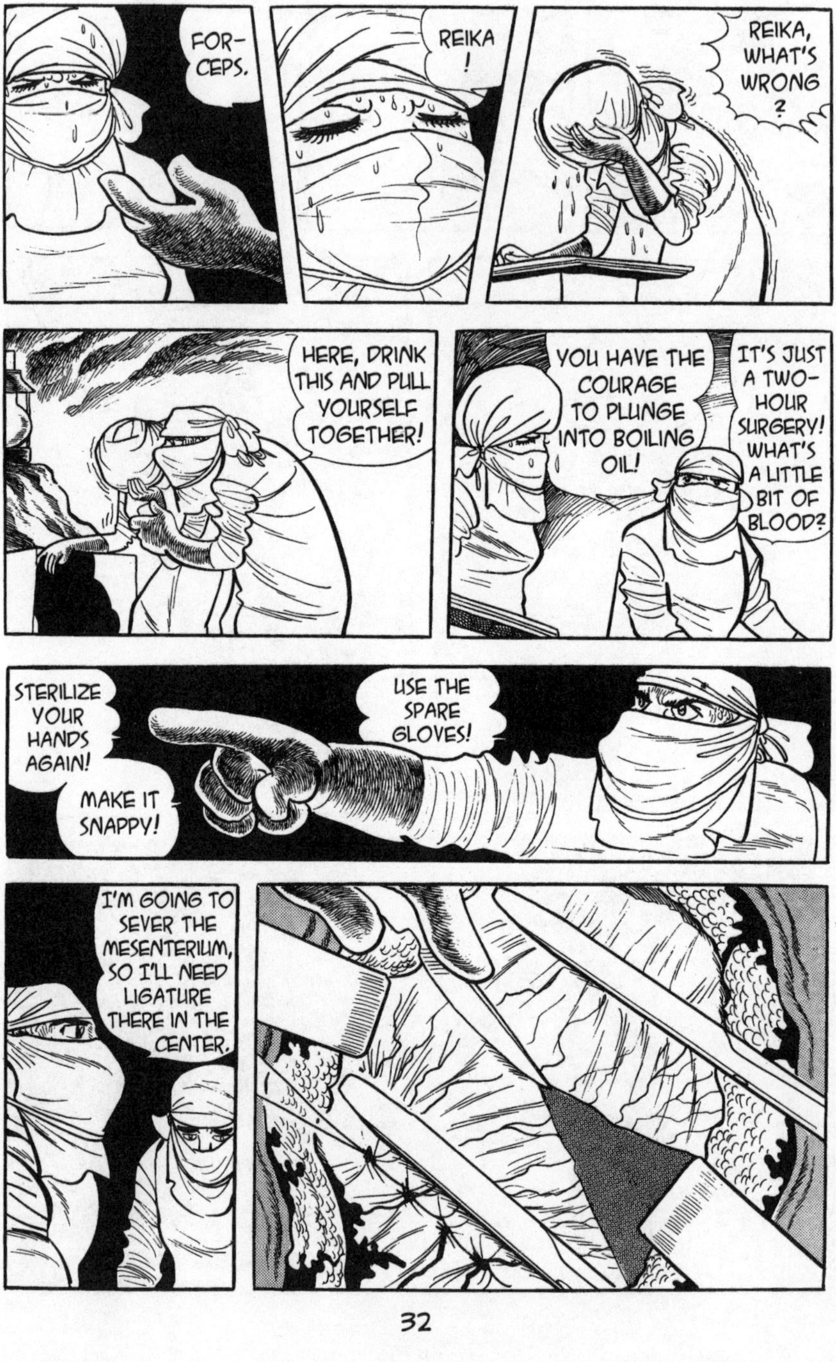
FOR-CEPS.
REIKA!
REIKA, WHAT'S WRONG?
HERE, DRINK THIS AND PULL YOURSELF TOGETHER!
YOU HAVE THE COURAGE TO PLUNGE INTO BOILING OIL!
IT'S JUST A TWO-HOUR SURGERY! WHAT'S A LITTLE BIT OF BLOOD?
STERILIZE YOUR HANDS AGAIN!
USE THE SPARE GLOVES!
MAKE IT SNAPPY!
I'M GOING TO SEVER THE MESENTERIUM, SO I'LL NEED LIGATURE THERE IN THE CENTER.

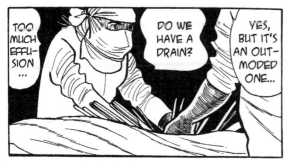

TOO MUCH EFFUSION...

DO WE HAVE A DRAIN?

YES, BUT IT'S AN OUTMODED ONE...

THAT'S FINE. USE IT. IT DOESN'T MATTER SO LONG AS IT WORKS.

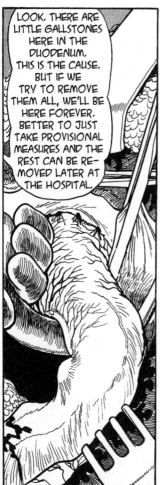

LOOK. THERE ARE LITTLE GALLSTONES HERE IN THE DUODENUM. THIS IS THE CAUSE. BUT IF WE TRY TO REMOVE THEM ALL, WE'LL BE HERE FOREVER. BETTER TO JUST TAKE PROVISIONAL MEASURES AND THE REST CAN BE REMOVED LATER AT THE HOSPITAL.

THE PANCREAS.

CAREFUL OF THE AORTA!

THERE'S SOME ADHESION IN THE CAUDAL PORTION. LET'S REMOVE IT.

FORCEPS!

33

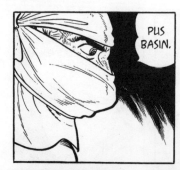

PUS
BASIN.

NOW WE
JUST NEED
A CON-
TINUOUS
SUTURE.

DRAIN
AND
TAMPO-
NADE.

TIC
TIC
TIC
TIC

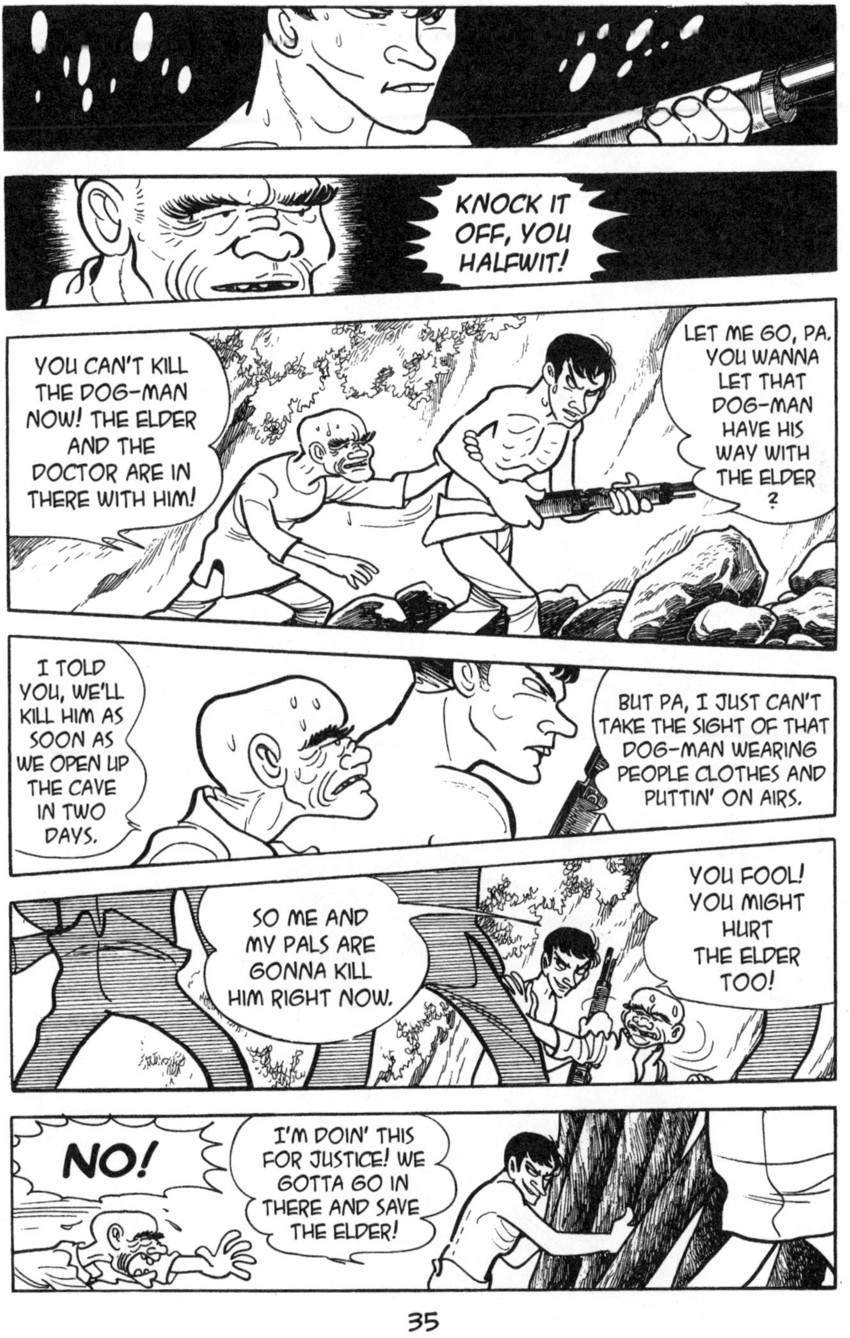
KNOCK IT OFF, YOU HALFWIT!
YOU CAN'T KILL THE DOG-MAN NOW! THE ELDER AND THE DOCTOR ARE IN THERE WITH HIM!
LET ME GO, PA. YOU WANNA LET THAT DOG-MAN HAVE HIS WAY WITH THE ELDER?
I TOLD YOU, WE'LL KILL HIM AS SOON AS WE OPEN UP THE CAVE IN TWO DAYS.
BUT PA, I JUST CAN'T TAKE THE SIGHT OF THAT DOG-MAN WEARING PEOPLE CLOTHES AND PUTTIN' ON AIRS.
SO ME AND MY PALS ARE GONNA KILL HIM RIGHT NOW.
YOU FOOL! YOU MIGHT HURT THE ELDER TOO!
NO!
I'M DOIN' THIS FOR JUSTICE! WE GOTTA GO IN THERE AND SAVE THE ELDER!

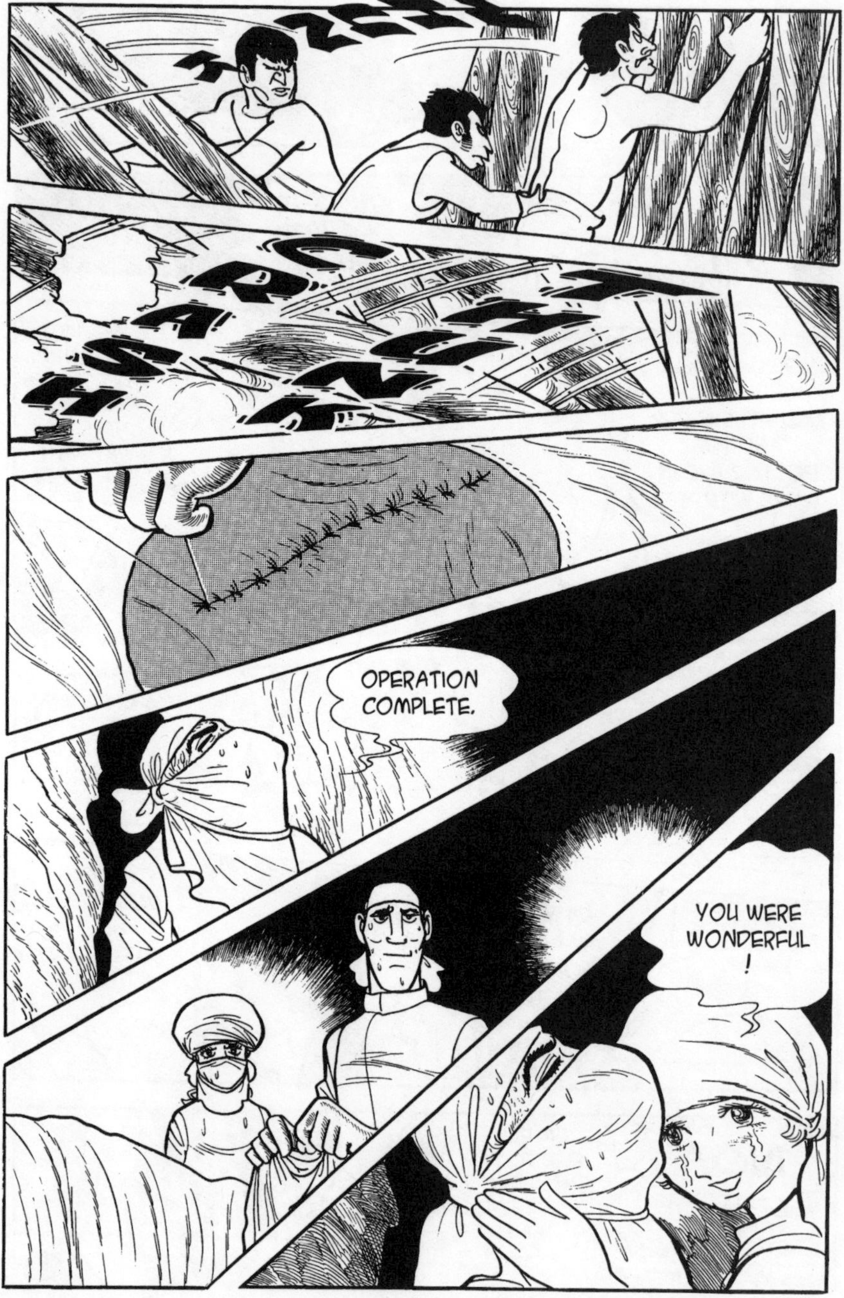
OPERATION COMPLETE.
YOU WERE WONDERFUL!

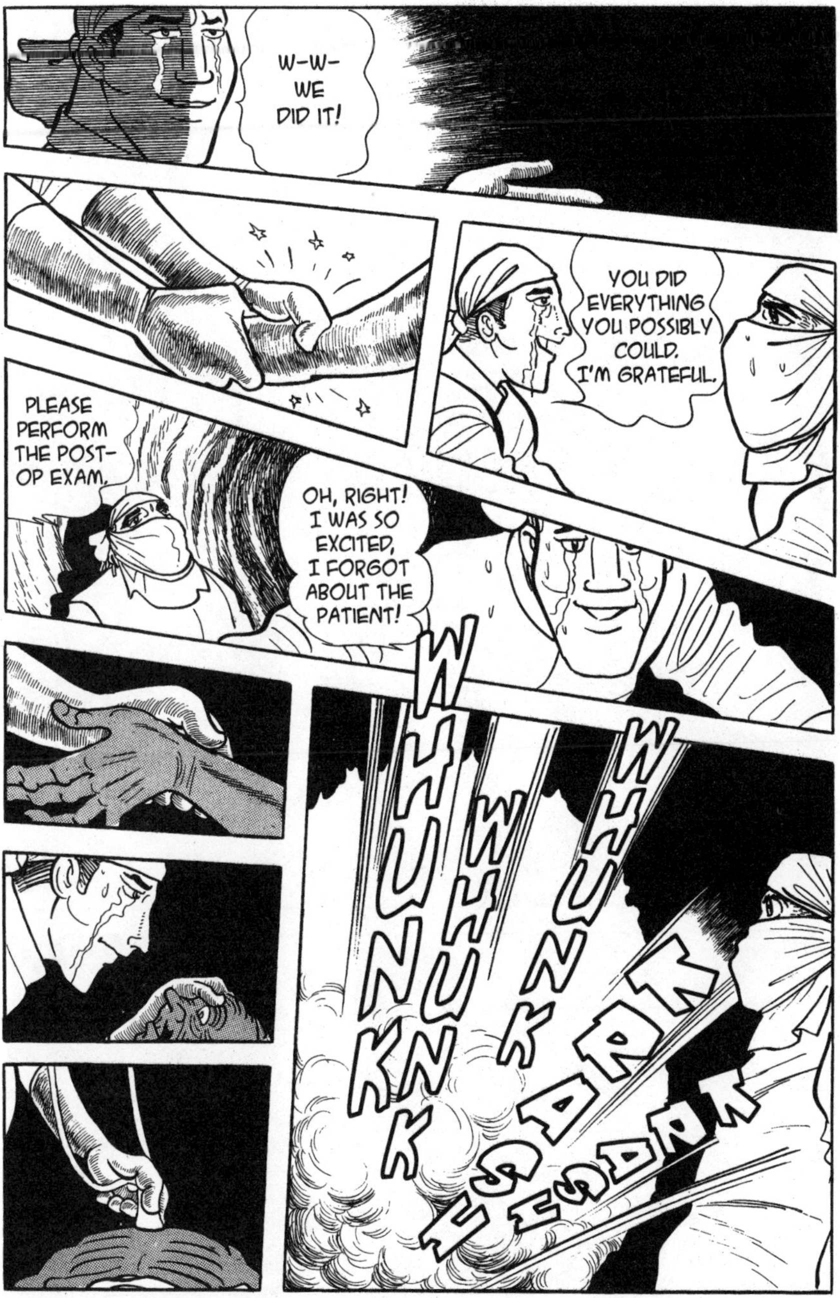
W-W-WE DID IT!
YOU DID EVERYTHING YOU POSSIBLY COULD. I'M GRATEFUL.
PLEASE PERFORM THE POST-OP EXAM.
OH, RIGHT! I WAS SO EXCITED, I FORGOT ABOUT THE PATIENT!
WHUNK
WHUNK
WHUNK
SPARK
SPARK

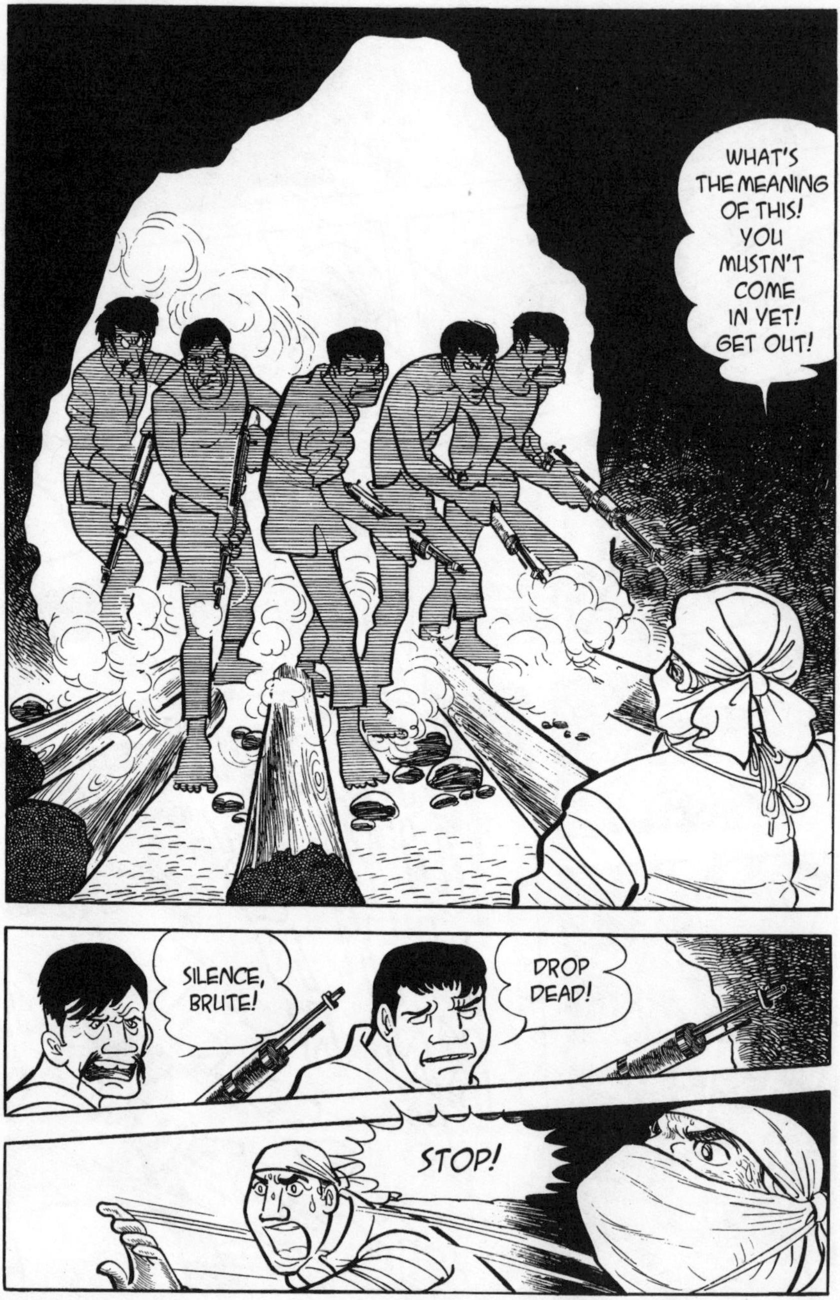
WHAT'S THE MEANING OF THIS! YOU MUSTN'T COME IN YET! GET OUT!
SILENCE, BRUTE!
DROP DEAD!
STOP!

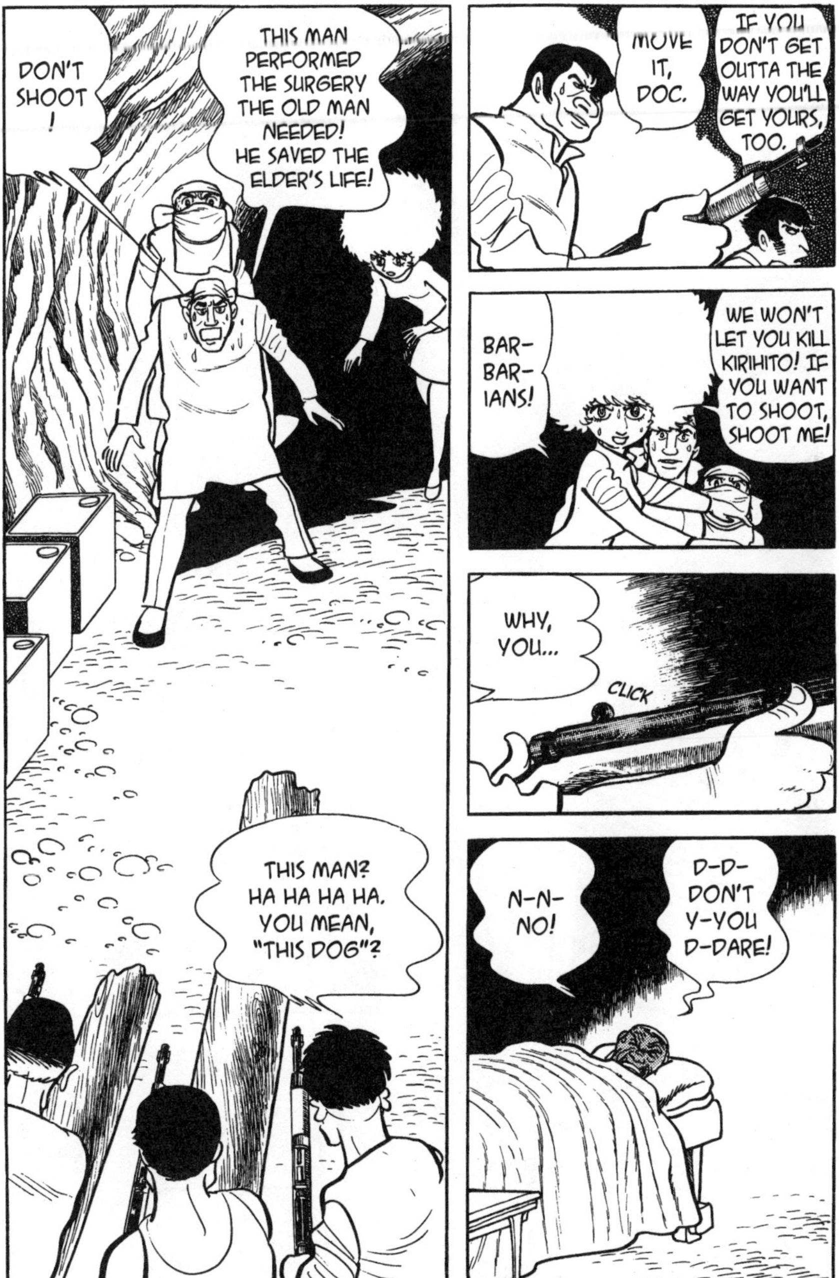
DON'T SHOOT!
THIS MAN PERFORMED THE SURGERY THE OLD MAN NEEDED! HE SAVED THE ELDER'S LIFE!
THIS MAN? HA HA HA HA. YOU MEAN, "THIS DOG"?
MOVE IT, DOC.
IF YOU DON'T GET OUTTA THE WAY YOU'LL GET YOURS, TOO.
BAR-BAR-IANS!
WE WON'T LET YOU KILL KIRIHITO! IF YOU WANT TO SHOOT, SHOOT ME!
WHY, YOU...
CLICK
N-N-NO!
D-D-DON'T Y-YOU D-DARE!

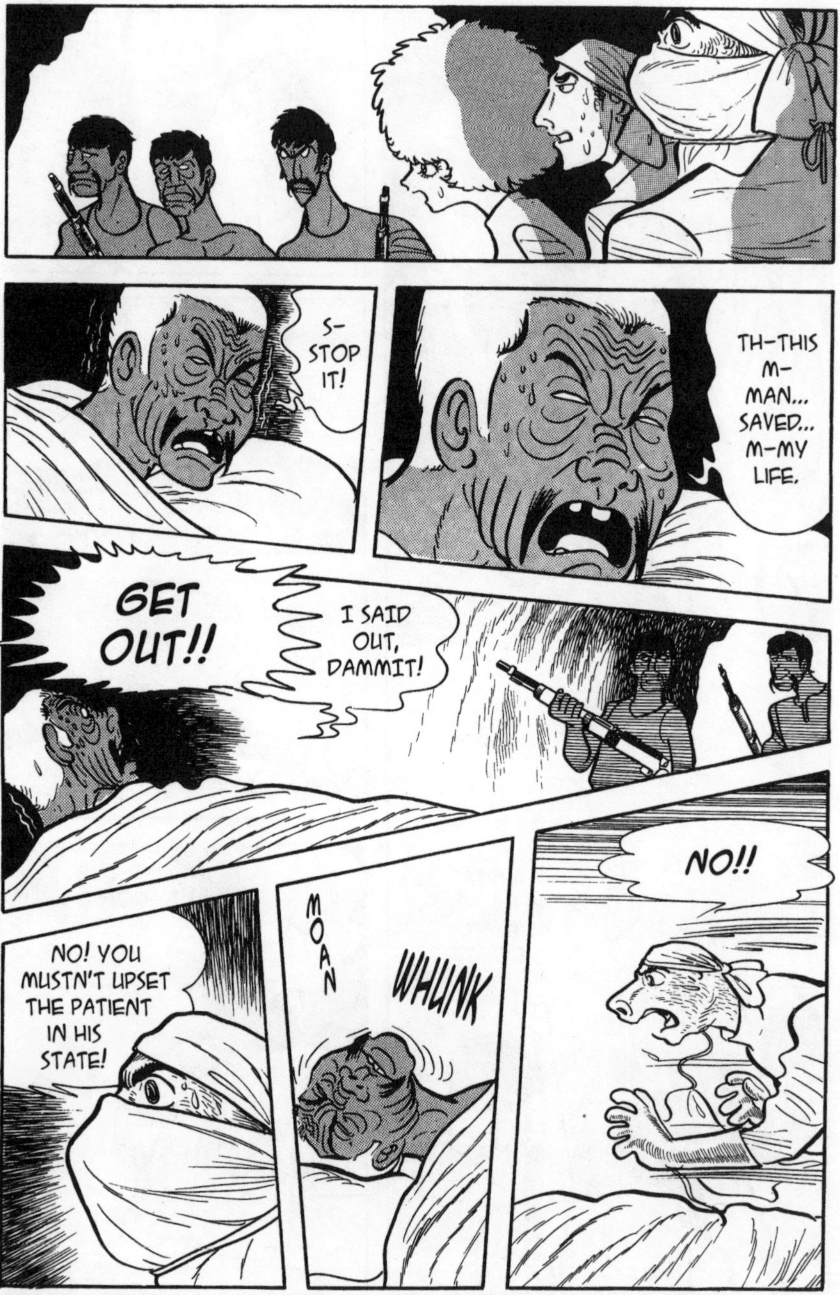
S-STOP IT!
TH-THIS M-MAN... SAVED... M-MY LIFE.
GET OUT!!
I SAID OUT, DAMMIT!
NO! YOU MUSTN'T UPSET THE PATIENT IN HIS STATE!
MOAN
WHUNK
NO!!

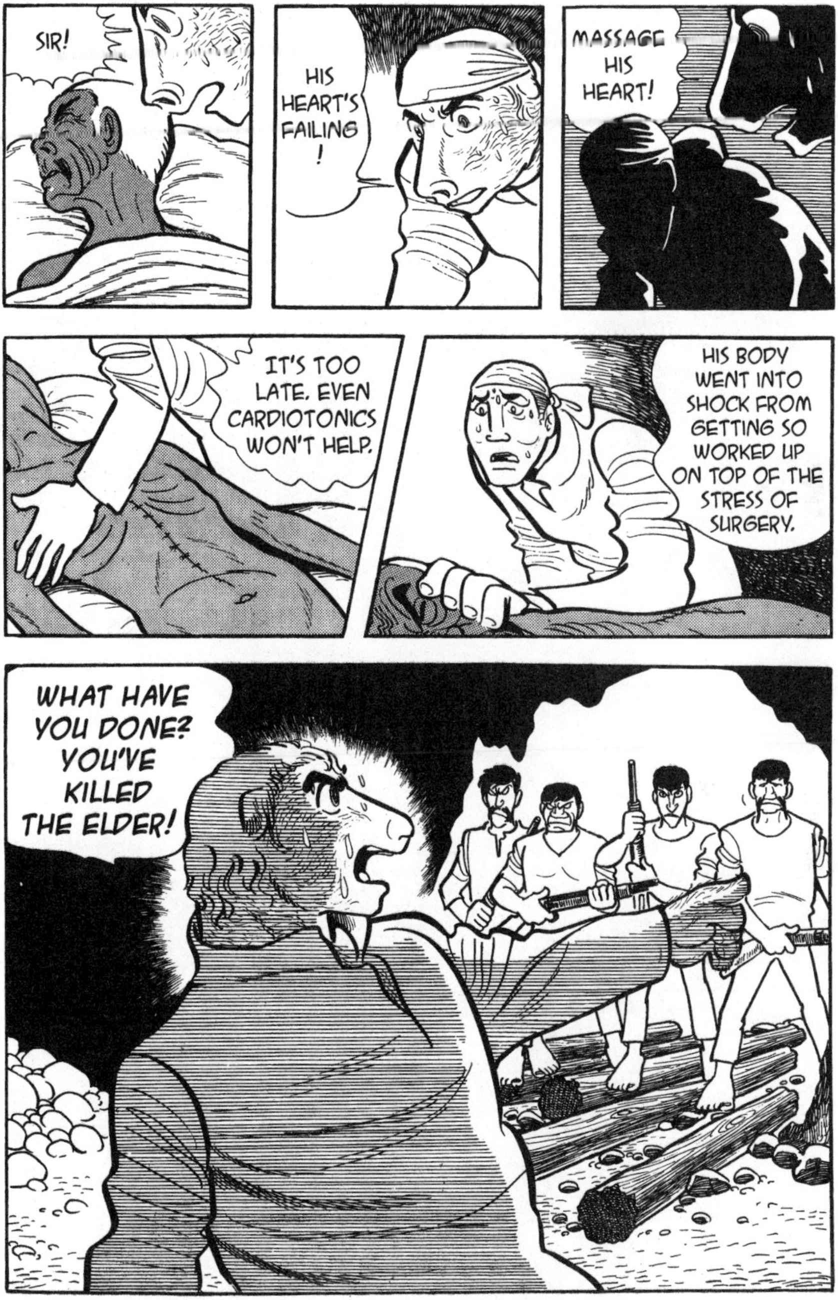
SIR!
HIS HEART'S FAILING!
MASSAGE HIS HEART!
IT'S TOO LATE. EVEN CARDIOTONICS WON'T HELP.
HIS BODY WENT INTO SHOCK FROM GETTING SO WORKED UP ON TOP OF THE STRESS OF SURGERY.
WHAT HAVE YOU DONE? YOU'VE KILLED THE ELDER!

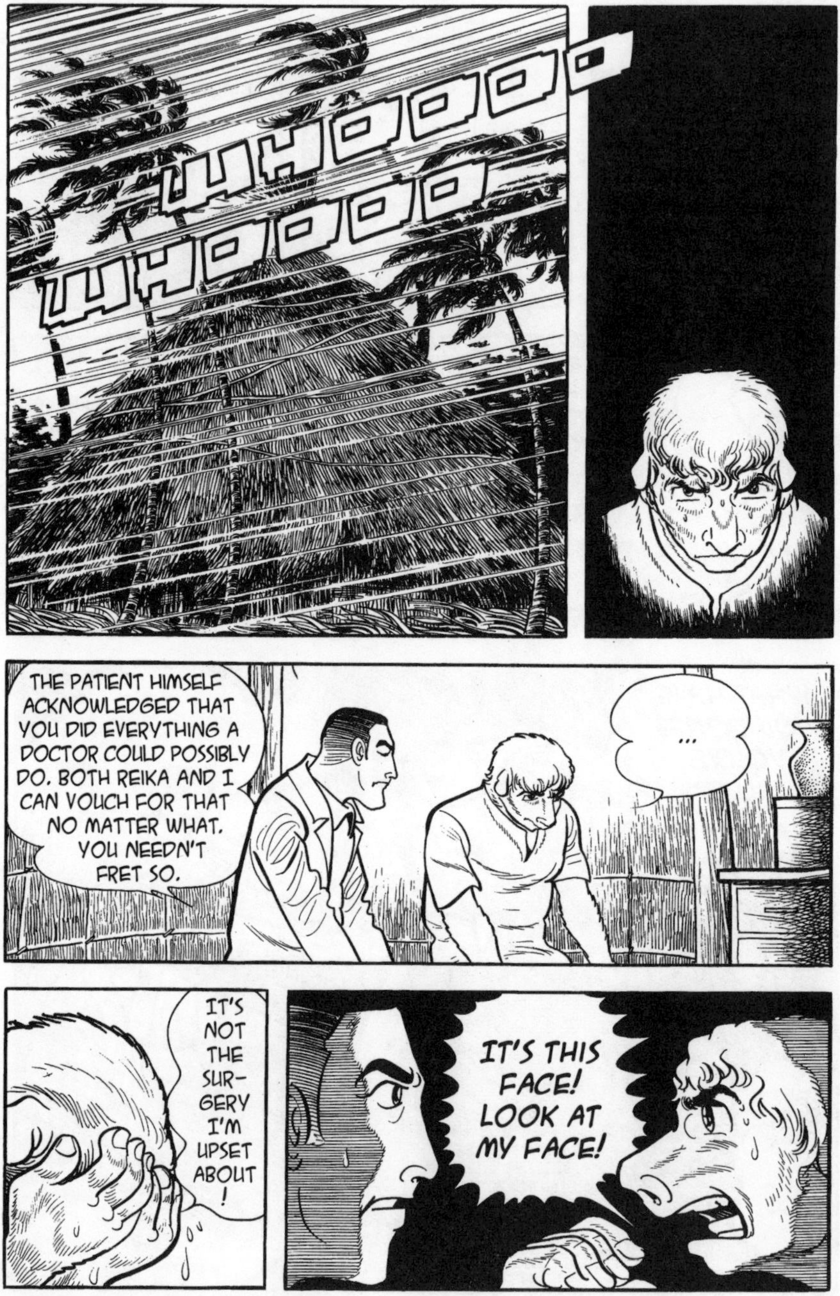
WHOOOOO
WHOOOOO
THE PATIENT HIMSELF ACKNOWLEDGED THAT YOU DID EVERYTHING A DOCTOR COULD POSSIBLY DO. BOTH REIKA AND I CAN VOUCH FOR THAT NO MATTER WHAT. YOU NEEDN'T FRET SO.
...
IT'S NOT THE SUR-GERY I'M UPSET ABOUT!
IT'S THIS FACE! LOOK AT MY FACE!

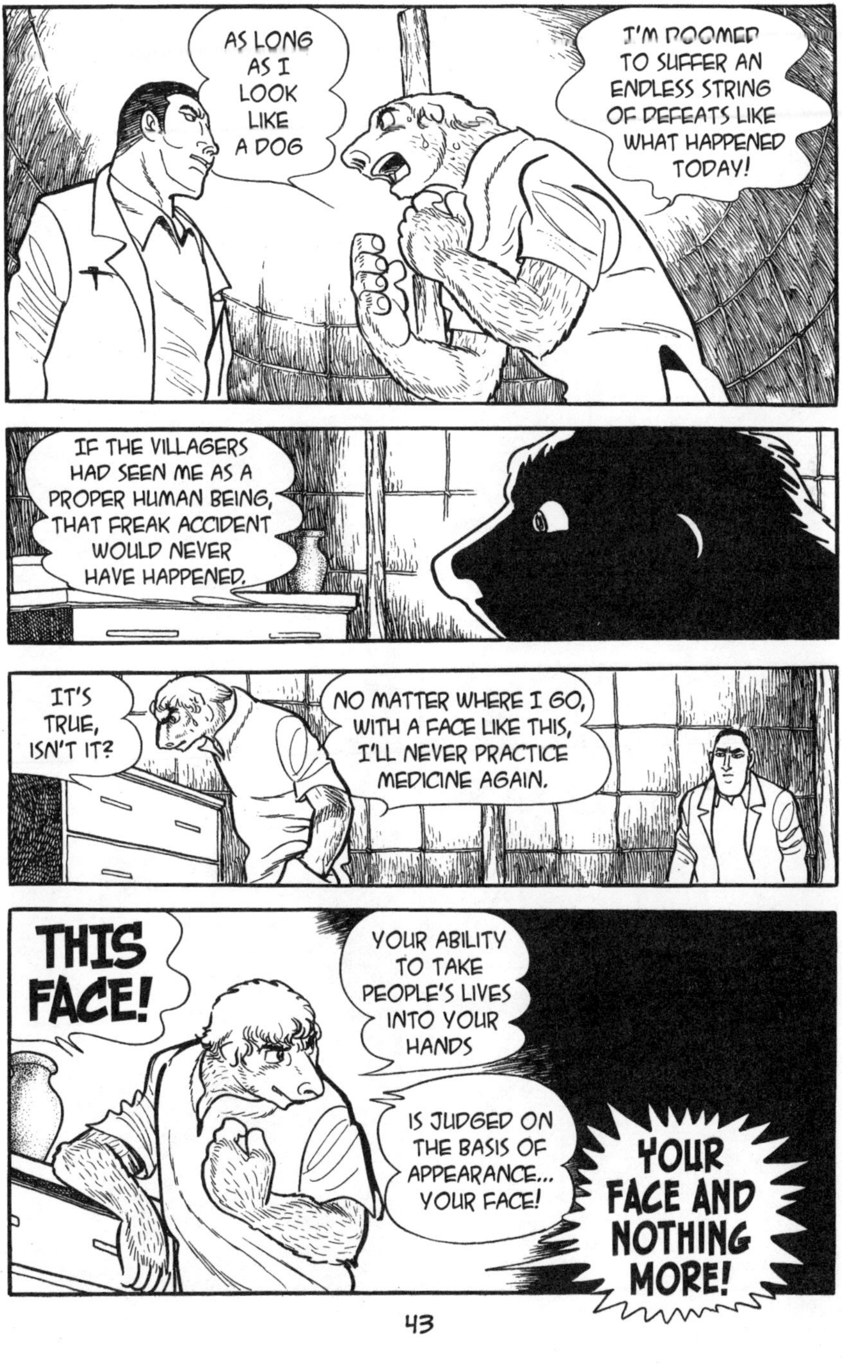
AS LONG AS I LOOK LIKE A DOG
I'M DOOMED TO SUFFER AN ENDLESS STRING OF DEFEATS LIKE WHAT HAPPENED TODAY!
IF THE VILLAGERS HAD SEEN ME AS A PROPER HUMAN BEING, THAT FREAK ACCIDENT WOULD NEVER HAVE HAPPENED.
IT'S TRUE, ISN'T IT?
NO MATTER WHERE I GO, WITH A FACE LIKE THIS, I'LL NEVER PRACTICE MEDICINE AGAIN.
THIS FACE!
YOUR ABILITY TO TAKE PEOPLE'S LIVES INTO YOUR HANDS
IS JUDGED ON THE BASIS OF APPEARANCE... YOUR FACE!
YOUR FACE AND NOTHING MORE!

WHEN I THINK ABOUT IT, EVEN BACK AT M UNIVERSITY PEOPLE WERE JUDGED BASED ON APPEARANCES.

SOME WERE NO BETTER THAN PIGS ON THE INSIDE!

I TEND TO BE A LITTLE BIT MORE OPTIMISTIC...

I THINK IT'S JUST A MATTER OF TIME BEFORE YOU GAIN THE VILLAGERS' TRUST AND RESPECT.

THERE ARE LOTS OF PEOPLE WHO WILL TAKE YOUR SIDE, TOO.

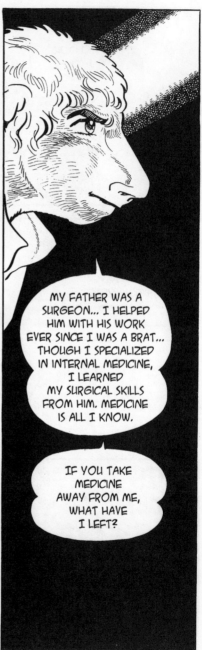

MY FATHER WAS A SURGEON... I HELPED HIM WITH HIS WORK EVER SINCE I WAS A BRAT... THOUGH I SPECIALIZED IN INTERNAL MEDICINE, I LEARNED MY SURGICAL SKILLS FROM HIM. MEDICINE IS ALL I KNOW.

IF YOU TAKE MEDICINE AWAY FROM ME, WHAT HAVE I LEFT?

44

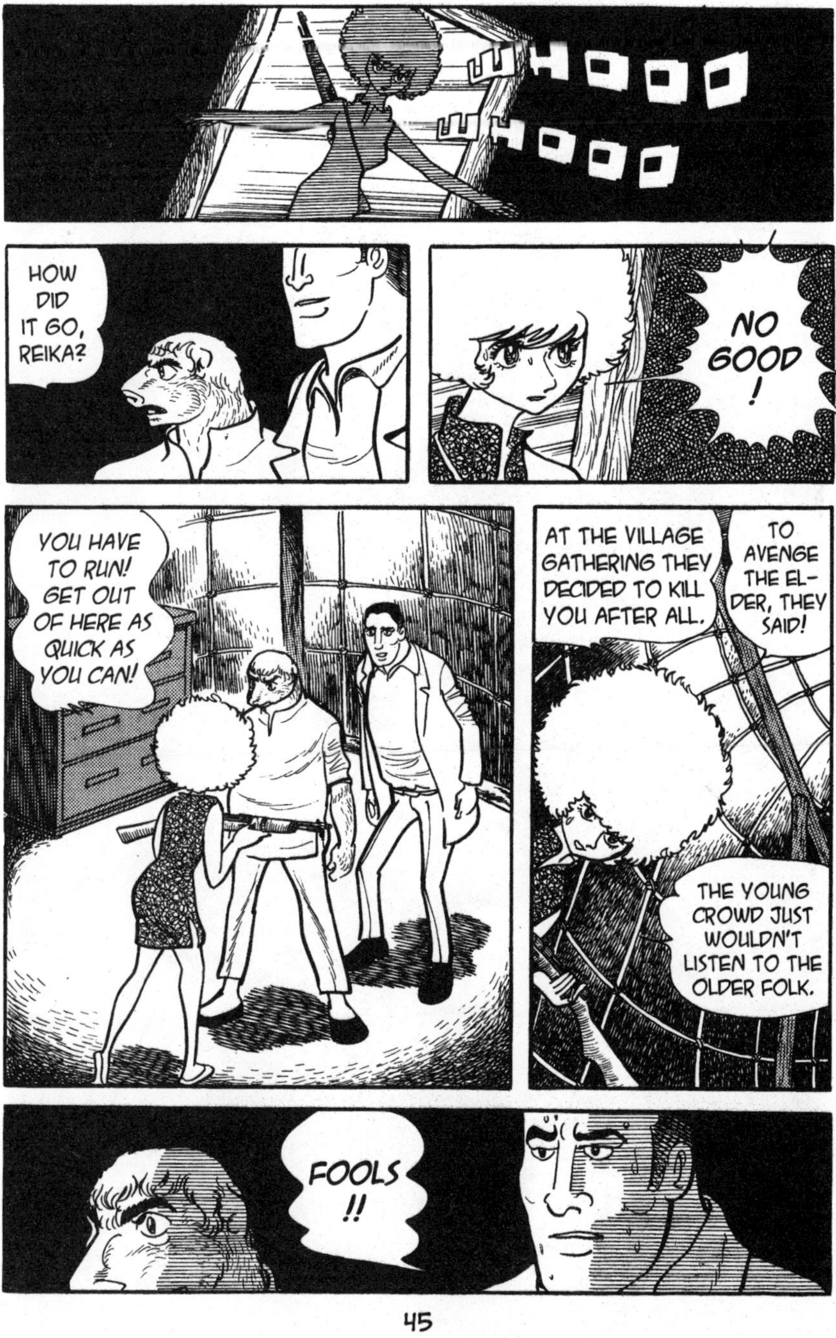
WHOOO
WHOOO
HOW DID IT GO, REIKA?
NO GOOD!
YOU HAVE TO RUN! GET OUT OF HERE AS QUICK AS YOU CAN!
AT THE VILLAGE GATHERING THEY DECIDED TO KILL YOU AFTER ALL.
TO AVENGE THE EL-DER, THEY SAID!
THE YOUNG CROWD JUST WOULDN'T LISTEN TO THE OLDER FOLK.
FOOLS!!

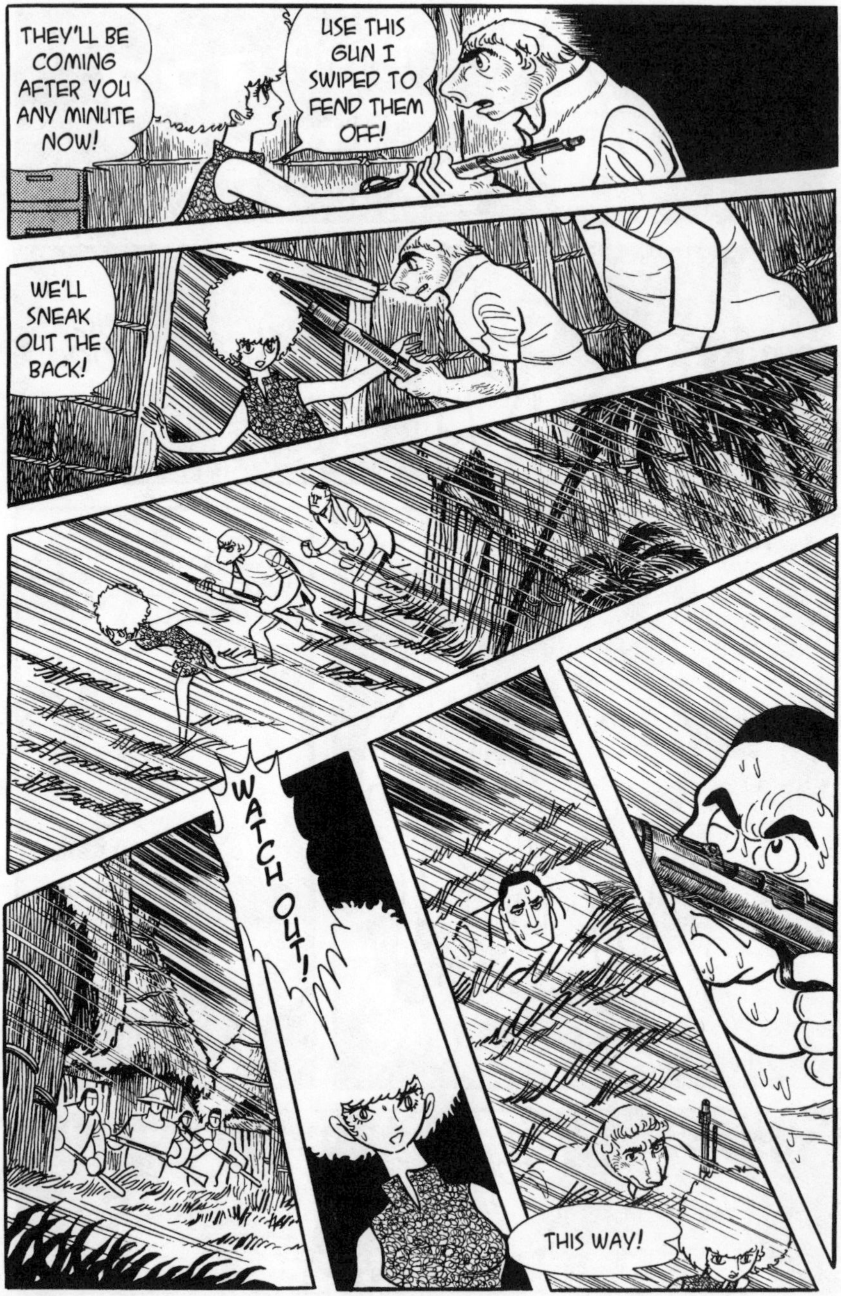
THEY'LL BE COMING AFTER YOU ANY MINUTE NOW!
USE THIS GUN I SWIPED TO FEND THEM OFF!
WE'LL SNEAK OUT THE BACK!
WATCH OUT!
THIS WAY!

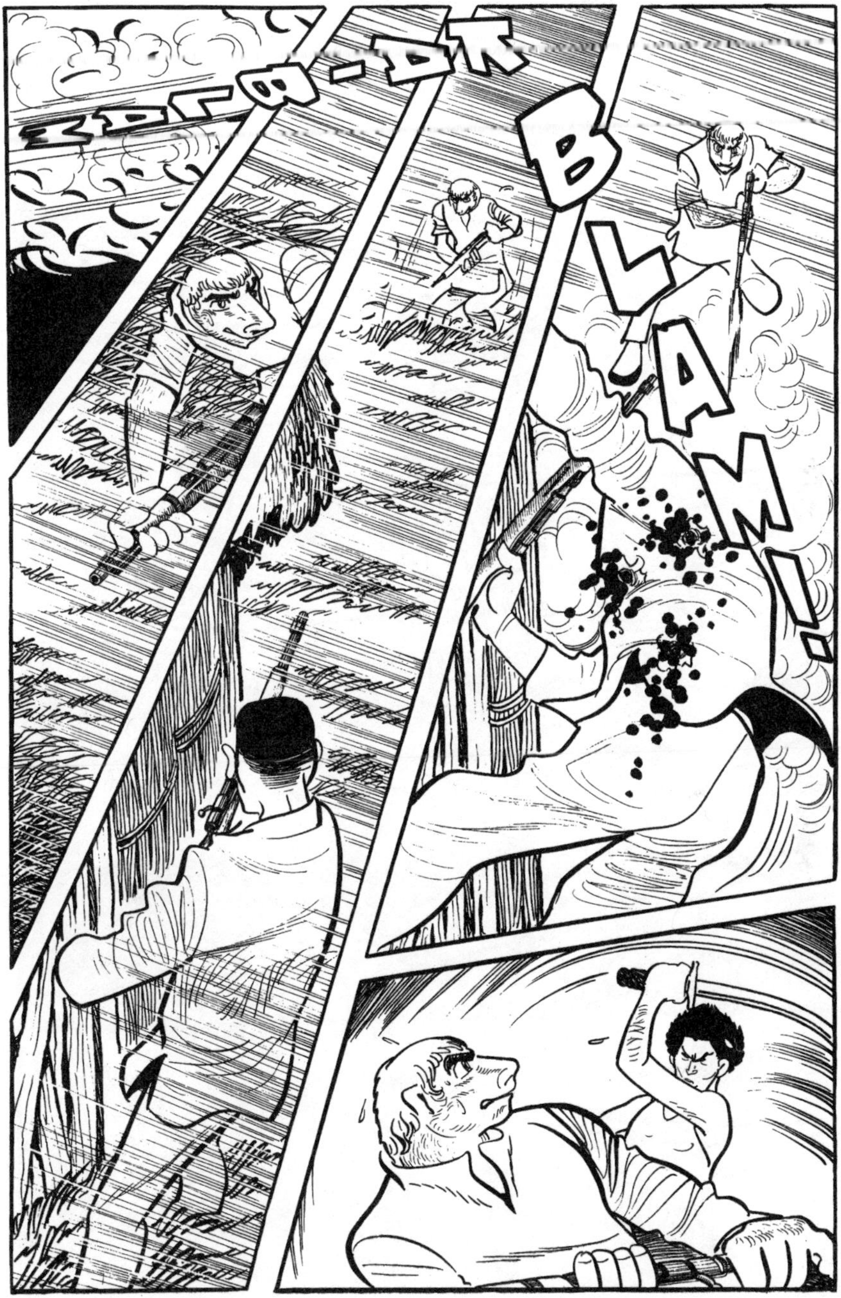
BLAM!

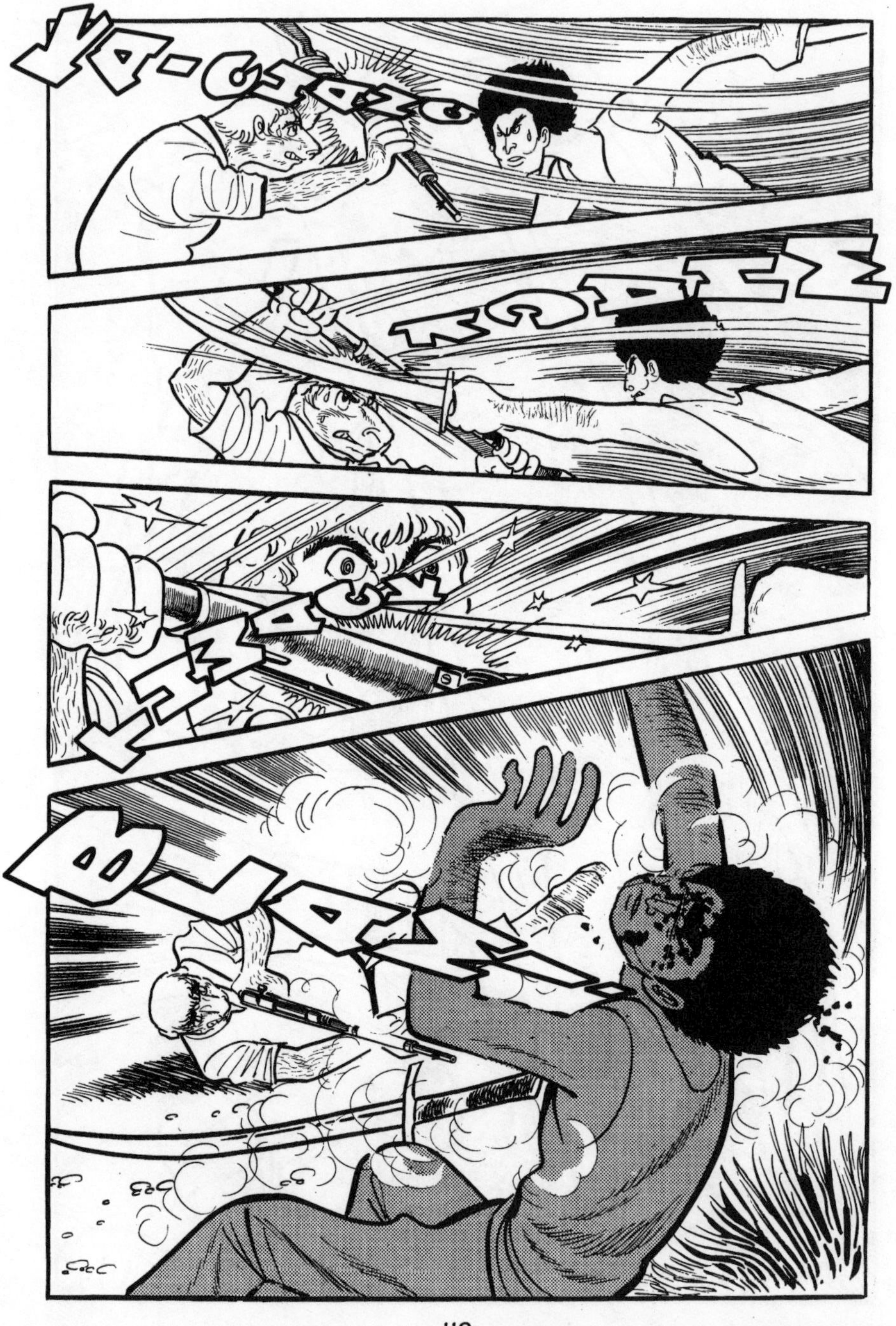
THWACK
BLAM!!

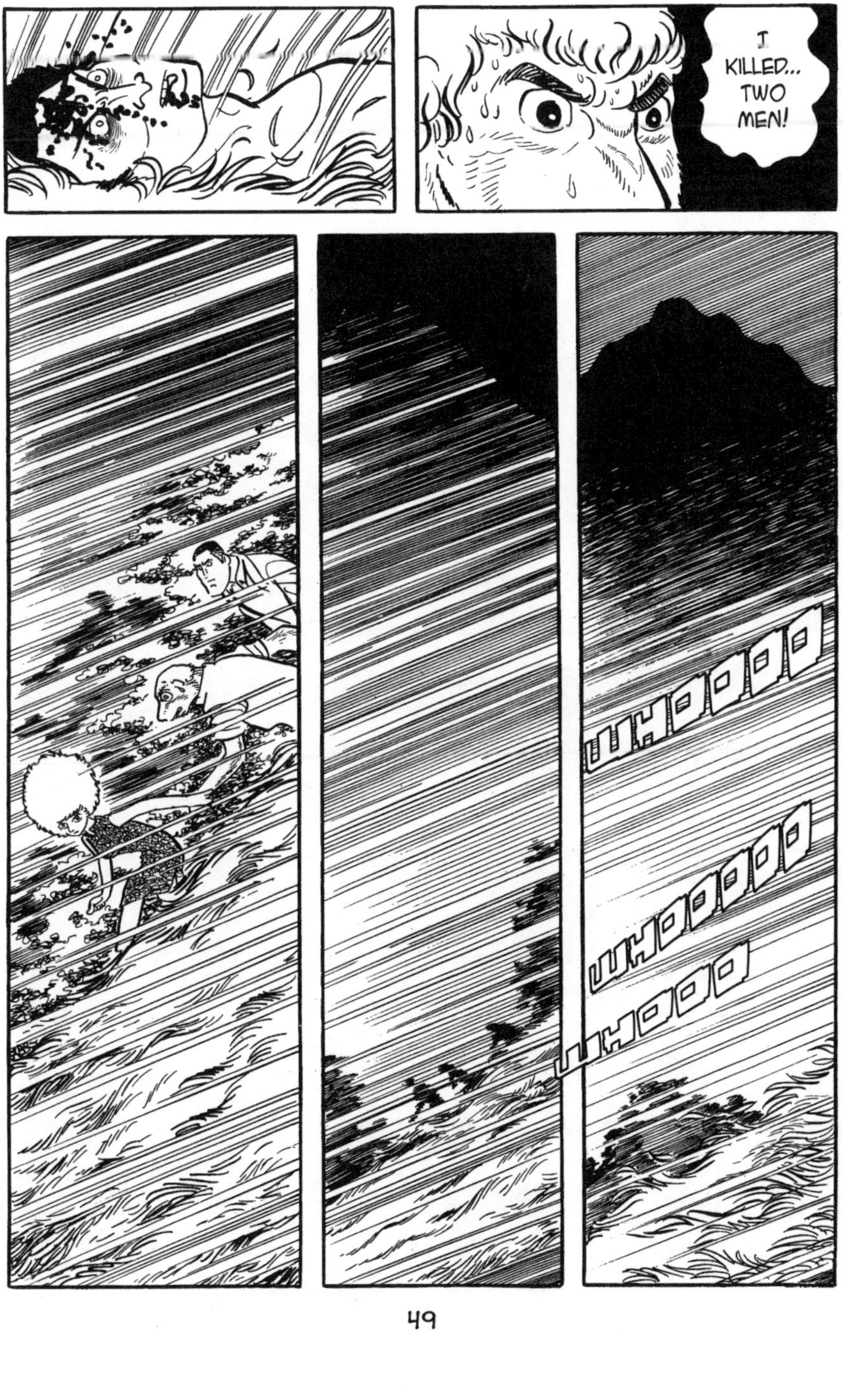
I KILLED... TWO MEN!
WHOOOO
WHOOOOO
WHOOO

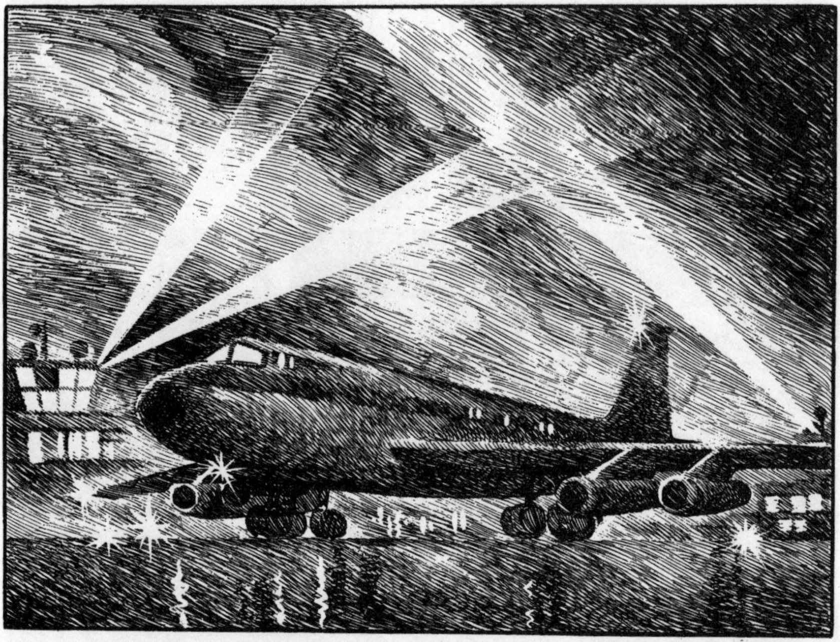

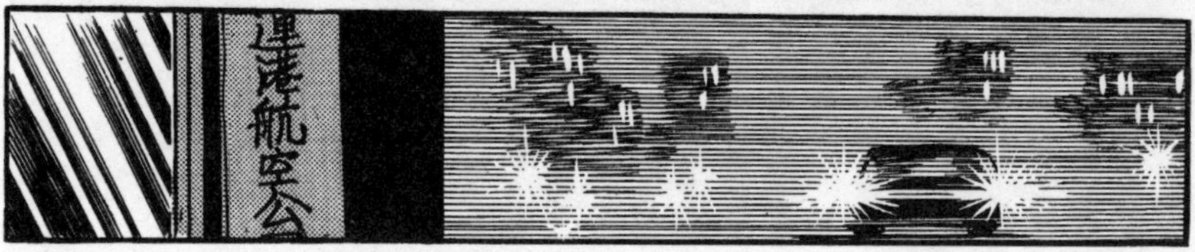

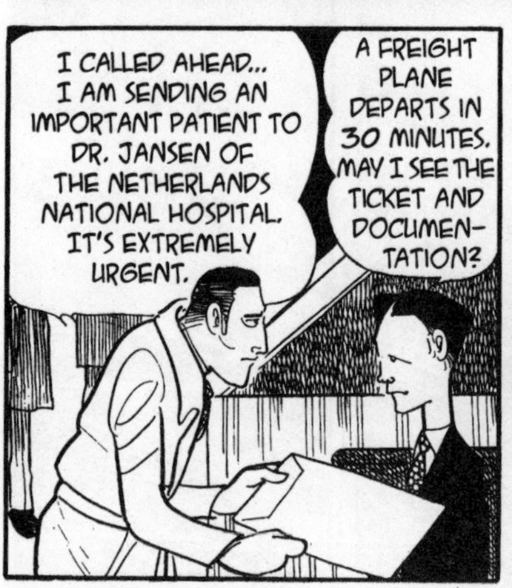
I CALLED AHEAD... I AM SENDING AN IMPORTANT PATIENT TO DR. JANSEN OF THE NETHERLANDS NATIONAL HOSPITAL. IT'S EXTREMELY URGENT.
A FREIGHT PLANE DEPARTS IN 30 MINUTES. MAY I SEE THE TICKET AND DOCUMENTATION?

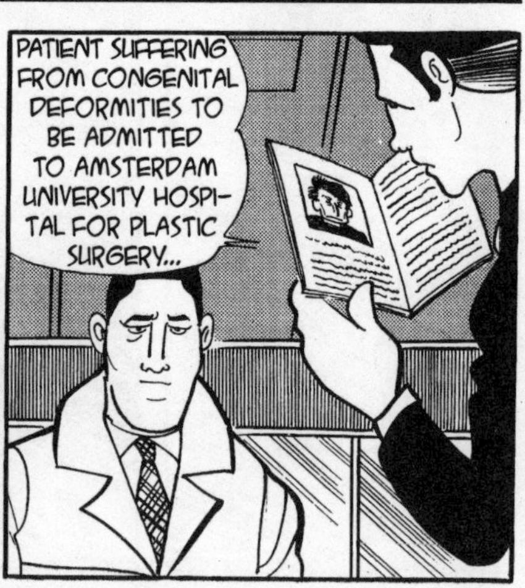
PATIENT SUFFERING FROM CONGENITAL DEFORMITIES TO BE ADMITTED TO AMSTERDAM UNIVERSITY HOSPITAL FOR PLASTIC SURGERY...

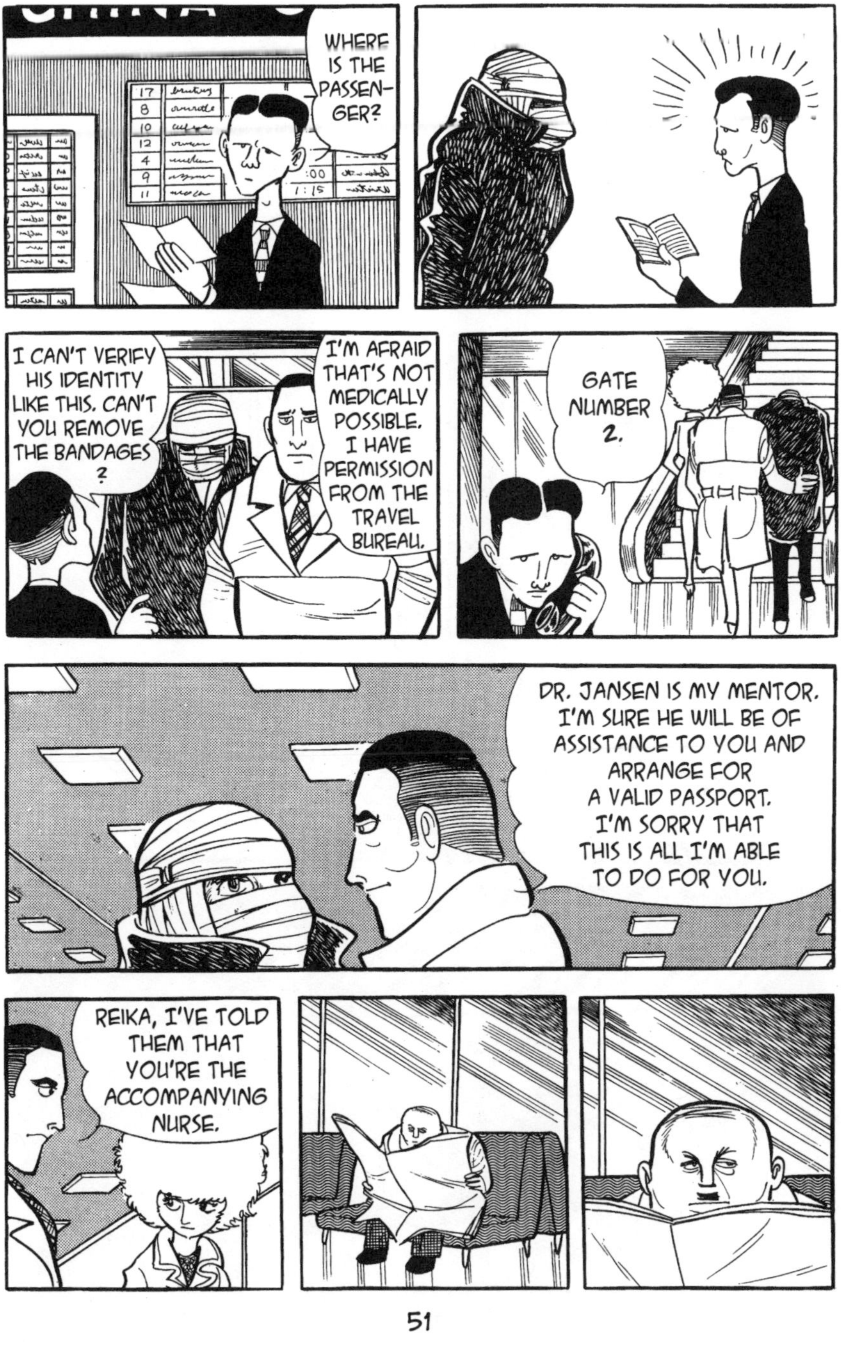
WHERE IS THE PASSENGER?
I CAN'T VERIFY HIS IDENTITY LIKE THIS. CAN'T YOU REMOVE THE BANDAGES?
I'M AFRAID THAT'S NOT MEDICALLY POSSIBLE. I HAVE PERMISSION FROM THE TRAVEL BUREAU.
GATE NUMBER 2.
DR. JANSEN IS MY MENTOR. I'M SURE HE WILL BE OF ASSISTANCE TO YOU AND ARRANGE FOR A VALID PASSPORT. I'M SORRY THAT THIS IS ALL I'M ABLE TO DO FOR YOU.
REIKA, I'VE TOLD THEM THAT YOU'RE THE ACCOMPANYING NURSE.

HULLO THERE. SO, YOU'LL BE TRAVELING ON THE FREIGHT PLANE?
I AM, TOO. MY, WHAT HAPPENED TO YOU?
9
8
7
I'M JAPANESE. MY NAME IS MURAKAMI. I'LL BE GETTING OFF IN BEIRUT... GUESS WE'LL BE TOGETHER UNTIL THEN!
POOR FELLOW
WHAT A CREEPY GUY.
TAKE CARE
VVVRRROOOOOMMM

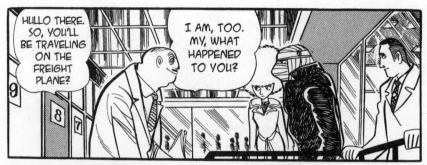

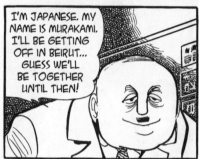

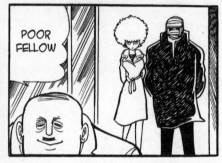

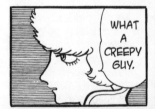

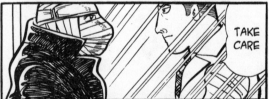

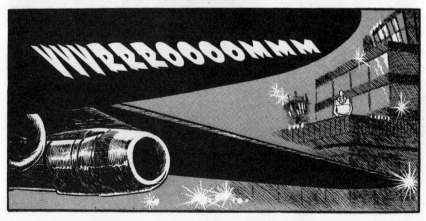

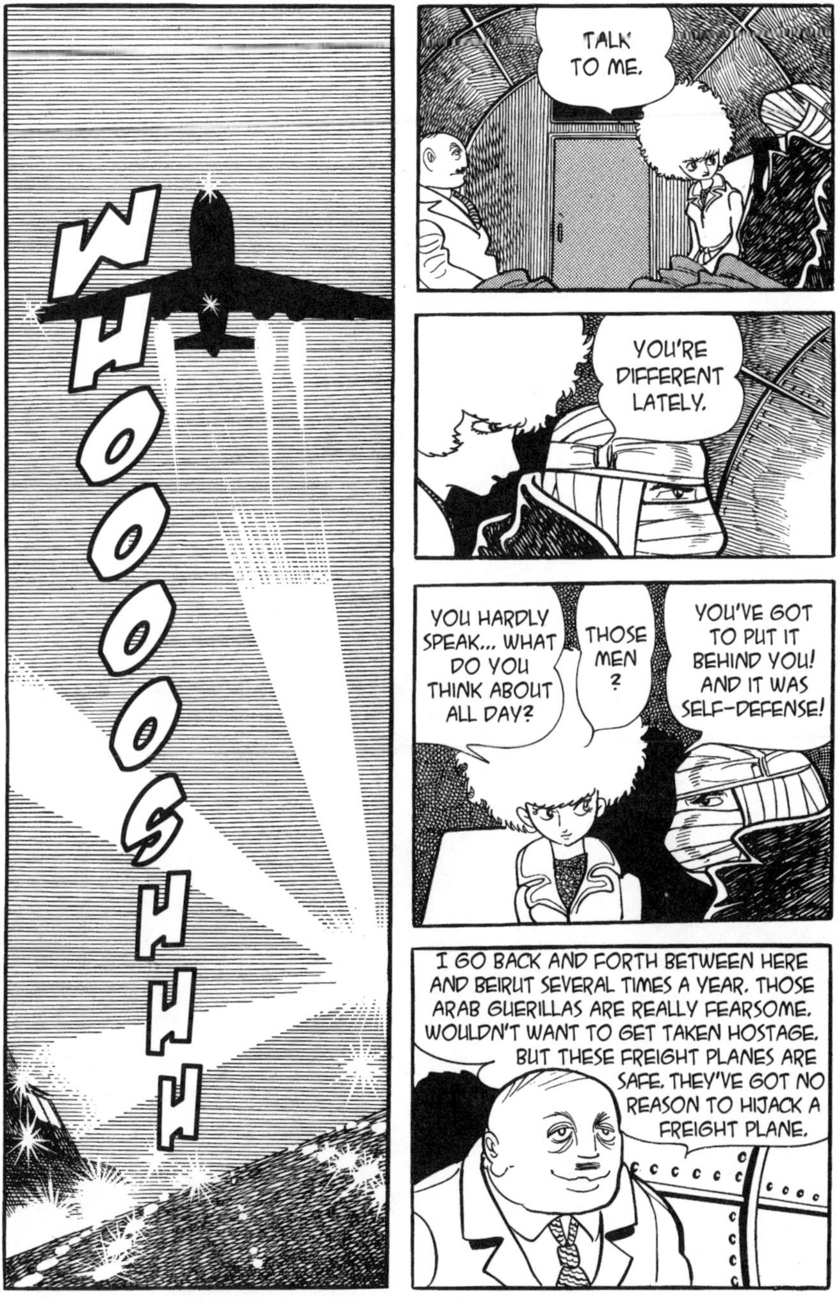
WHOOOOOSHHH
TALK TO ME.
YOU'RE DIFFERENT LATELY.
YOU HARDLY SPEAK... WHAT DO YOU THINK ABOUT ALL DAY?
THOSE MEN?
YOU'VE GOT TO PUT IT BEHIND YOU! AND IT WAS SELF-DEFENSE!
I GO BACK AND FORTH BETWEEN HERE AND BEIRUT SEVERAL TIMES A YEAR. THOSE ARAB GUERILLAS ARE REALLY FEARSOME. WOULDN'T WANT TO GET TAKEN HOSTAGE. BUT THESE FREIGHT PLANES ARE SAFE. THEY'VE GOT NO REASON TO HIJACK A FREIGHT PLANE.

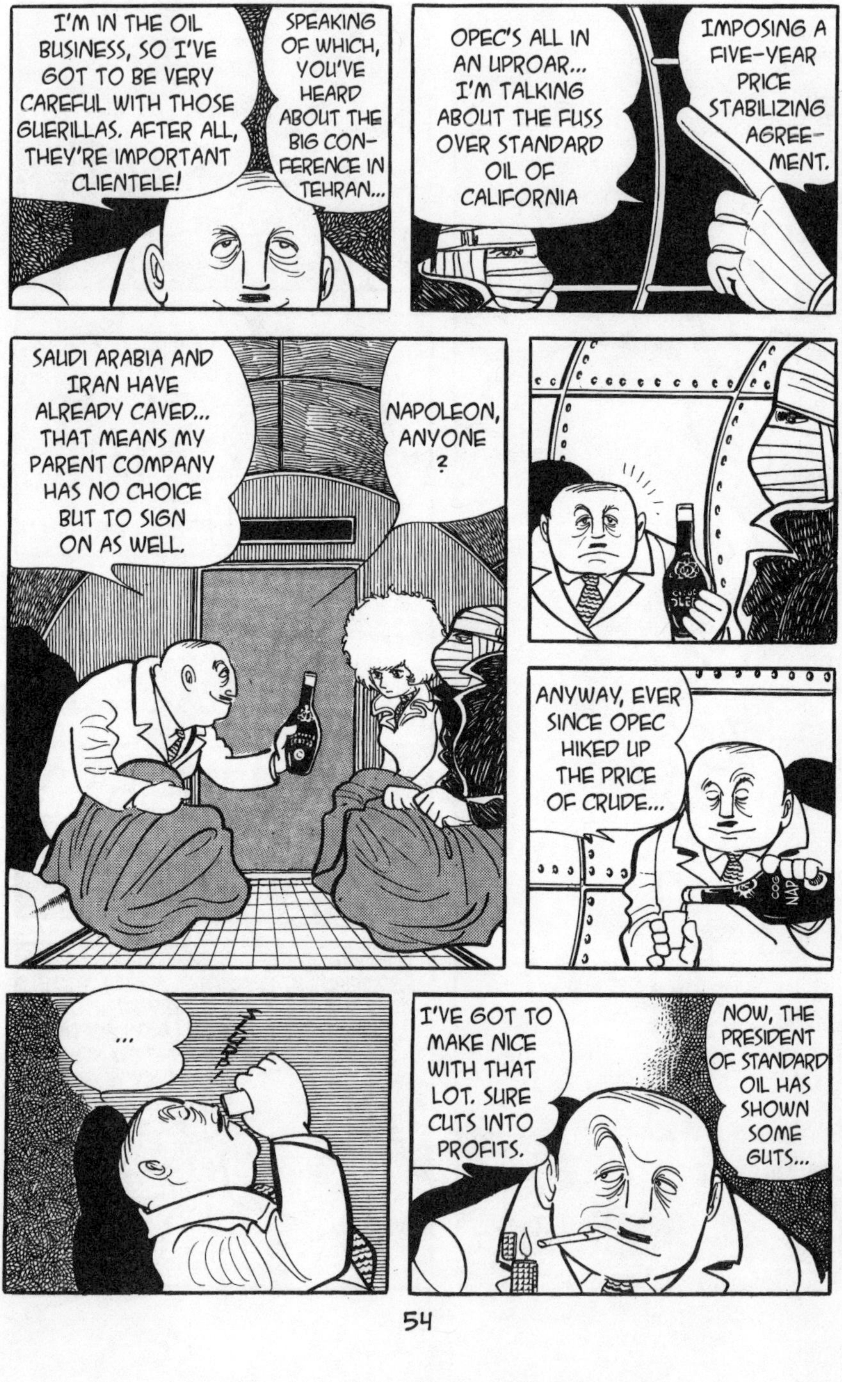

I'M IN THE OIL BUSINESS, SO I'VE GOT TO BE VERY CAREFUL WITH THOSE GUERILLAS. AFTER ALL, THEY'RE IMPORTANT CLIENTELE!
SPEAKING OF WHICH, YOU'VE HEARD ABOUT THE BIG CON-FERENCE IN TEHRAN...
OPEC'S ALL IN AN UPROAR... I'M TALKING ABOUT THE FUSS OVER STANDARD OIL OF CALIFORNIA
IMPOSING A FIVE-YEAR PRICE STABILIZING AGREE-MENT.
SAUDI ARABIA AND IRAN HAVE ALREADY CAVED... THAT MEANS MY PARENT COMPANY HAS NO CHOICE BUT TO SIGN ON AS WELL.
NAPOLEON, ANYONE ?
ANYWAY, EVER SINCE OPEC HIKED UP THE PRICE OF CRUDE...
...
I'VE GOT TO MAKE NICE WITH THAT LOT. SURE CUTS INTO PROFITS.
NOW, THE PRESIDENT OF STANDARD OIL HAS SHOWN SOME GUTS...

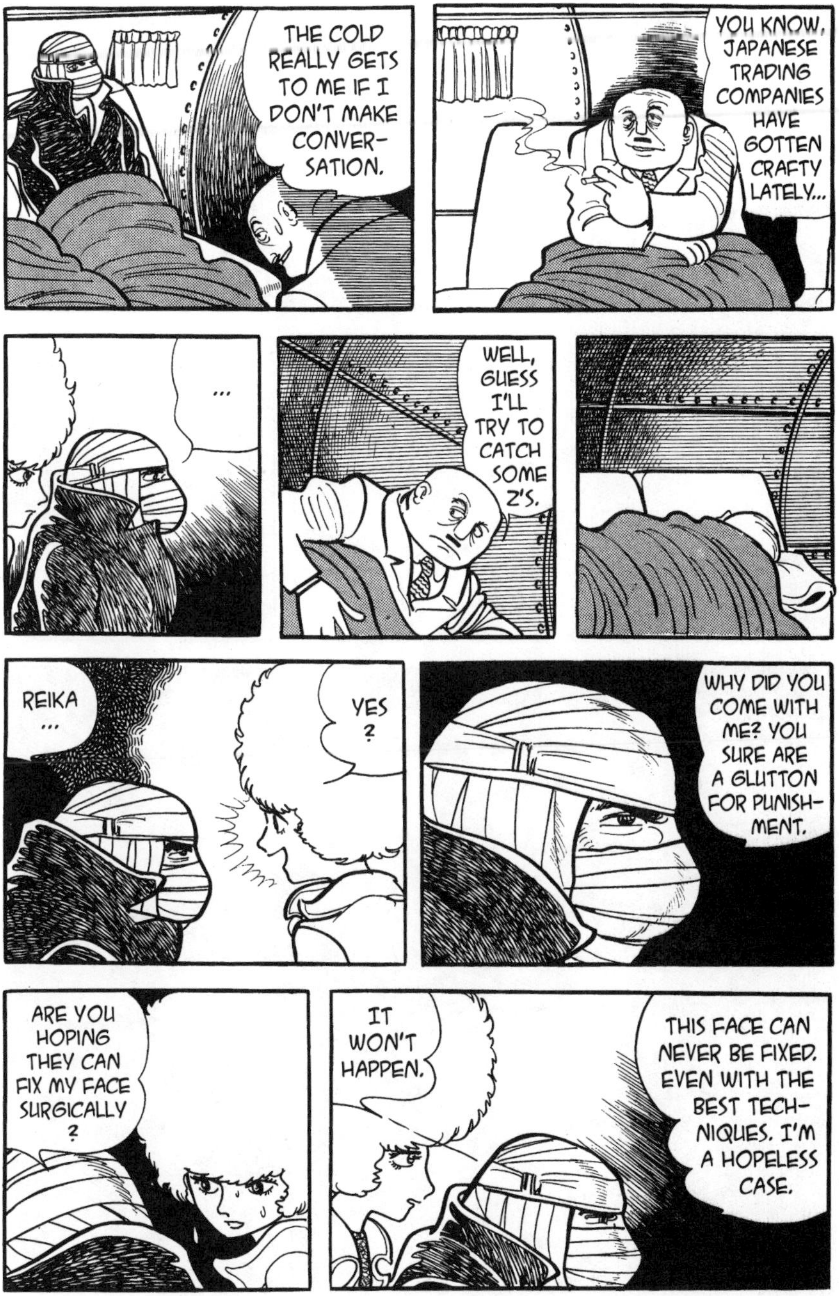
THE COLD REALLY GETS TO ME IF I DON'T MAKE CONVER-SATION.
YOU KNOW, JAPANESE TRADING COMPANIES HAVE GOTTEN CRAFTY LATELY...
...
WELL, GUESS I'LL TRY TO CATCH SOME Z'S.
REIKA ...
YES ?
WHY DID YOU COME WITH ME? YOU SURE ARE A GLUTTON FOR PUNISH-MENT.
ARE YOU HOPING THEY CAN FIX MY FACE SURGICALLY ?
IT WON'T HAPPEN.
THIS FACE CAN NEVER BE FIXED. EVEN WITH THE BEST TECH-NIQUES. I'M A HOPELESS CASE.

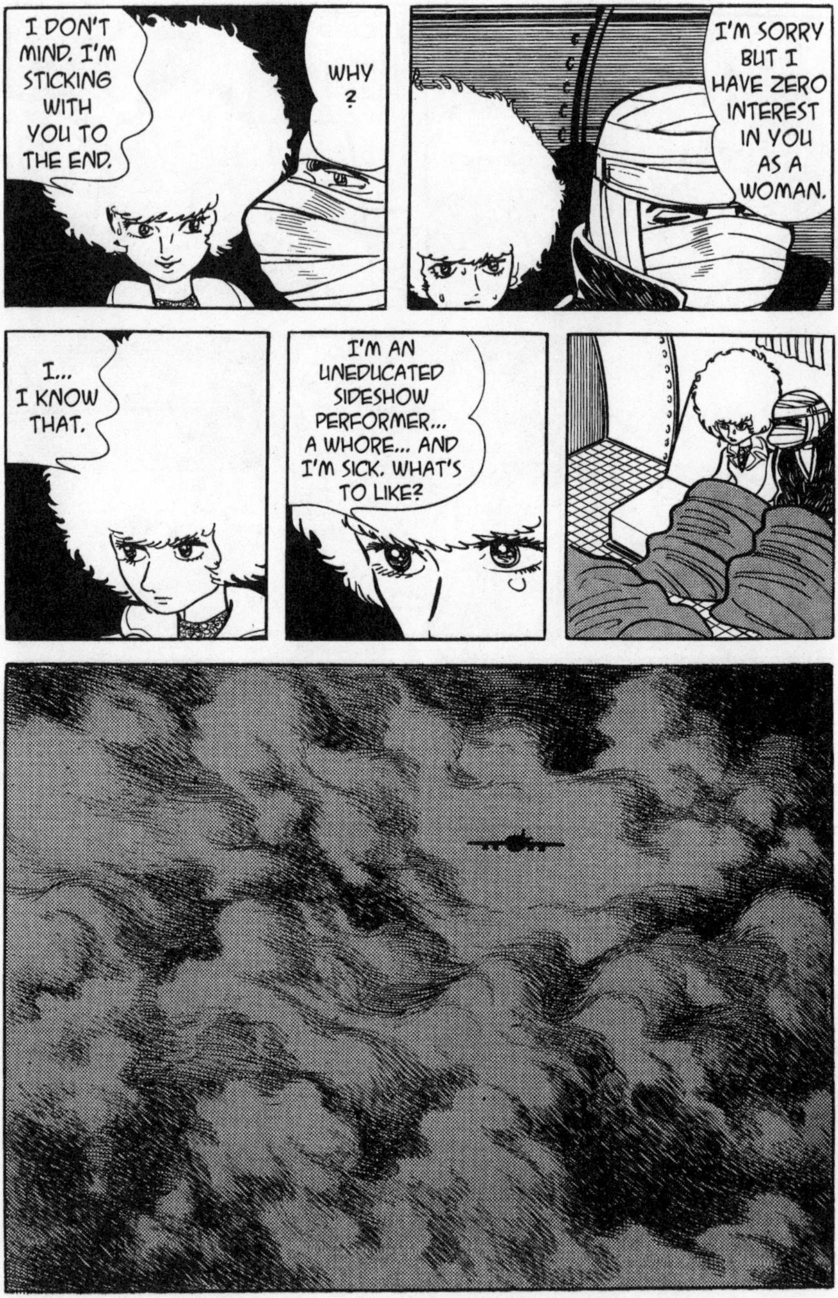
I DON'T MIND. I'M STICKING WITH YOU TO THE END.
WHY?
I'M SORRY BUT I HAVE ZERO INTEREST IN YOU AS A WOMAN.
I... I KNOW THAT.
I'M AN UNEDUCATED SIDESHOW PERFORMER... A WHORE... AND I'M SICK. WHAT'S TO LIKE?

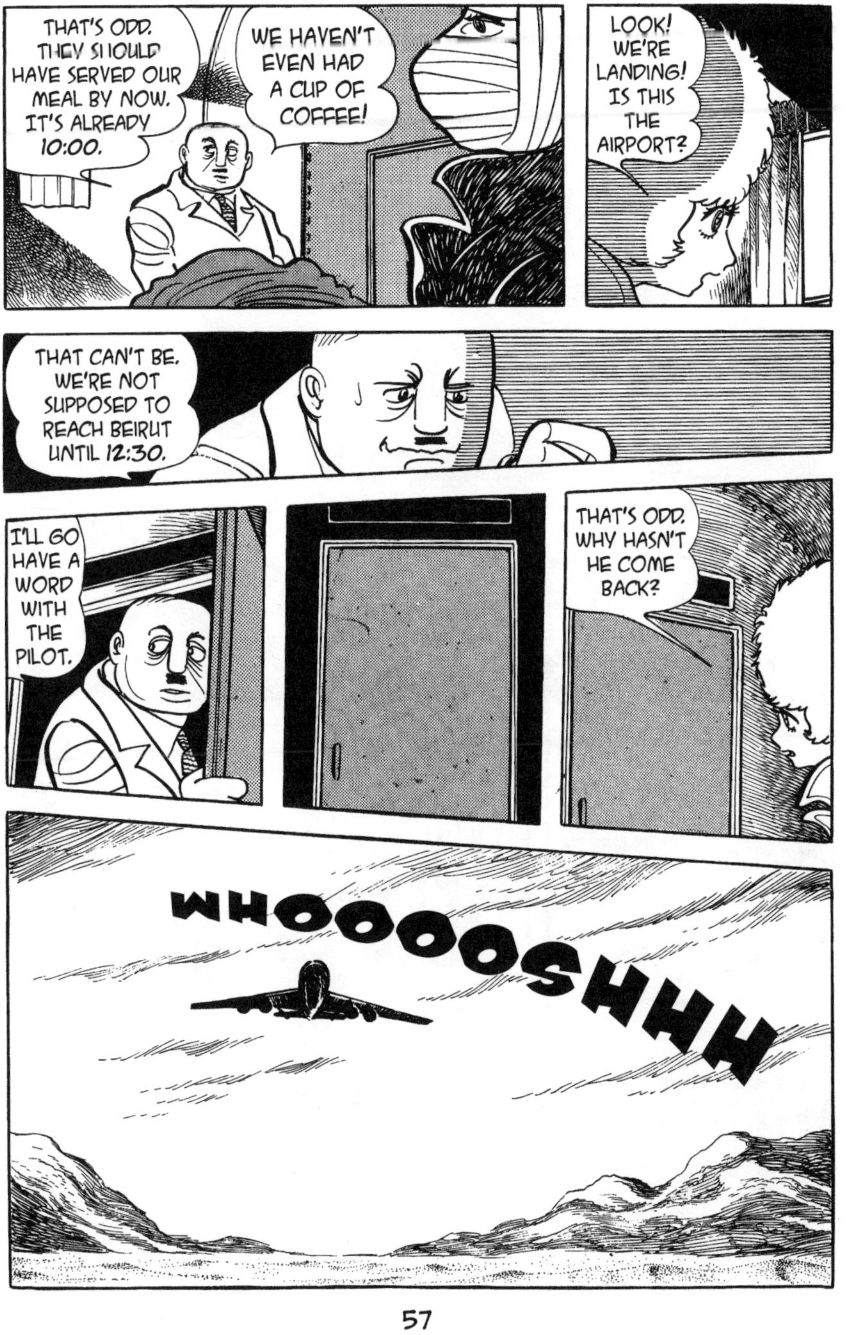
THAT'S ODD. THEY SHOULD HAVE SERVED OUR MEAL BY NOW. IT'S ALREADY 10:00.
WE HAVEN'T EVEN HAD A CUP OF COFFEE!
LOOK! WE'RE LANDING! IS THIS THE AIRPORT?
THAT CAN'T BE. WE'RE NOT SUPPOSED TO REACH BEIRUT UNTIL 12:30.
I'LL GO HAVE A WORD WITH THE PILOT.
THAT'S ODD. WHY HASN'T HE COME BACK?
WHOOOOOSHHH

HUSH

GET OUT!

WHAT'S GOING ON? WHERE ON EARTH ARE WE?

FRISK THEM.

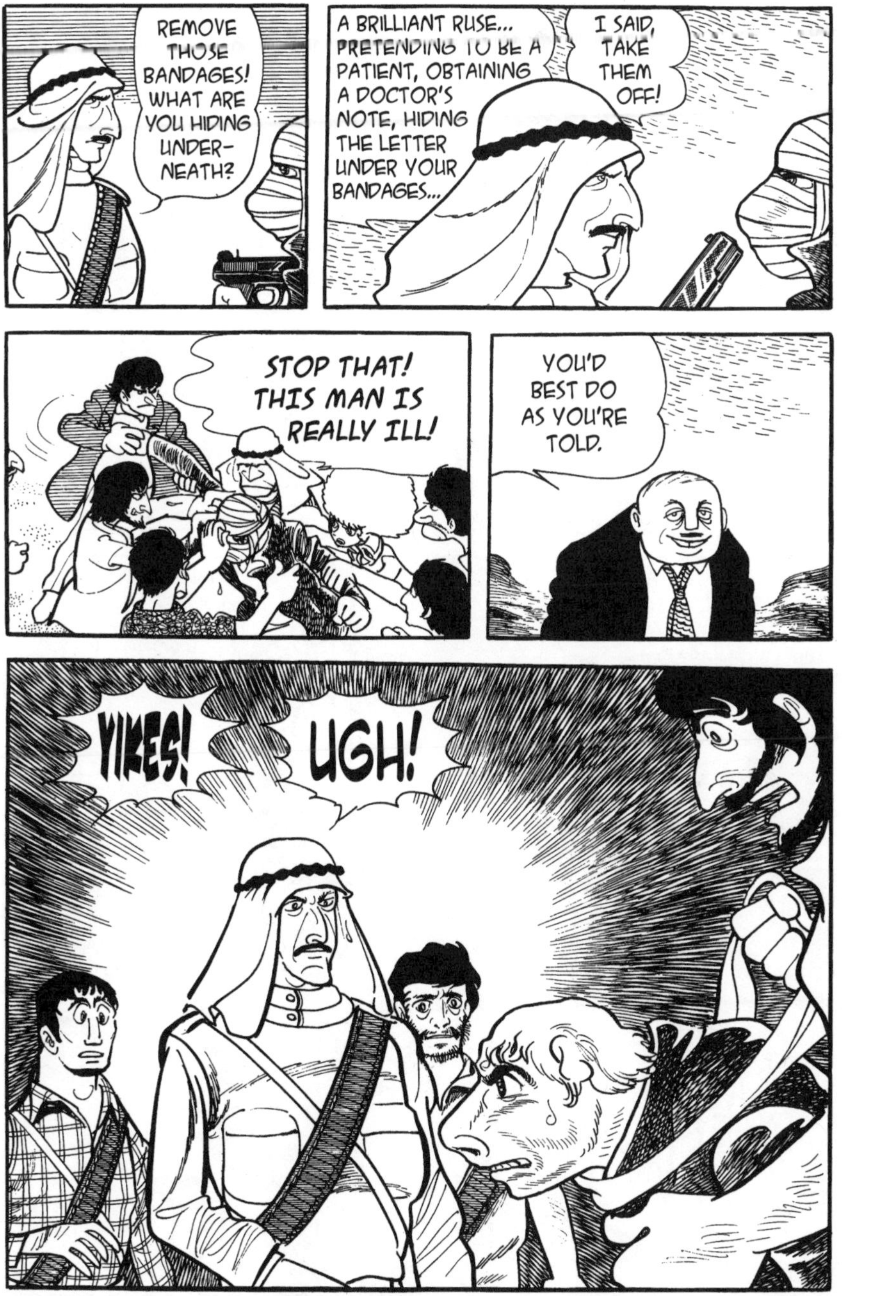
REMOVE THOSE BANDAGES! WHAT ARE YOU HIDING UNDER-NEATH?
A BRILLIANT RUSE... PRETENDING TO BE A PATIENT, OBTAINING A DOCTOR'S NOTE, HIDING THE LETTER UNDER YOUR BANDAGES...
I SAID, TAKE THEM OFF!
STOP THAT! THIS MAN IS REALLY ILL!
YOU'D BEST DO AS YOU'RE TOLD.
YIKES!
UGH!

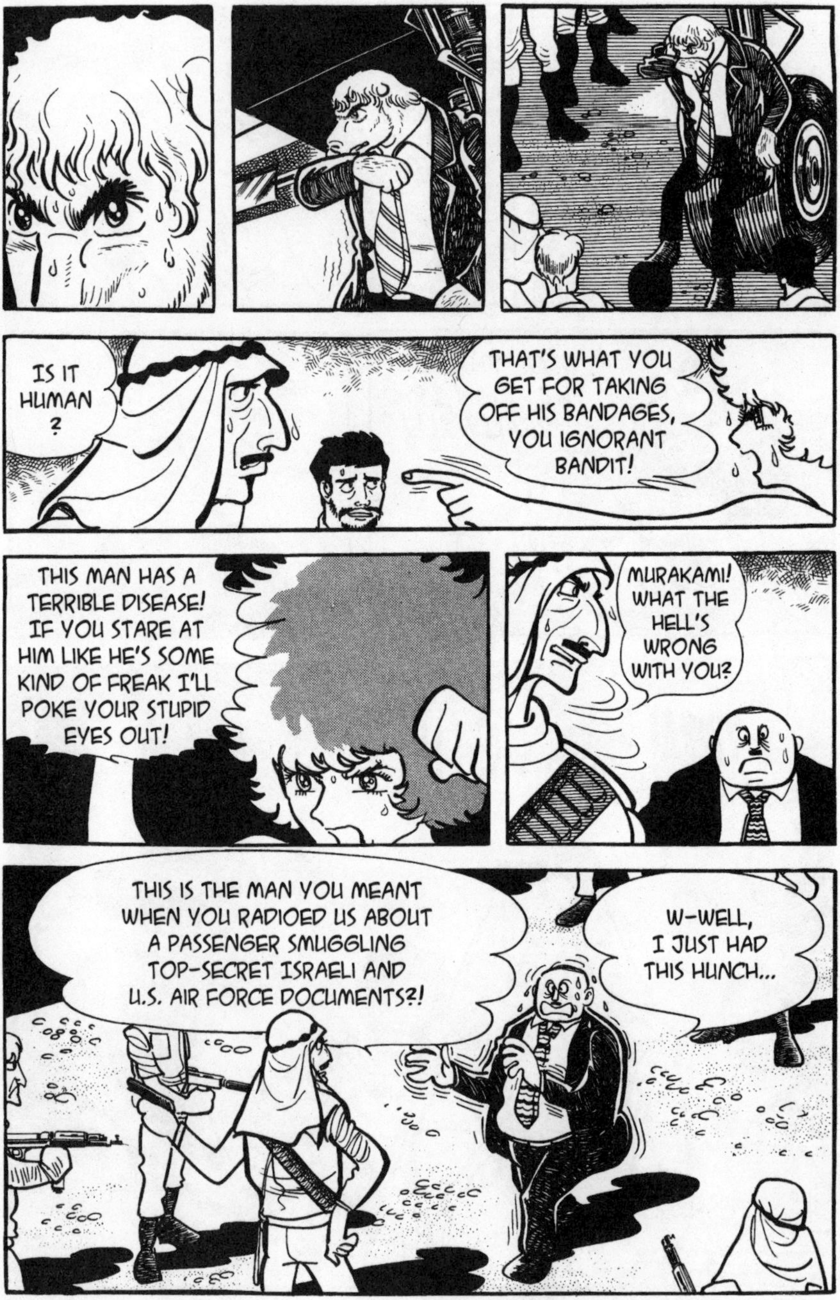
IS IT HUMAN ?
THAT'S WHAT YOU GET FOR TAKING OFF HIS BANDAGES, YOU IGNORANT BANDIT!
THIS MAN HAS A TERRIBLE DISEASE! IF YOU STARE AT HIM LIKE HE'S SOME KIND OF FREAK I'LL POKE YOUR STUPID EYES OUT!
MURAKAMI! WHAT THE HELL'S WRONG WITH YOU?
THIS IS THE MAN YOU MEANT WHEN YOU RADIOED US ABOUT A PASSENGER SMUGGLING TOP-SECRET ISRAELI AND U.S. AIR FORCE DOCUMENTS?!
W-WELL, I JUST HAD THIS HUNCH...

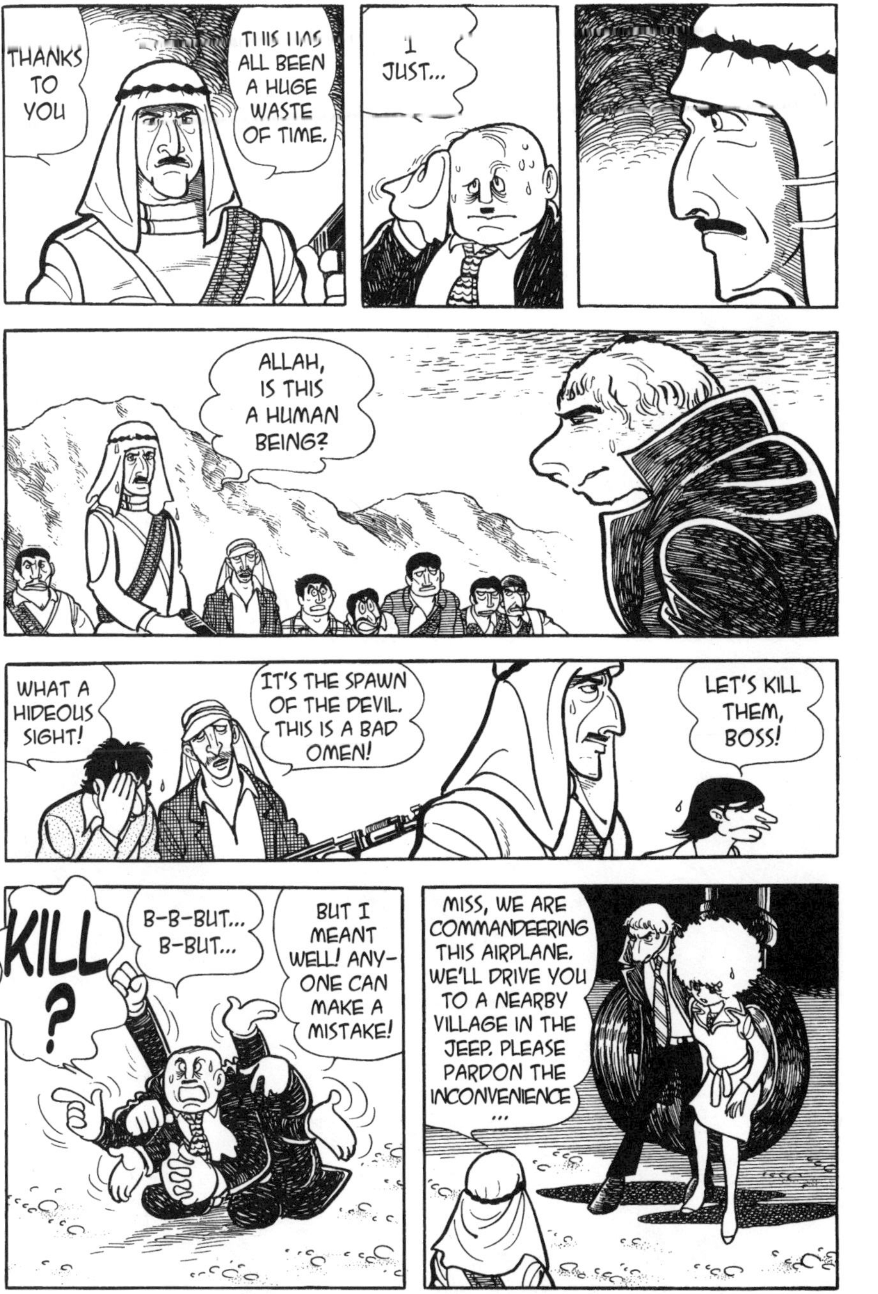
THANKS TO YOU
THIS HAS ALL BEEN A HUGE WASTE OF TIME.
I JUST...
ALLAH, IS THIS A HUMAN BEING?
WHAT A HIDEOUS SIGHT!
IT'S THE SPAWN OF THE DEVIL. THIS IS A BAD OMEN!
LET'S KILL THEM, BOSS!
KILL ?
B-B-BUT... B-BUT...
BUT I MEANT WELL! ANY-ONE CAN MAKE A MISTAKE!
MISS, WE ARE COMMANDEERING THIS AIRPLANE. WE'LL DRIVE YOU TO A NEARBY VILLAGE IN THE JEEP. PLEASE PARDON THE INCONVENIENCE ...

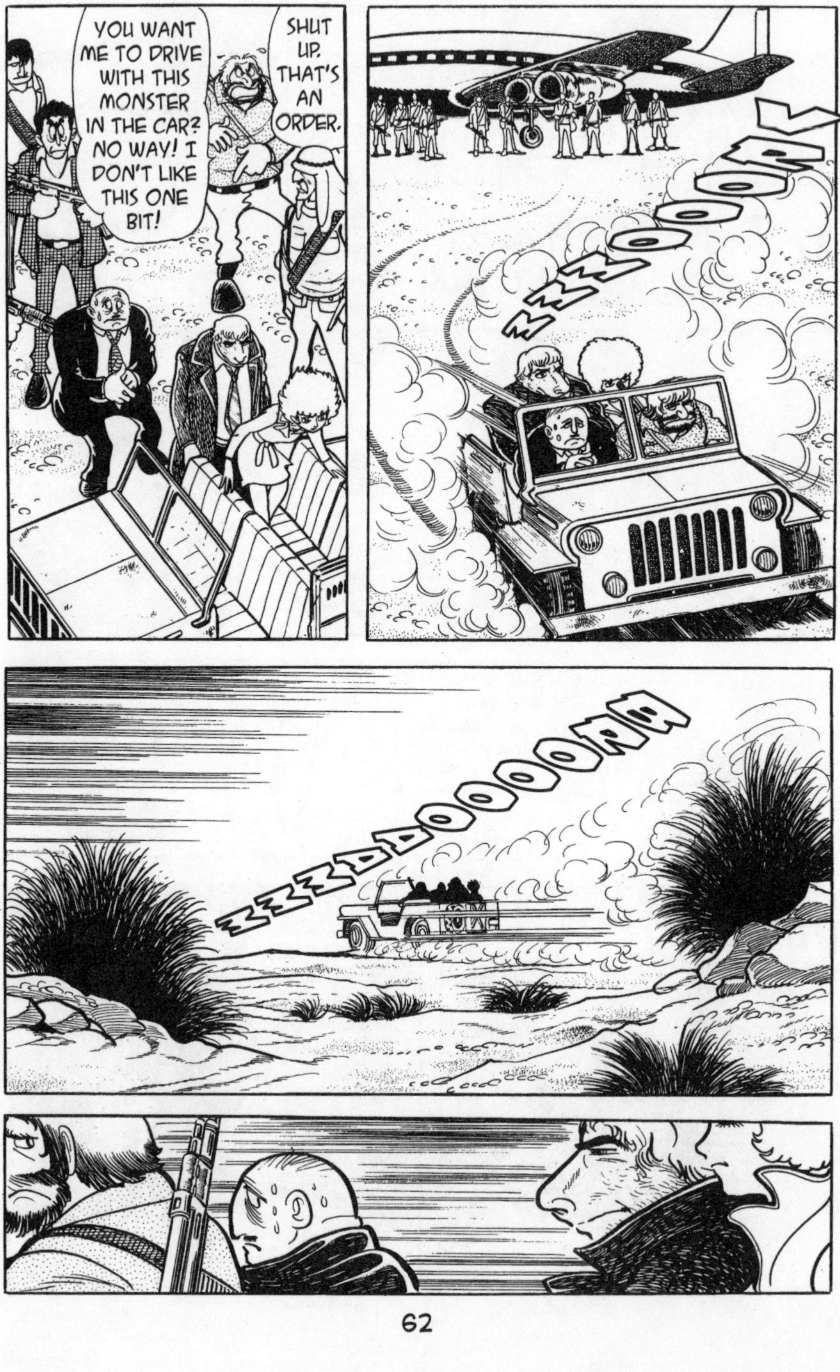
YOU WANT ME TO DRIVE WITH THIS MONSTER IN THE CAR? NO WAY! I DON'T LIKE THIS ONE BIT!
SHUT UP. THAT'S AN ORDER.
VROOOMMM

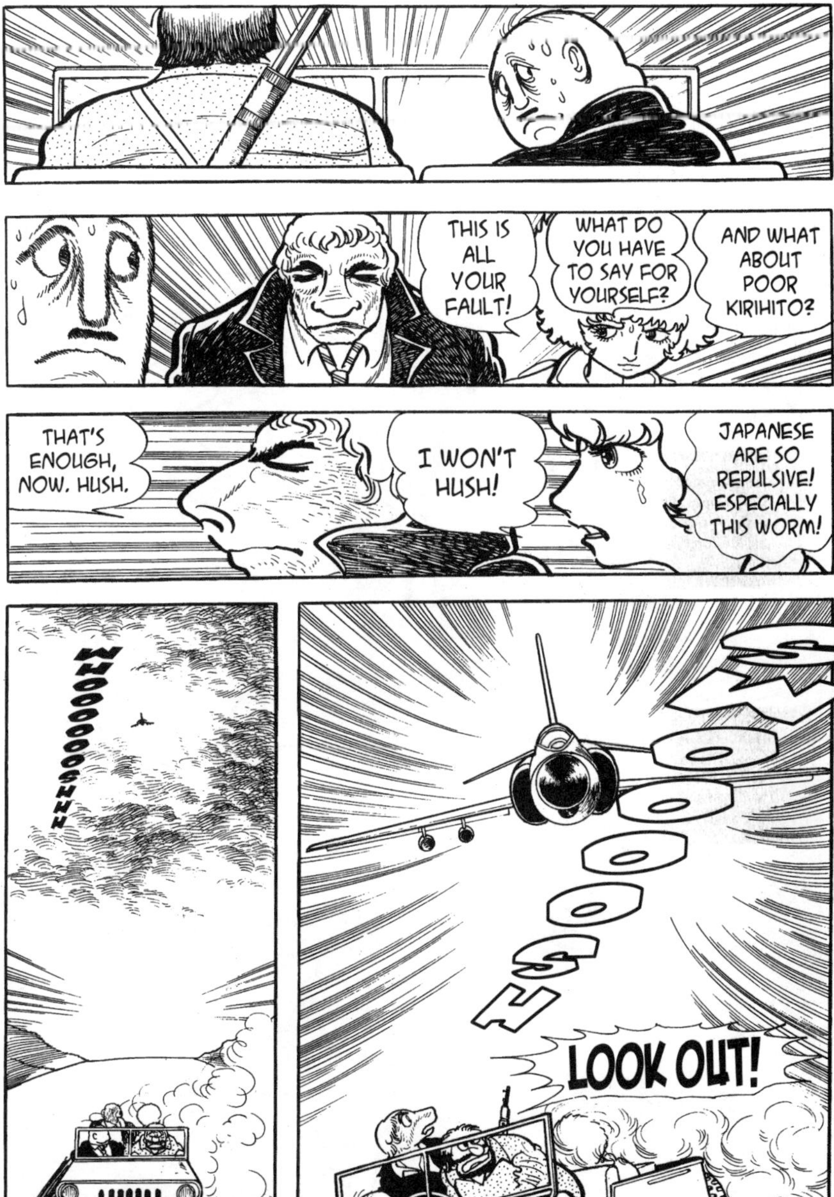
THIS IS ALL YOUR FAULT!
WHAT DO YOU HAVE TO SAY FOR YOURSELF?
AND WHAT ABOUT POOR KIRIHITO?
THAT'S ENOUGH, NOW. HUSH.
I WON'T HUSH!
JAPANESE ARE SO REPULSIVE! ESPECIALLY THIS WORM!
WHOOOOOOSHHH
SWOOOOSH
LOOK OUT!

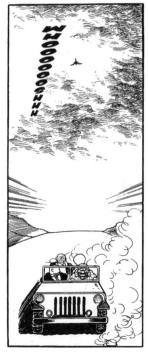

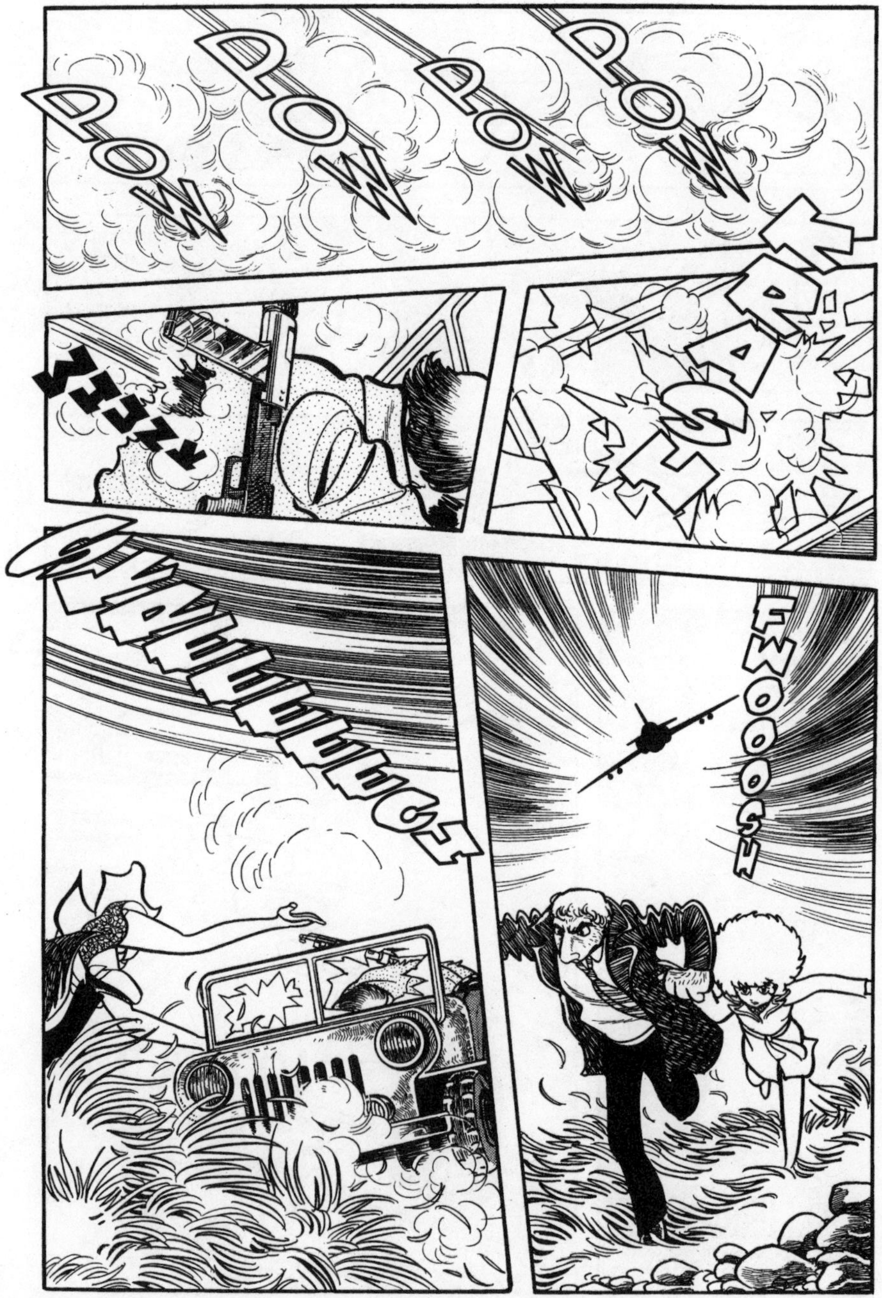
POW POW POW POW
KRASH
FWOOOOSH

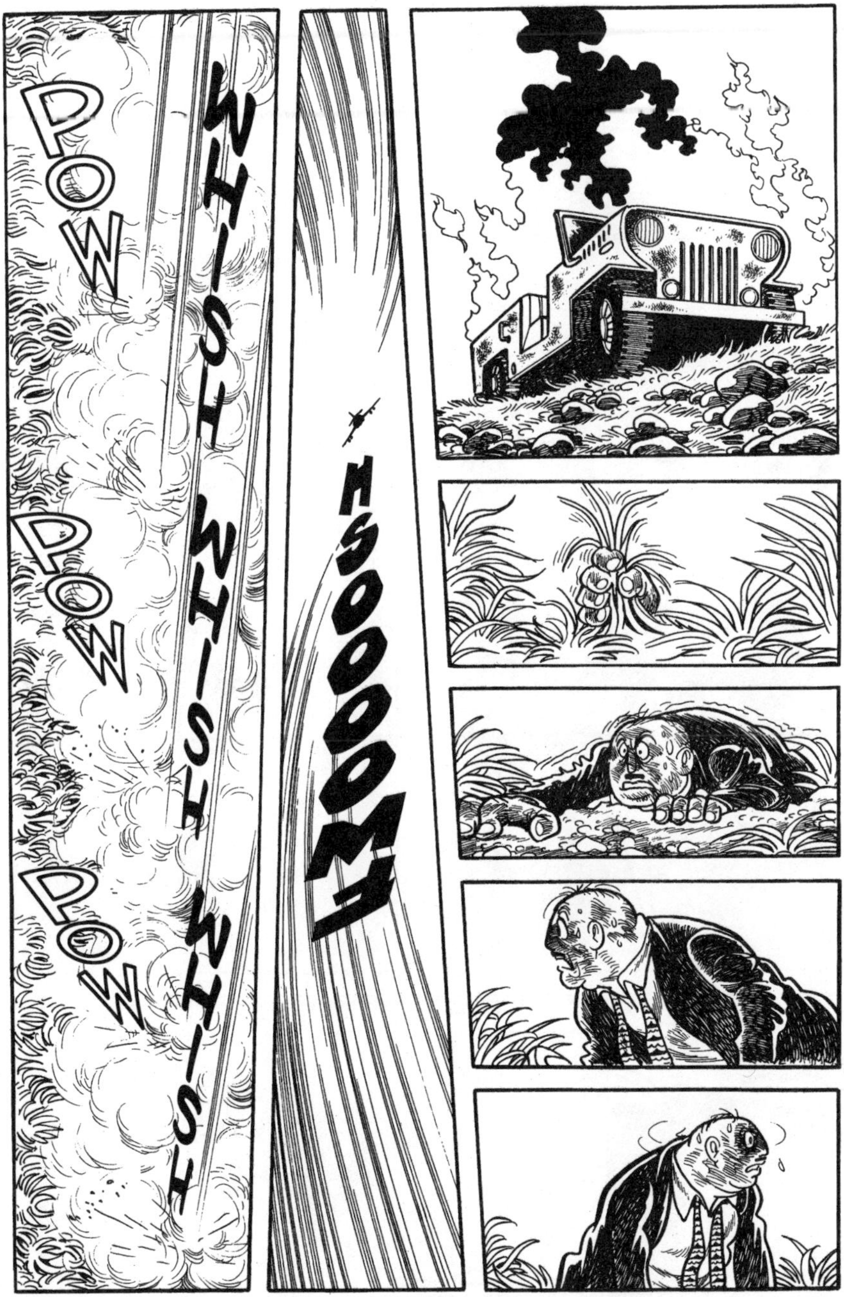
WOOOOSH
POW POW POW
WHISH WHISH WHISH

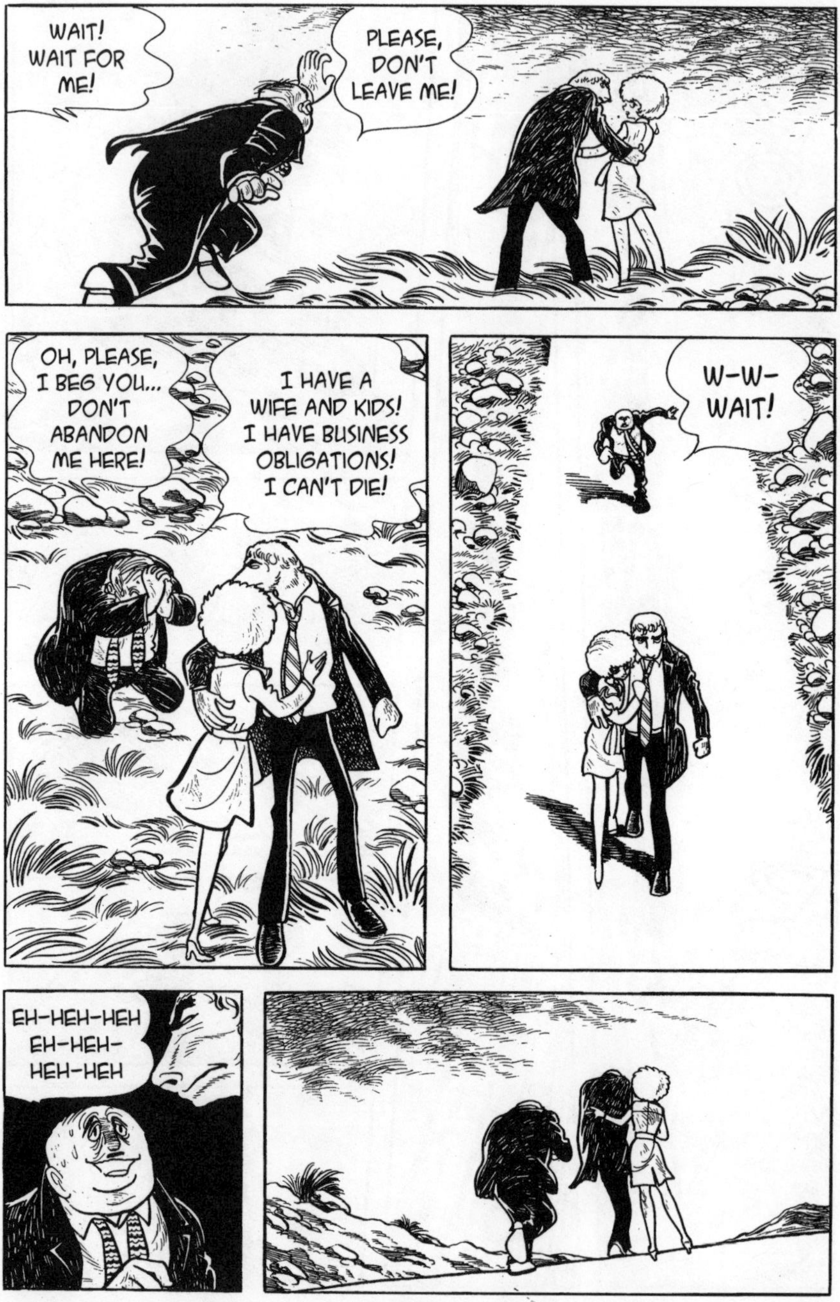
WAIT! WAIT FOR ME!
PLEASE, DON'T LEAVE ME!
OH, PLEASE, I BEG YOU... DON'T ABANDON ME HERE!
I HAVE A WIFE AND KIDS! I HAVE BUSINESS OBLIGATIONS! I CAN'T DIE!
W-W-WAIT!
EH-HEH-HEH EH-HEH-HEH-HEH

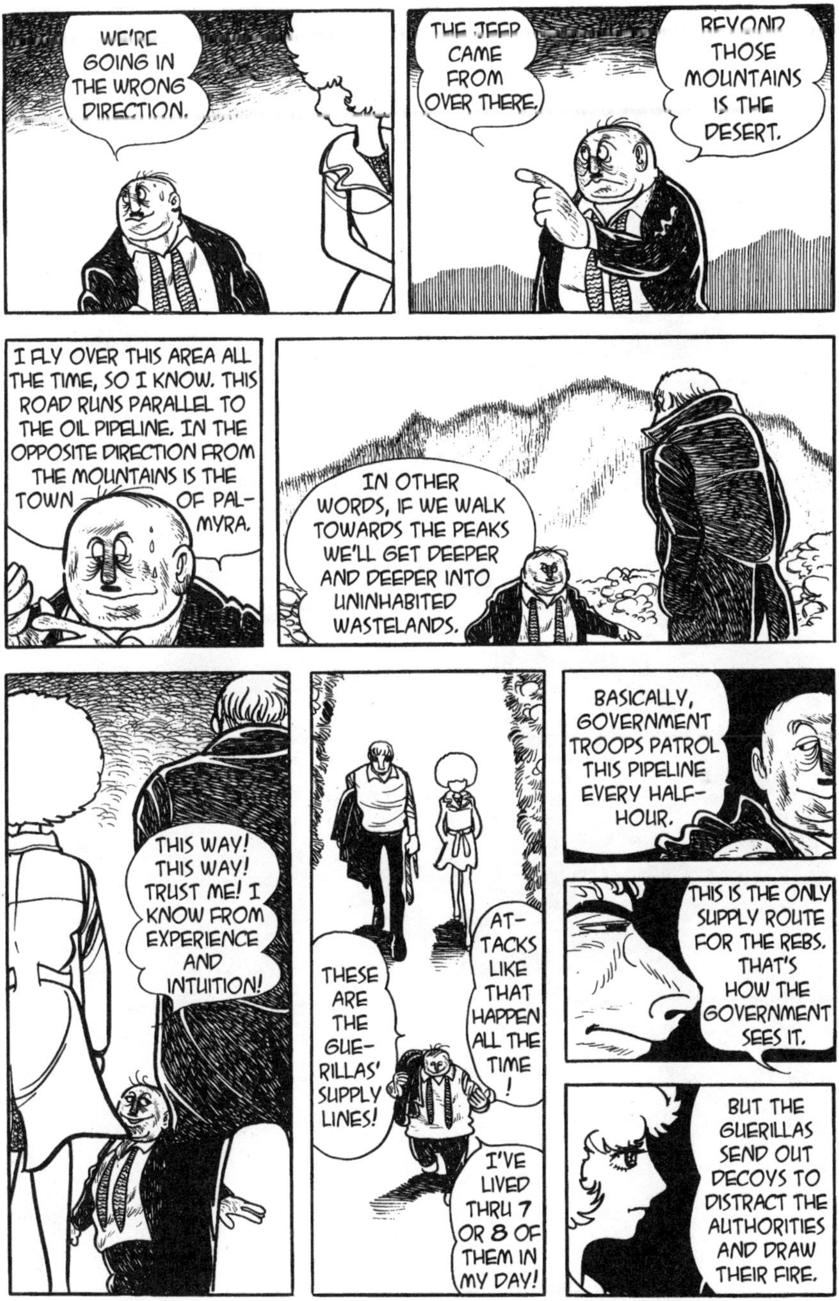
WE'RE GOING IN THE WRONG DIRECTION.
THE JEEP CAME FROM OVER THERE.
BEYOND THOSE MOUNTAINS IS THE DESERT.
I FLY OVER THIS AREA ALL THE TIME, SO I KNOW. THIS ROAD RUNS PARALLEL TO THE OIL PIPELINE. IN THE OPPOSITE DIRECTION FROM THE MOUNTAINS IS THE TOWN OF PAL-MYRA.
IN OTHER WORDS, IF WE WALK TOWARDS THE PEAKS WE'LL GET DEEPER AND DEEPER INTO UNINHABITED WASTELANDS.
THIS WAY! THIS WAY! TRUST ME! I KNOW FROM EXPERIENCE AND INTUITION!
THESE ARE THE GUE-RILLAS' SUPPLY LINES!
AT-TACKS LIKE THAT HAPPEN ALL THE TIME!
I'VE LIVED THRU 7 OR 8 OF THEM IN MY DAY!
BASICALLY, GOVERNMENT TROOPS PATROL THIS PIPELINE EVERY HALF-HOUR.
THIS IS THE ONLY SUPPLY ROUTE FOR THE REBS. THAT'S HOW THE GOVERNMENT SEES IT.
BUT THE GUERILLAS SEND OUT DECOYS TO DISTRACT THE AUTHORITIES AND DRAW THEIR FIRE.

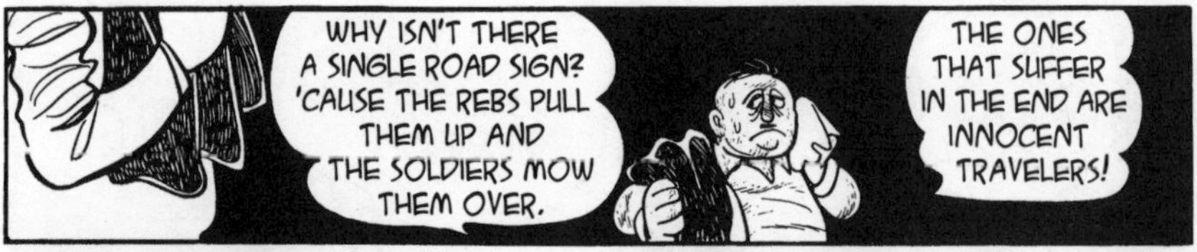
WHY ISN'T THERE A SINGLE ROAD SIGN? 'CAUSE THE REBS PULL THEM UP AND THE SOLDIERS MOW THEM OVER.
THE ONES THAT SUFFER IN THE END ARE INNOCENT TRAVELERS!

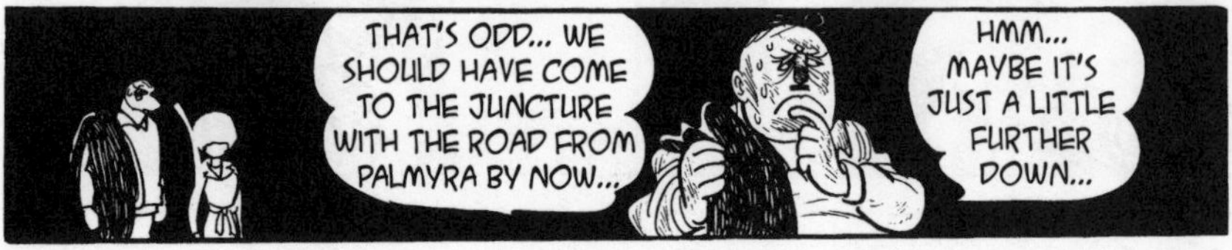
THAT'S ODD... WE SHOULD HAVE COME TO THE JUNCTURE WITH THE ROAD FROM PALMYRA BY NOW...
HMM... MAYBE IT'S JUST A LITTLE FURTHER DOWN...

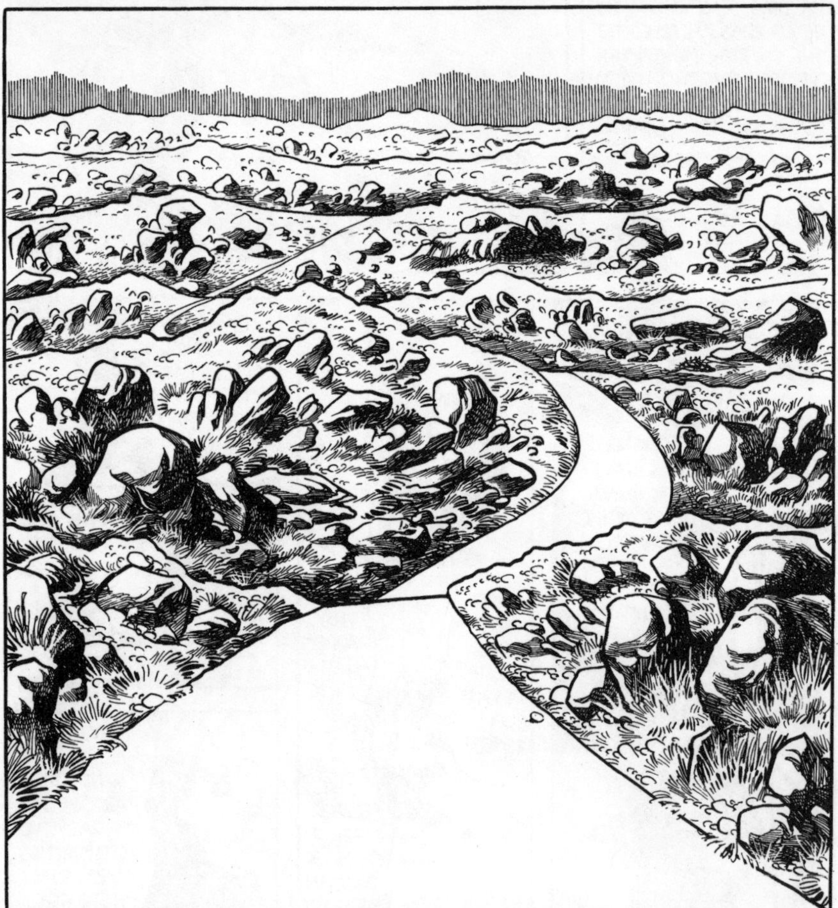

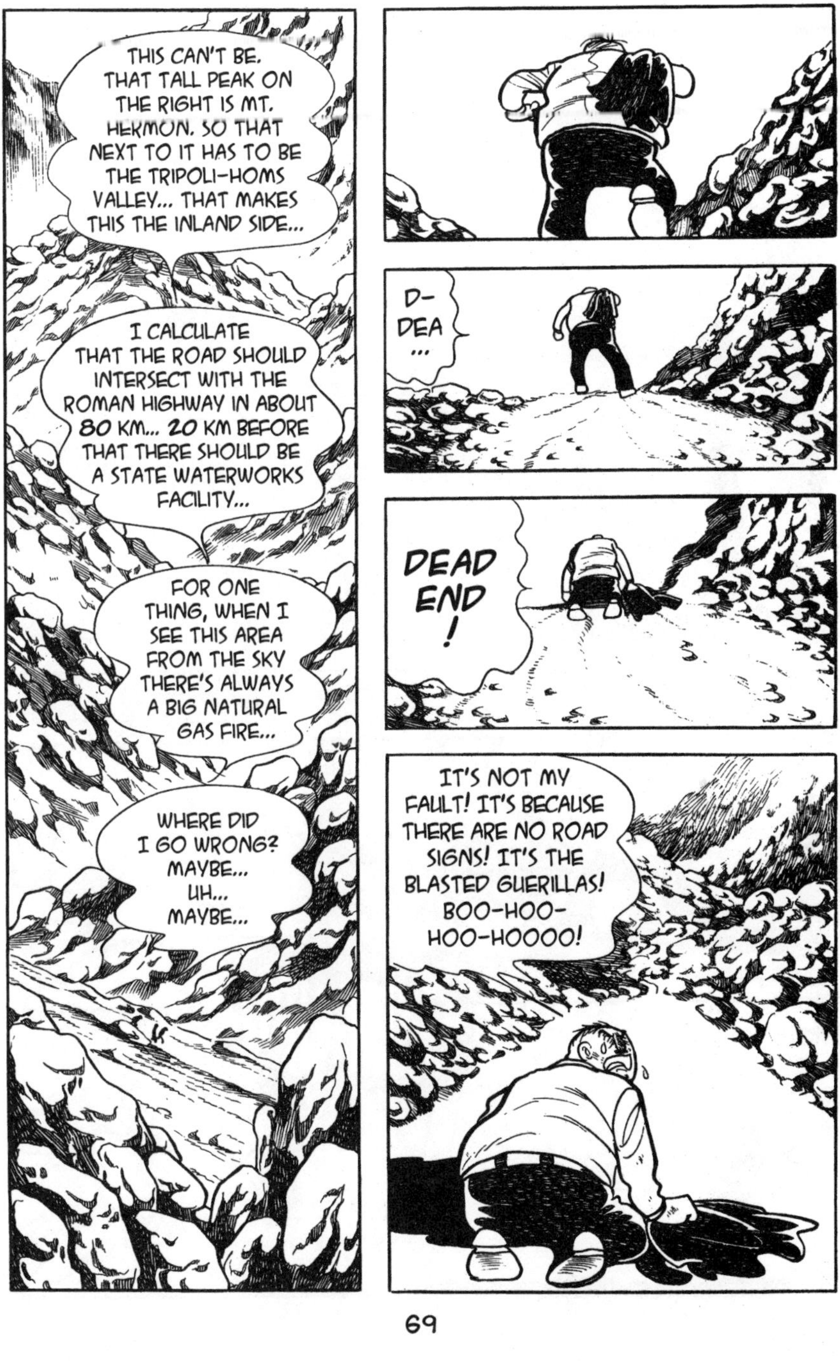
THIS CAN'T BE. THAT TALL PEAK ON THE RIGHT IS MT. HERMON. SO THAT NEXT TO IT HAS TO BE THE TRIPOLI-HOMS VALLEY... THAT MAKES THIS THE INLAND SIDE...
I CALCULATE THAT THE ROAD SHOULD INTERSECT WITH THE ROMAN HIGHWAY IN ABOUT 80 KM... 20 KM BEFORE THAT THERE SHOULD BE A STATE WATERWORKS FACILITY...
FOR ONE THING, WHEN I SEE THIS AREA FROM THE SKY THERE'S ALWAYS A BIG NATURAL GAS FIRE...
WHERE DID I GO WRONG? MAYBE... UH... MAYBE...
D-DEA...
DEAD END!
IT'S NOT MY FAULT! IT'S BECAUSE THERE ARE NO ROAD SIGNS! IT'S THE BLASTED GUERILLAS! BOO-HOO-HOO-HOOOO!

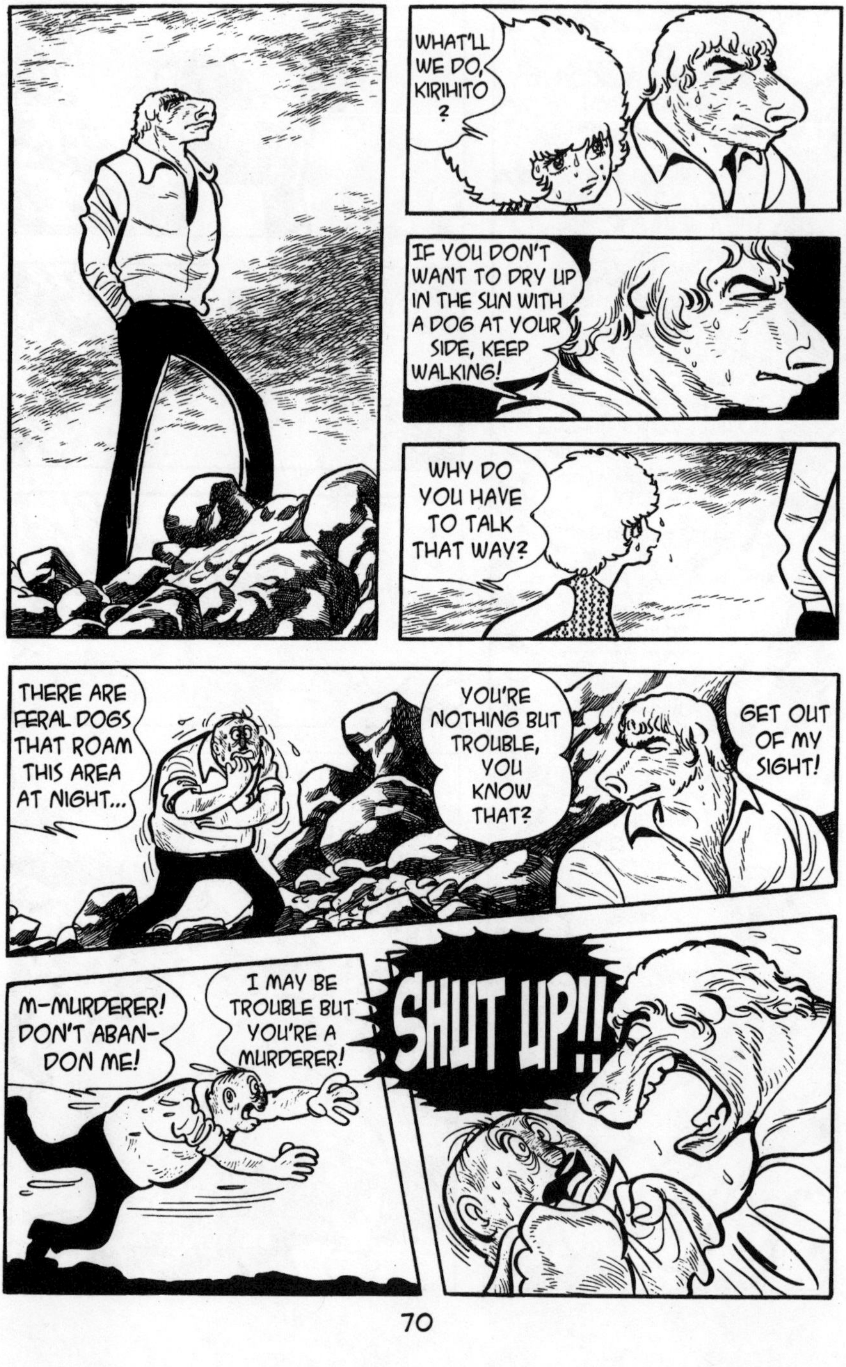
WHAT'LL WE DO, KIRIHITO ?
IF YOU DON'T WANT TO DRY UP IN THE SUN WITH A DOG AT YOUR SIDE, KEEP WALKING!
WHY DO YOU HAVE TO TALK THAT WAY?
THERE ARE FERAL DOGS THAT ROAM THIS AREA AT NIGHT...
YOU'RE NOTHING BUT TROUBLE, YOU KNOW THAT?
GET OUT OF MY SIGHT!
M-MURDERER! DON'T ABAN-DON ME!
I MAY BE TROUBLE BUT YOU'RE A MURDERER!
SHUT UP!!

STOP!

STOP THAT! YOU'VE REALLY CHANGED! YOU'RE LIKE A WILD ANIMAL!

THAT'S RIGHT! GO AHEAD AND SAY IT!

OR DOES THIS FACE MAKE YOU BITE YOUR TONGUE?

I'M AN ANIMAL! A DOG! I BELONG WITH A BITCH, NOT WITH THE LIKES OF YOU!

PLEASE, NOW, BE REASON-ABLE!

WHA..!

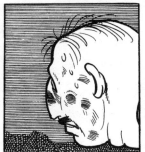

A LIGHT !

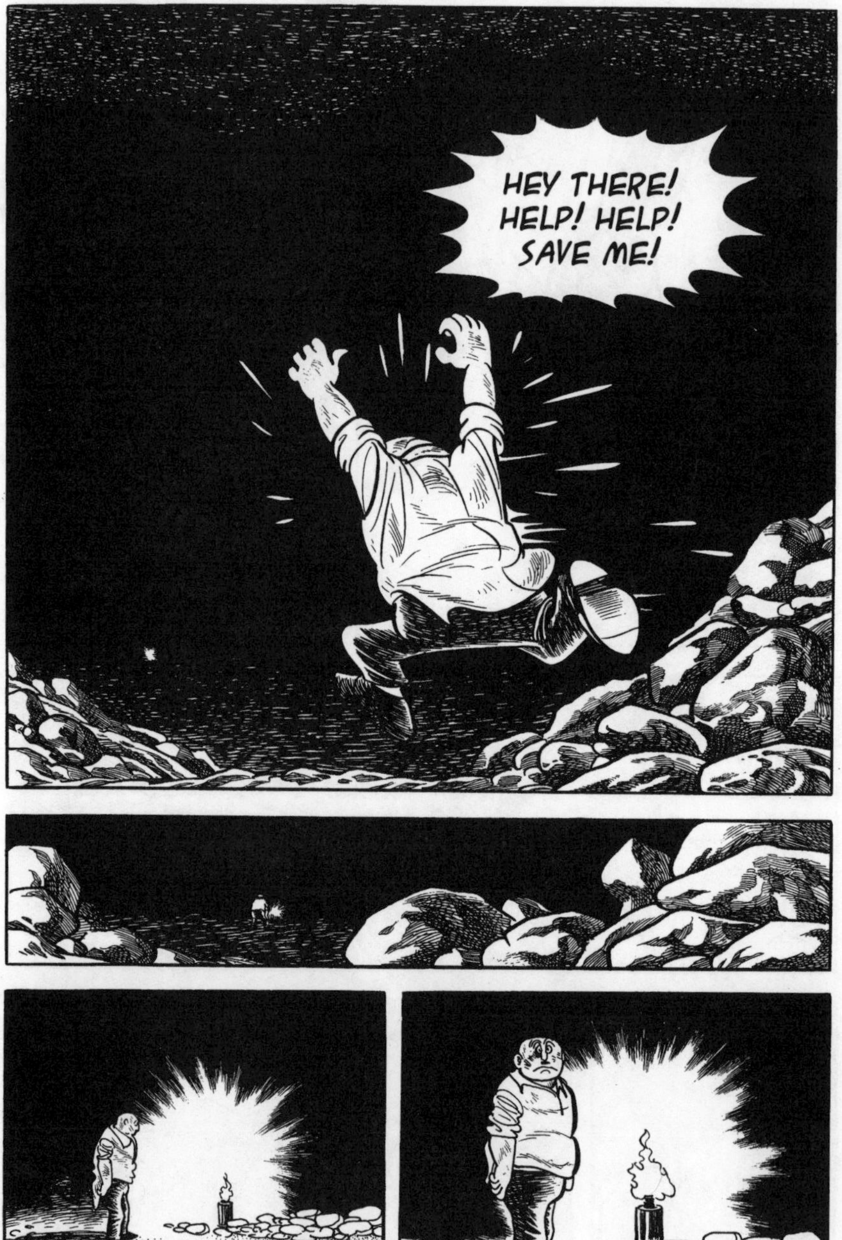
HEY THERE! HELP! HELP! SAVE ME!

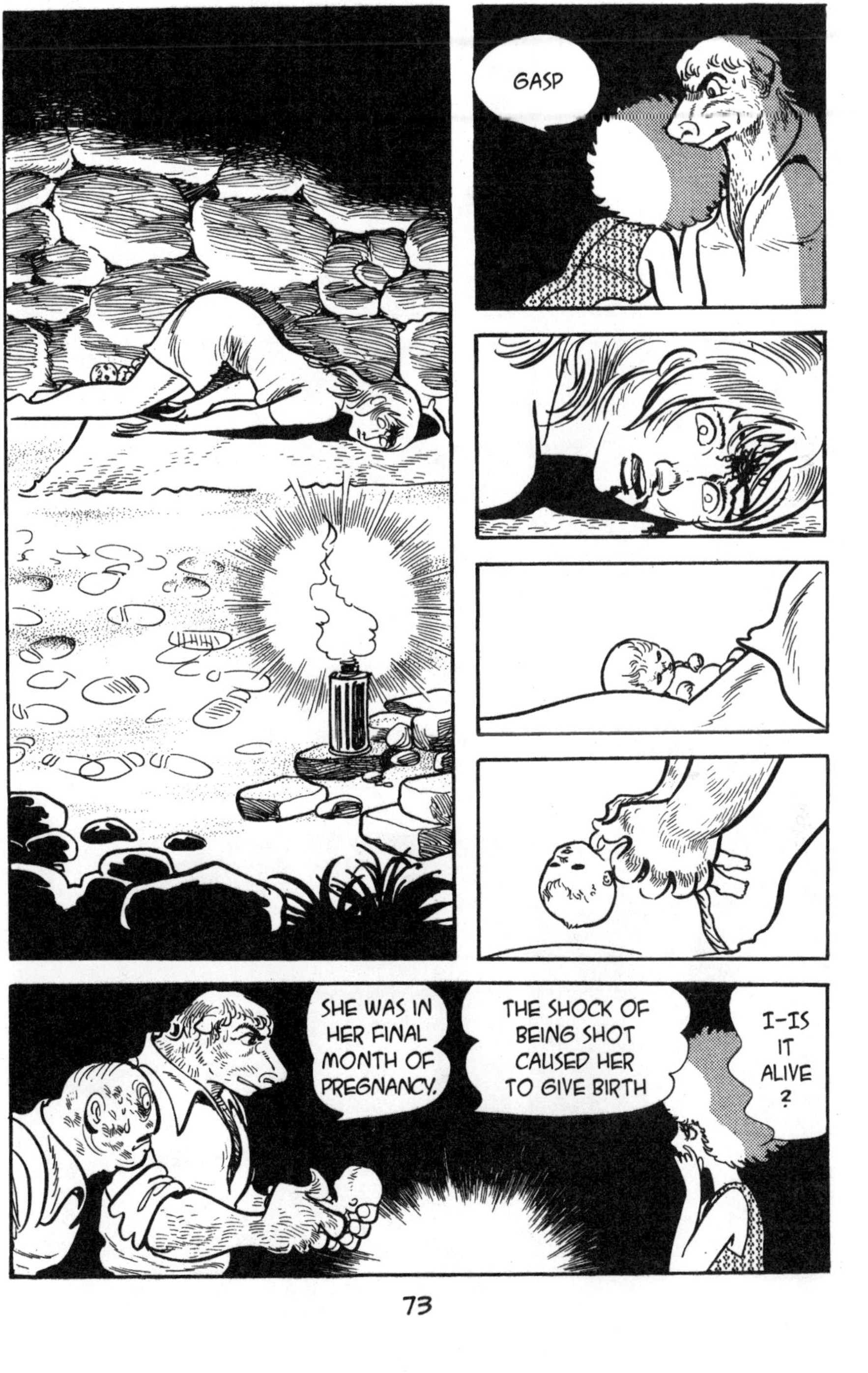
GASP
SHE WAS IN HER FINAL MONTH OF PREGNANCY.
THE SHOCK OF BEING SHOT CAUSED HER TO GIVE BIRTH
I-IS IT ALIVE ?

IT'S DEA...

NO! IT'S ALIVE!

SHE'S BEEN DEAD AROUND THREE DAYS. SOMEHOW THE BABY'S MANAGED TO STAY ALIVE.

HE'S LIMP WITH HUNGER. HE'S DYING.

WOULD SHE HAVE ANY BREAST MILK?

HE CAN'T DRINK THAT! SHE'S STARTING TO ROT!

WELL, ARE YOU SUGGESTING WE LEAVE HIM TO DIE?

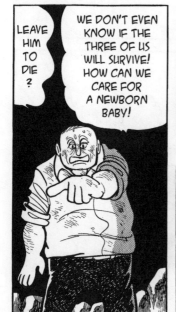

LEAVE HIM TO DIE?

WE DON'T EVEN KNOW IF THE THREE OF US WILL SURVIVE! HOW CAN WE CARE FOR A NEWBORN BABY!

SO, YOU WANT TO JUST SIT AND WATCH

AS THIS BABY GETS AS WEAK AS A KITTEN AND SLIPS INTO DEATH!

NO, I DON'T INTEND TO WATCH! I'M GETTING OUT OF HERE!

YOU PUT THAT BABY DOWN AND DO THE SAME!

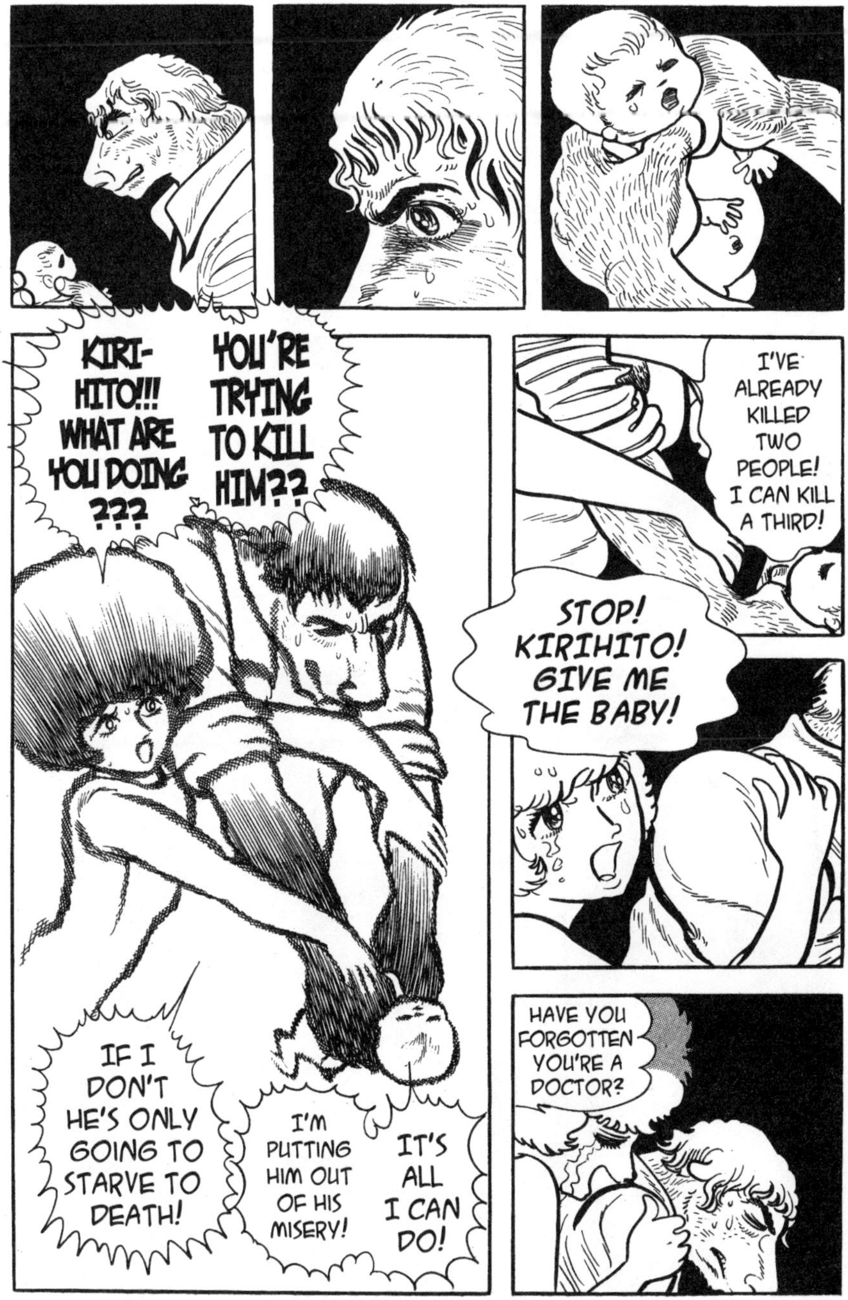
KIRI-HITO!!! WHAT ARE YOU DOING???
YOU'RE TRYING TO KILL HIM??
IF I DON'T HE'S ONLY GOING TO STARVE TO DEATH!
I'M PUTTING HIM OUT OF HIS MISERY!
IT'S ALL I CAN DO!
I'VE ALREADY KILLED TWO PEOPLE! I CAN KILL A THIRD!
STOP! KIRIHITO! GIVE ME THE BABY!
HAVE YOU FORGOTTEN YOU'RE A DOCTOR?

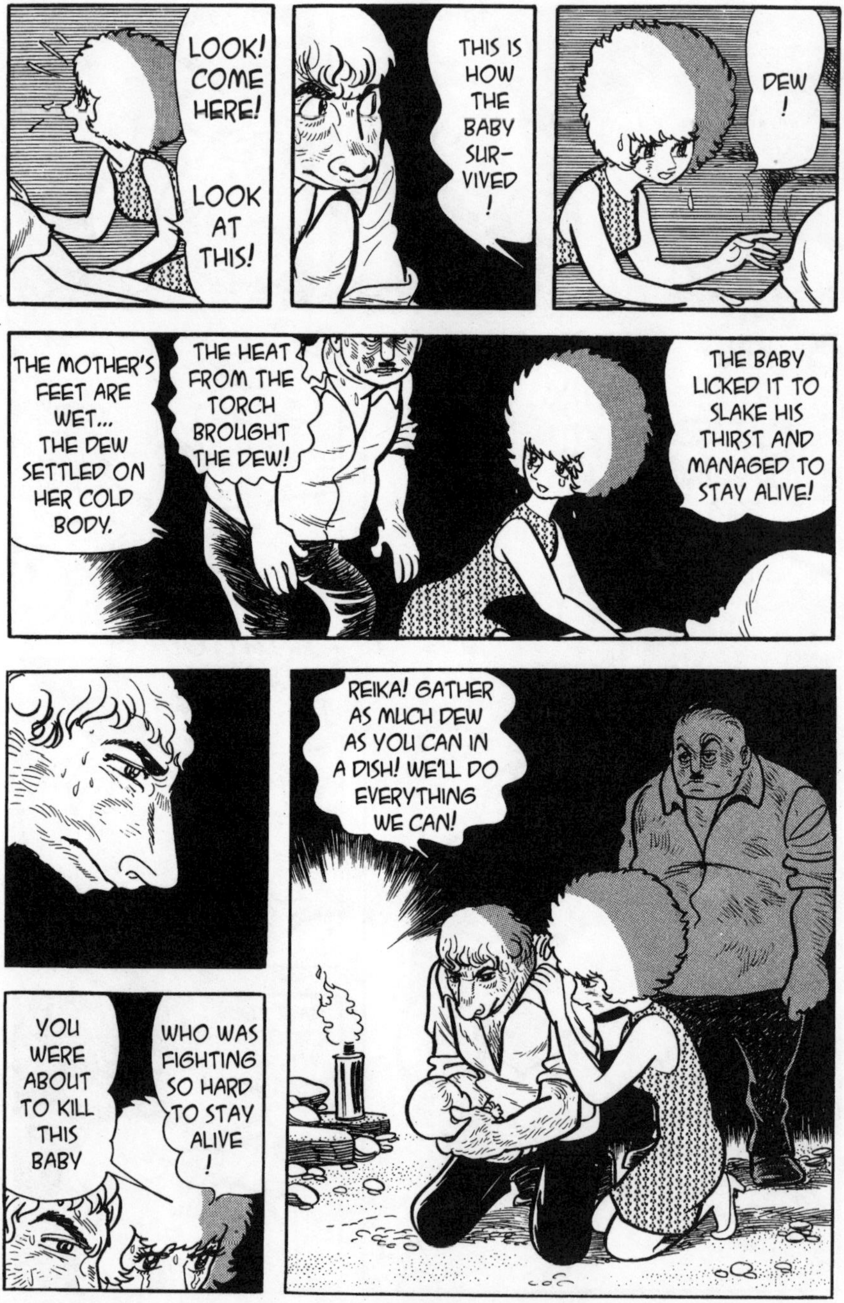
LOOK! COME HERE!
LOOK AT THIS!
THIS IS HOW THE BABY SUR-VIVED!
DEW!
THE MOTHER'S FEET ARE WET... THE DEW SETTLED ON HER COLD BODY.
THE HEAT FROM THE TORCH BROUGHT THE DEW!
THE BABY LICKED IT TO SLAKE HIS THIRST AND MANAGED TO STAY ALIVE!
YOU WERE ABOUT TO KILL THIS BABY
WHO WAS FIGHTING SO HARD TO STAY ALIVE!
REIKA! GATHER AS MUCH DEW AS YOU CAN IN A DISH! WE'LL DO EVERYTHING WE CAN!

CHAPTER 13

AT THE BAZAAR

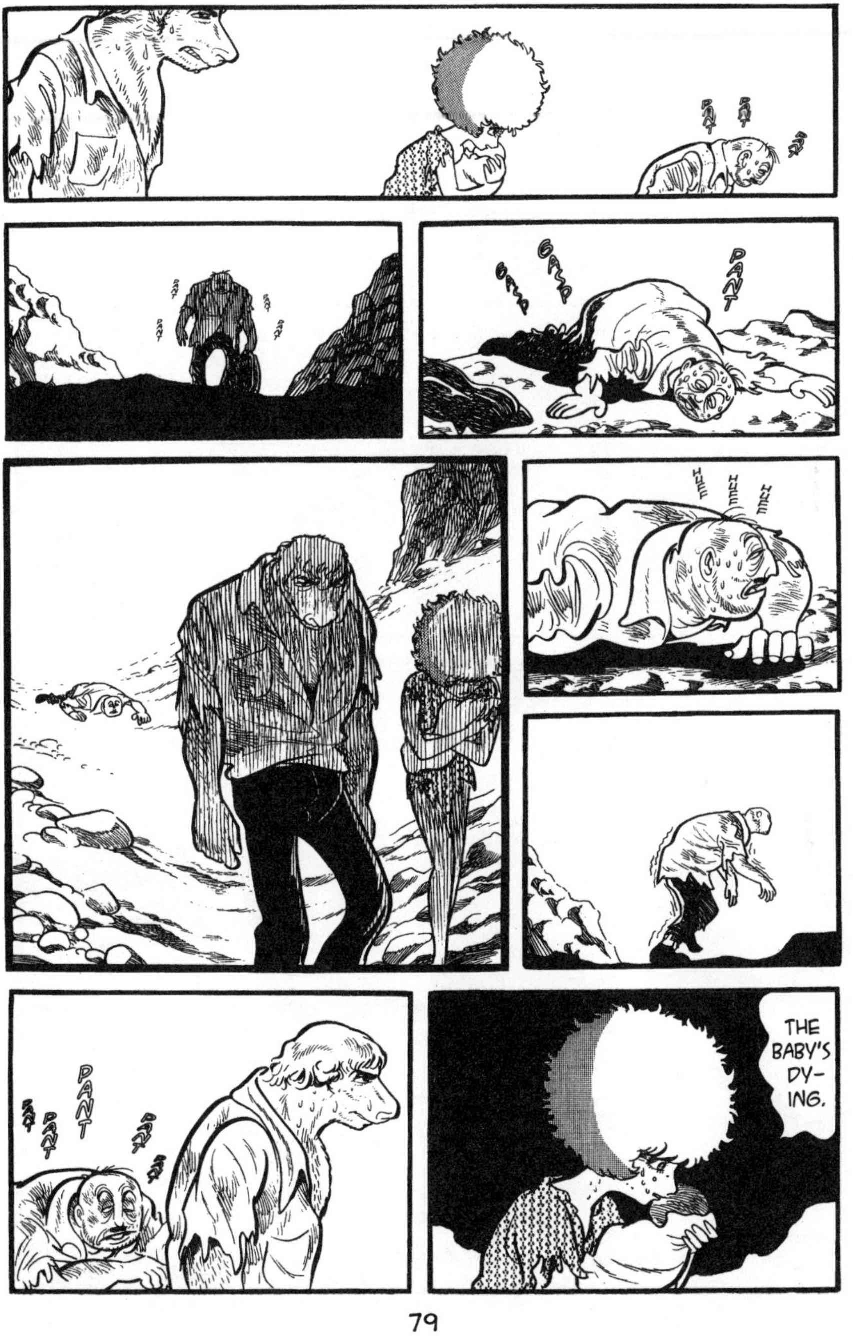
PANT
PANT
PANT
PANT
GASP
GASP
HUFF
HUFF
HUFF
THE BABY'S DY-ING.
PANT
PANT
PANT
PANT

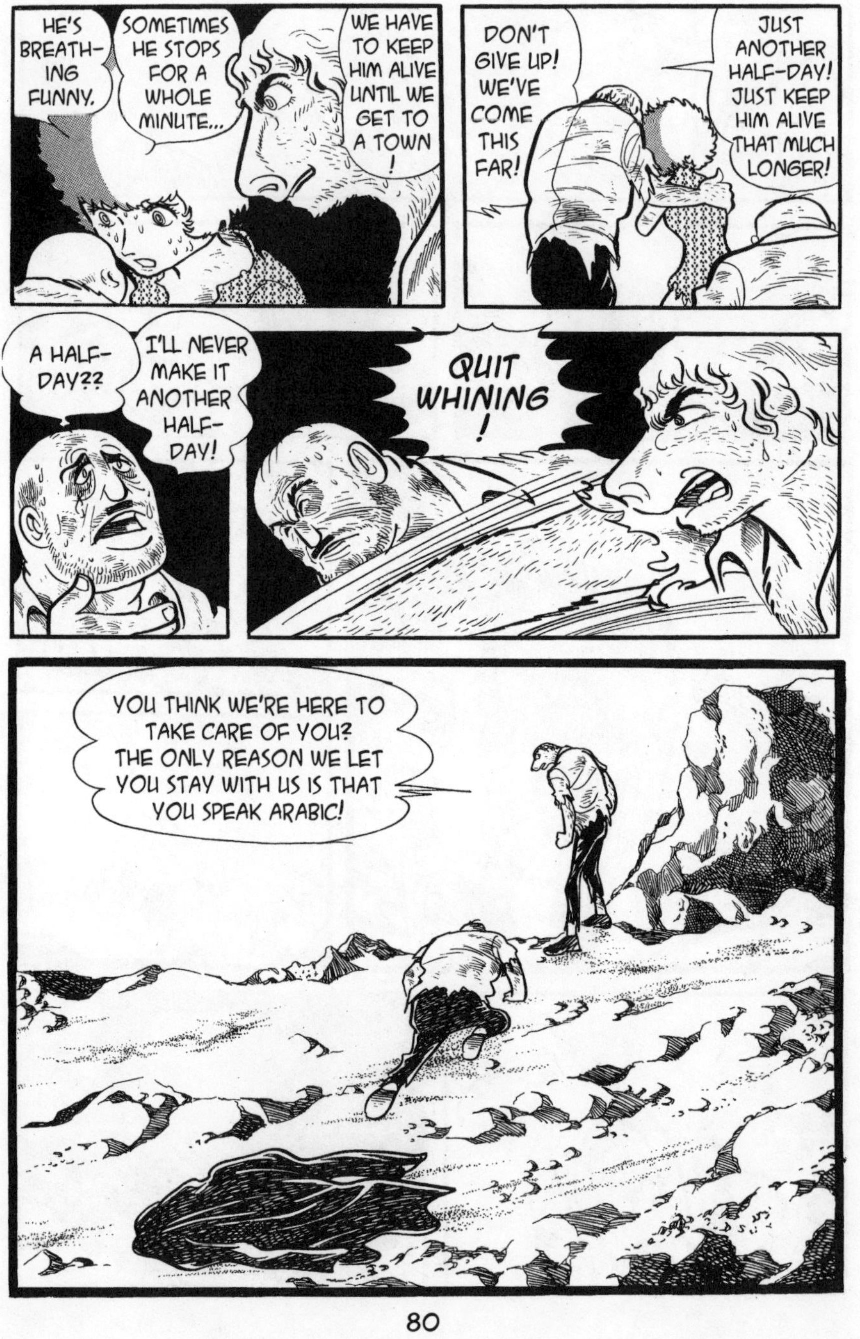
HE'S BREATHING FUNNY.
SOMETIMES HE STOPS FOR A WHOLE MINUTE...
WE HAVE TO KEEP HIM ALIVE UNTIL WE GET TO A TOWN!
DON'T GIVE UP! WE'VE COME THIS FAR!
JUST ANOTHER HALF-DAY! JUST KEEP HIM ALIVE THAT MUCH LONGER!
A HALF-DAY??
I'LL NEVER MAKE IT ANOTHER HALF-DAY!
QUIT WHINING!
YOU THINK WE'RE HERE TO TAKE CARE OF YOU? THE ONLY REASON WE LET YOU STAY WITH US IS THAT YOU SPEAK ARABIC!

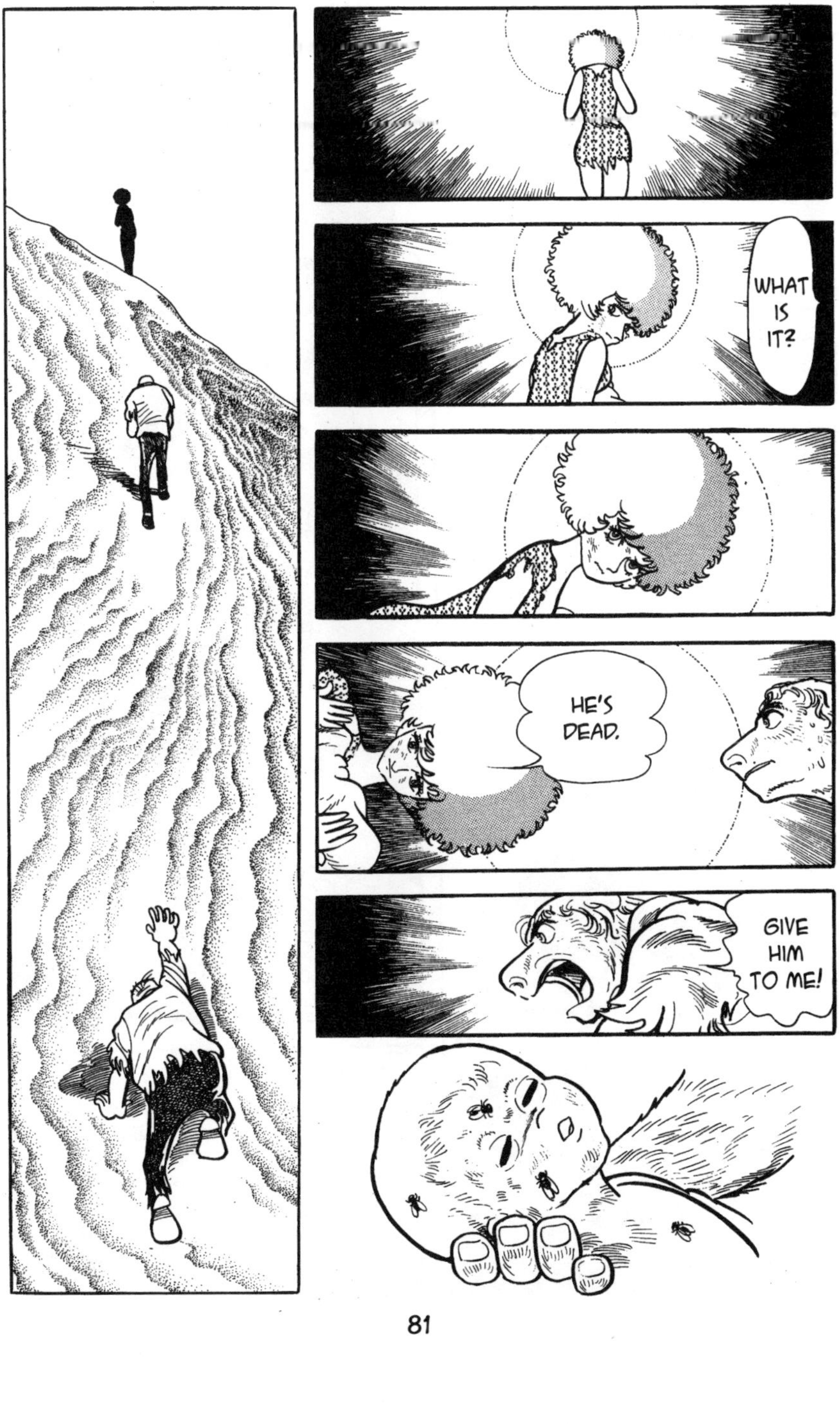
WHAT IS IT?
HE'S DEAD.
GIVE HIM TO ME!

DAMN...

DAMN!

DAMN! DAMN! DAMN!

THERE WAS NOTHING I COULD DO!

I COULDN'T DO ANYTHING TO KEEP THE BABY ALIVE!

SOME DOCTOR...

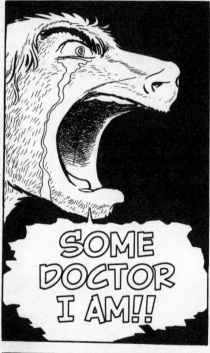

SOME DOCTOR I AM!!

LOOK AT ME. LOOK HOW WRETCHED, IMPOTENT, AND PATHETIC I AM.

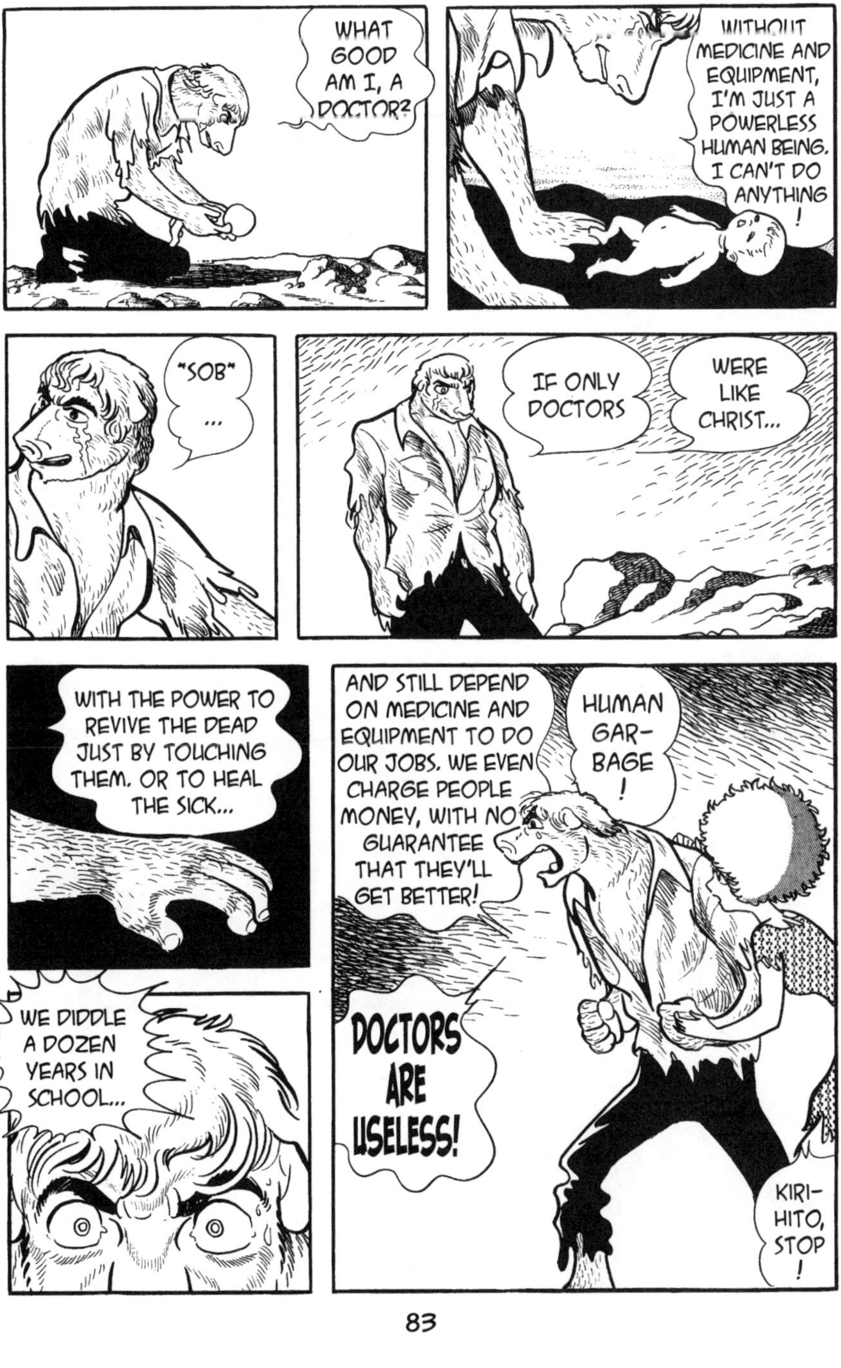

WHAT GOOD AM I, A DOCTOR?
WITHOUT MEDICINE AND EQUIPMENT, I'M JUST A POWERLESS HUMAN BEING. I CAN'T DO ANYTHING!
SOB ...
IF ONLY DOCTORS
WERE LIKE CHRIST...
WITH THE POWER TO REVIVE THE DEAD JUST BY TOUCHING THEM. OR TO HEAL THE SICK...
WE DIDDLE A DOZEN YEARS IN SCHOOL...
AND STILL DEPEND ON MEDICINE AND EQUIPMENT TO DO OUR JOBS. WE EVEN CHARGE PEOPLE MONEY, WITH NO GUARANTEE THAT THEY'LL GET BETTER!
HUMAN GAR-BAGE!
DOCTORS ARE USELESS!
KIRI-HITO, STOP!

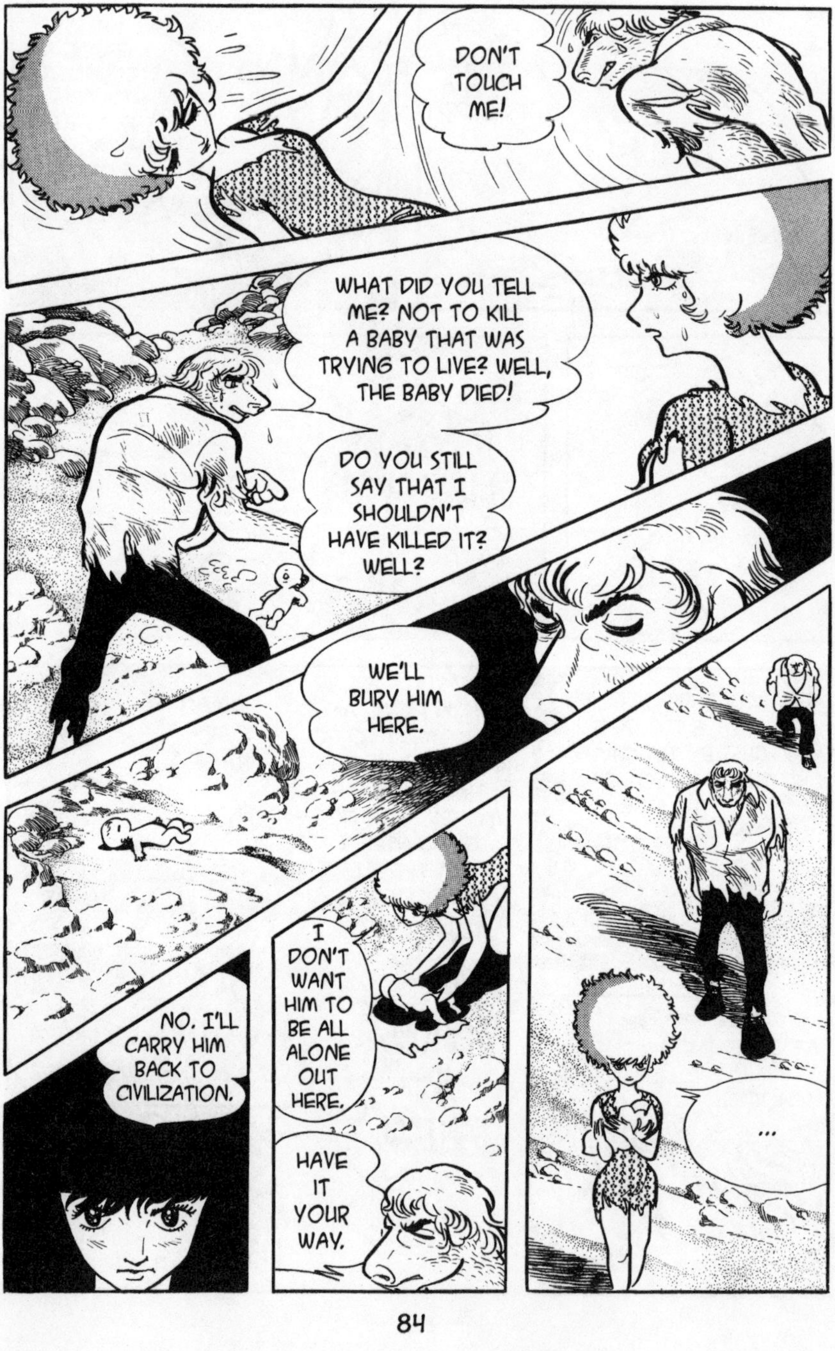
DON'T TOUCH ME!
WHAT DID YOU TELL ME? NOT TO KILL A BABY THAT WAS TRYING TO LIVE? WELL, THE BABY DIED!
DO YOU STILL SAY THAT I SHOULDN'T HAVE KILLED IT? WELL?
WE'LL BURY HIM HERE.
NO. I'LL CARRY HIM BACK TO CIVILIZATION.
I DON'T WANT HIM TO BE ALL ALONE OUT HERE.
HAVE IT YOUR WAY.
...

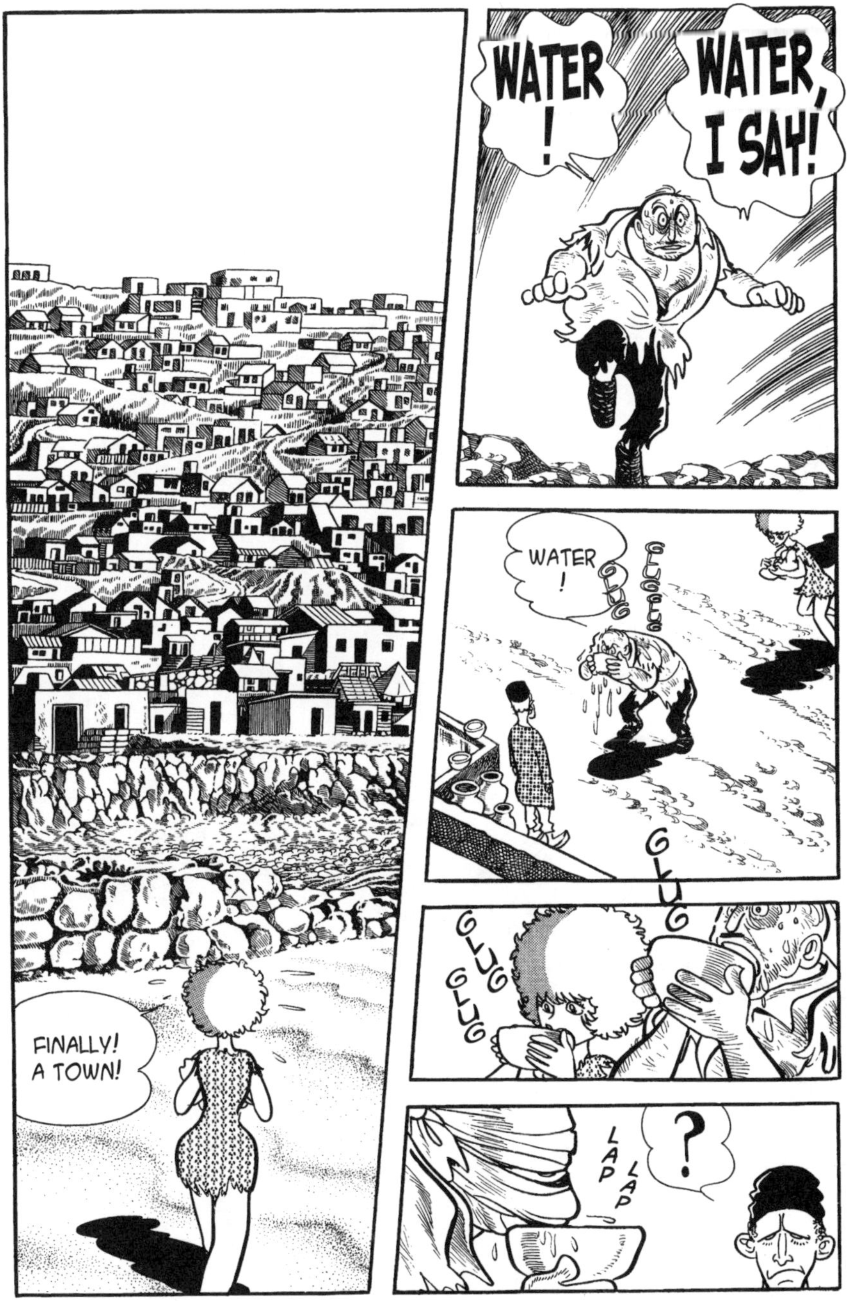
FINALLY! A TOWN!
WATER !
WATER, I SAY!
WATER !
GLUG
GLUGGUG
GLUG
GLUG GLUG GLUG
LAP LAP
?

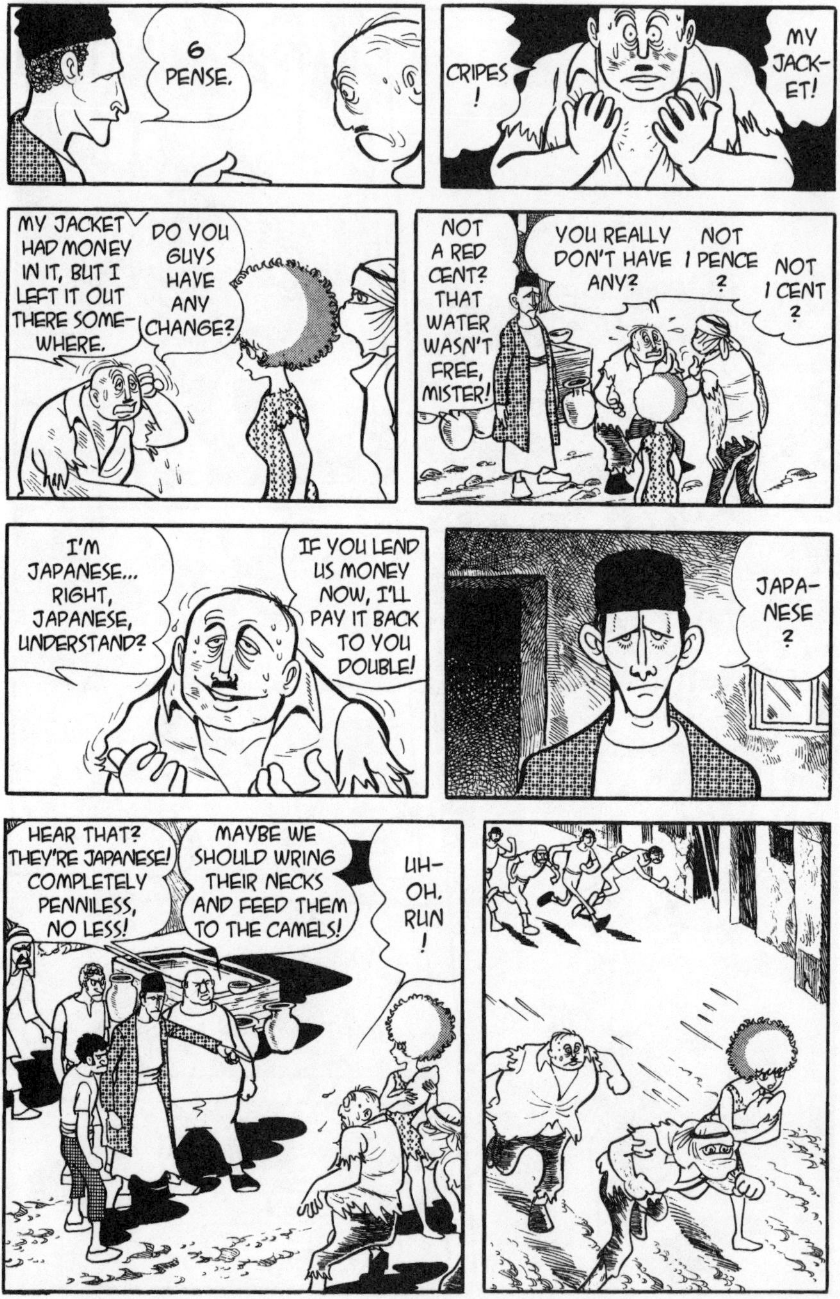
6 PENSE.
CRIPES!
MY JACKET!
MY JACKET HAD MONEY IN IT, BUT I LEFT IT OUT THERE SOMEWHERE.
DO YOU GUYS HAVE ANY CHANGE?
YOU REALLY DON'T HAVE ANY?
NOT 1 PENCE?
NOT 1 CENT?
NOT A RED CENT? THAT WATER WASN'T FREE, MISTER!
I'M JAPANESE... RIGHT, JAPANESE, UNDERSTAND?
IF YOU LEND US MONEY NOW, I'LL PAY IT BACK TO YOU DOUBLE!
JAPANESE?
HEAR THAT? THEY'RE JAPANESE! COMPLETELY PENNILESS, NO LESS!
MAYBE WE SHOULD WRING THEIR NECKS AND FEED THEM TO THE CAMELS!
UH-OH. RUN!

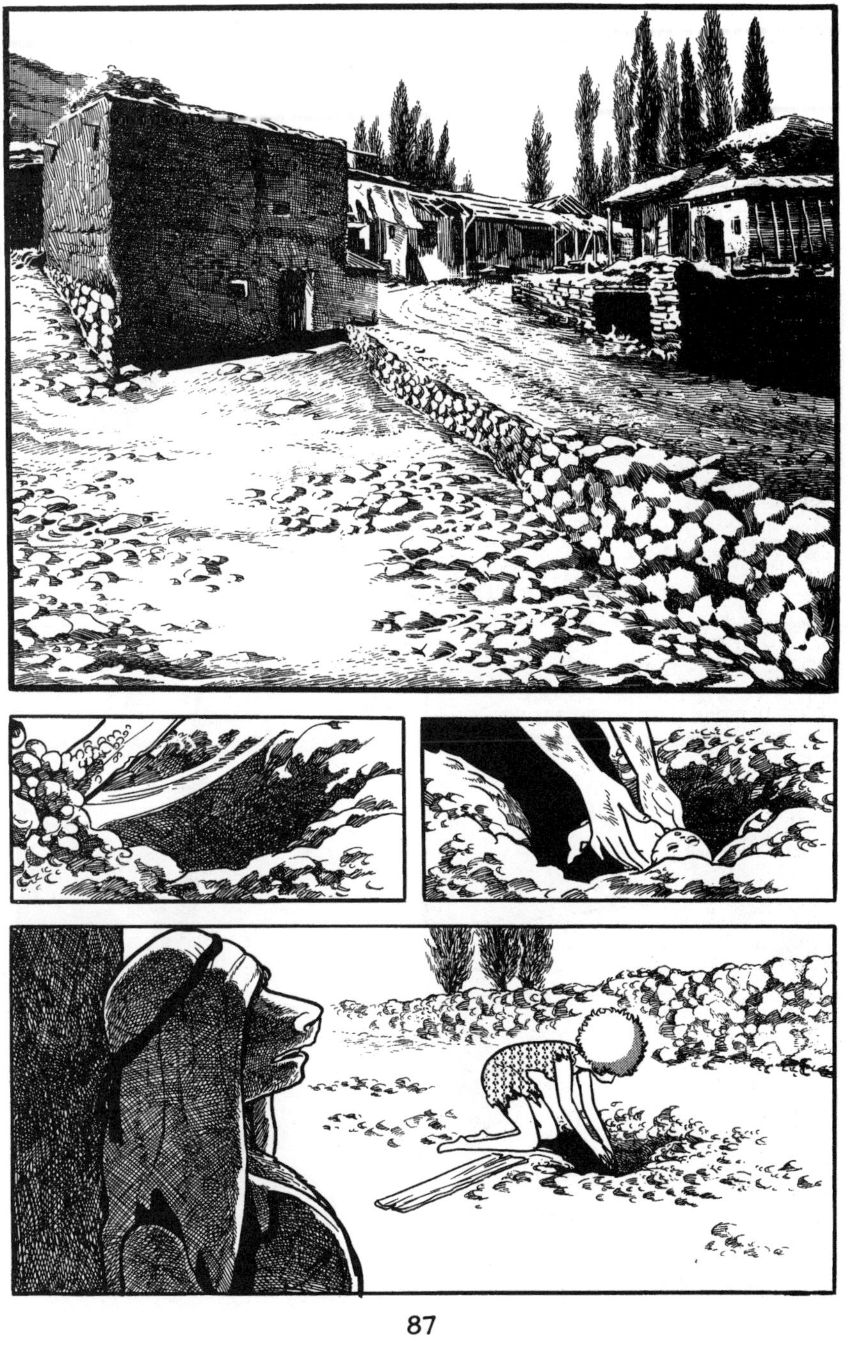

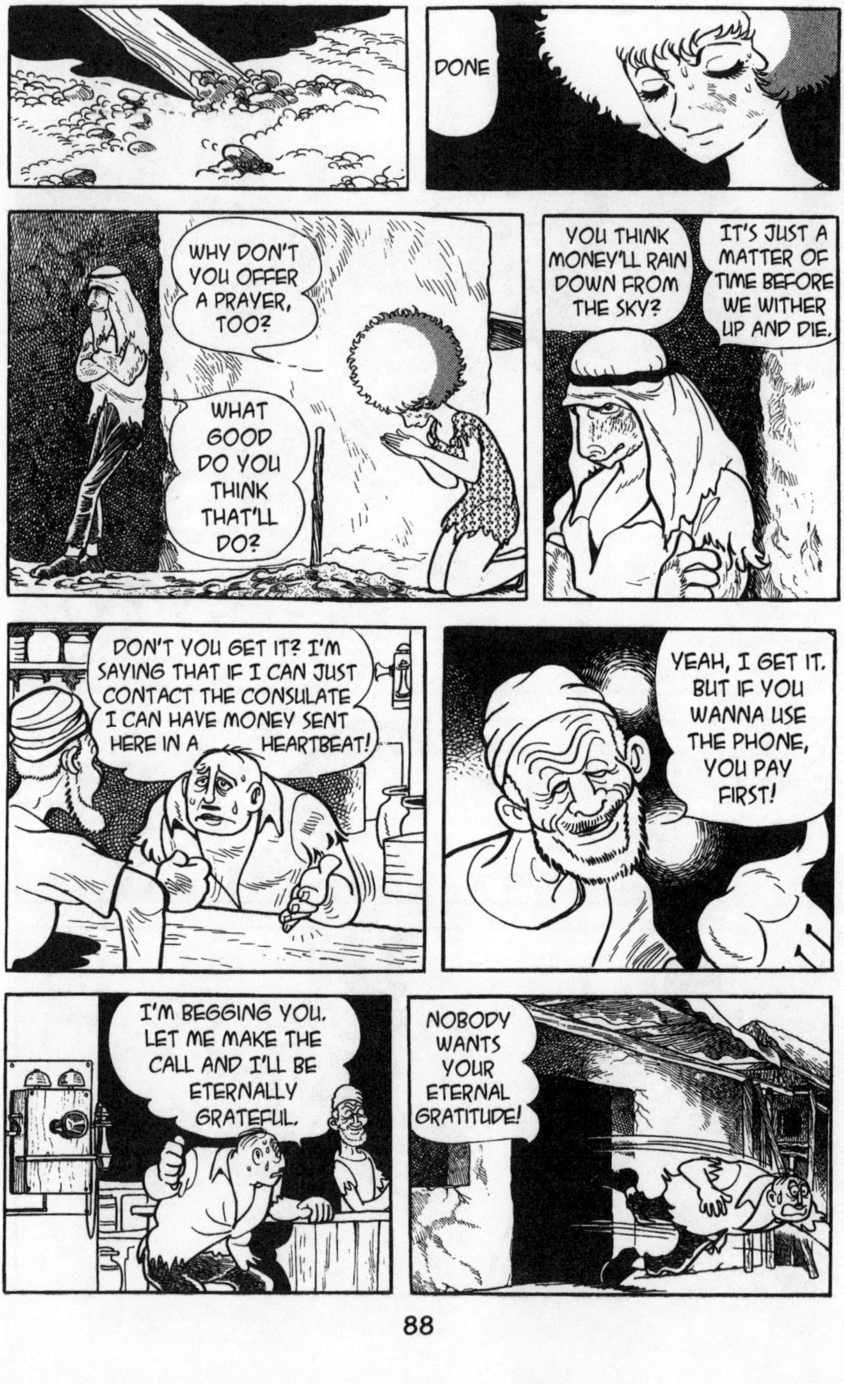
DONE
WHY DON'T YOU OFFER A PRAYER, TOO?
WHAT GOOD DO YOU THINK THAT'LL DO?
YOU THINK MONEY'LL RAIN DOWN FROM THE SKY?
IT'S JUST A MATTER OF TIME BEFORE WE WITHER UP AND DIE.
DON'T YOU GET IT? I'M SAYING THAT IF I CAN JUST CONTACT THE CONSULATE I CAN HAVE MONEY SENT HERE IN A HEARTBEAT!
YEAH, I GET IT. BUT IF YOU WANNA USE THE PHONE, YOU PAY FIRST!
I'M BEGGING YOU. LET ME MAKE THE CALL AND I'LL BE ETERNALLY GRATEFUL.
NOBODY WANTS YOUR ETERNAL GRATITUDE!

I'VE HAD IT!

YOU'LL BE SORRY FOR THIS!

SO, THEY WON'T EVEN LET YOU MAKE A PHONE CALL WITHOUT PAYING FIRST?

EVERYTHING'S ABOUT MONEY, MONEY, MONEY! THESE BLASTED STINGY MISERS!

ANYWAY, IF WE DON'T GET OUR HANDS ON SOME DOUGH WE WON'T BE ABLE TO EAT, LET ALONE GET OUT OF THIS PLACE.

ARE THEY REALLY THAT UN-CHARITABLE?

COME TO THINK OF IT, THE MOMENT YOU MENTIONED YOU WERE JAPANESE THEY TURNED CHILLY...

...

ANTI-JAPANESE SENTIMENT?

WHAT ON EARTH DID YOU GUYS DO TO THEM?

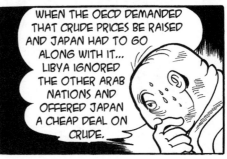

WHEN THE OECD DEMANDED THAT CRUDE PRICES BE RAISED AND JAPAN HAD TO GO ALONG WITH IT... LIBYA IGNORED THE OTHER ARAB NATIONS AND OFFERED JAPAN A CHEAP DEAL ON CRUDE.

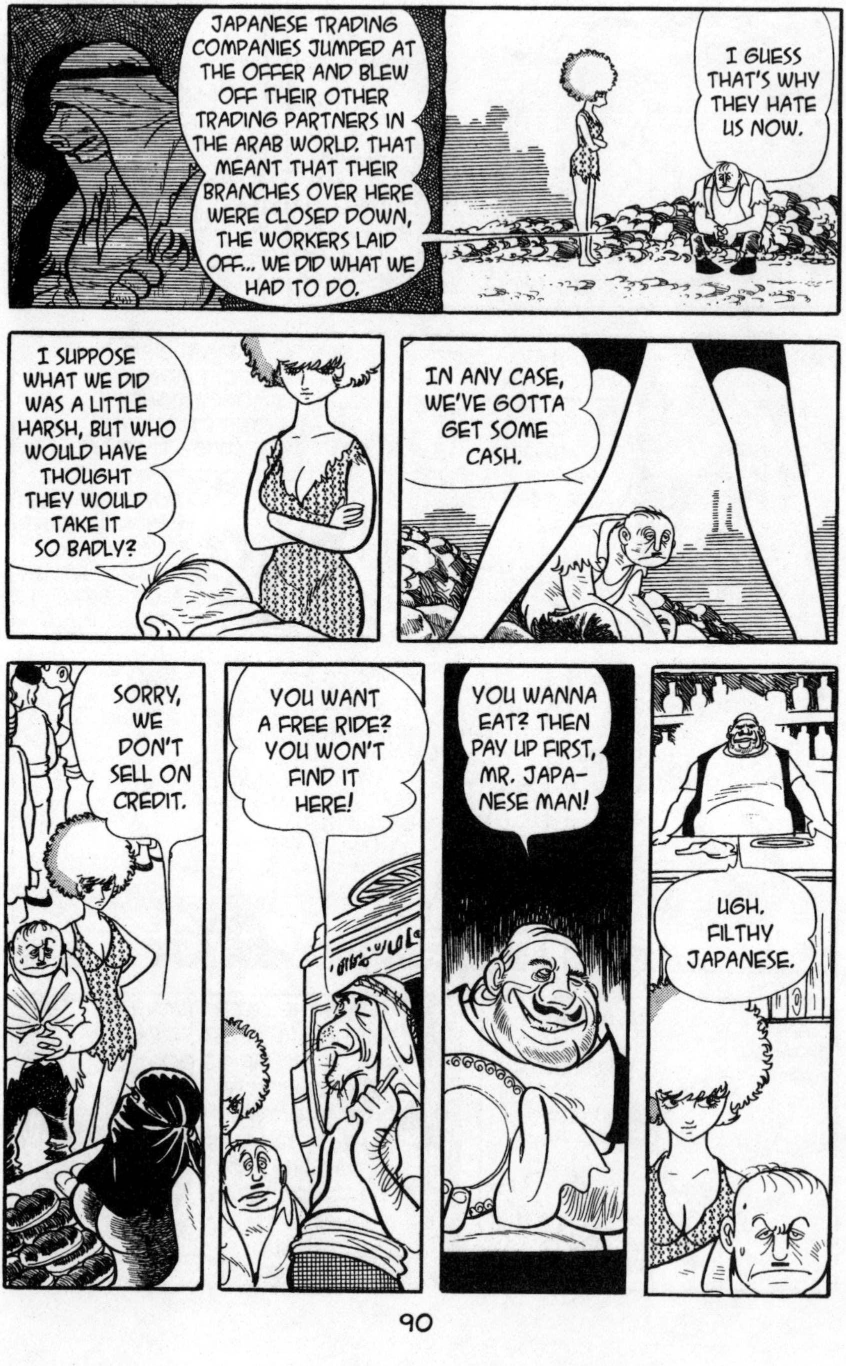
JAPANESE TRADING COMPANIES JUMPED AT THE OFFER AND BLEW OFF THEIR OTHER TRADING PARTNERS IN THE ARAB WORLD. THAT MEANT THAT THEIR BRANCHES OVER HERE WERE CLOSED DOWN, THE WORKERS LAID OFF... WE DID WHAT WE HAD TO DO.
I GUESS THAT'S WHY THEY HATE US NOW.
I SUPPOSE WHAT WE DID WAS A LITTLE HARSH, BUT WHO WOULD HAVE THOUGHT THEY WOULD TAKE IT SO BADLY?
IN ANY CASE, WE'VE GOTTA GET SOME CASH.
SORRY, WE DON'T SELL ON CREDIT.
YOU WANT A FREE RIDE? YOU WON'T FIND IT HERE!
YOU WANNA EAT? THEN PAY UP FIRST, MR. JAPA-NESE MAN!
UGH. FILTHY JAPANESE.

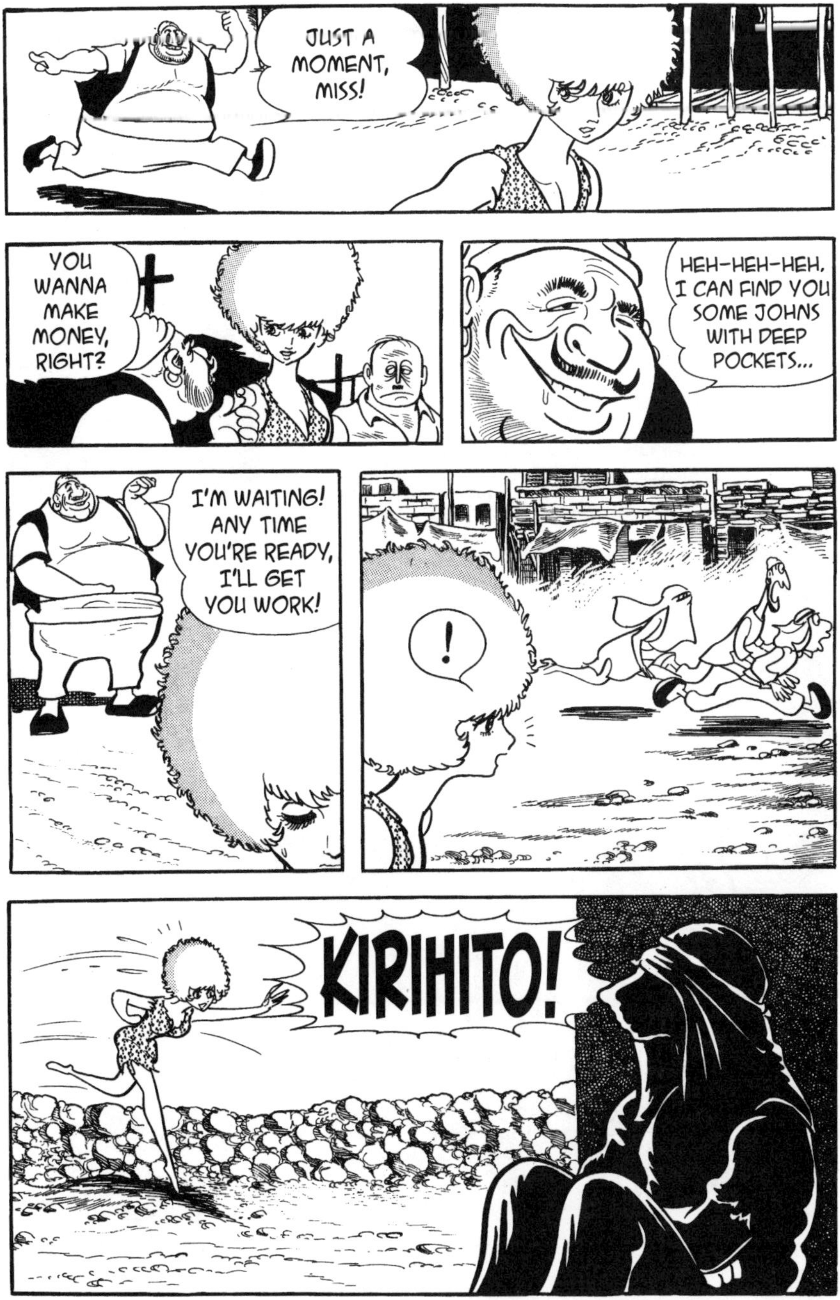
JUST A MOMENT, MISS!
YOU WANNA MAKE MONEY, RIGHT?
HEH-HEH-HEH. I CAN FIND YOU SOME JOHNS WITH DEEP POCKETS...
I'M WAITING! ANY TIME YOU'RE READY, I'LL GET YOU WORK!
!
KIRIHITO!

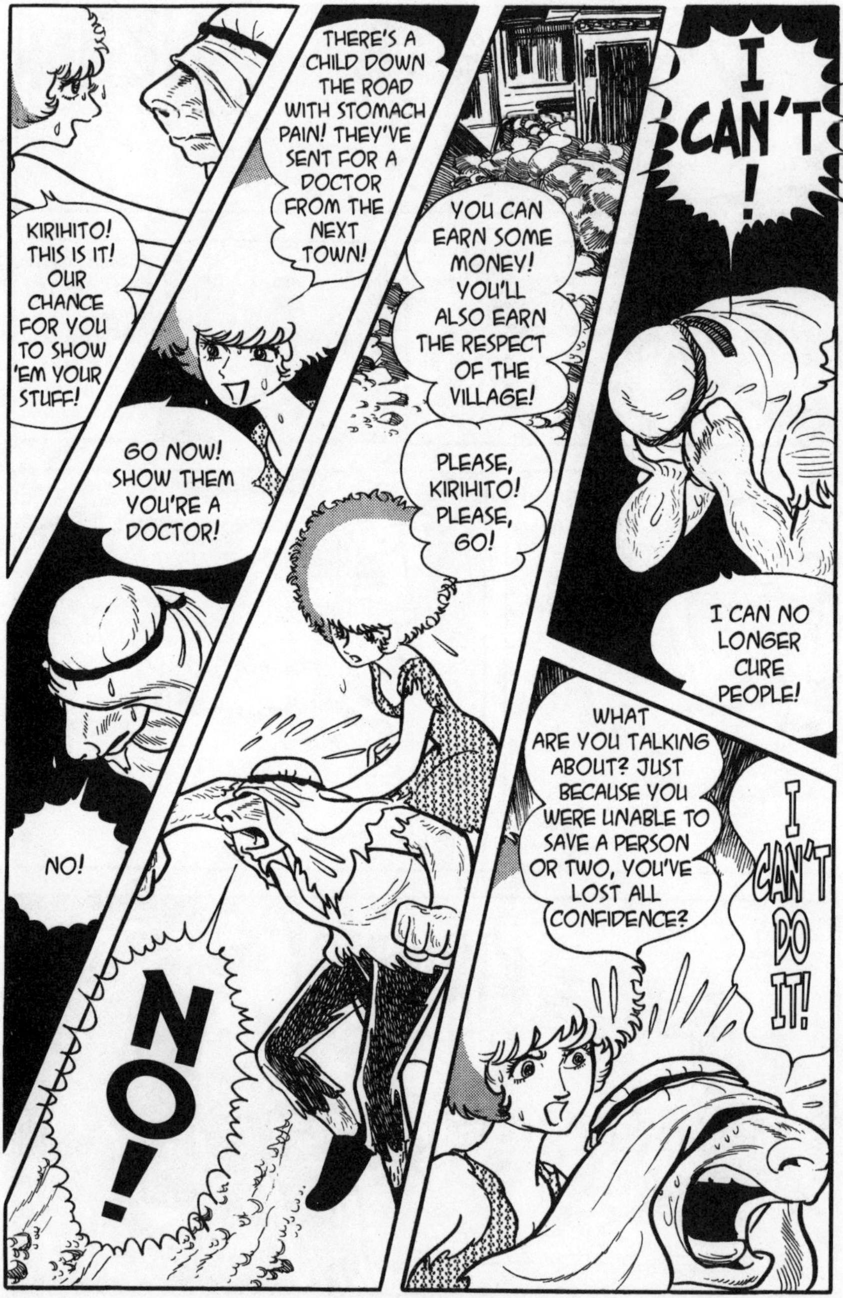
THERE'S A CHILD DOWN THE ROAD WITH STOMACH PAIN! THEY'VE SENT FOR A DOCTOR FROM THE NEXT TOWN!
KIRIHITO! THIS IS IT! OUR CHANCE FOR YOU TO SHOW 'EM YOUR STUFF!
GO NOW! SHOW THEM YOU'RE A DOCTOR!
NO!
YOU CAN EARN SOME MONEY! YOU'LL ALSO EARN THE RESPECT OF THE VILLAGE!
PLEASE, KIRIHITO! PLEASE, GO!
NO!
I CAN'T!
I CAN NO LONGER CURE PEOPLE!
WHAT ARE YOU TALKING ABOUT? JUST BECAUSE YOU WERE UNABLE TO SAVE A PERSON OR TWO, YOU'VE LOST ALL CONFIDENCE?
I CAN'T DO IT!

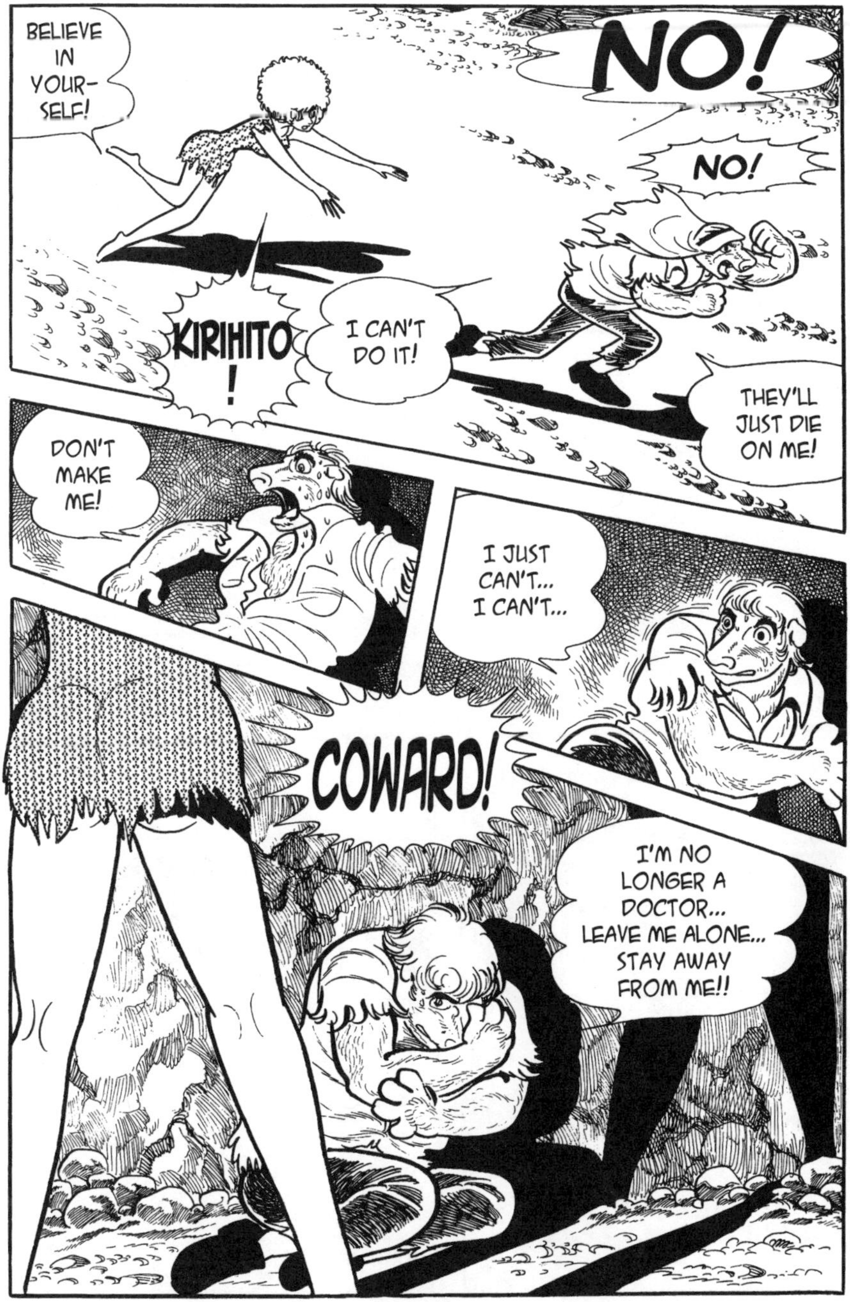
BELIEVE IN YOURSELF!
NO!
NO!
KIRIHITO!
I CAN'T DO IT!
THEY'LL JUST DIE ON ME!
DON'T MAKE ME!
I JUST CAN'T... I CAN'T...
COWARD!
I'M NO LONGER A DOCTOR... LEAVE ME ALONE... STAY AWAY FROM ME!!

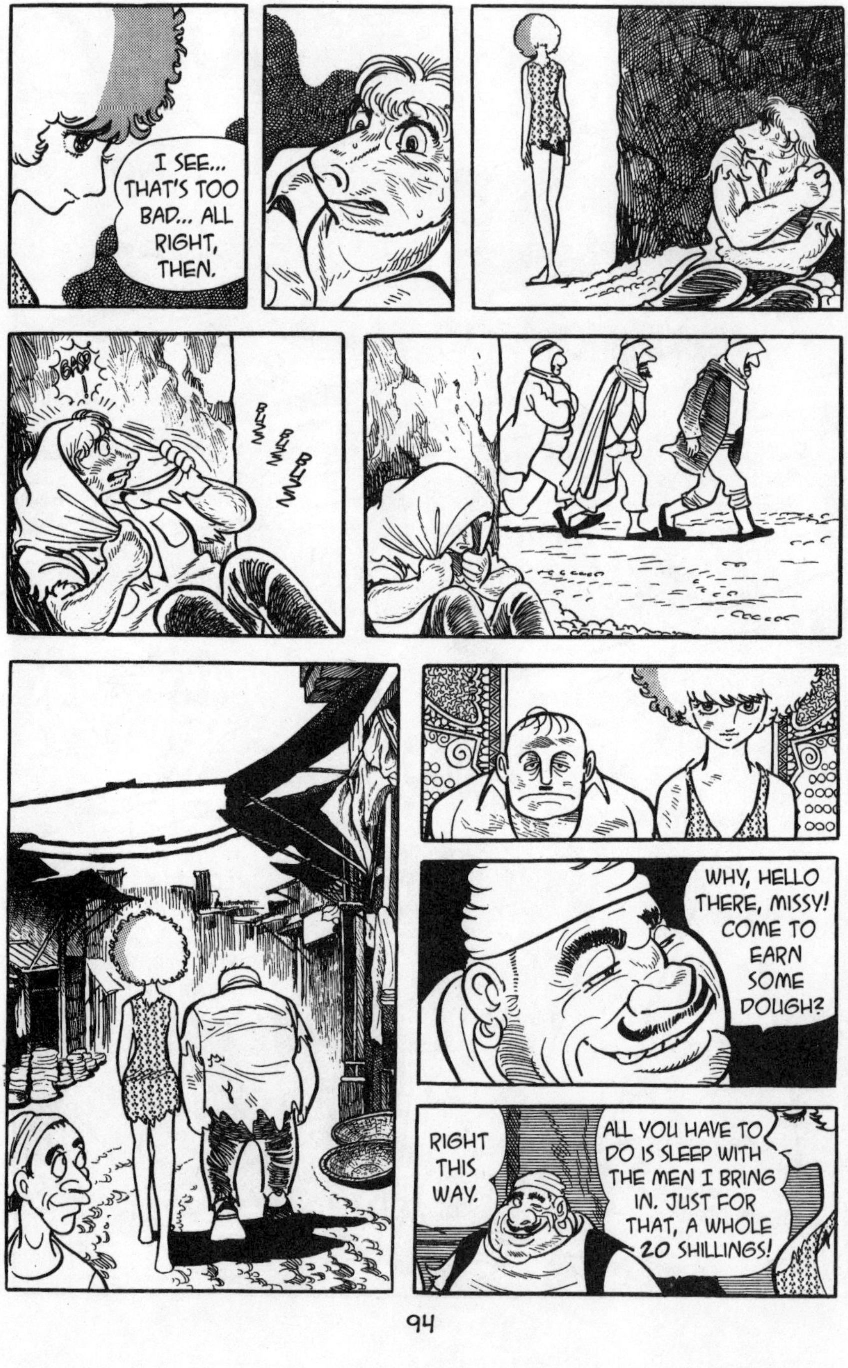
I SEE... THAT'S TOO BAD... ALL RIGHT, THEN.
GASP
BUZZ BUZZ BUZZ
WHY, HELLO THERE, MISSY! COME TO EARN SOME DOUGH?
RIGHT THIS WAY.
ALL YOU HAVE TO DO IS SLEEP WITH THE MEN I BRING IN. JUST FOR THAT, A WHOLE 20 SHILLINGS!

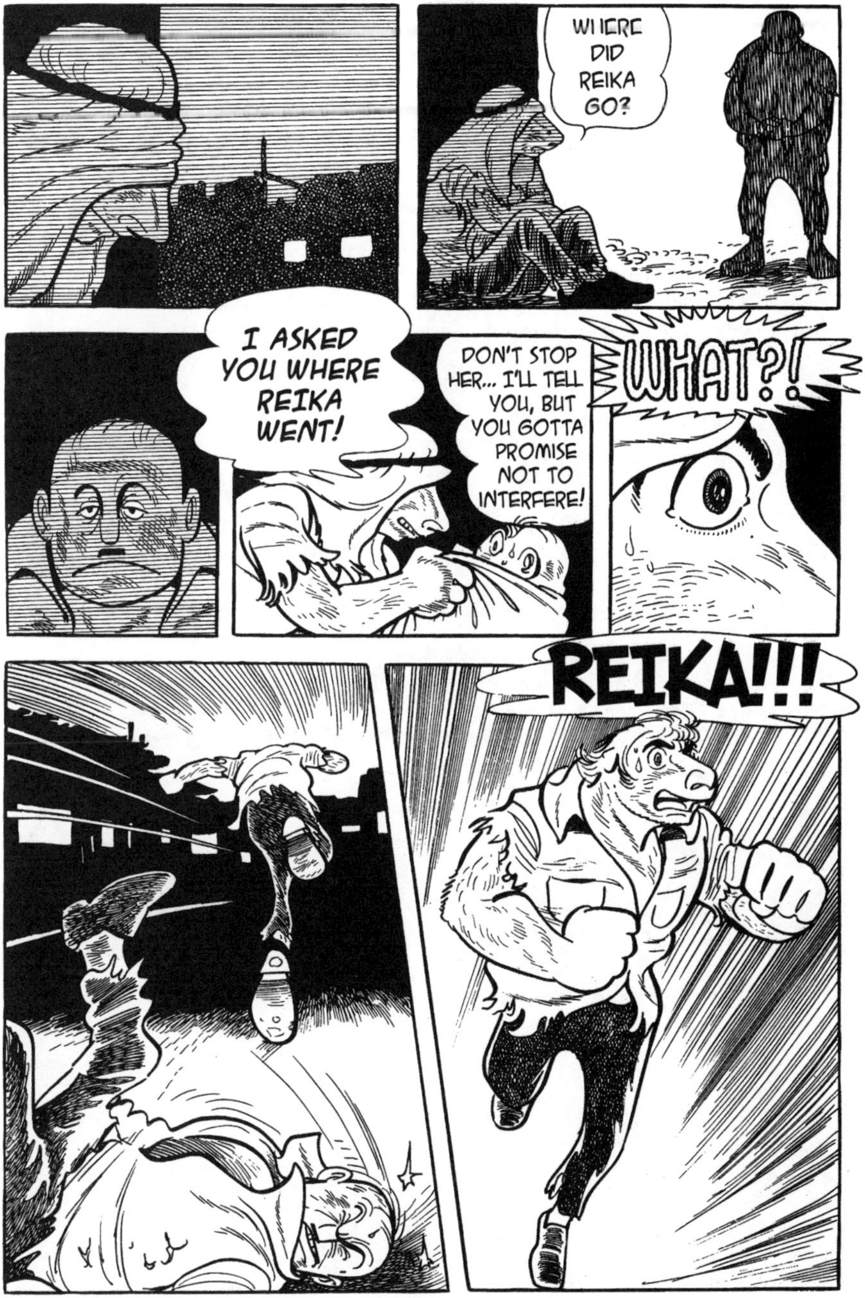
WHERE DID REIKA GO?
I ASKED YOU WHERE REIKA WENT!
DON'T STOP HER... I'LL TELL YOU, BUT YOU GOTTA PROMISE NOT TO INTERFERE!
WHAT?!
REIKA!!!

EEEEK!

GET OUT! I'LL KILL YOU IF YOU TOUCH MY REIKA AGAIN!

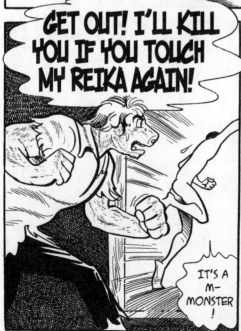

IT'S A M-MONSTER!

96

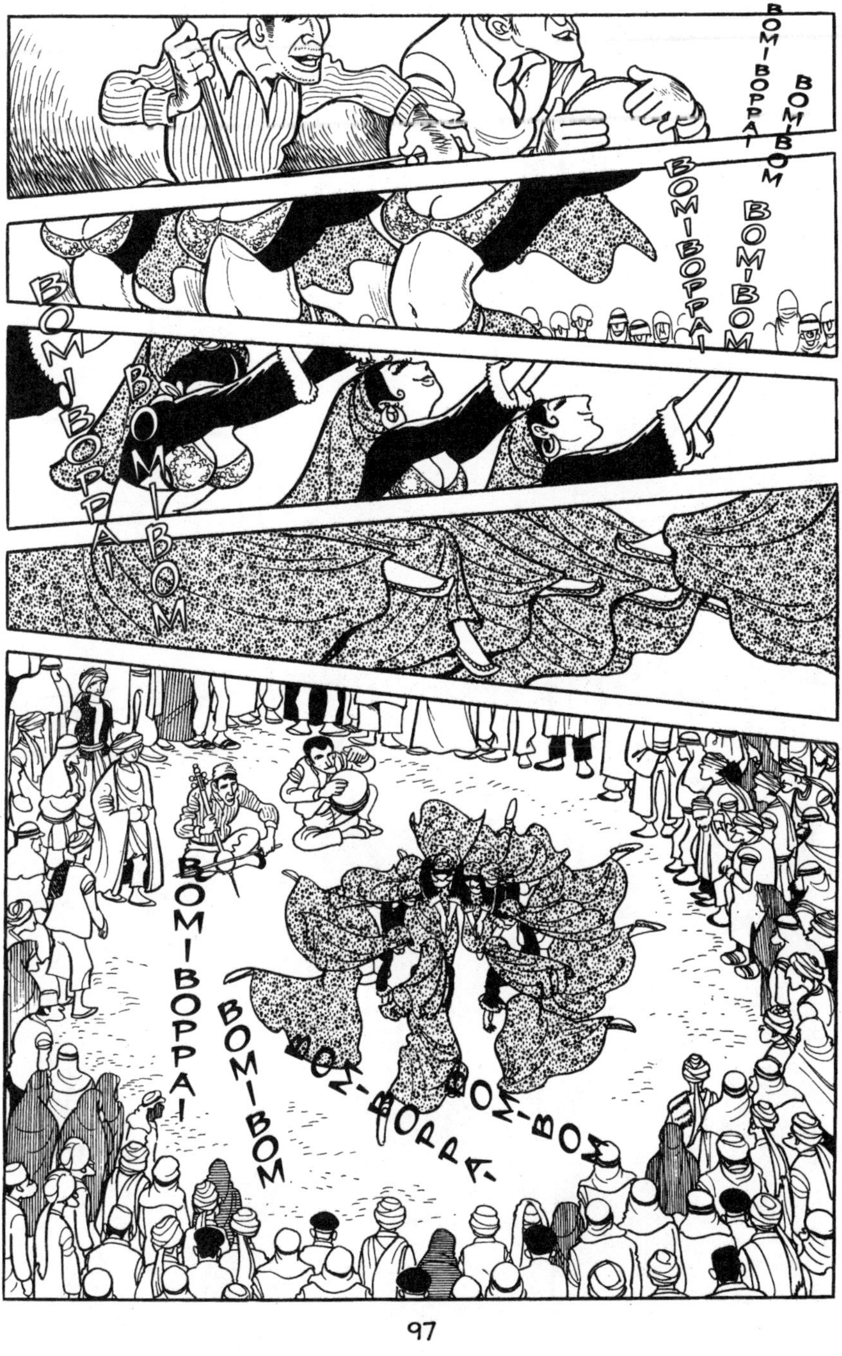
BOMIBOPPAI
BOMIBOM
BOMIBOPPAI
BOMIBOM
BOMIBOPPAI
BOMIBOM
BOMIBOPPAI
BOMIBOM
BOM-BOPPA-BOM-BOM

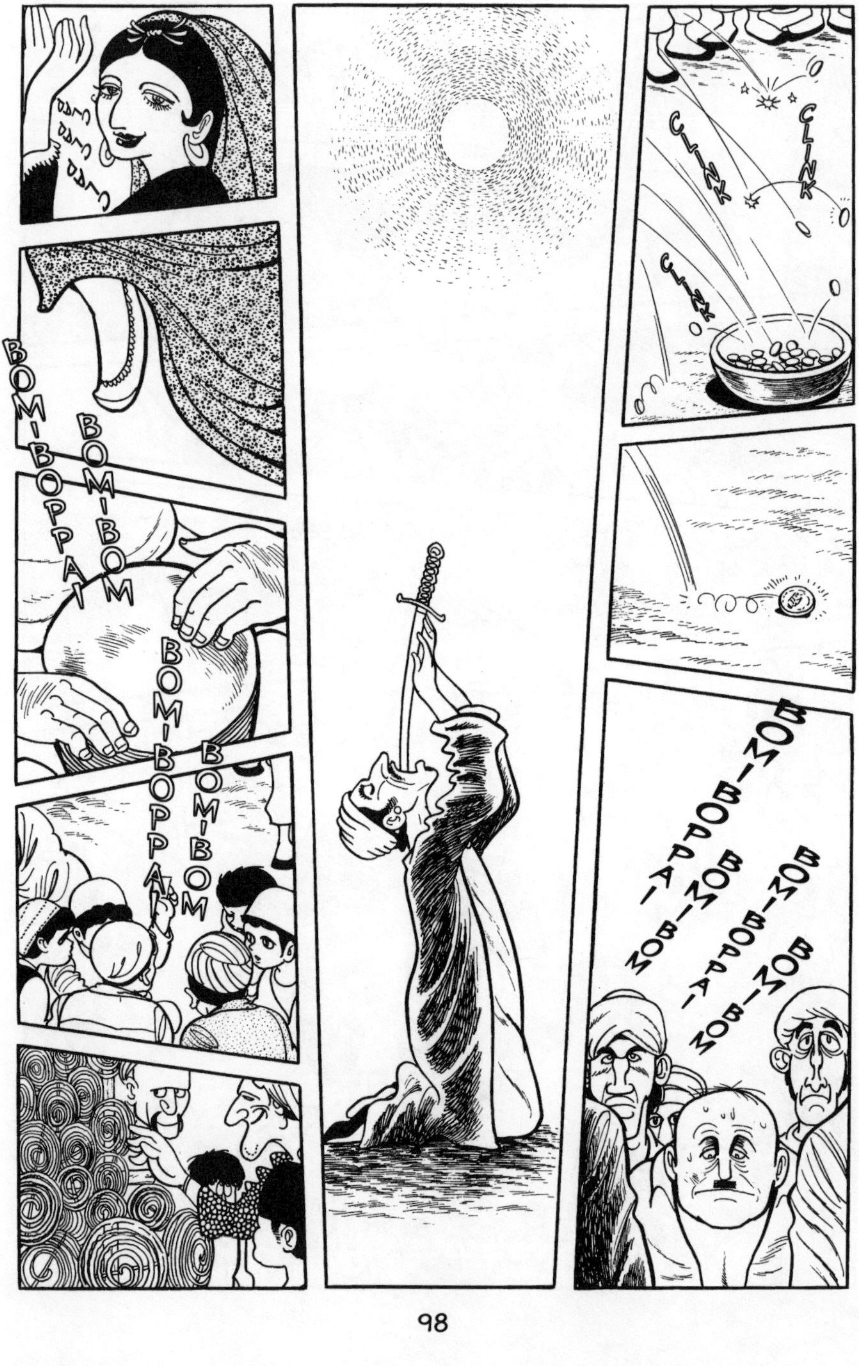
CLINK
CLINK
CLINK
BOMIBOPPAI
BOMIBOM
BOMIBOPPAI
BOMIBOM
CLAP CLAP CLAP
BOMIBOPPAI
BOMIBOM
BOMIBOPPAI
BOMIBOM

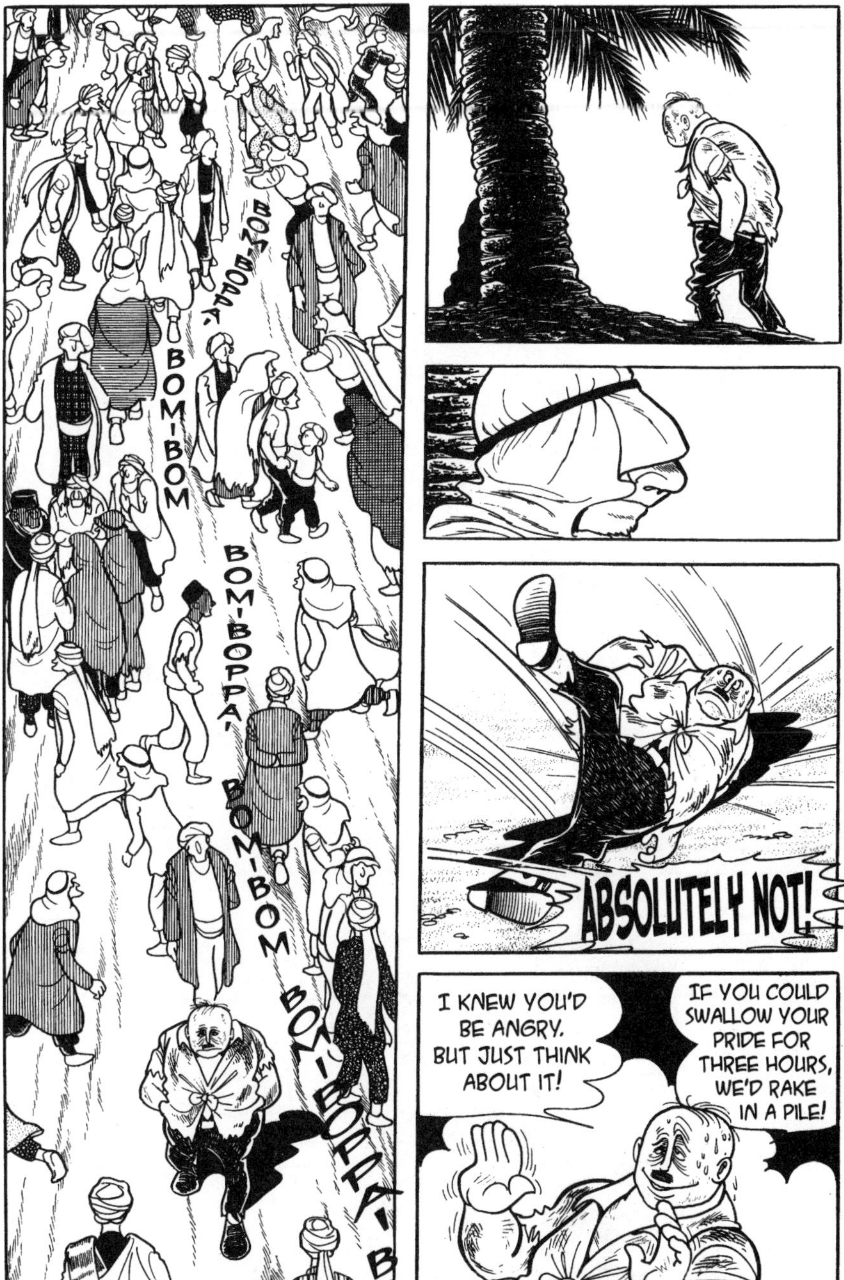
BOM-BOPPA
BOMI-BOM
BOMI-BOPPA
BOMI-BOM
BOMI-BOPPA-B
ABSOLUTELY NOT!
I KNEW YOU'D BE ANGRY. BUT JUST THINK ABOUT IT!
IF YOU COULD SWALLOW YOUR PRIDE FOR THREE HOURS, WE'D RAKE IN A PILE!

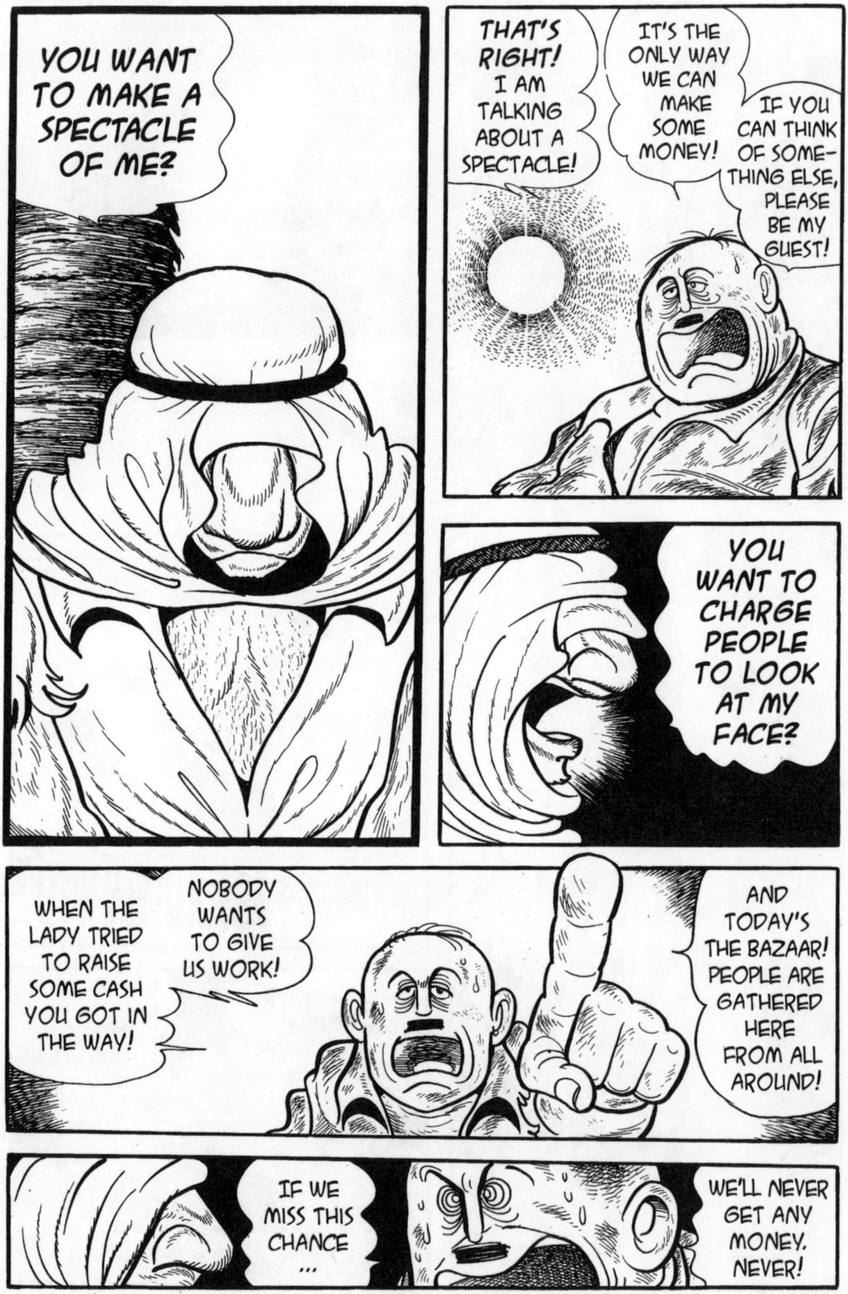
YOU WANT TO MAKE A SPECTACLE OF ME?
THAT'S RIGHT! I AM TALKING ABOUT A SPECTACLE!
IT'S THE ONLY WAY WE CAN MAKE SOME MONEY!
IF YOU CAN THINK OF SOME-THING ELSE, PLEASE BE MY GUEST!
YOU WANT TO CHARGE PEOPLE TO LOOK AT MY FACE?
WHEN THE LADY TRIED TO RAISE SOME CASH YOU GOT IN THE WAY!
NOBODY WANTS TO GIVE US WORK!
AND TODAY'S THE BAZAAR! PEOPLE ARE GATHERED HERE FROM ALL AROUND!
IF WE MISS THIS CHANCE ...
WE'LL NEVER GET ANY MONEY. NEVER!

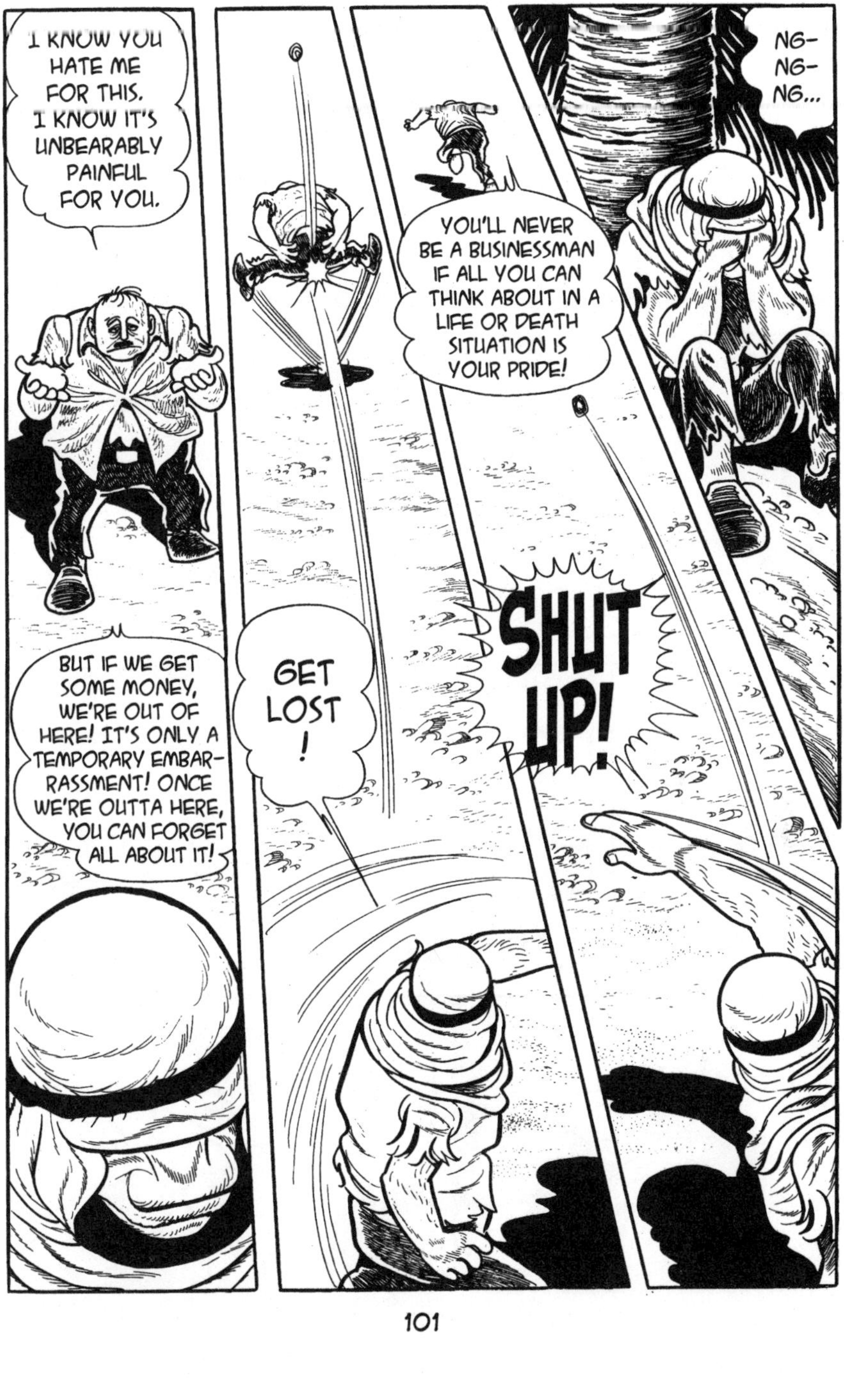
I KNOW YOU HATE ME FOR THIS. I KNOW IT'S UNBEARABLY PAINFUL FOR YOU.
BUT IF WE GET SOME MONEY, WE'RE OUT OF HERE! IT'S ONLY A TEMPORARY EMBARRASSMENT! ONCE WE'RE OUTTA HERE, YOU CAN FORGET ALL ABOUT IT!
GET LOST!
YOU'LL NEVER BE A BUSINESSMAN IF ALL YOU CAN THINK ABOUT IN A LIFE OR DEATH SITUATION IS YOUR PRIDE!
SHUT UP!
NG-NG-NG...

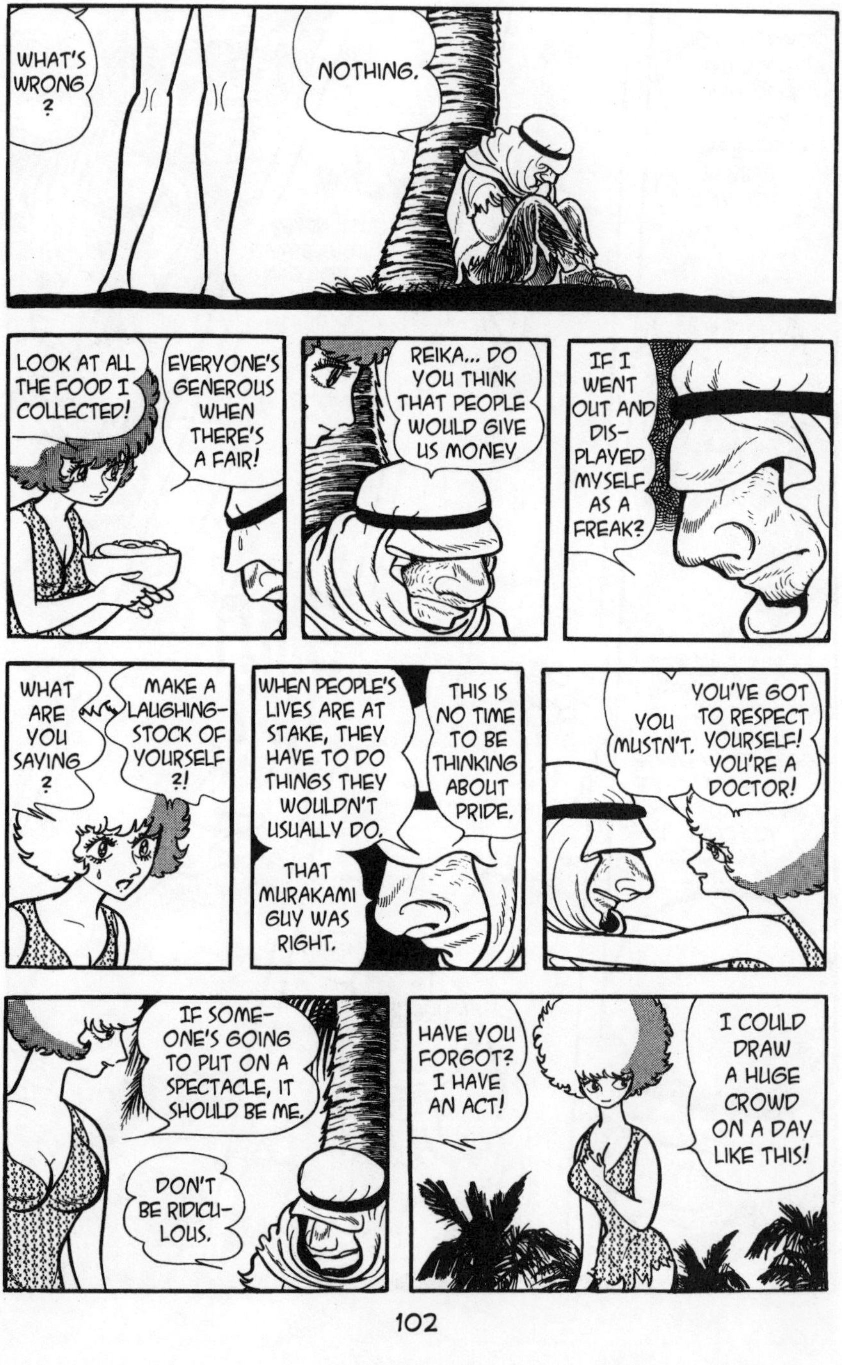
WHAT'S WRONG?
NOTHING.
LOOK AT ALL THE FOOD I COLLECTED!
EVERYONE'S GENEROUS WHEN THERE'S A FAIR!
REIKA... DO YOU THINK THAT PEOPLE WOULD GIVE US MONEY
IF I WENT OUT AND DIS-PLAYED MYSELF AS A FREAK?
WHAT ARE YOU SAYING?
MAKE A LAUGHING-STOCK OF YOURSELF?!
WHEN PEOPLE'S LIVES ARE AT STAKE, THEY HAVE TO DO THINGS THEY WOULDN'T USUALLY DO.
THIS IS NO TIME TO BE THINKING ABOUT PRIDE.
THAT MURAKAMI GUY WAS RIGHT.
YOU MUSTN'T.
YOU'VE GOT TO RESPECT YOURSELF! YOU'RE A DOCTOR!
IF SOME-ONE'S GOING TO PUT ON A SPECTACLE, IT SHOULD BE ME.
DON'T BE RIDICU-LOUS.
HAVE YOU FORGOT? I HAVE AN ACT!
I COULD DRAW A HUGE CROWD ON A DAY LIKE THIS!

HUH. SOUNDS IFFY...

I'LL DO IT IF WE GO 50-50.

THAT'S FINE. CAN YOU GET EVERYTHING READY RIGHT AWAY? BEFORE THE CROWD THINS?

WE'LL NEED A BIG POT FULL OF OIL, BREAD CRUMBS, WATER...

AND MAKE A SPOON BIG ENOUGH TO HOLD A PERSON.

A HUMAN SPOON?

THAT'S GONNA BE PRICY...

WHAT ARE WE DEEP FRYING?

ME.

OH-HO?

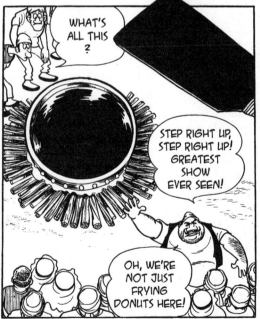

WHAT'S ALL THIS?

STEP RIGHT UP, STEP RIGHT UP! GREATEST SHOW EVER SEEN!

OH, WE'RE NOT JUST FRYING DONUTS HERE!

THAT'S RIGHT, A WOMAN. A LIVE WOMAN. DEEP FRIED!

YOU CAN'T BE SERIOUS...

YESSIREE! ONE HUMAN TEMPURA COMING UP!

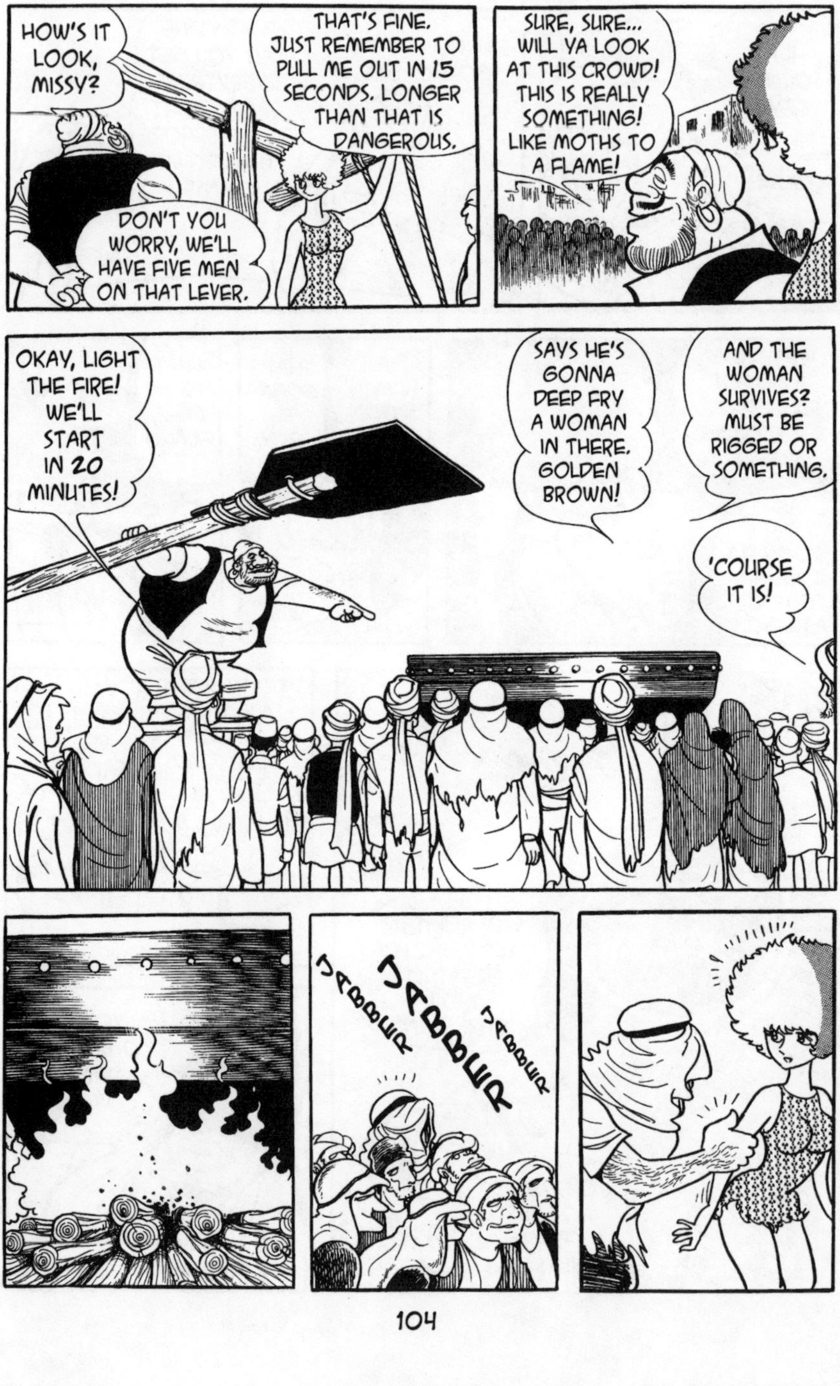
HOW'S IT LOOK, MISSY?
THAT'S FINE. JUST REMEMBER TO PULL ME OUT IN 15 SECONDS. LONGER THAN THAT IS DANGEROUS.
DON'T YOU WORRY, WE'LL HAVE FIVE MEN ON THAT LEVER.
SURE, SURE... WILL YA LOOK AT THIS CROWD! THIS IS REALLY SOMETHING! LIKE MOTHS TO A FLAME!
OKAY, LIGHT THE FIRE! WE'LL START IN 20 MINUTES!
SAYS HE'S GONNA DEEP FRY A WOMAN IN THERE. GOLDEN BROWN!
AND THE WOMAN SURVIVES? MUST BE RIGGED OR SOMETHING.
'COURSE IT IS!
JABBER
JABBER
JABBER

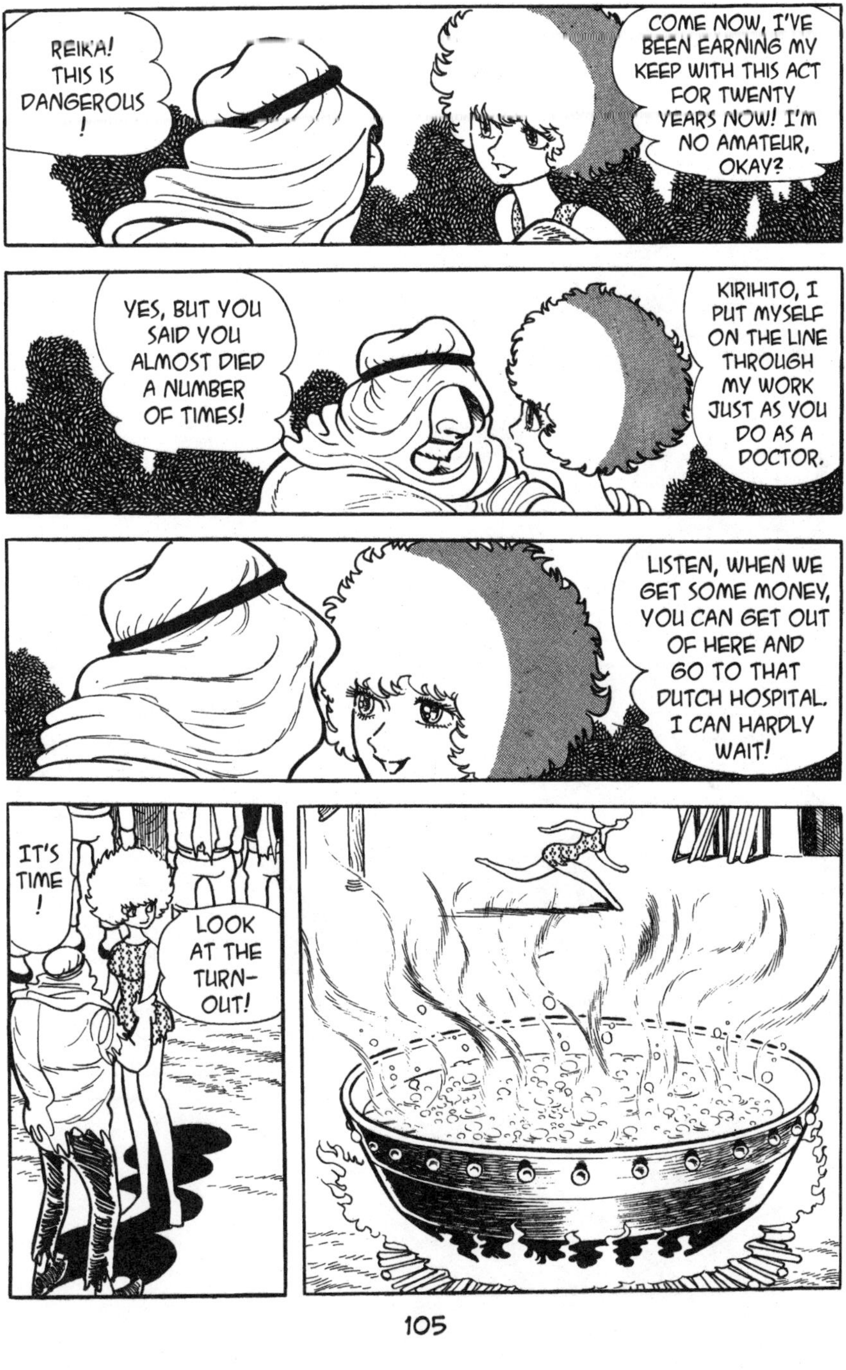
REIKA! THIS IS DANGEROUS!
COME NOW, I'VE BEEN EARNING MY KEEP WITH THIS ACT FOR TWENTY YEARS NOW! I'M NO AMATEUR, OKAY?
YES, BUT YOU SAID YOU ALMOST DIED A NUMBER OF TIMES!
KIRIHITO, I PUT MYSELF ON THE LINE THROUGH MY WORK JUST AS YOU DO AS A DOCTOR.
LISTEN, WHEN WE GET SOME MONEY, YOU CAN GET OUT OF HERE AND GO TO THAT DUTCH HOSPITAL. I CAN HARDLY WAIT!
IT'S TIME!
LOOK AT THE TURN-OUT!

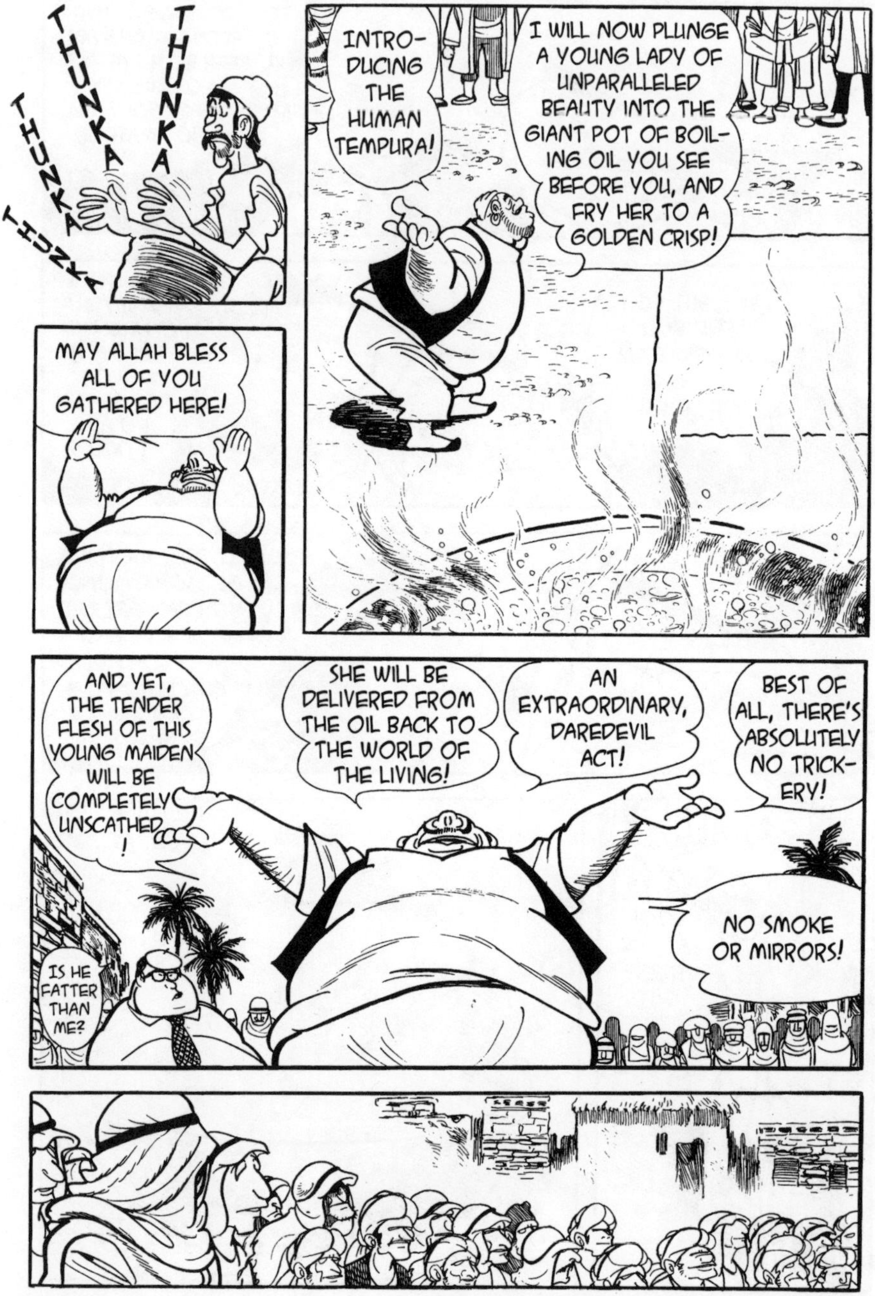
THUNKA
THUNKA
THUNKA
THUNKA
MAY ALLAH BLESS ALL OF YOU GATHERED HERE!
INTRO-DUCING THE HUMAN TEMPURA!
I WILL NOW PLUNGE A YOUNG LADY OF UNPARALLELED BEAUTY INTO THE GIANT POT OF BOIL-ING OIL YOU SEE BEFORE YOU, AND FRY HER TO A GOLDEN CRISP!
AND YET, THE TENDER FLESH OF THIS YOUNG MAIDEN WILL BE COMPLETELY UNSCATHED!
SHE WILL BE DELIVERED FROM THE OIL BACK TO THE WORLD OF THE LIVING!
AN EXTRAORDINARY, DAREDEVIL ACT!
BEST OF ALL, THERE'S ABSOLUTELY NO TRICK-ERY!
NO SMOKE OR MIRRORS!
IS HE FATTER THAN ME?

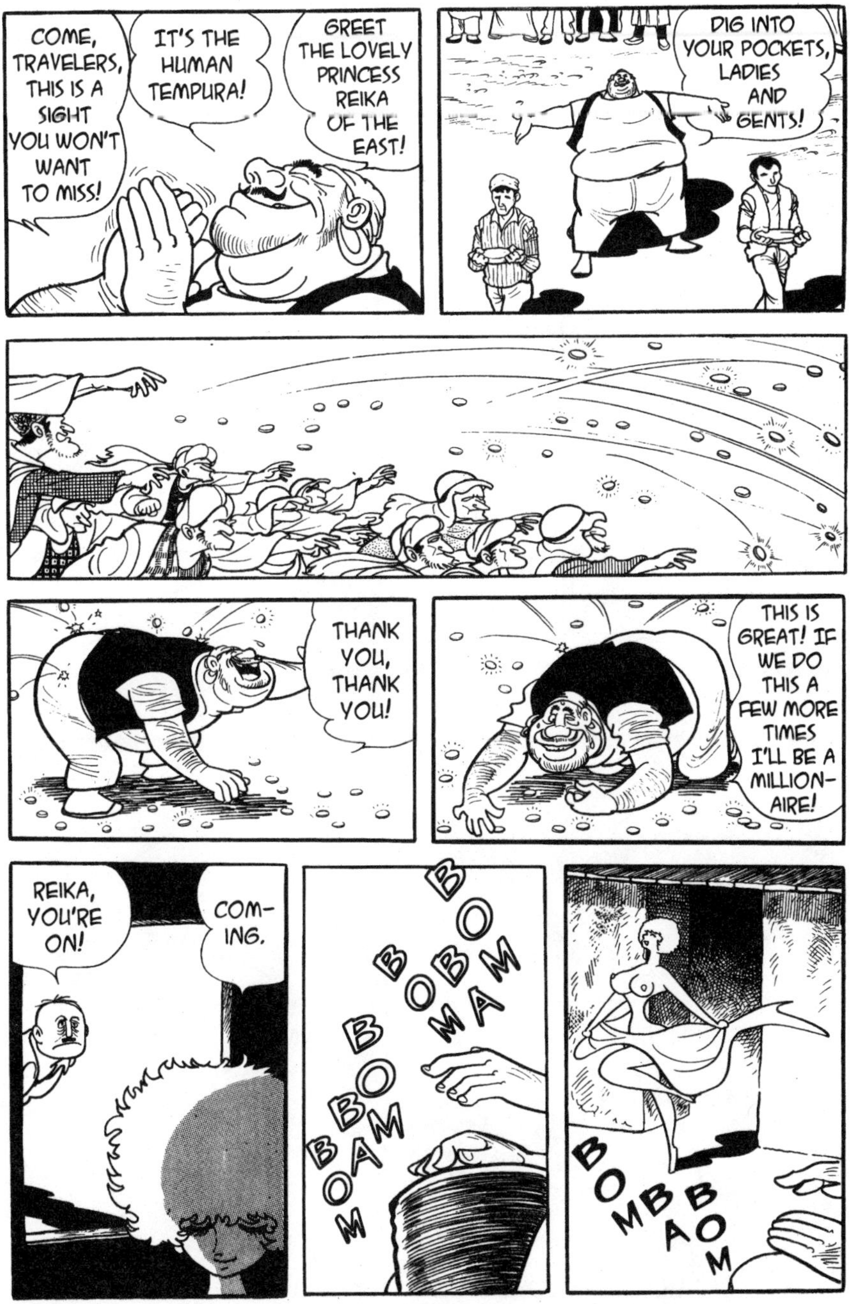
COME, TRAVELERS, THIS IS A SIGHT YOU WON'T WANT TO MISS!
IT'S THE HUMAN TEMPURA!
GREET THE LOVELY PRINCESS REIKA OF THE EAST!
DIG INTO YOUR POCKETS, LADIES AND GENTS!
THANK YOU, THANK YOU!
THIS IS GREAT! IF WE DO THIS A FEW MORE TIMES I'LL BE A MILLION-AIRE!
REIKA, YOU'RE ON!
COM-ING.

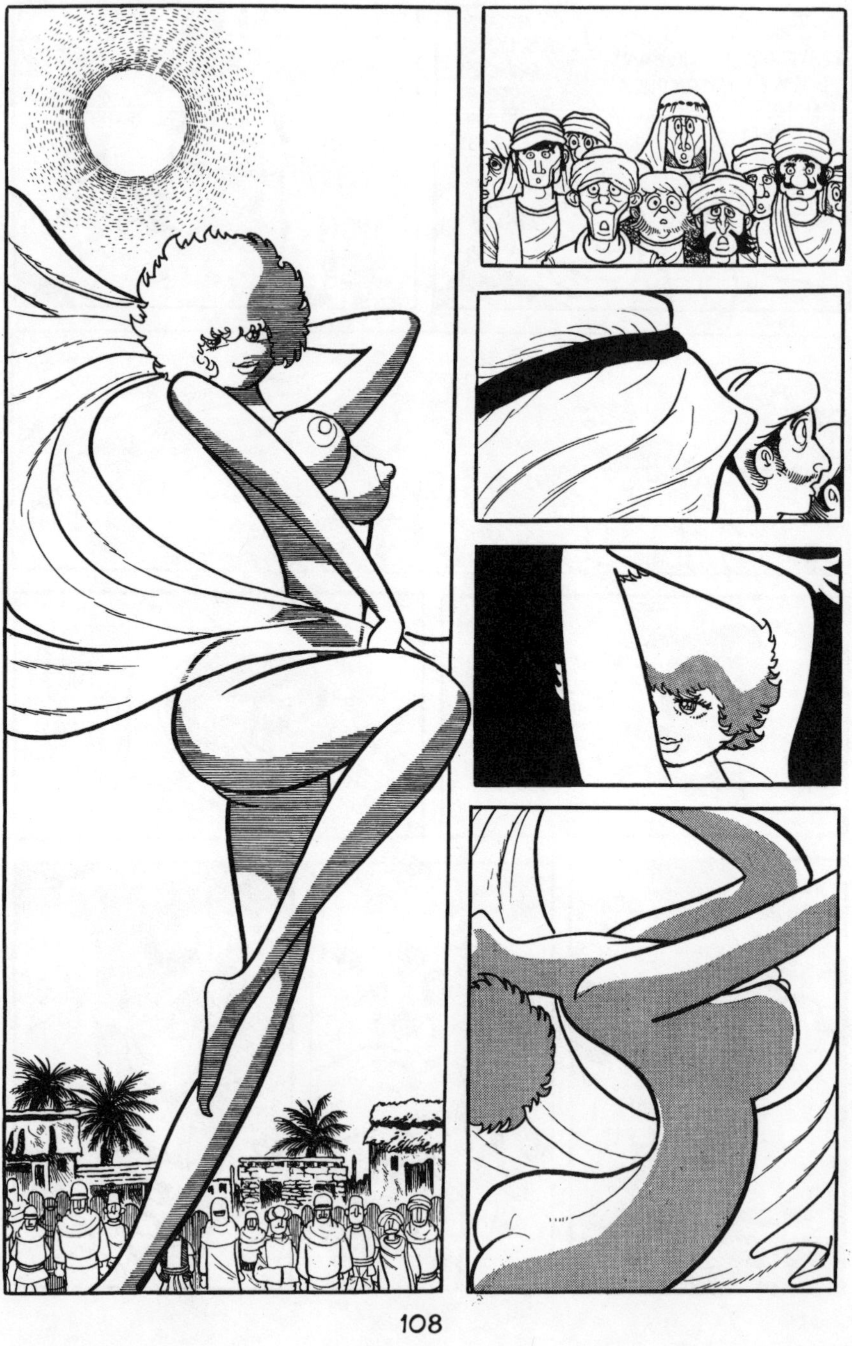

NOT YET.
BOMBABOM
BOMBABOM
BOMBABOM
BOMBABOM
BOMBABOMBABOM

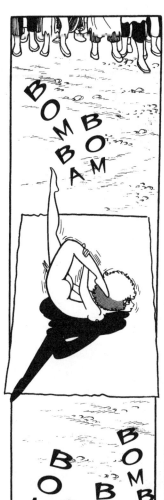

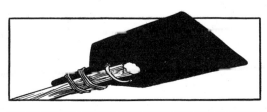

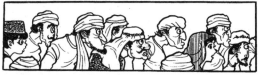

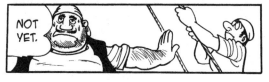

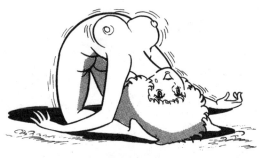

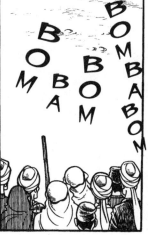

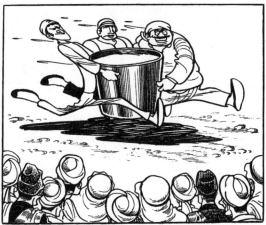

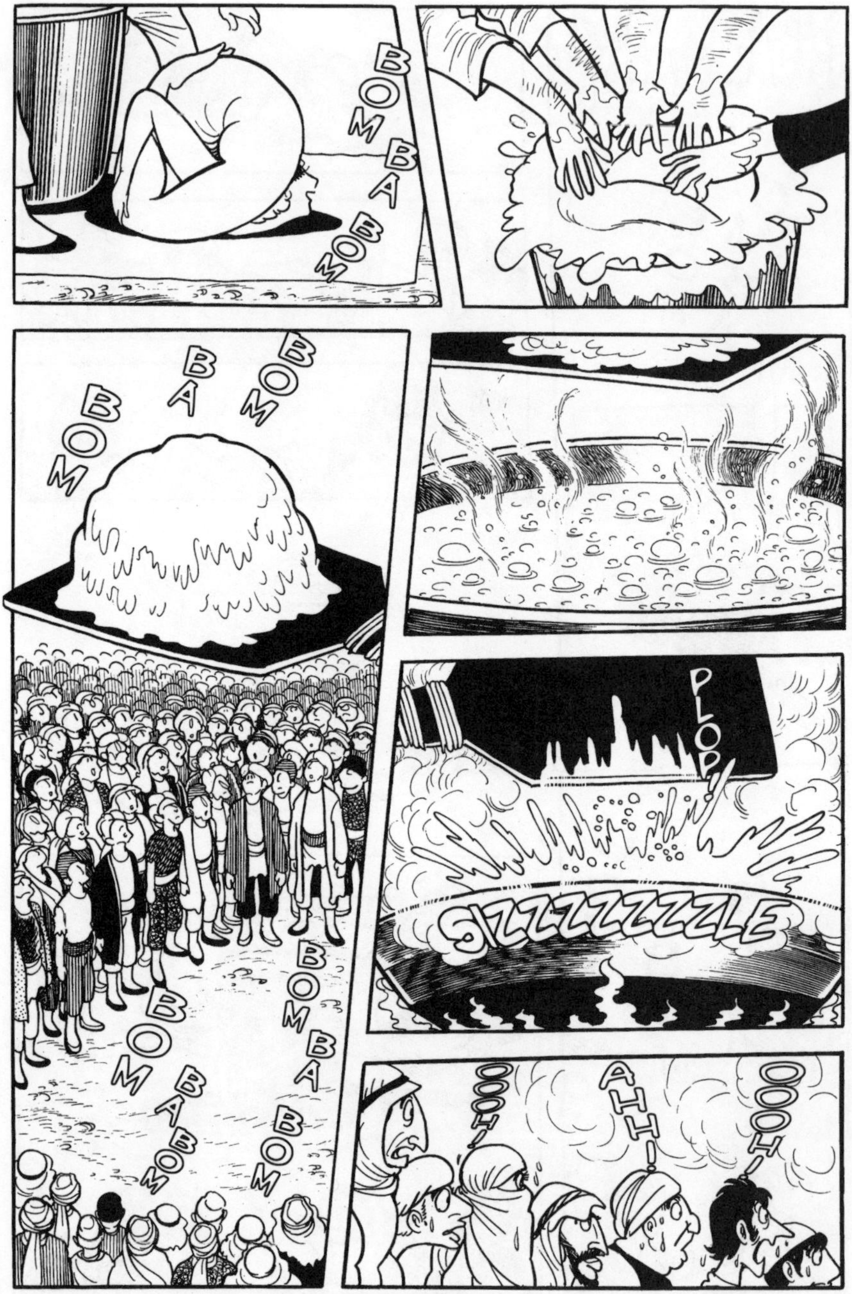
BOMBA BOM
PLOP!
SIZZZZZZLE
OOOH!
AHH!
OOOH!
BOM BA BOM
BOMBA BOM
BOM BABOM

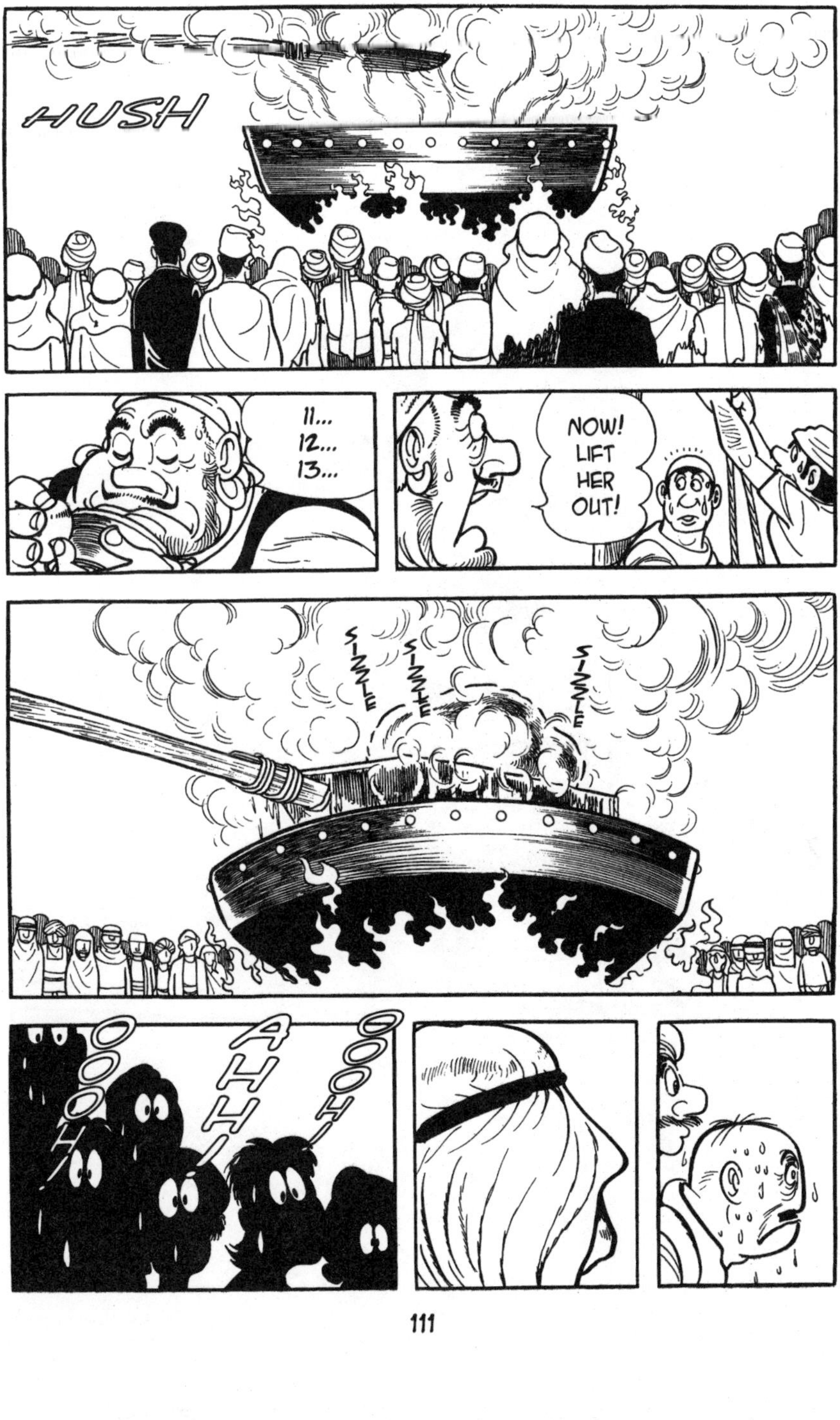
HUSH
11...
12...
13...
NOW! LIFT HER OUT!
SIZZLE
SIZZLE
SIZZLE
OOOH!
AHH!
OOOH!

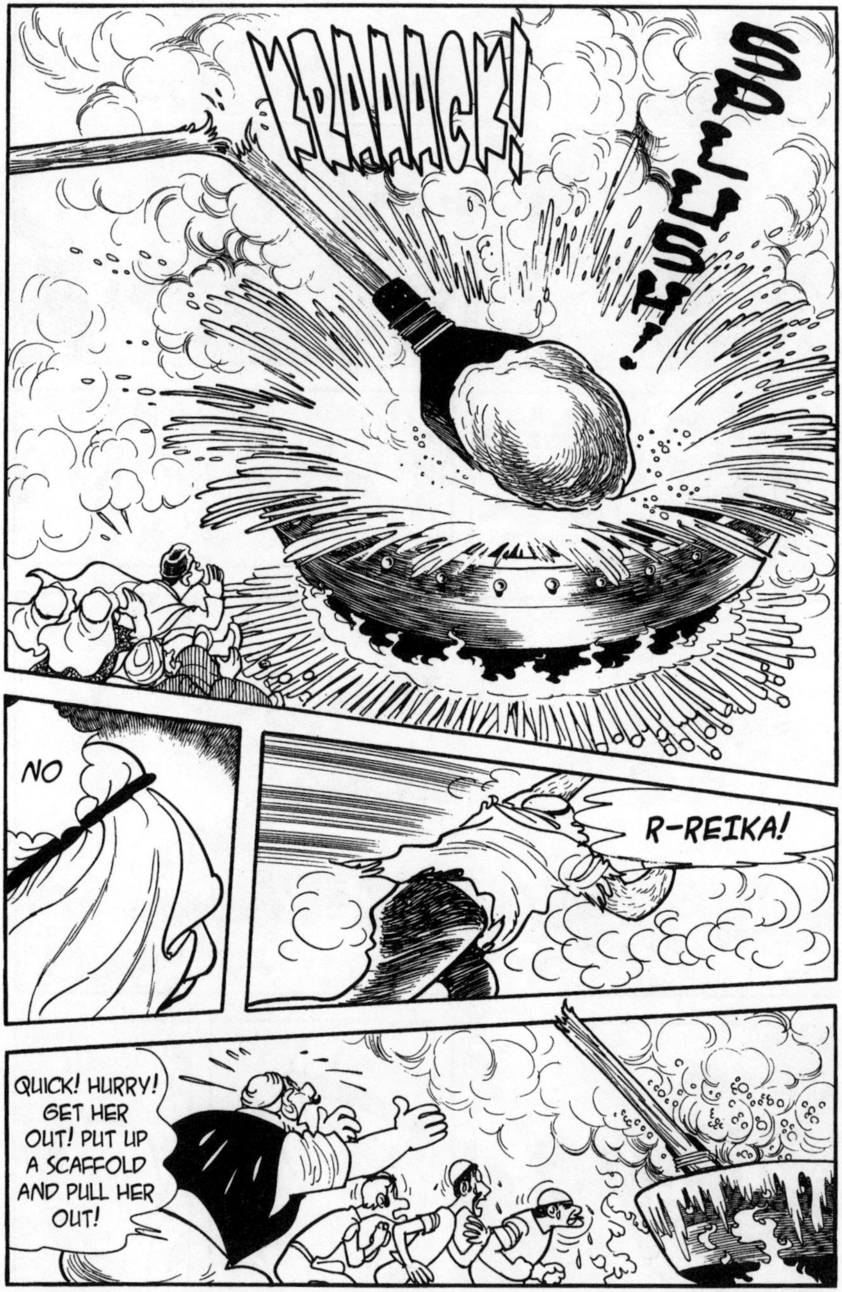
SPLUSH!
KRAAACK!
R-REIKA!
NO
QUICK! HURRY! GET HER OUT! PUT UP A SCAFFOLD AND PULL HER OUT!

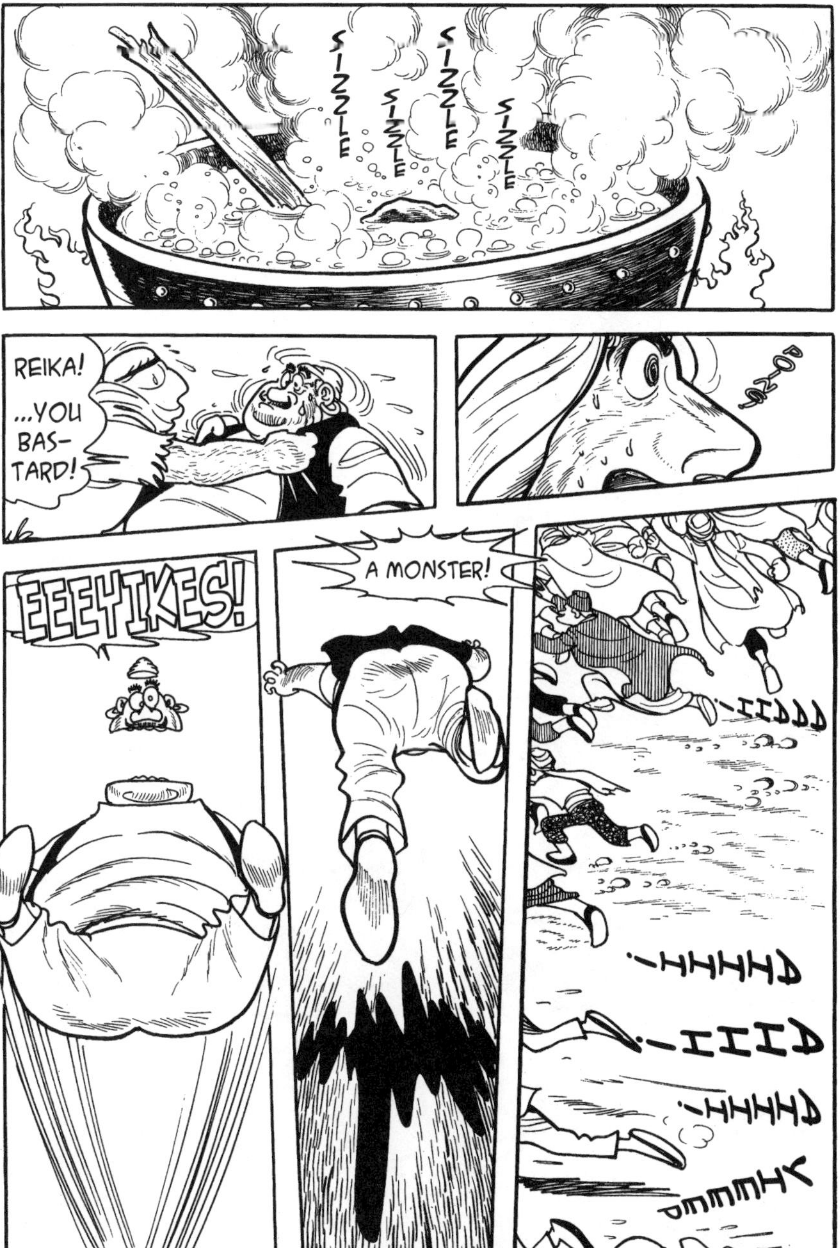
SIZZLE
SIZZLE
SIZZLE
SIZZLE
REIKA!
...YOU BAS-TARD!
AAAII-!
AHHHH!
AHHH-!
AHHHH!
A MONSTER!
EEEYIKES!

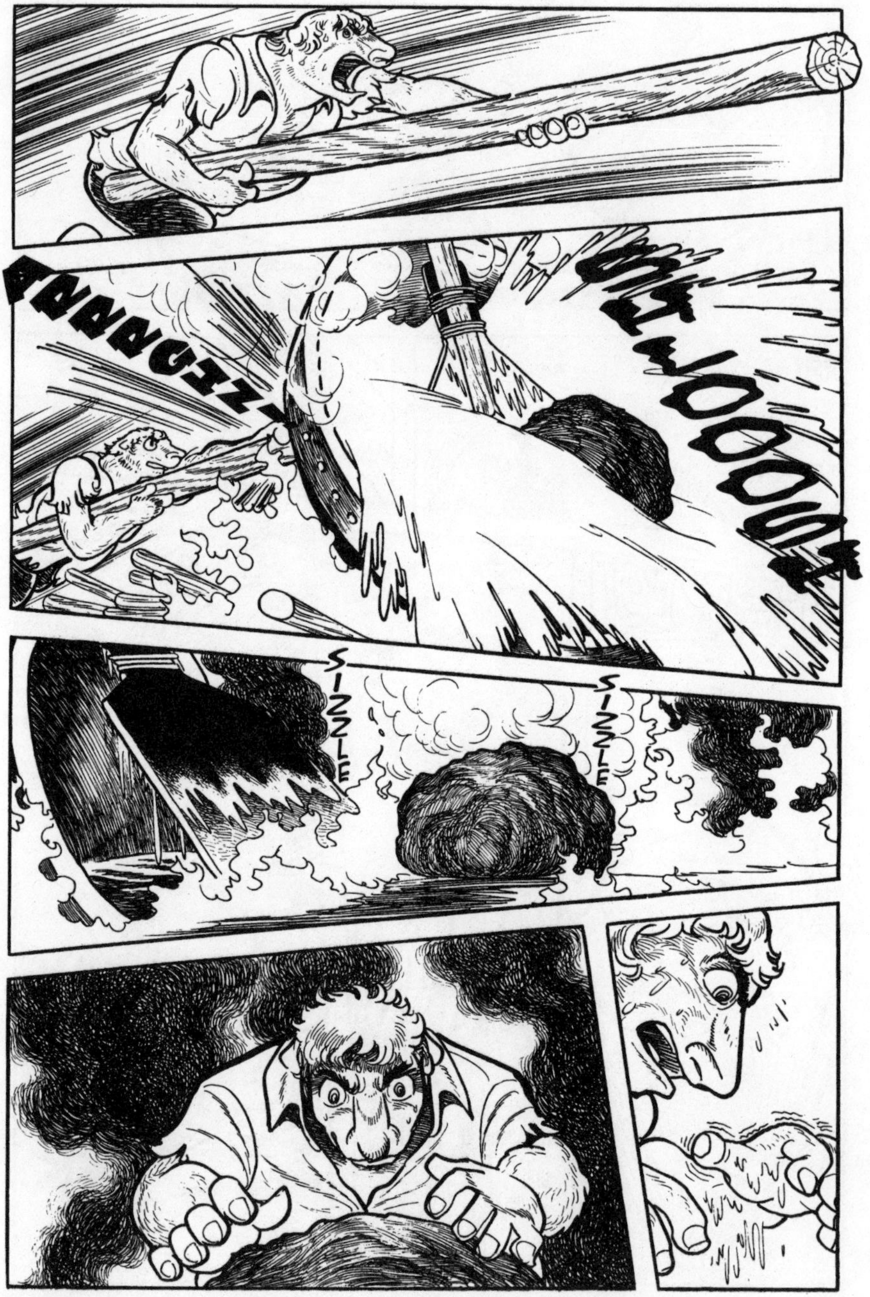
SIZZLE
SIZZLE

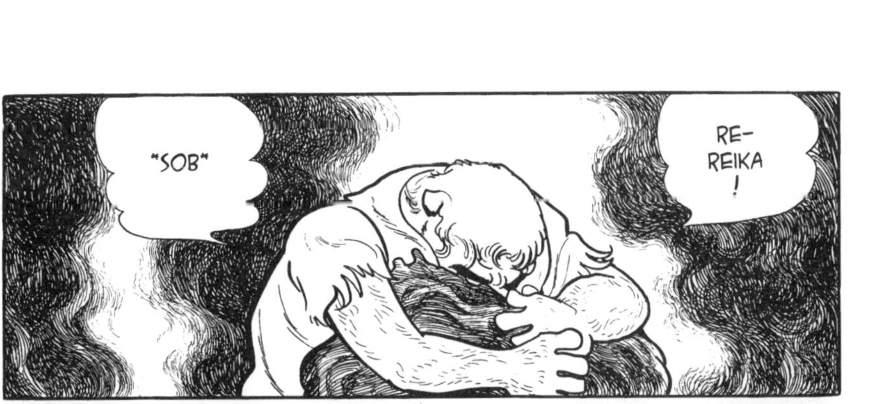
RE-REIKA!
SOB
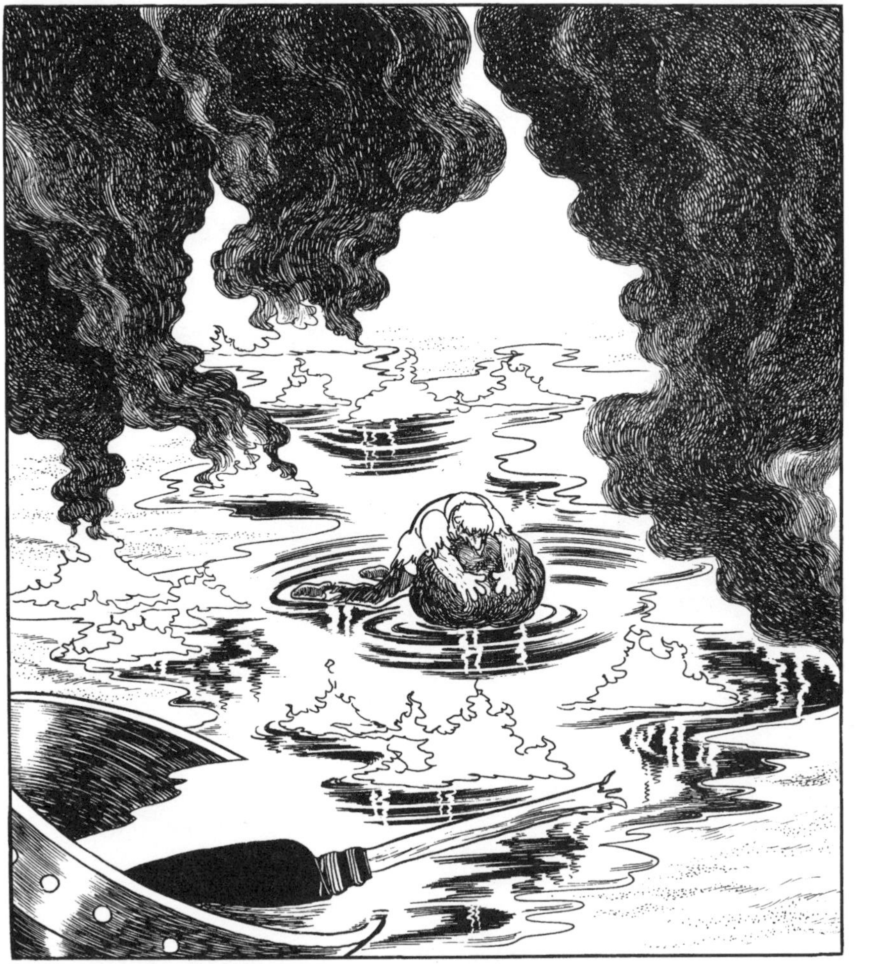

CHAPTER 14

FLASH

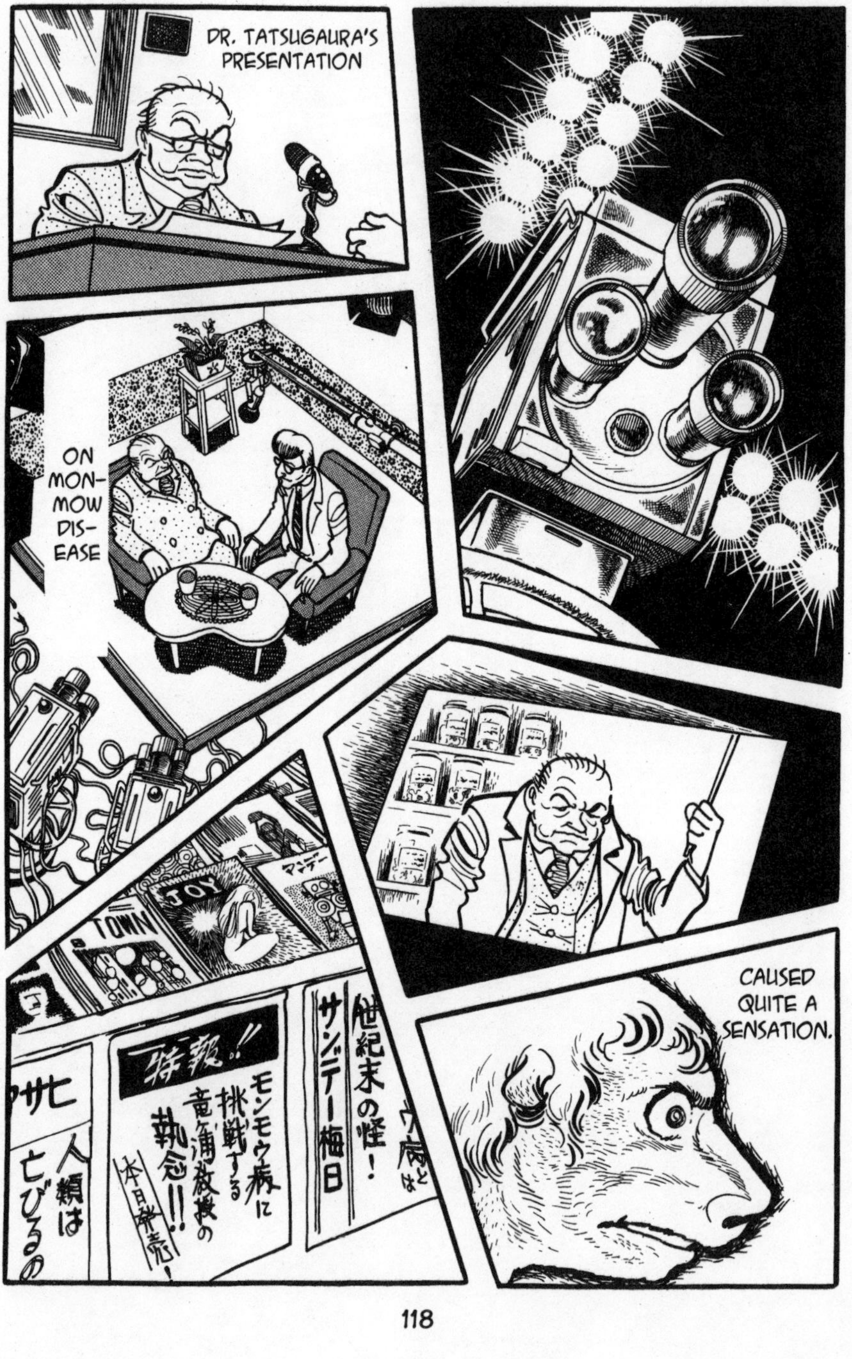
DR. TATSUGAURA'S PRESENTATION
ON MON-MOW DIS-EASE
JOY
TOWN
サンデー毎日
世紀末の怪!
特報!!
モンモウ病に挑戦する竜浦教授の執念!!
本日発売!
人類は亡びるの
CAUSED QUITE A SENSATION.

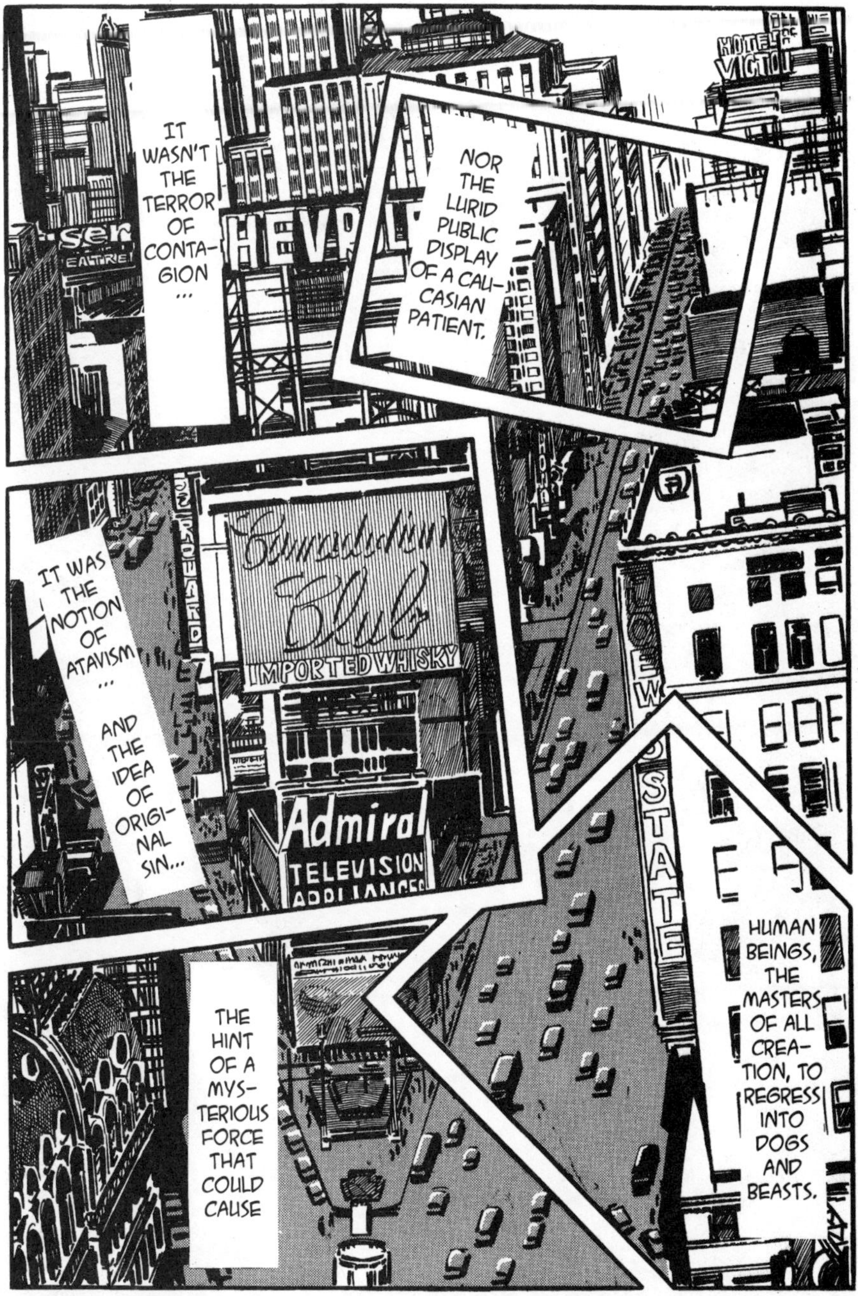
IT WASN'T THE TERROR OF CONTAGION ...
NOR THE LURID PUBLIC DISPLAY OF A CAUCASIAN PATIENT.
IMPORTED WHISKY
Admiral
TELEVISION
IT WAS THE NOTION OF ATAVISM ...
AND THE IDEA OF ORIGINAL SIN...
THE HINT OF A MYSTERIOUS FORCE THAT COULD CAUSE
HUMAN BEINGS, THE MASTERS OF ALL CREATION, TO REGRESS INTO DOGS AND BEASTS.

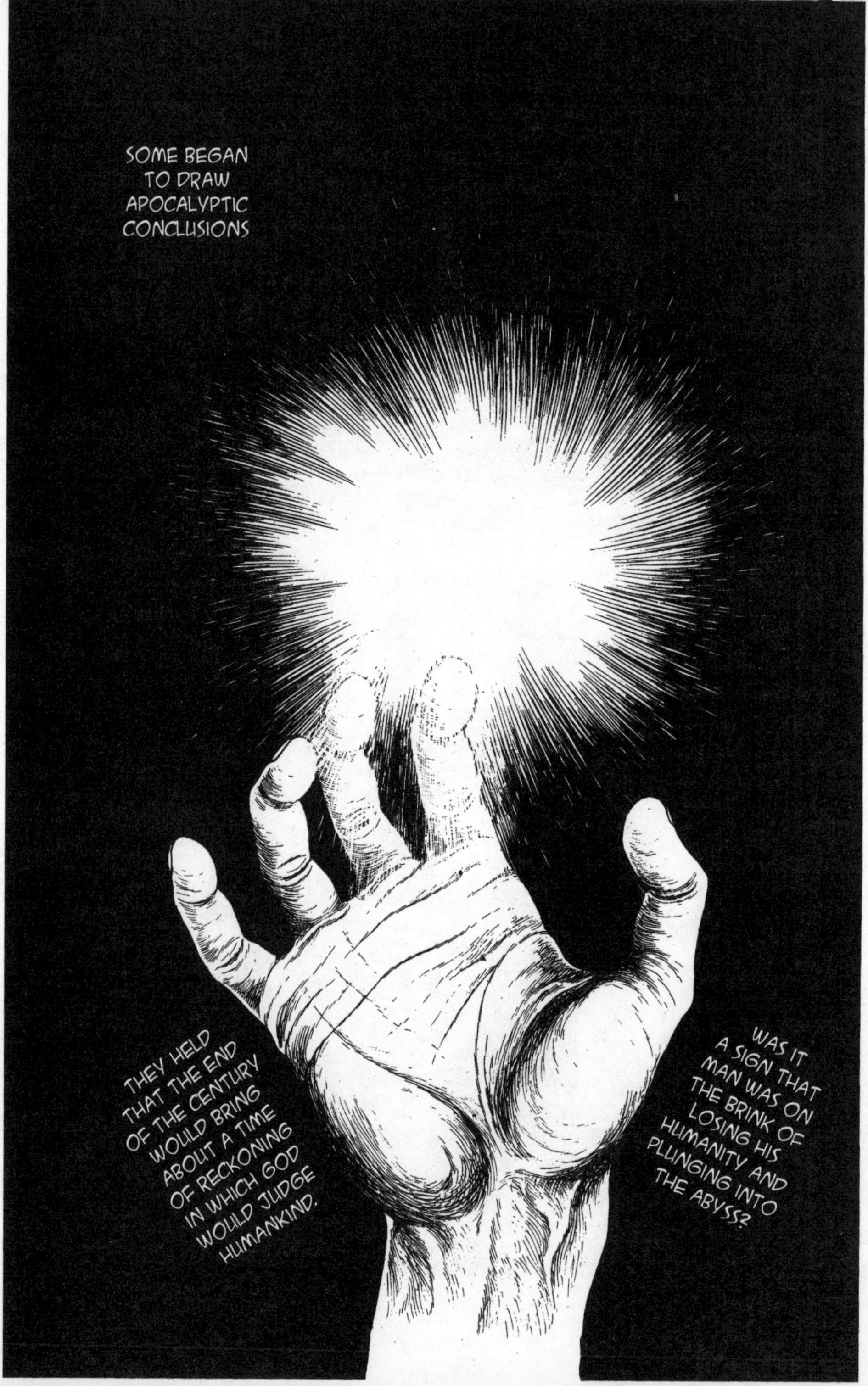
SOME BEGAN TO DRAW APOCALYPTIC CONCLUSIONS
WAS IT A SIGN THAT MAN WAS ON THE BRINK OF LOSING HIS HUMANITY AND PLUNGING INTO THE ABYSS?
THEY HELD THAT THE END OF THE CENTURY WOULD BRING ABOUT A TIME OF RECKONING IN WHICH GOD WOULD JUDGE HUMANKIND.

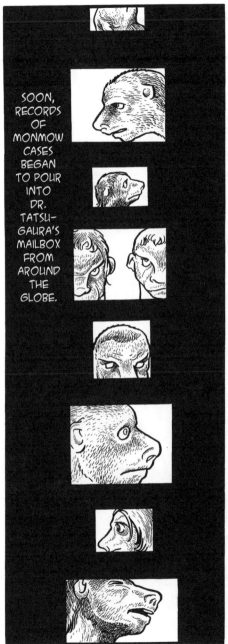

SOON, RECORDS OF MONMOW CASES BEGAN TO POUR INTO DR. TATSU-GAURA'S MAILBOX FROM AROUND THE GLOBE.

SHOCKINGLY, THERE SEEMED TO BE VICTIMS IN ALMOST EVERY COUNTRY. IN PARTICULAR, THERE WAS A SURGE IN REPORTS FROM CHRISTIAN NATIONS.

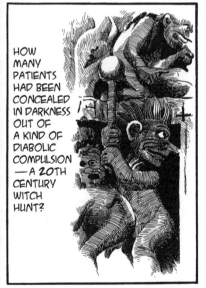

HOW MANY PATIENTS HAD BEEN CONCEALED IN DARKNESS OUT OF A KIND OF DIABOLIC COMPULSION —A 20TH CENTURY WITCH HUNT?

IN MEDICAL CIRCLES WORLDWIDE—PARTICULARLY IN THE U.S., WHICH WAS QUICK TO REACT—SCHOLARS RACED TO GATHER DATA AND LEARN MORE ABOUT THE STRANGE DISEASE.

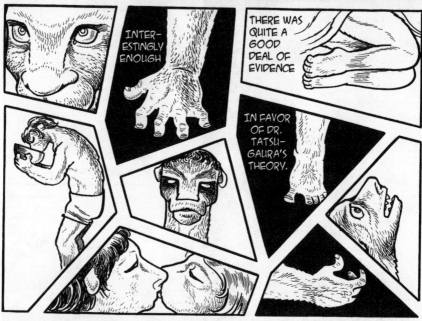

INTER-ESTINGLY ENOUGH

THERE WAS QUITE A GOOD DEAL OF EVIDENCE

IN FAVOR OF DR. TATSU-GAURA'S THEORY.

RESEARCHERS ANNOUNCED THAT THEY HAD ISO-LATED THE PATHO-GEN. AND YET...

NONE OF THE FINDINGS PROVED FINAL.

IN FACT, THERE WERE QUITE A NUMBER OF GROUPS

WHO ARGUED THAT MONMOW WASN'T INFECTIOUS.

DR. TATSUGAURA WAS INVITED TO SPEAK AT SCHOOLS ALL OVER THE WORLD.

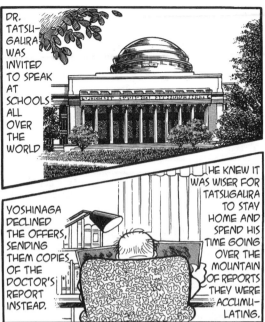

YOSHINAGA DECLINED THE OFFERS, SENDING THEM COPIES OF THE DOCTOR'S REPORT INSTEAD.

HE KNEW IT WAS WISER FOR TATSUGAURA TO STAY HOME AND SPEND HIS TIME GOING OVER THE MOUNTAIN OF REPORTS THEY WERE ACCUMULATING.

AFTER ALL, PREPARING FOR THE JMA ELECTIONS WAS MORE IMPORTANT.

MORE AIR MAIL? WHERE'S THIS ONE FROM?

SYRIA.

HOW ABOUT THAT? IT'S FROM THE JAPANESE EMBASSY IN SYRIA!

WHAT'S IT ABOUT?

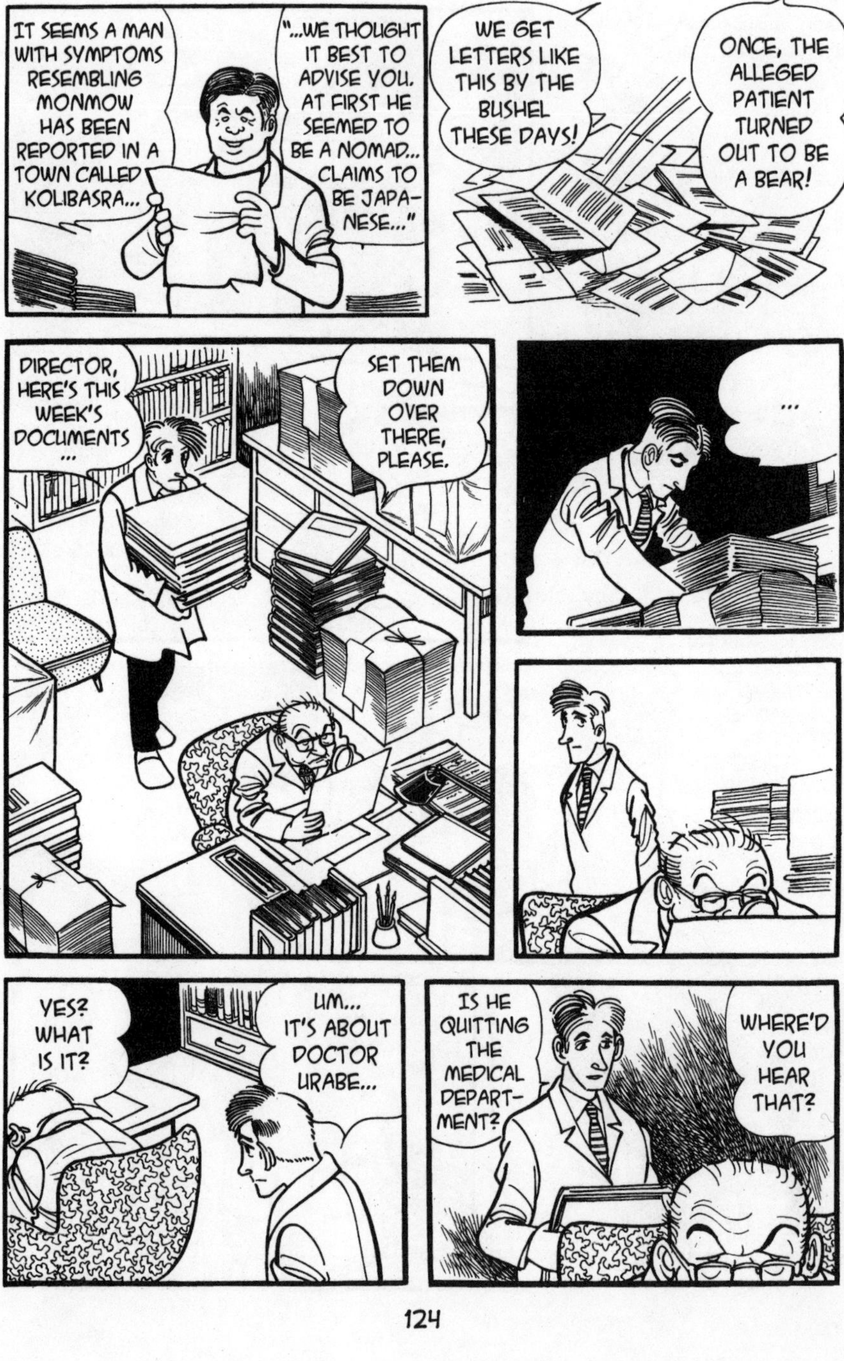
IT SEEMS A MAN WITH SYMPTOMS RESEMBLING MONMOW HAS BEEN REPORTED IN A TOWN CALLED KOLIBASRA...
"...WE THOUGHT IT BEST TO ADVISE YOU. AT FIRST HE SEEMED TO BE A NOMAD... CLAIMS TO BE JAPANESE..."
WE GET LETTERS LIKE THIS BY THE BUSHEL THESE DAYS!
ONCE, THE ALLEGED PATIENT TURNED OUT TO BE A BEAR!
DIRECTOR, HERE'S THIS WEEK'S DOCUMENTS ...
SET THEM DOWN OVER THERE, PLEASE.
...
YES? WHAT IS IT?
UM... IT'S ABOUT DOCTOR URABE...
IS HE QUITTING THE MEDICAL DEPARTMENT?
WHERE'D YOU HEAR THAT?

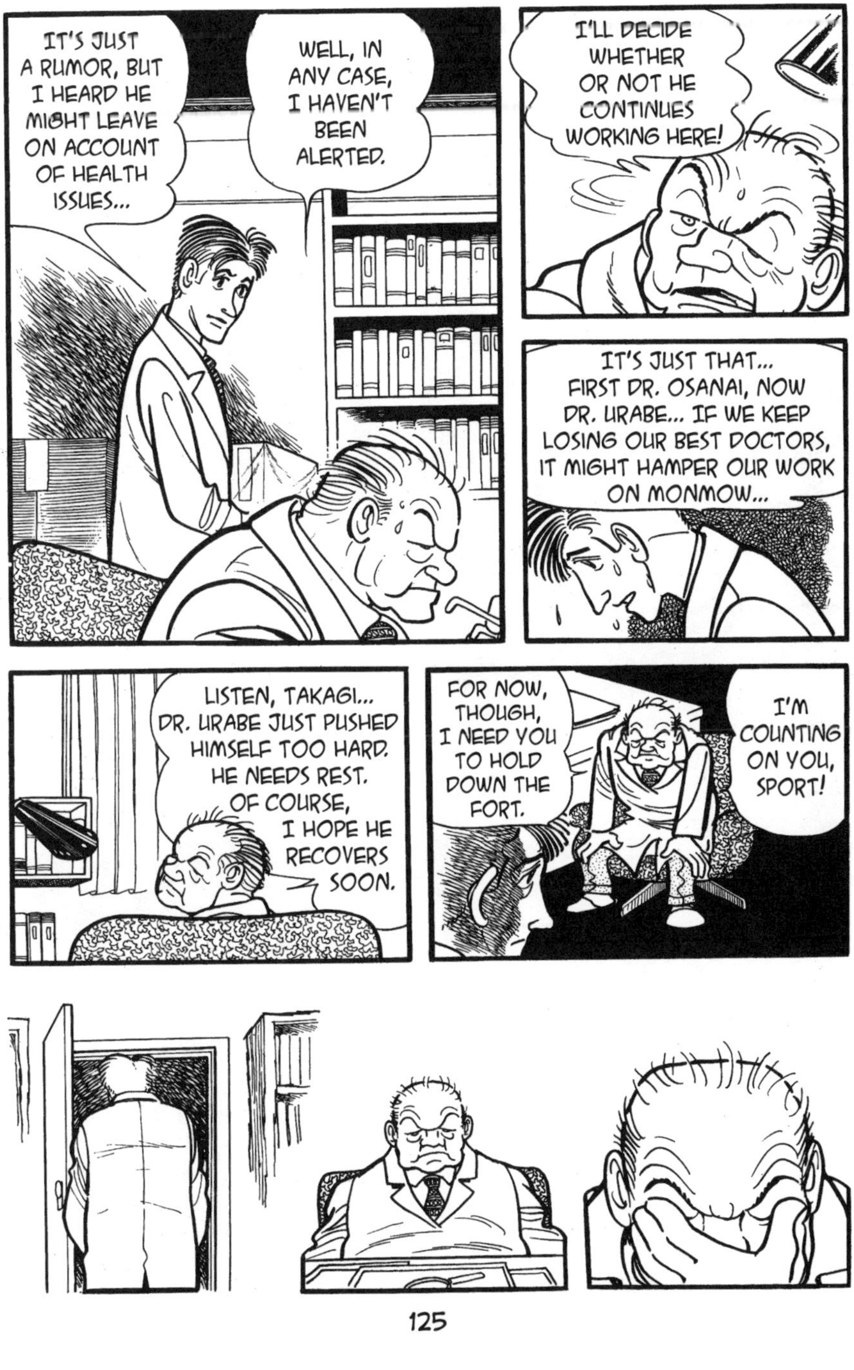
IT'S JUST A RUMOR, BUT I HEARD HE MIGHT LEAVE ON ACCOUNT OF HEALTH ISSUES...
WELL, IN ANY CASE, I HAVEN'T BEEN ALERTED.
I'LL DECIDE WHETHER OR NOT HE CONTINUES WORKING HERE!
IT'S JUST THAT... FIRST DR. OSANAI, NOW DR. URABE... IF WE KEEP LOSING OUR BEST DOCTORS, IT MIGHT HAMPER OUR WORK ON MONMOW...
LISTEN, TAKAGI... DR. URABE JUST PUSHED HIMSELF TOO HARD. HE NEEDS REST. OF COURSE, I HOPE HE RECOVERS SOON.
FOR NOW, THOUGH, I NEED YOU TO HOLD DOWN THE FORT.
I'M COUNTING ON YOU, SPORT!

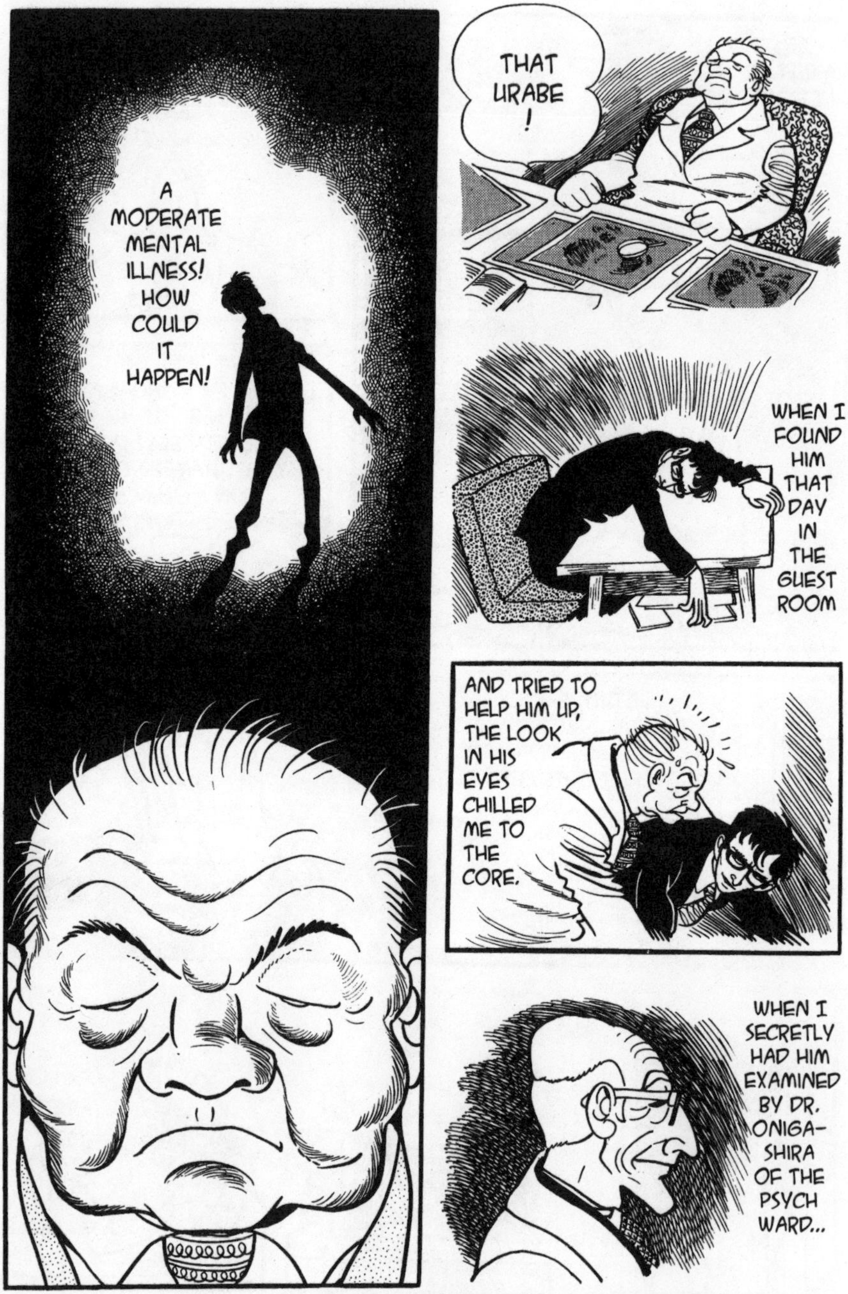
THAT URABE !
WHEN I FOUND HIM THAT DAY IN THE GUEST ROOM
AND TRIED TO HELP HIM UP, THE LOOK IN HIS EYES CHILLED ME TO THE CORE.
WHEN I SECRETLY HAD HIM EXAMINED BY DR. ONIGA-SHIRA OF THE PSYCH WARD...
A MODERATE MENTAL ILLNESS! HOW COULD IT HAPPEN!

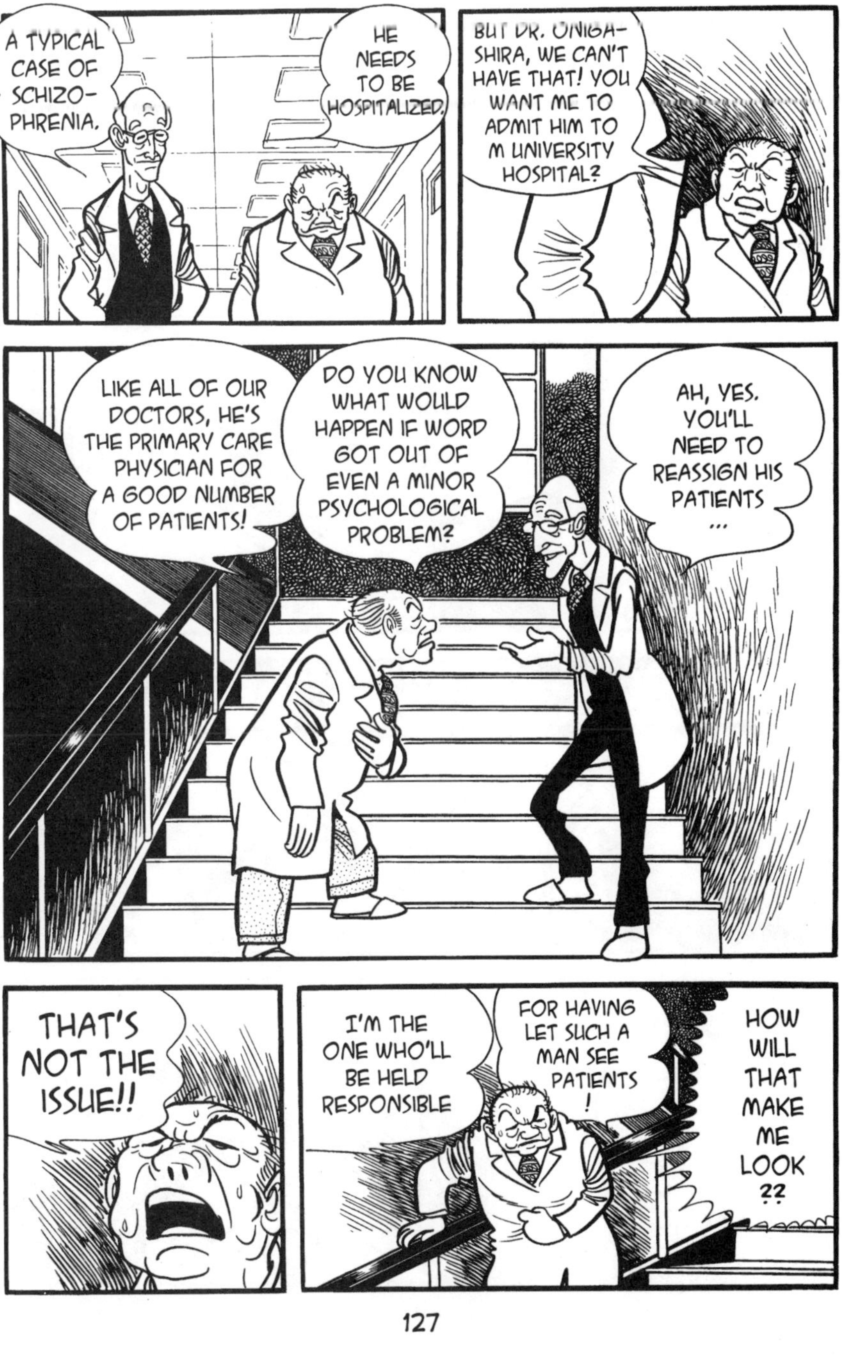
A TYPICAL CASE OF SCHIZO-PHRENIA.
HE NEEDS TO BE HOSPITALIZED.
BUT DR. ONIGA-SHIRA, WE CAN'T HAVE THAT! YOU WANT ME TO ADMIT HIM TO M UNIVERSITY HOSPITAL?
LIKE ALL OF OUR DOCTORS, HE'S THE PRIMARY CARE PHYSICIAN FOR A GOOD NUMBER OF PATIENTS!
DO YOU KNOW WHAT WOULD HAPPEN IF WORD GOT OUT OF EVEN A MINOR PSYCHOLOGICAL PROBLEM?
AH, YES. YOU'LL NEED TO REASSIGN HIS PATIENTS ...
THAT'S NOT THE ISSUE!!
I'M THE ONE WHO'LL BE HELD RESPONSIBLE
FOR HAVING LET SUCH A MAN SEE PATIENTS!
HOW WILL THAT MAKE ME LOOK??

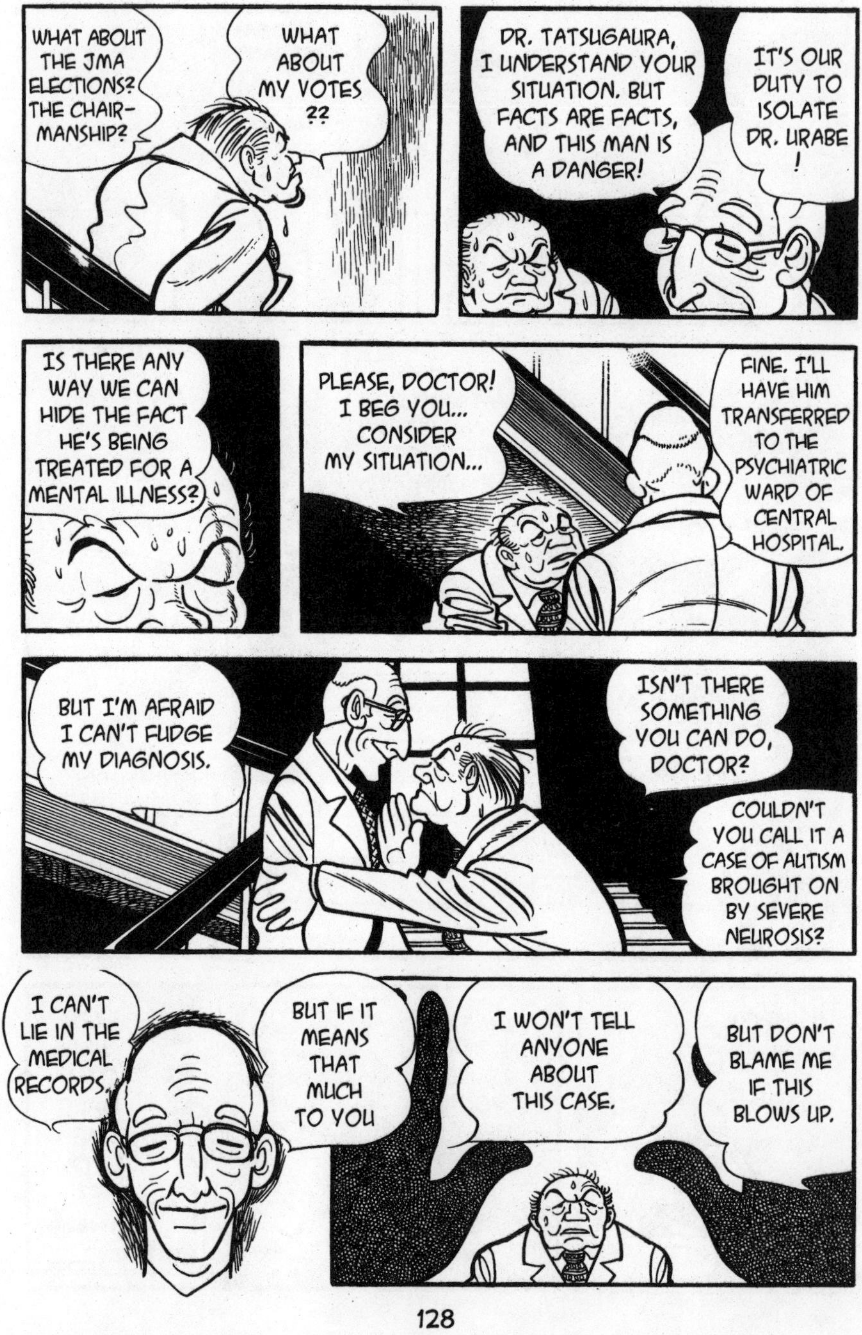
WHAT ABOUT THE JMA ELECTIONS? THE CHAIR-MANSHIP?
WHAT ABOUT MY VOTES ??
DR. TATSUGAURA, I UNDERSTAND YOUR SITUATION. BUT FACTS ARE FACTS, AND THIS MAN IS A DANGER!
IT'S OUR DUTY TO ISOLATE DR. URABE !
IS THERE ANY WAY WE CAN HIDE THE FACT HE'S BEING TREATED FOR A MENTAL ILLNESS?
PLEASE, DOCTOR! I BEG YOU... CONSIDER MY SITUATION...
FINE. I'LL HAVE HIM TRANSFERRED TO THE PSYCHIATRIC WARD OF CENTRAL HOSPITAL.
BUT I'M AFRAID I CAN'T FUDGE MY DIAGNOSIS.
ISN'T THERE SOMETHING YOU CAN DO, DOCTOR?
COULDN'T YOU CALL IT A CASE OF AUTISM BROUGHT ON BY SEVERE NEUROSIS?
I CAN'T LIE IN THE MEDICAL RECORDS.
BUT IF IT MEANS THAT MUCH TO YOU
I WON'T TELL ANYONE ABOUT THIS CASE.
BUT DON'T BLAME ME IF THIS BLOWS UP.

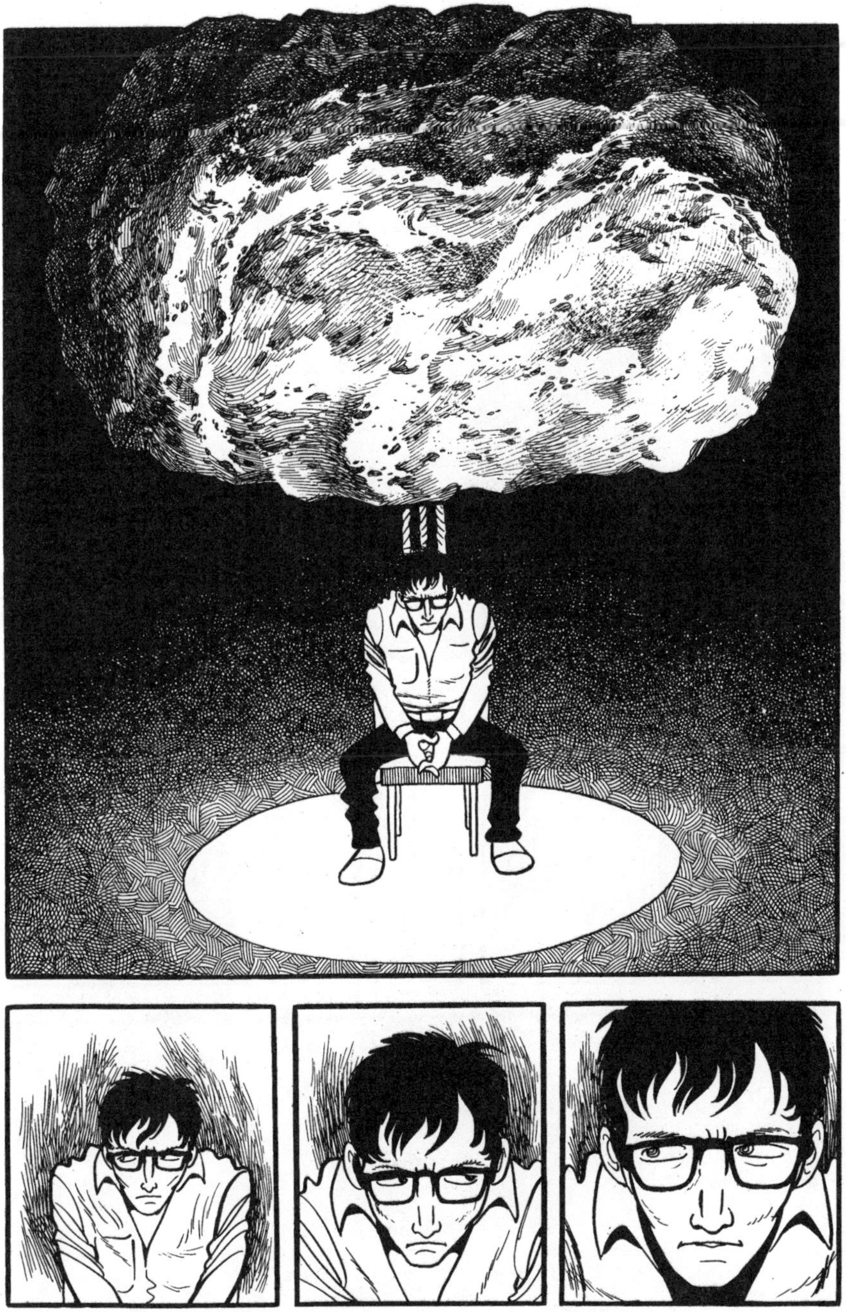

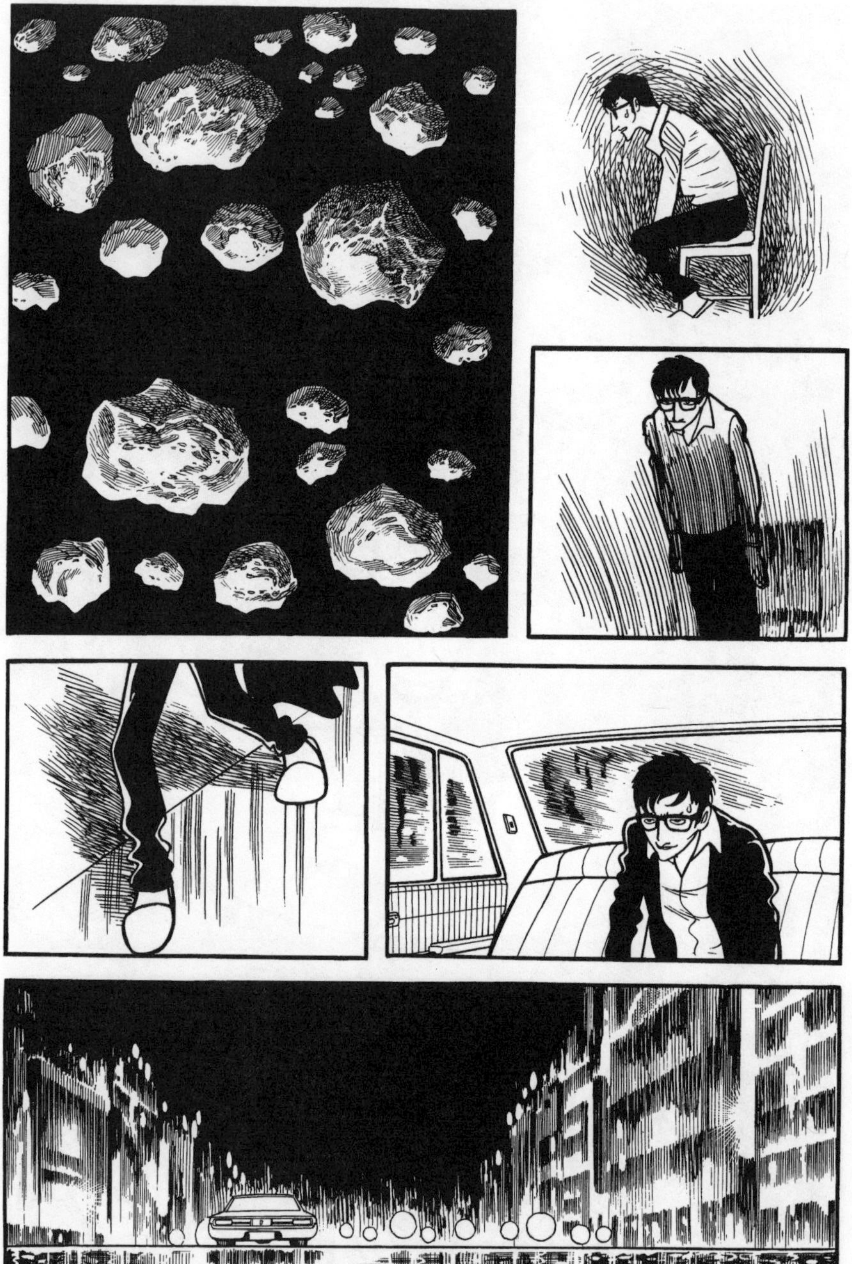

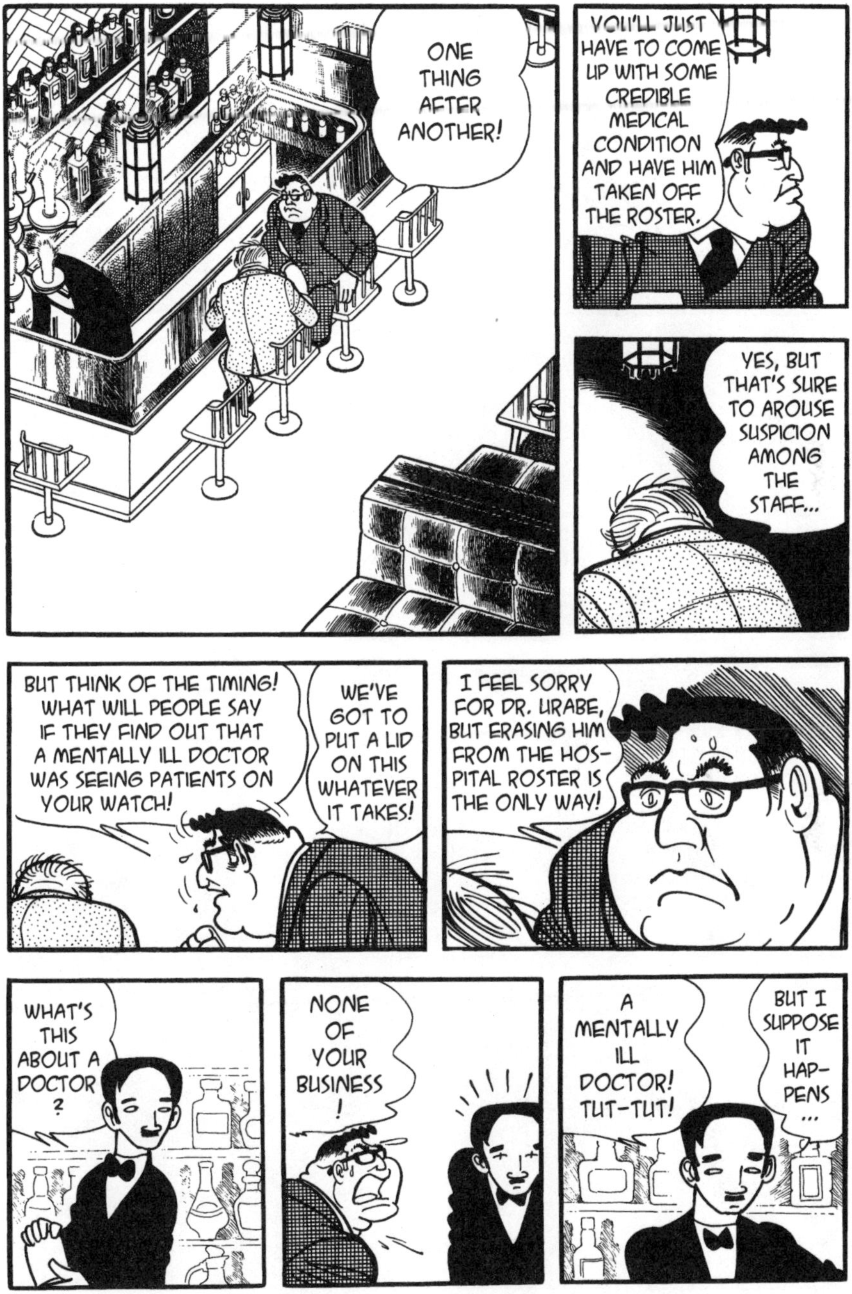
ONE THING AFTER ANOTHER!
YOU'LL JUST HAVE TO COME UP WITH SOME CREDIBLE MEDICAL CONDITION AND HAVE HIM TAKEN OFF THE ROSTER.
YES, BUT THAT'S SURE TO AROUSE SUSPICION AMONG THE STAFF...
BUT THINK OF THE TIMING! WHAT WILL PEOPLE SAY IF THEY FIND OUT THAT A MENTALLY ILL DOCTOR WAS SEEING PATIENTS ON YOUR WATCH!
WE'VE GOT TO PUT A LID ON THIS WHATEVER IT TAKES!
I FEEL SORRY FOR DR. URABE, BUT ERASING HIM FROM THE HOSPITAL ROSTER IS THE ONLY WAY!
WHAT'S THIS ABOUT A DOCTOR ?
NONE OF YOUR BUSINESS !
A MENTALLY ILL DOCTOR! TUT-TUT!
BUT I SUPPOSE IT HAPPENS ...

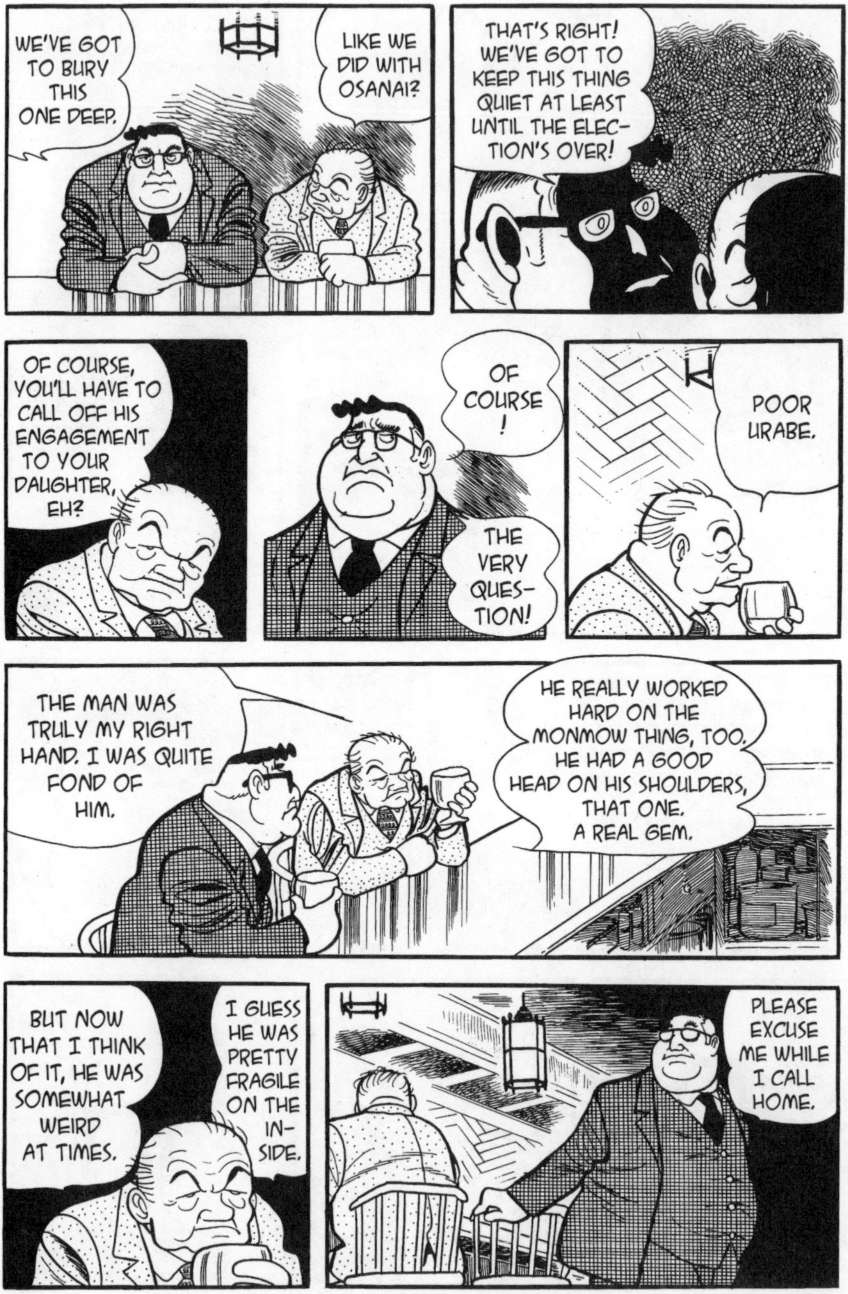
WE'VE GOT TO BURY THIS ONE DEEP.
LIKE WE DID WITH OSANAI?
THAT'S RIGHT! WE'VE GOT TO KEEP THIS THING QUIET AT LEAST UNTIL THE ELEC-TION'S OVER!
OF COURSE, YOU'LL HAVE TO CALL OFF HIS ENGAGEMENT TO YOUR DAUGHTER, EH?
OF COURSE!
THE VERY QUES-TION!
POOR URABE.
THE MAN WAS TRULY MY RIGHT HAND. I WAS QUITE FOND OF HIM.
HE REALLY WORKED HARD ON THE MONMOW THING, TOO. HE HAD A GOOD HEAD ON HIS SHOULDERS, THAT ONE. A REAL GEM.
BUT NOW THAT I THINK OF IT, HE WAS SOMEWHAT WEIRD AT TIMES.
I GUESS HE WAS PRETTY FRAGILE ON THE IN-SIDE.
PLEASE EXCUSE ME WHILE I CALL HOME.

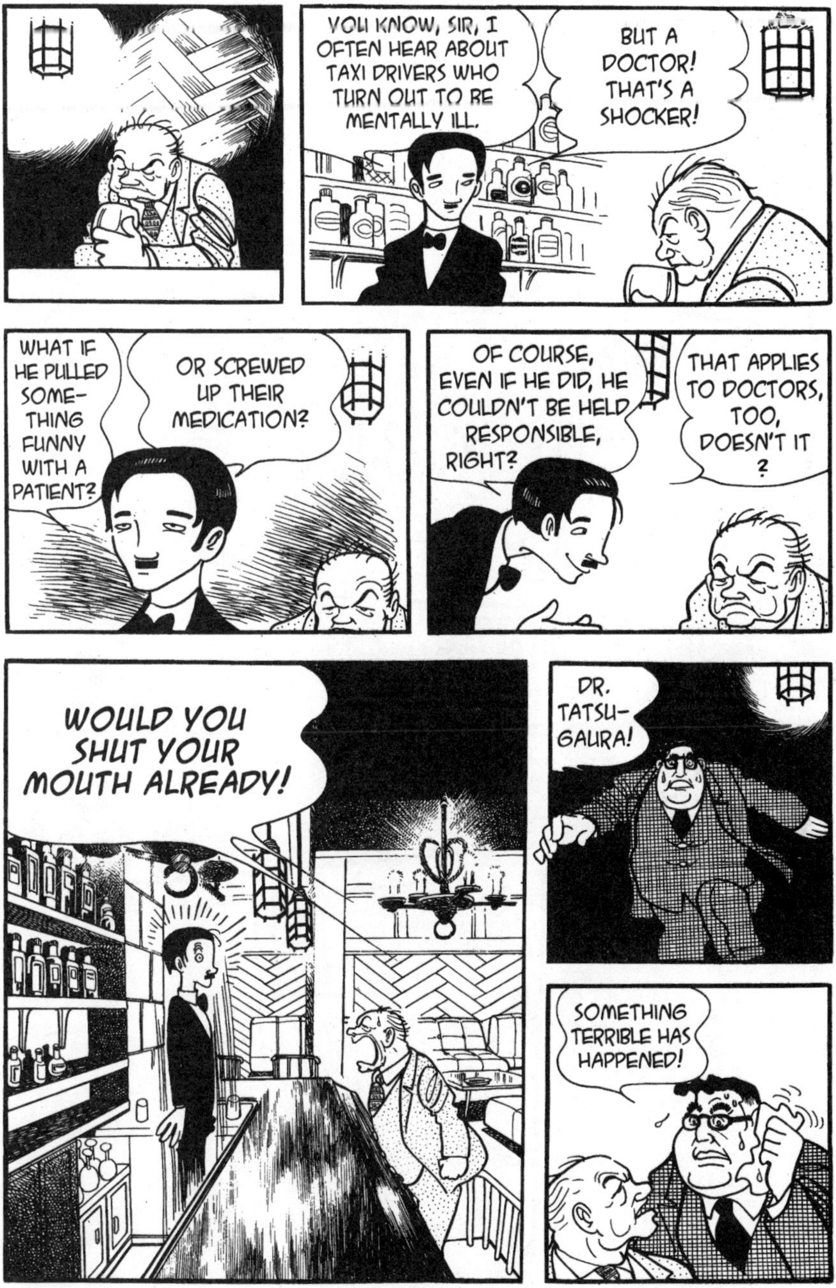
YOU KNOW, SIR, I OFTEN HEAR ABOUT TAXI DRIVERS WHO TURN OUT TO BE MENTALLY ILL.
BUT A DOCTOR! THAT'S A SHOCKER!
WHAT IF HE PULLED SOME-THING FUNNY WITH A PATIENT?
OR SCREWED UP THEIR MEDICATION?
OF COURSE, EVEN IF HE DID, HE COULDN'T BE HELD RESPONSIBLE, RIGHT?
THAT APPLIES TO DOCTORS, TOO, DOESN'T IT?
WOULD YOU SHUT YOUR MOUTH ALREADY!
DR. TATSU-GAURA!
SOMETHING TERRIBLE HAS HAPPENED!

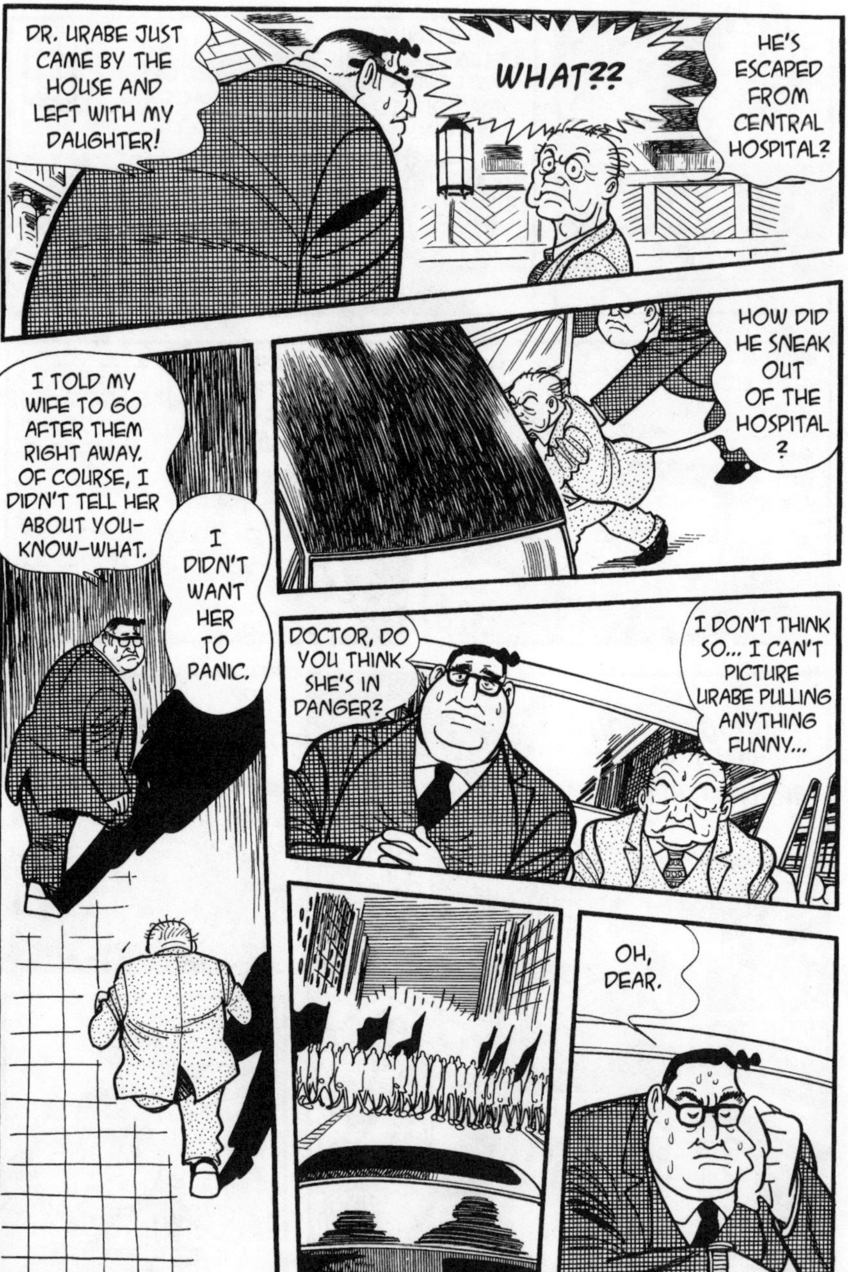
DR. URABE JUST CAME BY THE HOUSE AND LEFT WITH MY DAUGHTER!
WHAT??
HE'S ESCAPED FROM CENTRAL HOSPITAL?
HOW DID HE SNEAK OUT OF THE HOSPITAL ?
I TOLD MY WIFE TO GO AFTER THEM RIGHT AWAY. OF COURSE, I DIDN'T TELL HER ABOUT YOU-KNOW-WHAT.
I DIDN'T WANT HER TO PANIC.
DOCTOR, DO YOU THINK SHE'S IN DANGER?
I DON'T THINK SO... I CAN'T PICTURE URABE PULLING ANYTHING FUNNY...
OH, DEAR.

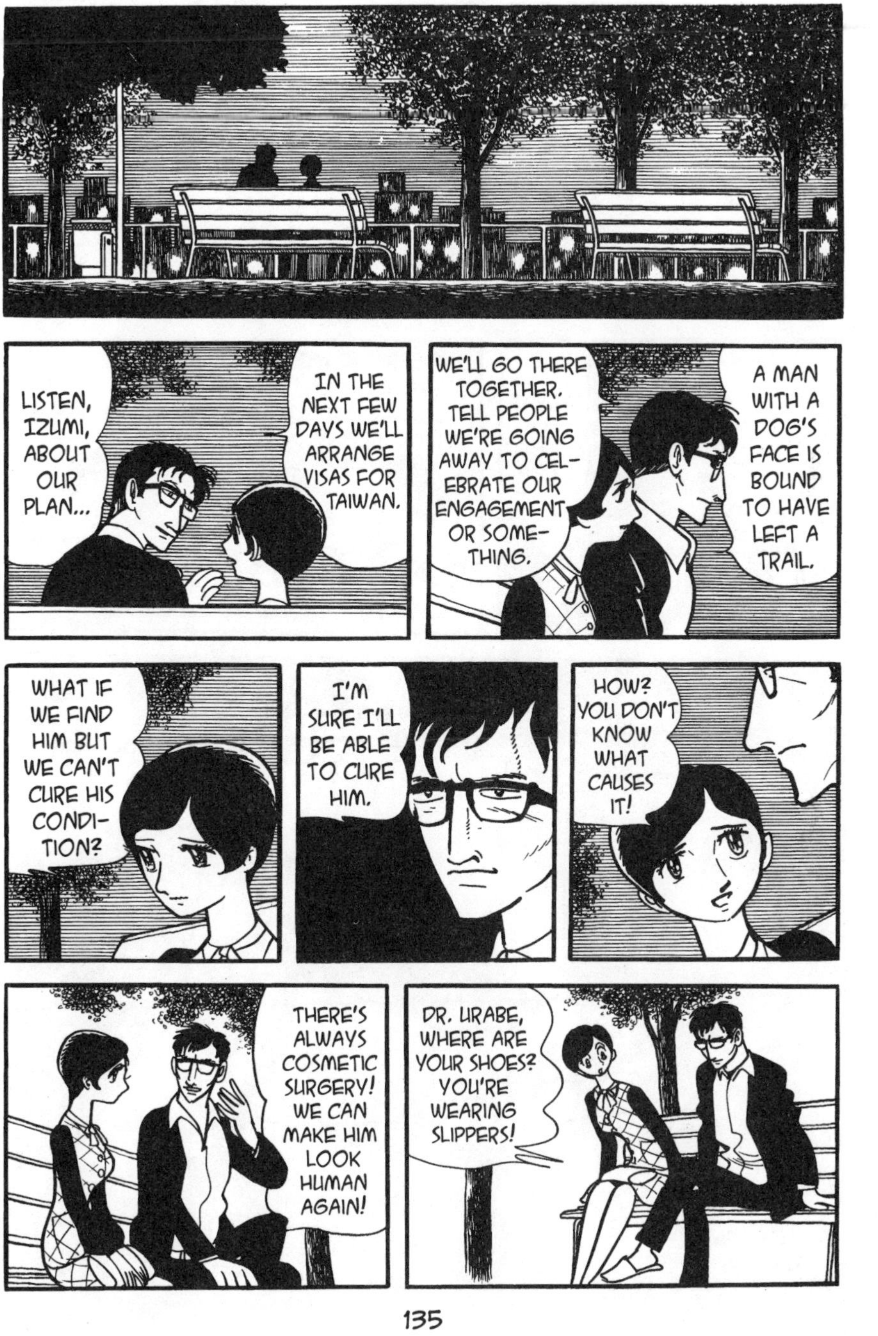
LISTEN, IZUMI, ABOUT OUR PLAN...
IN THE NEXT FEW DAYS WE'LL ARRANGE VISAS FOR TAIWAN.
WE'LL GO THERE TOGETHER. TELL PEOPLE WE'RE GOING AWAY TO CEL-EBRATE OUR ENGAGEMENT OR SOME-THING.
A MAN WITH A DOG'S FACE IS BOUND TO HAVE LEFT A TRAIL.
WHAT IF WE FIND HIM BUT WE CAN'T CURE HIS CONDI-TION?
I'M SURE I'LL BE ABLE TO CURE HIM.
HOW? YOU DON'T KNOW WHAT CAUSES IT!
THERE'S ALWAYS COSMETIC SURGERY! WE CAN MAKE HIM LOOK HUMAN AGAIN!
DR. URABE, WHERE ARE YOUR SHOES? YOU'RE WEARING SLIPPERS!

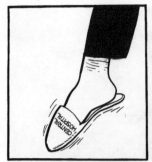

WHY, THEY'RE FROM CENTRAL HOSPITAL!

HOW ODD!

ODD, IN- DEED!

I ESCAPED FROM C. H. TO COME HERE.

WHAT DID YOU JUST SAY ?

THEY'VE ALL GANGED UP

AND LABELED ME MENTALLY ILL! LOCKED ME IN THE FUNNY FARM!

B-BUT WHY?

HEH HEH HEH HEH... HEH HEH HEH...

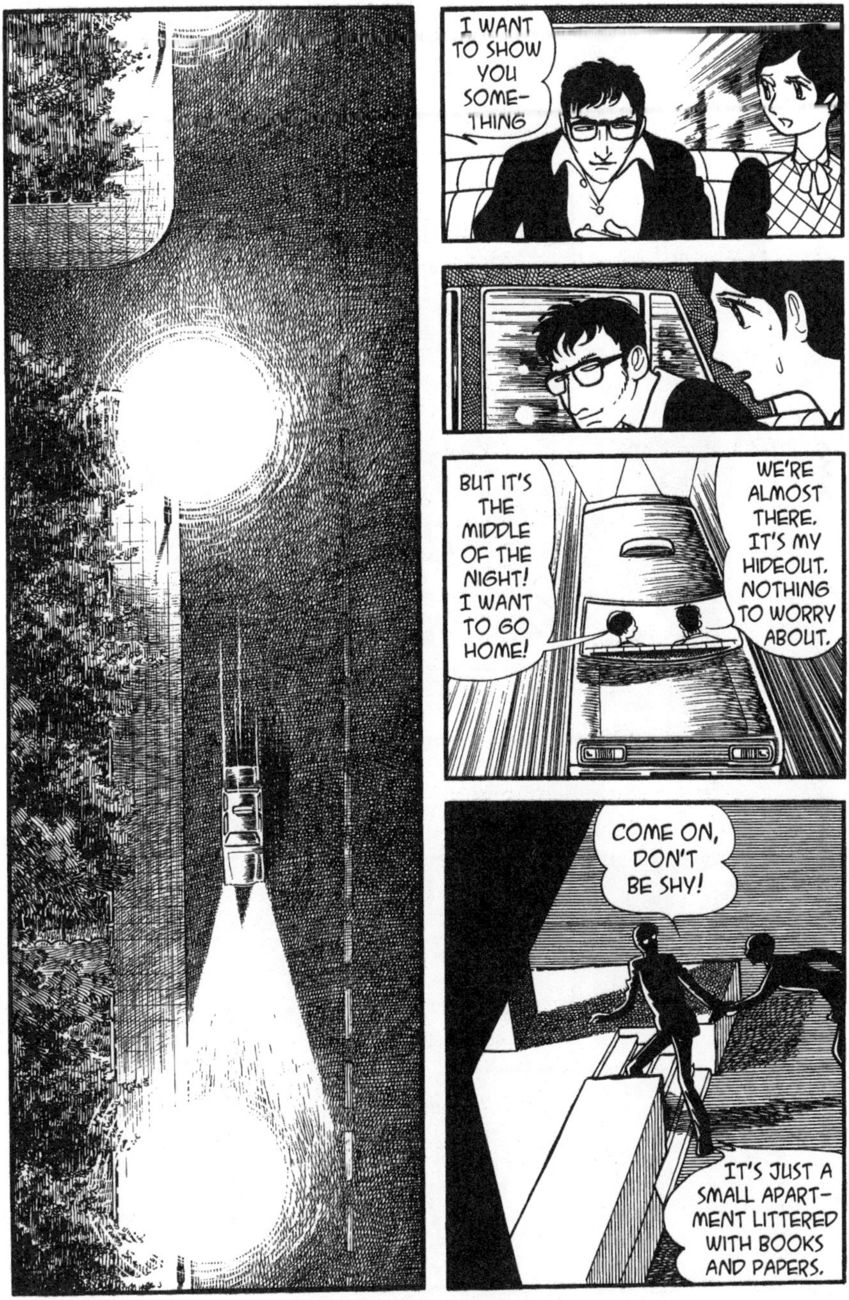
I WANT TO SHOW YOU SOME-THING
WE'RE ALMOST THERE. IT'S MY HIDEOUT. NOTHING TO WORRY ABOUT.
BUT IT'S THE MIDDLE OF THE NIGHT! I WANT TO GO HOME!
COME ON, DON'T BE SHY!
IT'S JUST A SMALL APART-MENT LITTERED WITH BOOKS AND PAPERS.

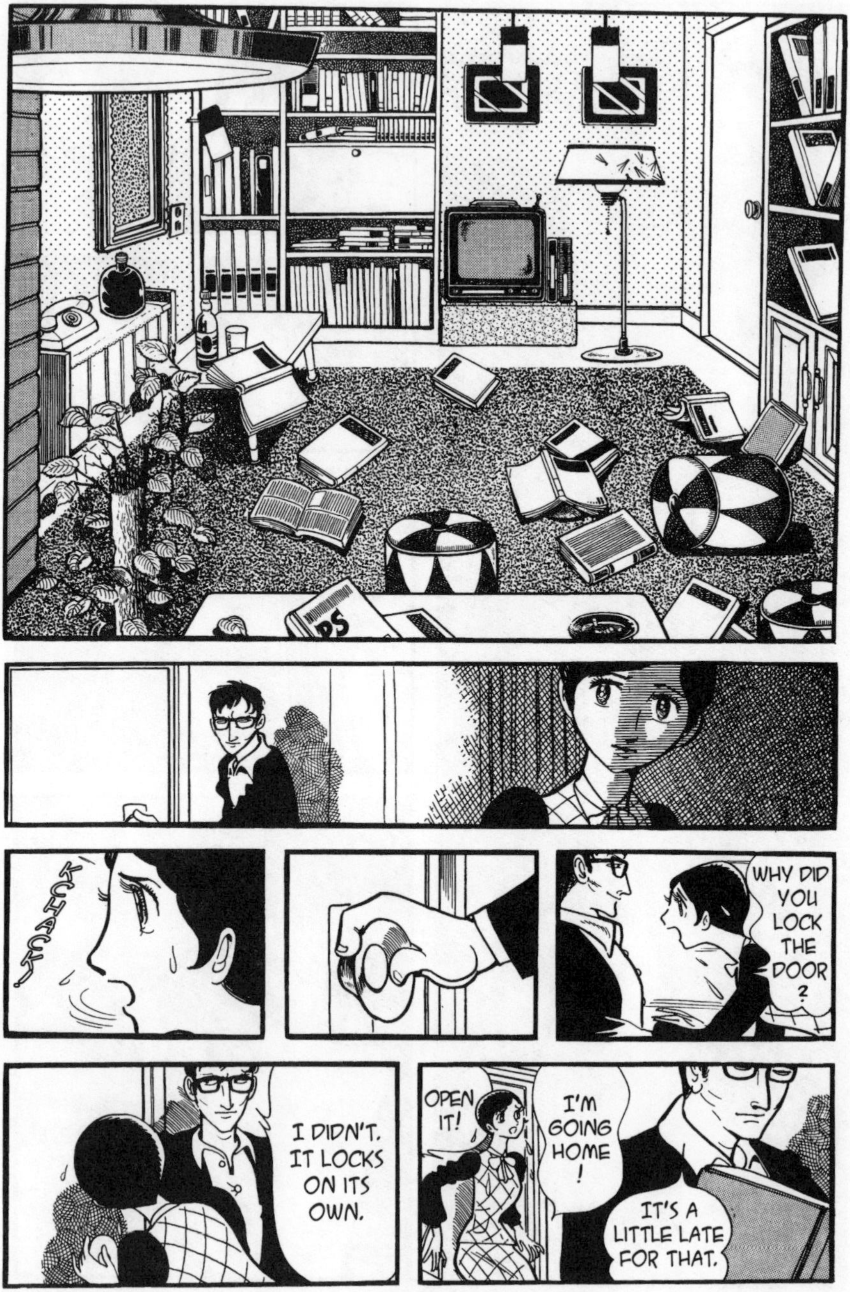
PS
KCHACK
WHY DID YOU LOCK THE DOOR?
I DIDN'T. IT LOCKS ON ITS OWN.
OPEN IT!
I'M GOING HOME!
IT'S A LITTLE LATE FOR THAT.

COME LOOK, THESE BOOKS WILL ASSUAGE YOUR FEARS.

SEE HERE ...

PLEASE ...

PLEASE LET ME GO!

JACOBSON (COLUMBIA UNIVERSITY) REPORTS TWENTY SUCCESSFUL CASES...

RATTLE RATTLE RATTLE

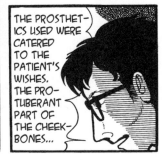

THE PROSTHET- ICS USED WERE CATERED TO THE PATIENT'S WISHES. THE PRO- TUBERANT PART OF THE CHEEK- BONES...

KA-CHAKK

HELLO? HELLO?

MOTHER? IT'S ME! I'M AT DR. URABE'S PLACE. TELL DADDY TO COME PICK ME UP!

WHAT? DADDY WENT LOOKING FOR ME? WITH DR. TATSU- GAURA?

HOW LONG AGO?

WHAT?

MOTHER, ARE YOU SERIOUS?

B-BUT...

WHAT?

YES?

MM-HMM.

...

THE MAXILLOMAN-DIBULAR RESECTIONING IS USUALLY DONE TO TREAT KREBS.... THE OPERATION ITSELF ISN'T DIFFICULT.

OF COURSE, WITH KREBS CYCLE, THE PROCEDURE IS MEAN-INGLESS IF THE DISEASE HAS METASTASIZED, SO IT'S PREFERABLE NOT TO GO TO SUCH EXTREMES

140

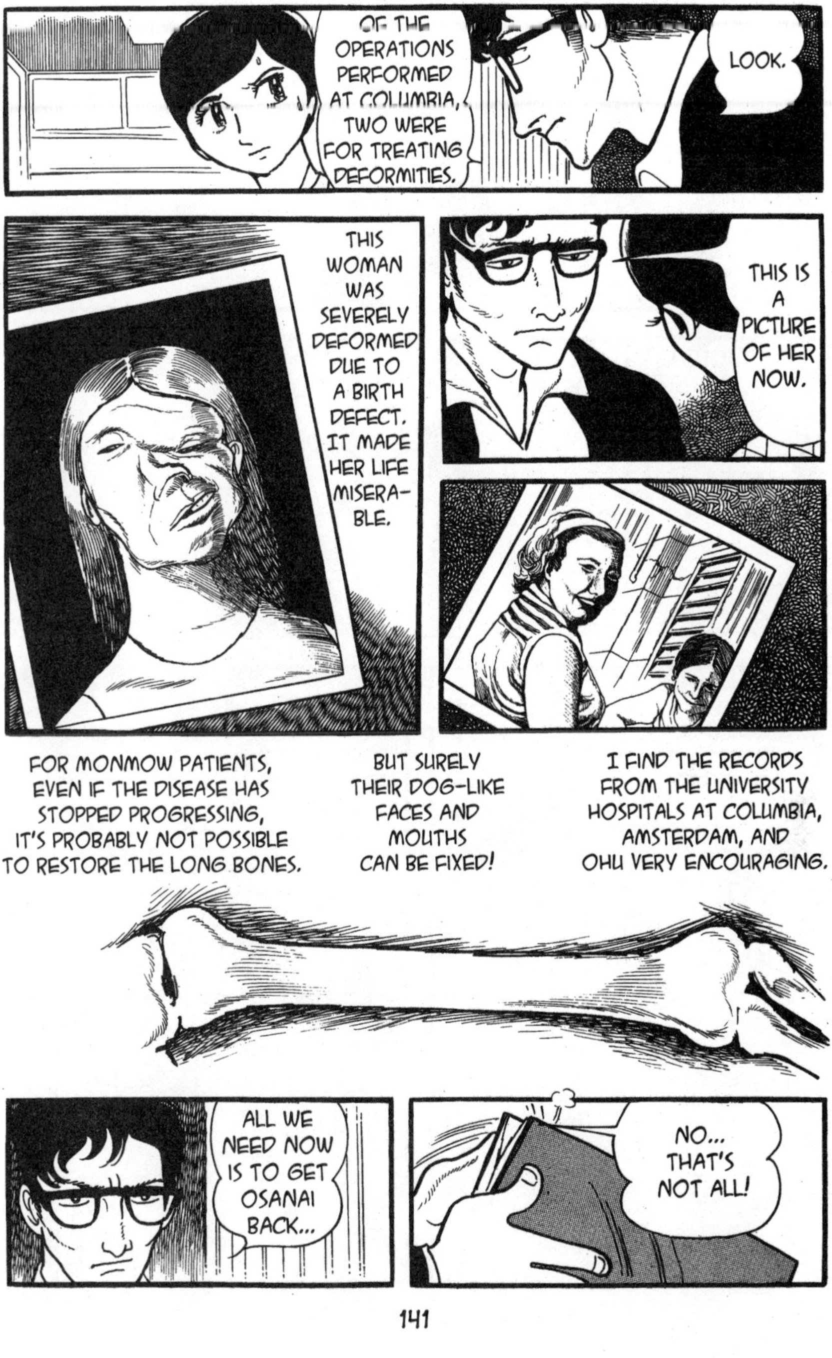
OF THE OPERATIONS PERFORMED AT COLUMBIA, TWO WERE FOR TREATING DEFORMITIES.
LOOK.
THIS WOMAN WAS SEVERELY DEFORMED DUE TO A BIRTH DEFECT. IT MADE HER LIFE MISERA-BLE.
THIS IS A PICTURE OF HER NOW.
FOR MONMOW PATIENTS, EVEN IF THE DISEASE HAS STOPPED PROGRESSING, IT'S PROBABLY NOT POSSIBLE TO RESTORE THE LONG BONES.
BUT SURELY THEIR DOG-LIKE FACES AND MOUTHS CAN BE FIXED!
I FIND THE RECORDS FROM THE UNIVERSITY HOSPITALS AT COLUMBIA, AMSTERDAM, AND OHU VERY ENCOURAGING.
ALL WE NEED NOW IS TO GET OSANAI BACK...
NO... THAT'S NOT ALL!

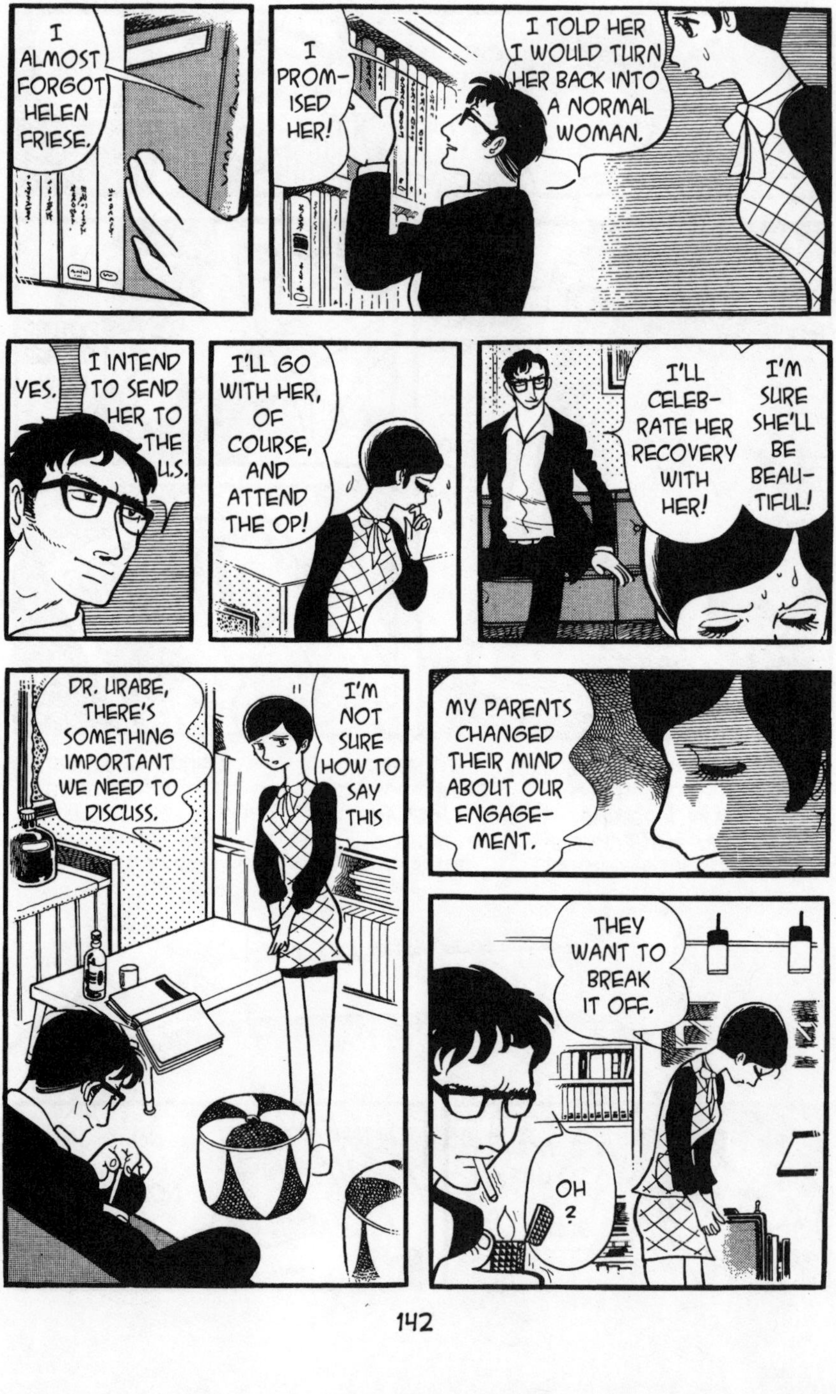
I ALMOST FORGOT HELEN FRIESE.
I PROM-ISED HER!
I TOLD HER I WOULD TURN HER BACK INTO A NORMAL WOMAN.
YES.
I INTEND TO SEND HER TO THE U.S.
I'LL GO WITH HER, OF COURSE, AND ATTEND THE OP!
I'LL CELEB-RATE HER RECOVERY WITH HER!
I'M SURE SHE'LL BE BEAU-TIFUL!
DR. URABE, THERE'S SOMETHING IMPORTANT WE NEED TO DISCUSS.
I'M NOT SURE HOW TO SAY THIS
MY PARENTS CHANGED THEIR MIND ABOUT OUR ENGAGE-MENT.
THEY WANT TO BREAK IT OFF.
OH?

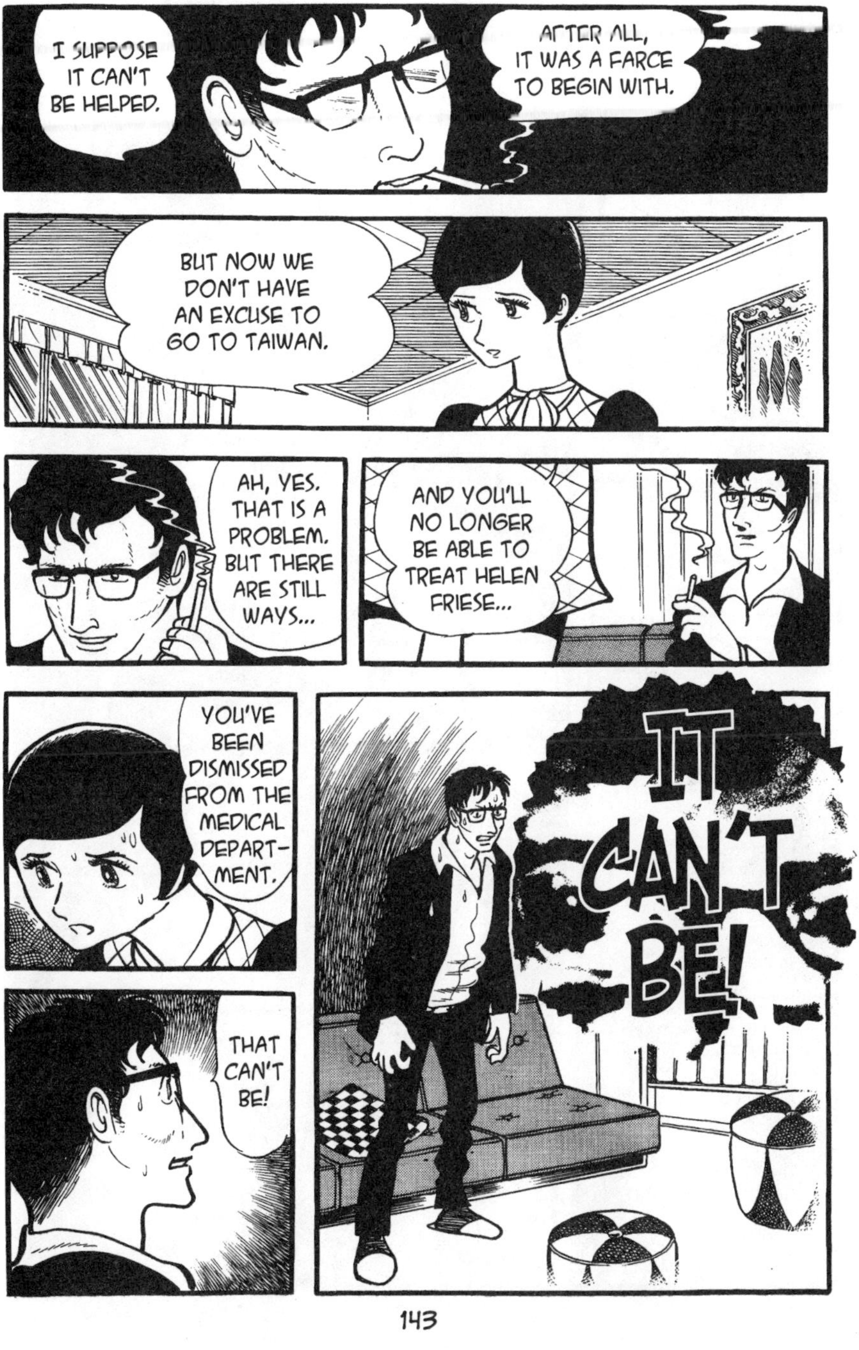
I SUPPOSE IT CAN'T BE HELPED.
AFTER ALL, IT WAS A FARCE TO BEGIN WITH.
BUT NOW WE DON'T HAVE AN EXCUSE TO GO TO TAIWAN.
AH, YES. THAT IS A PROBLEM. BUT THERE ARE STILL WAYS...
AND YOU'LL NO LONGER BE ABLE TO TREAT HELEN FRIESE...
YOU'VE BEEN DISMISSED FROM THE MEDICAL DEPART-MENT.
THAT CAN'T BE!
IT CAN'T BE!

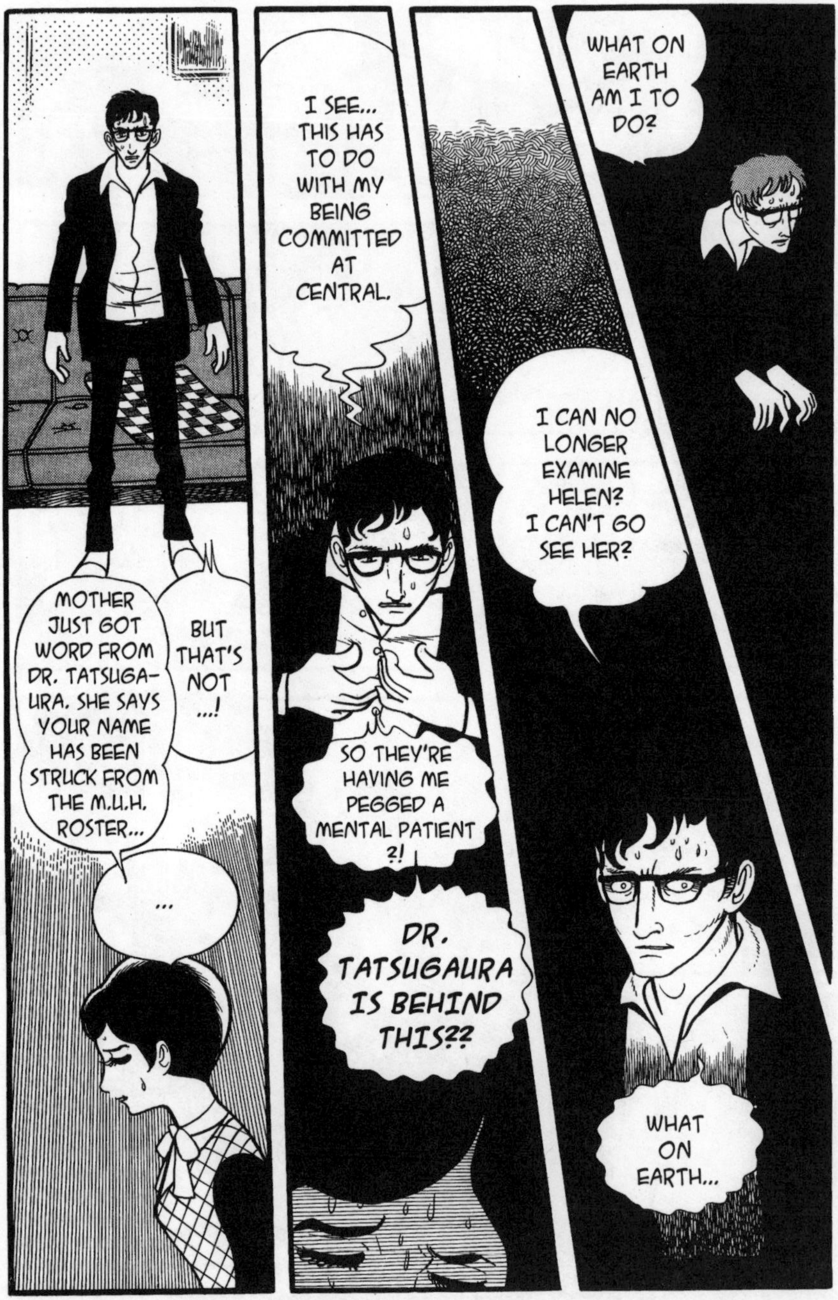
MOTHER JUST GOT WORD FROM DR. TATSUGAURA. SHE SAYS YOUR NAME HAS BEEN STRUCK FROM THE M.U.H. ROSTER...
BUT THAT'S NOT ...!
...
I SEE... THIS HAS TO DO WITH MY BEING COMMITTED AT CENTRAL.
SO THEY'RE HAVING ME PEGGED A MENTAL PATIENT ?!
DR. TATSUGAURA IS BEHIND THIS??
I CAN NO LONGER EXAMINE HELEN? I CAN'T GO SEE HER?
WHAT ON EARTH...
WHAT ON EARTH AM I TO DO?

144

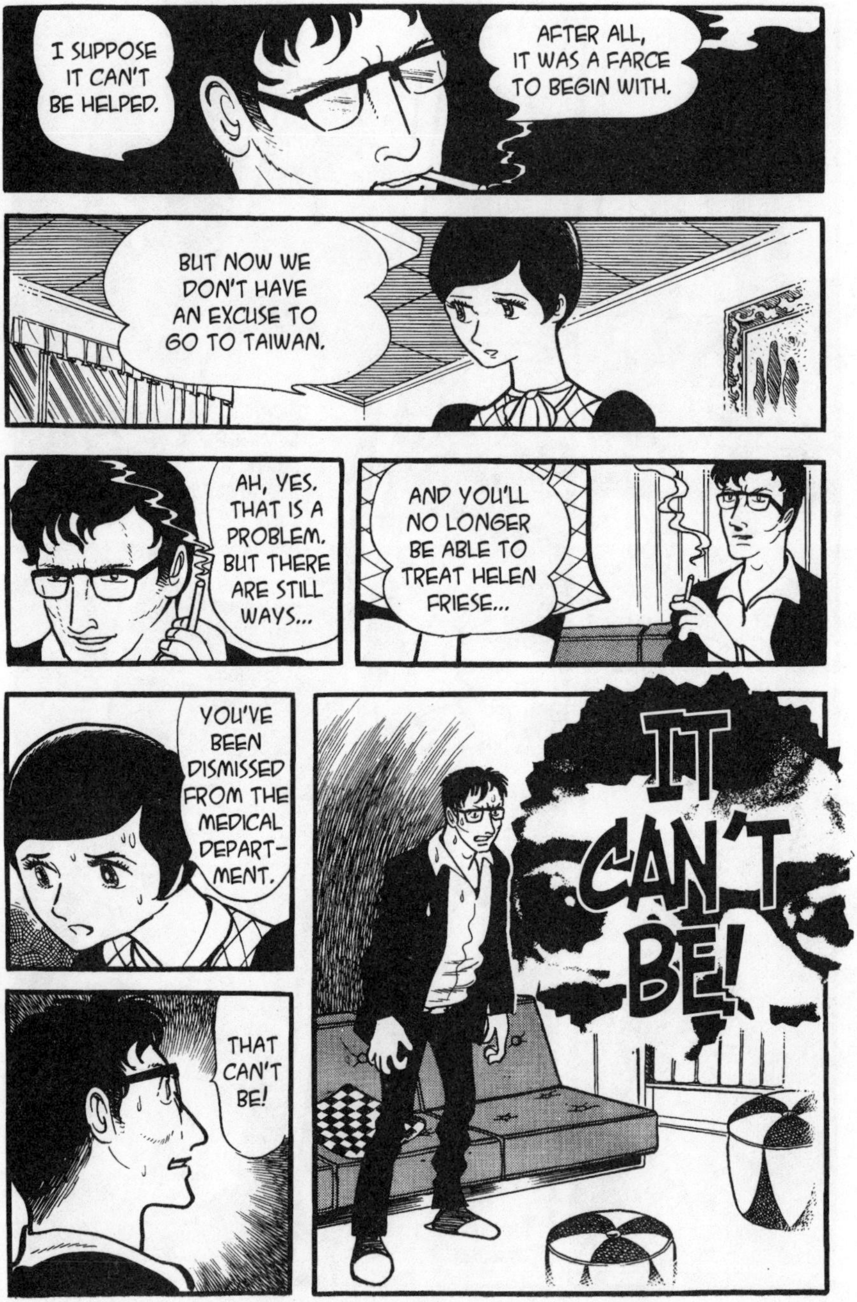
I SUPPOSE IT CAN'T BE HELPED.
AFTER ALL, IT WAS A FARCE TO BEGIN WITH.
BUT NOW WE DON'T HAVE AN EXCUSE TO GO TO TAIWAN.
AND YOU'LL NO LONGER BE ABLE TO TREAT HELEN FRIESE...
AH, YES. THAT IS A PROBLEM. BUT THERE ARE STILL WAYS...
YOU'VE BEEN DISMISSED FROM THE MEDICAL DEPART-MENT.
THAT CAN'T BE!
IT CAN'T BE!

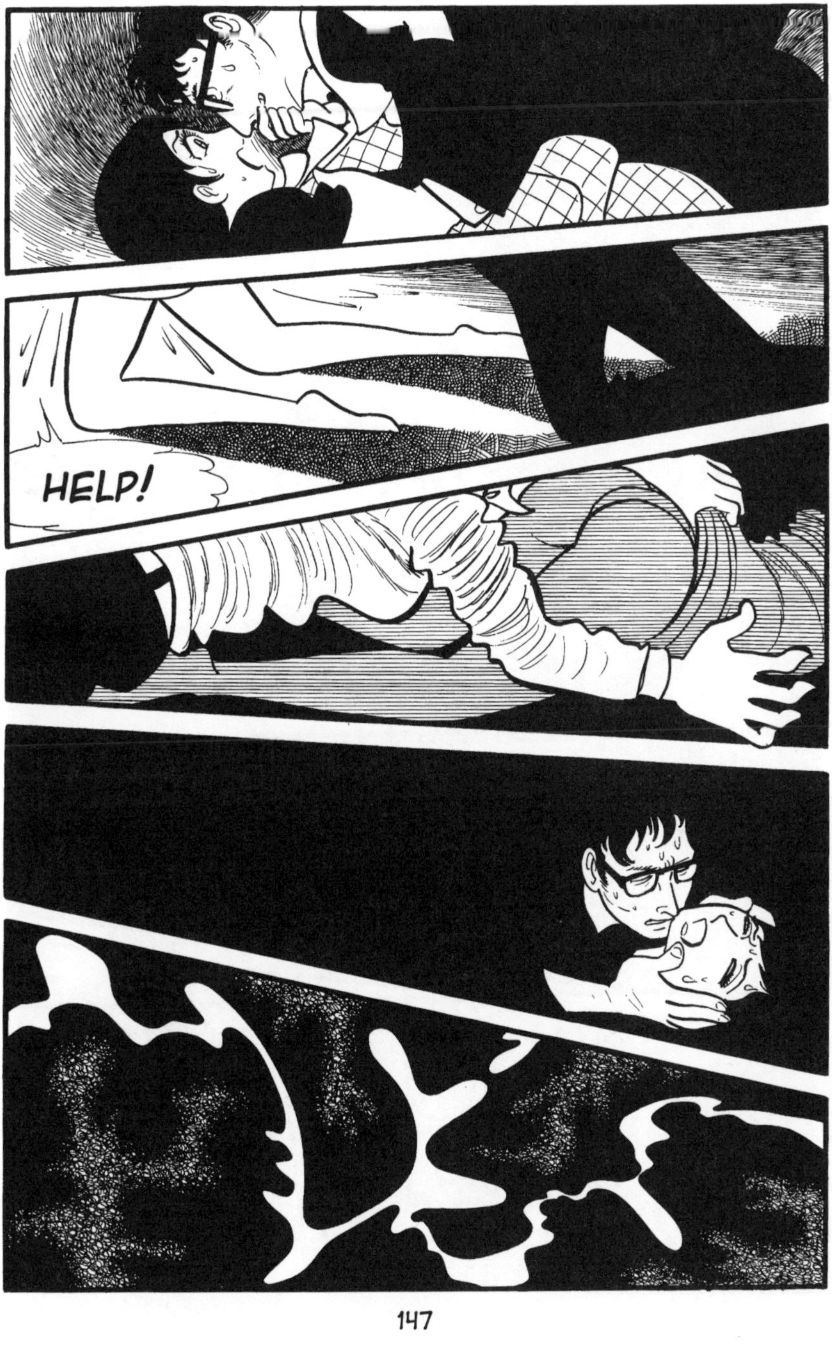
HELP!

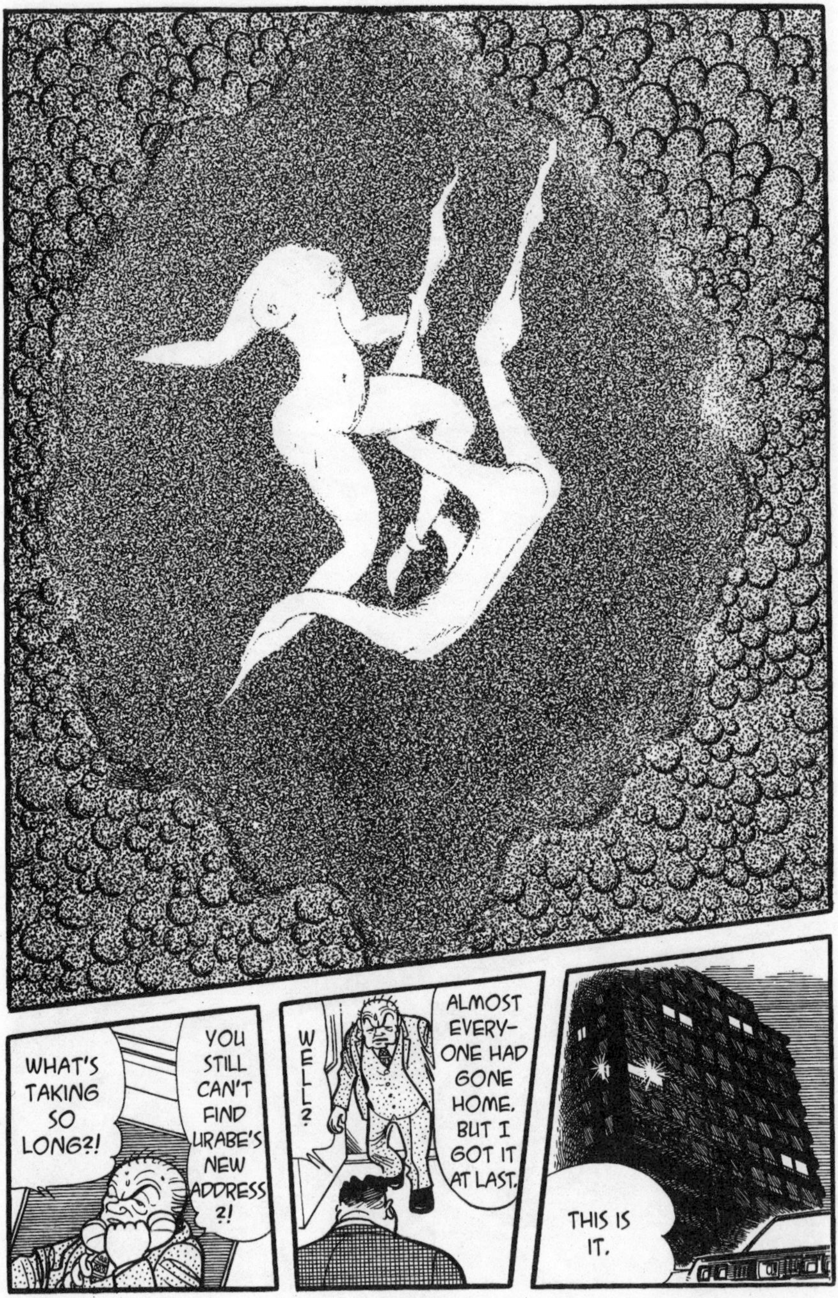
WHAT'S TAKING SO LONG?!
YOU STILL CAN'T FIND URABE'S NEW ADDRESS?!
WELL?
ALMOST EVERY-ONE HAD GONE HOME. BUT I GOT IT AT LAST.
THIS IS IT.

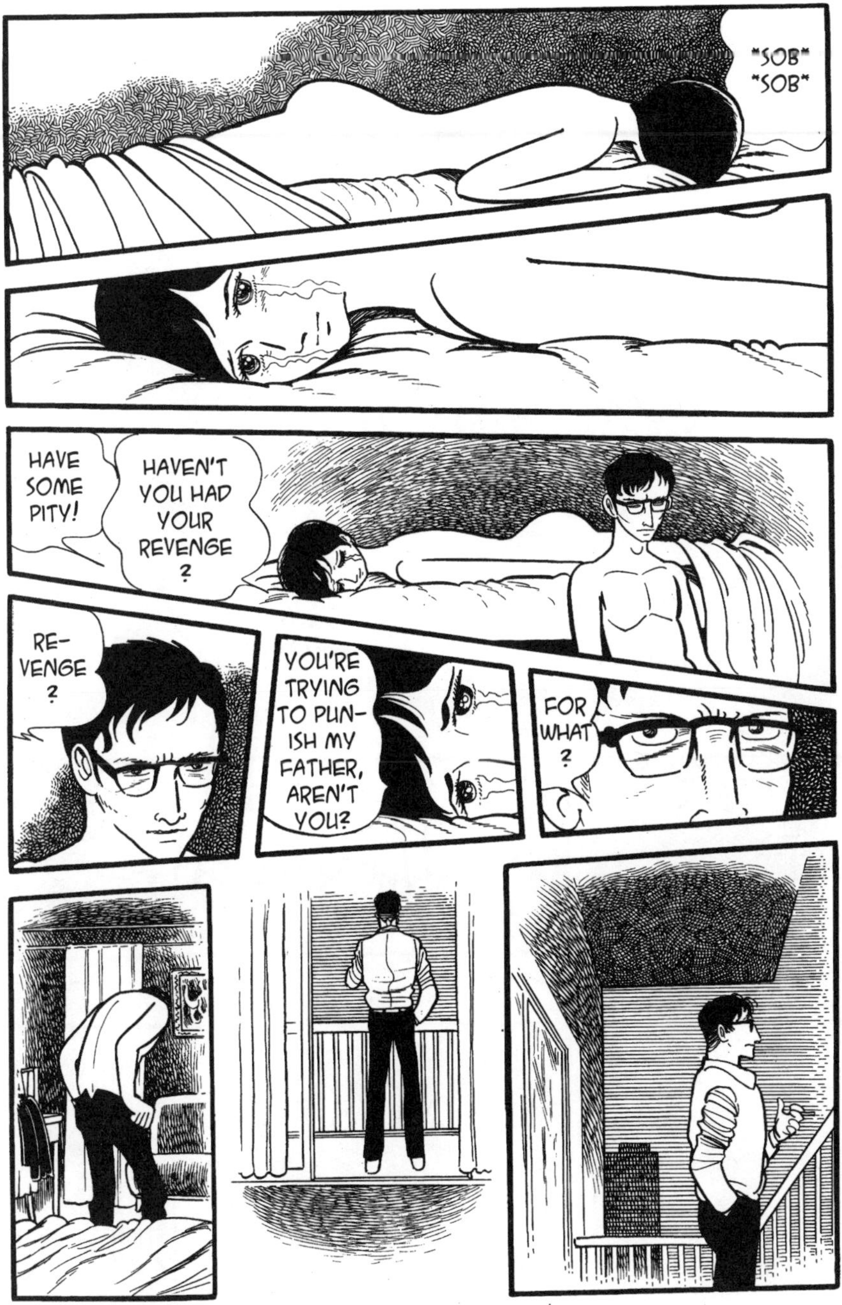
SOB
SOB
HAVE SOME PITY!
HAVEN'T YOU HAD YOUR REVENGE?
RE-VENGE?
YOU'RE TRYING TO PUN-ISH MY FATHER, AREN'T YOU?
FOR WHAT?

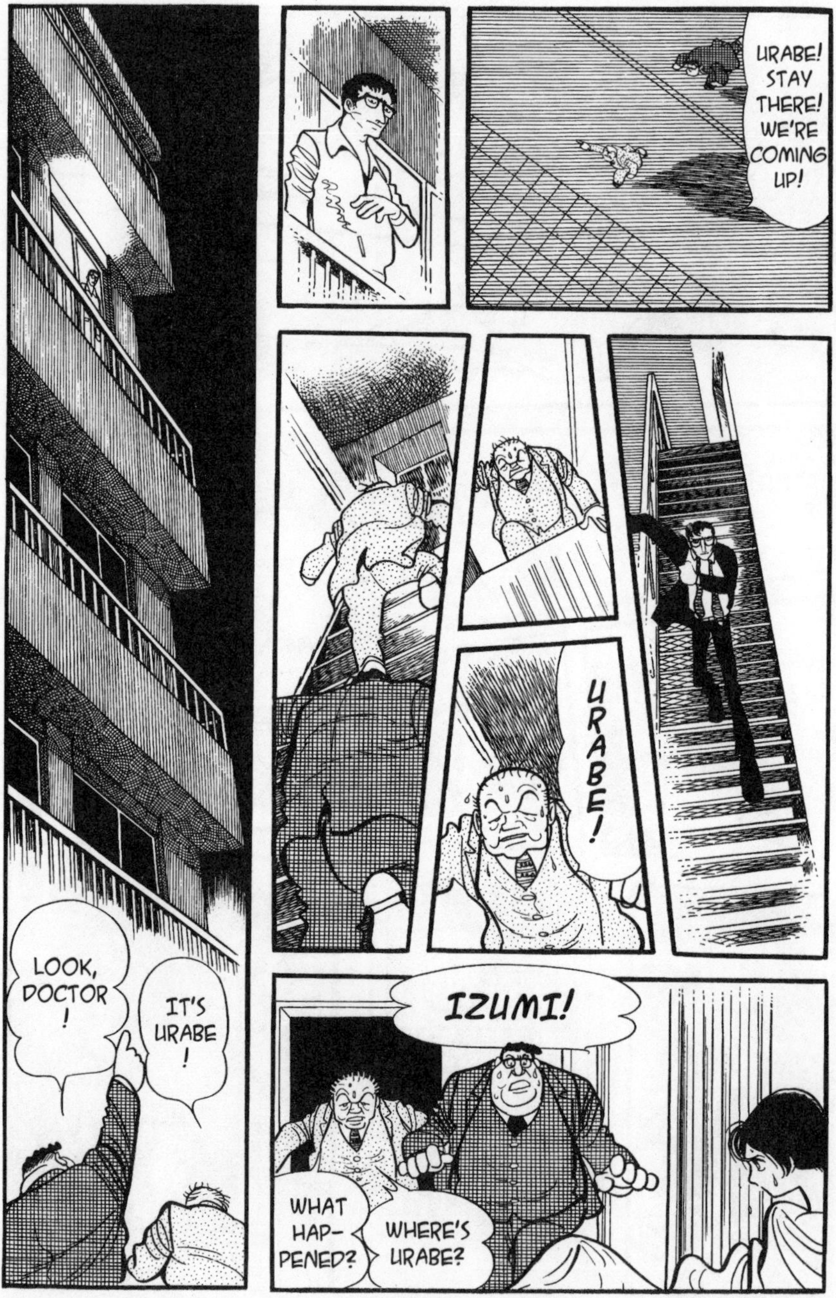
LOOK, DOCTOR!
IT'S URABE!
URABE! STAY THERE! WE'RE COMING UP!
URABE!
IZUMI!
WHAT HAPPENED?
WHERE'S URABE?

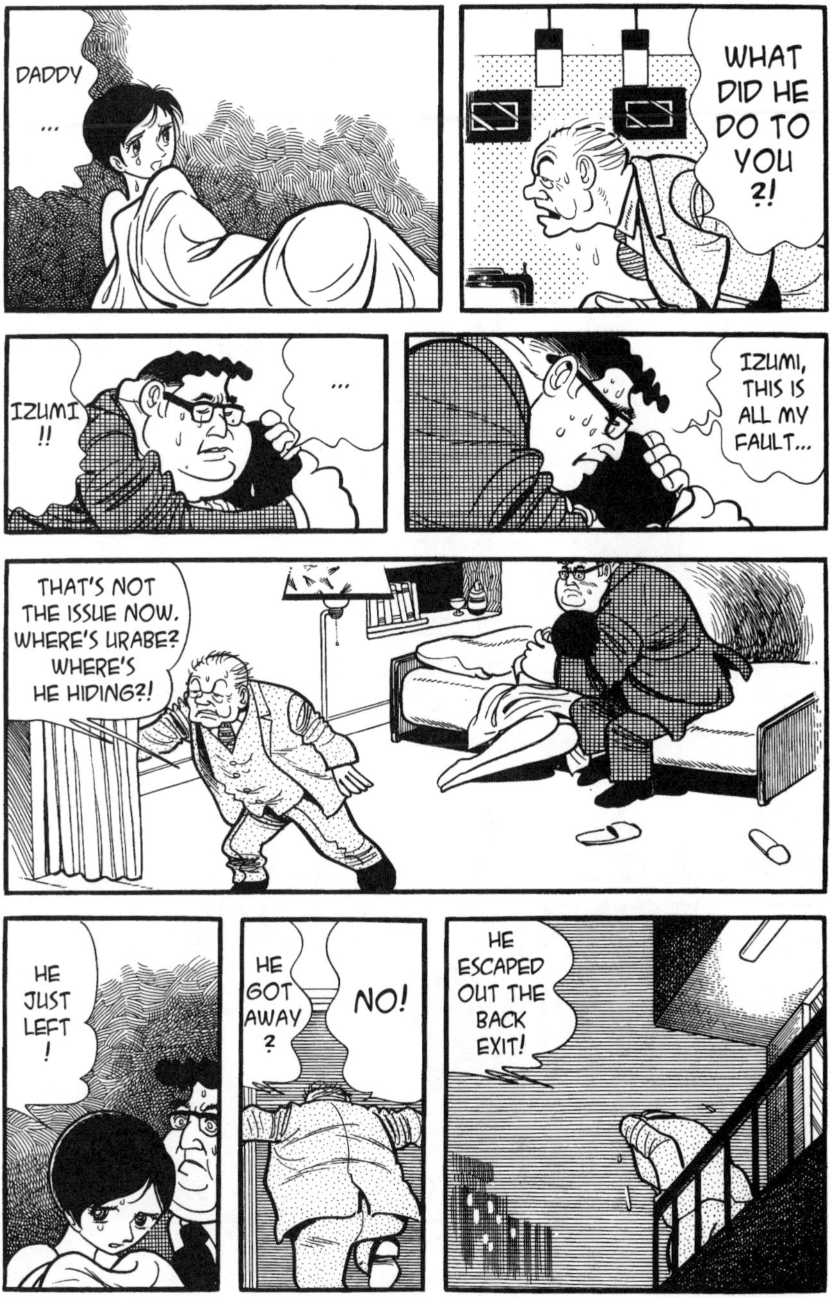
DADDY ...
WHAT DID HE DO TO YOU ?!
IZUMI !!
...
IZUMI, THIS IS ALL MY FAULT...
THAT'S NOT THE ISSUE NOW. WHERE'S URABE? WHERE'S HE HIDING?!
HE JUST LEFT !
HE GOT AWAY ?
NO!
HE ESCAPED OUT THE BACK EXIT!

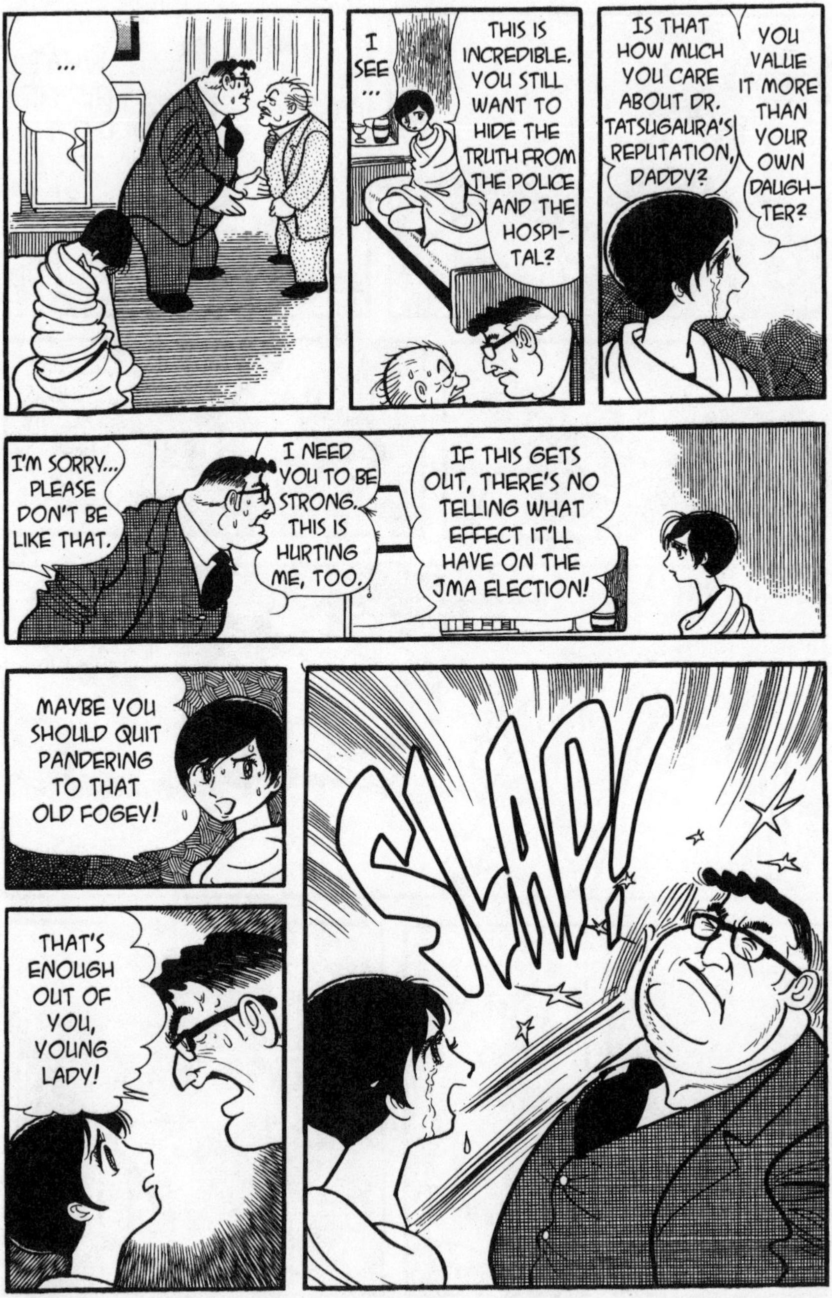
...
I SEE ...
THIS IS INCREDIBLE. YOU STILL WANT TO HIDE THE TRUTH FROM THE POLICE AND THE HOSPITAL?
IS THAT HOW MUCH YOU CARE ABOUT DR. TATSUGAURA'S REPUTATION, DADDY?
YOU VALUE IT MORE THAN YOUR OWN DAUGHTER?
I'M SORRY... PLEASE DON'T BE LIKE THAT.
I NEED YOU TO BE STRONG. THIS IS HURTING ME, TOO.
IF THIS GETS OUT, THERE'S NO TELLING WHAT EFFECT IT'LL HAVE ON THE JMA ELECTION!
MAYBE YOU SHOULD QUIT PANDERING TO THAT OLD FOGEY!
THAT'S ENOUGH OUT OF YOU, YOUNG LADY!
SLAP!

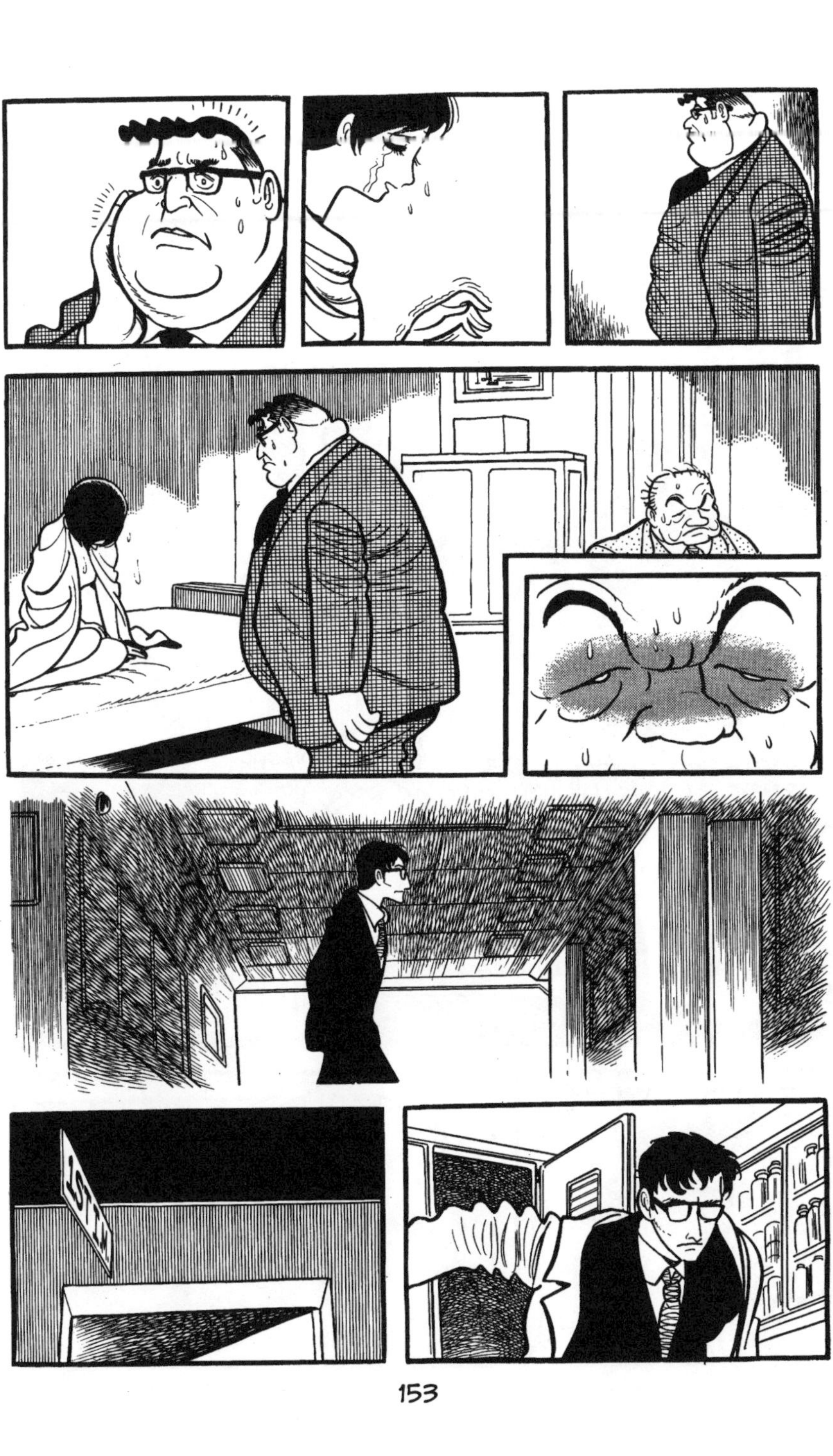
1ST I.M.

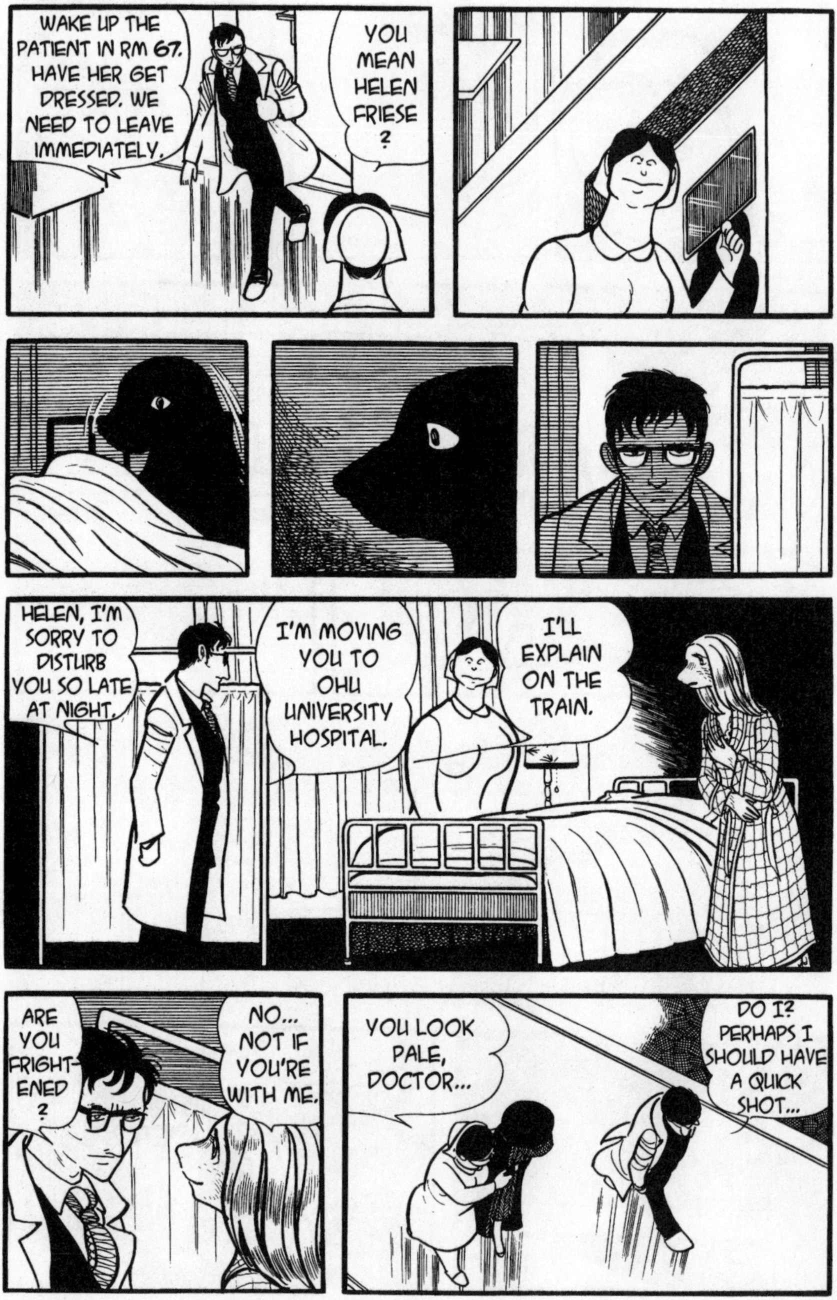
WAKE UP THE PATIENT IN RM 67. HAVE HER GET DRESSED. WE NEED TO LEAVE IMMEDIATELY.
YOU MEAN HELEN FRIESE ?
HELEN, I'M SORRY TO DISTURB YOU SO LATE AT NIGHT.
I'M MOVING YOU TO OHU UNIVERSITY HOSPITAL.
I'LL EXPLAIN ON THE TRAIN.
ARE YOU FRIGHT-ENED ?
NO... NOT IF YOU'RE WITH ME.
YOU LOOK PALE, DOCTOR...
DO I? PERHAPS I SHOULD HAVE A QUICK SHOT...

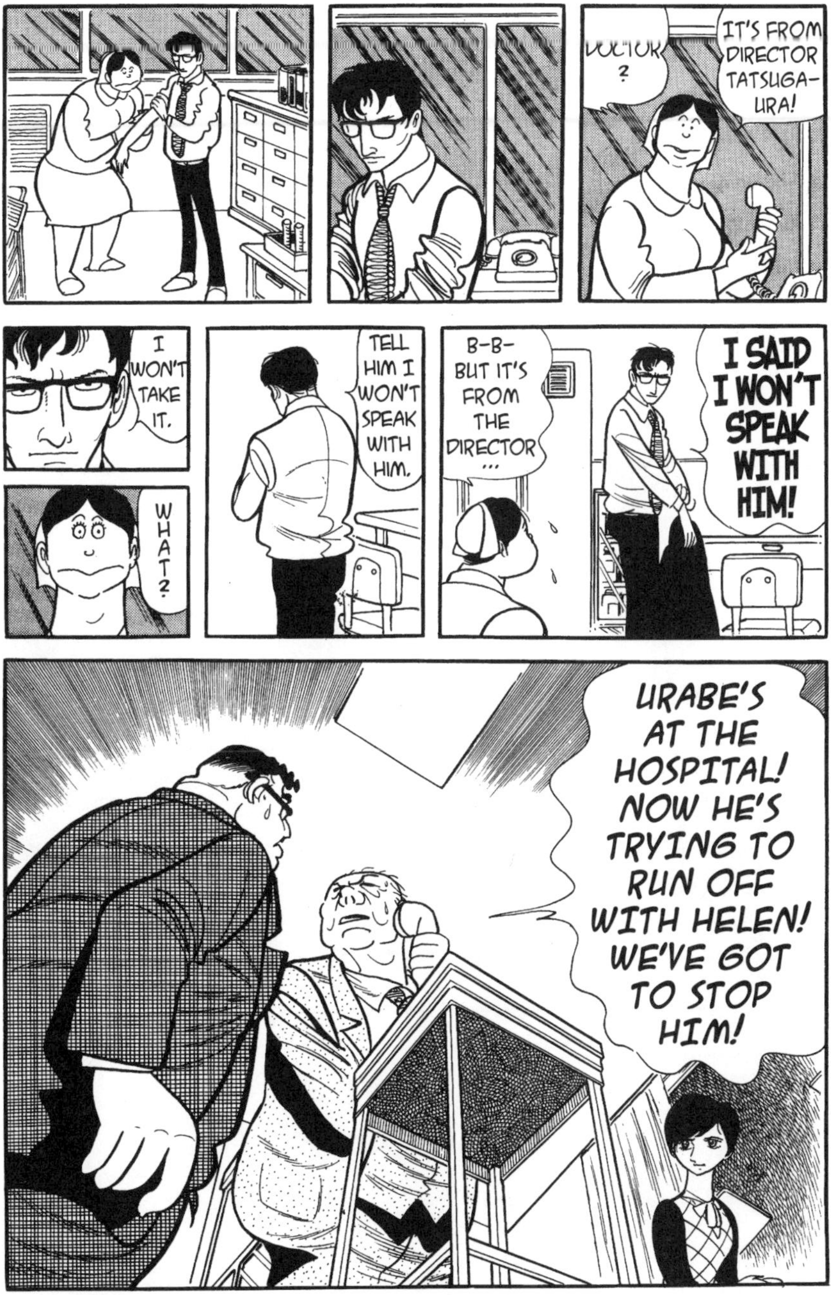
DOCTOR?
IT'S FROM DIRECTOR TATSUGAURA!
I WON'T TAKE IT.
WHAT?
TELL HIM I WON'T SPEAK WITH HIM.
B-B-BUT IT'S FROM THE DIRECTOR...
I SAID I WON'T SPEAK WITH HIM!
URABE'S AT THE HOSPITAL! NOW HE'S TRYING TO RUN OFF WITH HELEN! WE'VE GOT TO STOP HIM!

CHAPTER 15

VISIONS OF MARY

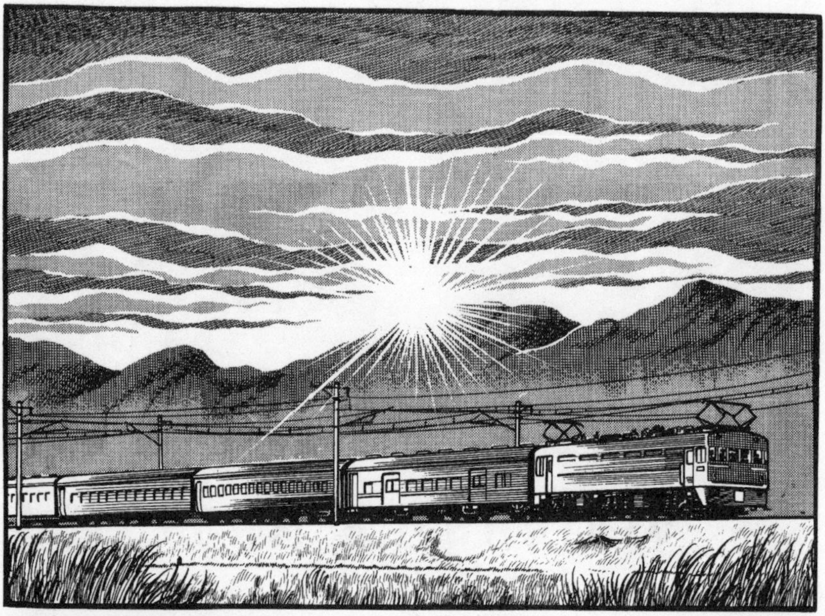

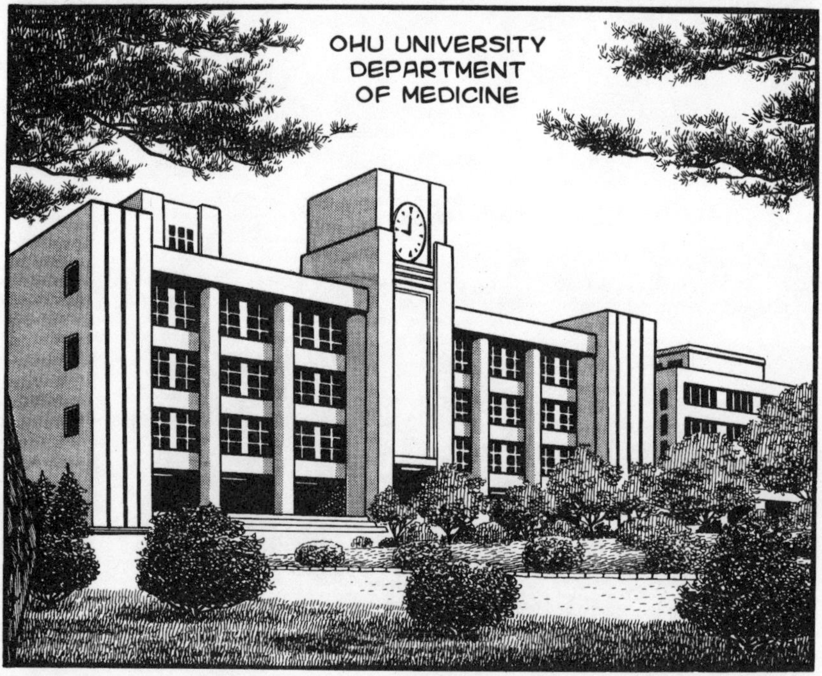
OHU UNIVERSITY
DEPARTMENT
OF MEDICINE

I'VE NEVER SEEN A MONMOW PATIENT BEFORE, DR. URABE.

WILL YOU CONDUCT THE SURGERY, DR. YAMA-GATA?

LET'S NOT BE HASTY, NOW.

YOU JUST ARRIVED THIS MORNING!

BUT...

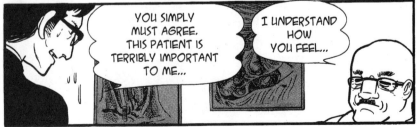

YOU SIMPLY MUST AGREE. THIS PATIENT IS TERRIBLY IMPORTANT TO ME...

I UNDERSTAND HOW YOU FEEL...

159

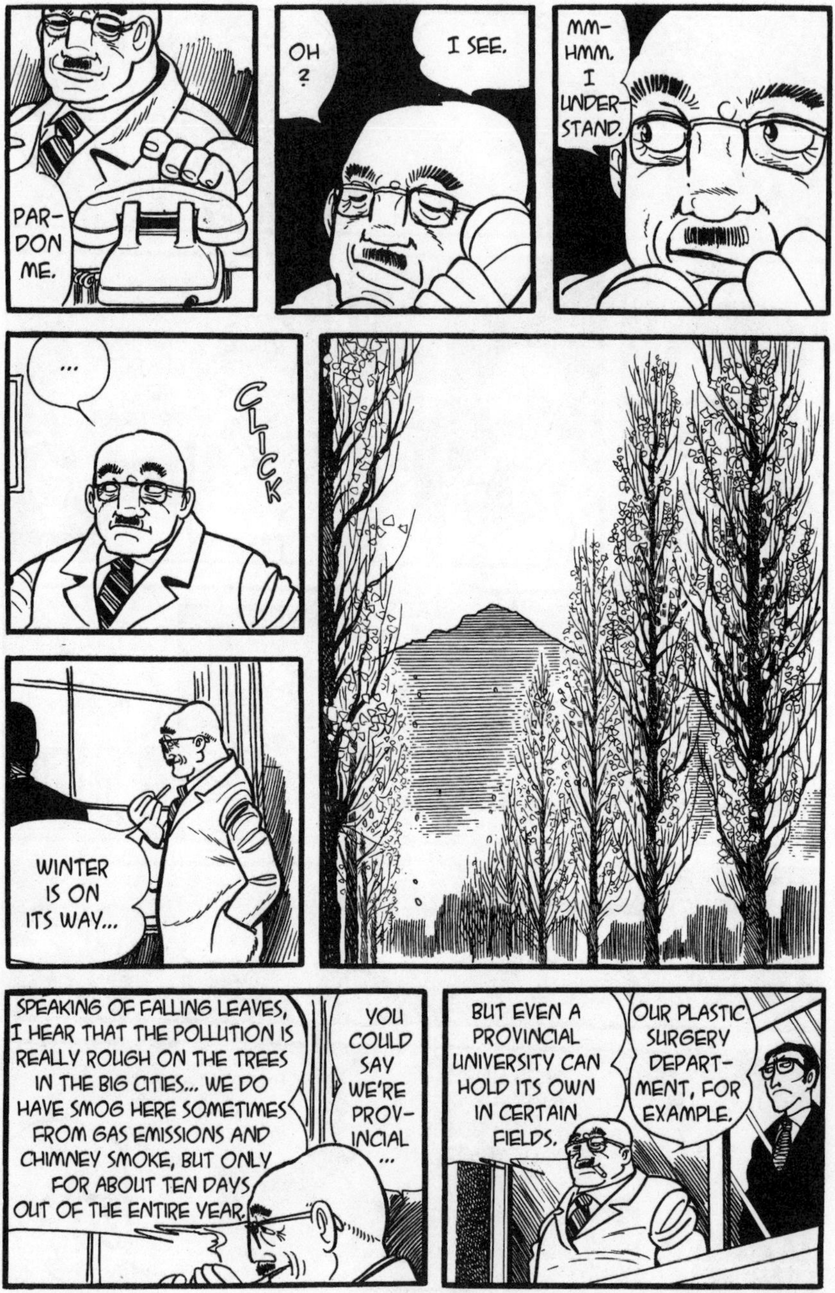
PAR-
DON
ME.
OH
?
I SEE.
MM-
HMM.
I
UNDER-
STAND.
...
CLICK
WINTER
IS ON
ITS WAY...
SPEAKING OF FALLING LEAVES, I HEAR THAT THE POLLUTION IS REALLY ROUGH ON THE TREES IN THE BIG CITIES... WE DO HAVE SMOG HERE SOMETIMES FROM GAS EMISSIONS AND CHIMNEY SMOKE, BUT ONLY FOR ABOUT TEN DAYS OUT OF THE ENTIRE YEAR.
YOU COULD SAY WE'RE PROV-INCIAL ...
BUT EVEN A PROVINCIAL UNIVERSITY CAN HOLD ITS OWN IN CERTAIN FIELDS.
OUR PLASTIC SURGERY DEPART-MENT, FOR EXAMPLE.

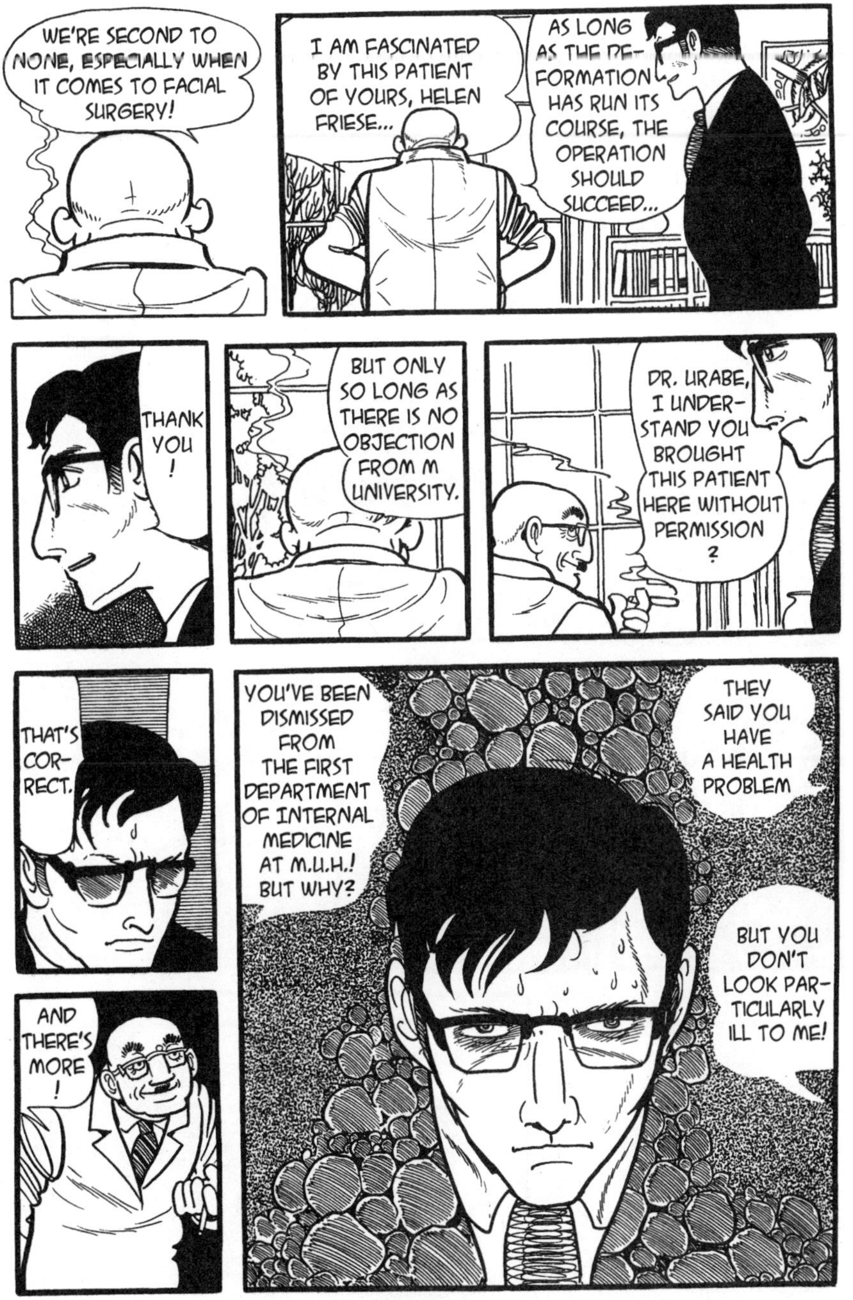
WE'RE SECOND TO NONE, ESPECIALLY WHEN IT COMES TO FACIAL SURGERY!
I AM FASCINATED BY THIS PATIENT OF YOURS, HELEN FRIESE...
AS LONG AS THE DEFORMATION HAS RUN ITS COURSE, THE OPERATION SHOULD SUCCEED...
THANK YOU!
BUT ONLY SO LONG AS THERE IS NO OBJECTION FROM M UNIVERSITY.
DR. URABE, I UNDERSTAND YOU BROUGHT THIS PATIENT HERE WITHOUT PERMISSION?
THAT'S CORRECT.
AND THERE'S MORE!
YOU'VE BEEN DISMISSED FROM THE FIRST DEPARTMENT OF INTERNAL MEDICINE AT M.U.H.! BUT WHY?
THEY SAID YOU HAVE A HEALTH PROBLEM
BUT YOU DON'T LOOK PARTICULARLY ILL TO ME!

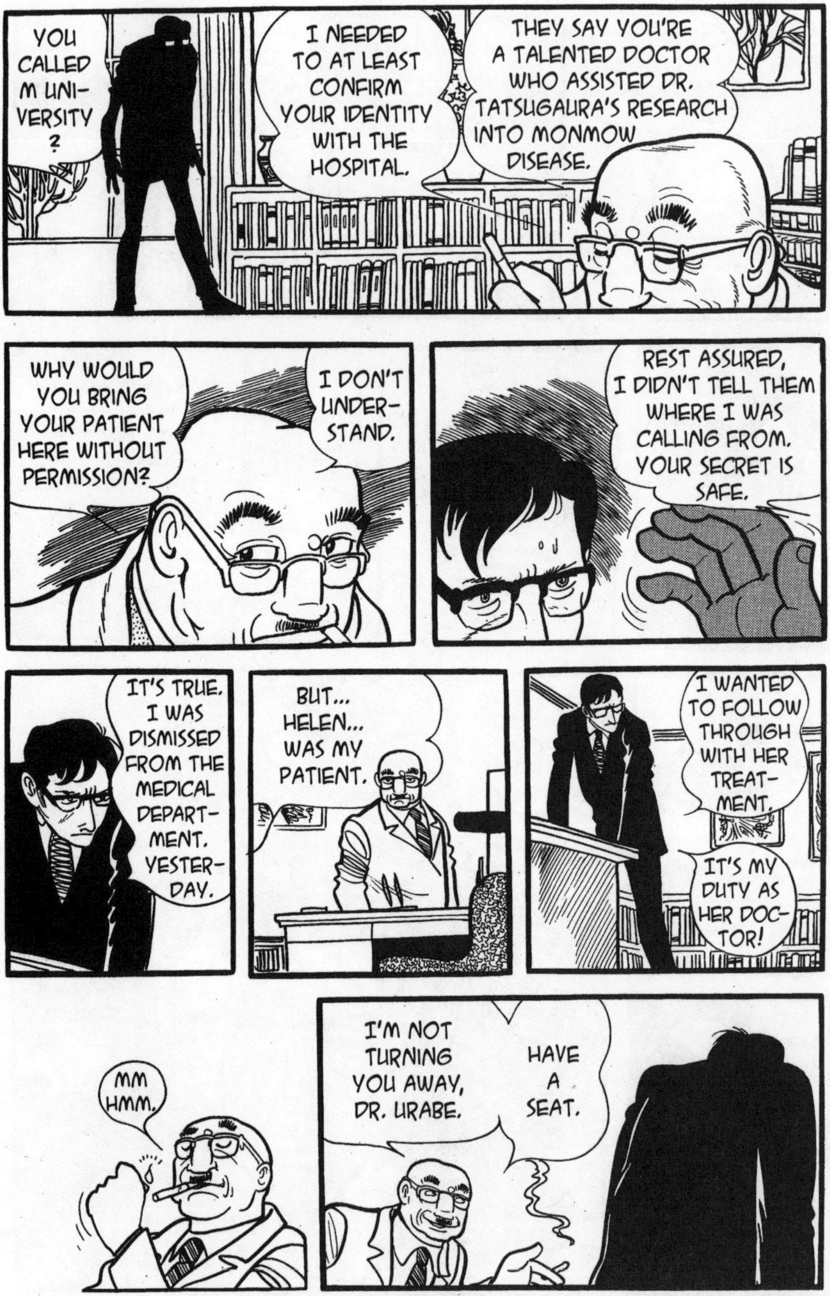
YOU CALLED M UNI-VERSITY?
I NEEDED TO AT LEAST CONFIRM YOUR IDENTITY WITH THE HOSPITAL.
THEY SAY YOU'RE A TALENTED DOCTOR WHO ASSISTED DR. TATSUGAURA'S RESEARCH INTO MONMOW DISEASE.
WHY WOULD YOU BRING YOUR PATIENT HERE WITHOUT PERMISSION?
I DON'T UNDER-STAND.
REST ASSURED, I DIDN'T TELL THEM WHERE I WAS CALLING FROM. YOUR SECRET IS SAFE.
IT'S TRUE. I WAS DISMISSED FROM THE MEDICAL DEPART-MENT. YESTER-DAY.
BUT... HELEN... WAS MY PATIENT.
I WANTED TO FOLLOW THROUGH WITH HER TREAT-MENT.
IT'S MY DUTY AS HER DOC-TOR!
MM HMM.
I'M NOT TURNING YOU AWAY, DR. URABE.
HAVE A SEAT.

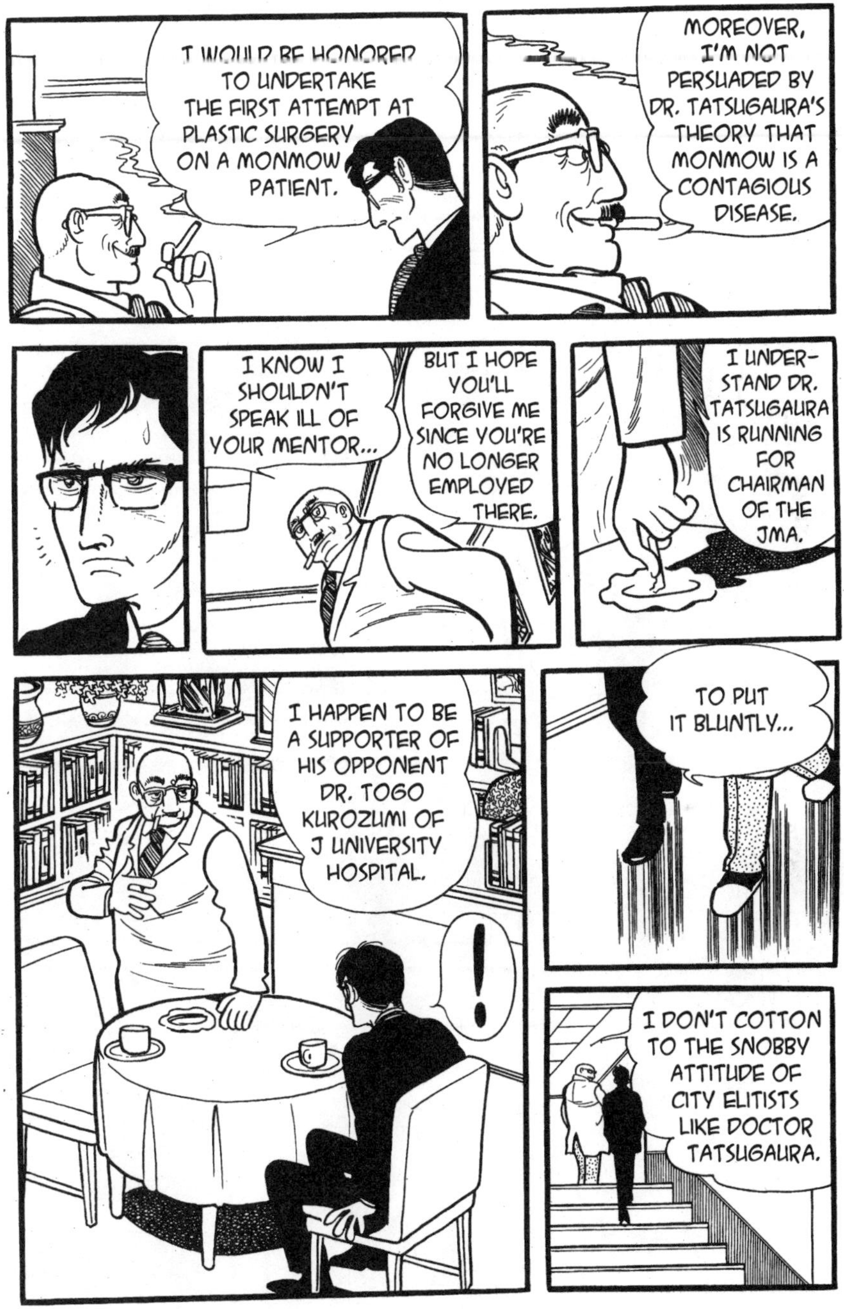
I WOULD BE HONORED TO UNDERTAKE THE FIRST ATTEMPT AT PLASTIC SURGERY ON A MONMOW PATIENT.
MOREOVER, I'M NOT PERSUADED BY DR. TATSUGAURA'S THEORY THAT MONMOW IS A CONTAGIOUS DISEASE.
I KNOW I SHOULDN'T SPEAK ILL OF YOUR MENTOR...
BUT I HOPE YOU'LL FORGIVE ME SINCE YOU'RE NO LONGER EMPLOYED THERE.
I UNDERSTAND DR. TATSUGAURA IS RUNNING FOR CHAIRMAN OF THE JMA.
I HAPPEN TO BE A SUPPORTER OF HIS OPPONENT DR. TOGO KUROZUMI OF J UNIVERSITY HOSPITAL.
!
TO PUT IT BLUNTLY...
I DON'T COTTON TO THE SNOBBY ATTITUDE OF CITY ELITISTS LIKE DOCTOR TATSUGAURA.

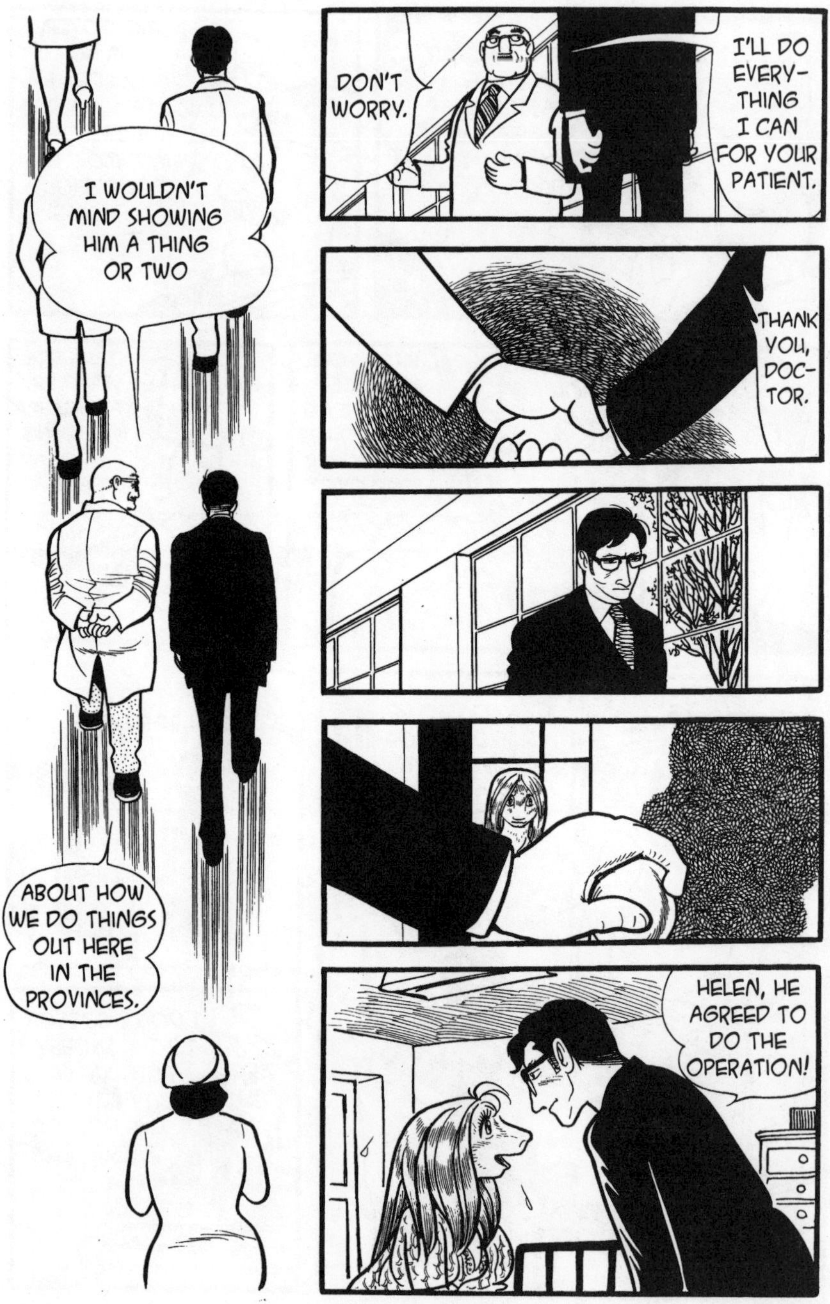
I WOULDN'T MIND SHOWING HIM A THING OR TWO
ABOUT HOW WE DO THINGS OUT HERE IN THE PROVINCES.
DON'T WORRY.
I'LL DO EVERY-THING I CAN FOR YOUR PATIENT.
THANK YOU, DOC-TOR.
HELEN, HE AGREED TO DO THE OPERATION!

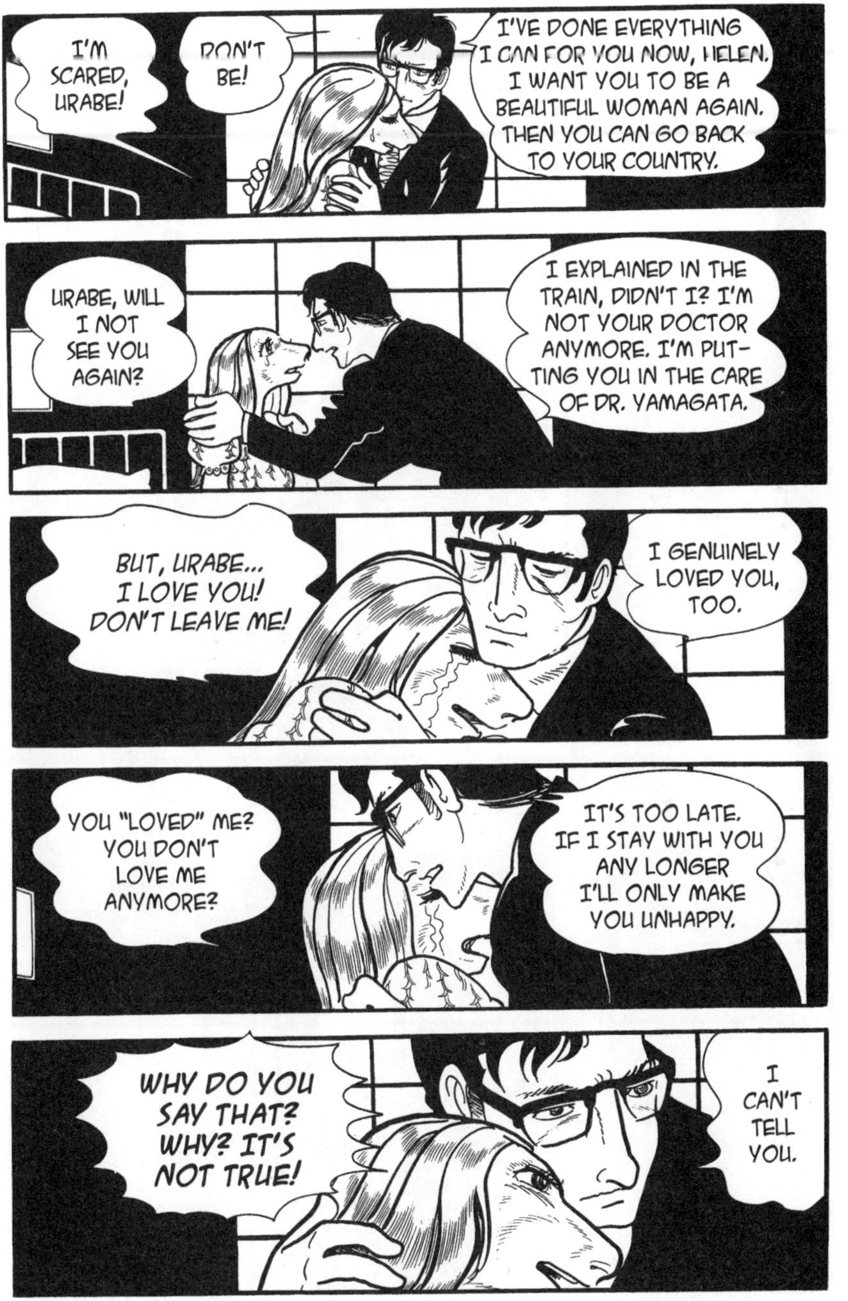
I'M SCARED, URABE!
DON'T BE!
I'VE DONE EVERYTHING I CAN FOR YOU NOW, HELEN. I WANT YOU TO BE A BEAUTIFUL WOMAN AGAIN. THEN YOU CAN GO BACK TO YOUR COUNTRY.
URABE, WILL I NOT SEE YOU AGAIN?
I EXPLAINED IN THE TRAIN, DIDN'T I? I'M NOT YOUR DOCTOR ANYMORE. I'M PUTTING YOU IN THE CARE OF DR. YAMAGATA.
BUT, URABE... I LOVE YOU! DON'T LEAVE ME!
I GENUINELY LOVED YOU, TOO.
YOU "LOVED" ME? YOU DON'T LOVE ME ANYMORE?
IT'S TOO LATE. IF I STAY WITH YOU ANY LONGER I'LL ONLY MAKE YOU UNHAPPY.
WHY DO YOU SAY THAT? WHY? IT'S NOT TRUE!
I CAN'T TELL YOU.

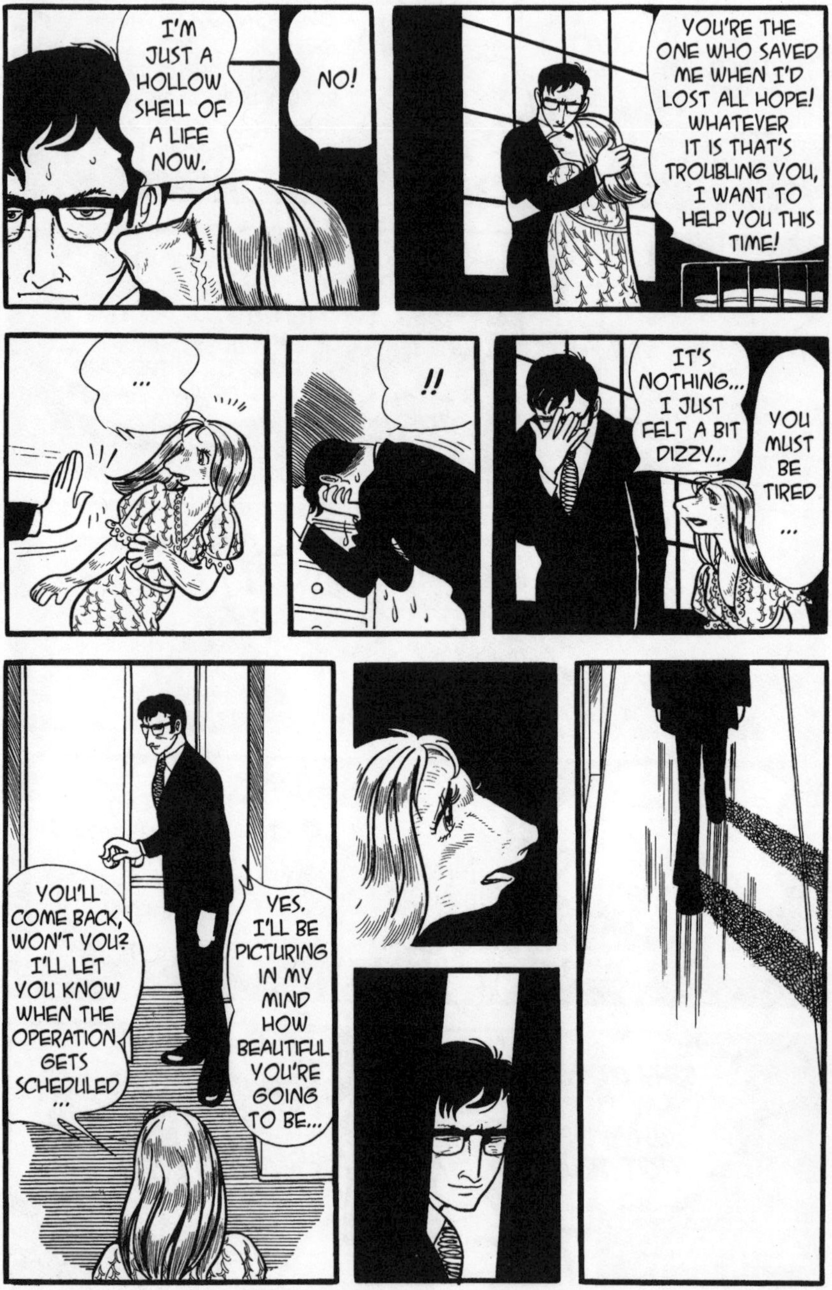

I'M JUST A HOLLOW SHELL OF A LIFE NOW.
NO!
YOU'RE THE ONE WHO SAVED ME WHEN I'D LOST ALL HOPE! WHATEVER IT IS THAT'S TROUBLING YOU, I WANT TO HELP YOU THIS TIME!
...
!!
IT'S NOTHING... I JUST FELT A BIT DIZZY...
YOU MUST BE TIRED ...
YOU'LL COME BACK, WON'T YOU? I'LL LET YOU KNOW WHEN THE OPERATION GETS SCHEDULED ...
YES. I'LL BE PICTURING IN MY MIND HOW BEAUTIFUL YOU'RE GOING TO BE...

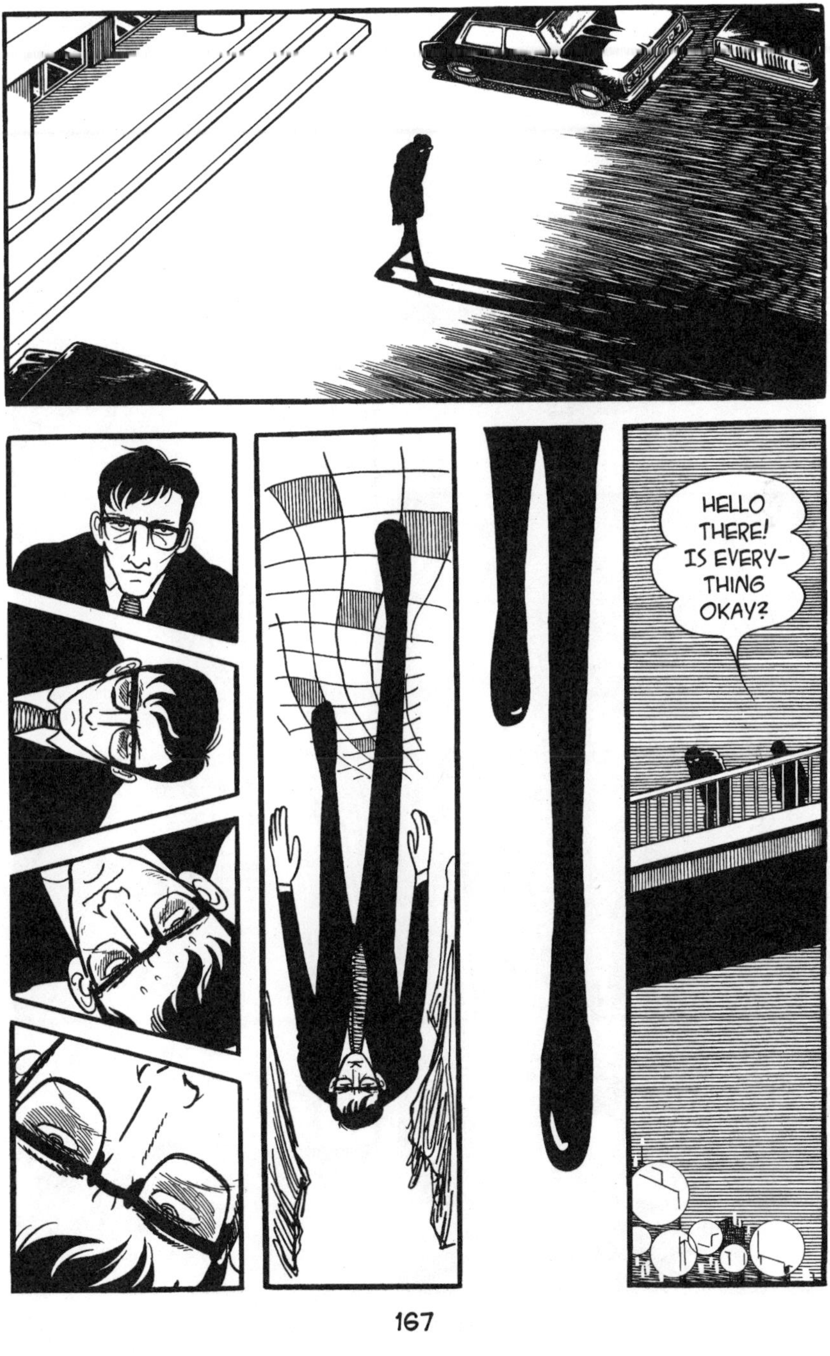
HELLO THERE! IS EVERYTHING OKAY?

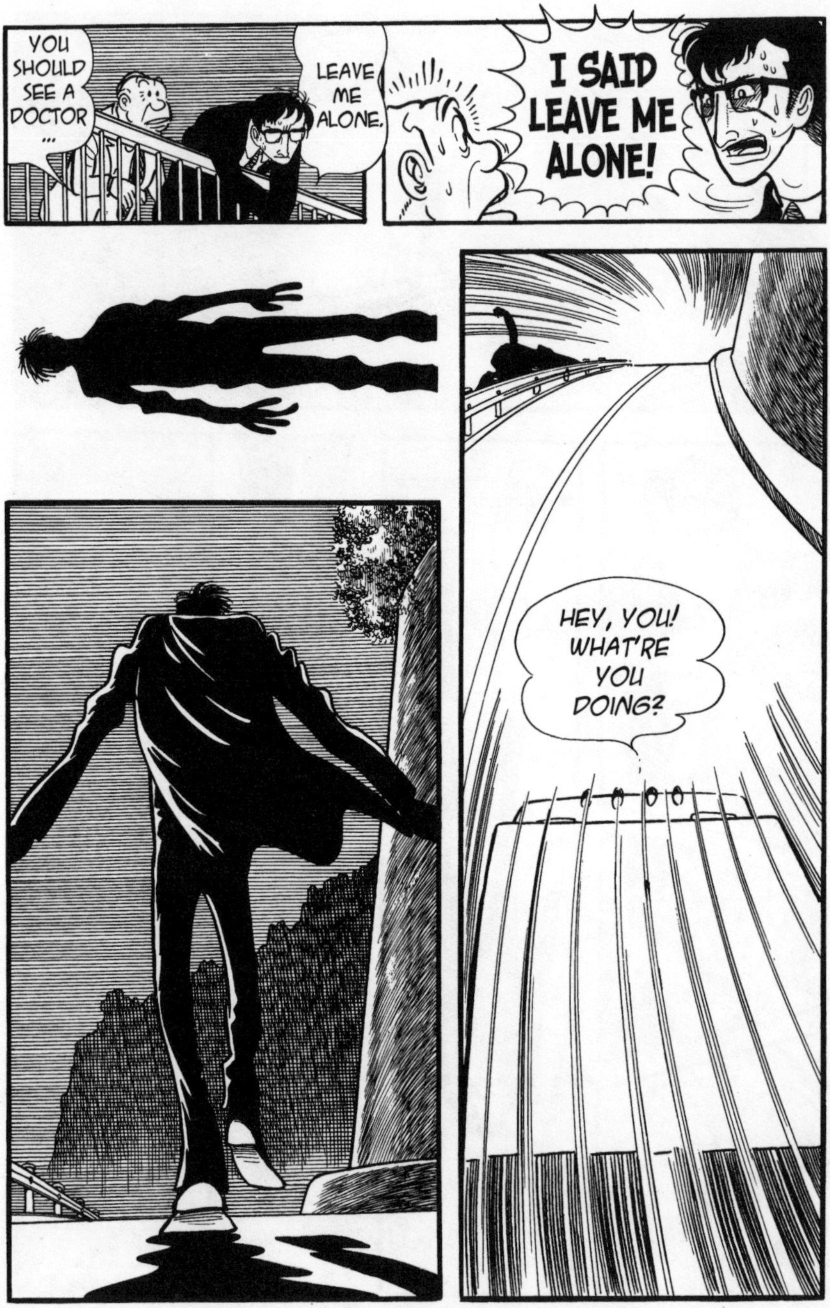
YOU SHOULD SEE A DOCTOR ...
LEAVE ME ALONE.
I SAID LEAVE ME ALONE!
HEY, YOU! WHAT'RE YOU DOING?

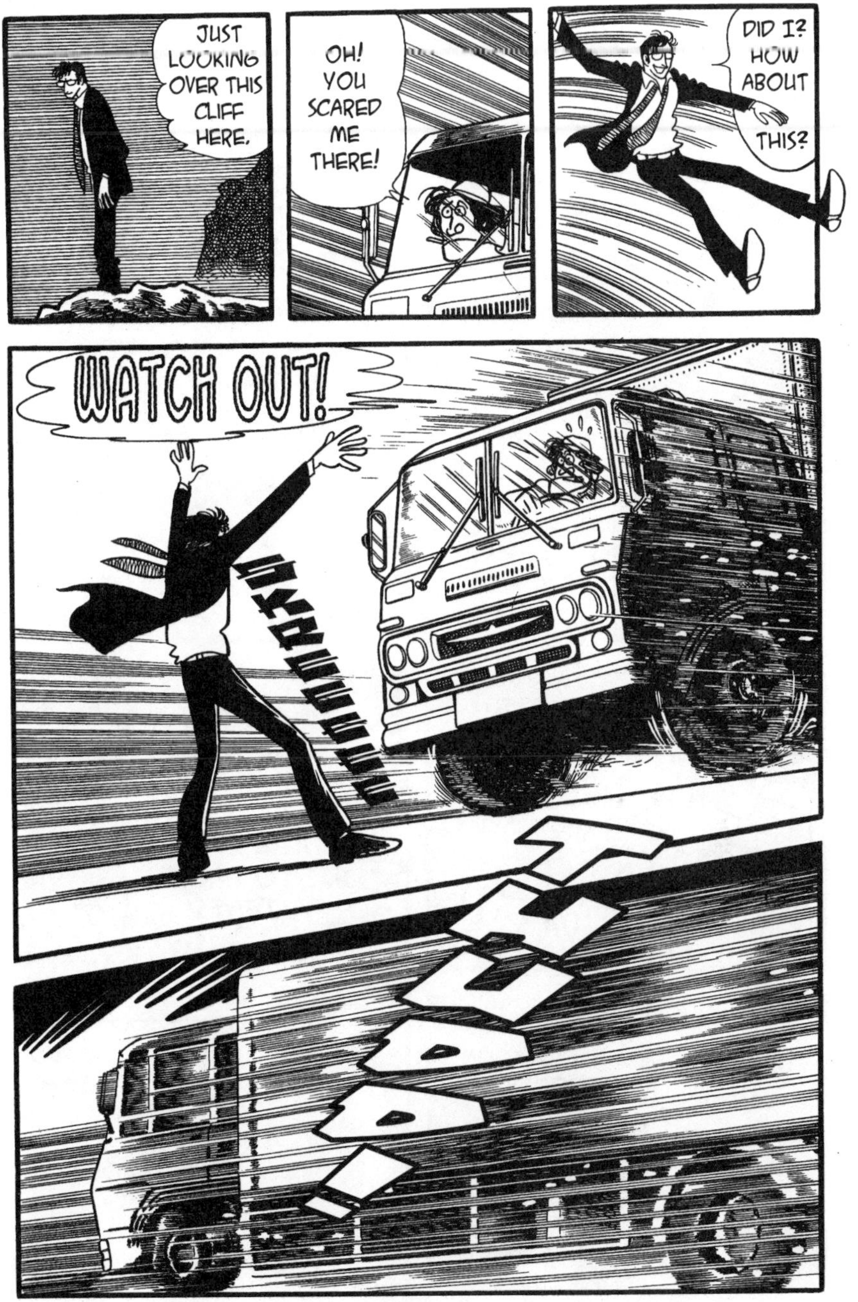
JUST LOOKING OVER THIS CLIFF HERE.
OH! YOU SCARED ME THERE!
DID I? HOW ABOUT THIS?
WATCH OUT!
THUDD!

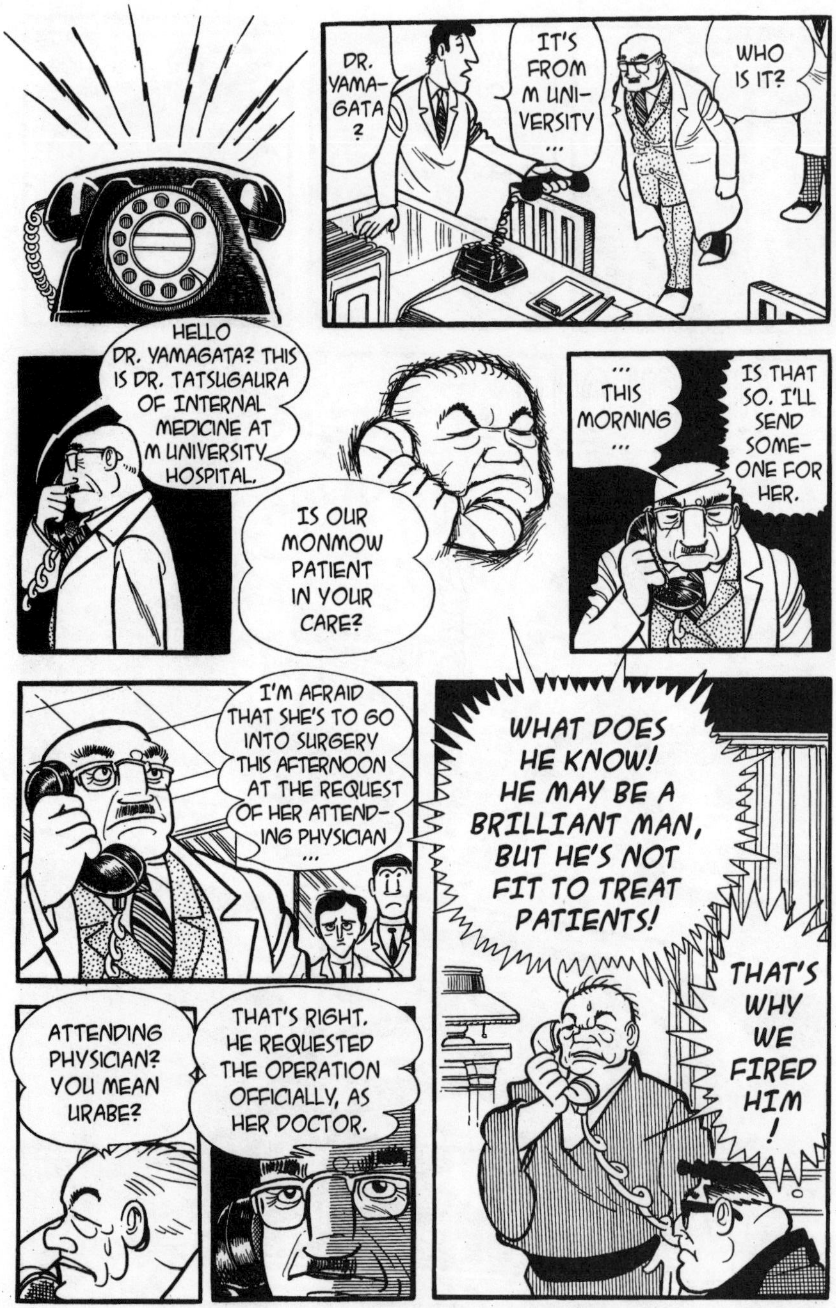
DR. YAMAGATA?
IT'S FROM M UNIVERSITY ...
WHO IS IT?
HELLO DR. YAMAGATA? THIS IS DR. TATSUGAURA OF INTERNAL MEDICINE AT M UNIVERSITY HOSPITAL.
IS OUR MONMOW PATIENT IN YOUR CARE?
... THIS MORNING ...
IS THAT SO. I'LL SEND SOMEONE FOR HER.
I'M AFRAID THAT SHE'S TO GO INTO SURGERY THIS AFTERNOON AT THE REQUEST OF HER ATTENDING PHYSICIAN ...
ATTENDING PHYSICIAN? YOU MEAN URABE?
THAT'S RIGHT. HE REQUESTED THE OPERATION OFFICIALLY, AS HER DOCTOR.
WHAT DOES HE KNOW! HE MAY BE A BRILLIANT MAN, BUT HE'S NOT FIT TO TREAT PATIENTS!
THAT'S WHY WE FIRED HIM!

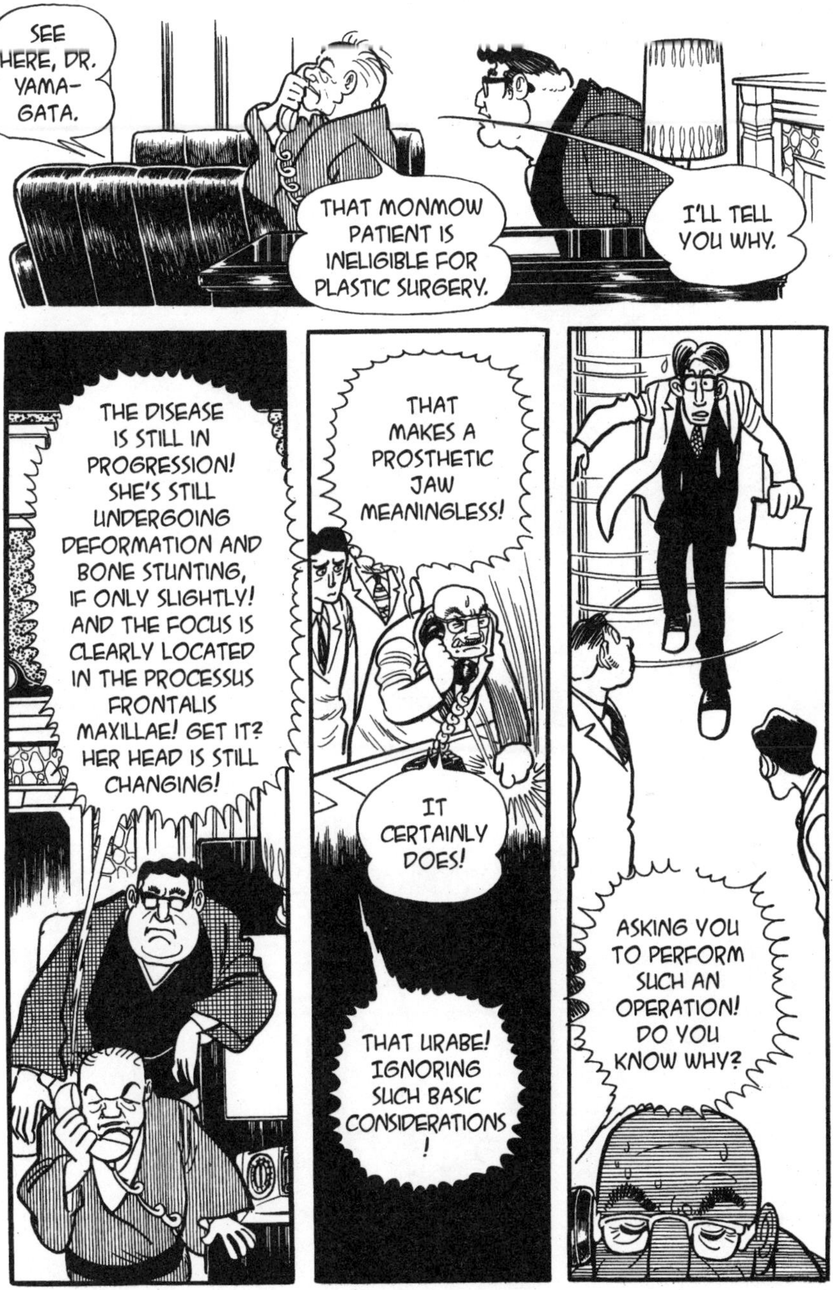
SEE HERE, DR. YAMA-GATA.
THAT MONMOW PATIENT IS INELIGIBLE FOR PLASTIC SURGERY.
I'LL TELL YOU WHY.
THE DISEASE IS STILL IN PROGRESSION! SHE'S STILL UNDERGOING DEFORMATION AND BONE STUNTING, IF ONLY SLIGHTLY! AND THE FOCUS IS CLEARLY LOCATED IN THE PROCESSUS FRONTALIS MAXILLAE! GET IT? HER HEAD IS STILL CHANGING!
THAT MAKES A PROSTHETIC JAW MEANINGLESS!
IT CERTAINLY DOES!
THAT URABE! IGNORING SUCH BASIC CONSIDERATIONS!
ASKING YOU TO PERFORM SUCH AN OPERATION! DO YOU KNOW WHY?

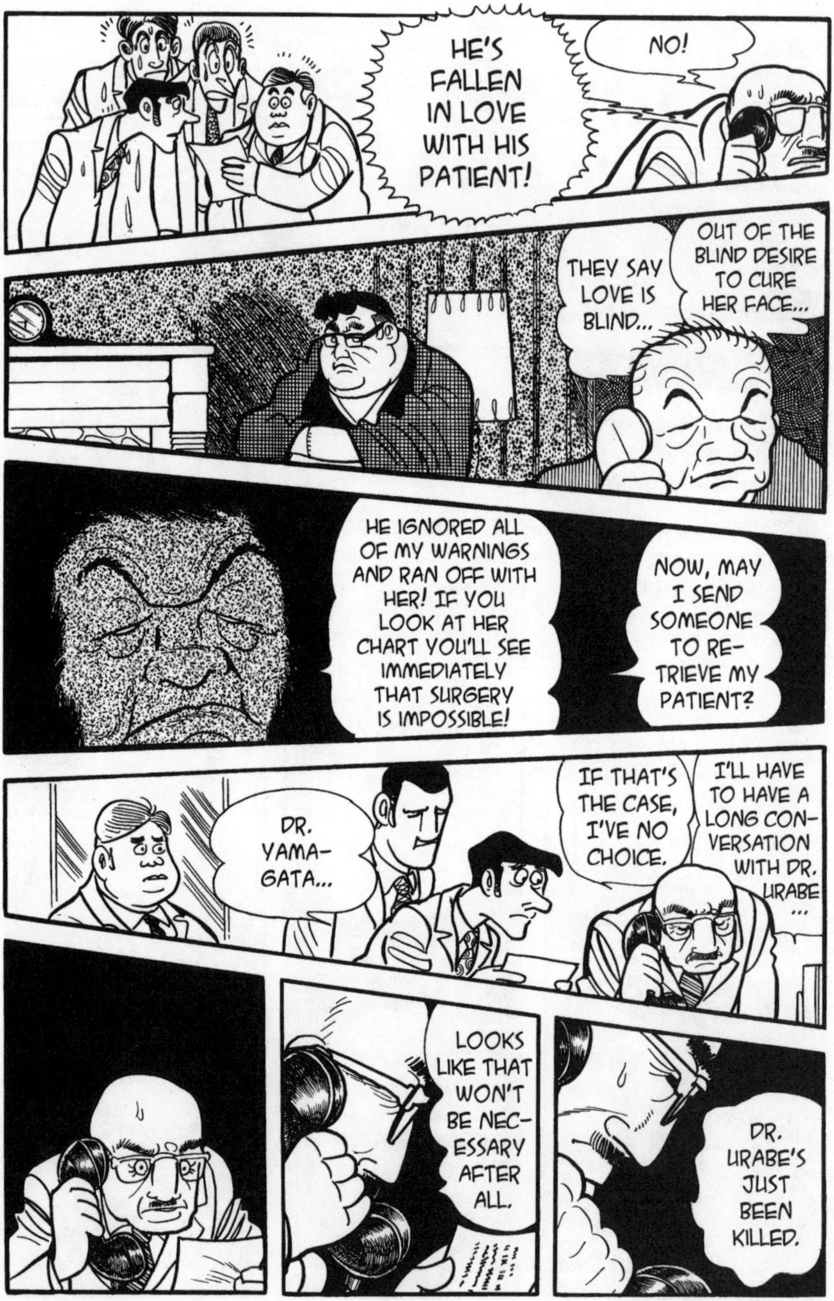
HE'S FALLEN IN LOVE WITH HIS PATIENT!
NO!
THEY SAY LOVE IS BLIND...
OUT OF THE BLIND DESIRE TO CURE HER FACE...
HE IGNORED ALL OF MY WARNINGS AND RAN OFF WITH HER! IF YOU LOOK AT HER CHART YOU'LL SEE IMMEDIATELY THAT SURGERY IS IMPOSSIBLE!
NOW, MAY I SEND SOMEONE TO RE-TRIEVE MY PATIENT?
DR. YAMA-GATA...
IF THAT'S THE CASE, I'VE NO CHOICE.
I'LL HAVE TO HAVE A LONG CON-VERSATION WITH DR. URABE ...
LOOKS LIKE THAT WON'T BE NEC-ESSARY AFTER ALL.
DR. URABE'S JUST BEEN KILLED.

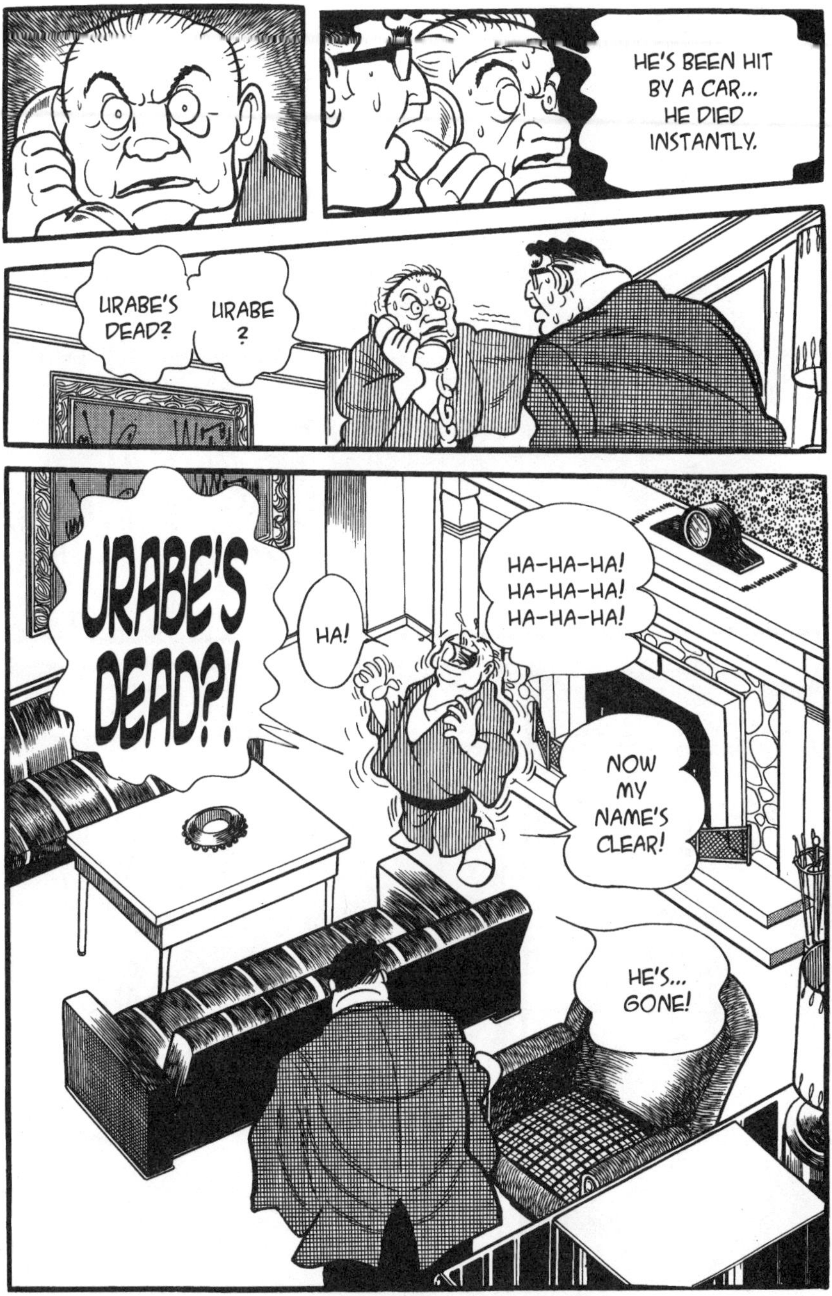
HE'S BEEN HIT BY A CAR... HE DIED INSTANTLY.
URABE ?
URABE'S DEAD?
URABE'S DEAD?!
HA!
HA-HA-HA! HA-HA-HA! HA-HA-HA!
NOW MY NAME'S CLEAR!
HE'S... GONE!

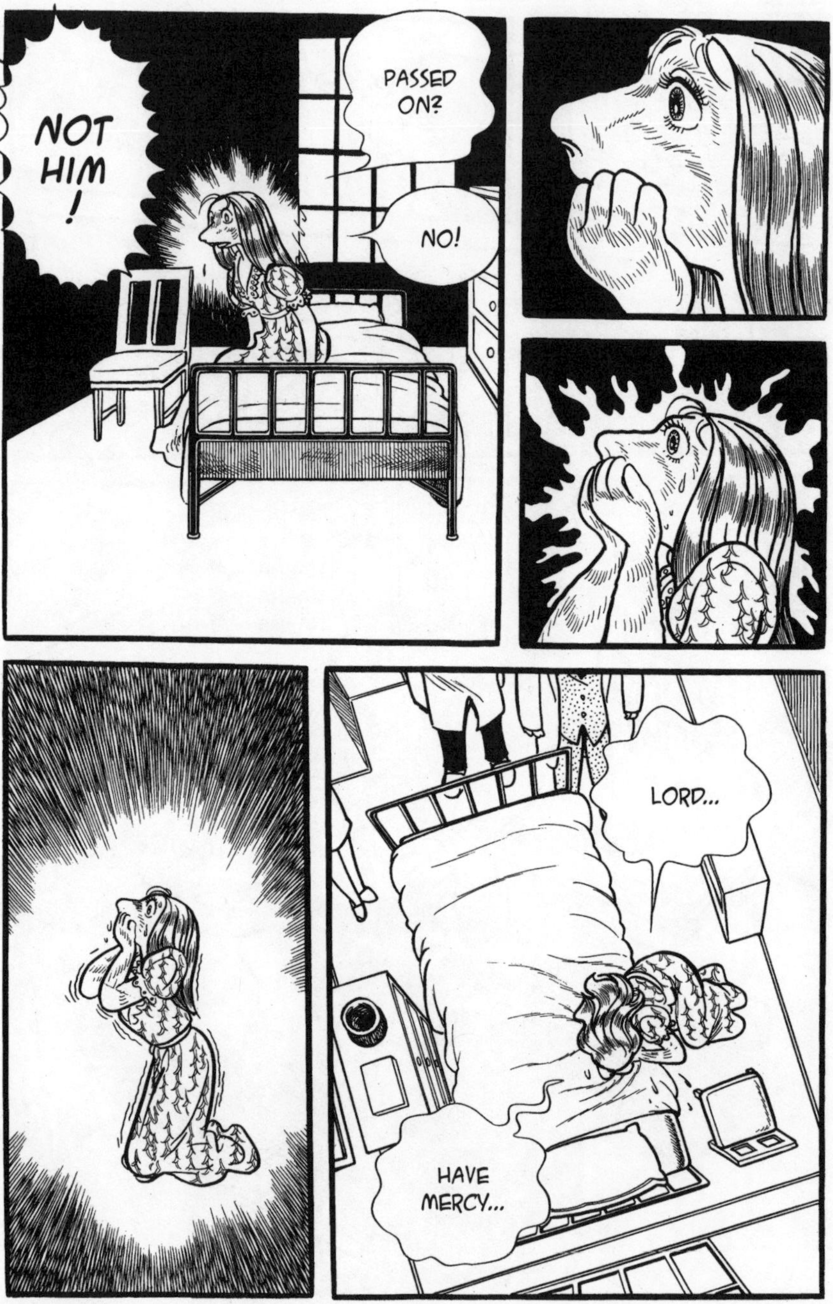
PASSED ON?
NO!
NOT HIM!
LORD...
HAVE MERCY...

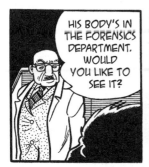

HIS BODY'S IN THE FORENSICS DEPARTMENT. WOULD YOU LIKE TO SEE IT?

...

PLEASE LEAVE ME ALONE... PLEASE...

GET THE PATIENT READY TO RETURN TO M UNIVERSITY HOSPITAL...

THE SURGERY HAS BEEN CANCELLED.

TOO BAD! THIS WAS OUR CHANCE TO PUT OHU UNIVERSITY ON THE MAP!

WHOEVER WISHES TO COME AFTER ME MUST DENY HIMSELF, TAKE UP HIS CROSS, AND FOLLOW ME. FOR WHOEVER WISHES TO SAVE HIS LIFE WILL LOSE IT, BUT WHOEVER LOSES HIS LIFE FOR MY SAKE WILL SAVE IT. WHAT PROFIT IS THERE FOR ONE TO GAIN THE WHOLE WORLD AND FORFEIT HIS LIFE? WHAT COULD ONE GIVE IN EXCHANGE FOR HIS LIFE?

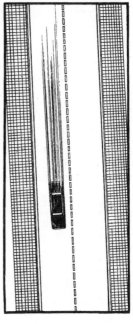

175

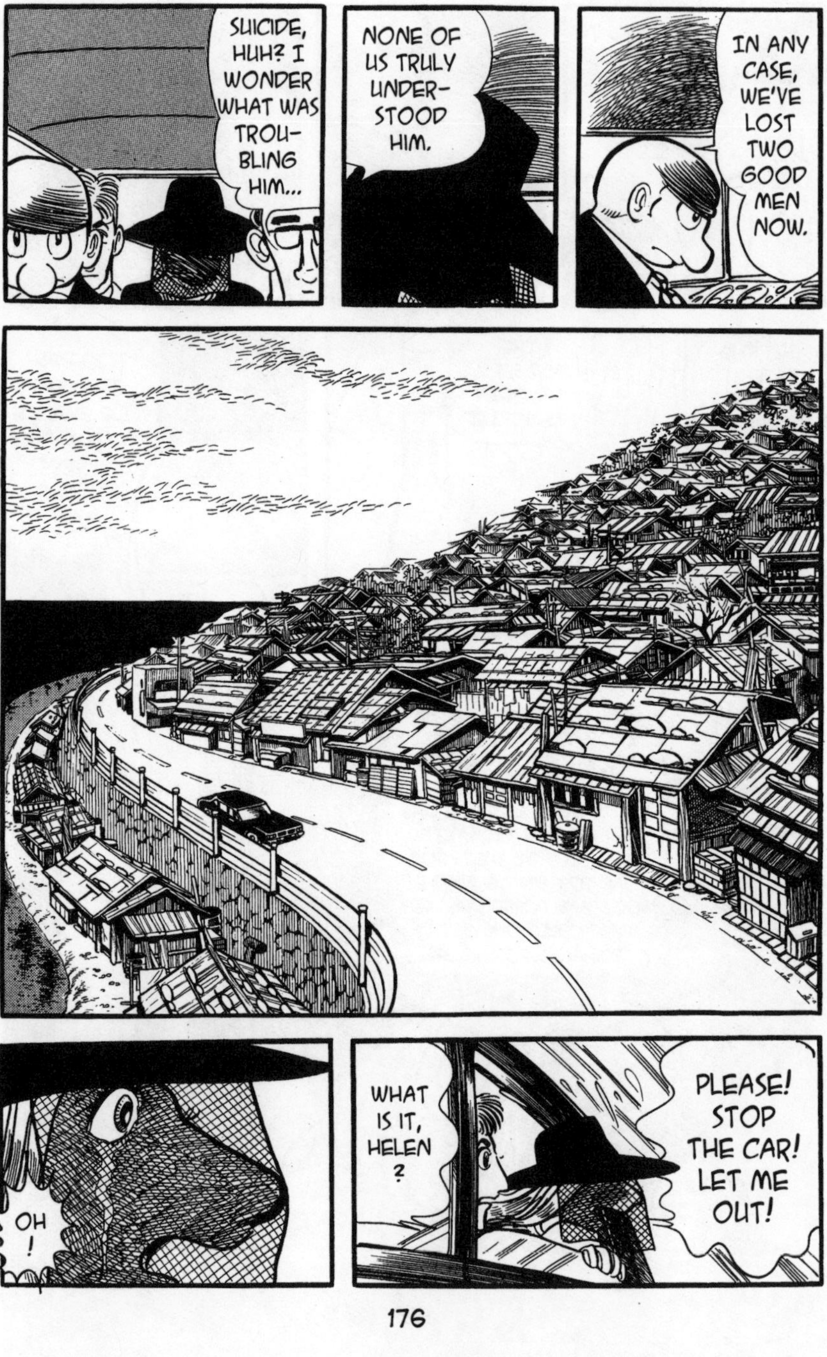
SUICIDE, HUH? I WONDER WHAT WAS TROUBLING HIM...
NONE OF US TRULY UNDERSTOOD HIM.
IN ANY CASE, WE'VE LOST TWO GOOD MEN NOW.
OH!
WHAT IS IT, HELEN?
PLEASE! STOP THE CAR! LET ME OUT!

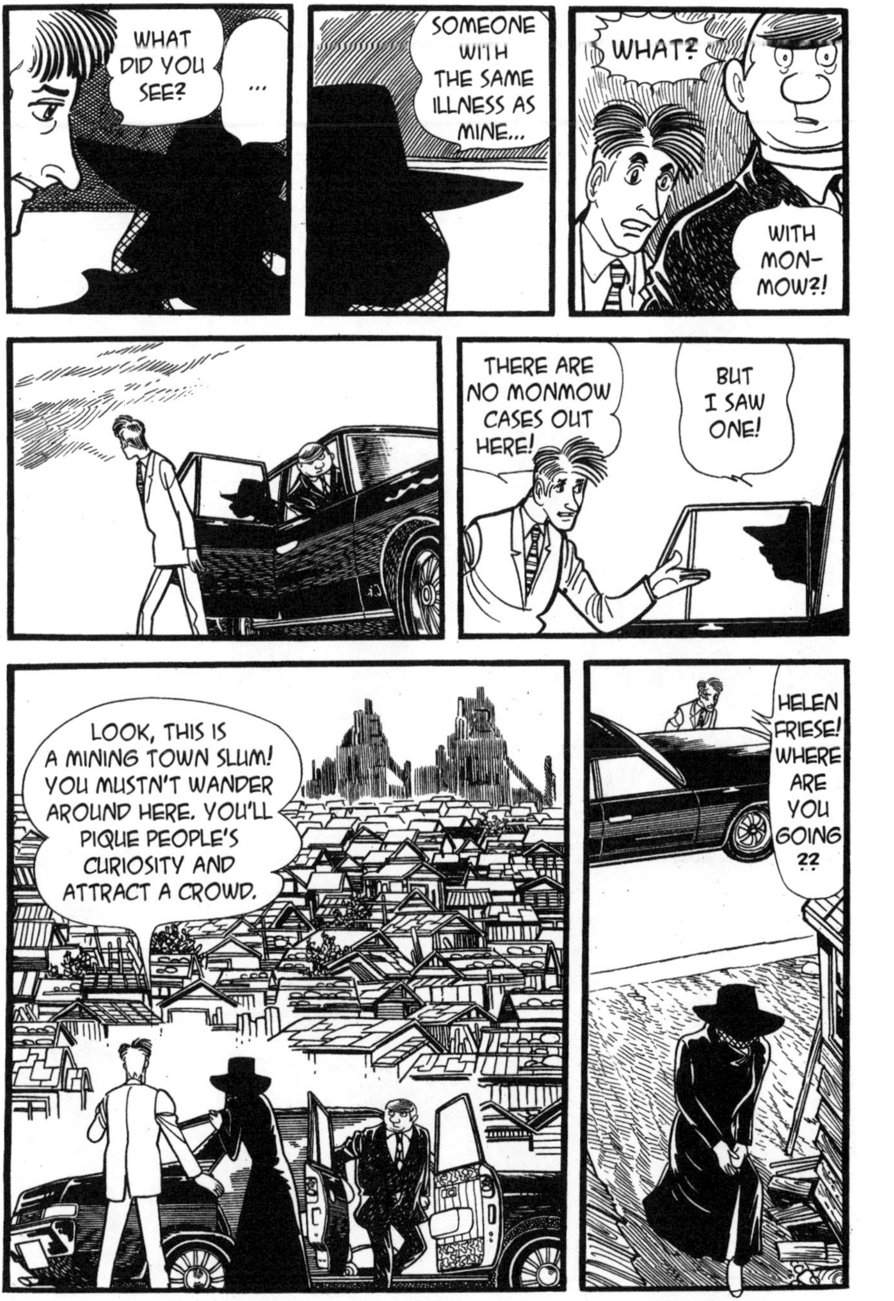
WHAT DID YOU SEE?
...
SOMEONE WITH THE SAME ILLNESS AS MINE...
WHAT?
WITH MON-MOW?!
THERE ARE NO MONMOW CASES OUT HERE!
BUT I SAW ONE!
LOOK, THIS IS A MINING TOWN SLUM! YOU MUSTN'T WANDER AROUND HERE. YOU'LL PIQUE PEOPLE'S CURIOSITY AND ATTRACT A CROWD.
HELEN FRIESE! WHERE ARE YOU GOING??

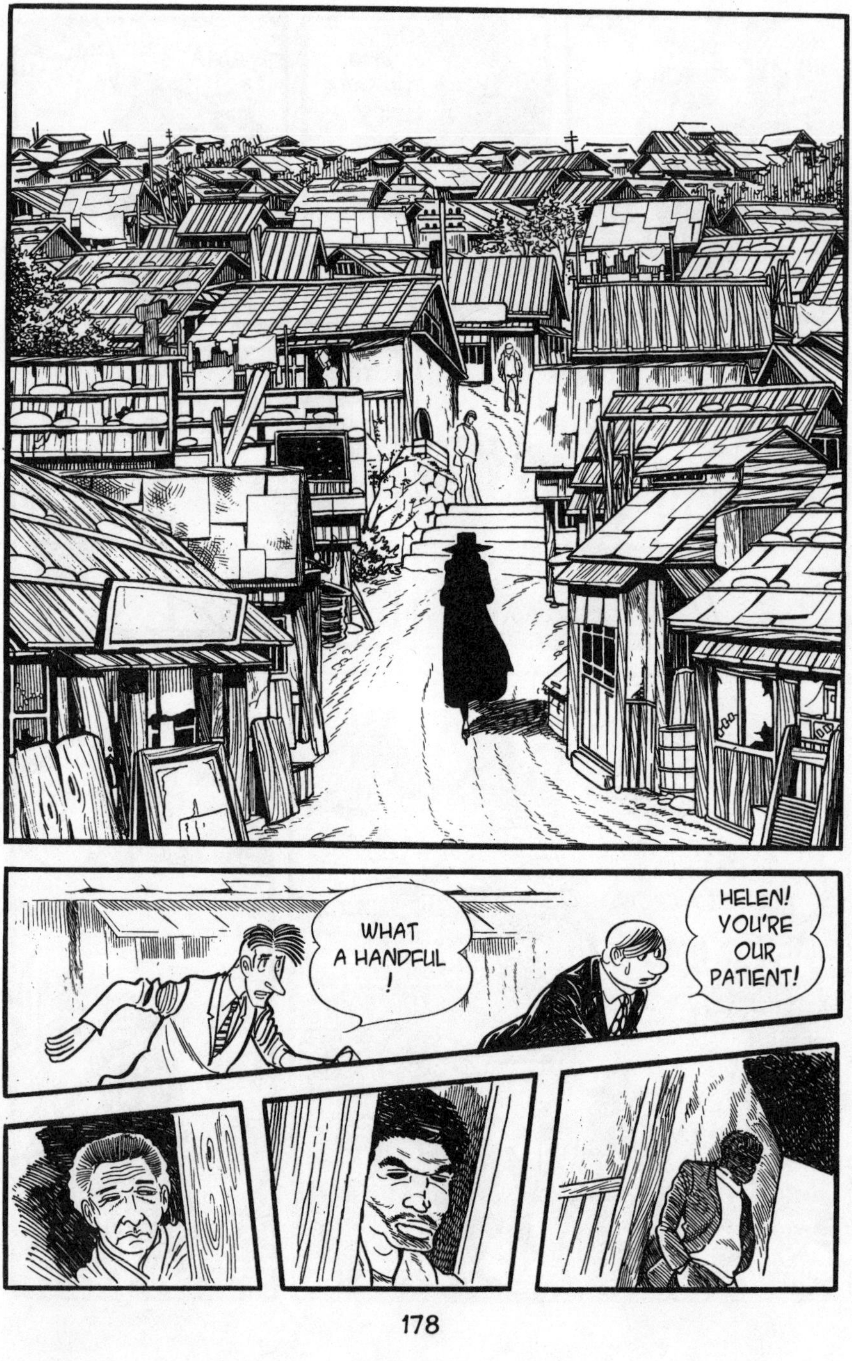
HELEN! YOU'RE OUR PATIENT!
WHAT A HANDFUL!

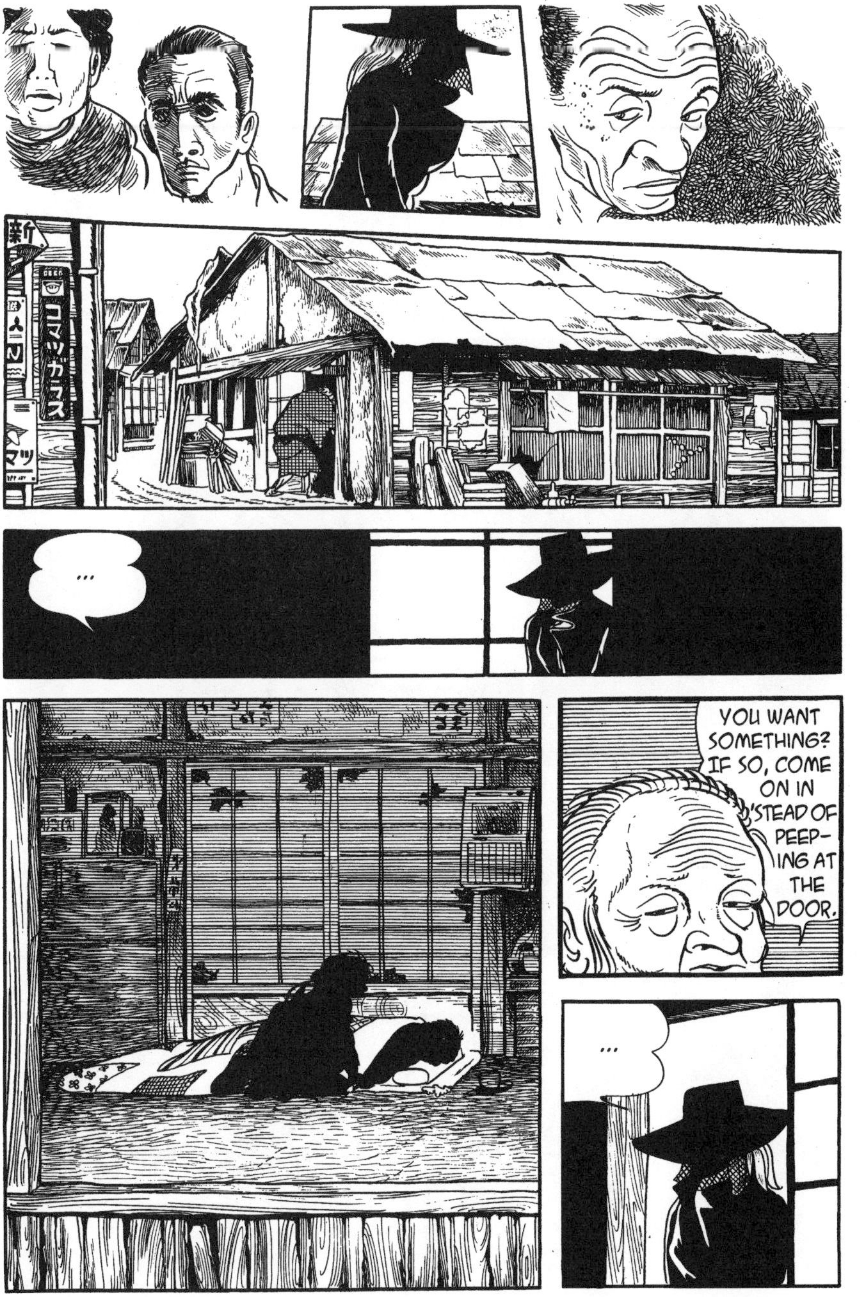
新
コマツガラス
マツ
...
YOU WANT SOMETHING? IF SO, COME ON IN 'STEAD OF PEEPING AT THE DOOR.
...

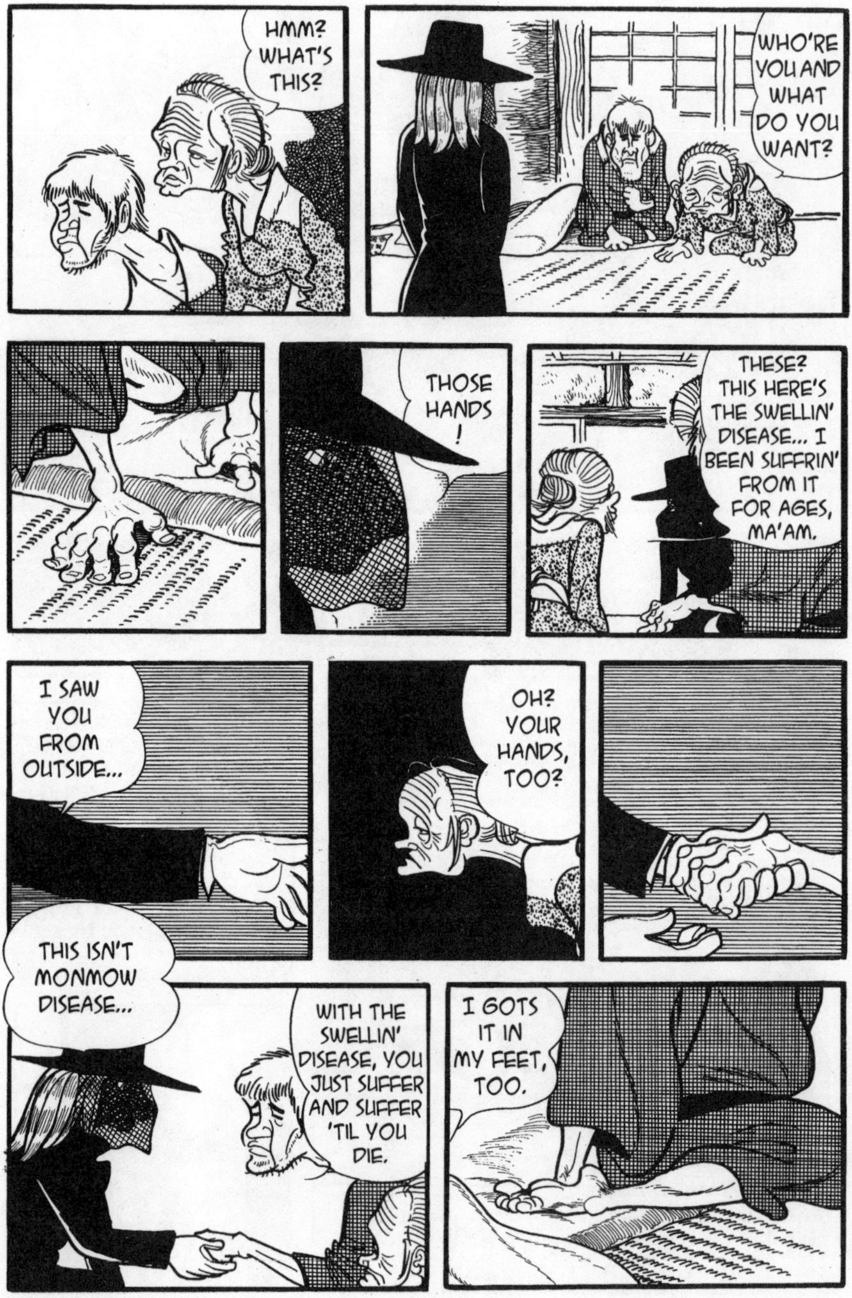
HMM? WHAT'S THIS?
WHO'RE YOU AND WHAT DO YOU WANT?
THOSE HANDS!
THESE? THIS HERE'S THE SWELLIN' DISEASE... I BEEN SUFFRIN' FROM IT FOR AGES, MA'AM.
I SAW YOU FROM OUTSIDE...
OH? YOUR HANDS, TOO?
THIS ISN'T MONMOW DISEASE...
WITH THE SWELLIN' DISEASE, YOU JUST SUFFER AND SUFFER 'TIL YOU DIE.
I GOTS IT IN MY FEET, TOO.

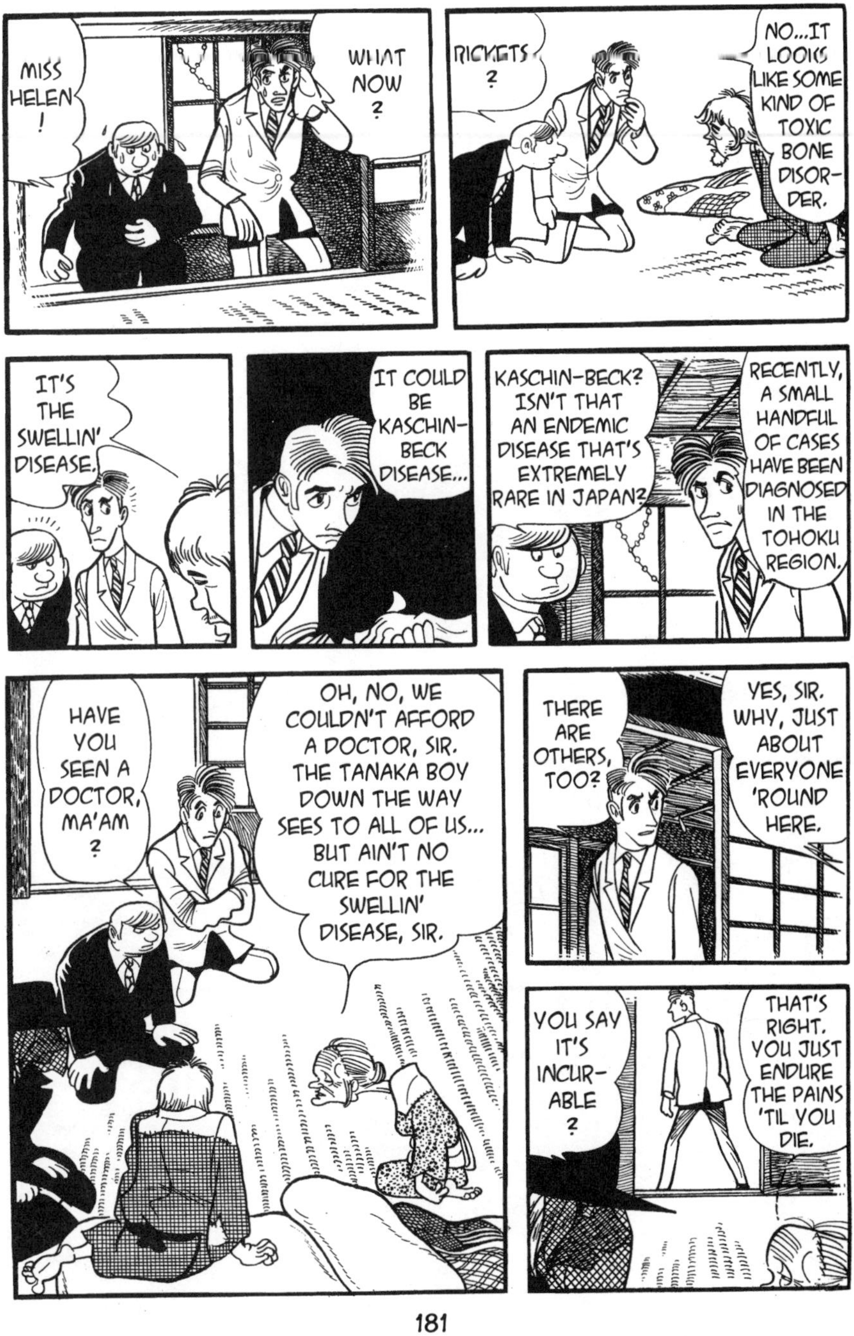

MISS HELEN!
WHAT NOW?
RICKETS?
NO...IT LOOKS LIKE SOME KIND OF TOXIC BONE DISORDER.
IT'S THE SWELLIN' DISEASE.
IT COULD BE KASCHIN-BECK DISEASE...
KASCHIN-BECK? ISN'T THAT AN ENDEMIC DISEASE THAT'S EXTREMELY RARE IN JAPAN?
RECENTLY, A SMALL HANDFUL OF CASES HAVE BEEN DIAGNOSED IN THE TOHOKU REGION.
HAVE YOU SEEN A DOCTOR, MA'AM?
OH, NO, WE COULDN'T AFFORD A DOCTOR, SIR. THE TANAKA BOY DOWN THE WAY SEES TO ALL OF US... BUT AIN'T NO CURE FOR THE SWELLIN' DISEASE, SIR.
THERE ARE OTHERS, TOO?
YES, SIR. WHY, JUST ABOUT EVERYONE 'ROUND HERE.
YOU SAY IT'S INCURABLE?
THAT'S RIGHT. YOU JUST ENDURE THE PAINS 'TIL YOU DIE.

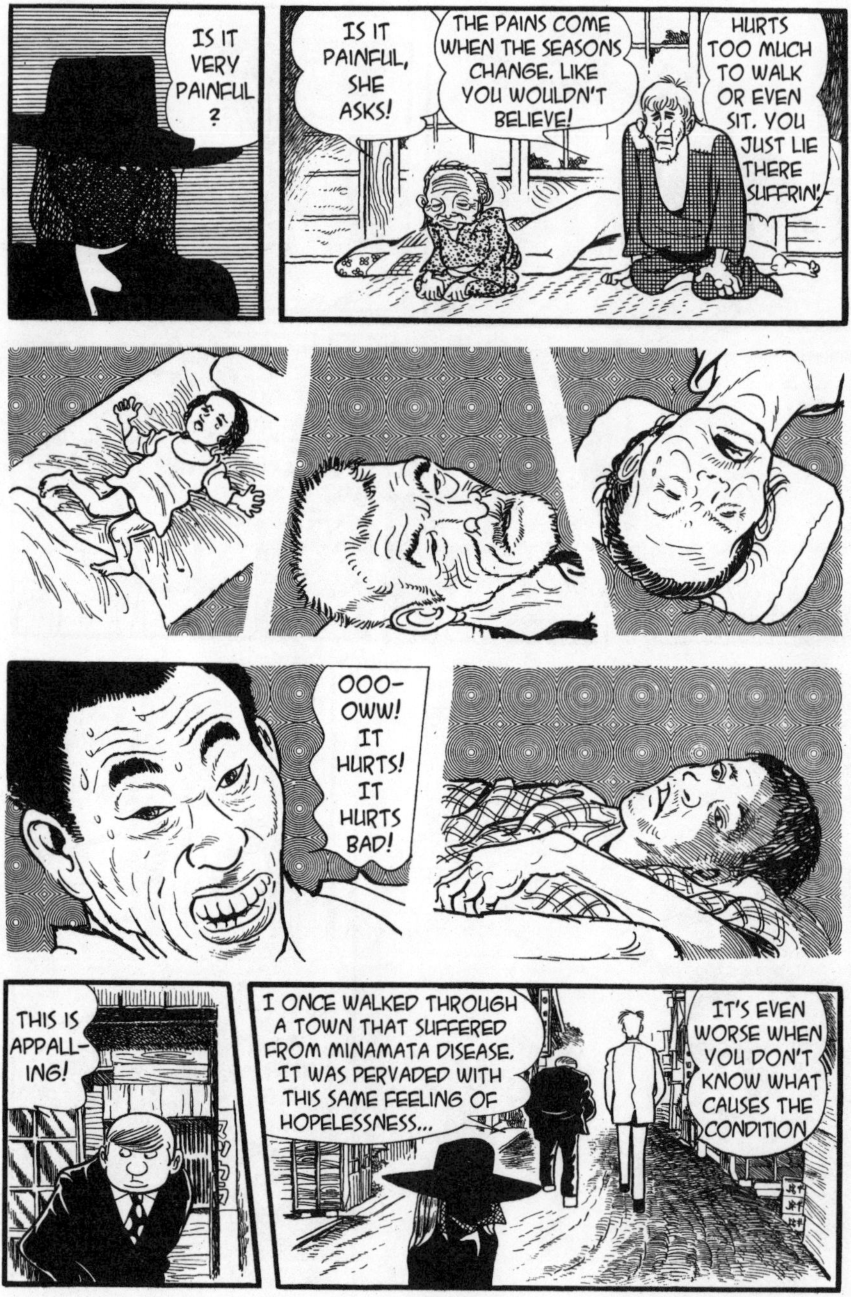
IS IT VERY PAINFUL ?
IS IT PAINFUL, SHE ASKS!
THE PAINS COME WHEN THE SEASONS CHANGE. LIKE YOU WOULDN'T BELIEVE!
HURTS TOO MUCH TO WALK OR EVEN SIT. YOU JUST LIE THERE SUFFRIN'.
OOO-OWW! IT HURTS! IT HURTS BAD!
THIS IS APPALL-ING!
I ONCE WALKED THROUGH A TOWN THAT SUFFERED FROM MINAMATA DISEASE. IT WAS PERVADED WITH THIS SAME FEELING OF HOPELESSNESS...
IT'S EVEN WORSE WHEN YOU DON'T KNOW WHAT CAUSES THE CONDITION

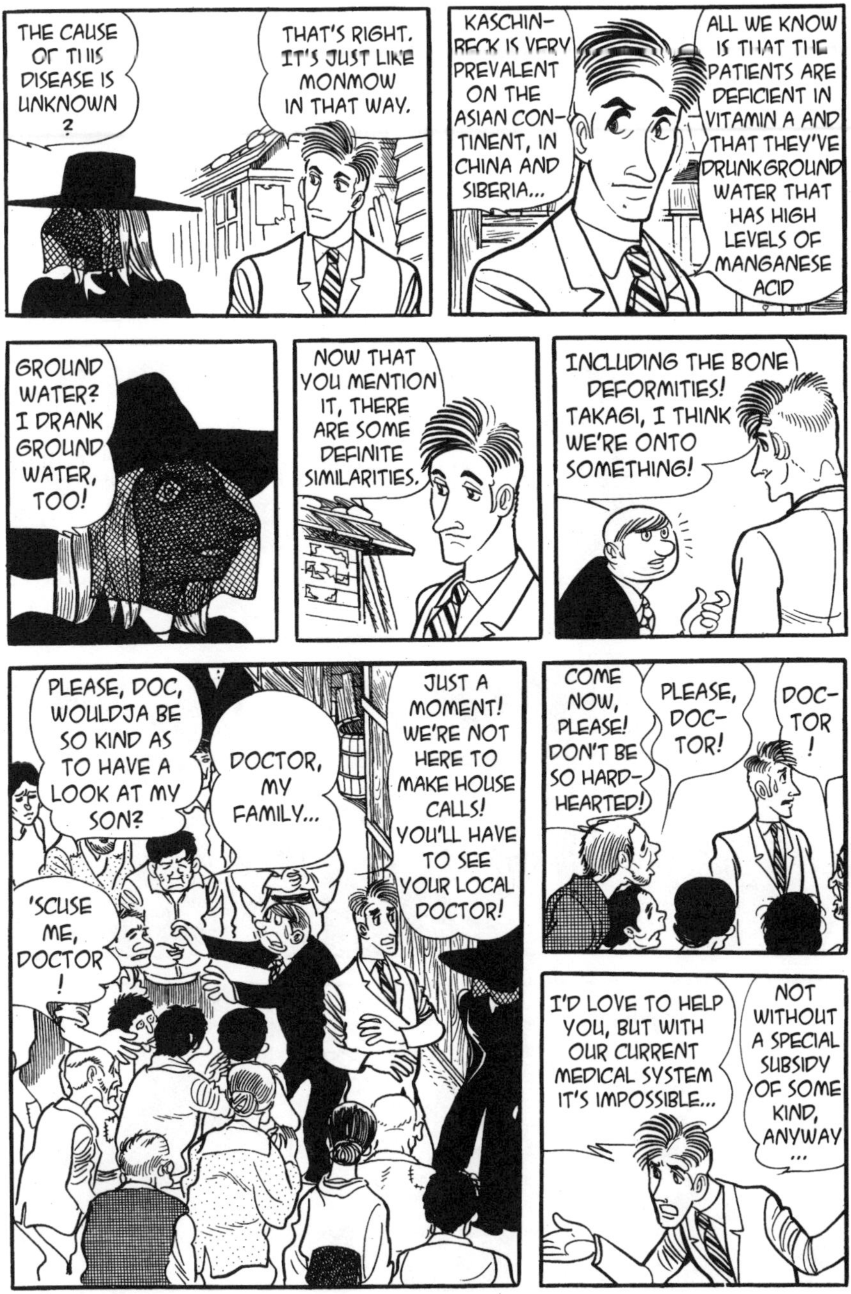
THE CAUSE OF THIS DISEASE IS UNKNOWN?
THAT'S RIGHT. IT'S JUST LIKE MONMOW IN THAT WAY.
KASCHIN-BECK IS VERY PREVALENT ON THE ASIAN CONTINENT, IN CHINA AND SIBERIA...
ALL WE KNOW IS THAT THE PATIENTS ARE DEFICIENT IN VITAMIN A AND THAT THEY'VE DRUNK GROUND WATER THAT HAS HIGH LEVELS OF MANGANESE ACID
GROUND WATER? I DRANK GROUND WATER, TOO!
NOW THAT YOU MENTION IT, THERE ARE SOME DEFINITE SIMILARITIES.
INCLUDING THE BONE DEFORMITIES! TAKAGI, I THINK WE'RE ONTO SOMETHING!
PLEASE, DOC, WOULDJA BE SO KIND AS TO HAVE A LOOK AT MY SON?
DOCTOR, MY FAMILY...
'SCUSE ME, DOCTOR!
JUST A MOMENT! WE'RE NOT HERE TO MAKE HOUSE CALLS! YOU'LL HAVE TO SEE YOUR LOCAL DOCTOR!
COME NOW, PLEASE! DON'T BE SO HARD-HEARTED!
PLEASE, DOCTOR!
DOCTOR!
I'D LOVE TO HELP YOU, BUT WITH OUR CURRENT MEDICAL SYSTEM IT'S IMPOSSIBLE...
NOT WITHOUT A SPECIAL SUBSIDY OF SOME KIND, ANYWAY...

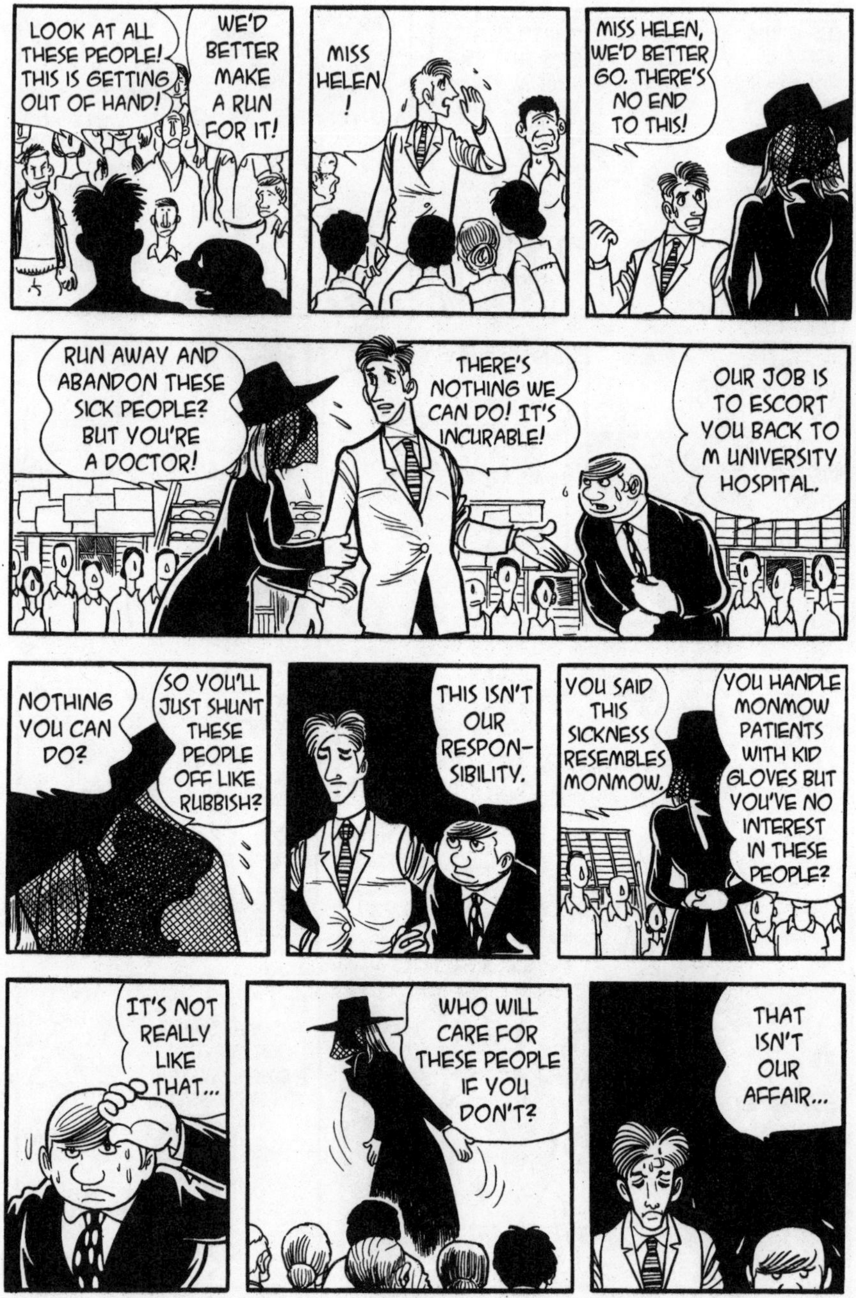
LOOK AT ALL THESE PEOPLE! THIS IS GETTING OUT OF HAND!
WE'D BETTER MAKE A RUN FOR IT!
MISS HELEN!
MISS HELEN, WE'D BETTER GO. THERE'S NO END TO THIS!
RUN AWAY AND ABANDON THESE SICK PEOPLE? BUT YOU'RE A DOCTOR!
THERE'S NOTHING WE CAN DO! IT'S INCURABLE!
OUR JOB IS TO ESCORT YOU BACK TO M UNIVERSITY HOSPITAL.
NOTHING YOU CAN DO?
SO YOU'LL JUST SHUNT THESE PEOPLE OFF LIKE RUBBISH?
THIS ISN'T OUR RESPON-SIBILITY.
YOU SAID THIS SICKNESS RESEMBLES MONMOW.
YOU HANDLE MONMOW PATIENTS WITH KID GLOVES BUT YOU'VE NO INTEREST IN THESE PEOPLE?
IT'S NOT REALLY LIKE THAT...
WHO WILL CARE FOR THESE PEOPLE IF YOU DON'T?
THAT ISN'T OUR AFFAIR...

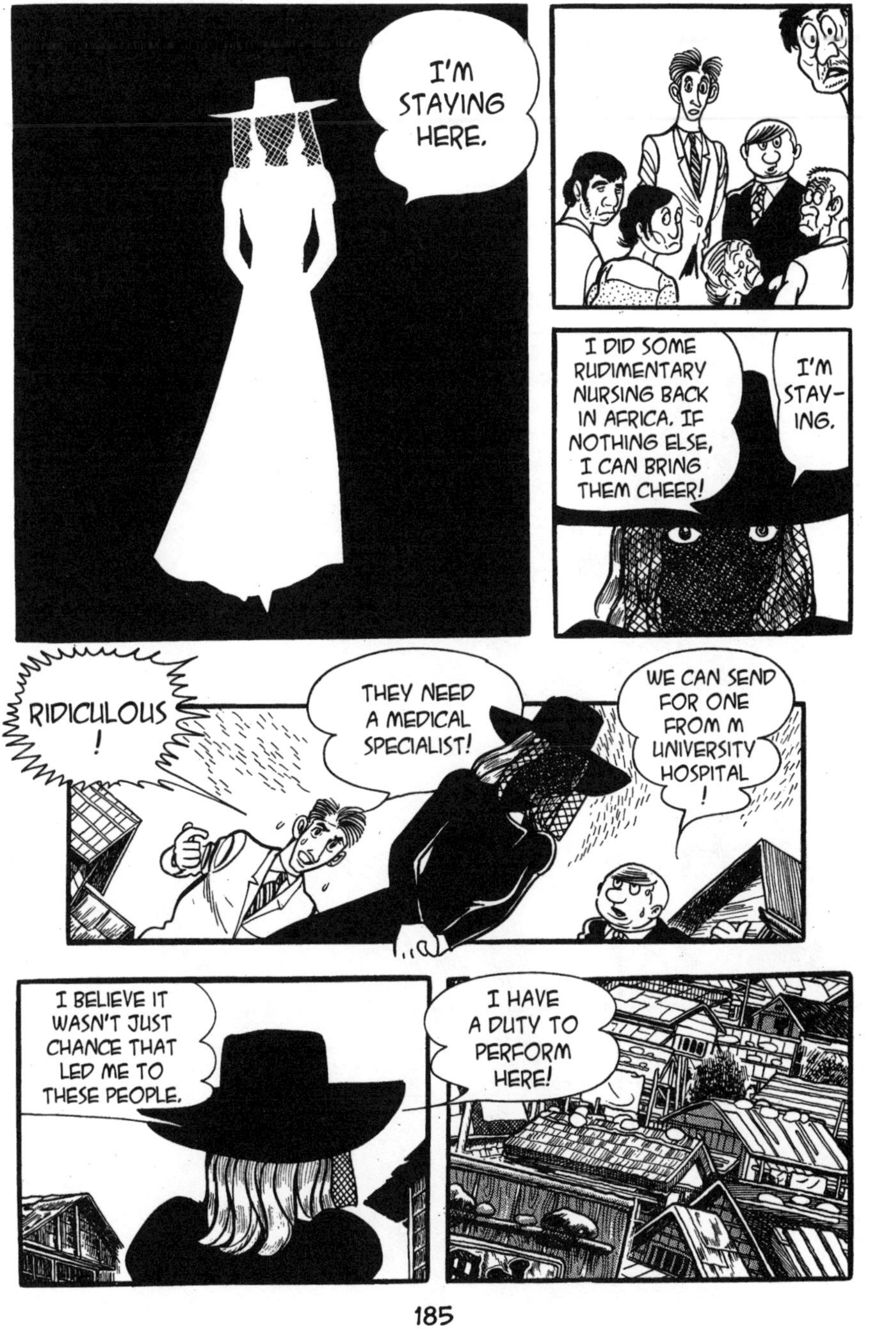
I'M STAYING HERE.
I DID SOME RUDIMENTARY NURSING BACK IN AFRICA. IF NOTHING ELSE, I CAN BRING THEM CHEER!
I'M STAY-ING.
RIDICULOUS!
THEY NEED A MEDICAL SPECIALIST!
WE CAN SEND FOR ONE FROM M UNIVERSITY HOSPITAL!
I BELIEVE IT WASN'T JUST CHANCE THAT LED ME TO THESE PEOPLE.
I HAVE A DUTY TO PERFORM HERE!

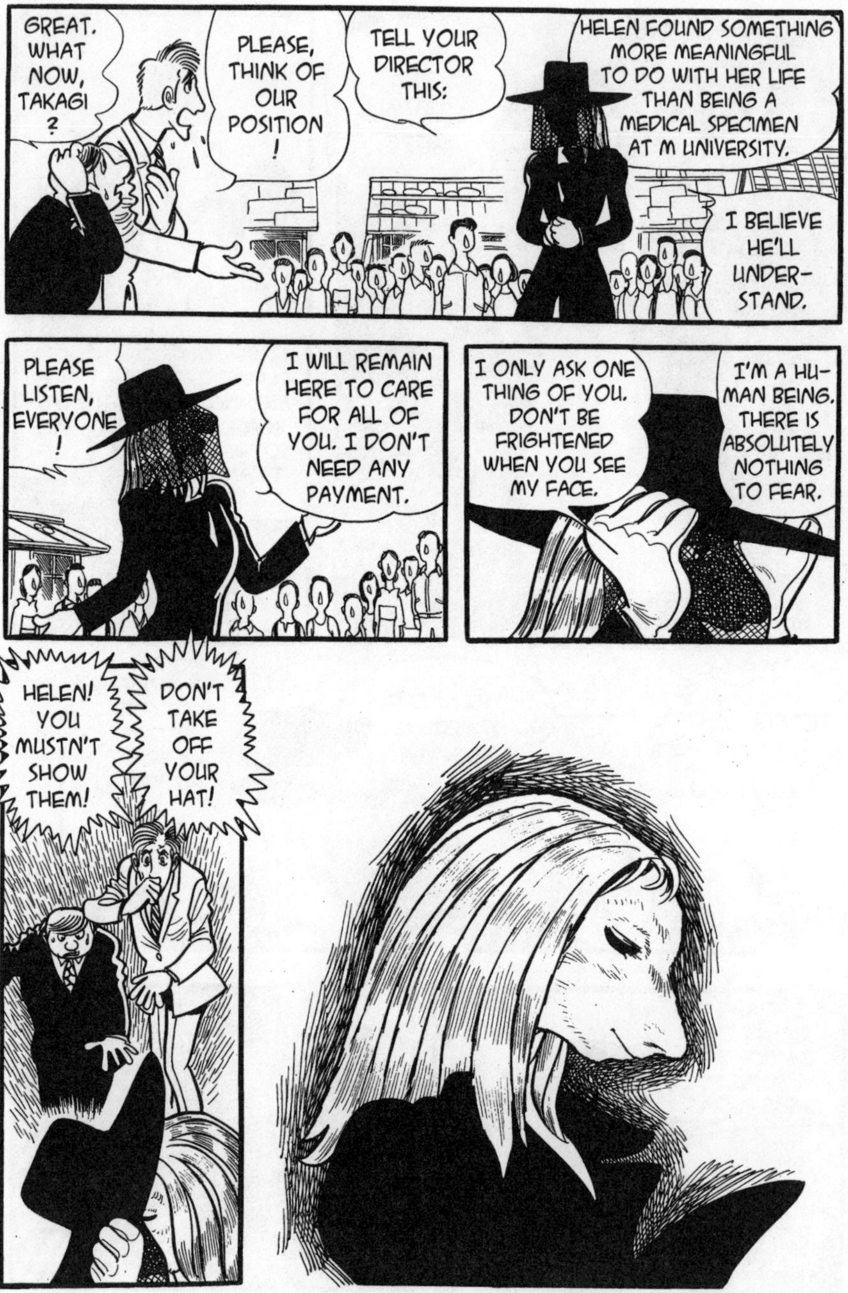

GREAT. WHAT NOW, TAKAGI?
PLEASE, THINK OF OUR POSITION!
TELL YOUR DIRECTOR THIS:
HELEN FOUND SOMETHING MORE MEANINGFUL TO DO WITH HER LIFE THAN BEING A MEDICAL SPECIMEN AT M UNIVERSITY.
I BELIEVE HE'LL UNDERSTAND.
PLEASE LISTEN, EVERYONE!
I WILL REMAIN HERE TO CARE FOR ALL OF YOU. I DON'T NEED ANY PAYMENT.
I ONLY ASK ONE THING OF YOU. DON'T BE FRIGHTENED WHEN YOU SEE MY FACE.
I'M A HUMAN BEING. THERE IS ABSOLUTELY NOTHING TO FEAR.
HELEN! YOU MUSTN'T SHOW THEM!
DON'T TAKE OFF YOUR HAT!

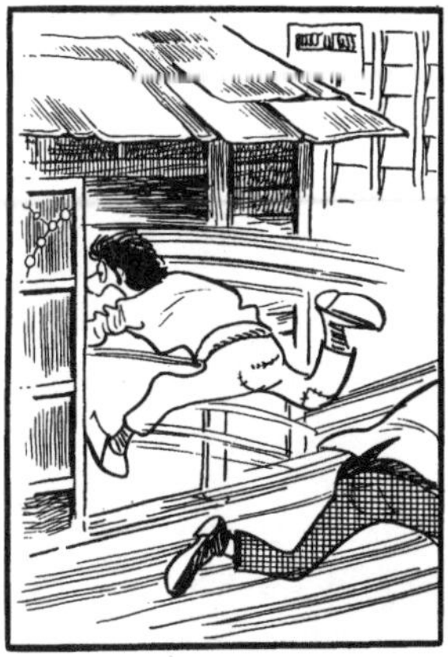

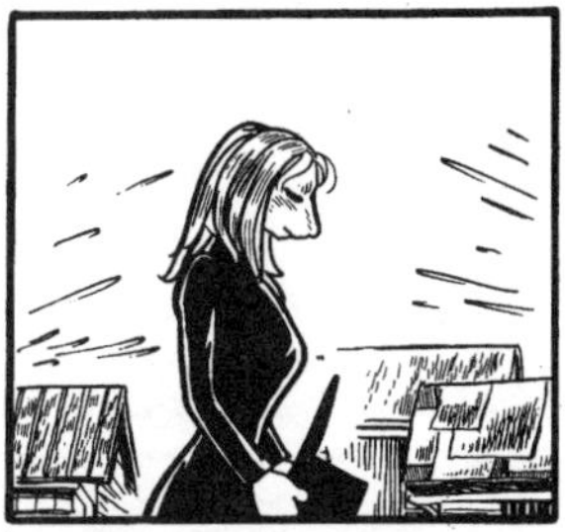

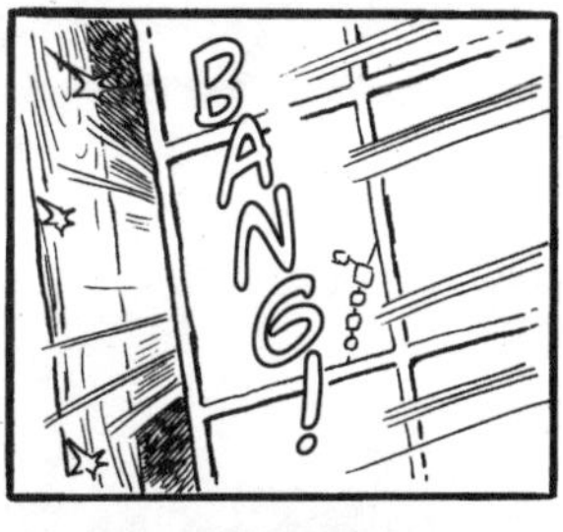
BANG!

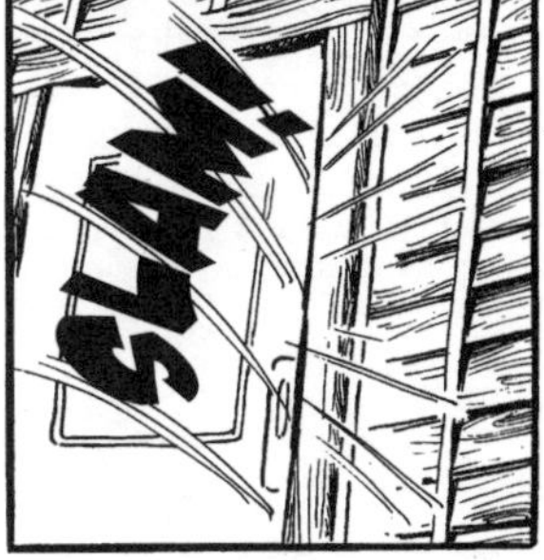
SLAM!

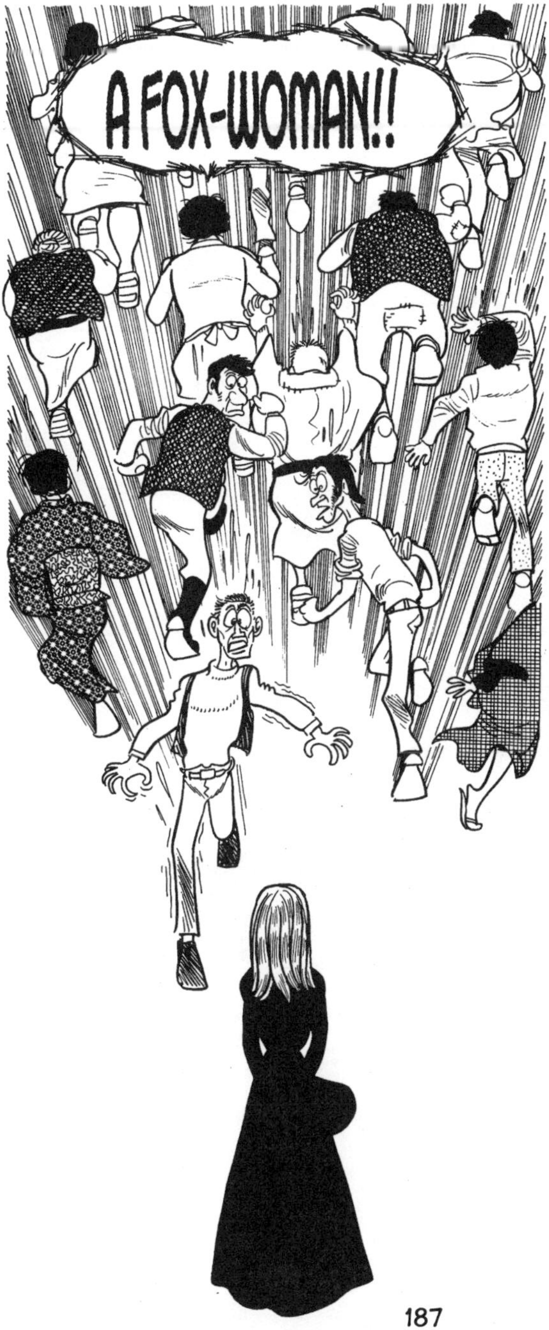
A FOX-WOMAN!!

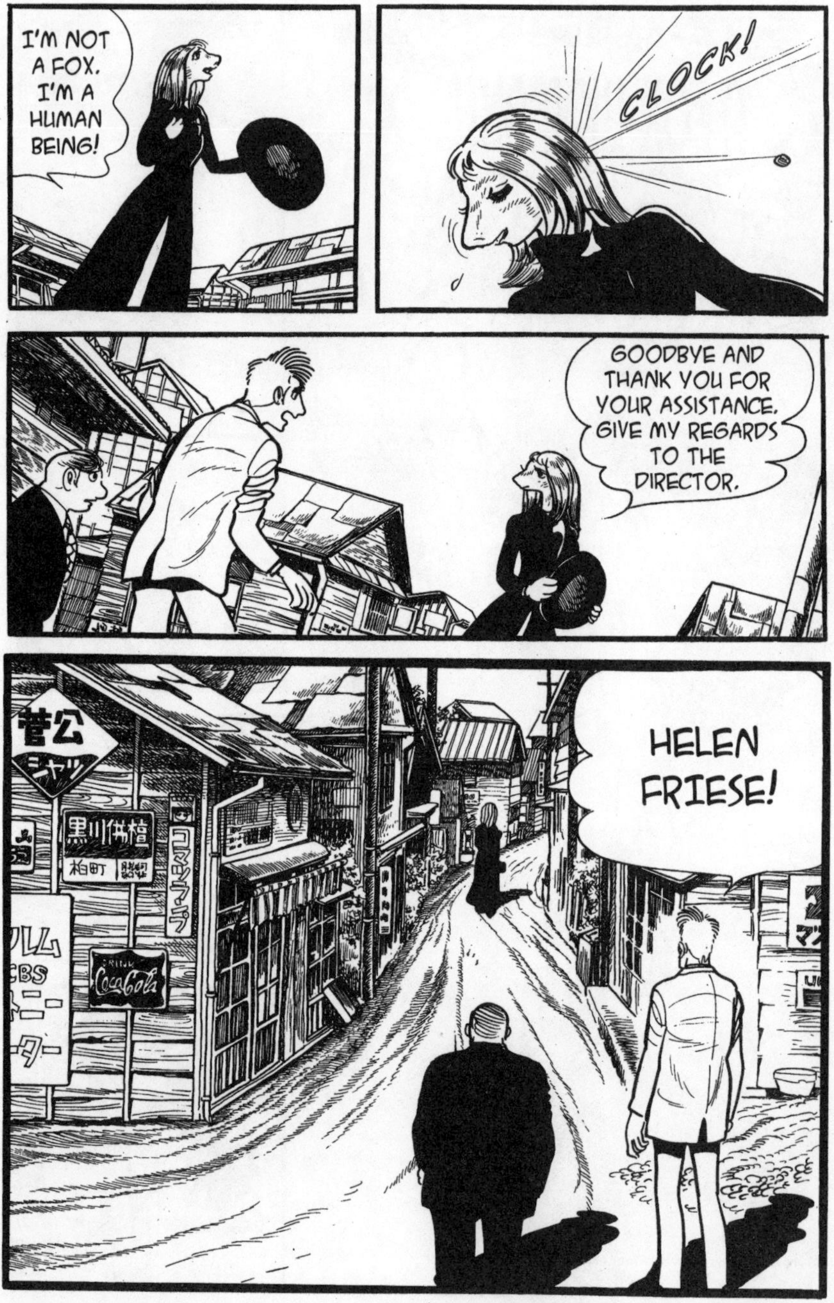
I'M NOT A FOX. I'M A HUMAN BEING!
CLOCK!
GOODBYE AND THANK YOU FOR YOUR ASSISTANCE. GIVE MY REGARDS TO THE DIRECTOR.
HELEN FRIESE!
Coca-Cola
CBS

CHAPTER 16

THE JOURNEY HOME

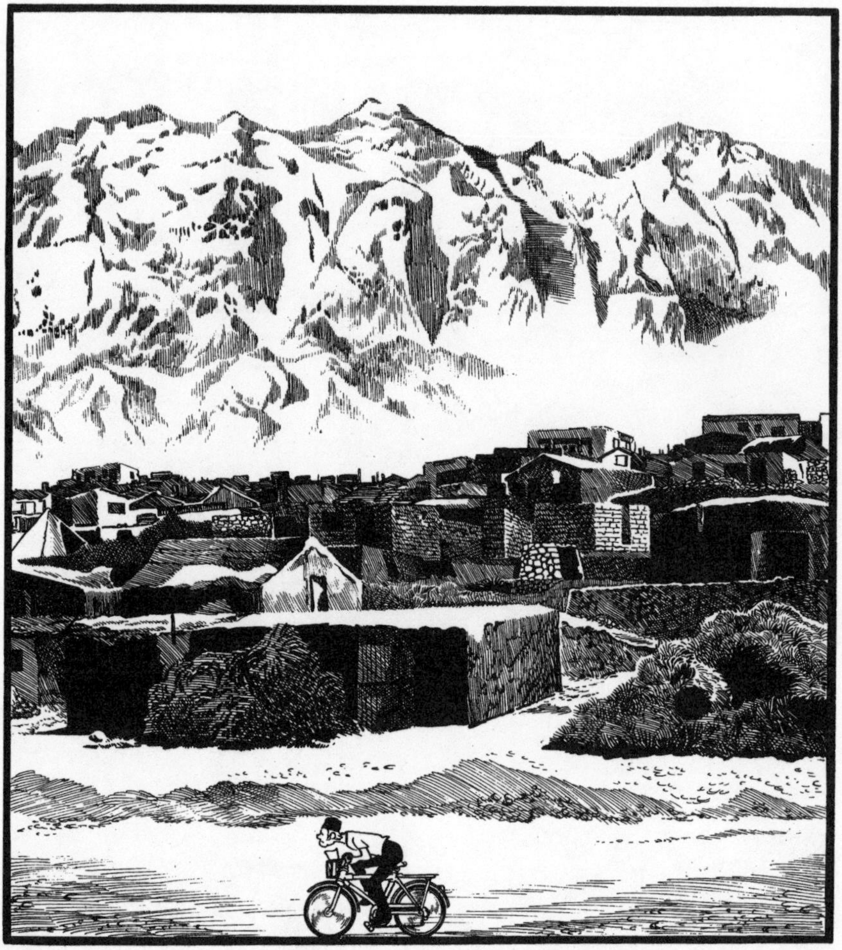
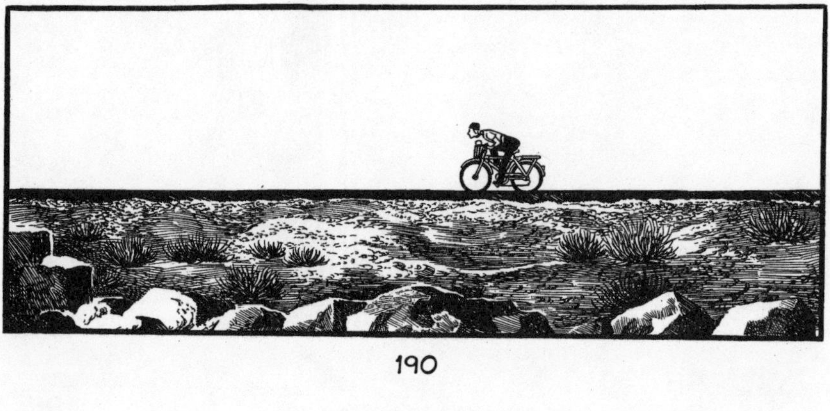

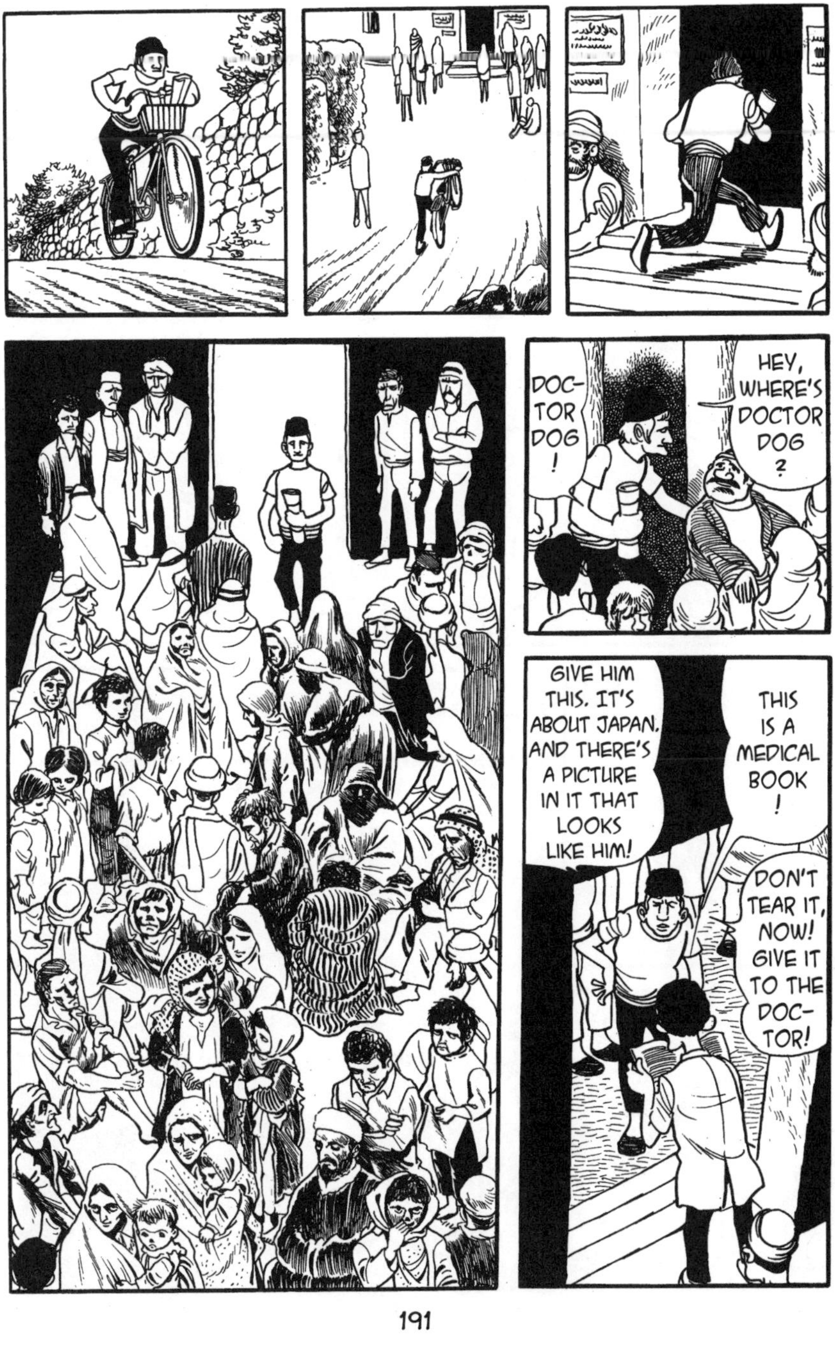
HEY, WHERE'S DOCTOR DOG ?
DOC-TOR DOG !
THIS IS A MEDICAL BOOK !
GIVE HIM THIS. IT'S ABOUT JAPAN. AND THERE'S A PICTURE IN IT THAT LOOKS LIKE HIM!
DON'T TEAR IT, NOW! GIVE IT TO THE DOC-TOR!

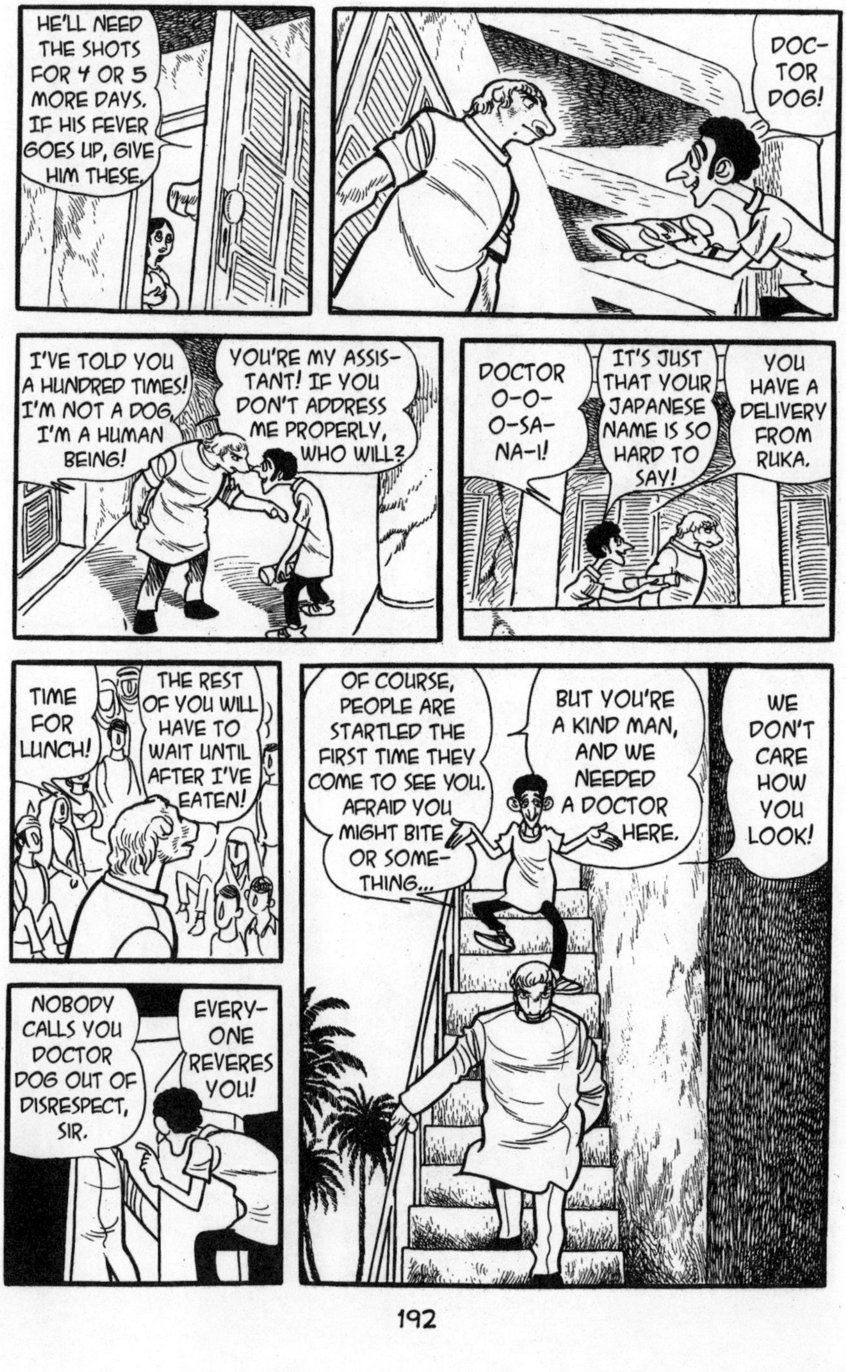
HE'LL NEED THE SHOTS FOR 4 OR 5 MORE DAYS. IF HIS FEVER GOES UP, GIVE HIM THESE.
DOC-TOR DOG!
I'VE TOLD YOU A HUNDRED TIMES! I'M NOT A DOG. I'M A HUMAN BEING!
YOU'RE MY ASSIS-TANT! IF YOU DON'T ADDRESS ME PROPERLY, WHO WILL?
DOCTOR O-O-O-SA-NA-I!
IT'S JUST THAT YOUR JAPANESE NAME IS SO HARD TO SAY!
YOU HAVE A DELIVERY FROM RUKA.
TIME FOR LUNCH!
THE REST OF YOU WILL HAVE TO WAIT UNTIL AFTER I'VE EATEN!
NOBODY CALLS YOU DOCTOR DOG OUT OF DISRESPECT, SIR.
EVERY-ONE REVERES YOU!
OF COURSE, PEOPLE ARE STARTLED THE FIRST TIME THEY COME TO SEE YOU. AFRAID YOU MIGHT BITE OR SOME-THING...
BUT YOU'RE A KIND MAN, AND WE NEEDED A DOCTOR HERE.
WE DON'T CARE HOW YOU LOOK!

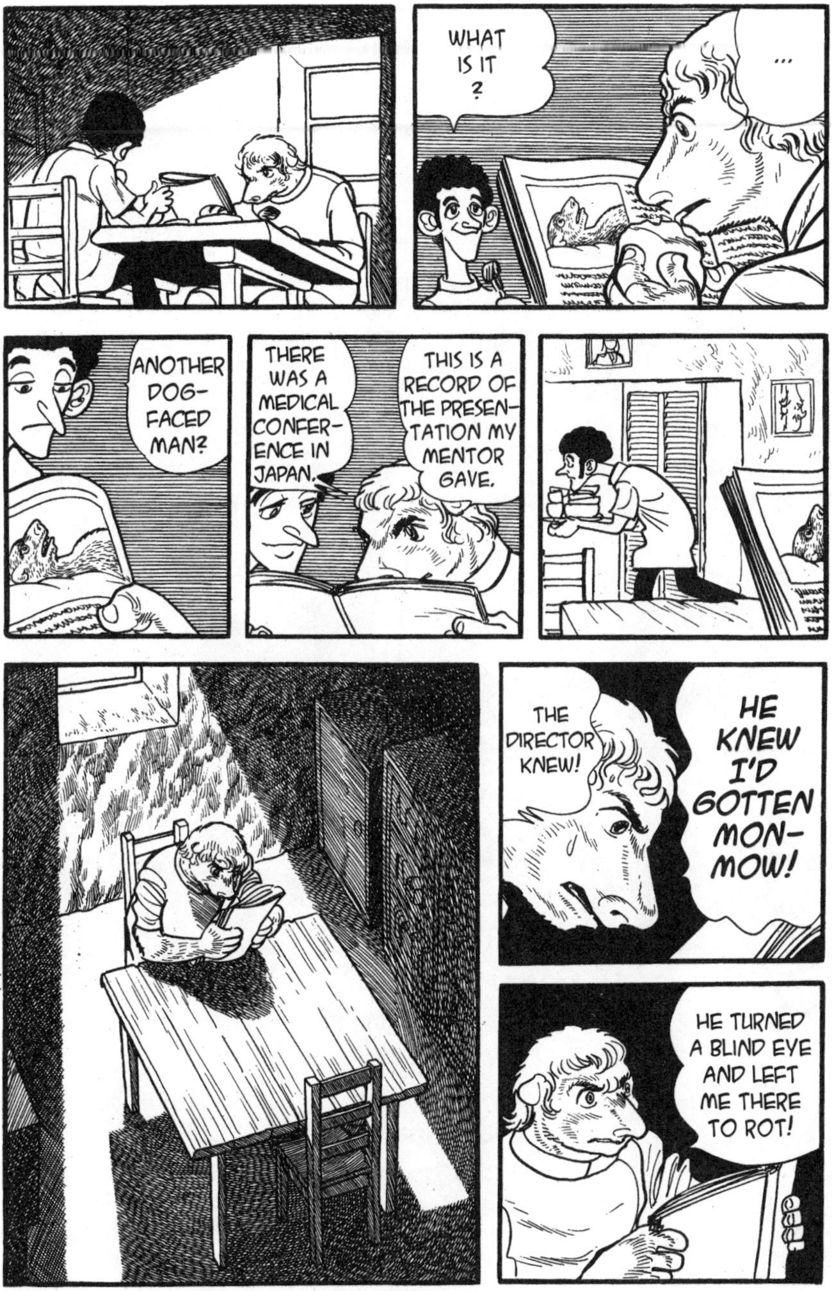
...
WHAT IS IT ?
THIS IS A RECORD OF THE PRESENTATION MY MENTOR GAVE.
THERE WAS A MEDICAL CONFERENCE IN JAPAN.
ANOTHER DOG-FACED MAN?
HE KNEW I'D GOTTEN MONMOW!
THE DIRECTOR KNEW!
HE TURNED A BLIND EYE AND LEFT ME THERE TO ROT!

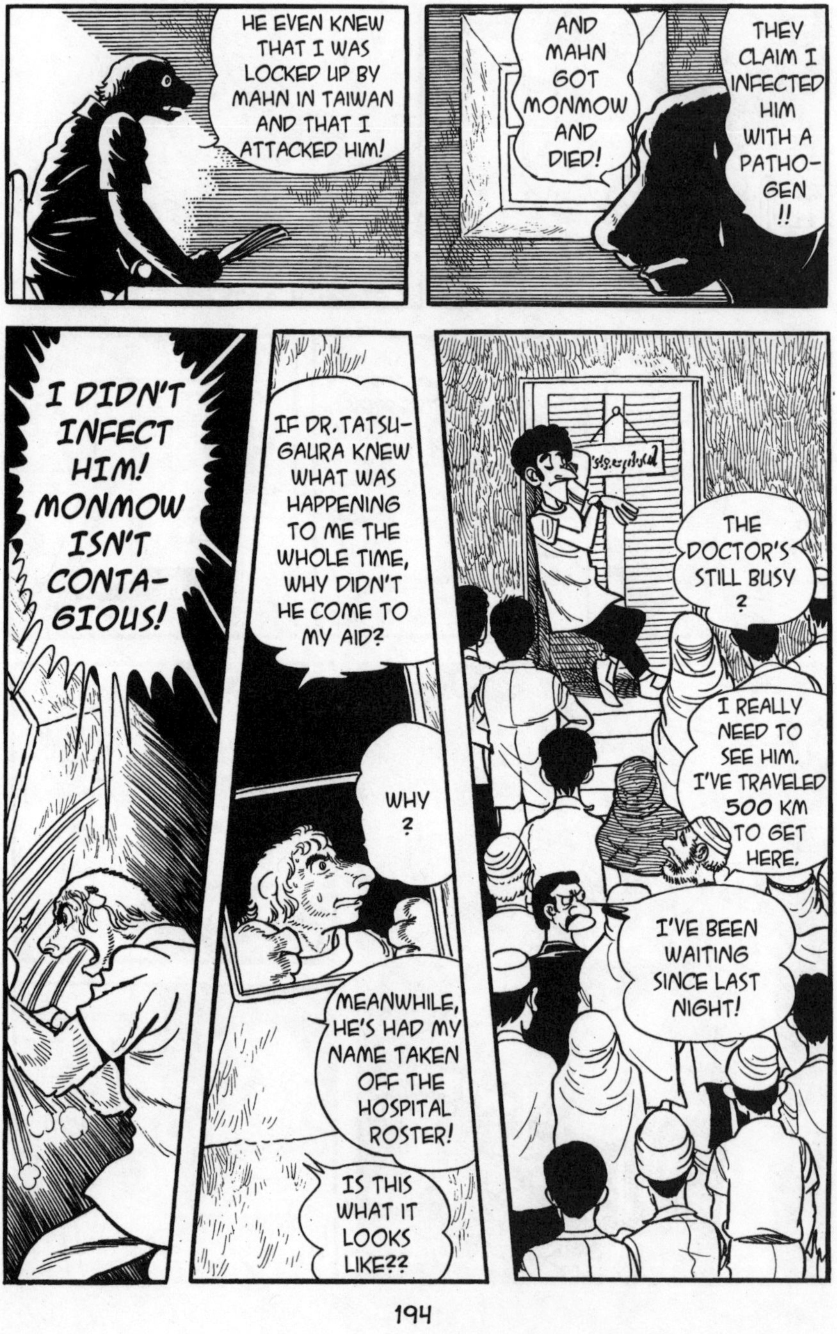
HE EVEN KNEW THAT I WAS LOCKED UP BY MAHN IN TAIWAN AND THAT I ATTACKED HIM!
AND MAHN GOT MONMOW AND DIED!
THEY CLAIM I INFECTED HIM WITH A PATHO-GEN !!
I DIDN'T INFECT HIM! MONMOW ISN'T CONTA-GIOUS!
IF DR. TATSU-GAURA KNEW WHAT WAS HAPPENING TO ME THE WHOLE TIME, WHY DIDN'T HE COME TO MY AID?
WHY ?
MEANWHILE, HE'S HAD MY NAME TAKEN OFF THE HOSPITAL ROSTER!
IS THIS WHAT IT LOOKS LIKE??
THE DOCTOR'S STILL BUSY ?
I REALLY NEED TO SEE HIM. I'VE TRAVELED 500 KM TO GET HERE.
I'VE BEEN WAITING SINCE LAST NIGHT!

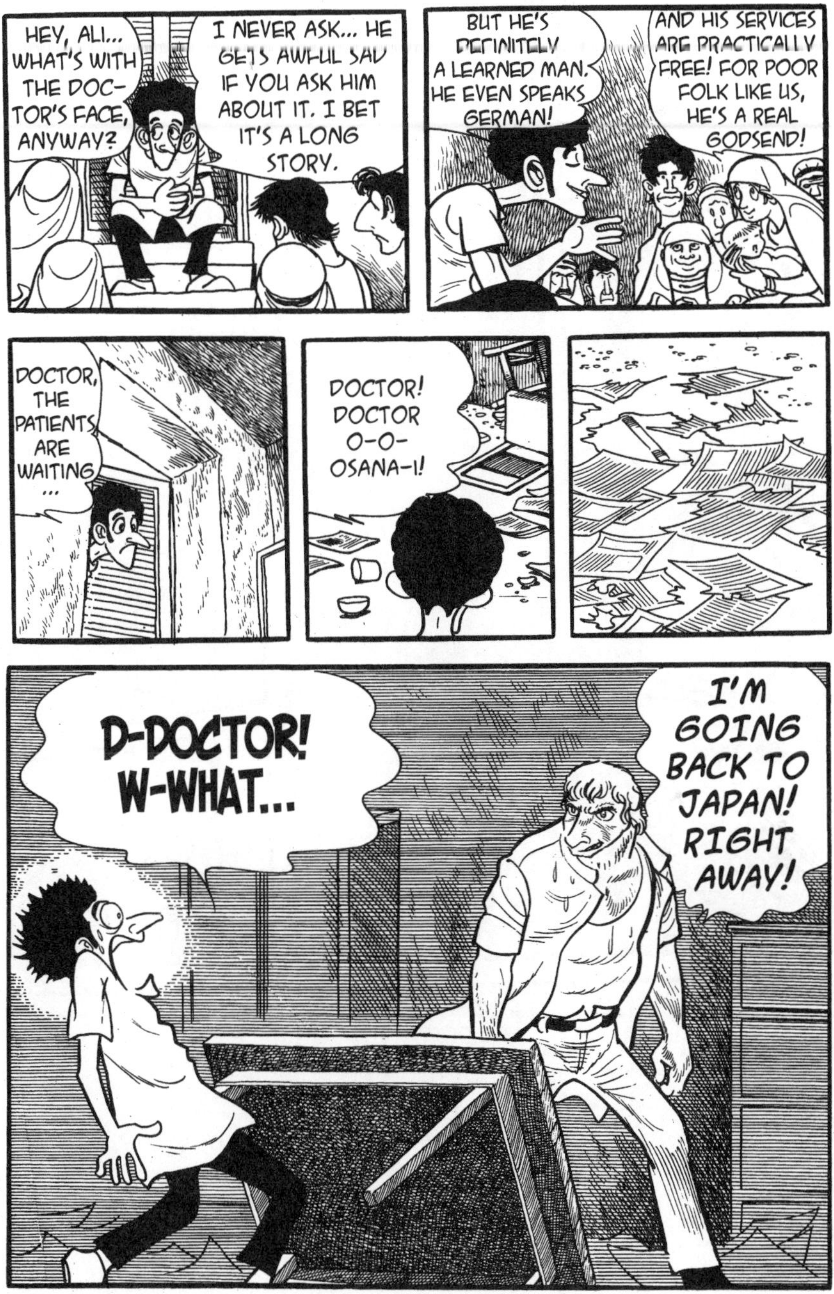
HEY, ALI... WHAT'S WITH THE DOCTOR'S FACE, ANYWAY?
I NEVER ASK... HE GETS AWFUL SAD IF YOU ASK HIM ABOUT IT. I BET IT'S A LONG STORY.
BUT HE'S DEFINITELY A LEARNED MAN. HE EVEN SPEAKS GERMAN!
AND HIS SERVICES ARE PRACTICALLY FREE! FOR POOR FOLK LIKE US, HE'S A REAL GODSEND!
DOCTOR, THE PATIENTS ARE WAITING...
DOCTOR! DOCTOR O-O-OSANA-I!
D-DOCTOR! W-WHAT...
I'M GOING BACK TO JAPAN! RIGHT AWAY!

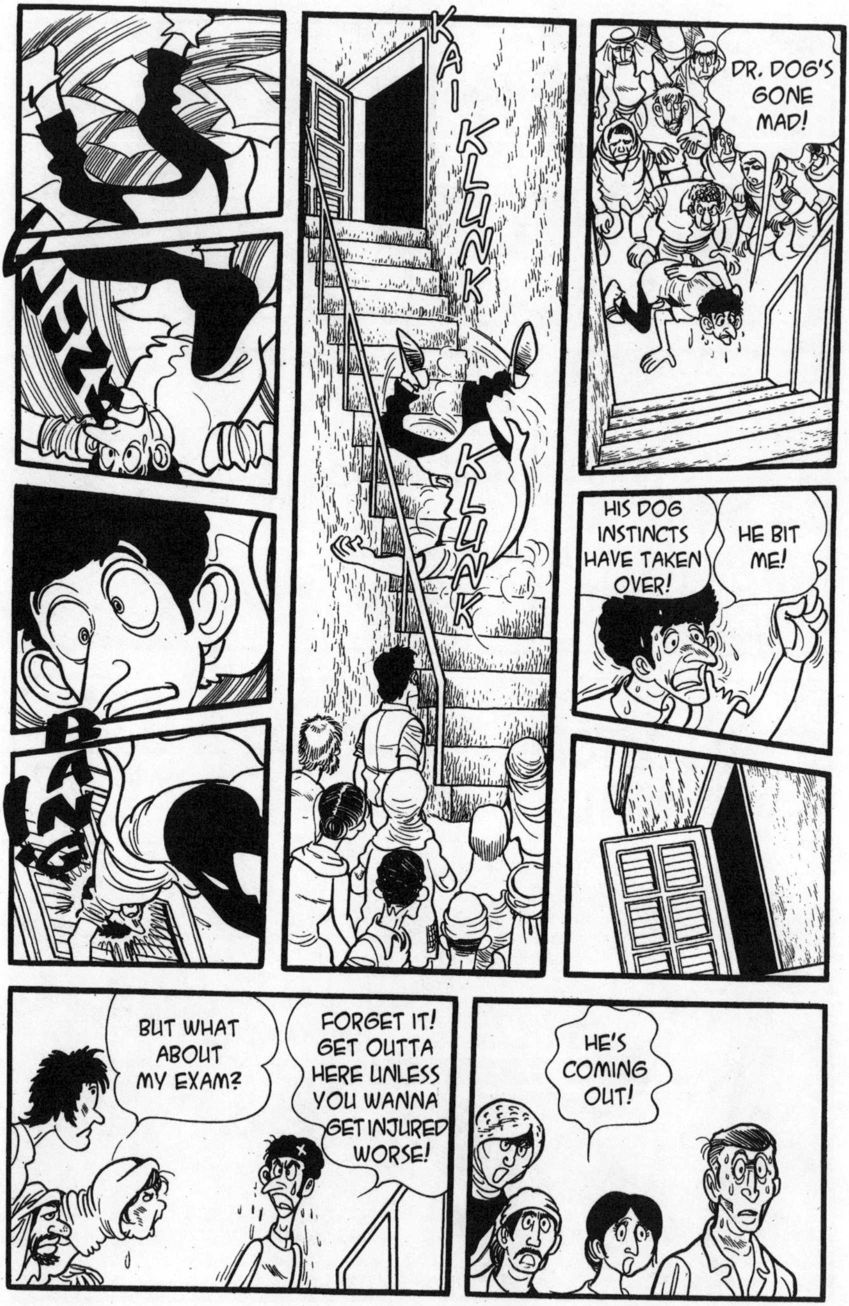
BANG!
KA-KLUNK
KLUNK
KLUNK
DR. DOG'S GONE MAD!
HIS DOG INSTINCTS HAVE TAKEN OVER!
HE BIT ME!
BUT WHAT ABOUT MY EXAM?
FORGET IT! GET OUTTA HERE UNLESS YOU WANNA GET INJURED WORSE!
HE'S COMING OUT!

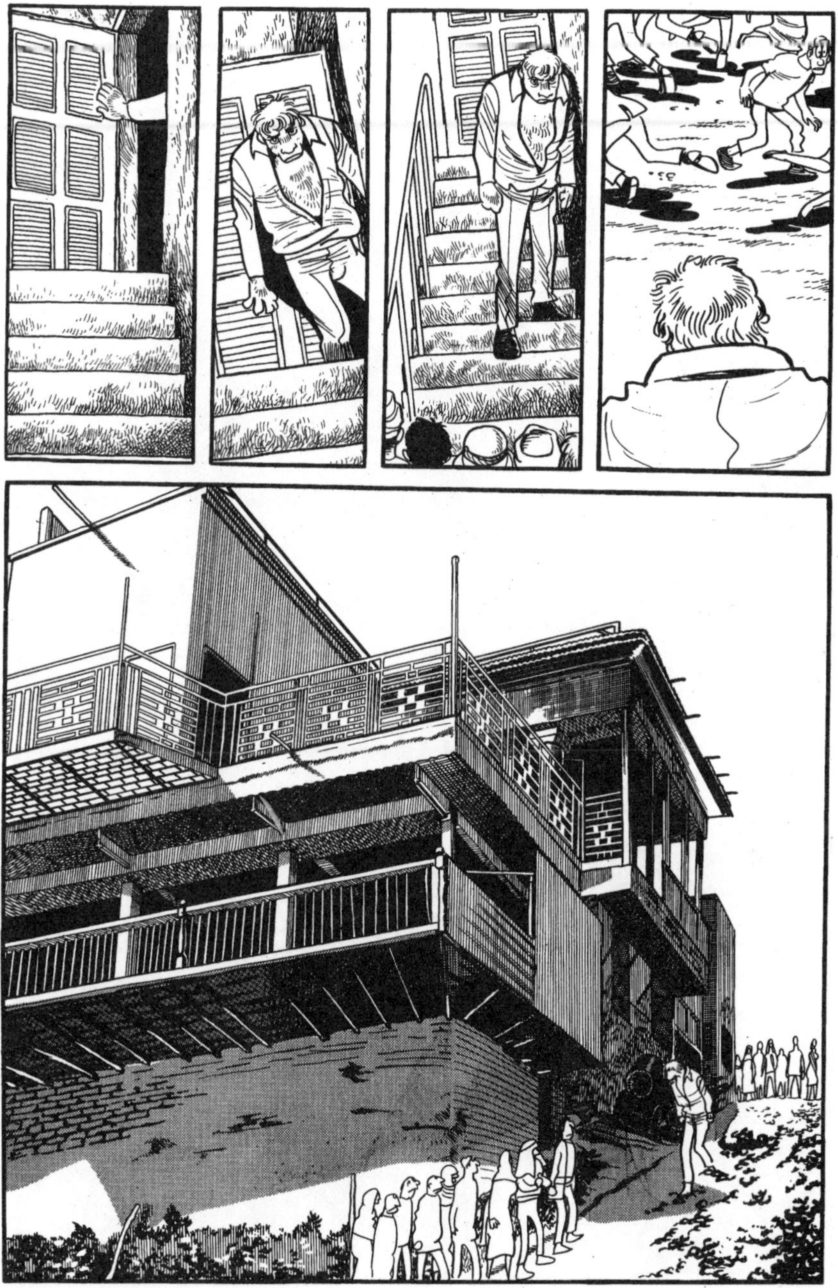

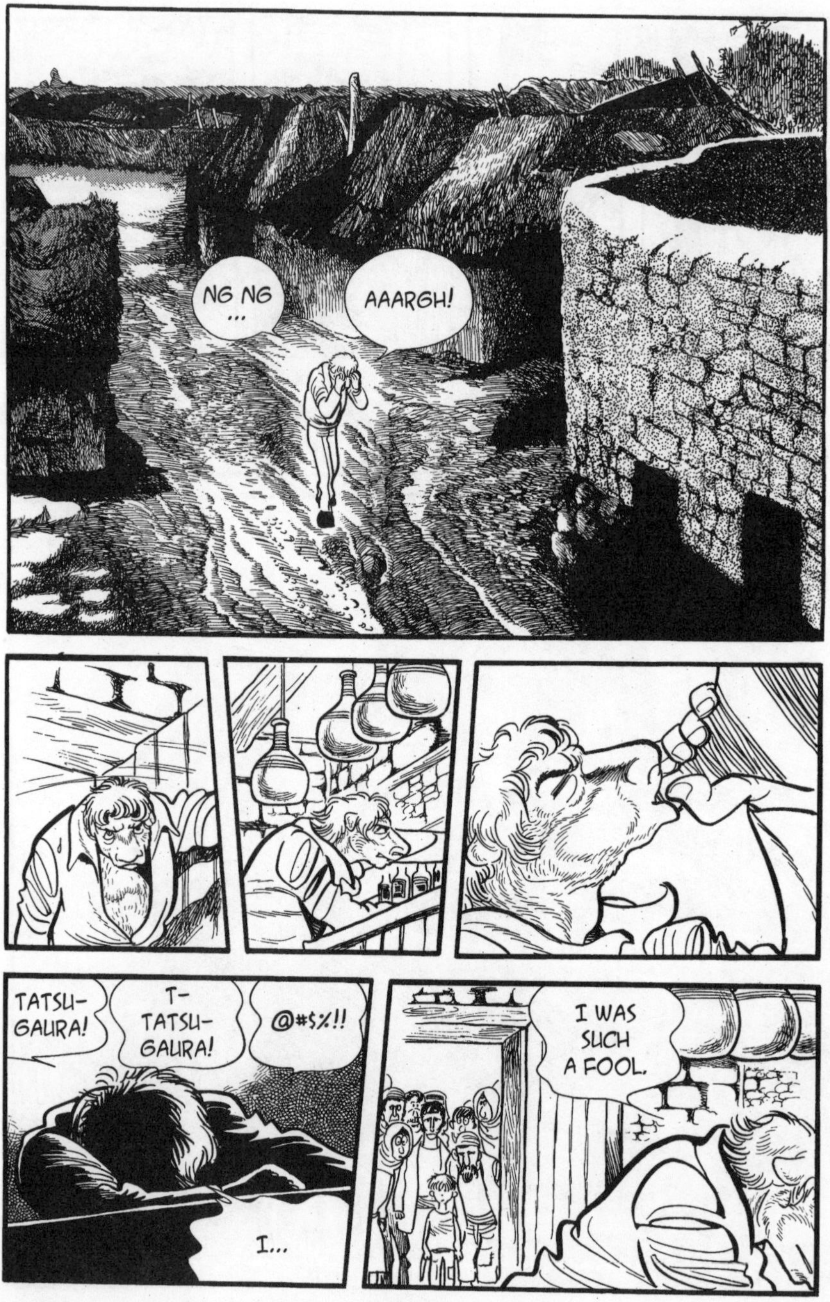
NG NG ...
AAARGH!
TATSU-GAURA!
T-TATSU-GAURA!
@#$%!!
I...
I WAS SUCH A FOOL.

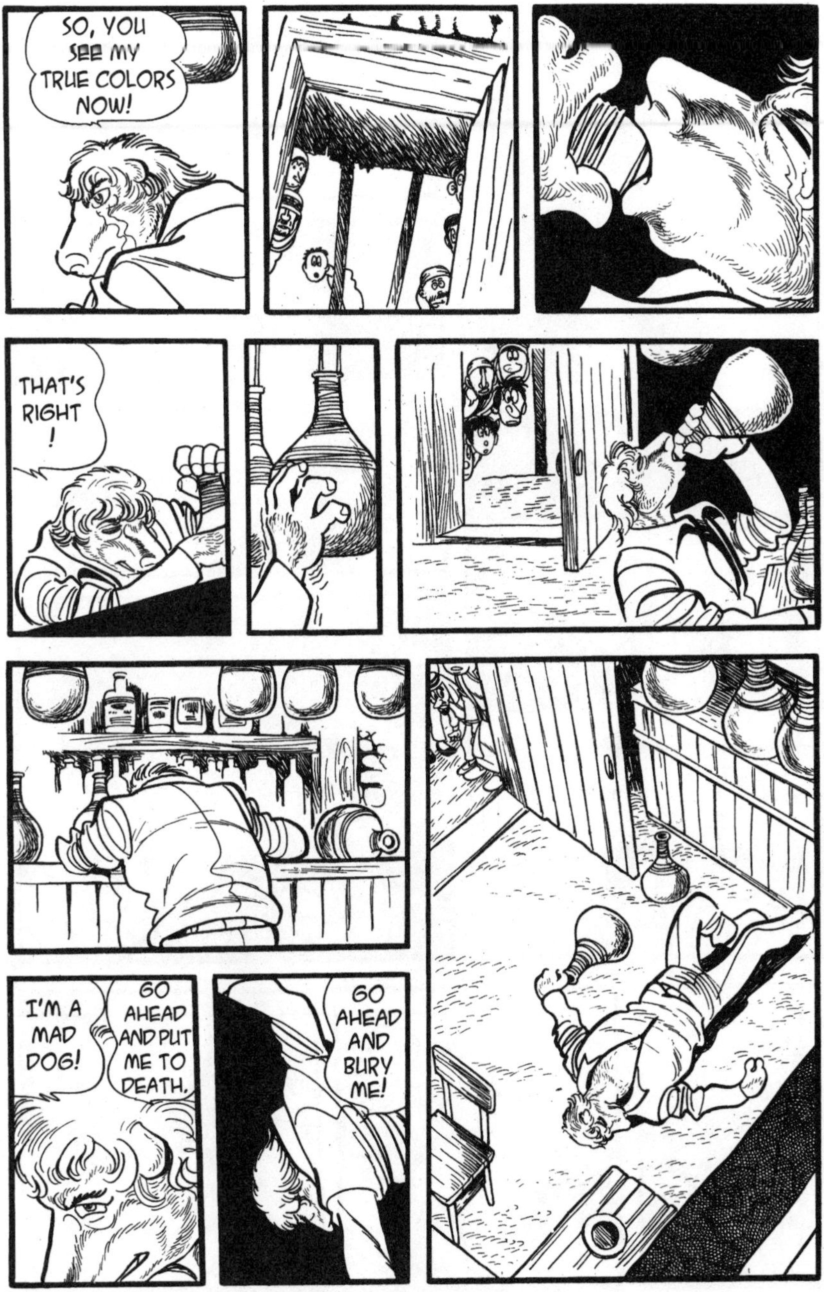
SO, YOU SEE MY TRUE COLORS NOW!
THAT'S RIGHT !
I'M A MAD DOG!
GO AHEAD AND PUT ME TO DEATH.
GO AHEAD AND BURY ME!

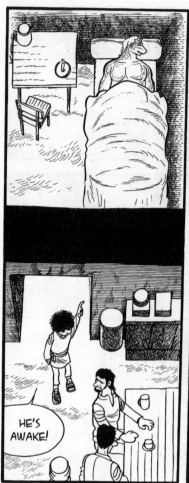

HE'S
AWAKE!

SIGH

ARE THEY
HAVING
A VILLAGE
MEETING
?

YES.

AH.

DECID-
ING
WHAT
TO DO
WITH ME.

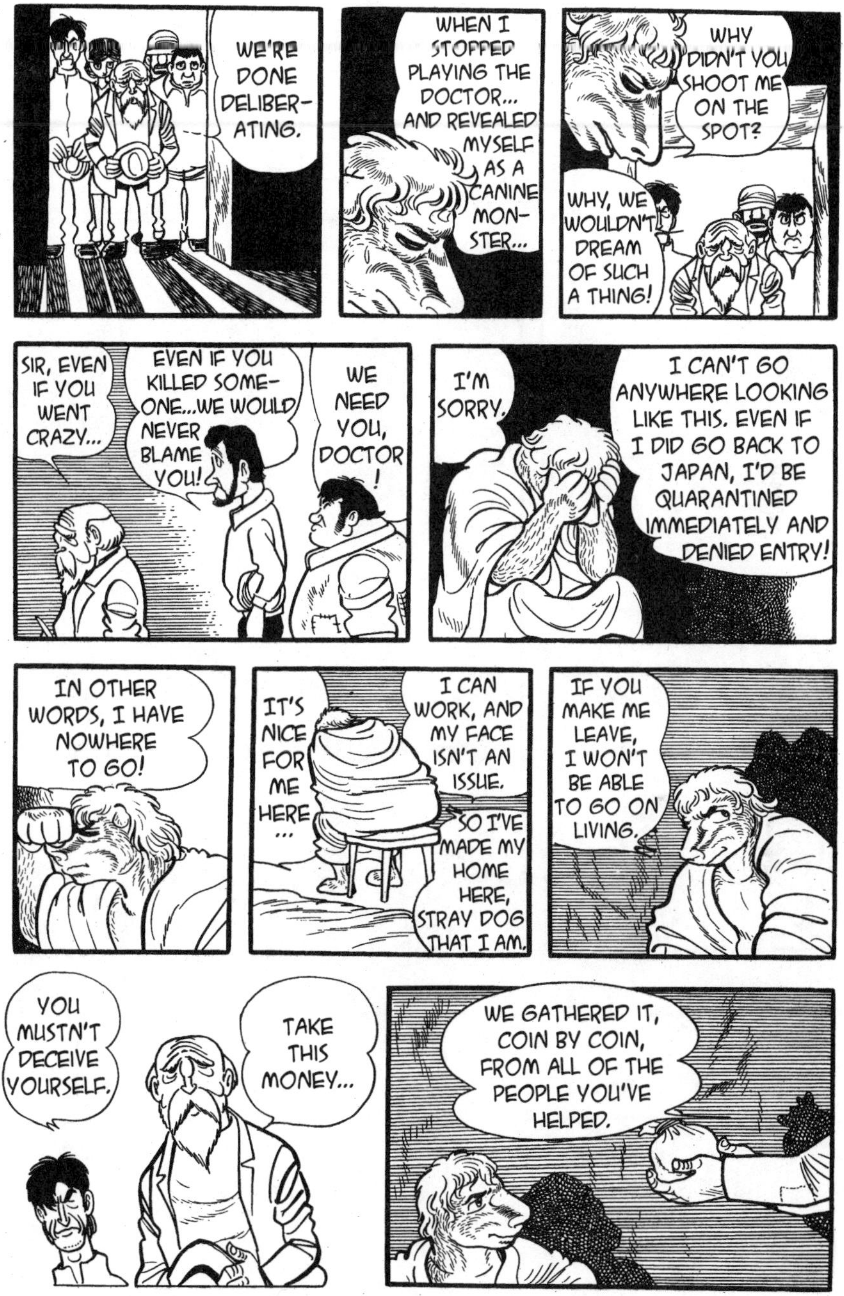
WE'RE DONE DELIBER-ATING.
WHEN I STOPPED PLAYING THE DOCTOR... AND REVEALED MYSELF AS A CANINE MON-STER...
WHY DIDN'T YOU SHOOT ME ON THE SPOT?
WHY, WE WOULDN'T DREAM OF SUCH A THING!
SIR, EVEN IF YOU WENT CRAZY...
EVEN IF YOU KILLED SOME-ONE...WE WOULD NEVER BLAME YOU!
WE NEED YOU, DOCTOR!
I'M SORRY.
I CAN'T GO ANYWHERE LOOKING LIKE THIS. EVEN IF I DID GO BACK TO JAPAN, I'D BE QUARANTINED IMMEDIATELY AND DENIED ENTRY!
IN OTHER WORDS, I HAVE NOWHERE TO GO!
IT'S NICE FOR ME HERE...
I CAN WORK, AND MY FACE ISN'T AN ISSUE.
SO I'VE MADE MY HOME HERE, STRAY DOG THAT I AM.
IF YOU MAKE ME LEAVE, I WON'T BE ABLE TO GO ON LIVING.
YOU MUSTN'T DECEIVE YOURSELF.
TAKE THIS MONEY...
WE GATHERED IT, COIN BY COIN, FROM ALL OF THE PEOPLE YOU'VE HELPED.

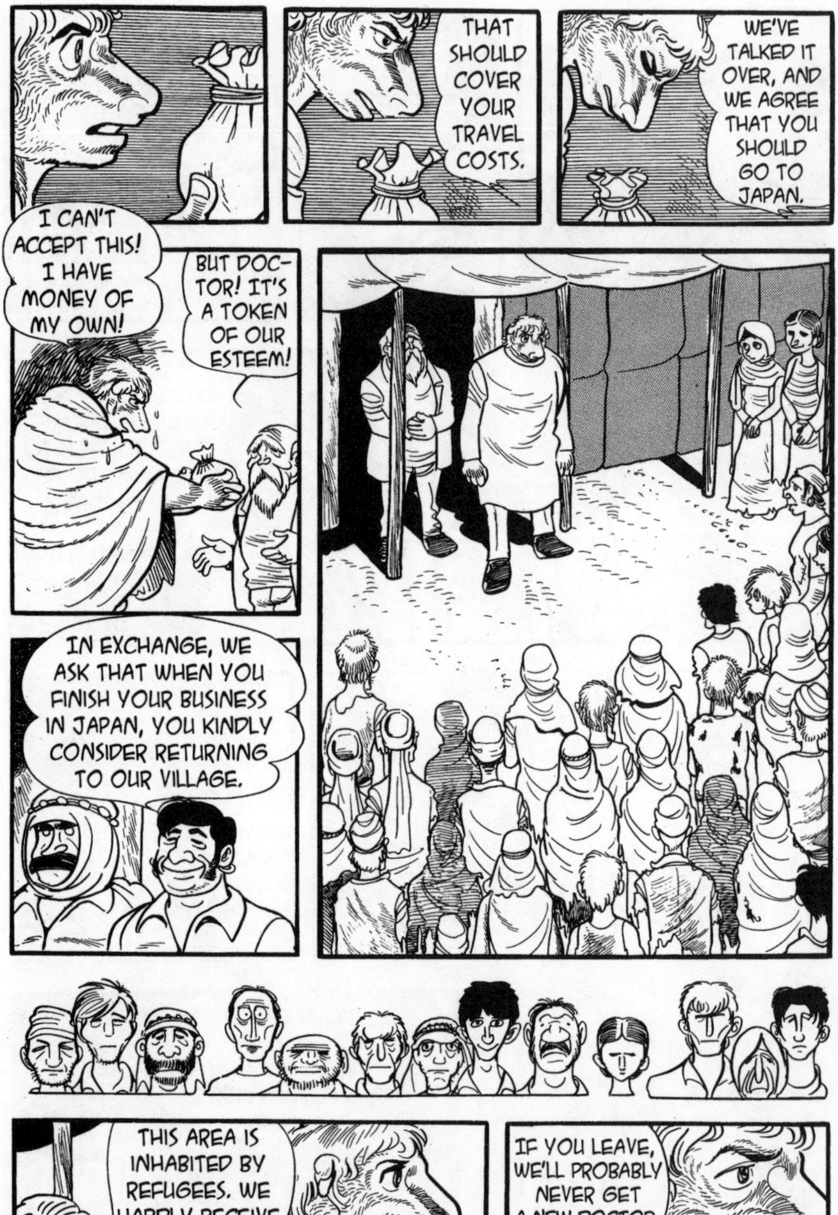
WE'VE TALKED IT OVER, AND WE AGREE THAT YOU SHOULD GO TO JAPAN.
THAT SHOULD COVER YOUR TRAVEL COSTS.
I CAN'T ACCEPT THIS! I HAVE MONEY OF MY OWN!
BUT DOC-TOR! IT'S A TOKEN OF OUR ESTEEM!
IN EXCHANGE, WE ASK THAT WHEN YOU FINISH YOUR BUSINESS IN JAPAN, YOU KINDLY CONSIDER RETURNING TO OUR VILLAGE.
IF YOU LEAVE, WE'LL PROBABLY NEVER GET A NEW DOCTOR TO COME OUT HERE.
THIS AREA IS INHABITED BY REFUGEES. WE HARDLY RECEIVE ANY GOVERN-MENT AID.

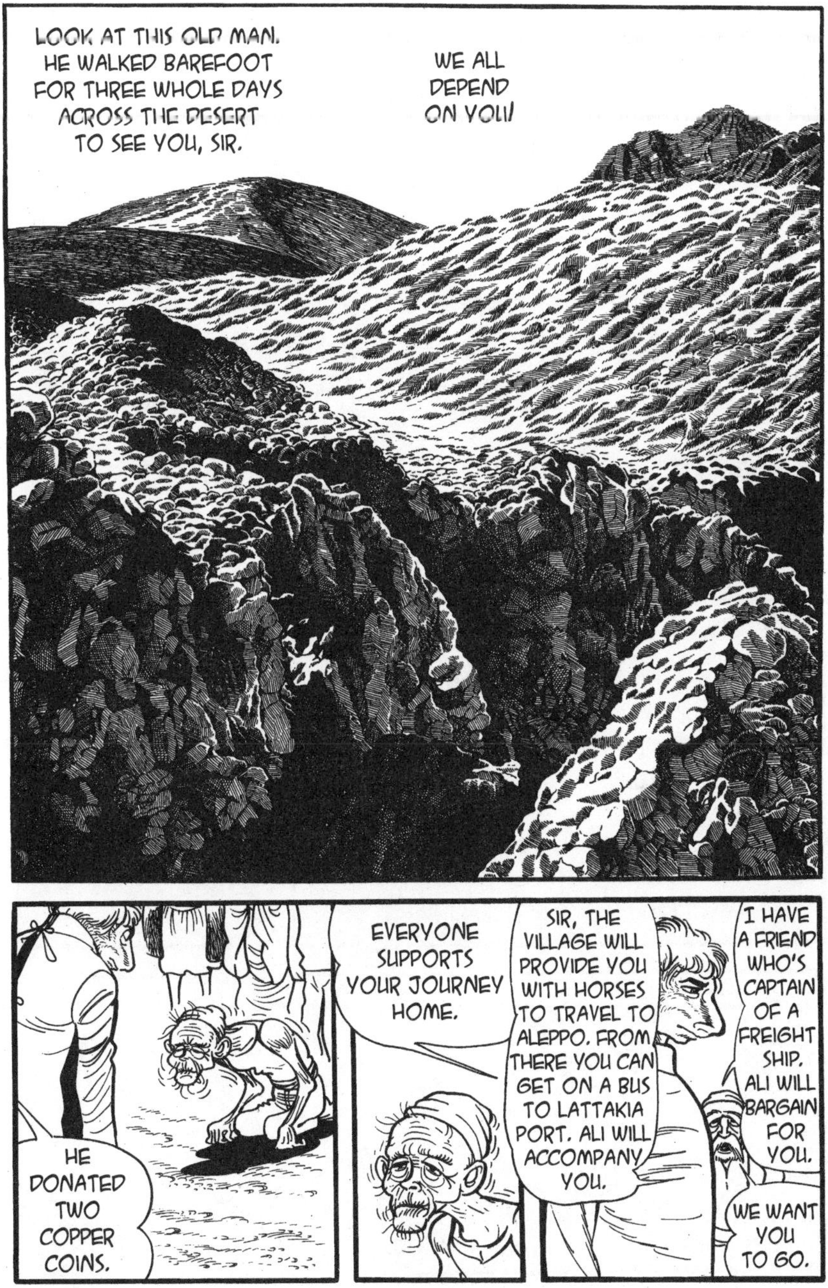
LOOK AT THIS OLD MAN. HE WALKED BAREFOOT FOR THREE WHOLE DAYS ACROSS THE DESERT TO SEE YOU, SIR.
WE ALL DEPEND ON YOU!
HE DONATED TWO COPPER COINS.
EVERYONE SUPPORTS YOUR JOURNEY HOME.
SIR, THE VILLAGE WILL PROVIDE YOU WITH HORSES TO TRAVEL TO ALEPPO. FROM THERE YOU CAN GET ON A BUS TO LATTAKIA PORT. ALI WILL ACCOMPANY YOU.
I HAVE A FRIEND WHO'S CAPTAIN OF A FREIGHT SHIP. ALI WILL BARGAIN FOR YOU.
WE WANT YOU TO GO.

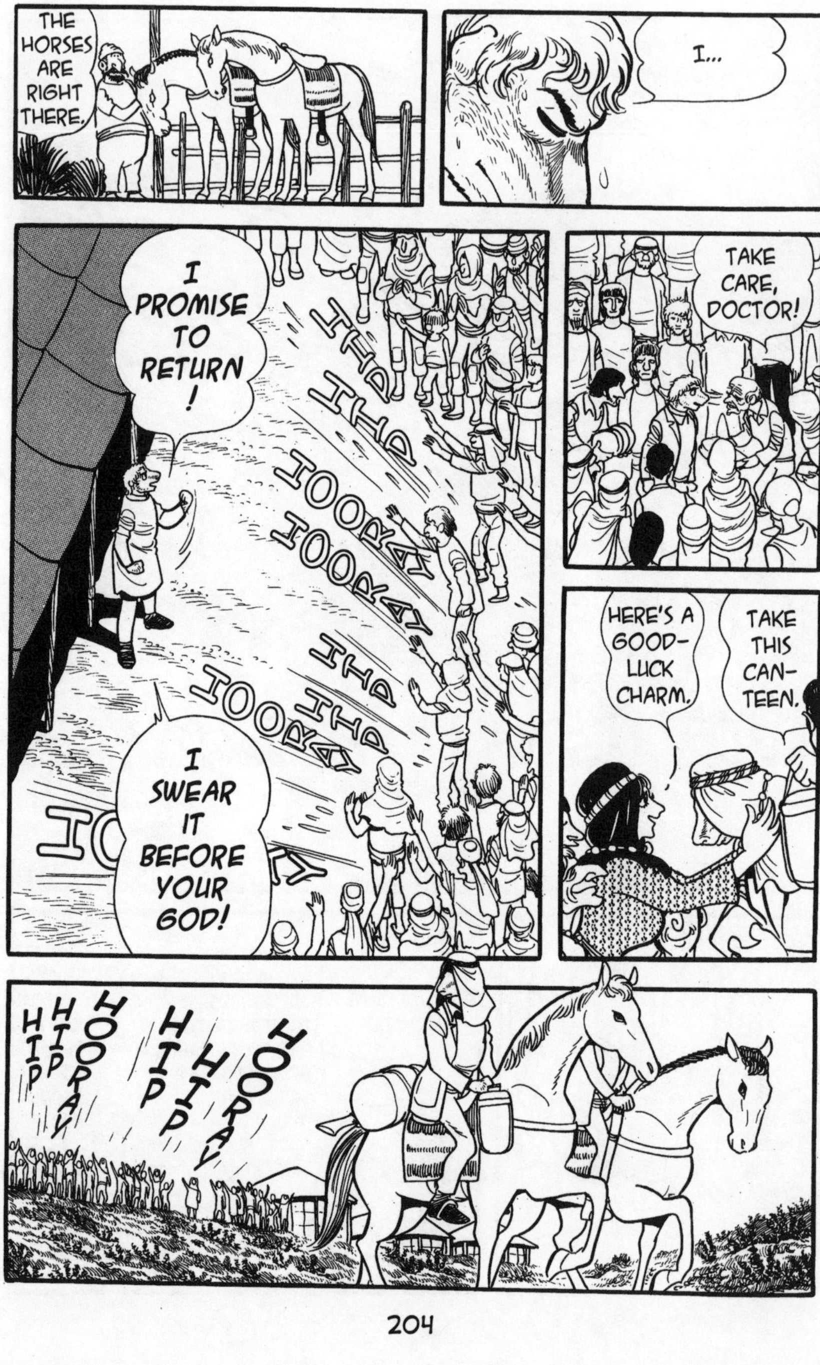
THE HORSES ARE RIGHT THERE.
I...
I PROMISE TO RETURN!
HIP HIP HOORAY HOORAY
HIP HIP HOORAY
I SWEAR IT BEFORE YOUR GOD!
TAKE CARE, DOCTOR!
HERE'S A GOOD-LUCK CHARM.
TAKE THIS CAN-TEEN.
HIP HIP HOORAY
HIP HIP HOORAY

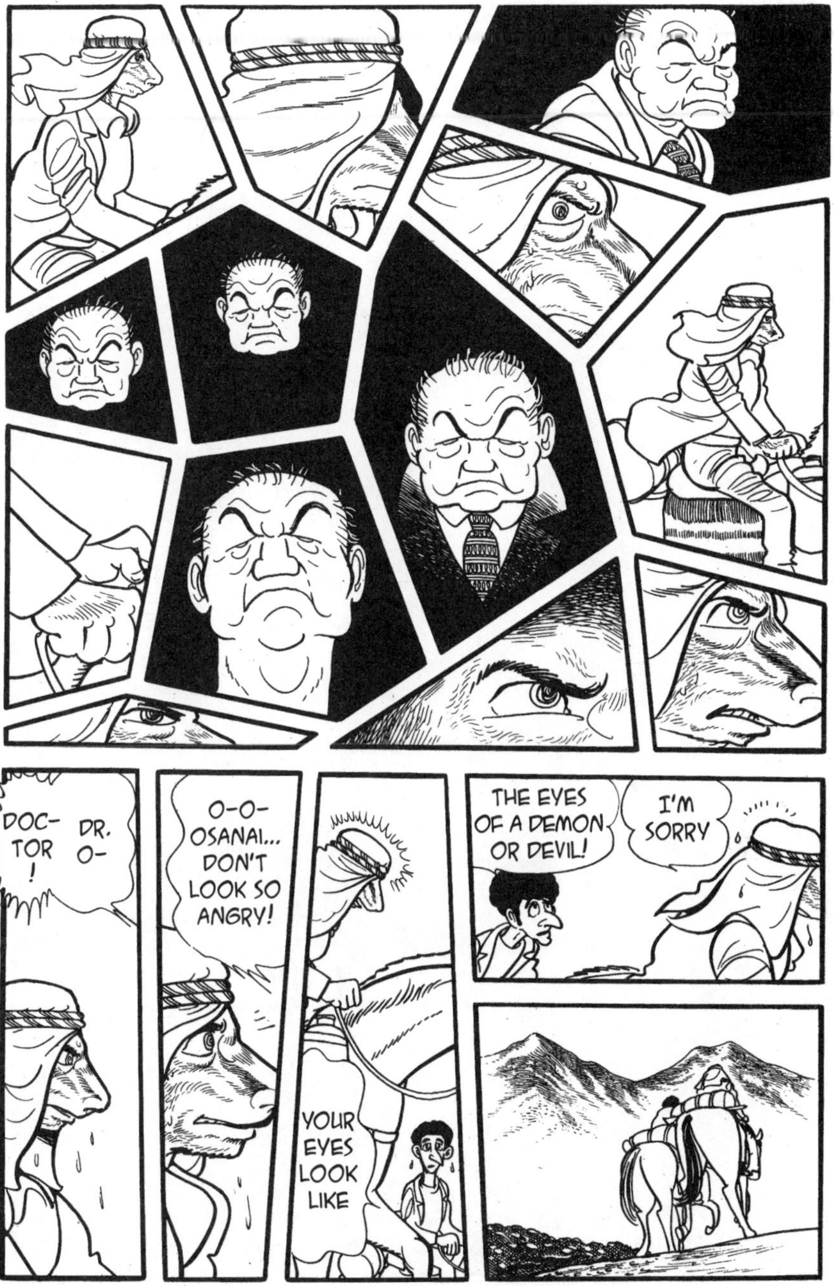

DOC-TOR!
DR. O-
O-O-OSANAI... DON'T LOOK SO ANGRY!
YOUR EYES LOOK LIKE
THE EYES OF A DEMON OR DEVIL!
I'M SORRY

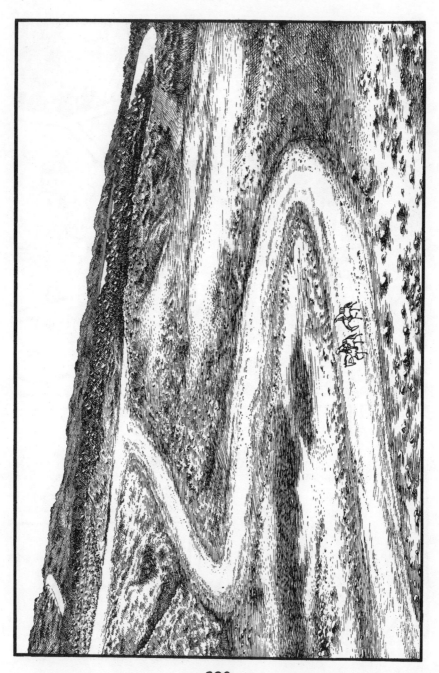

CHAPTER 17

ENCOUNTERS
PART 1

YOU CALL YOURSELVES MEMBERS OF THIS DEPARTMENT??

I ASKED YOU TO ASSUME RESPONSIBILITY FOR A PATIENT OF M UNIVERSITY HOSPITAL.

YOU SAY YOU LEFT HER IN SOME VILLAGE? EVEN A CHILD WOULDN'T MAKE SUCH A LAME EXCUSE!

JUST WHAT DO YOU INTEND TO DO ABOUT THIS?!

WE COULD PETITION THE LOCAL CLINIC OR POLICE AND ASK THEM TO TAKE HER INTO CUSTODY...

YOU WANT TO ESCALATE THINGS FURTHER? DO YOU REALIZE HOW HARD I'VE BEEN WORKING TO KEEP ALL OF THESE SCANDALS AROUND HERE UNDER WRAPS?

BUT I DON'T THINK HAVING HELEN FRIESE TAKEN INTO CUSTODY WOULD AFFECT YOUR REPUTATION, DOCTOR...

YOU CLEARLY DON'T REALIZE HOW PERSISTENT THE YOUNG DOCTORS LEAGUE HAS BECOME.

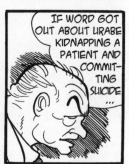

IF WORD GOT OUT ABOUT URABE KIDNAPPING A PATIENT AND COMMITTING SUICIDE...

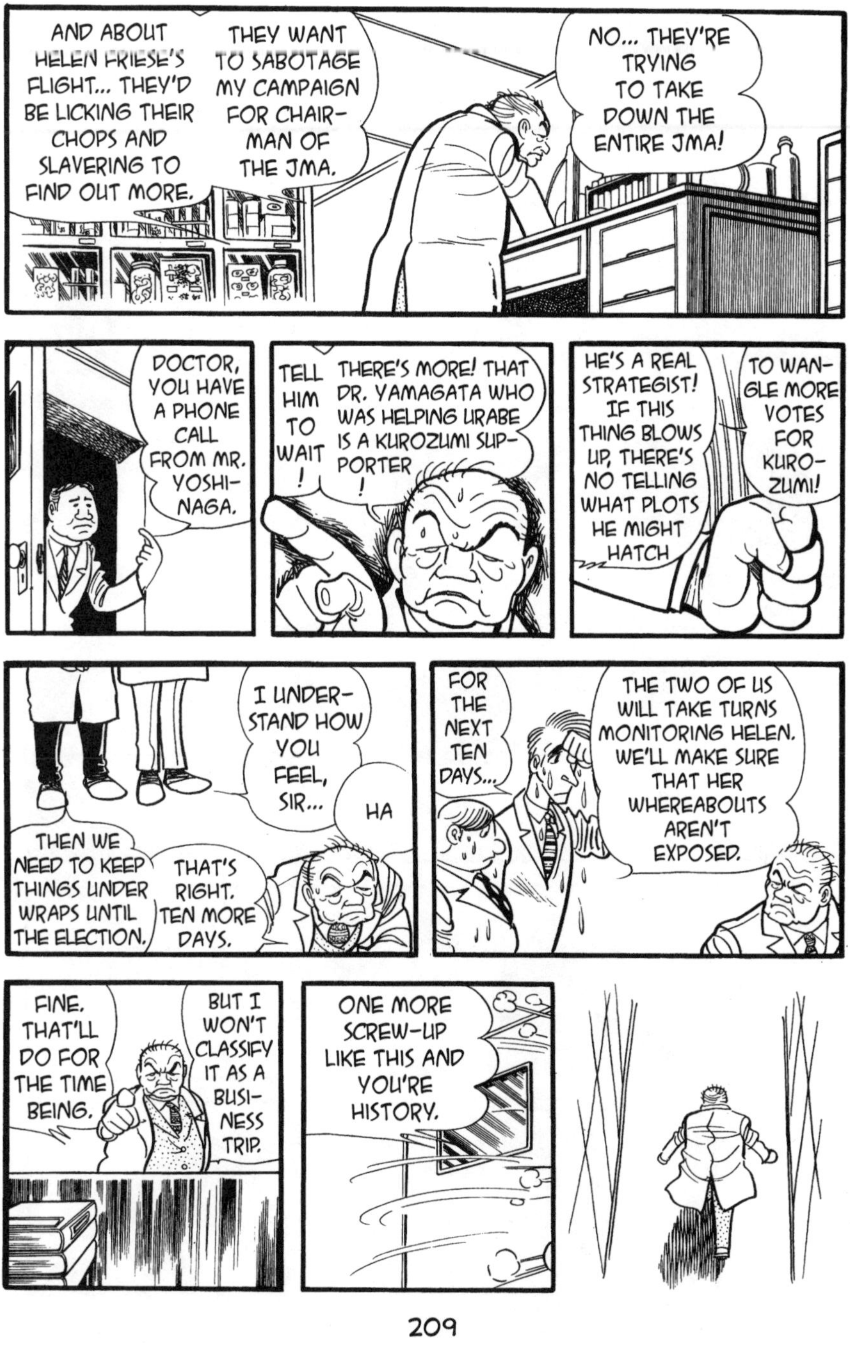
AND ABOUT HELEN FRIESE'S FLIGHT... THEY'D BE LICKING THEIR CHOPS AND SLAVERING TO FIND OUT MORE.
THEY WANT TO SABOTAGE MY CAMPAIGN FOR CHAIR-MAN OF THE JMA.
NO... THEY'RE TRYING TO TAKE DOWN THE ENTIRE JMA!
DOCTOR, YOU HAVE A PHONE CALL FROM MR. YOSHI-NAGA.
TELL HIM TO WAIT!
THERE'S MORE! THAT DR. YAMAGATA WHO WAS HELPING URABE IS A KUROZUMI SUP-PORTER!
HE'S A REAL STRATEGIST! IF THIS THING BLOWS UP, THERE'S NO TELLING WHAT PLOTS HE MIGHT HATCH
TO WAN-GLE MORE VOTES FOR KURO-ZUMI!
I UNDER-STAND HOW YOU FEEL, SIR...
HA
THEN WE NEED TO KEEP THINGS UNDER WRAPS UNTIL THE ELECTION.
THAT'S RIGHT. TEN MORE DAYS.
FOR THE NEXT TEN DAYS...
THE TWO OF US WILL TAKE TURNS MONITORING HELEN. WE'LL MAKE SURE THAT HER WHEREABOUTS AREN'T EXPOSED.
FINE. THAT'LL DO FOR THE TIME BEING.
BUT I WON'T CLASSIFY IT AS A BUSI-NESS TRIP.
ONE MORE SCREW-UP LIKE THIS AND YOU'RE HISTORY.

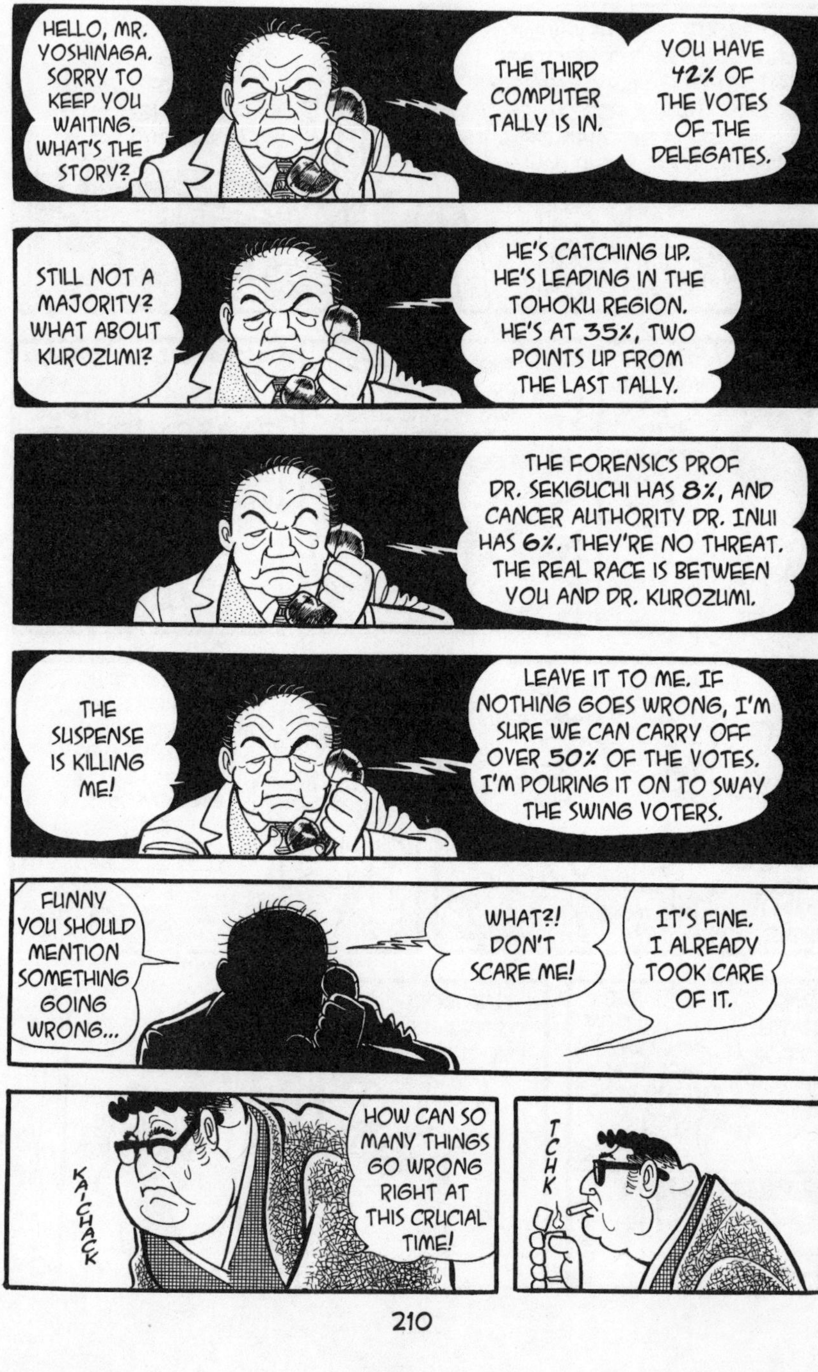
HELLO, MR. YOSHINAGA. SORRY TO KEEP YOU WAITING. WHAT'S THE STORY?
THE THIRD COMPUTER TALLY IS IN.
YOU HAVE 42% OF THE VOTES OF THE DELEGATES.
STILL NOT A MAJORITY? WHAT ABOUT KUROZUMI?
HE'S CATCHING UP. HE'S LEADING IN THE TOHOKU REGION. HE'S AT 35%, TWO POINTS UP FROM THE LAST TALLY.
THE FORENSICS PROF DR. SEKIGUCHI HAS 8%, AND CANCER AUTHORITY DR. INUI HAS 6%. THEY'RE NO THREAT. THE REAL RACE IS BETWEEN YOU AND DR. KUROZUMI.
THE SUSPENSE IS KILLING ME!
LEAVE IT TO ME. IF NOTHING GOES WRONG, I'M SURE WE CAN CARRY OFF OVER 50% OF THE VOTES. I'M POURING IT ON TO SWAY THE SWING VOTERS.
FUNNY YOU SHOULD MENTION SOMETHING GOING WRONG...
WHAT?! DON'T SCARE ME!
IT'S FINE. I ALREADY TOOK CARE OF IT.
KA-CHACK
HOW CAN SO MANY THINGS GO WRONG RIGHT AT THIS CRUCIAL TIME!
TCHK

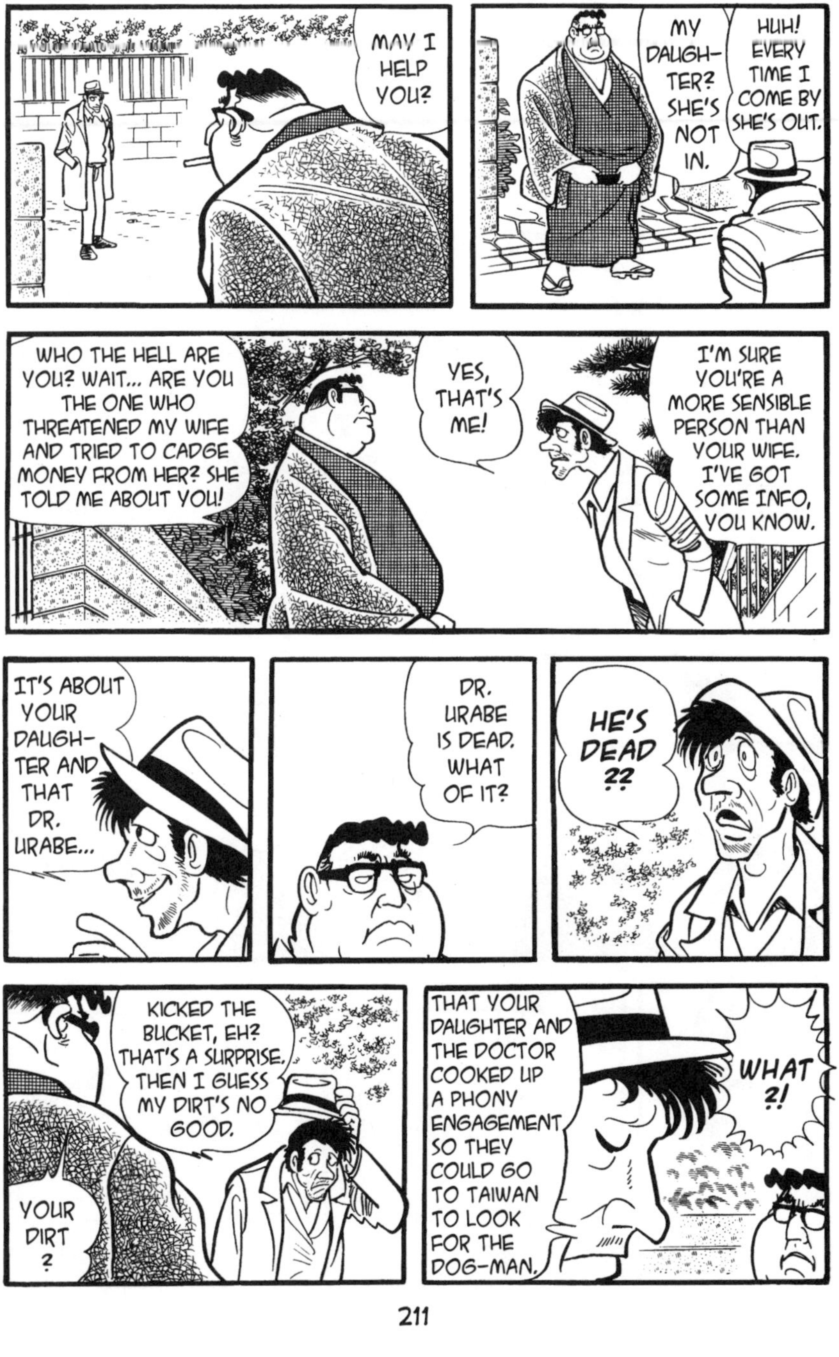
MAY I HELP YOU?
MY DAUGHTER? SHE'S NOT IN.
HUH! EVERY TIME I COME BY SHE'S OUT.
WHO THE HELL ARE YOU? WAIT... ARE YOU THE ONE WHO THREATENED MY WIFE AND TRIED TO CADGE MONEY FROM HER? SHE TOLD ME ABOUT YOU!
YES, THAT'S ME!
I'M SURE YOU'RE A MORE SENSIBLE PERSON THAN YOUR WIFE. I'VE GOT SOME INFO, YOU KNOW.
IT'S ABOUT YOUR DAUGHTER AND THAT DR. URABE...
DR. URABE IS DEAD. WHAT OF IT?
HE'S DEAD ??
KICKED THE BUCKET, EH? THAT'S A SURPRISE. THEN I GUESS MY DIRT'S NO GOOD.
YOUR DIRT ?
THAT YOUR DAUGHTER AND THE DOCTOR COOKED UP A PHONY ENGAGEMENT SO THEY COULD GO TO TAIWAN TO LOOK FOR THE DOG-MAN.
WHAT ?!

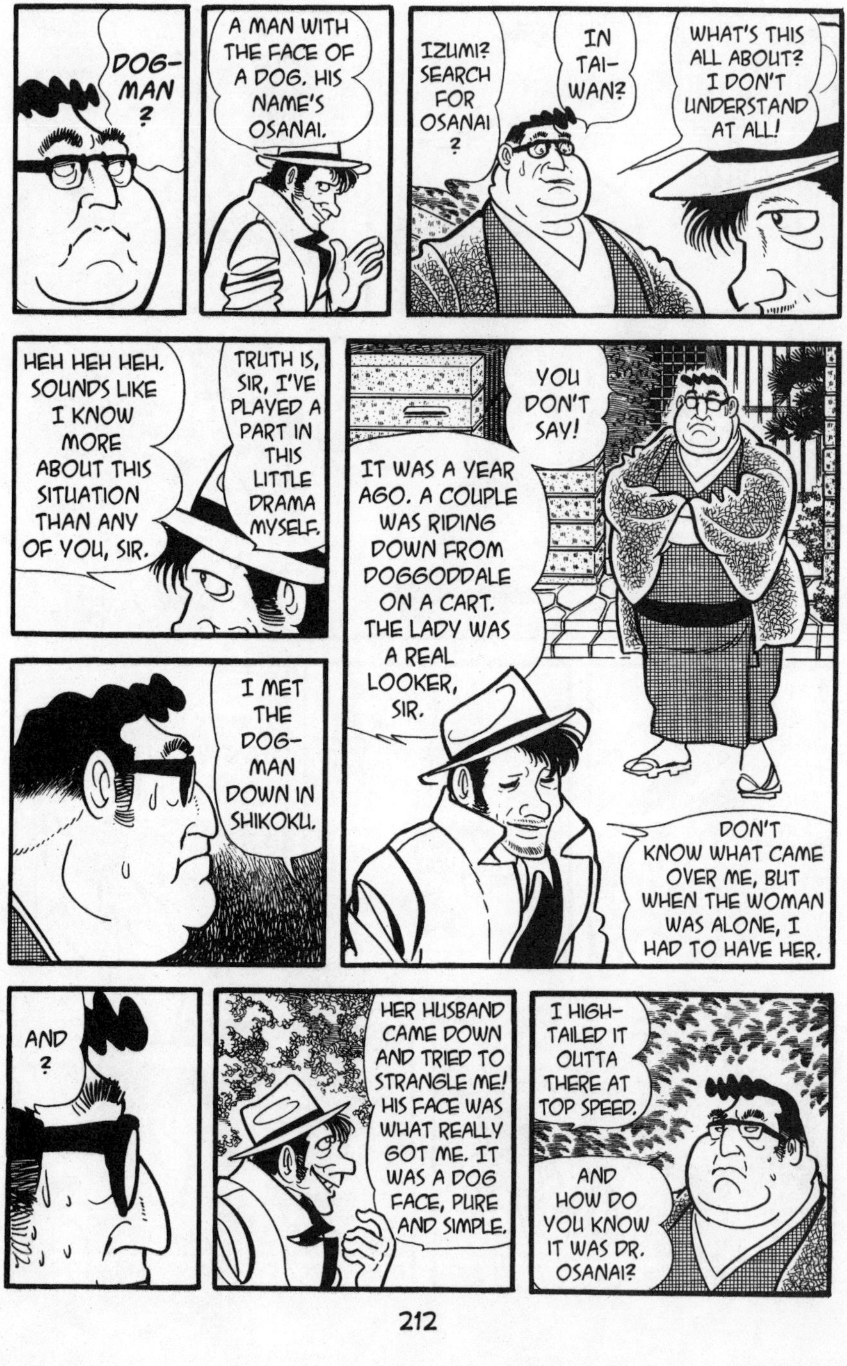
DOG-MAN?
A MAN WITH THE FACE OF A DOG. HIS NAME'S OSANAI.
IZUMI? SEARCH FOR OSANAI?
IN TAIWAN?
WHAT'S THIS ALL ABOUT? I DON'T UNDERSTAND AT ALL!
HEH HEH HEH. SOUNDS LIKE I KNOW MORE ABOUT THIS SITUATION THAN ANY OF YOU, SIR.
TRUTH IS, SIR, I'VE PLAYED A PART IN THIS LITTLE DRAMA MYSELF.
I MET THE DOG-MAN DOWN IN SHIKOKU.
YOU DON'T SAY!
IT WAS A YEAR AGO. A COUPLE WAS RIDING DOWN FROM DOGGODDALE ON A CART. THE LADY WAS A REAL LOOKER, SIR.
DON'T KNOW WHAT CAME OVER ME, BUT WHEN THE WOMAN WAS ALONE, I HAD TO HAVE HER.
AND?
HER HUSBAND CAME DOWN AND TRIED TO STRANGLE ME! HIS FACE WAS WHAT REALLY GOT ME. IT WAS A DOG FACE, PURE AND SIMPLE.
I HIGH-TAILED IT OUTTA THERE AT TOP SPEED.
AND HOW DO YOU KNOW IT WAS DR. OSANAI?

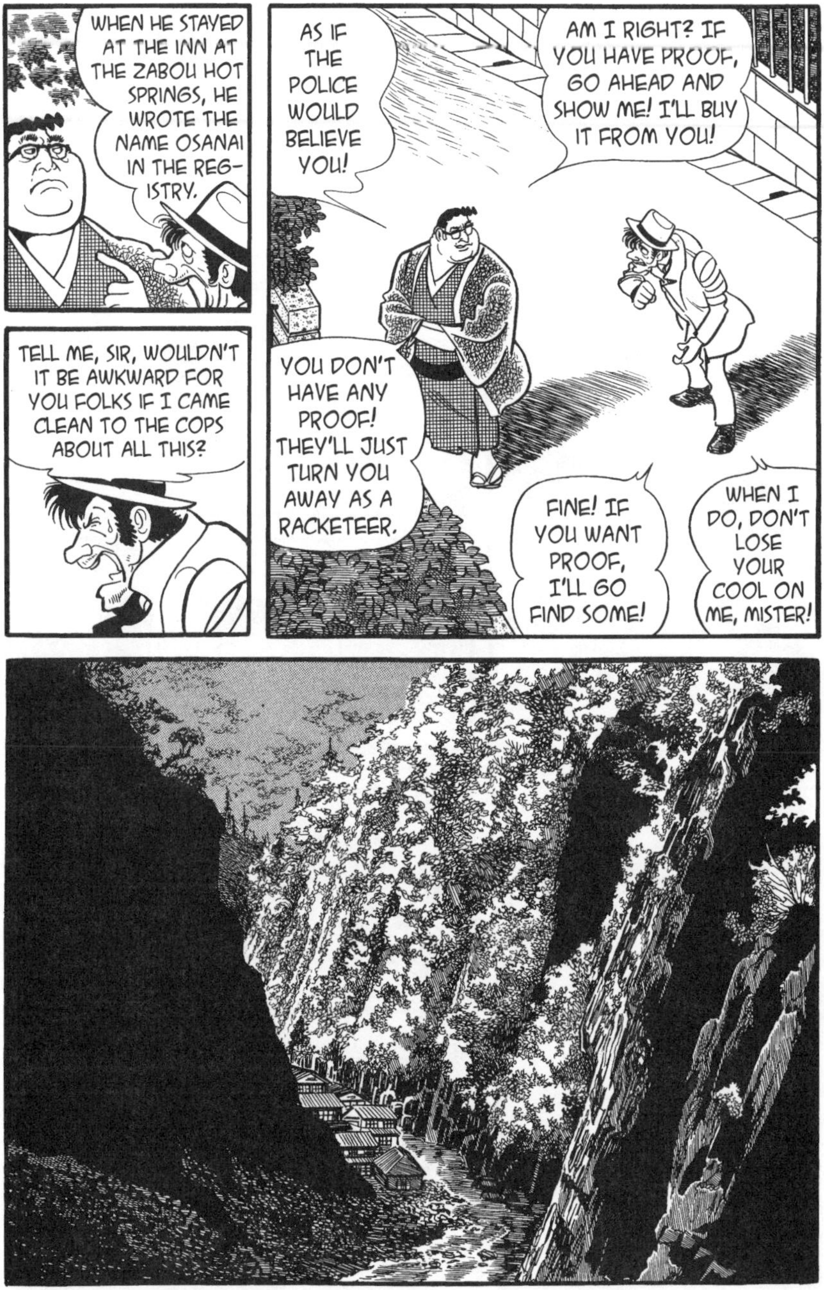
WHEN HE STAYED AT THE INN AT THE ZABOU HOT SPRINGS, HE WROTE THE NAME OSANAI IN THE REG-ISTRY.
TELL ME, SIR, WOULDN'T IT BE AWKWARD FOR YOU FOLKS IF I CAME CLEAN TO THE COPS ABOUT ALL THIS?
AS IF THE POLICE WOULD BELIEVE YOU!
YOU DON'T HAVE ANY PROOF! THEY'LL JUST TURN YOU AWAY AS A RACKETEER.
AM I RIGHT? IF YOU HAVE PROOF, GO AHEAD AND SHOW ME! I'LL BUY IT FROM YOU!
FINE! IF YOU WANT PROOF, I'LL GO FIND SOME!
WHEN I DO, DON'T LOSE YOUR COOL ON ME, MISTER!

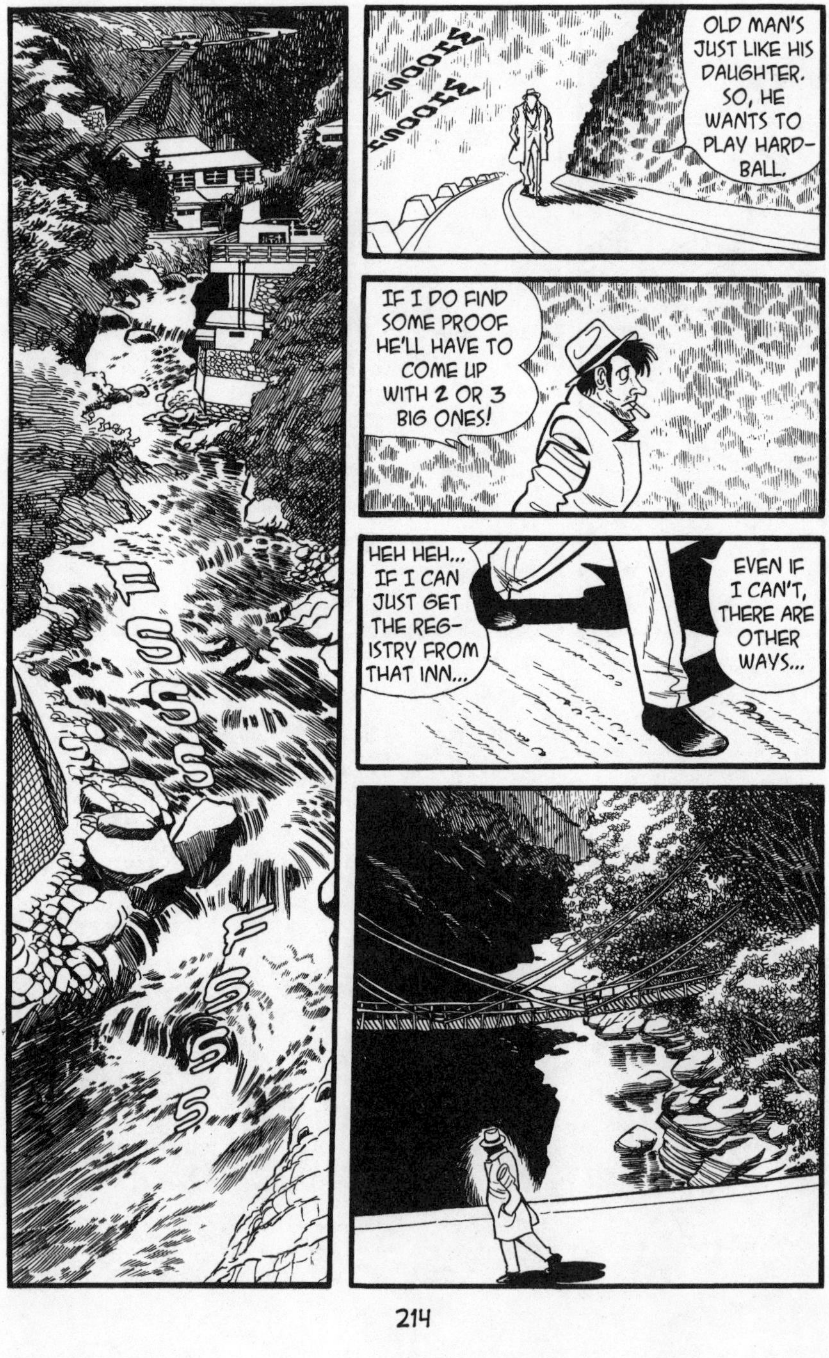
FSSS
FSSSS
WHOOSH
WHOOSH
OLD MAN'S JUST LIKE HIS DAUGHTER. SO, HE WANTS TO PLAY HARD-BALL.
IF I DO FIND SOME PROOF HE'LL HAVE TO COME UP WITH 2 OR 3 BIG ONES!
HEH HEH... IF I CAN JUST GET THE REG-ISTRY FROM THAT INN...
EVEN IF I CAN'T, THERE ARE OTHER WAYS...

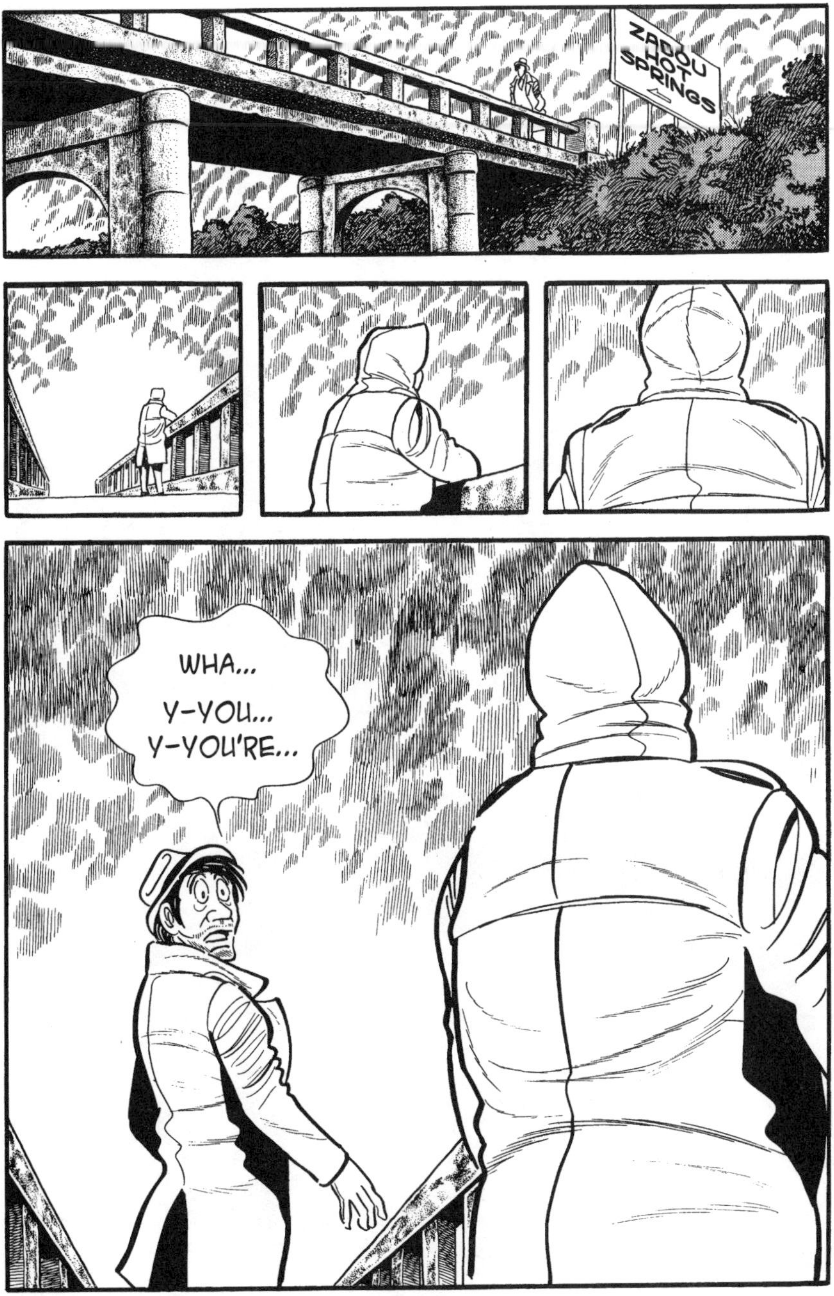
ZADOU HOT SPRINGS
WHA... Y-YOU... Y-YOU'RE...

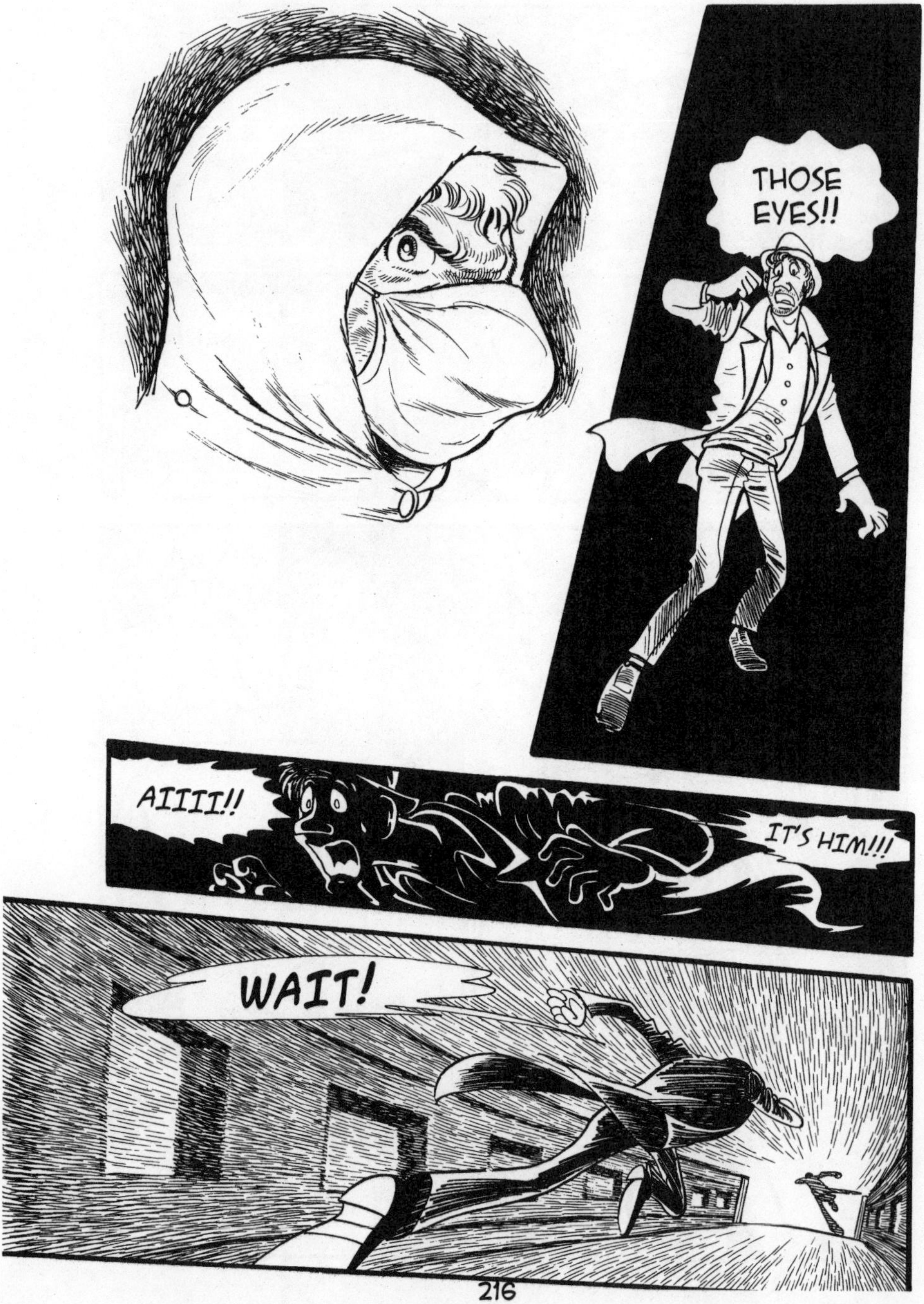
THOSE EYES!!
AIIII!!
IT'S HIM!!!
WAIT!

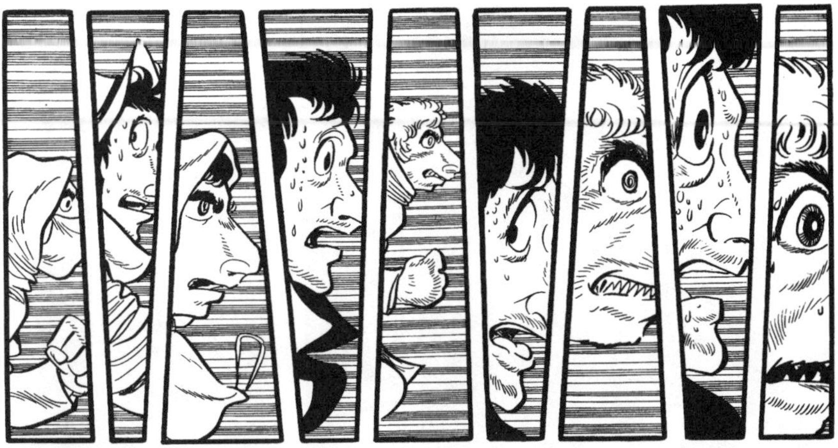
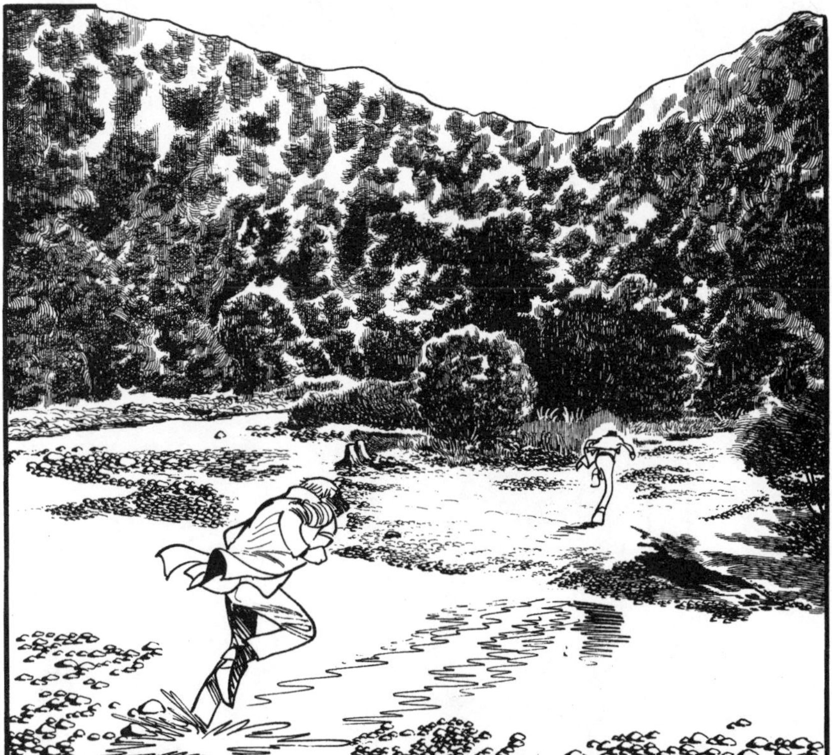

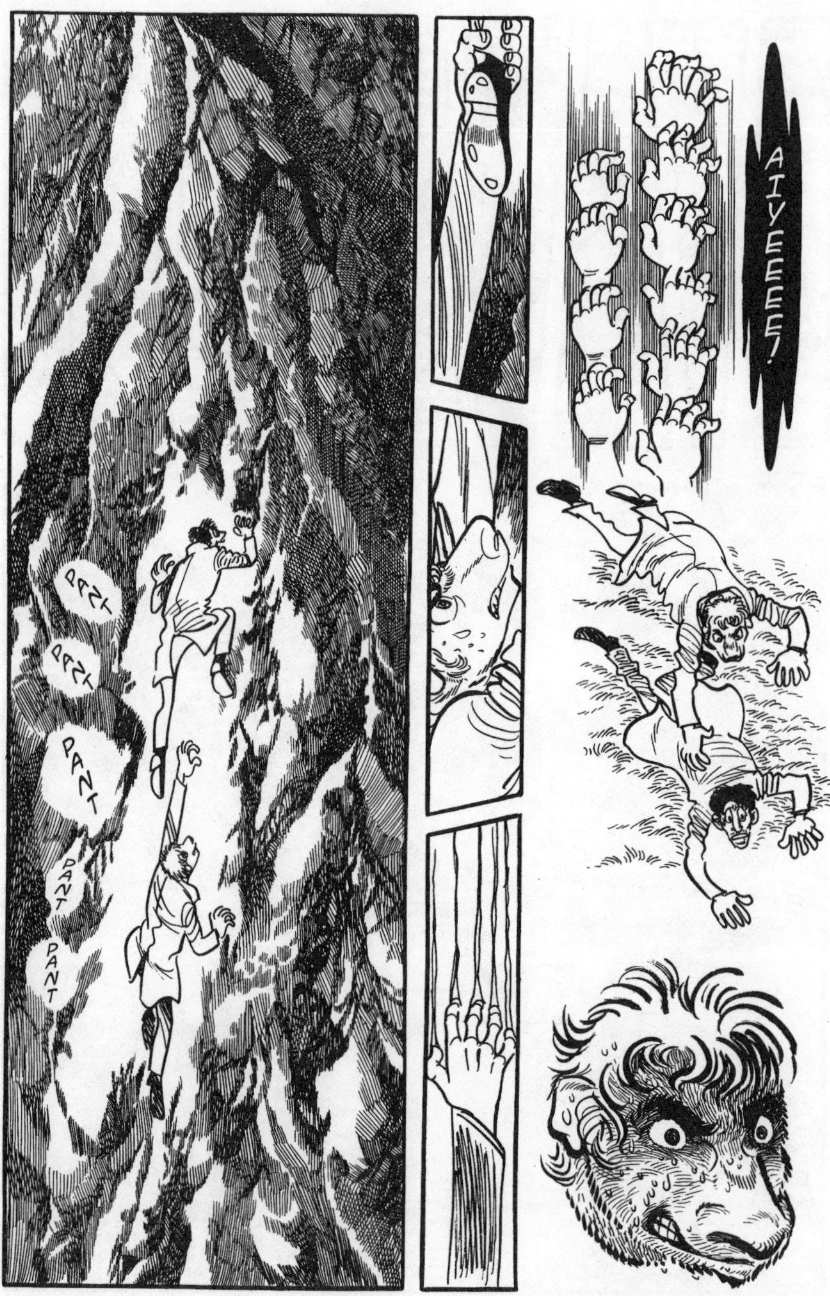
AIYEEEE!
PANT
PANT
PANT
PANT

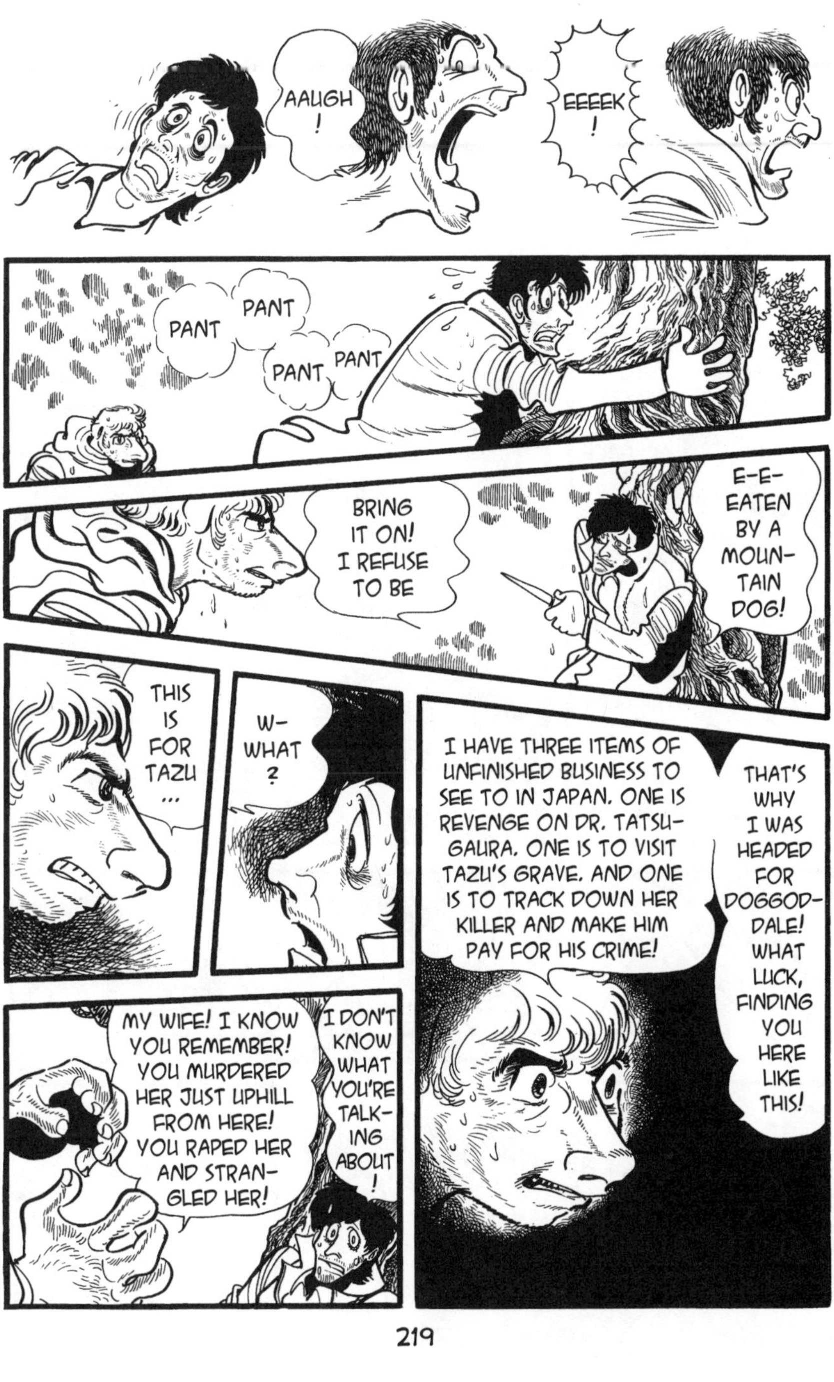
AAUGH!
EEEEK!
PANT PANT PANT PANT
BRING IT ON! I REFUSE TO BE
E-E-EATEN BY A MOUNTAIN DOG!
THIS IS FOR TAZU...
W-WHAT?
MY WIFE! I KNOW YOU REMEMBER! YOU MURDERED HER JUST UPHILL FROM HERE! YOU RAPED HER AND STRANGLED HER!
I DON'T KNOW WHAT YOU'RE TALKING ABOUT!
I HAVE THREE ITEMS OF UNFINISHED BUSINESS TO SEE TO IN JAPAN. ONE IS REVENGE ON DR. TATSUGAURA. ONE IS TO VISIT TAZU'S GRAVE. AND ONE IS TO TRACK DOWN HER KILLER AND MAKE HIM PAY FOR HIS CRIME!
THAT'S WHY I WAS HEADED FOR DOGGODDALE! WHAT LUCK, FINDING YOU HERE LIKE THIS!

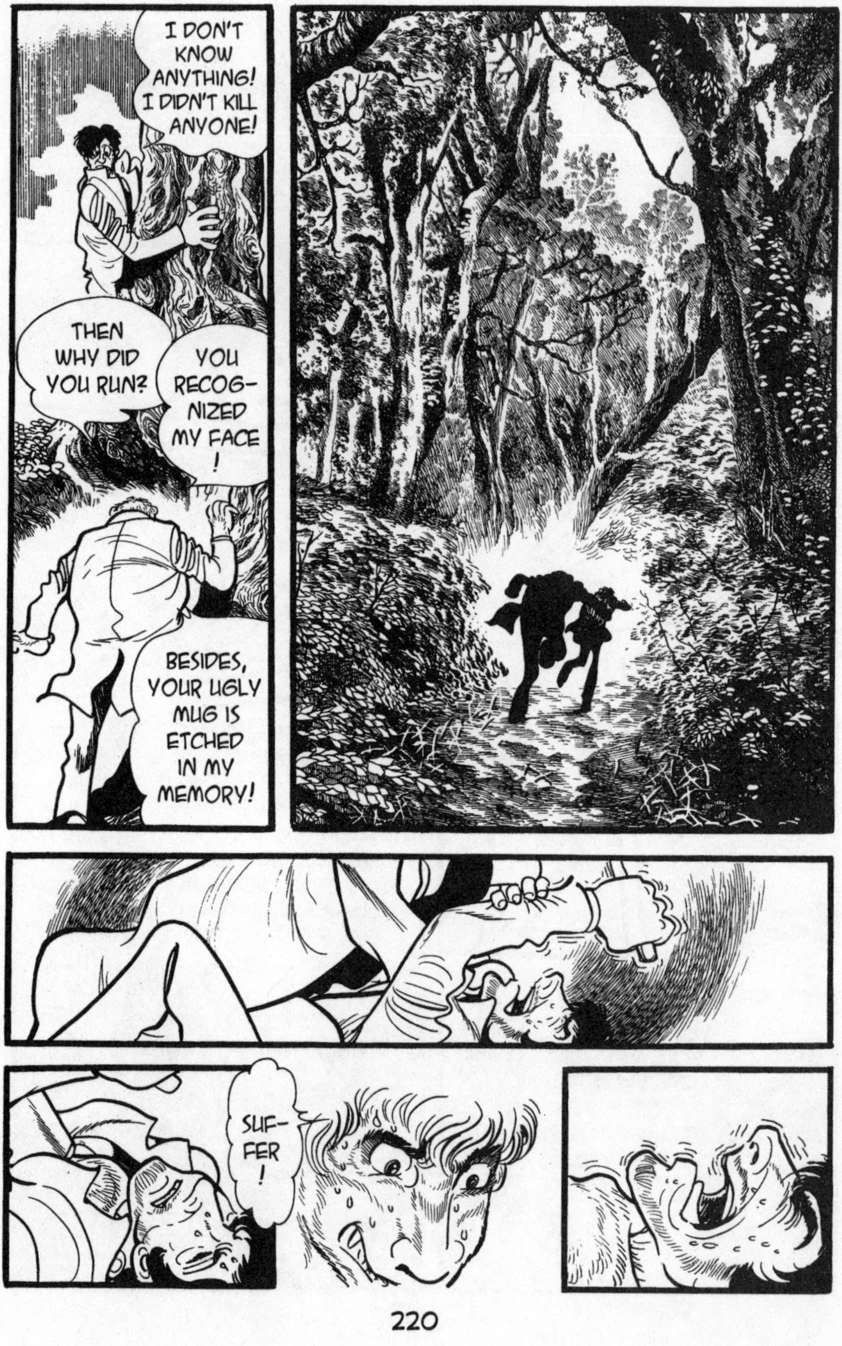
I DON'T KNOW ANYTHING! I DIDN'T KILL ANYONE!
THEN WHY DID YOU RUN?
YOU RECOGNIZED MY FACE!
BESIDES, YOUR UGLY MUG IS ETCHED IN MY MEMORY!
SUF-FER!

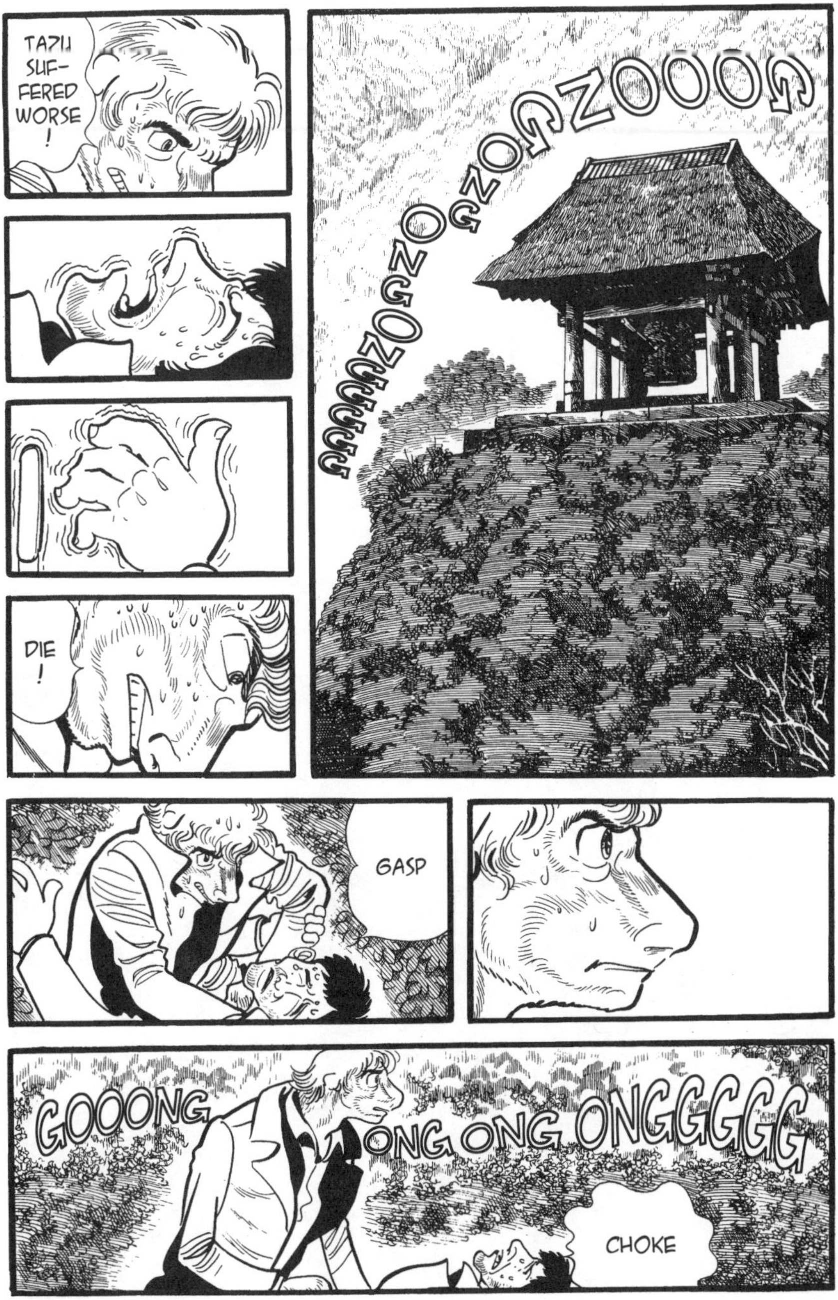
GGGGGGONGONGONGONGZOOOG
TAJU SUF-FERED WORSE!
DIE!
GASP
GOOOONG ONG ONG ONGGGGGG
CHOKE

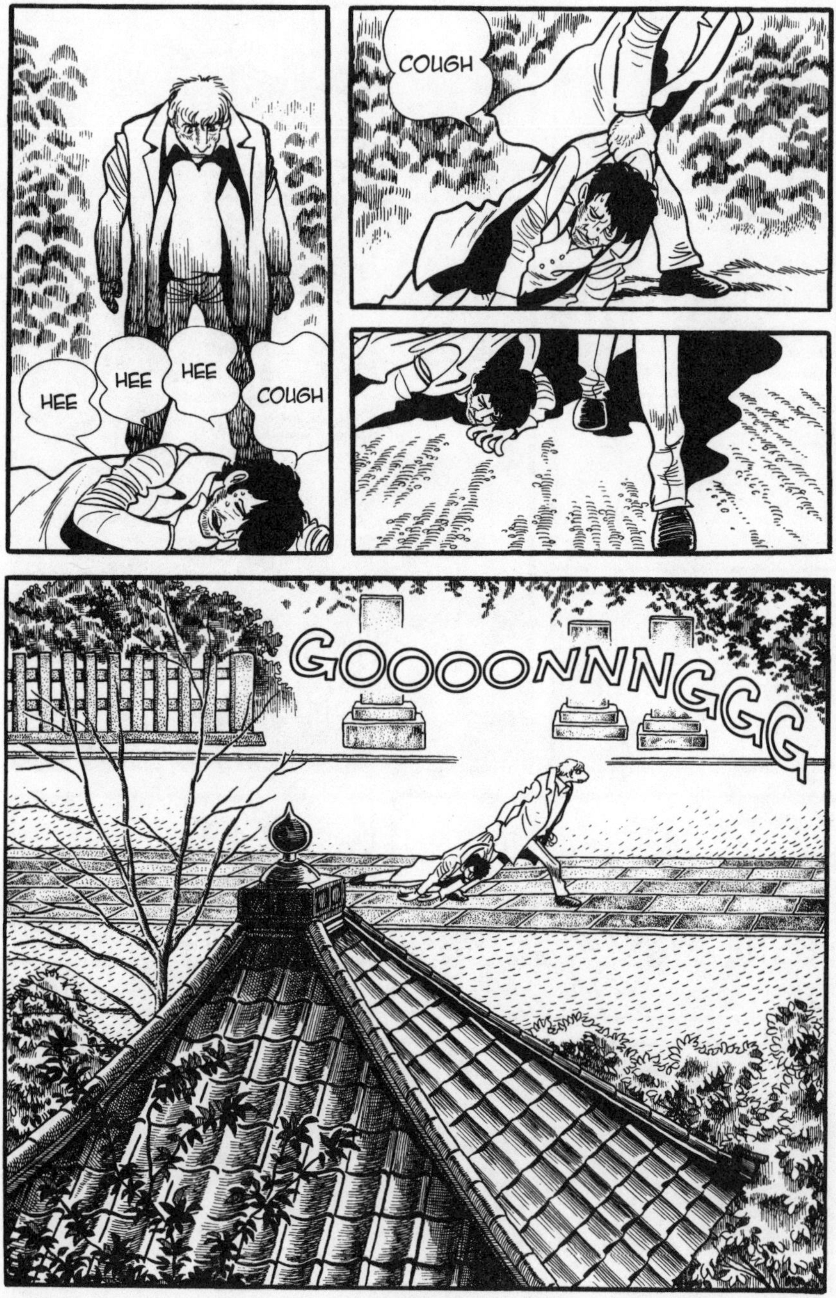
COUGH
COUGH
HEE
HEE
HEE
GOOOONNNGGG

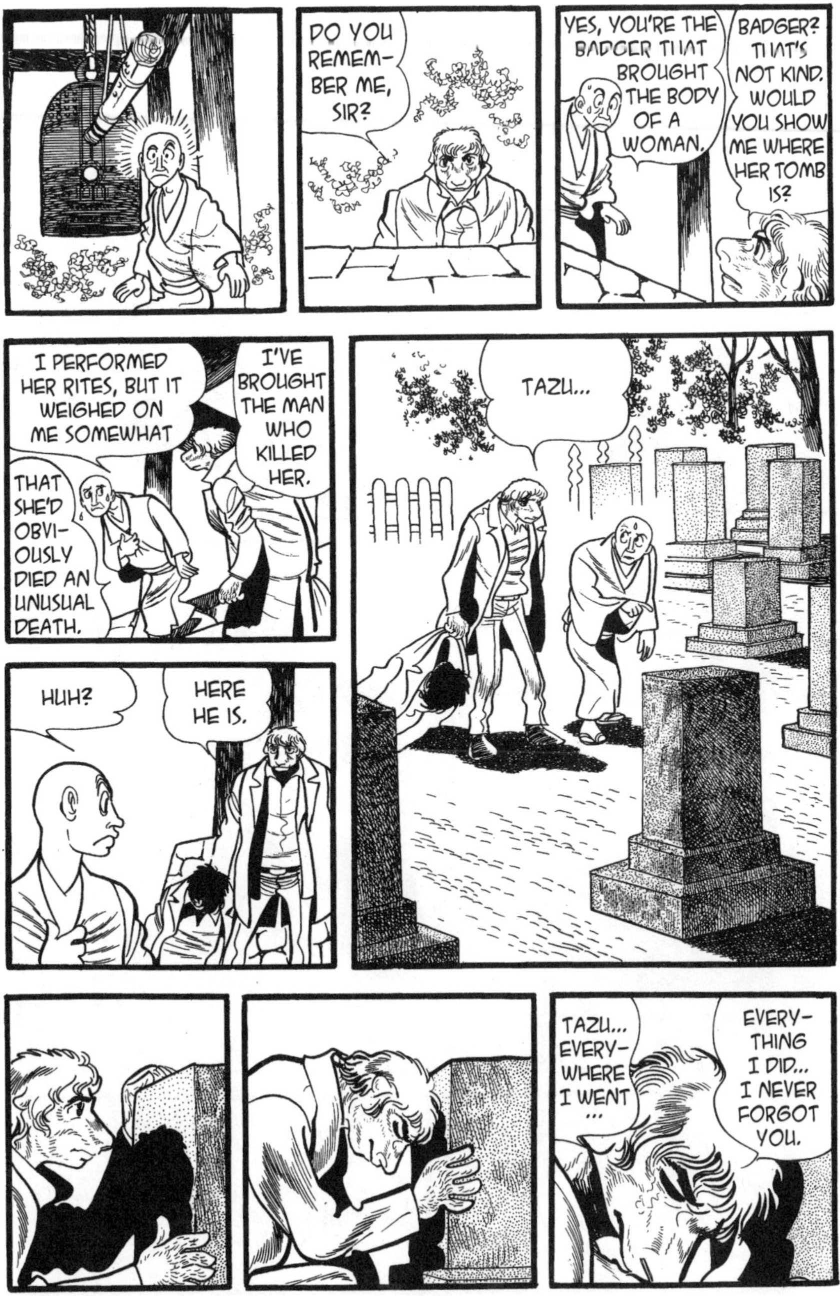
DO YOU REMEMBER ME, SIR?
YES, YOU'RE THE BADGER THAT BROUGHT THE BODY OF A WOMAN.
BADGER? THAT'S NOT KIND. WOULD YOU SHOW ME WHERE HER TOMB IS?
I PERFORMED HER RITES, BUT IT WEIGHED ON ME SOMEWHAT
THAT SHE'D OBVIOUSLY DIED AN UNUSUAL DEATH.
I'VE BROUGHT THE MAN WHO KILLED HER.
HUH?
HERE HE IS.
TAZU...
TAZU... EVERYWHERE I WENT ...
EVERYTHING I DID... I NEVER FORGOT YOU.

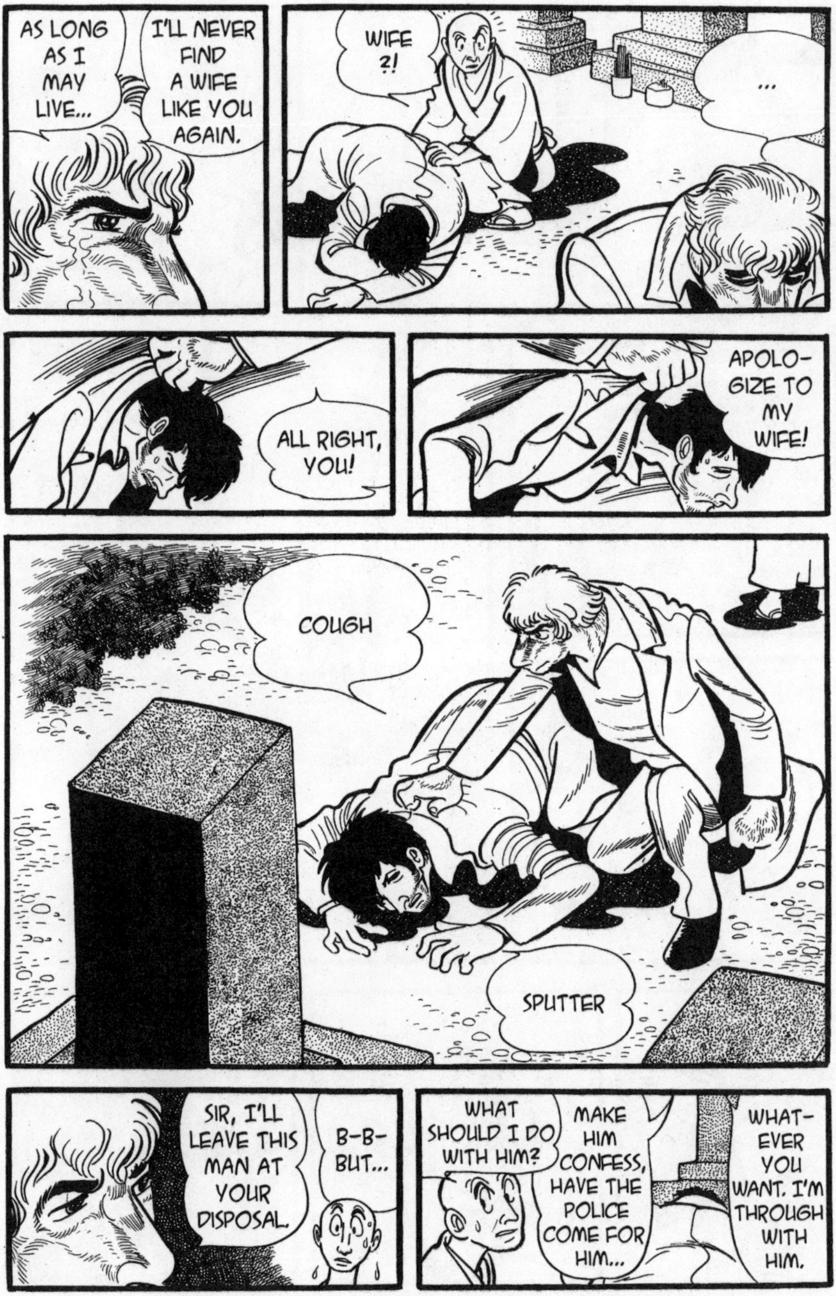
AS LONG AS I MAY LIVE...
I'LL NEVER FIND A WIFE LIKE YOU AGAIN.
WIFE ?!
...
ALL RIGHT, YOU!
APOLOGIZE TO MY WIFE!
COUGH
SPUTTER
SIR, I'LL LEAVE THIS MAN AT YOUR DISPOSAL.
B-B-BUT...
WHAT SHOULD I DO WITH HIM?
MAKE HIM CONFESS, HAVE THE POLICE COME FOR HIM...
WHATEVER YOU WANT. I'M THROUGH WITH HIM.

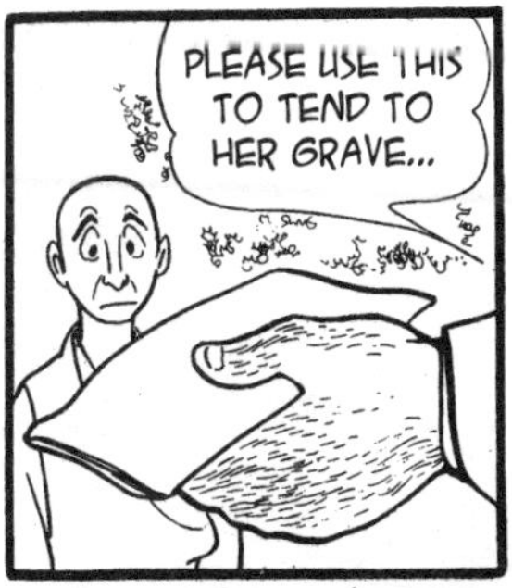
PLEASE USE THIS TO TEND TO HER GRAVE...

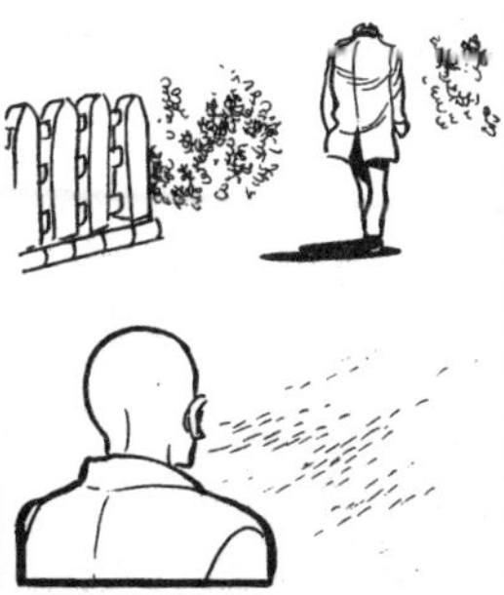

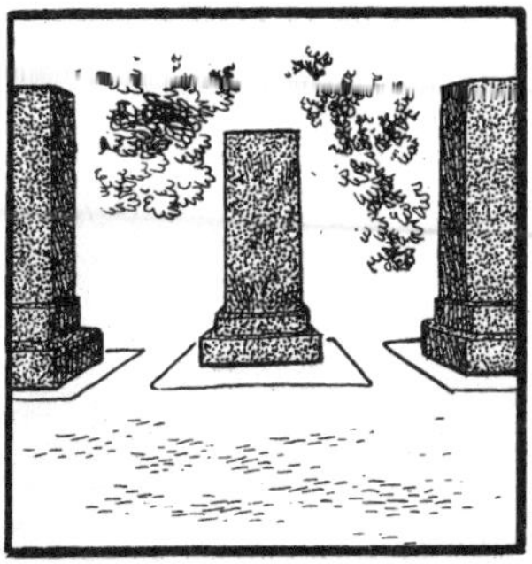

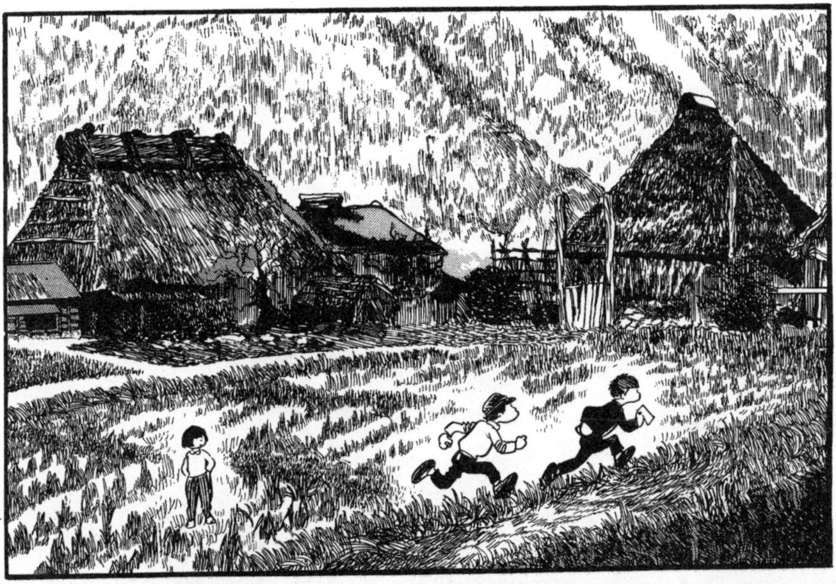

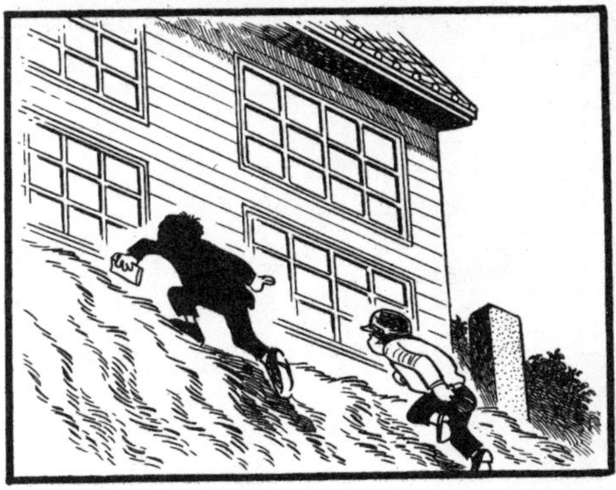

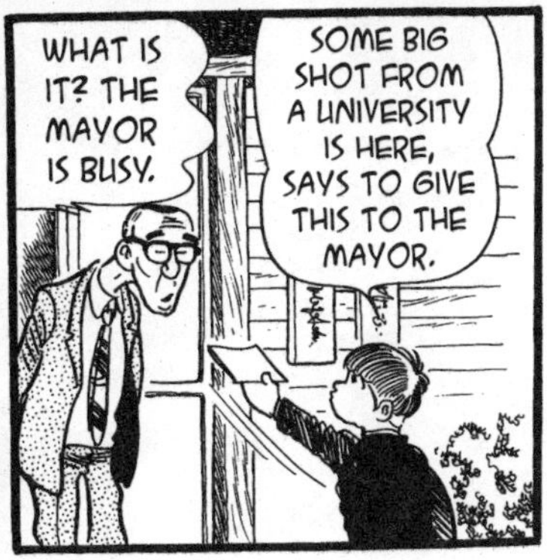
WHAT IS IT? THE MAYOR IS BUSY.
SOME BIG SHOT FROM A UNIVERSITY IS HERE, SAYS TO GIVE THIS TO THE MAYOR.

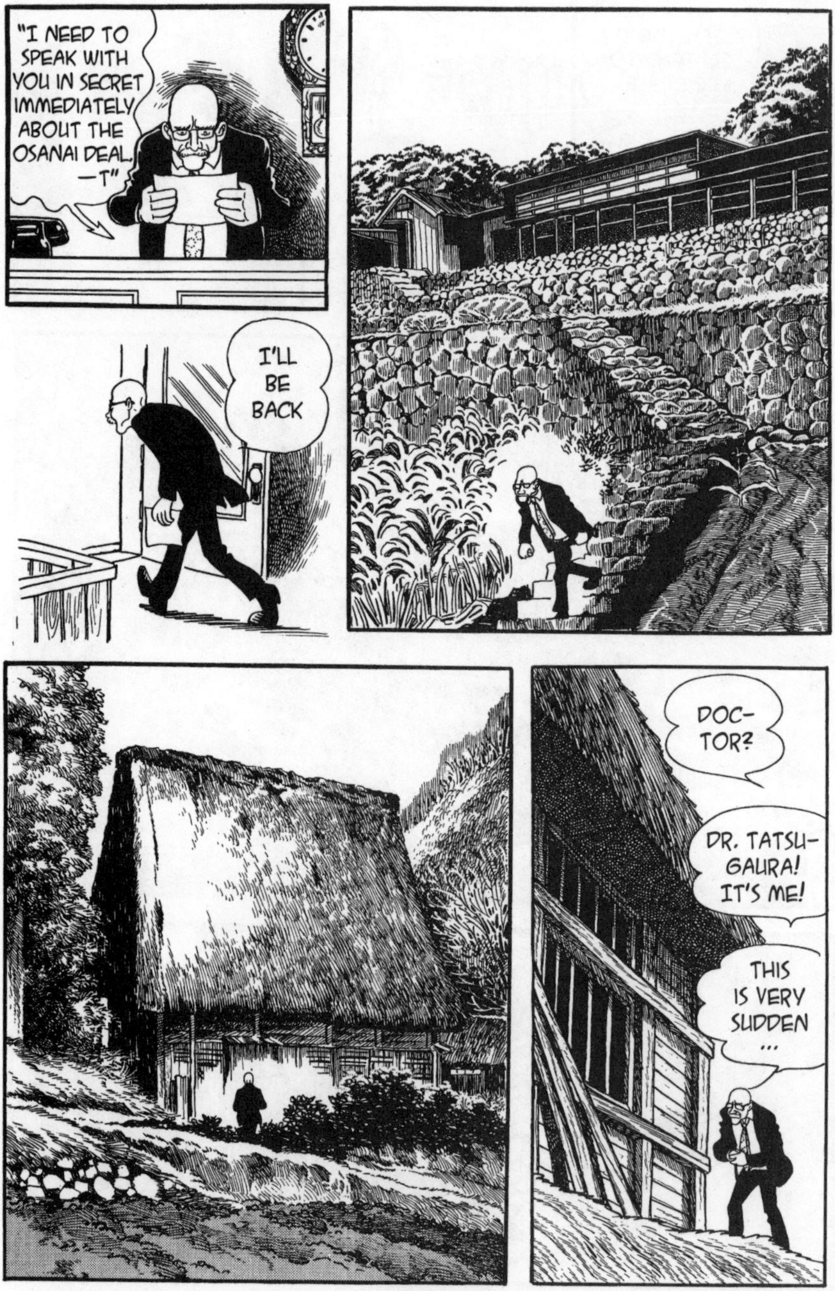
"I NEED TO SPEAK WITH YOU IN SECRET IMMEDIATELY ABOUT THE OSANAI DEAL. —T"
I'LL BE BACK
DOC-TOR?
DR. TATSU-GAURA! IT'S ME!
THIS IS VERY SUDDEN ...

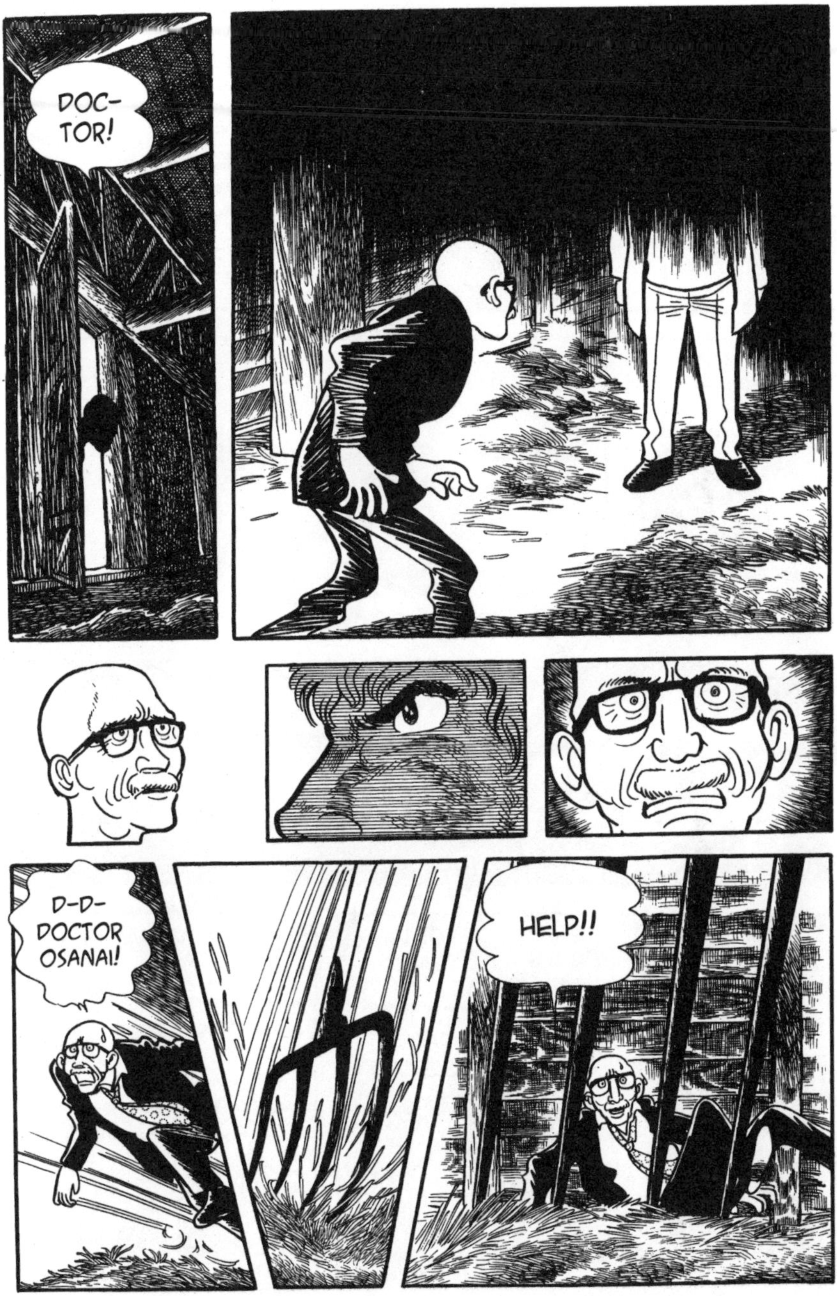
DOC-
TOR!
D-D-
DOCTOR
OSANAI!
HELP!!

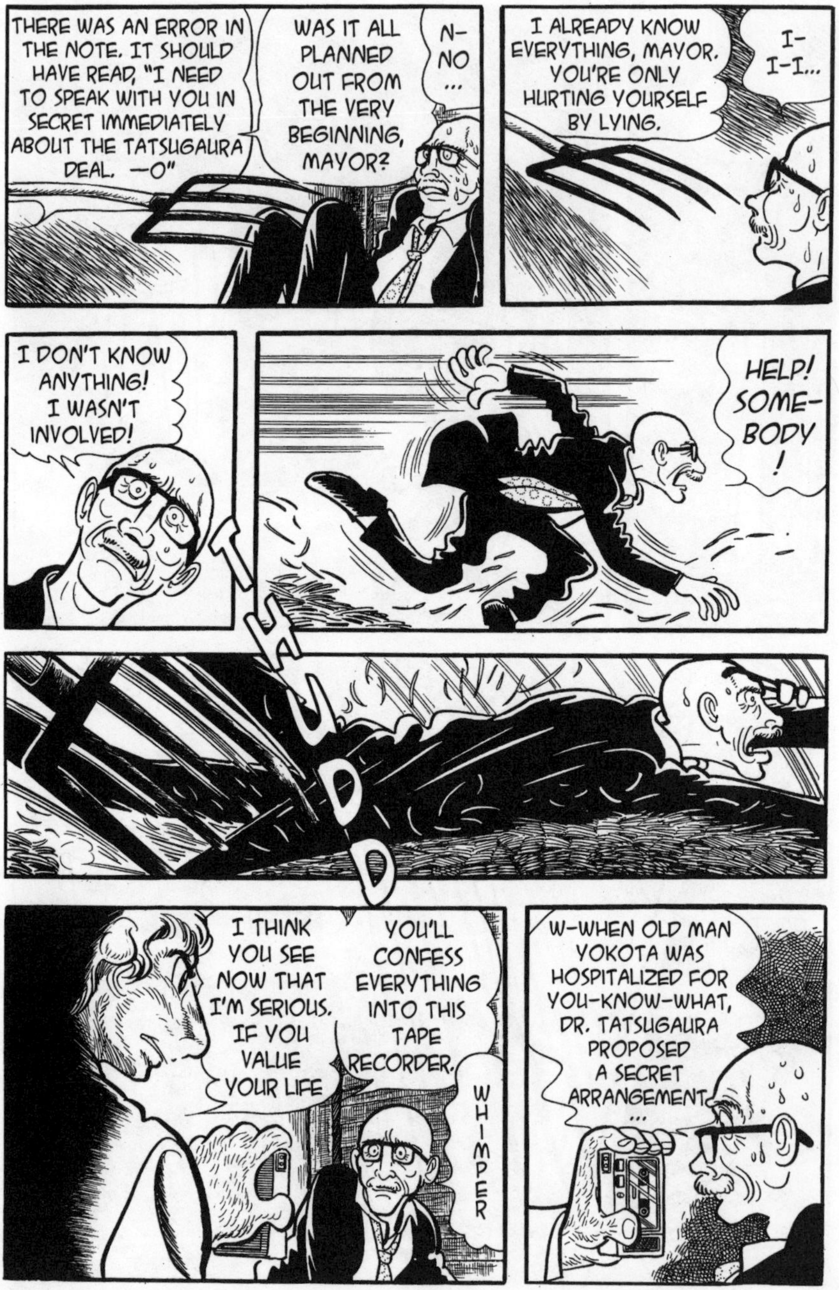
THERE WAS AN ERROR IN THE NOTE. IT SHOULD HAVE READ, "I NEED TO SPEAK WITH YOU IN SECRET IMMEDIATELY ABOUT THE TATSUGAURA DEAL. —O"
WAS IT ALL PLANNED OUT FROM THE VERY BEGINNING, MAYOR?
N-NO ...
I ALREADY KNOW EVERYTHING, MAYOR. YOU'RE ONLY HURTING YOURSELF BY LYING.
I- I-I...
I DON'T KNOW ANYTHING! I WASN'T INVOLVED!
HELP! SOME-BODY!
THUDD
I THINK YOU SEE NOW THAT I'M SERIOUS. IF YOU VALUE YOUR LIFE
YOU'LL CONFESS EVERYTHING INTO THIS TAPE RECORDER.
WHIMPER
W-WHEN OLD MAN YOKOTA WAS HOSPITALIZED FOR YOU-KNOW-WHAT, DR. TATSUGAURA PROPOSED A SECRET ARRANGEMENT ...

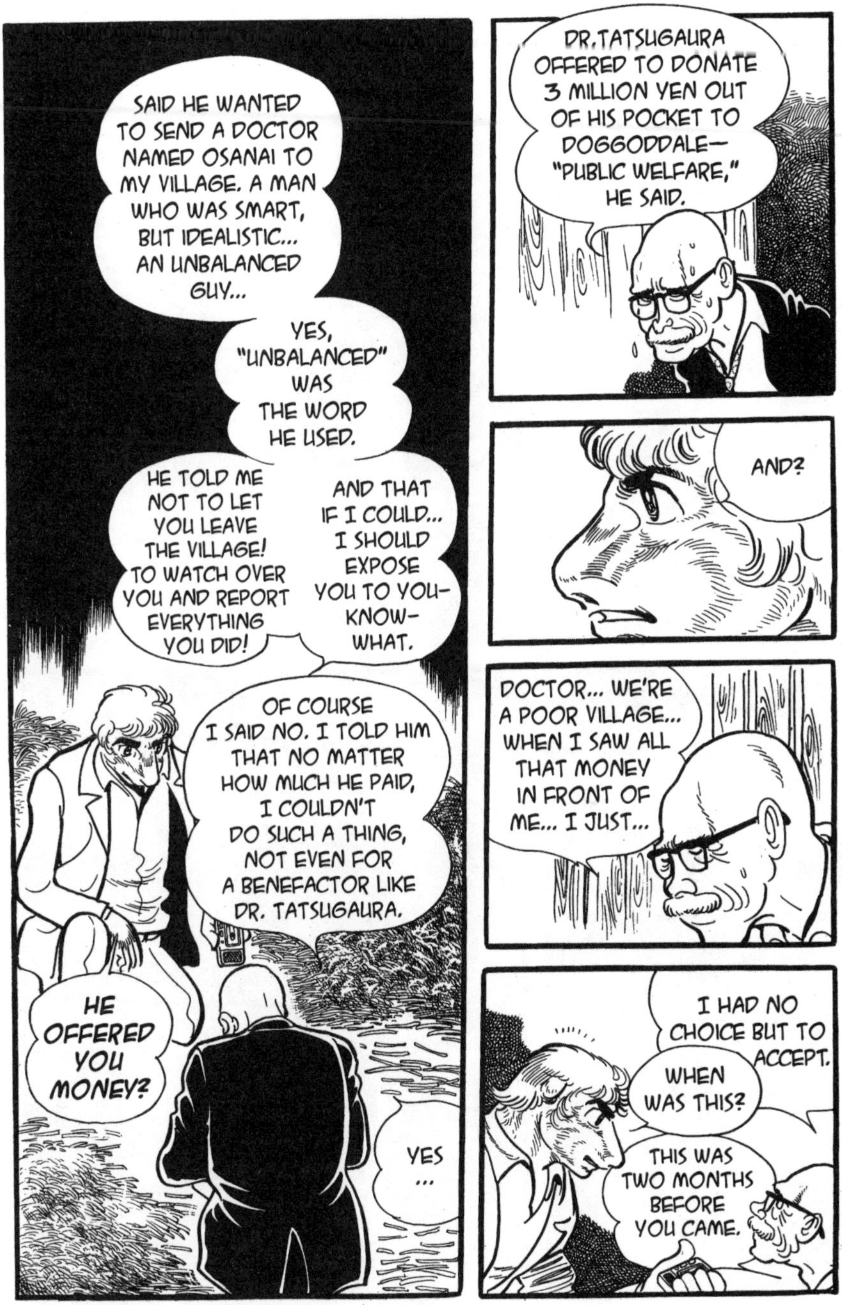
SAID HE WANTED TO SEND A DOCTOR NAMED OSANAI TO MY VILLAGE. A MAN WHO WAS SMART, BUT IDEALISTIC... AN UNBALANCED GUY...
YES, "UNBALANCED" WAS THE WORD HE USED.
HE TOLD ME NOT TO LET YOU LEAVE THE VILLAGE! TO WATCH OVER YOU AND REPORT EVERYTHING YOU DID!
AND THAT IF I COULD... I SHOULD EXPOSE YOU TO YOU-KNOW-WHAT.
OF COURSE I SAID NO. I TOLD HIM THAT NO MATTER HOW MUCH HE PAID, I COULDN'T DO SUCH A THING, NOT EVEN FOR A BENEFACTOR LIKE DR. TATSUGAURA.
HE OFFERED YOU MONEY?
YES ...
DR.TATSUGAURA OFFERED TO DONATE 3 MILLION YEN OUT OF HIS POCKET TO DOGGODDALE— "PUBLIC WELFARE," HE SAID.
AND?
DOCTOR... WE'RE A POOR VILLAGE... WHEN I SAW ALL THAT MONEY IN FRONT OF ME... I JUST...
I HAD NO CHOICE BUT TO ACCEPT.
WHEN WAS THIS?
THIS WAS TWO MONTHS BEFORE YOU CAME.

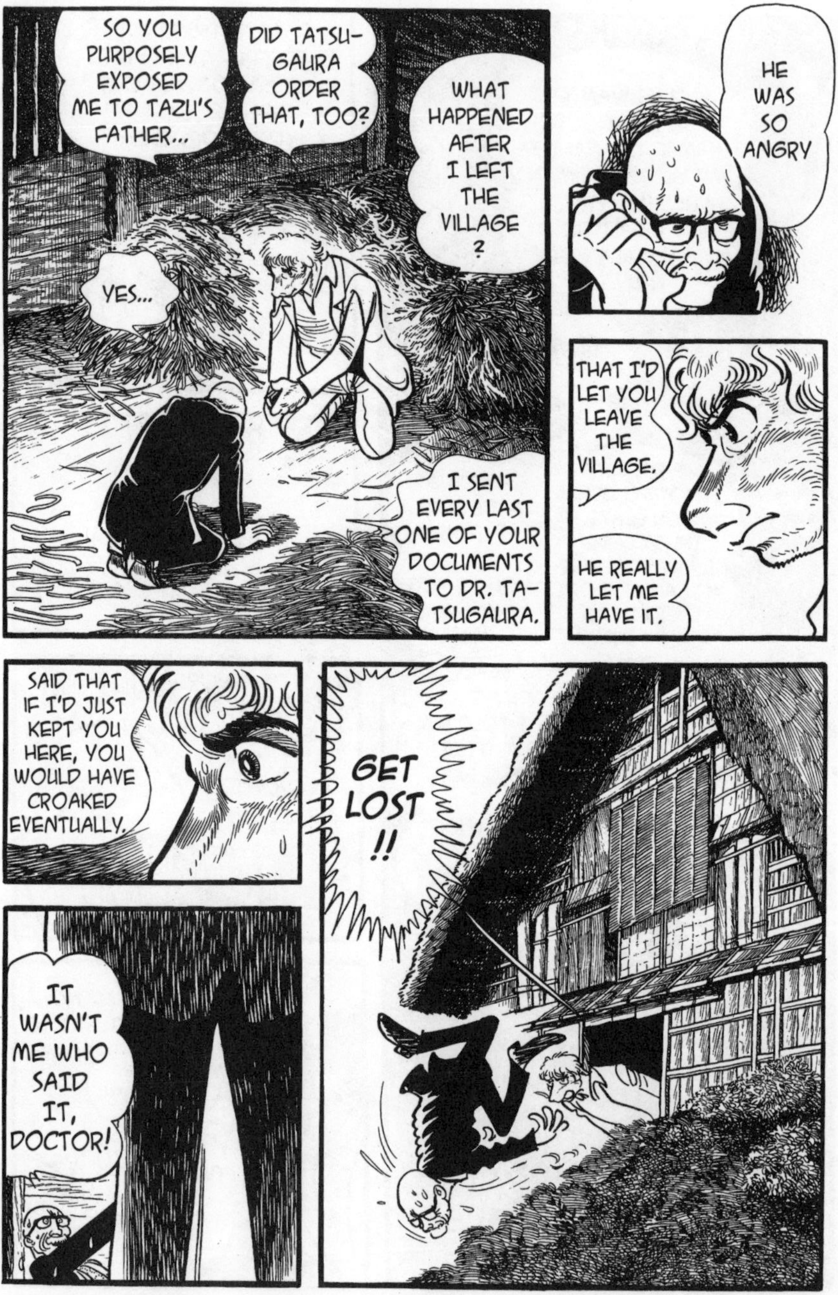
SO YOU PURPOSELY EXPOSED ME TO TAZU'S FATHER...
YES...
DID TATSU-GAURA ORDER THAT, TOO?
I SENT EVERY LAST ONE OF YOUR DOCUMENTS TO DR. TA-TSUGAURA.
WHAT HAPPENED AFTER I LEFT THE VILLAGE ?
HE WAS SO ANGRY
THAT I'D LET YOU LEAVE THE VILLAGE.
HE REALLY LET ME HAVE IT.
SAID THAT IF I'D JUST KEPT YOU HERE, YOU WOULD HAVE CROAKED EVENTUALLY.
IT WASN'T ME WHO SAID IT, DOCTOR!
GET LOST !!

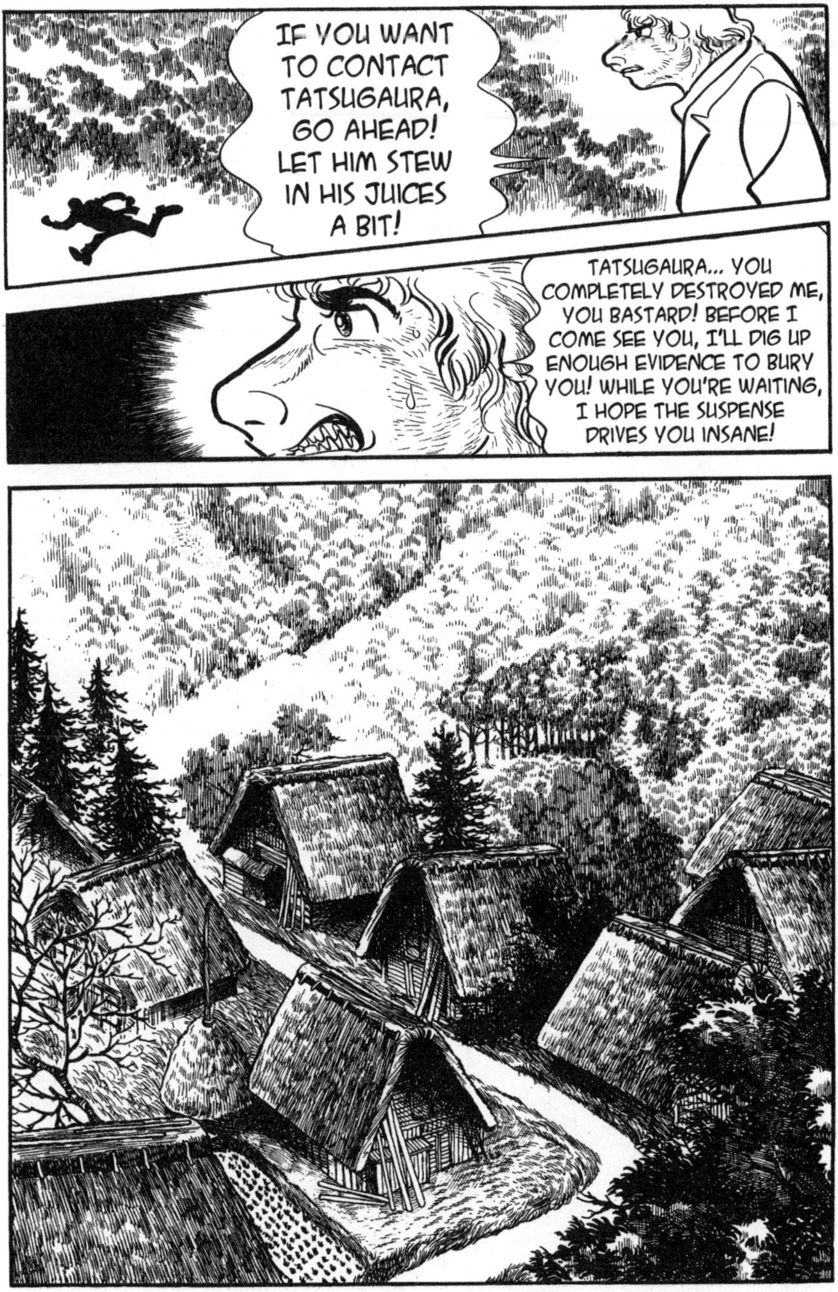
IF YOU WANT TO CONTACT TATSUGAURA, GO AHEAD! LET HIM STEW IN HIS JUICES A BIT!
TATSUGAURA... YOU COMPLETELY DESTROYED ME, YOU BASTARD! BEFORE I COME SEE YOU, I'LL DIG UP ENOUGH EVIDENCE TO BURY YOU! WHILE YOU'RE WAITING, I HOPE THE SUSPENSE DRIVES YOU INSANE!

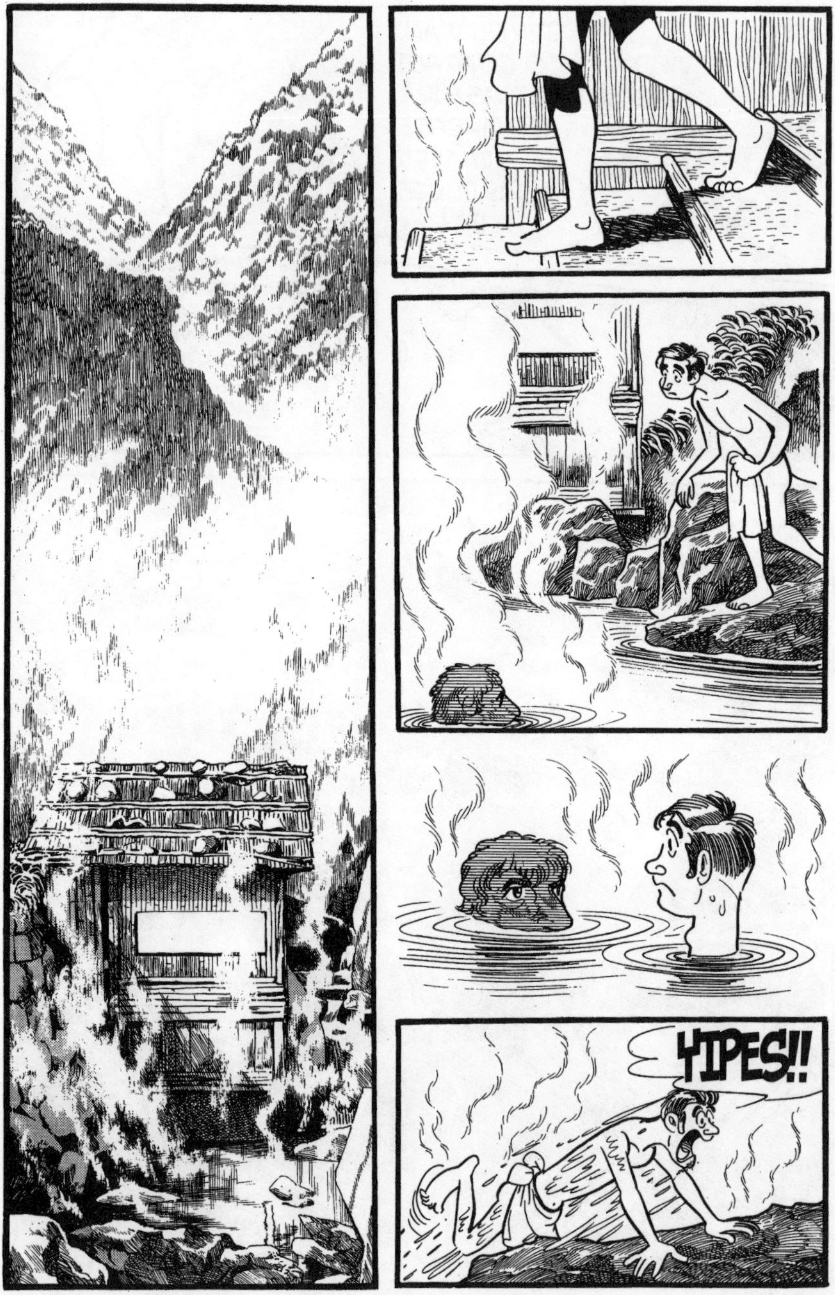
YIPES!!

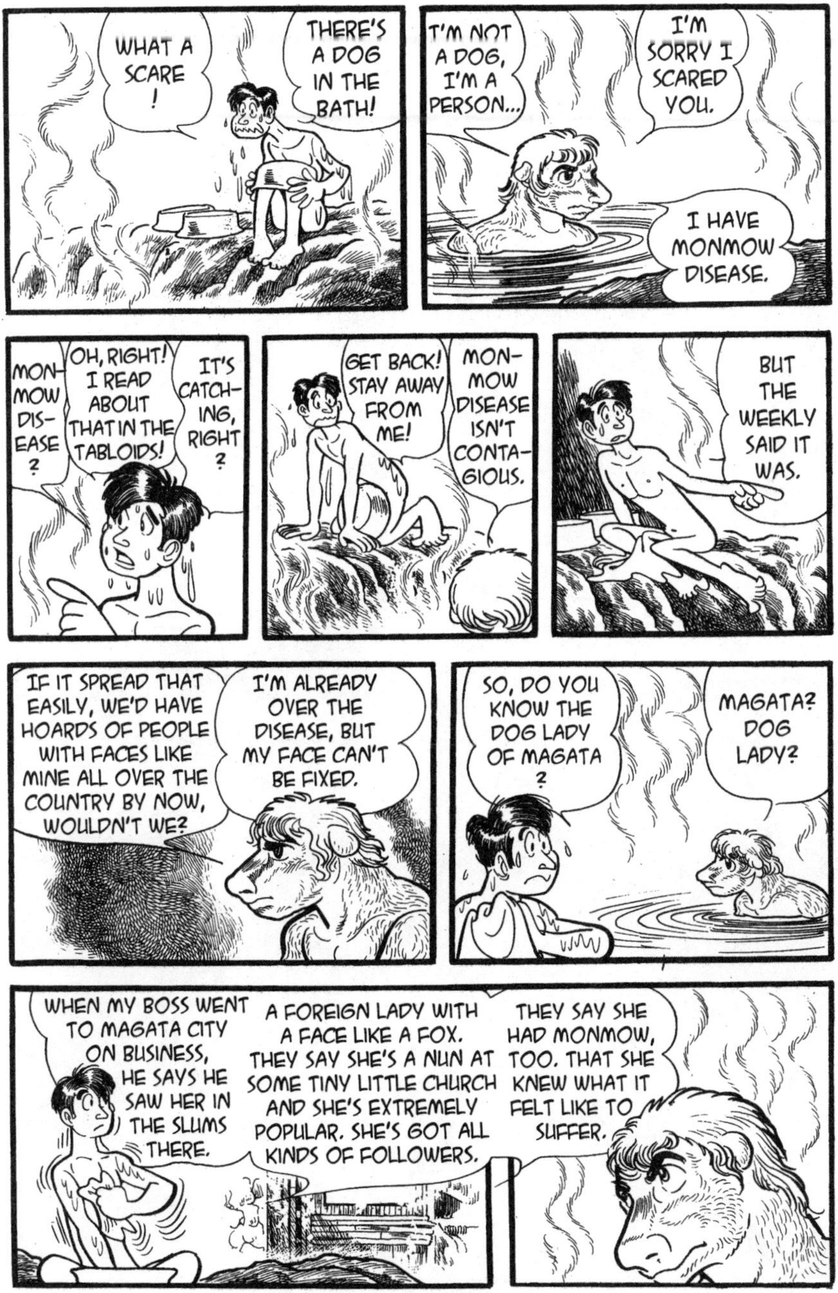
WHAT A SCARE!
THERE'S A DOG IN THE BATH!
I'M NOT A DOG, I'M A PERSON...
I'M SORRY I SCARED YOU.
I HAVE MONMOW DISEASE.
MON-MOW DIS-EASE?
OH, RIGHT! I READ ABOUT THAT IN THE TABLOIDS!
IT'S CATCHING, RIGHT?
GET BACK! STAY AWAY FROM ME!
MON-MOW DISEASE ISN'T CONTA-GIOUS.
BUT THE WEEKLY SAID IT WAS.
IF IT SPREAD THAT EASILY, WE'D HAVE HOARDS OF PEOPLE WITH FACES LIKE MINE ALL OVER THE COUNTRY BY NOW, WOULDN'T WE?
I'M ALREADY OVER THE DISEASE, BUT MY FACE CAN'T BE FIXED.
SO, DO YOU KNOW THE DOG LADY OF MAGATA?
MAGATA? DOG LADY?
WHEN MY BOSS WENT TO MAGATA CITY ON BUSINESS, HE SAYS HE SAW HER IN THE SLUMS THERE.
A FOREIGN LADY WITH A FACE LIKE A FOX. THEY SAY SHE'S A NUN AT SOME TINY LITTLE CHURCH AND SHE'S EXTREMELY POPULAR. SHE'S GOT ALL KINDS OF FOLLOWERS.
THEY SAY SHE HAD MONMOW, TOO. THAT SHE KNEW WHAT IT FELT LIKE TO SUFFER.

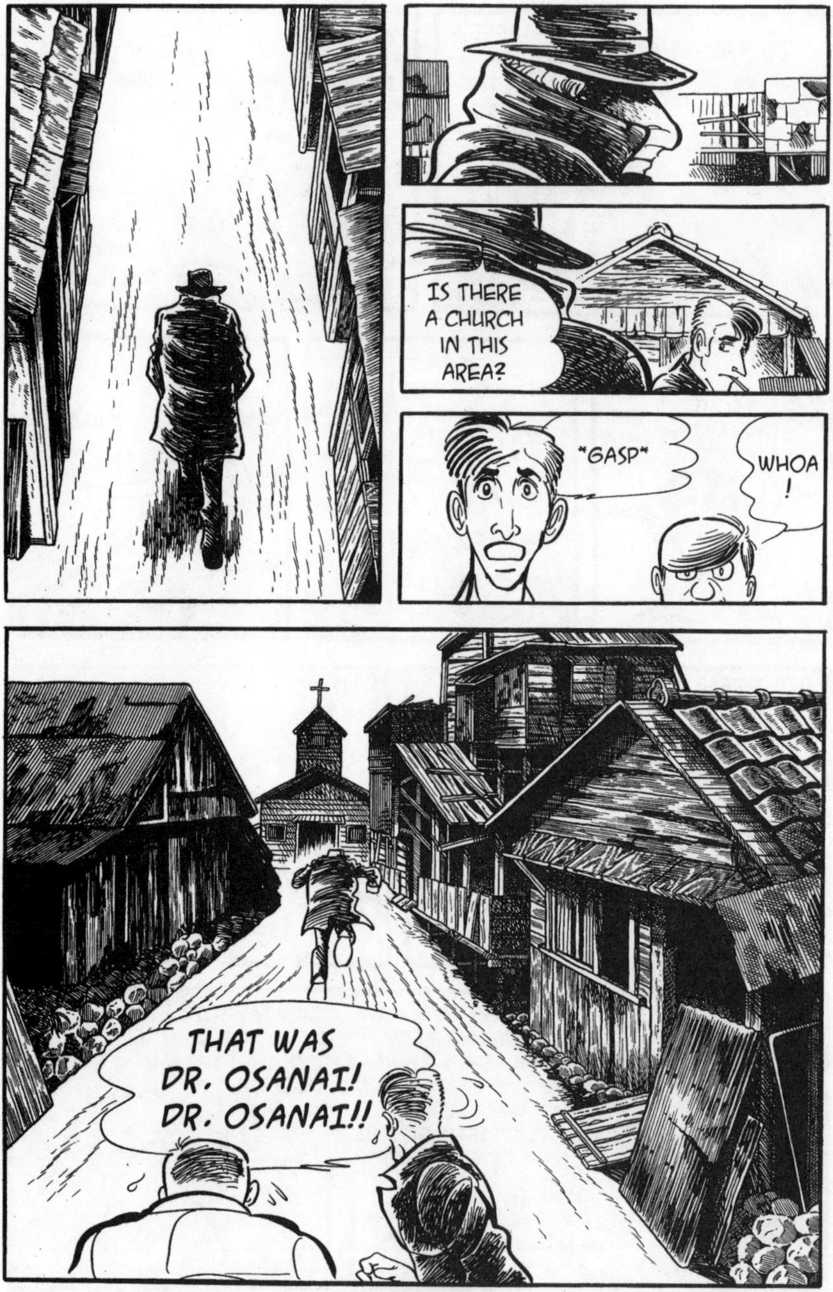
IS THERE A CHURCH IN THIS AREA?
WHOA !
GASP
THAT WAS DR. OSANAI! DR. OSANAI!!

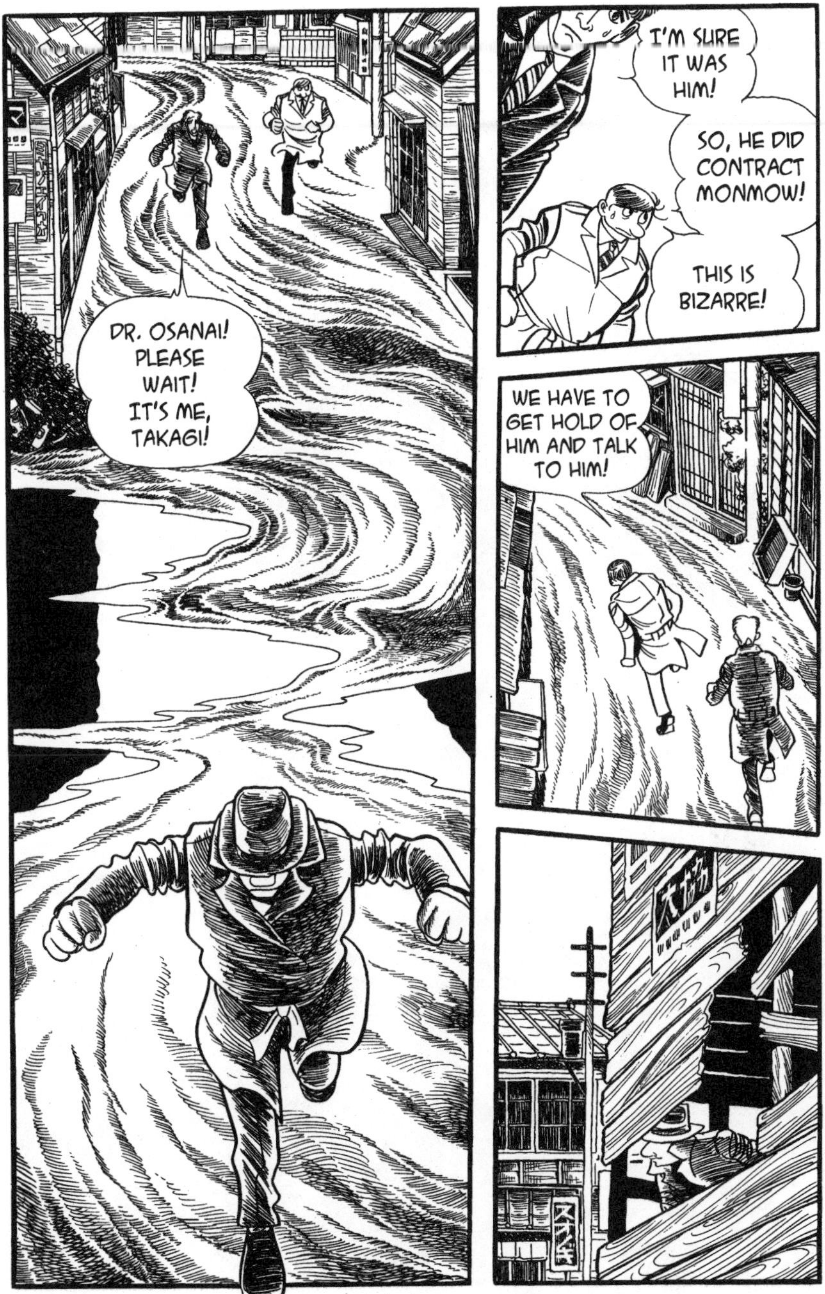
DR. OSANAI! PLEASE WAIT! IT'S ME, TAKAGI!
I'M SURE IT WAS HIM!
SO, HE DID CONTRACT MONMOW!
THIS IS BIZARRE!
WE HAVE TO GET HOLD OF HIM AND TALK TO HIM!

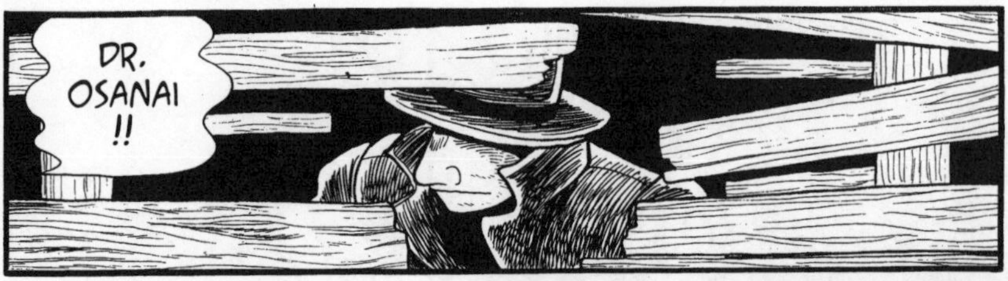
DR. OSANAI !!

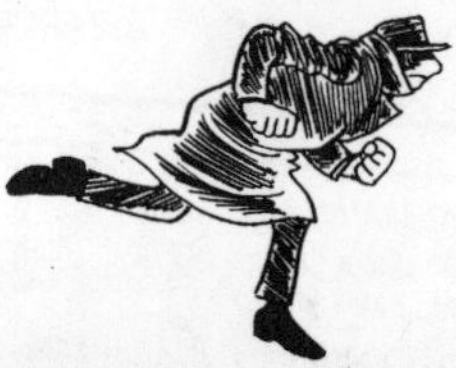

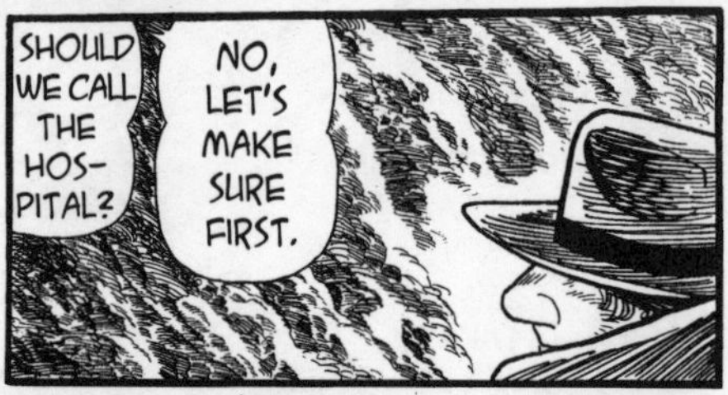
SHOULD WE CALL THE HOS-PITAL?
NO, LET'S MAKE SURE FIRST.

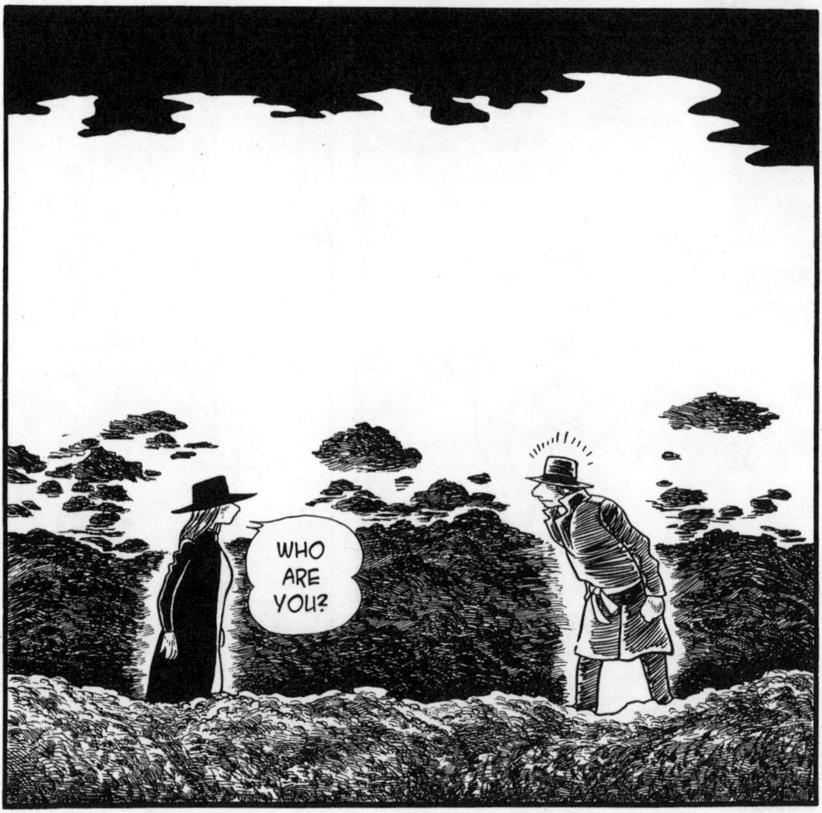
WHO ARE YOU?

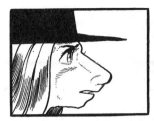

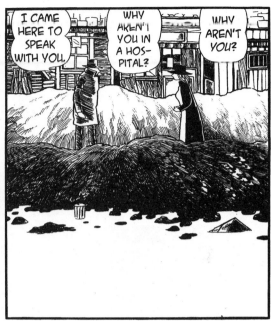

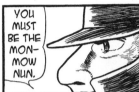

YOU MUST BE THE MON-MOW NUN.
YES. ARE YOU AFFLICTED TOO?
I CAME HERE TO SPEAK WITH YOU.
WHY AREN'T YOU IN A HOSPITAL?
WHY AREN'T YOU?

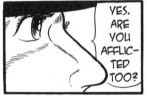

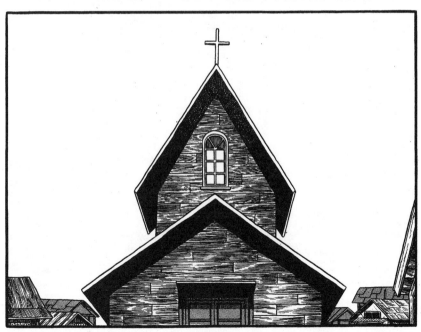

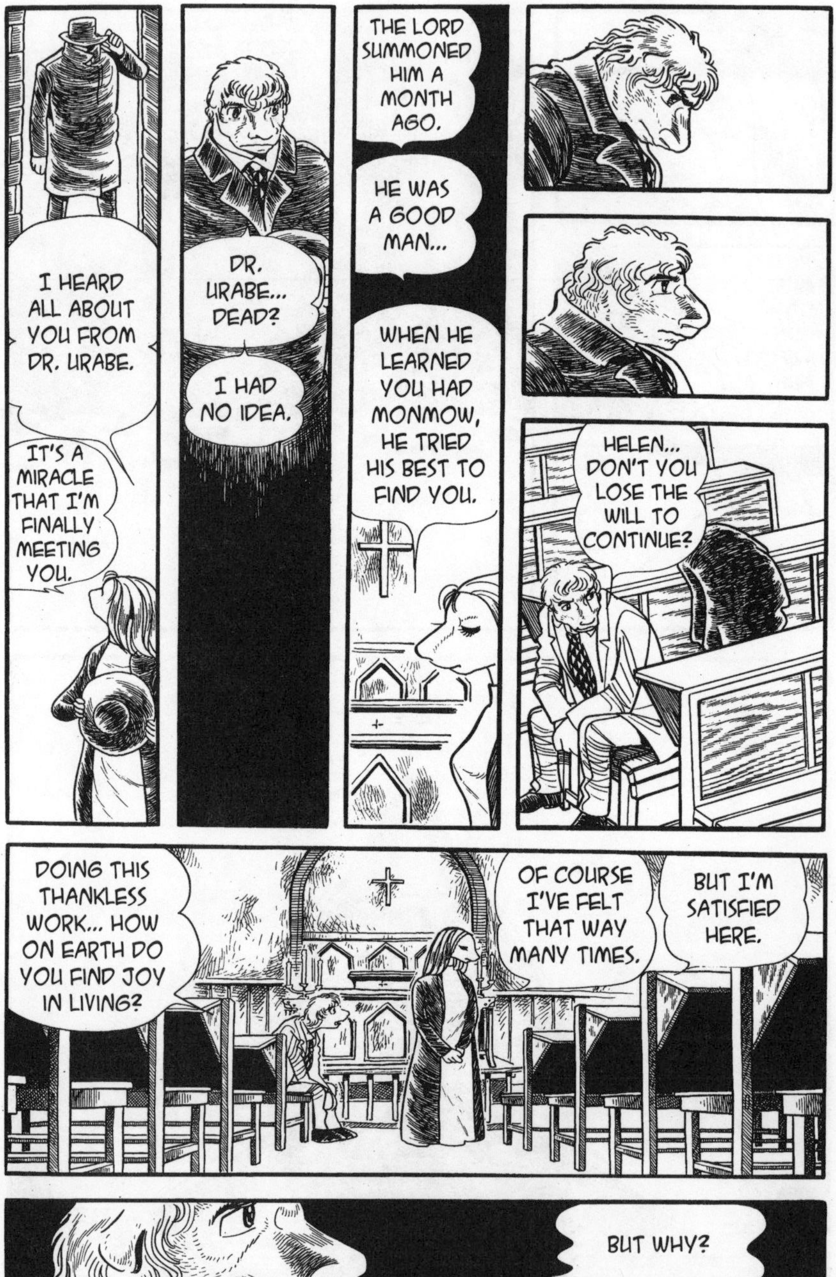
I HEARD ALL ABOUT YOU FROM DR. URABE.
IT'S A MIRACLE THAT I'M FINALLY MEETING YOU.
DR. URABE... DEAD?
I HAD NO IDEA.
THE LORD SUMMONED HIM A MONTH AGO.
HE WAS A GOOD MAN...
WHEN HE LEARNED YOU HAD MONMOW, HE TRIED HIS BEST TO FIND YOU.
HELEN... DON'T YOU LOSE THE WILL TO CONTINUE?
DOING THIS THANKLESS WORK... HOW ON EARTH DO YOU FIND JOY IN LIVING?
OF COURSE I'VE FELT THAT WAY MANY TIMES.
BUT I'M SATISFIED HERE.
BUT WHY?

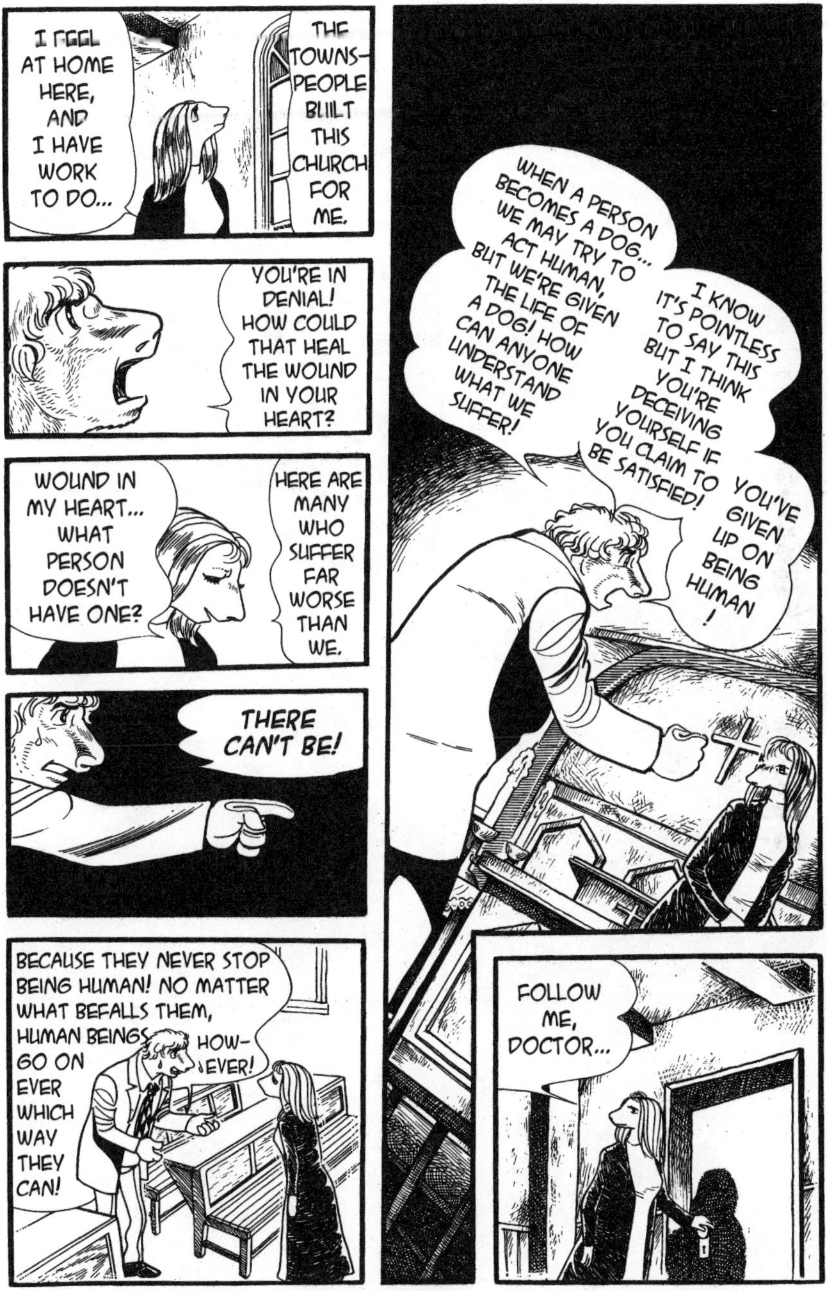

I FEEL AT HOME HERE, AND I HAVE WORK TO DO...
THE TOWNSPEOPLE BUILT THIS CHURCH FOR ME.
YOU'RE IN DENIAL! HOW COULD THAT HEAL THE WOUND IN YOUR HEART?
WOUND IN MY HEART... WHAT PERSON DOESN'T HAVE ONE?
HERE ARE MANY WHO SUFFER FAR WORSE THAN WE.
THERE CAN'T BE!
BECAUSE THEY NEVER STOP BEING HUMAN! NO MATTER WHAT BEFALLS THEM, HUMAN BEINGS GO ON EVER WHICH WAY THEY CAN!
HOW-EVER!
WHEN A PERSON BECOMES A DOG... WE MAY TRY TO ACT HUMAN, BUT WE'RE GIVEN THE LIFE OF A DOG! HOW CAN ANYONE UNDERSTAND WHAT WE SUFFER!
I KNOW IT'S POINTLESS TO SAY THIS BUT I THINK YOU'RE DECEIVING YOURSELF IF YOU CLAIM TO BE SATISFIED!
YOU'VE GIVEN UP ON BEING HUMAN!
FOLLOW ME, DOCTOR...

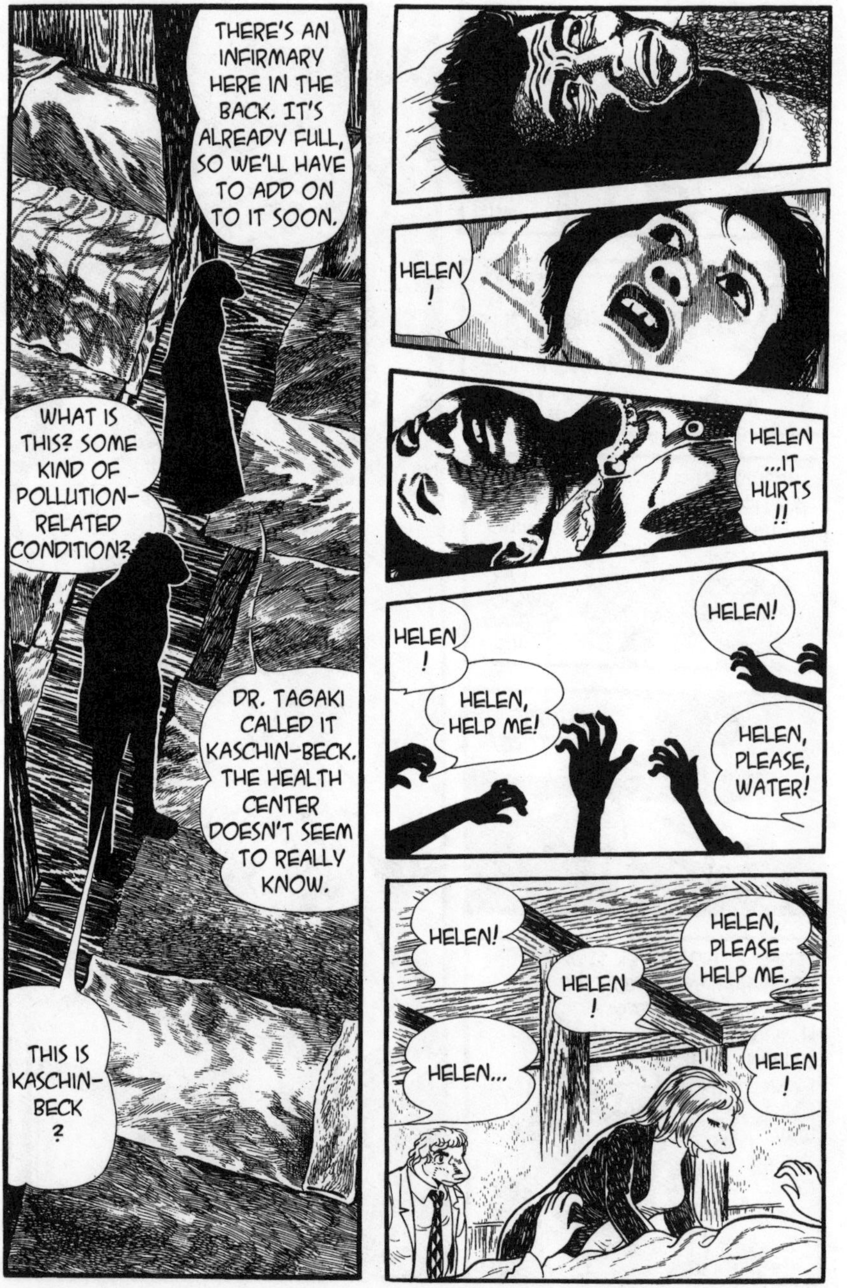
THERE'S AN INFIRMARY HERE IN THE BACK. IT'S ALREADY FULL, SO WE'LL HAVE TO ADD ON TO IT SOON.
WHAT IS THIS? SOME KIND OF POLLUTION-RELATED CONDITION?
DR. TAGAKI CALLED IT KASCHIN-BECK. THE HEALTH CENTER DOESN'T SEEM TO REALLY KNOW.
THIS IS KASCHIN-BECK?
HELEN!
HELEN ...IT HURTS!!
HELEN!
HELEN, HELP ME!
HELEN!
HELEN, PLEASE, WATER!
HELEN!
HELEN!
HELEN, PLEASE HELP ME.
HELEN...
HELEN!

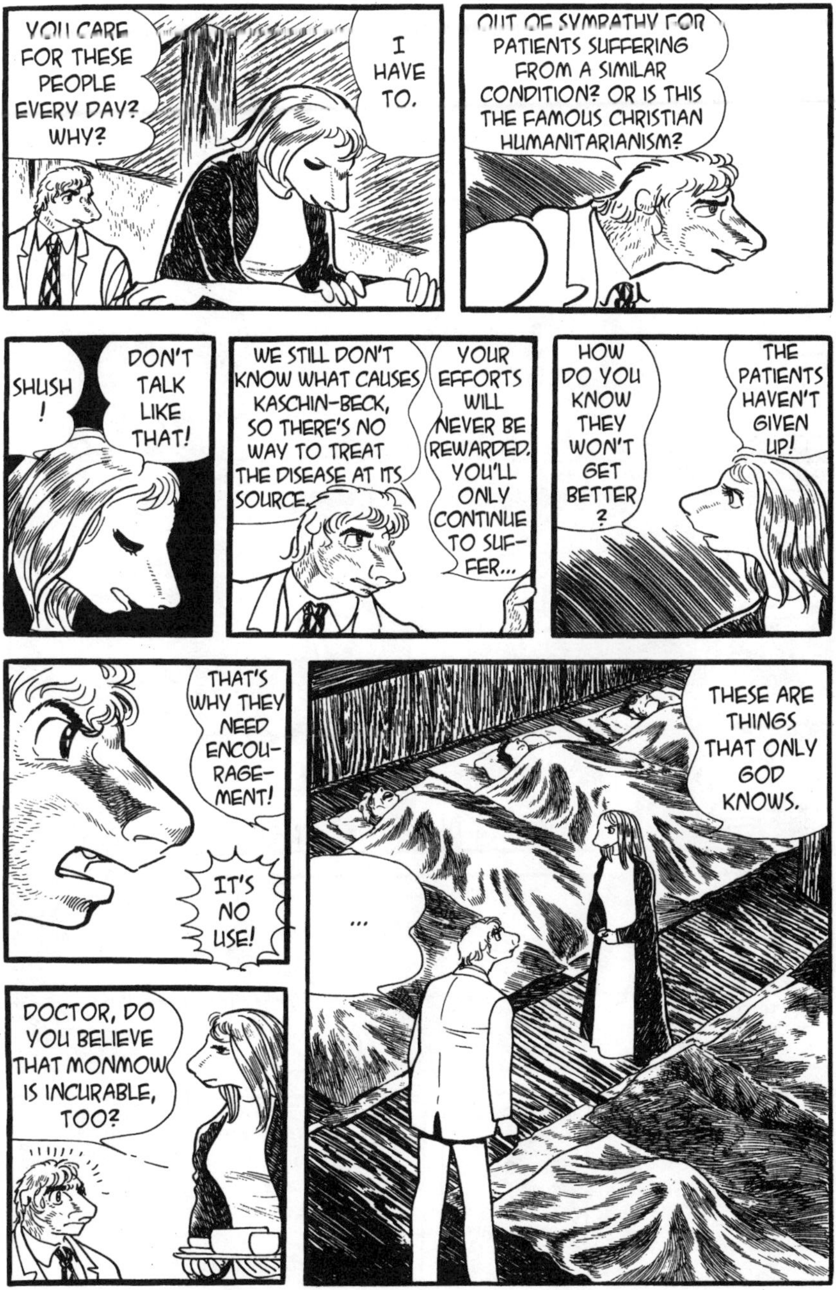
YOU CARE FOR THESE PEOPLE EVERY DAY? WHY?
I HAVE TO.
OUT OF SYMPATHY FOR PATIENTS SUFFERING FROM A SIMILAR CONDITION? OR IS THIS THE FAMOUS CHRISTIAN HUMANITARIANISM?
SHUSH!
DON'T TALK LIKE THAT!
WE STILL DON'T KNOW WHAT CAUSES KASCHIN-BECK, SO THERE'S NO WAY TO TREAT THE DISEASE AT ITS SOURCE.
YOUR EFFORTS WILL NEVER BE REWARDED. YOU'LL ONLY CONTINUE TO SUFFER...
HOW DO YOU KNOW THEY WON'T GET BETTER?
THE PATIENTS HAVEN'T GIVEN UP!
THAT'S WHY THEY NEED ENCOURAGEMENT!
IT'S NO USE!
DOCTOR, DO YOU BELIEVE THAT MONMOW IS INCURABLE, TOO?
THESE ARE THINGS THAT ONLY GOD KNOWS.
...

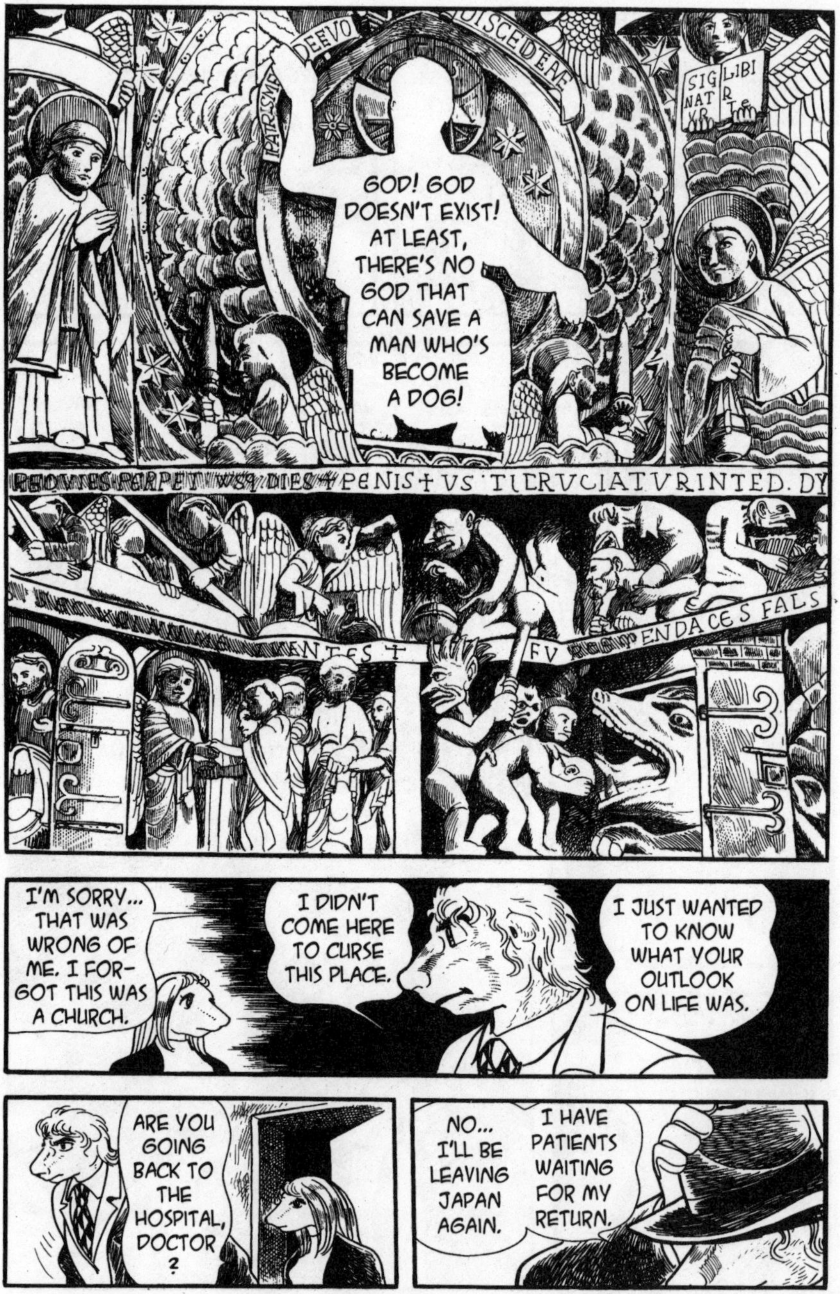

GOD! GOD DOESN'T EXIST! AT LEAST, THERE'S NO GOD THAT CAN SAVE A MAN WHO'S BECOME A DOG!
I'M SORRY... THAT WAS WRONG OF ME. I FOR-GOT THIS WAS A CHURCH.
I DIDN'T COME HERE TO CURSE THIS PLACE.
I JUST WANTED TO KNOW WHAT YOUR OUTLOOK ON LIFE WAS.
ARE YOU GOING BACK TO THE HOSPITAL, DOCTOR?
NO... I'LL BE LEAVING JAPAN AGAIN.
I HAVE PATIENTS WAITING FOR MY RETURN.

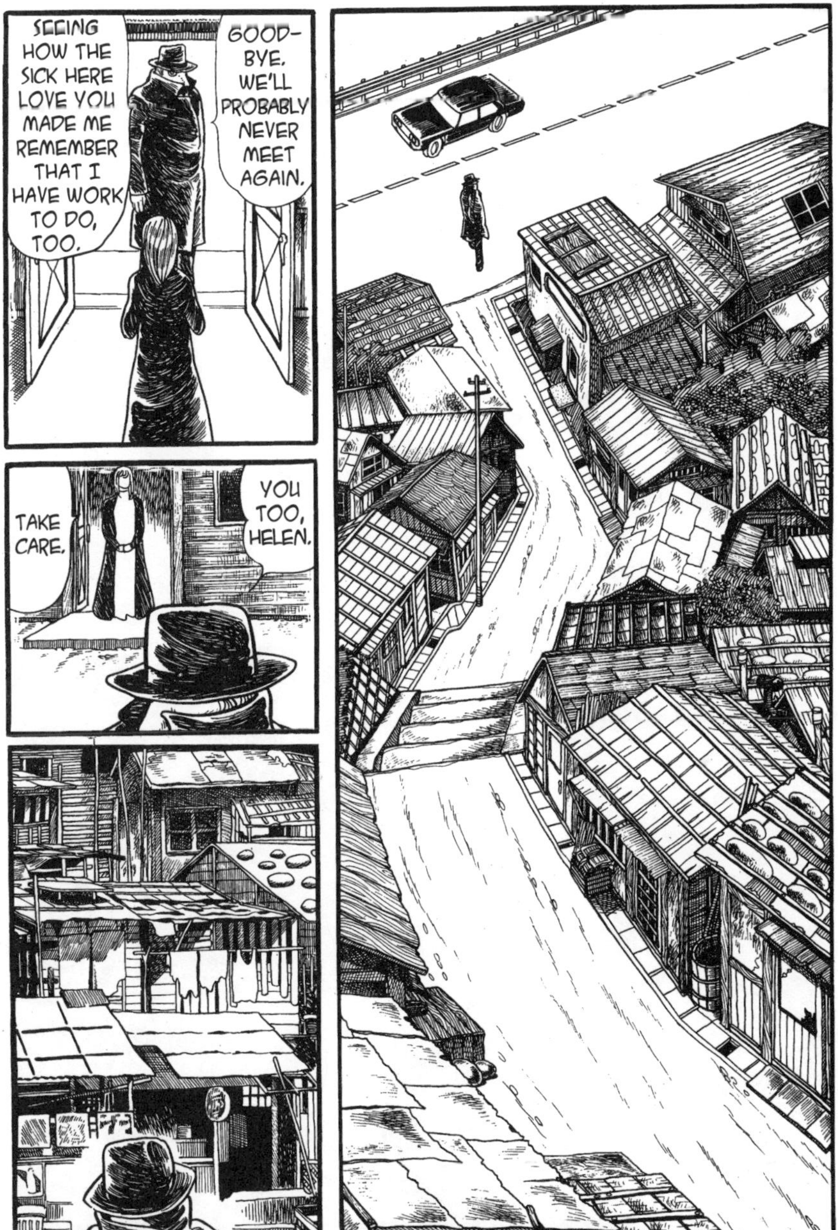
SEEING HOW THE SICK HERE LOVE YOU MADE ME REMEMBER THAT I HAVE WORK TO DO, TOO.
GOOD-BYE. WE'LL PROBABLY NEVER MEET AGAIN.
TAKE CARE.
YOU TOO, HELEN.

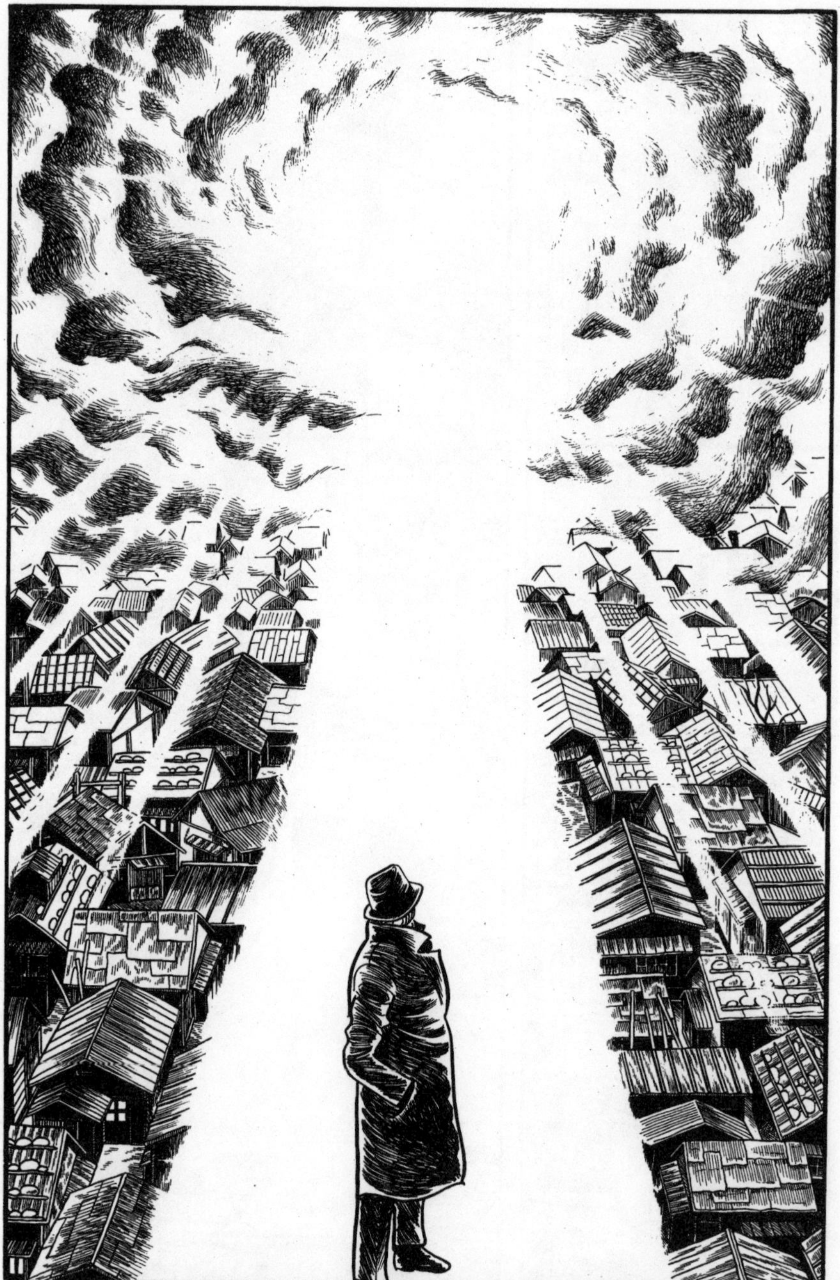

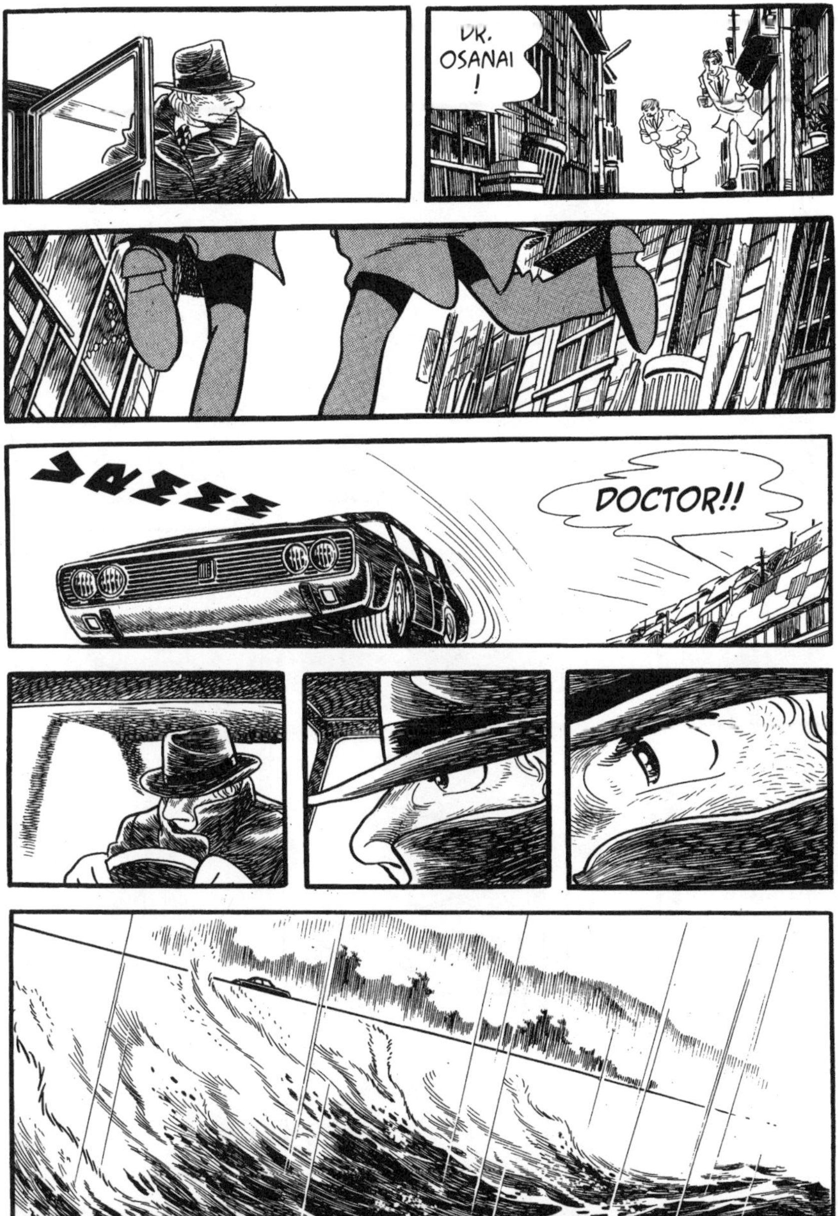
DR. OSANAI!
VRZZZ
DOCTOR!!

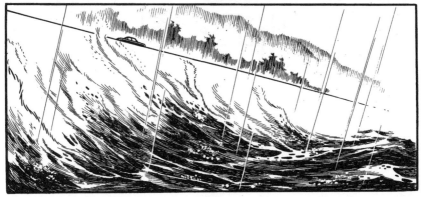

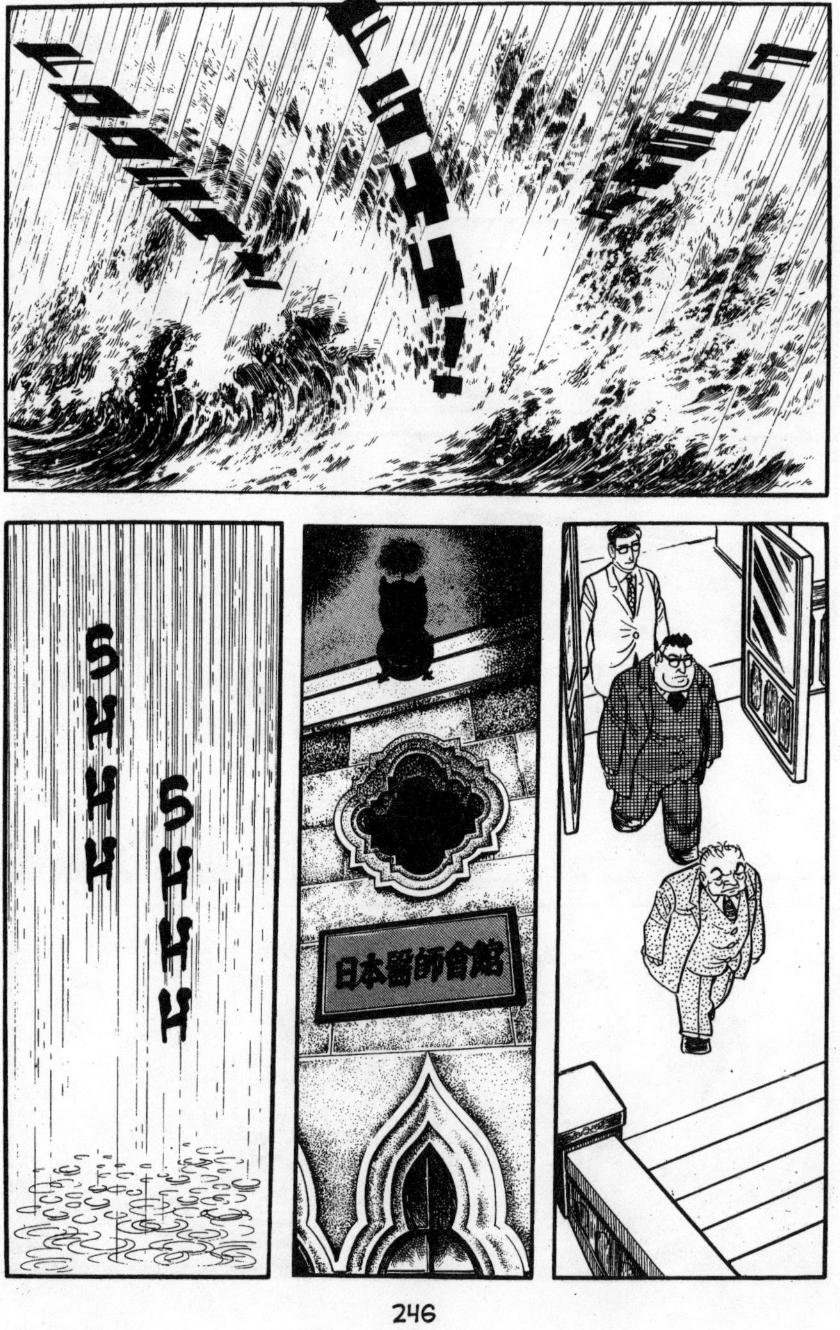
SHHHH
SHHHH
日本醫師會館

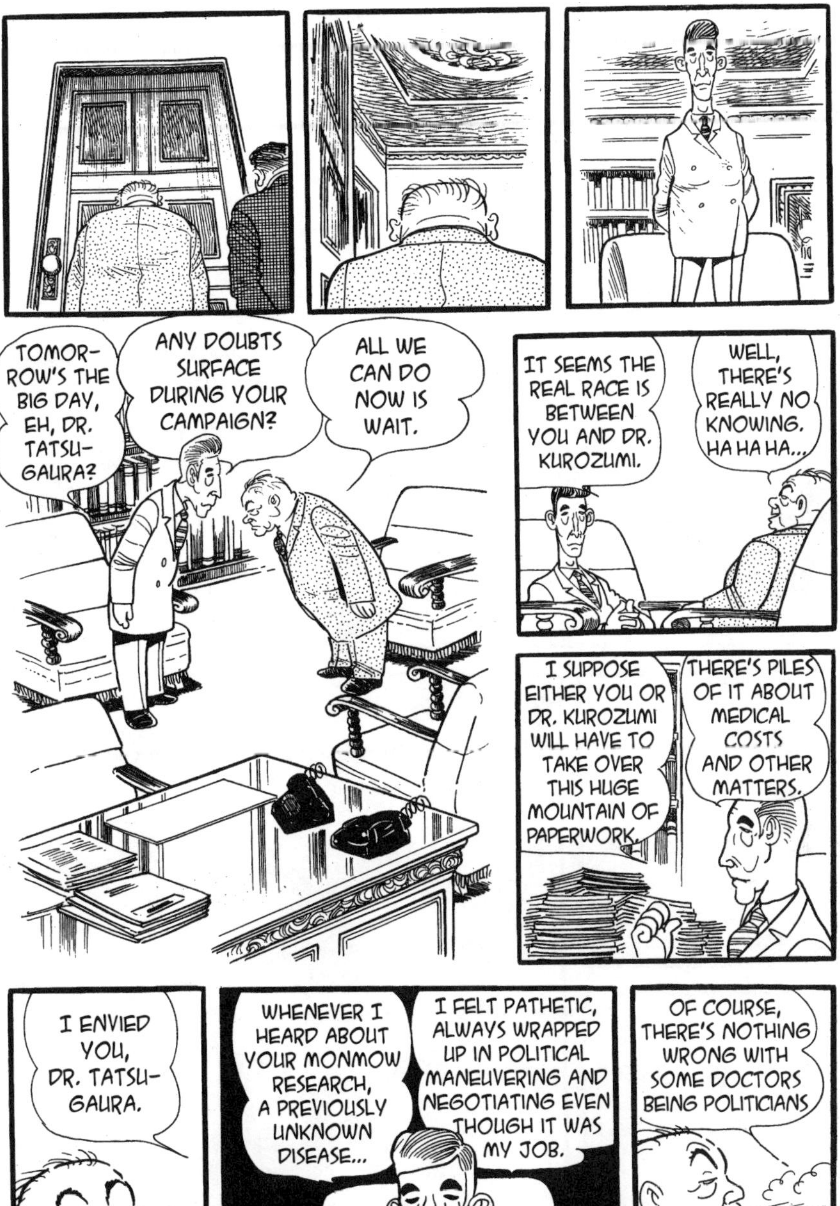

TOMORROW'S THE BIG DAY, EH, DR. TATSUGAURA?
ANY DOUBTS SURFACE DURING YOUR CAMPAIGN?
ALL WE CAN DO NOW IS WAIT.
IT SEEMS THE REAL RACE IS BETWEEN YOU AND DR. KUROZUMI.
WELL, THERE'S REALLY NO KNOWING. HA HA HA...
I SUPPOSE EITHER YOU OR DR. KUROZUMI WILL HAVE TO TAKE OVER THIS HUGE MOUNTAIN OF PAPERWORK.
THERE'S PILES OF IT ABOUT MEDICAL COSTS AND OTHER MATTERS.
I ENVIED YOU, DR. TATSUGAURA.
WHENEVER I HEARD ABOUT YOUR MONMOW RESEARCH, A PREVIOUSLY UNKNOWN DISEASE...
I FELT PATHETIC, ALWAYS WRAPPED UP IN POLITICAL MANEUVERING AND NEGOTIATING EVEN THOUGH IT WAS MY JOB.
OF COURSE, THERE'S NOTHING WRONG WITH SOME DOCTORS BEING POLITICIANS

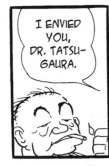

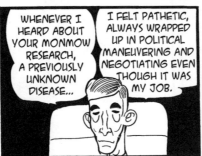

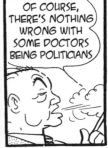

BUT IT'S A SHAME THAT MEN WITH IMPRESSIVE SCHOLARLY ACHIEVEMENTS LIKE YOU AND DR. KUROZUMI NEED TO GIVE IT ALL UP FOR POLITICS.

AS FAR AS MONMOW GOES, THE YOUNG FOLK WILL HAVE A CHANCE TO RUN WITH THE BALL NOW.

IT'S FINE FOR A DOCTOR LIKE ME WITH NO SPECIAL TALENTS TO SPEND ALL HIS TIME ORGANIZING MEETINGS AND CONFERRING ABOUT THIS AND THAT.

BUT YOU'RE DIFFERENT!

THIS JOB CAN BE QUITE TAXING PSYCHOLOGICALLY.

FOR ONE THING, THE UNION HAS NO IDEA HOW THINGS REALLY WORK

AND THE COUNCIL MEMBERS ALL WANT TO DO EVERYTHING THEIR OWN WAY

CHAIRMAN, IT SOUNDS LIKE YOU THINK I'D BE BETTER OFF SHUT UP IN A LABORATORY UNTIL THE END OF MY DAYS! HA HA HA HA.

OF COURSE, A DOCTOR CAN'T ALWAYS STAY IN HIS IVORY TOWER

ARGH!! NGNGG!

W-WHAT'S WRONG, DR. TATSU-GAURA?

UGH!

248

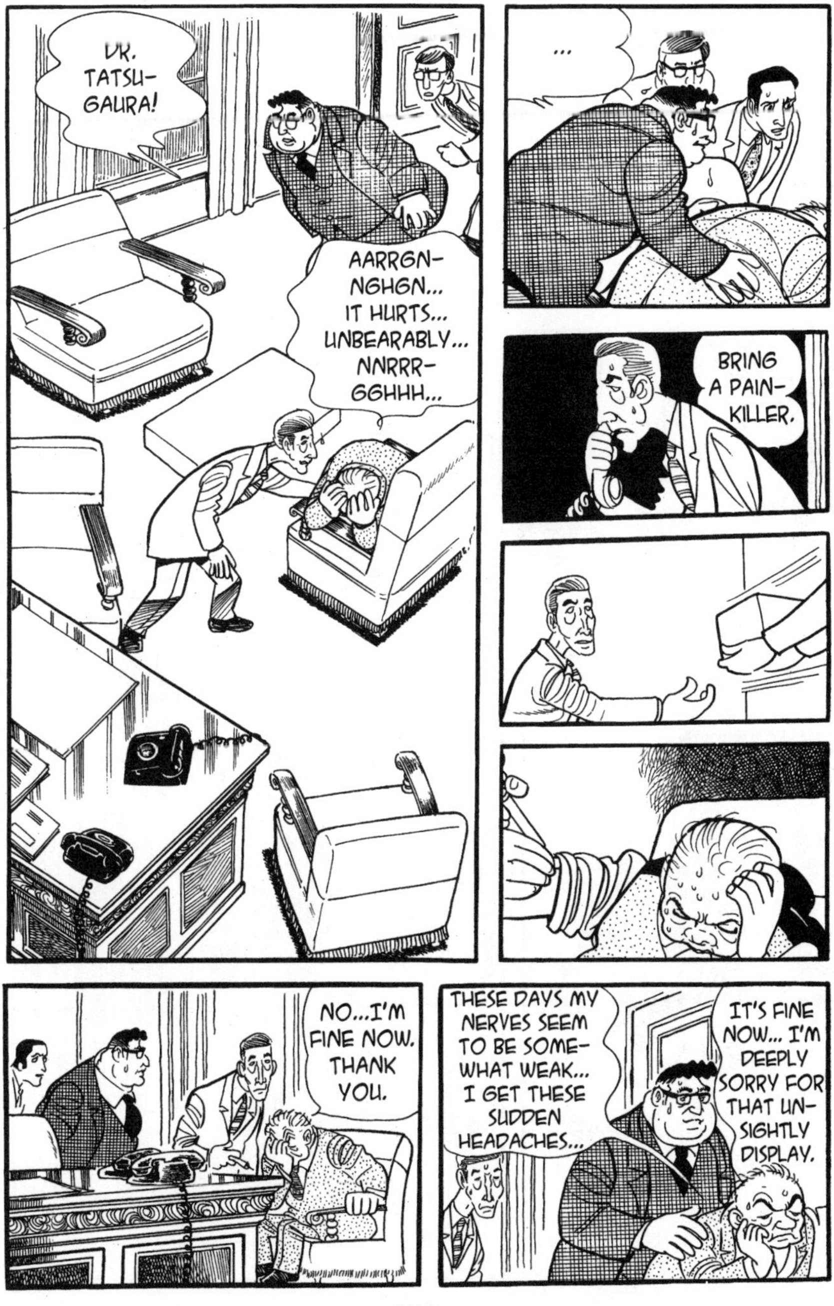
DR. TATSU-GAURA!
AARRGN-NGHGN... IT HURTS... UNBEARABLY... NNRRR-GGHHH...
...
BRING A PAIN-KILLER.
NO...I'M FINE NOW. THANK YOU.
THESE DAYS MY NERVES SEEM TO BE SOME-WHAT WEAK... I GET THESE SUDDEN HEADACHES...
IT'S FINE NOW... I'M DEEPLY SORRY FOR THAT UN-SIGHTLY DISPLAY.

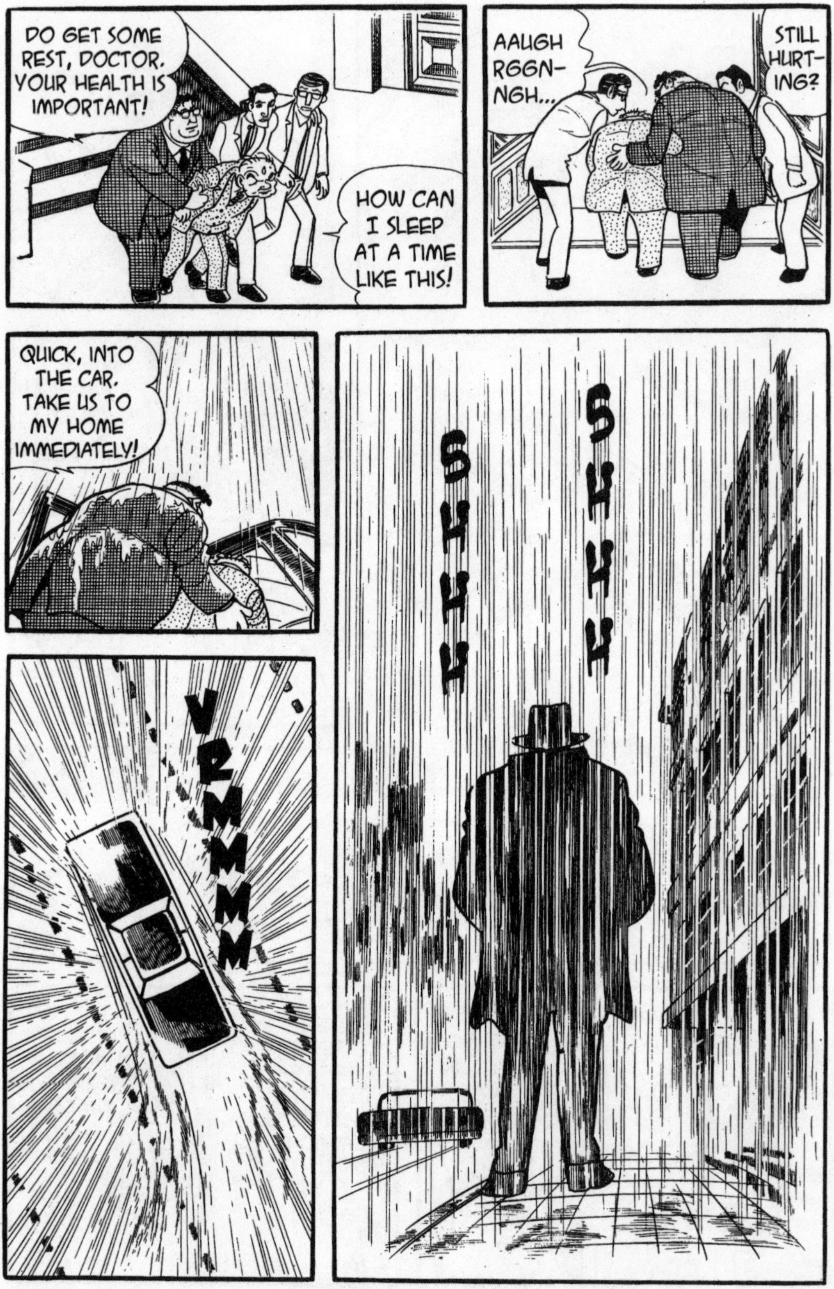
DO GET SOME REST, DOCTOR. YOUR HEALTH IS IMPORTANT!
HOW CAN I SLEEP AT A TIME LIKE THIS!
AAUGH RGGN-NGH...
STILL HURT-ING?
QUICK, INTO THE CAR. TAKE US TO MY HOME IMMEDIATELY!
VRMMMMM
SHHHH
SHHHH

HEY!
A WEREWOLF!

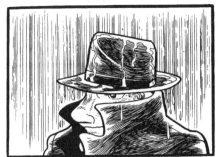

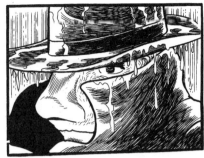

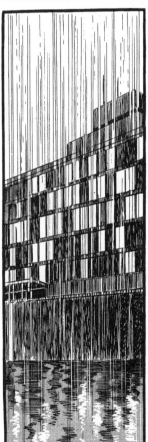

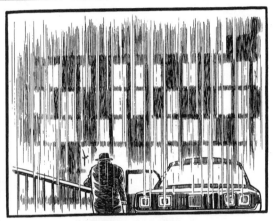

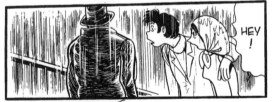

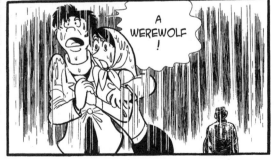

CHAPTER 18

ENCOUNTERS
PART 2

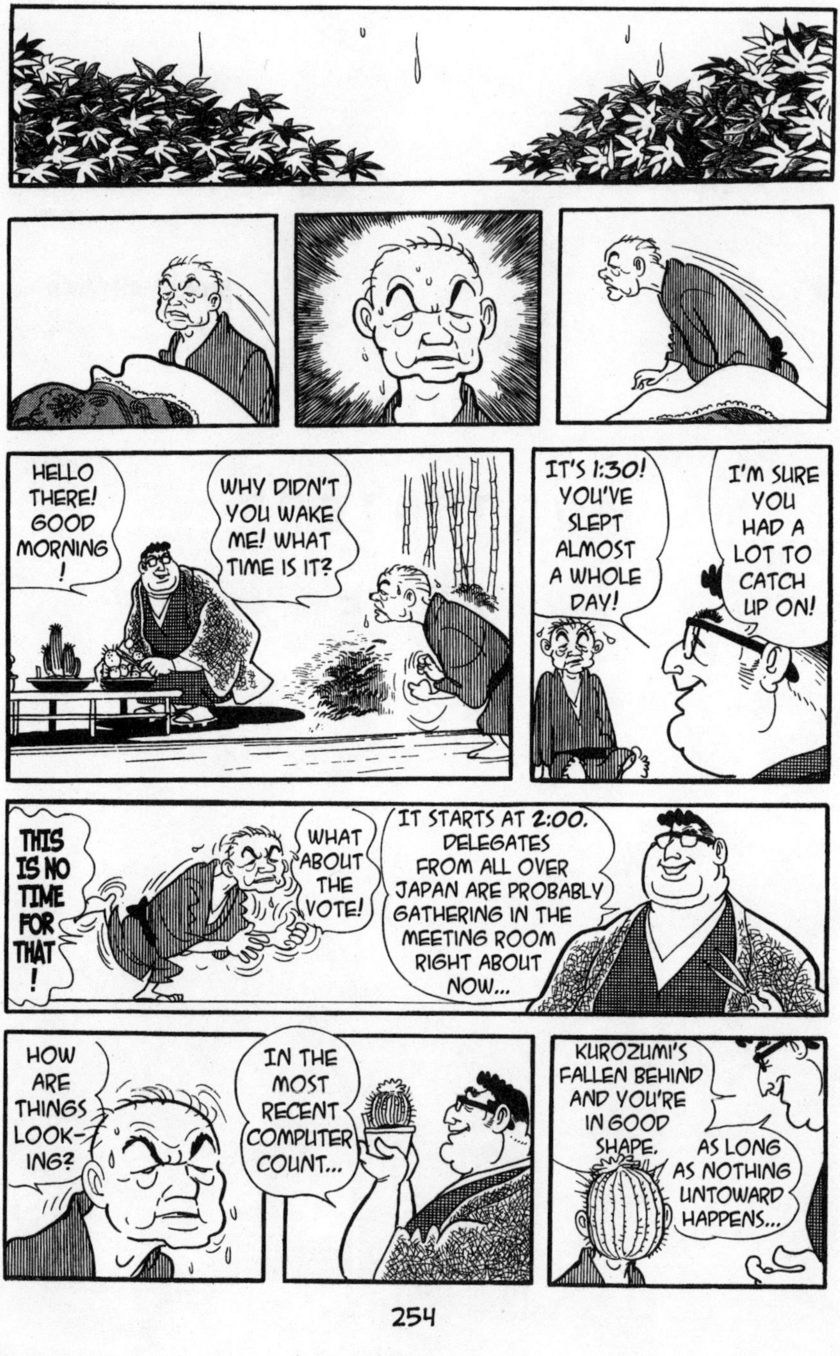
HELLO THERE! GOOD MORNING!
WHY DIDN'T YOU WAKE ME! WHAT TIME IS IT?
IT'S 1:30! YOU'VE SLEPT ALMOST A WHOLE DAY!
I'M SURE YOU HAD A LOT TO CATCH UP ON!
THIS IS NO TIME FOR THAT!
WHAT ABOUT THE VOTE!
IT STARTS AT 2:00. DELEGATES FROM ALL OVER JAPAN ARE PROBABLY GATHERING IN THE MEETING ROOM RIGHT ABOUT NOW...
HOW ARE THINGS LOOK-ING?
IN THE MOST RECENT COMPUTER COUNT...
KUROZUMI'S FALLEN BEHIND AND YOU'RE IN GOOD SHAPE.
AS LONG AS NOTHING UNTOWARD HAPPENS...

THIS ELECTION IS A SURE THING!
I HOPE SO...
THE VOTES FOR CHAIRMAN WILL NOW BE CAST BY THE DELEGATES FROM EACH PREFECTURAL ELECTORATE. WHEN YOUR NAME IS CALLED, PLEASE BRING YOUR COMPLETED BALLOT TO THE BALLOT BOX ON THE PLATFORM.

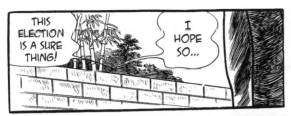

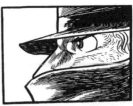

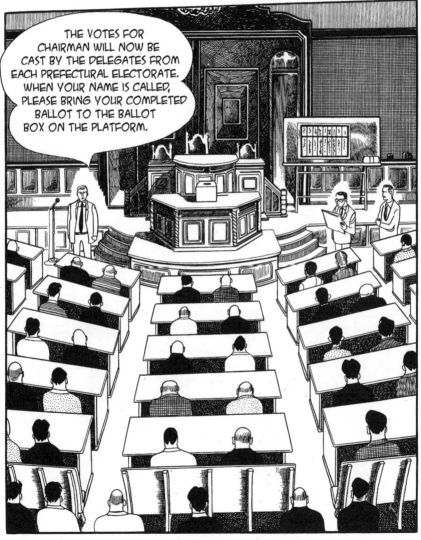

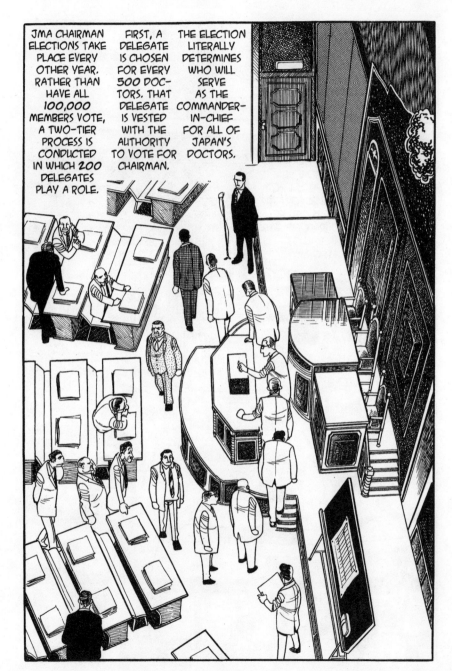

JMA CHAIRMAN ELECTIONS TAKE PLACE EVERY OTHER YEAR. RATHER THAN HAVE ALL 100,000 MEMBERS VOTE, A TWO-TIER PROCESS IS CONDUCTED IN WHICH **200** DELEGATES PLAY A ROLE.

FIRST, A DELEGATE IS CHOSEN FOR EVERY 500 DOC-TORS. THAT DELEGATE IS VESTED WITH THE AUTHORITY TO VOTE FOR CHAIRMAN.

THE ELECTION LITERALLY DETERMINES WHO WILL SERVE AS THE COMMANDER-IN-CHIEF FOR ALL OF JAPAN'S DOCTORS.

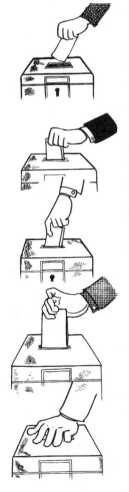

WAIT JUST A MOMENT, EVERYONE.

257

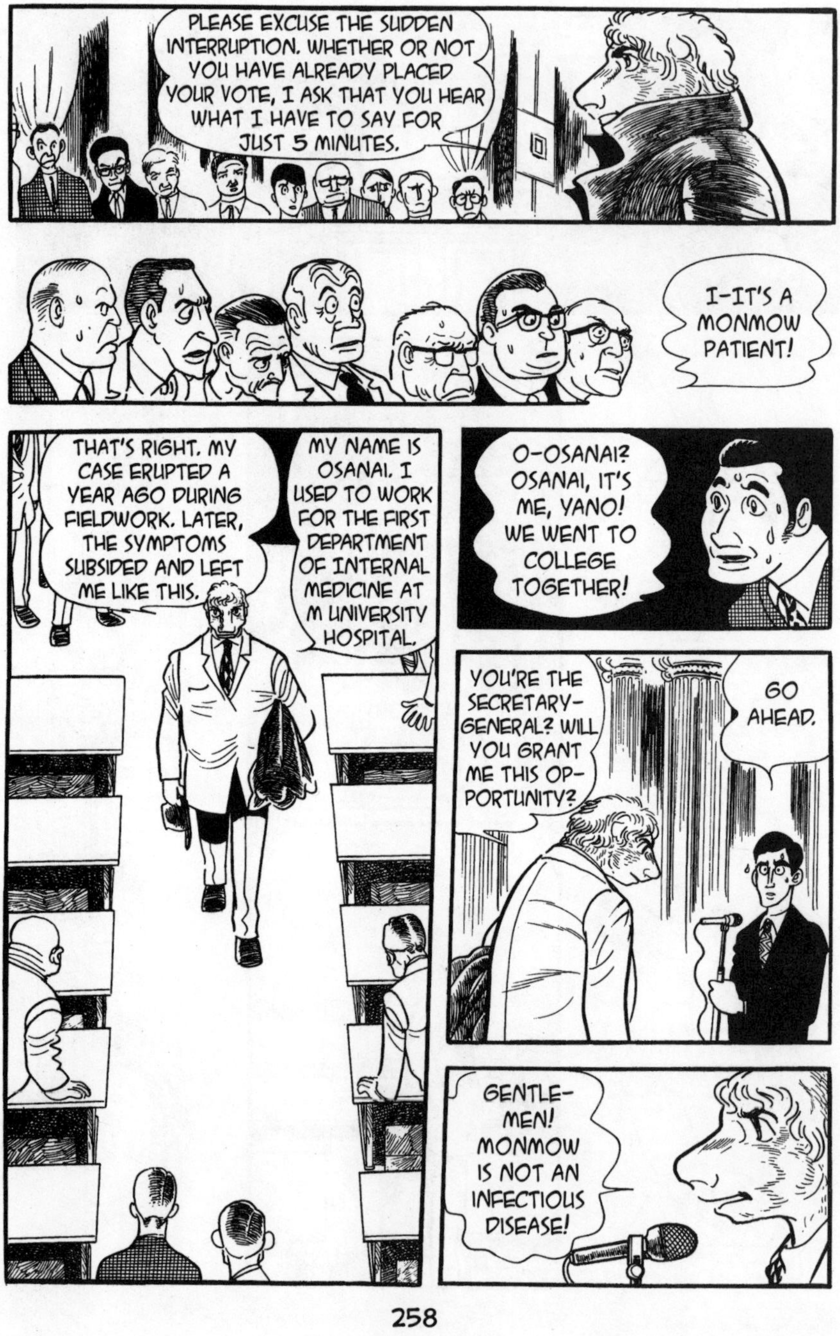
PLEASE EXCUSE THE SUDDEN INTERRUPTION. WHETHER OR NOT YOU HAVE ALREADY PLACED YOUR VOTE, I ASK THAT YOU HEAR WHAT I HAVE TO SAY FOR JUST 5 MINUTES.
I-IT'S A MONMOW PATIENT!
THAT'S RIGHT. MY CASE ERUPTED A YEAR AGO DURING FIELDWORK. LATER, THE SYMPTOMS SUBSIDED AND LEFT ME LIKE THIS.
MY NAME IS OSANAI. I USED TO WORK FOR THE FIRST DEPARTMENT OF INTERNAL MEDICINE AT M UNIVERSITY HOSPITAL.
O-OSANAI? OSANAI, IT'S ME, YANO! WE WENT TO COLLEGE TOGETHER!
YOU'RE THE SECRETARY-GENERAL? WILL YOU GRANT ME THIS OP-PORTUNITY?
GO AHEAD.
GENTLE-MEN! MONMOW IS NOT AN INFECTIOUS DISEASE!

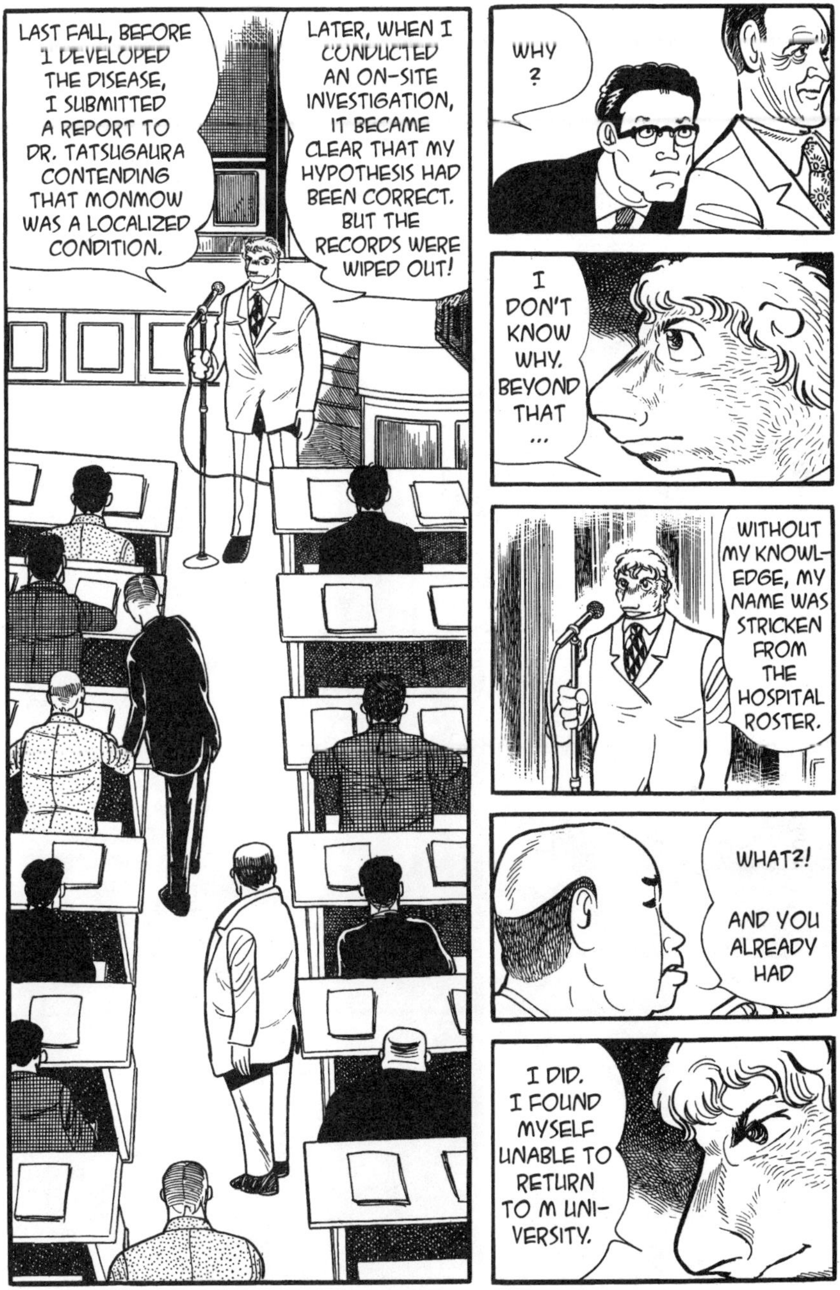
LAST FALL, BEFORE I DEVELOPED THE DISEASE, I SUBMITTED A REPORT TO DR. TATSUGAURA CONTENDING THAT MONMOW WAS A LOCALIZED CONDITION.
LATER, WHEN I CONDUCTED AN ON-SITE INVESTIGATION, IT BECAME CLEAR THAT MY HYPOTHESIS HAD BEEN CORRECT. BUT THE RECORDS WERE WIPED OUT!
WHY ?
I DON'T KNOW WHY. BEYOND THAT ...
WITHOUT MY KNOWL-EDGE, MY NAME WAS STRICKEN FROM THE HOSPITAL ROSTER.
WHAT?!
AND YOU ALREADY HAD
I DID. I FOUND MYSELF UNABLE TO RETURN TO M UNI-VERSITY.

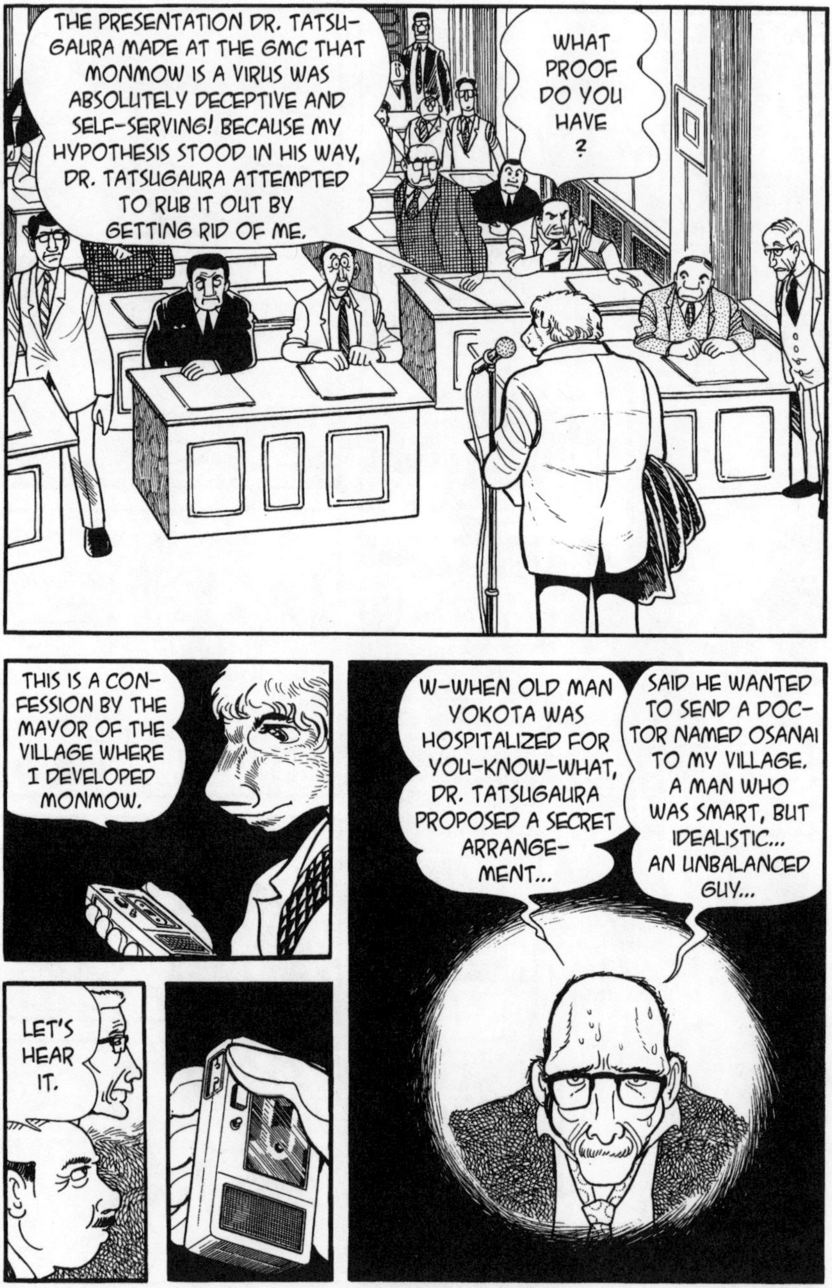
THE PRESENTATION DR. TATSUGAURA MADE AT THE GMC THAT MONMOW IS A VIRUS WAS ABSOLUTELY DECEPTIVE AND SELF-SERVING! BECAUSE MY HYPOTHESIS STOOD IN HIS WAY, DR. TATSUGAURA ATTEMPTED TO RUB IT OUT BY GETTING RID OF ME.
WHAT PROOF DO YOU HAVE?
THIS IS A CONFESSION BY THE MAYOR OF THE VILLAGE WHERE I DEVELOPED MONMOW.
LET'S HEAR IT.
W-WHEN OLD MAN YOKOTA WAS HOSPITALIZED FOR YOU-KNOW-WHAT, DR. TATSUGAURA PROPOSED A SECRET ARRANGEMENT...
SAID HE WANTED TO SEND A DOCTOR NAMED OSANAI TO MY VILLAGE. A MAN WHO WAS SMART, BUT IDEALISTIC... AN UNBALANCED GUY...

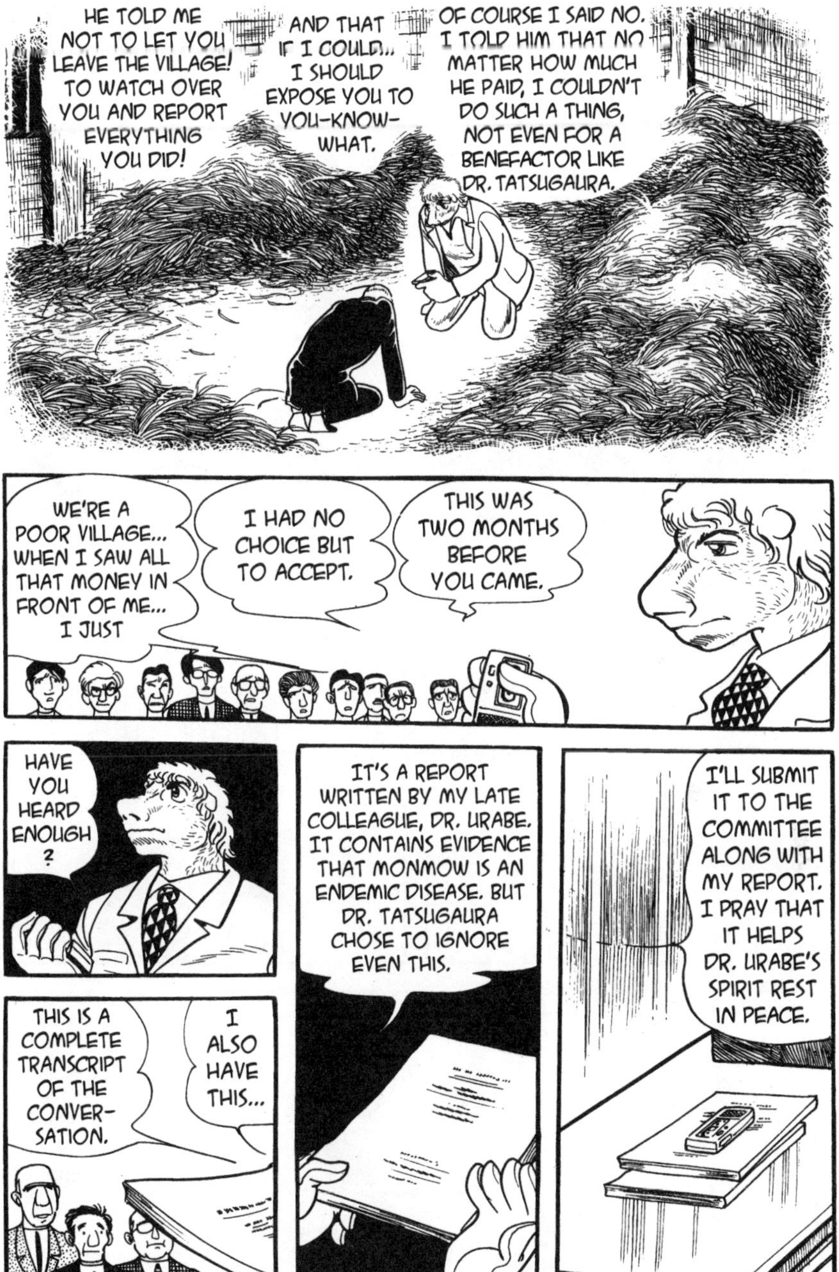
HE TOLD ME NOT TO LET YOU LEAVE THE VILLAGE! TO WATCH OVER YOU AND REPORT EVERYTHING YOU DID!
AND THAT IF I COULD... I SHOULD EXPOSE YOU TO YOU-KNOW-WHAT.
OF COURSE I SAID NO. I TOLD HIM THAT NO MATTER HOW MUCH HE PAID, I COULDN'T DO SUCH A THING, NOT EVEN FOR A BENEFACTOR LIKE DR. TATSUGAURA.
WE'RE A POOR VILLAGE... WHEN I SAW ALL THAT MONEY IN FRONT OF ME... I JUST
I HAD NO CHOICE BUT TO ACCEPT.
THIS WAS TWO MONTHS BEFORE YOU CAME.
HAVE YOU HEARD ENOUGH?
THIS IS A COMPLETE TRANSCRIPT OF THE CONVERSATION.
I ALSO HAVE THIS...
IT'S A REPORT WRITTEN BY MY LATE COLLEAGUE, DR. URABE. IT CONTAINS EVIDENCE THAT MONMOW IS AN ENDEMIC DISEASE. BUT DR. TATSUGAURA CHOSE TO IGNORE EVEN THIS.
I'LL SUBMIT IT TO THE COMMITTEE ALONG WITH MY REPORT. I PRAY THAT IT HELPS DR. URABE'S SPIRIT REST IN PEACE.

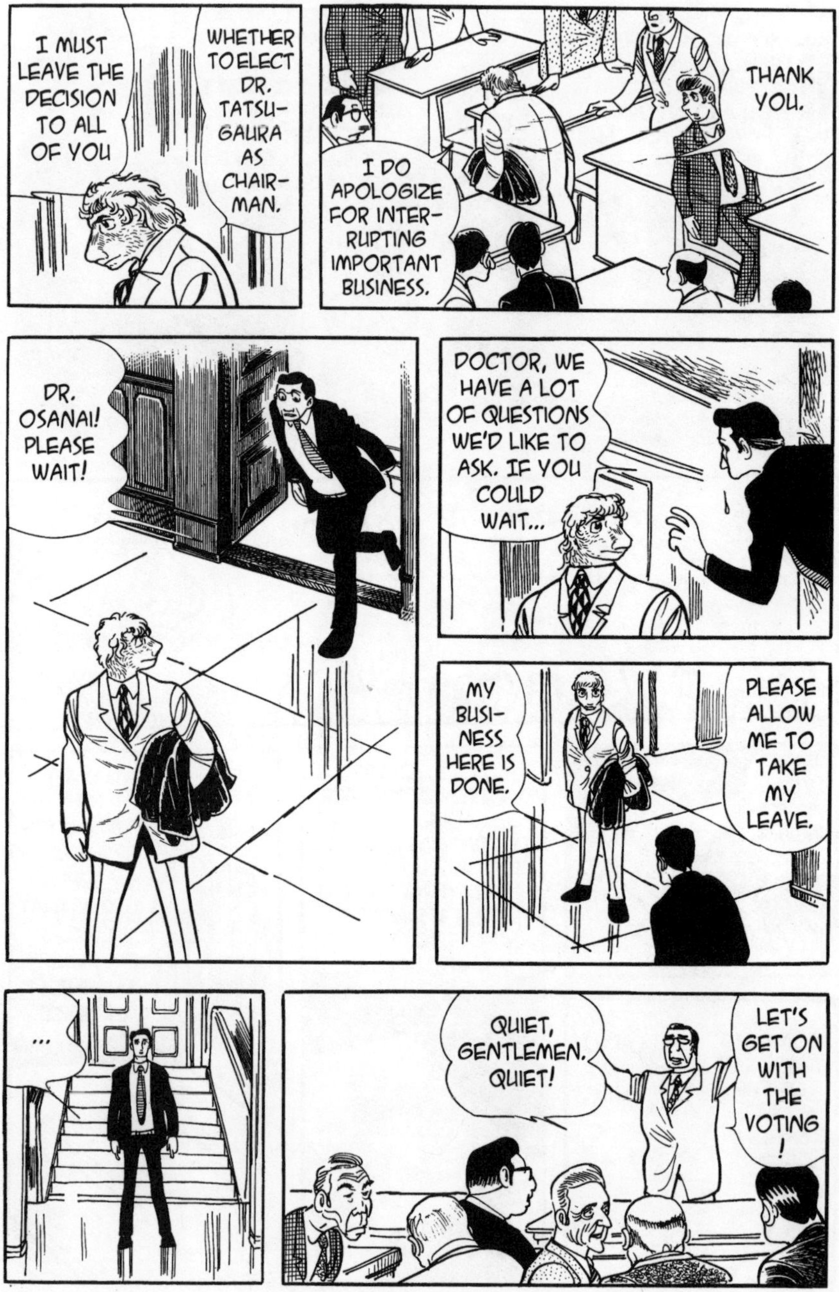
I MUST LEAVE THE DECISION TO ALL OF YOU
WHETHER TO ELECT DR. TATSUGAURA AS CHAIRMAN.
THANK YOU.
I DO APOLOGIZE FOR INTERRUPTING IMPORTANT BUSINESS.
DR. OSANAI! PLEASE WAIT!
DOCTOR, WE HAVE A LOT OF QUESTIONS WE'D LIKE TO ASK. IF YOU COULD WAIT...
MY BUSINESS HERE IS DONE.
PLEASE ALLOW ME TO TAKE MY LEAVE.
...
QUIET, GENTLEMEN. QUIET!
LET'S GET ON WITH THE VOTING!

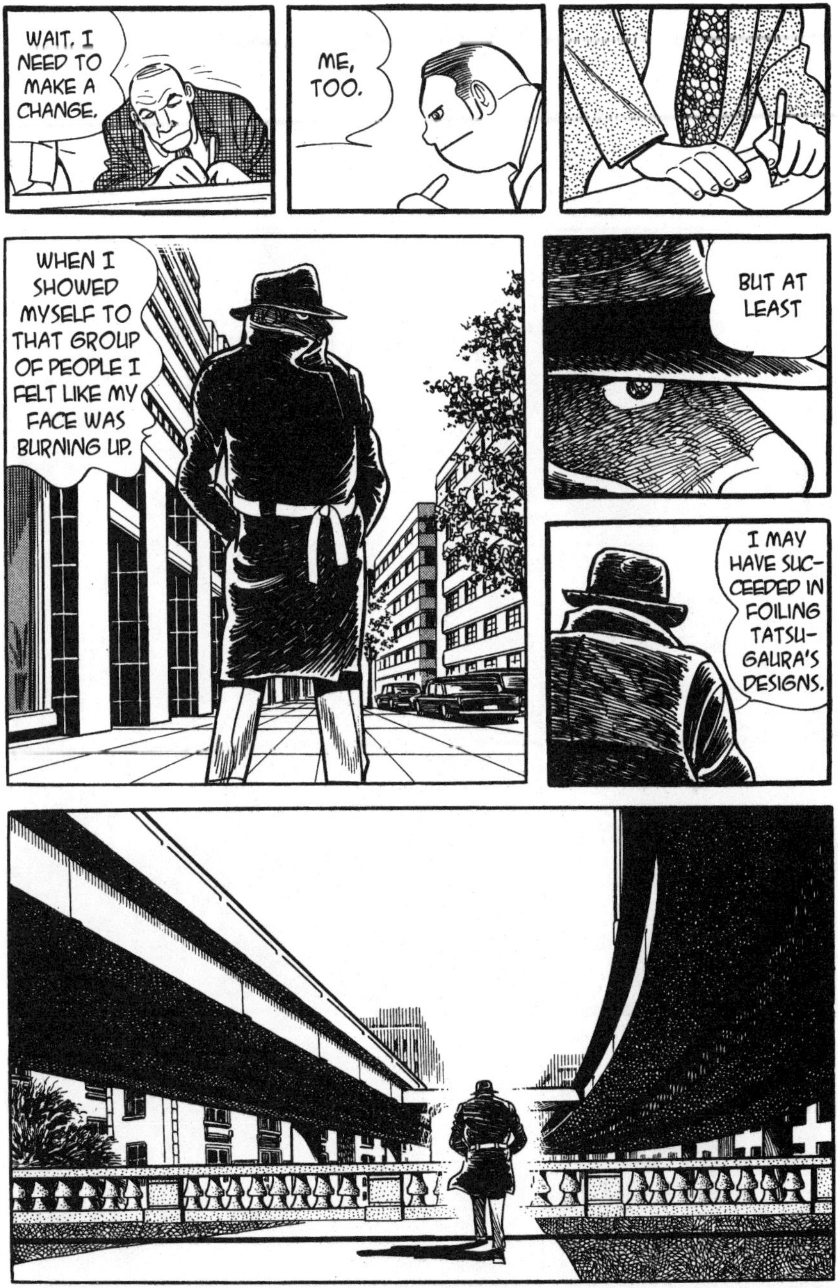
WAIT. I NEED TO MAKE A CHANGE.
ME, TOO.
WHEN I SHOWED MYSELF TO THAT GROUP OF PEOPLE I FELT LIKE MY FACE WAS BURNING UP.
BUT AT LEAST
I MAY HAVE SUC-CEEDED IN FOILING TATSU-GAURA'S DESIGNS.

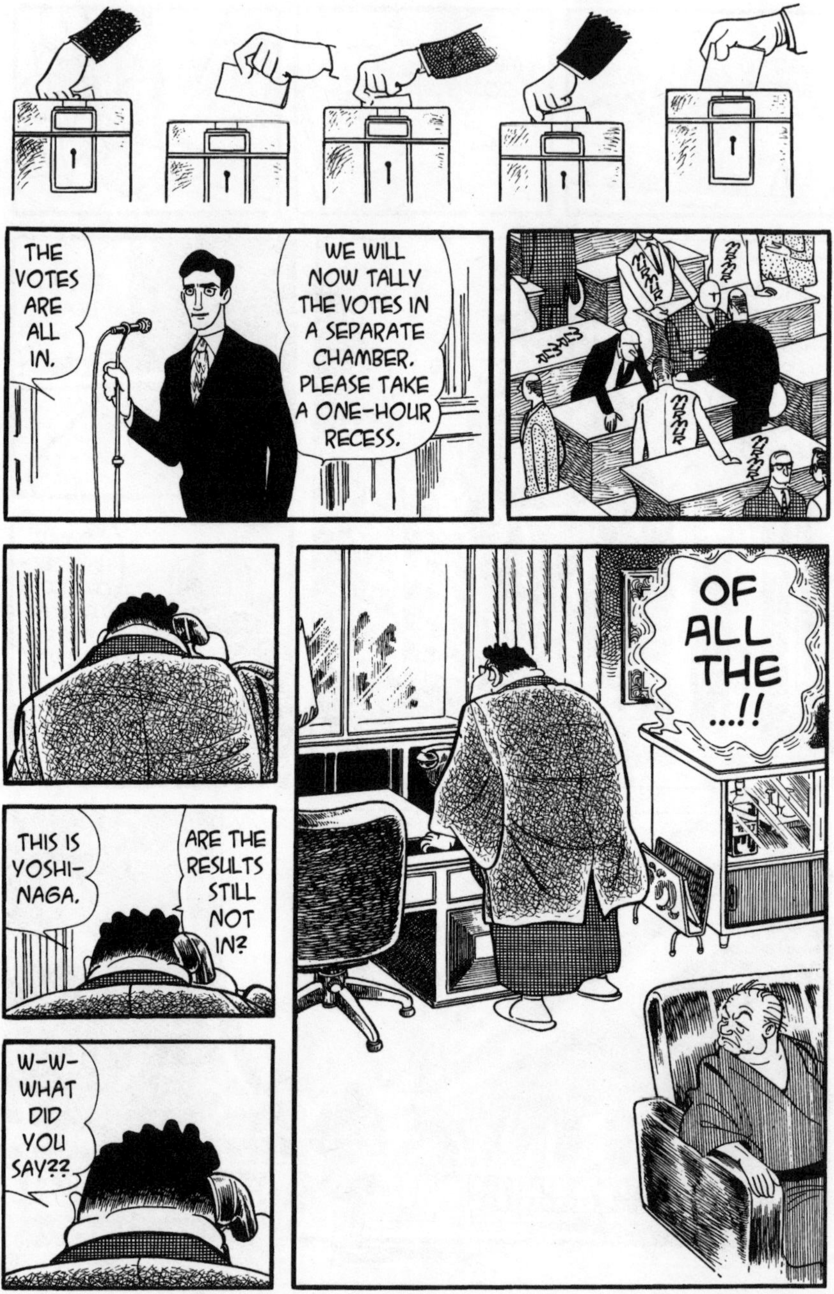
THE VOTES ARE ALL IN.
WE WILL NOW TALLY THE VOTES IN A SEPARATE CHAMBER. PLEASE TAKE A ONE-HOUR RECESS.
THIS IS YOSHI-NAGA.
ARE THE RESULTS STILL NOT IN?
W-W-WHAT DID YOU SAY??
OF ALL THE ....!!

WHAT'S WRONG?
...
DR. OSANAI ...
DR. OSANAI??
DR. OSANAI... WHAT?!
WHERE IS HE?
HE SHOWED UP AT THE JMA...
JM ...
SAY THAT AGAIN?
DR. OSANAI APPEARED AT THE JMA JUST NOW AND INTERRUPTED THE VOTING.
HE TOLD THEM WHAT HAPPENED IN DOG-GOD-DALE...
IS THAT TRUE?!

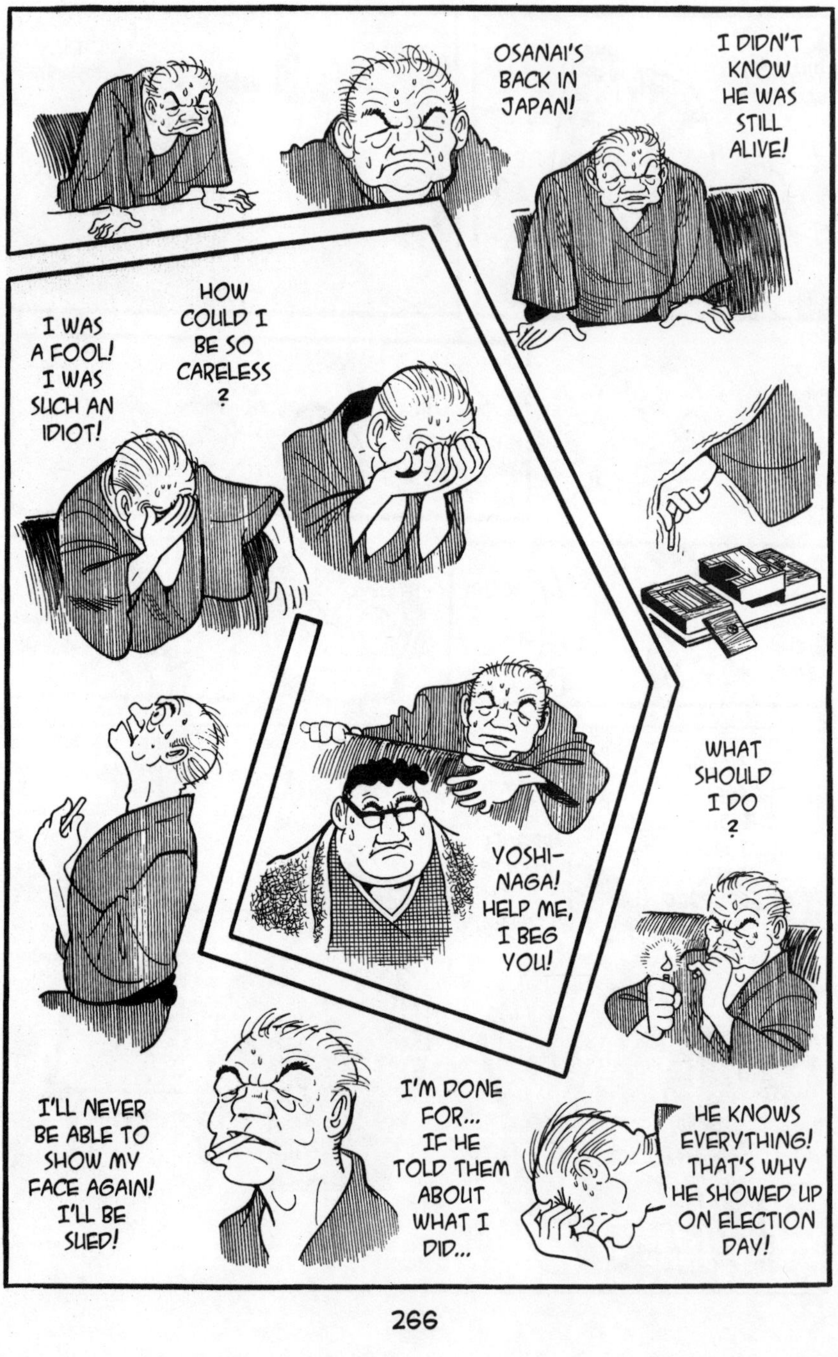
I DIDN'T KNOW HE WAS STILL ALIVE!
OSANAI'S BACK IN JAPAN!
HOW COULD I BE SO CARELESS?
I WAS A FOOL! I WAS SUCH AN IDIOT!
WHAT SHOULD I DO?
YOSHI-NAGA! HELP ME, I BEG YOU!
HE KNOWS EVERYTHING! THAT'S WHY HE SHOWED UP ON ELECTION DAY!
I'M DONE FOR... IF HE TOLD THEM ABOUT WHAT I DID...
I'LL NEVER BE ABLE TO SHOW MY FACE AGAIN! I'LL BE SUED!

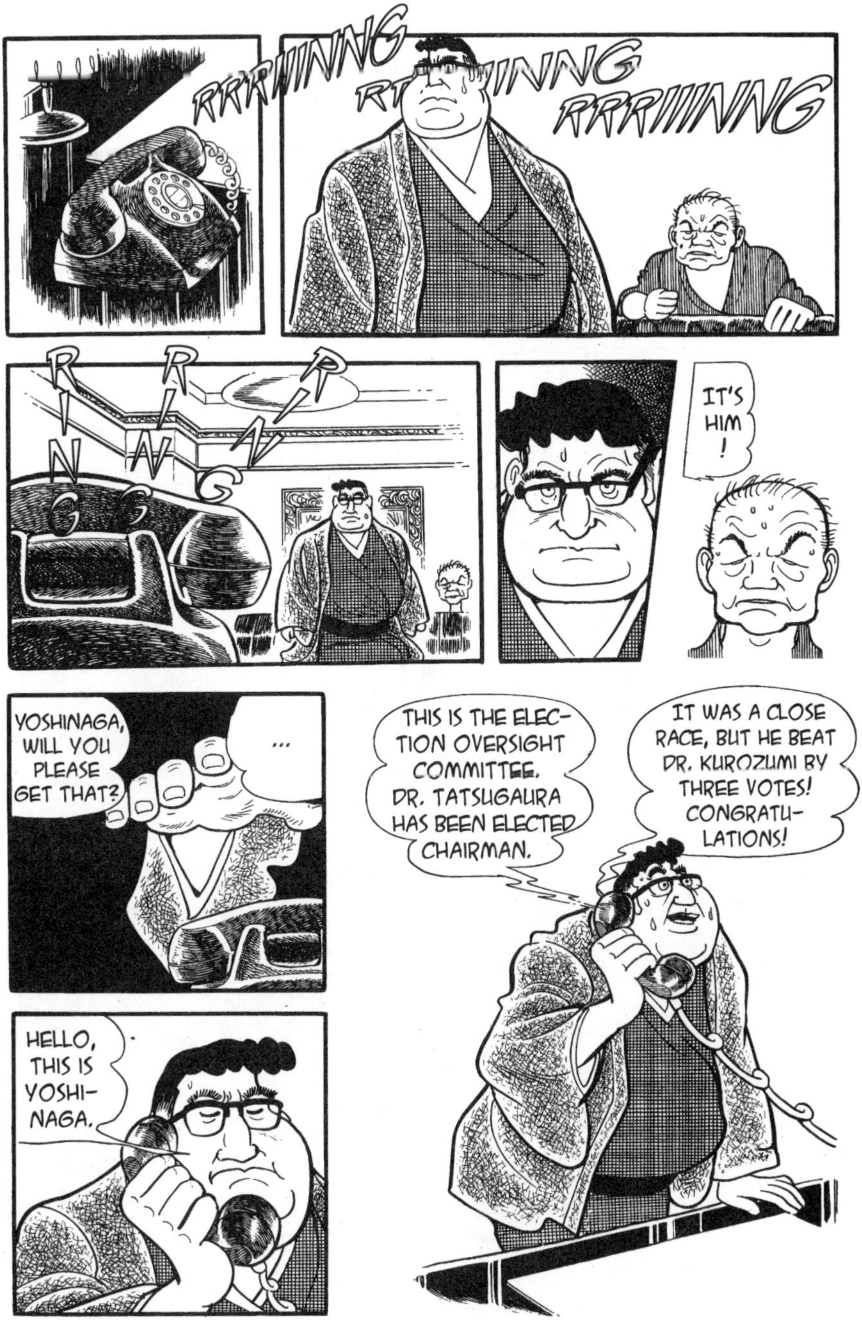

RRRIIINNG
RRRIIINNG
RING
RING
RING
IT'S HIM!
YOSHINAGA, WILL YOU PLEASE GET THAT?
...
HELLO, THIS IS YOSHINAGA.
THIS IS THE ELECTION OVERSIGHT COMMITTEE. DR. TATSUGAURA HAS BEEN ELECTED CHAIRMAN.
IT WAS A CLOSE RACE, BUT HE BEAT DR. KUROZUMI BY THREE VOTES! CONGRATULATIONS!

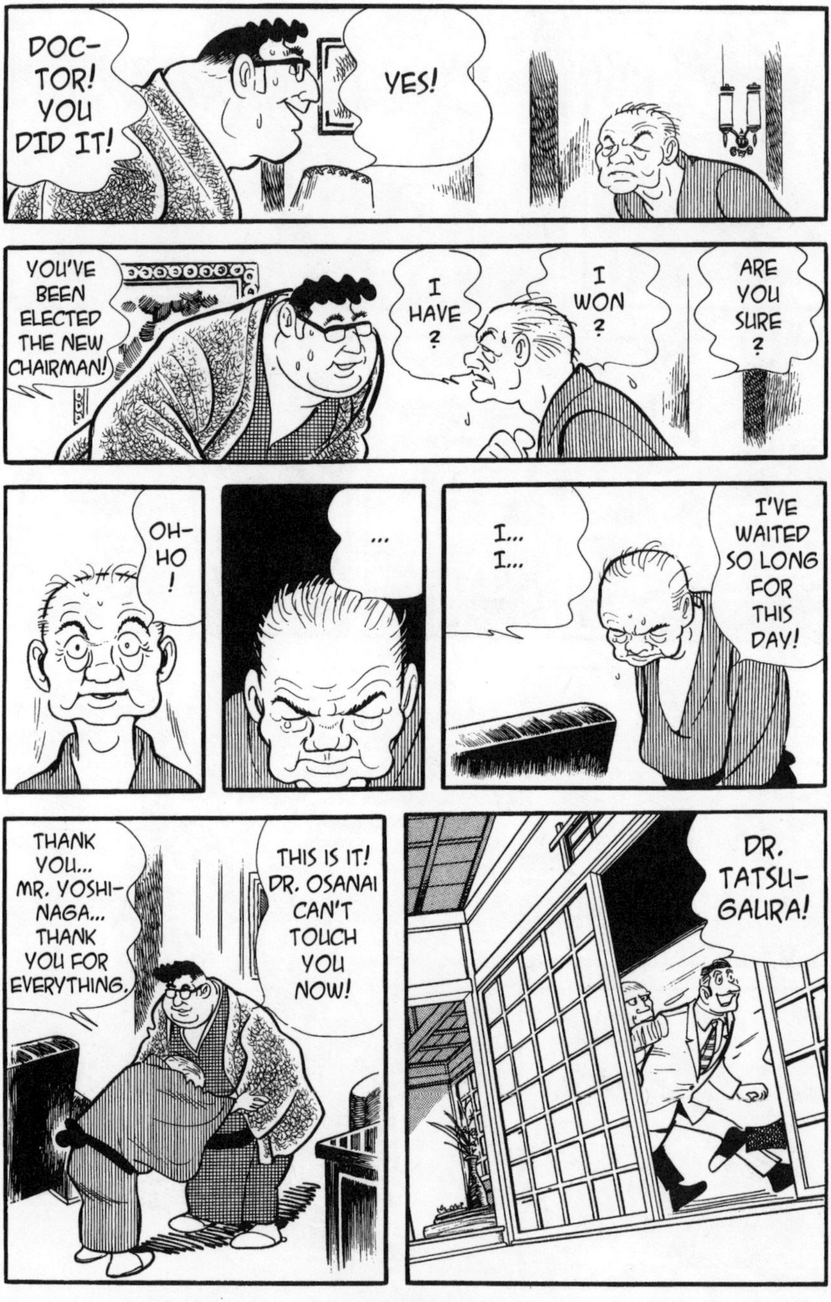
DOC-TOR! YOU DID IT!
YES!
YOU'VE BEEN ELECTED THE NEW CHAIRMAN!
I HAVE?
I WON?
ARE YOU SURE?
OH-HO!
...
I... I...
I'VE WAITED SO LONG FOR THIS DAY!
THANK YOU... MR. YOSHI-NAGA... THANK YOU FOR EVERYTHING.
THIS IS IT! DR. OSANAI CAN'T TOUCH YOU NOW!
DR. TATSU-GAURA!

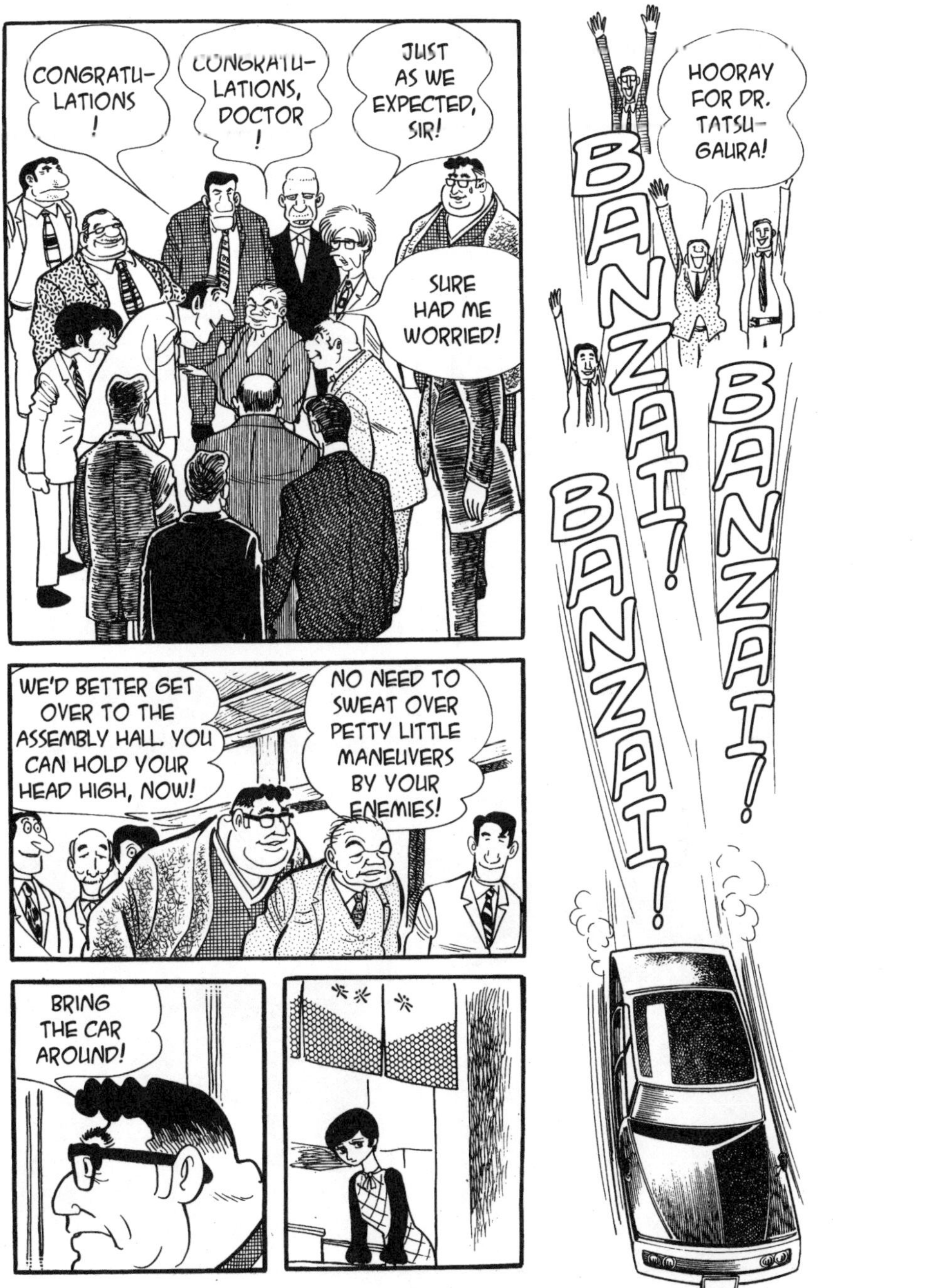
CONGRATULATIONS!
CONGRATULATIONS, DOCTOR!
JUST AS WE EXPECTED, SIR!
SURE HAD ME WORRIED!
WE'D BETTER GET OVER TO THE ASSEMBLY HALL. YOU CAN HOLD YOUR HEAD HIGH, NOW!
NO NEED TO SWEAT OVER PETTY LITTLE MANEUVERS BY YOUR ENEMIES!
BRING THE CAR AROUND!
HOORAY FOR DR. TATSUGAURA!
BANZAI!
BANZAI!
BANZAI!

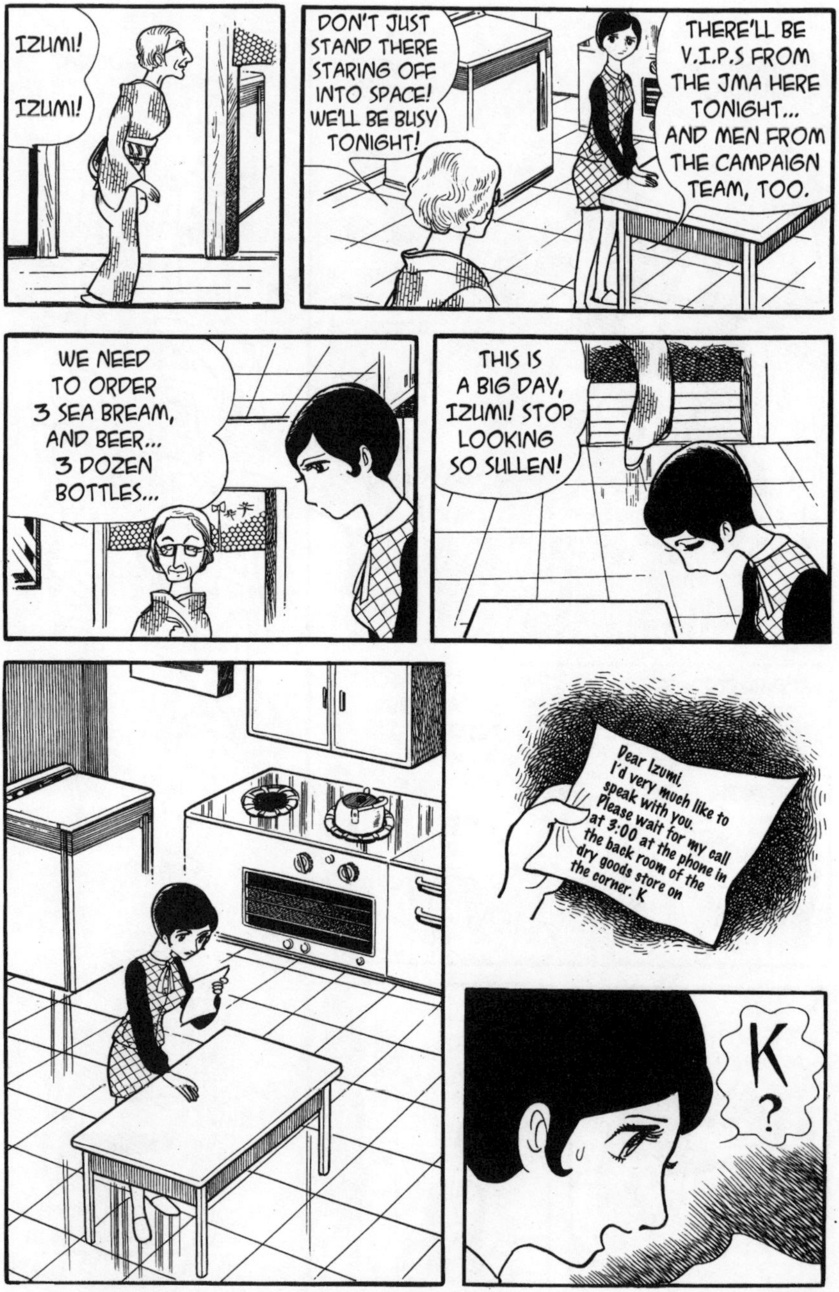
IZUMI!
IZUMI!
DON'T JUST STAND THERE STARING OFF INTO SPACE! WE'LL BE BUSY TONIGHT!
THERE'LL BE V.I.P.S FROM THE JMA HERE TONIGHT... AND MEN FROM THE CAMPAIGN TEAM, TOO.
WE NEED TO ORDER 3 SEA BREAM, AND BEER... 3 DOZEN BOTTLES...
THIS IS A BIG DAY, IZUMI! STOP LOOKING SO SULLEN!
Dear Izumi, I'd very much like to speak with you. Please wait for my call at 3:00 at the phone in the back room of the dry goods store on the corner. K
K ?

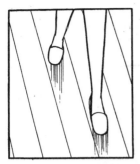

EXCUSE ME... I'M HERE ABOUT A PHONE CALL...

AH, YES! MISS YOSHINAGA! I UNDERSTAND. PLEASE, COME IN.

RRRING!

KCHAK

HELLO ...

OH!! KIRI- HITO!!

271

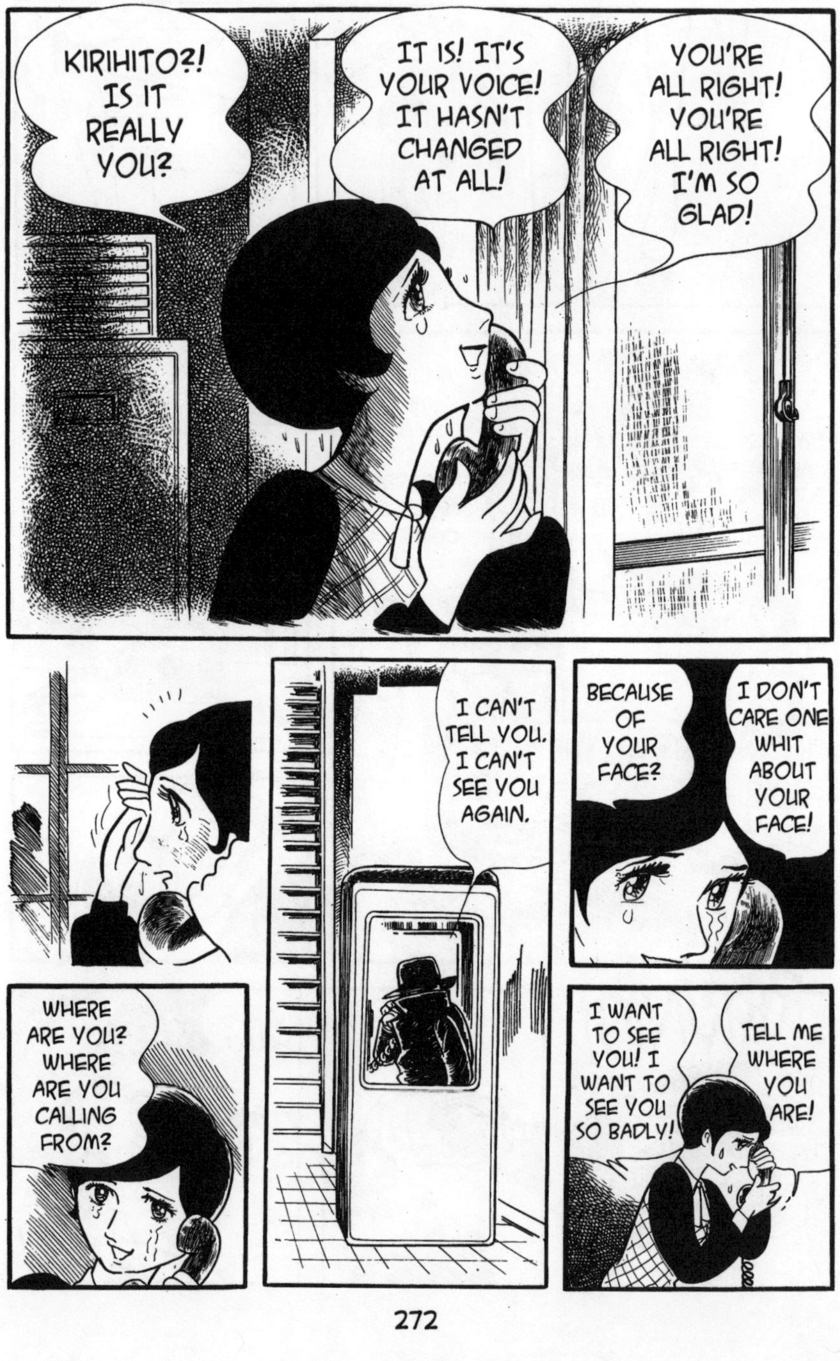
KIRIHITO?! IS IT REALLY YOU?
IT IS! IT'S YOUR VOICE! IT HASN'T CHANGED AT ALL!
YOU'RE ALL RIGHT! YOU'RE ALL RIGHT! I'M SO GLAD!
I CAN'T TELL YOU. I CAN'T SEE YOU AGAIN.
BECAUSE OF YOUR FACE?
I DON'T CARE ONE WHIT ABOUT YOUR FACE!
WHERE ARE YOU? WHERE ARE YOU CALLING FROM?
I WANT TO SEE YOU! I WANT TO SEE YOU SO BADLY!
TELL ME WHERE YOU ARE!

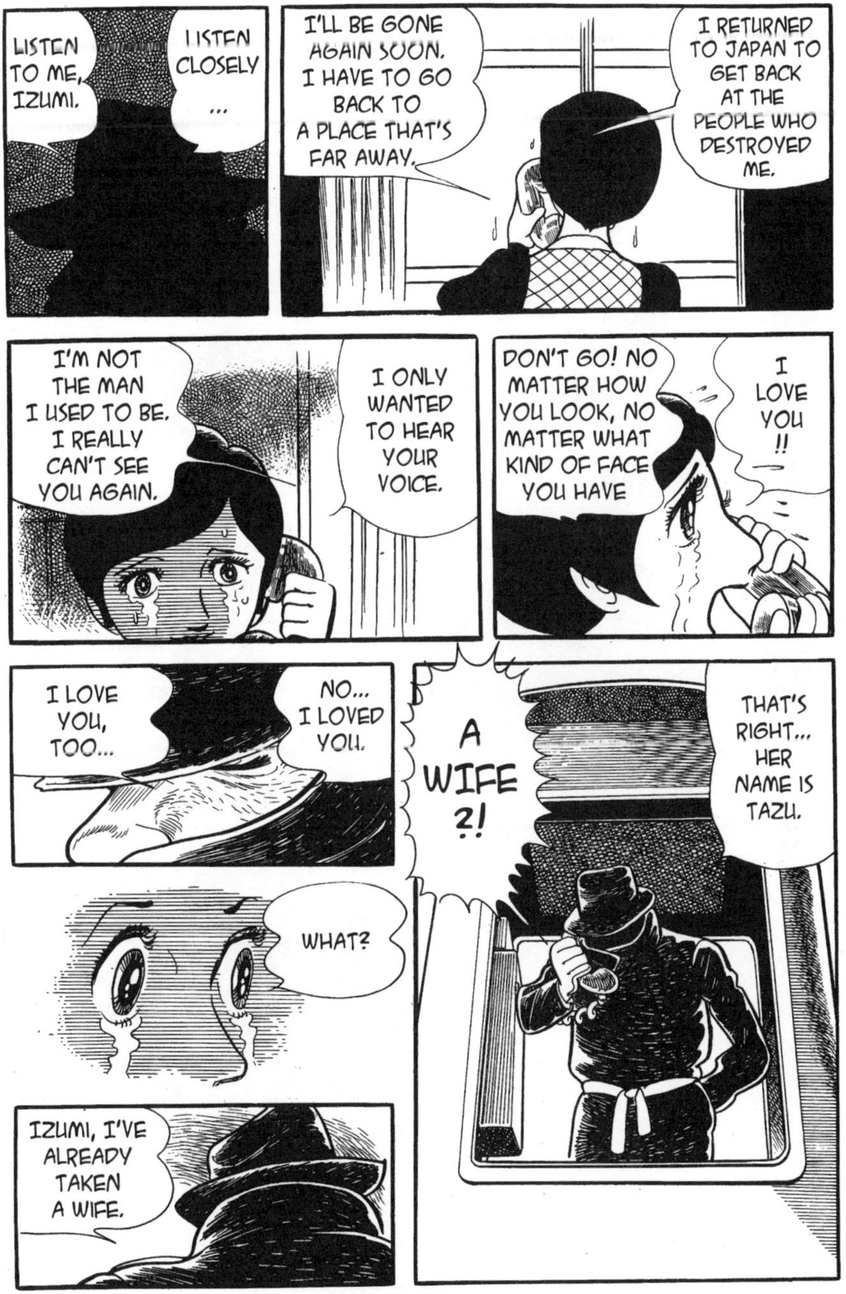
LISTEN TO ME, IZUMI.
LISTEN CLOSELY ...
I'LL BE GONE AGAIN SOON. I HAVE TO GO BACK TO A PLACE THAT'S FAR AWAY.
I RETURNED TO JAPAN TO GET BACK AT THE PEOPLE WHO DESTROYED ME.
I'M NOT THE MAN I USED TO BE. I REALLY CAN'T SEE YOU AGAIN.
I ONLY WANTED TO HEAR YOUR VOICE.
DON'T GO! NO MATTER HOW YOU LOOK, NO MATTER WHAT KIND OF FACE YOU HAVE
I LOVE YOU !!
I LOVE YOU, TOO...
NO... I LOVED YOU.
WHAT?
IZUMI, I'VE ALREADY TAKEN A WIFE.
A WIFE ?!
THAT'S RIGHT... HER NAME IS TAZU.

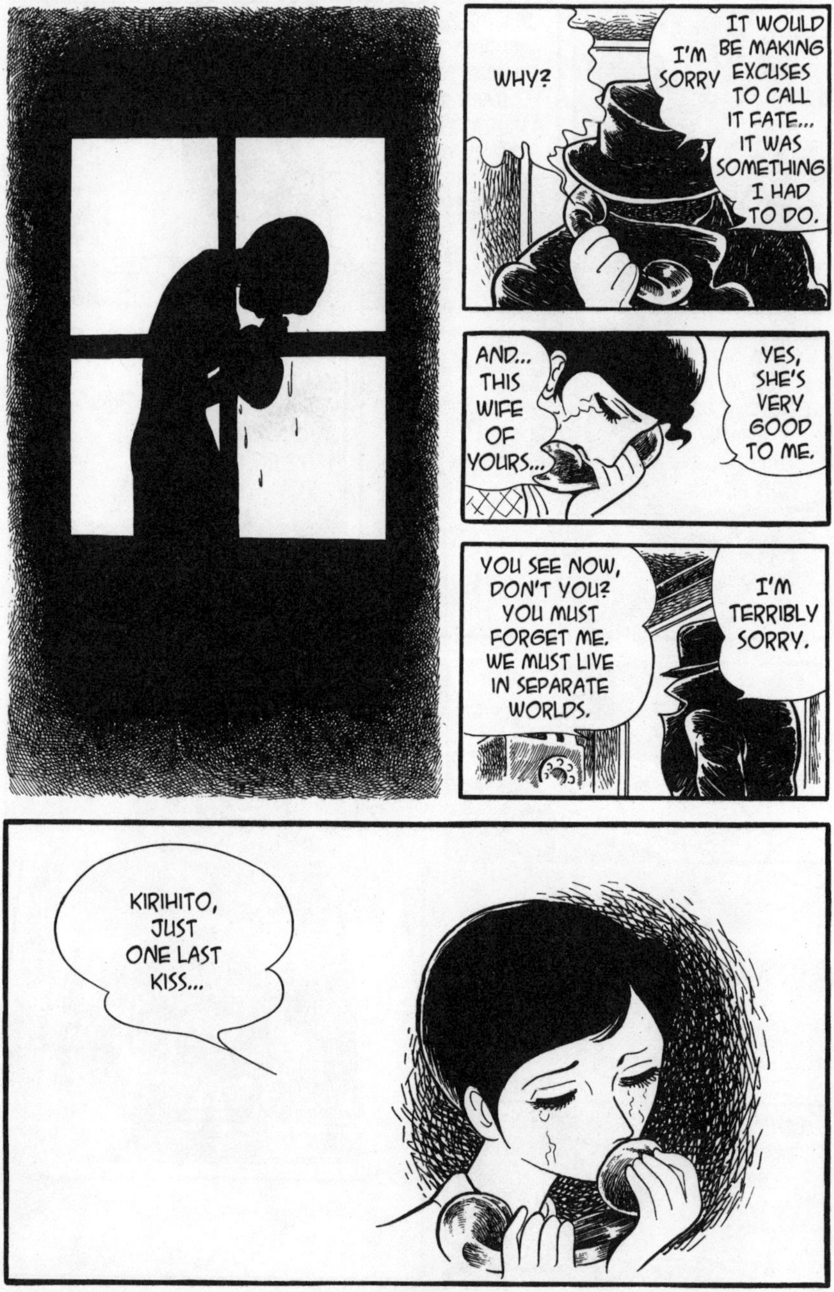
WHY?
I'M SORRY
IT WOULD BE MAKING EXCUSES TO CALL IT FATE... IT WAS SOMETHING I HAD TO DO.
AND... THIS WIFE OF YOURS...
YES, SHE'S VERY GOOD TO ME.
YOU SEE NOW, DON'T YOU? YOU MUST FORGET ME. WE MUST LIVE IN SEPARATE WORLDS.
I'M TERRIBLY SORRY.
KIRIHITO, JUST ONE LAST KISS...

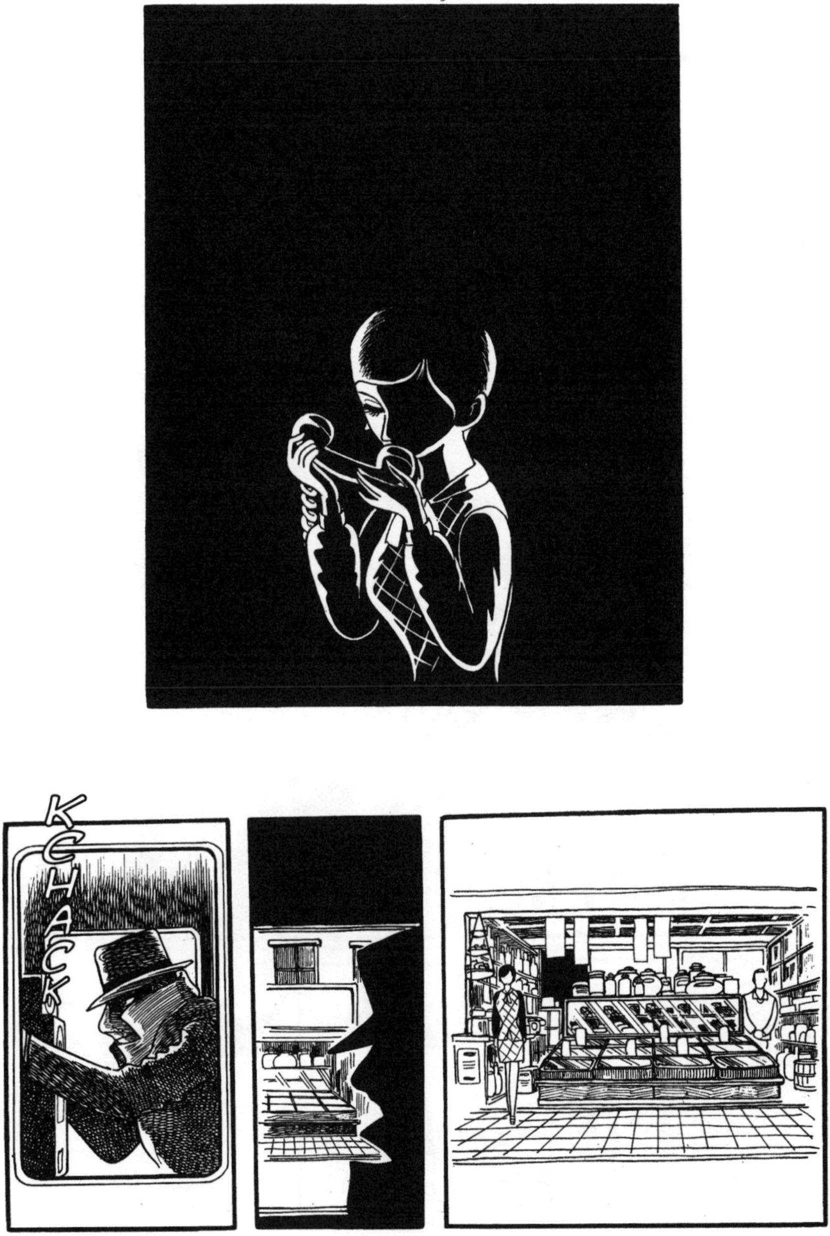
KCHACK

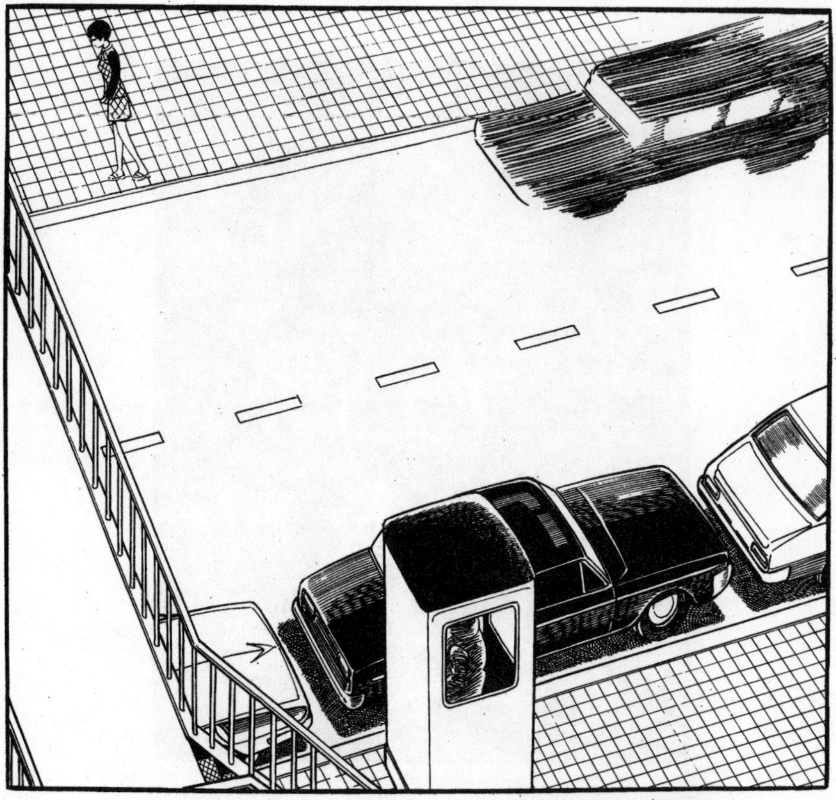

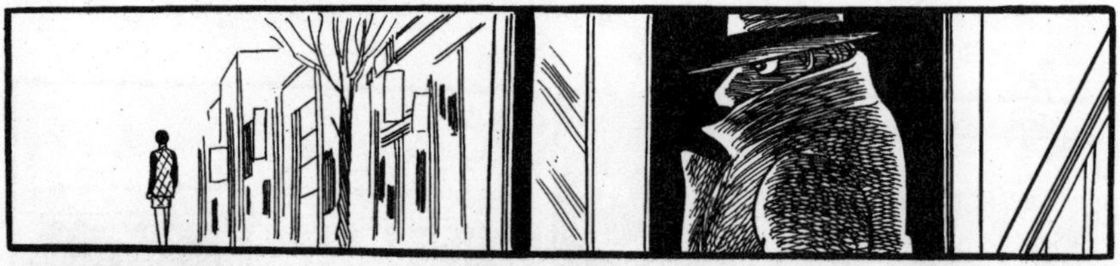

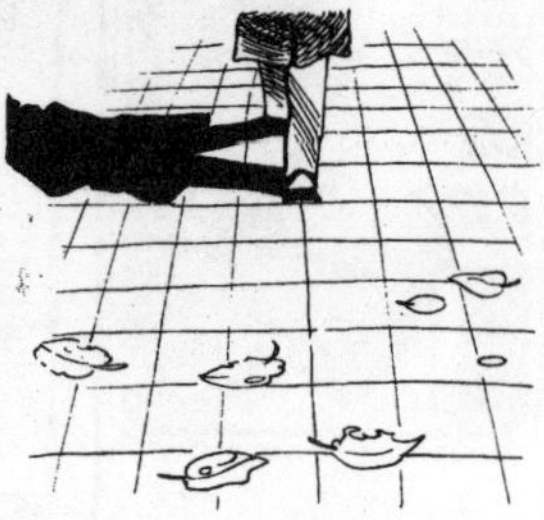

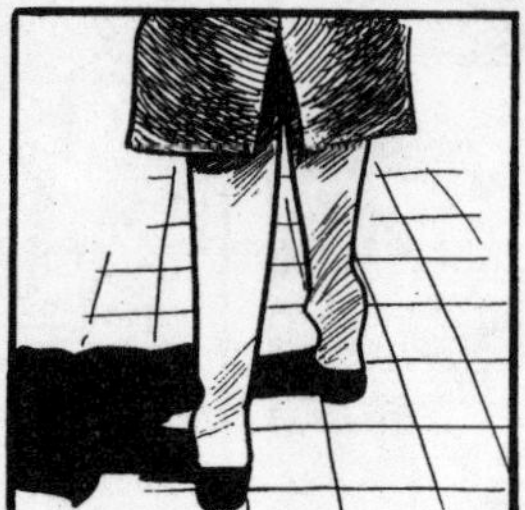

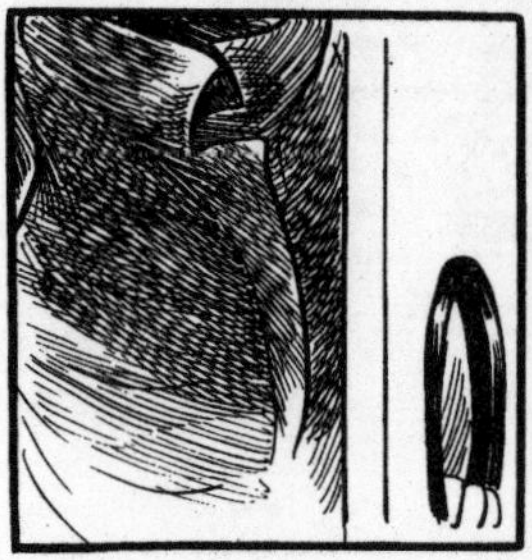

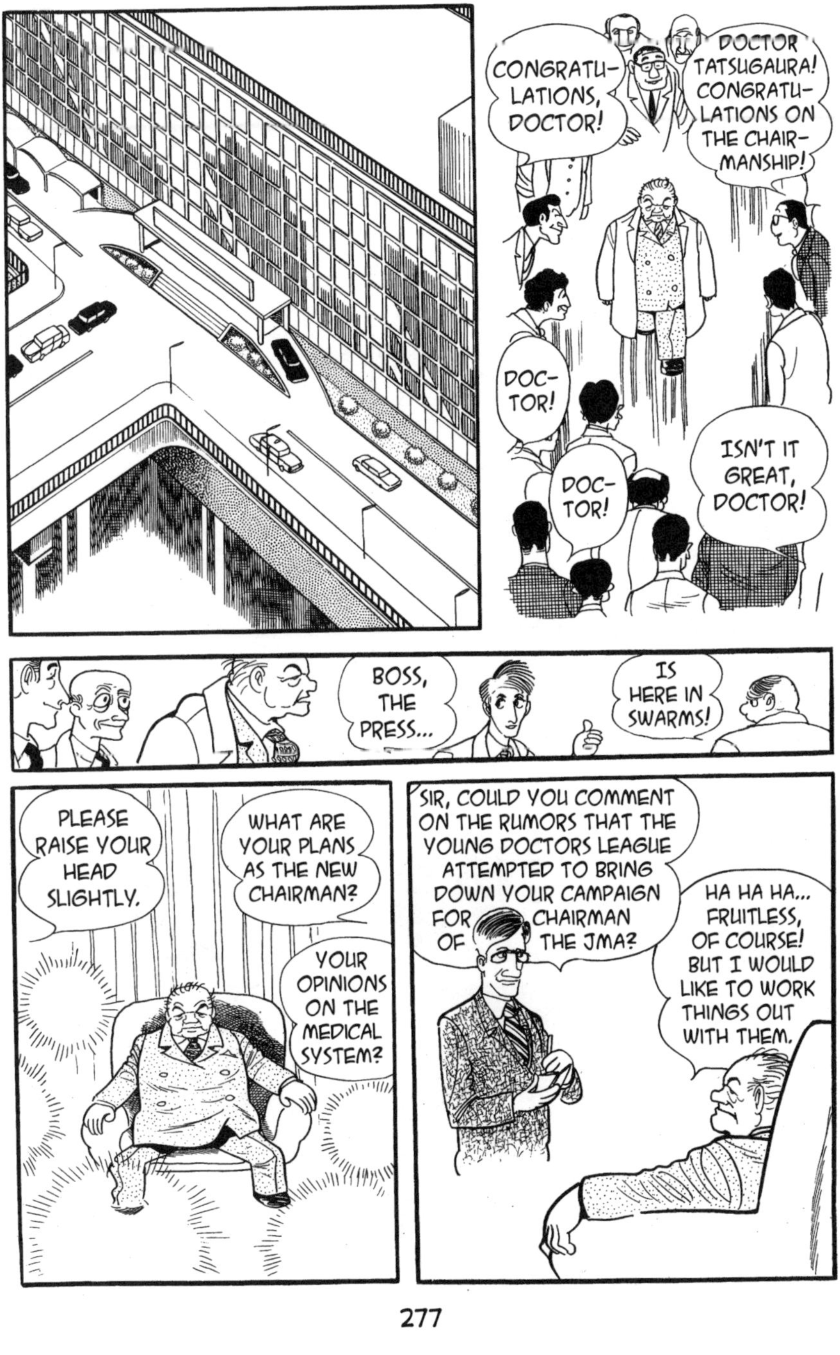
CONGRATULATIONS, DOCTOR!
DOCTOR TATSUGAURA! CONGRATULATIONS ON THE CHAIRMANSHIP!
DOC-TOR!
DOC-TOR!
ISN'T IT GREAT, DOCTOR!
BOSS, THE PRESS...
IS HERE IN SWARMS!
PLEASE RAISE YOUR HEAD SLIGHTLY.
WHAT ARE YOUR PLANS AS THE NEW CHAIRMAN?
YOUR OPINIONS ON THE MEDICAL SYSTEM?
SIR, COULD YOU COMMENT ON THE RUMORS THAT THE YOUNG DOCTORS LEAGUE ATTEMPTED TO BRING DOWN YOUR CAMPAIGN FOR CHAIRMAN OF THE JMA?
HA HA HA... FRUITLESS, OF COURSE! BUT I WOULD LIKE TO WORK THINGS OUT WITH THEM.

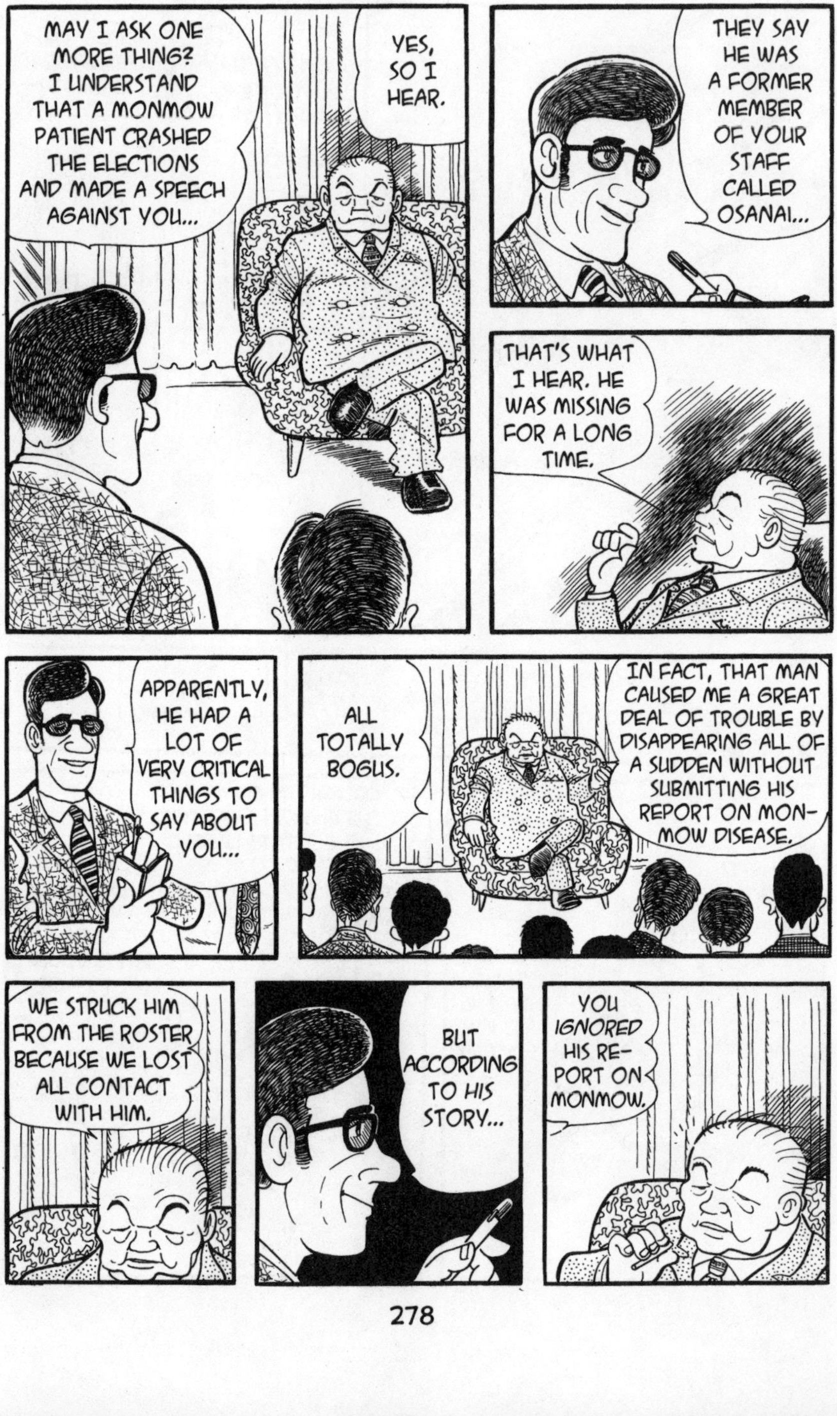
MAY I ASK ONE MORE THING? I UNDERSTAND THAT A MONMOW PATIENT CRASHED THE ELECTIONS AND MADE A SPEECH AGAINST YOU...
YES, SO I HEAR.
THEY SAY HE WAS A FORMER MEMBER OF YOUR STAFF CALLED OSANAI...
THAT'S WHAT I HEAR. HE WAS MISSING FOR A LONG TIME.
APPARENTLY, HE HAD A LOT OF VERY CRITICAL THINGS TO SAY ABOUT YOU...
ALL TOTALLY BOGUS.
IN FACT, THAT MAN CAUSED ME A GREAT DEAL OF TROUBLE BY DISAPPEARING ALL OF A SUDDEN WITHOUT SUBMITTING HIS REPORT ON MON-MOW DISEASE.
WE STRUCK HIM FROM THE ROSTER BECAUSE WE LOST ALL CONTACT WITH HIM.
BUT ACCORDING TO HIS STORY...
YOU IGNORED HIS RE-PORT ON MONMOW.

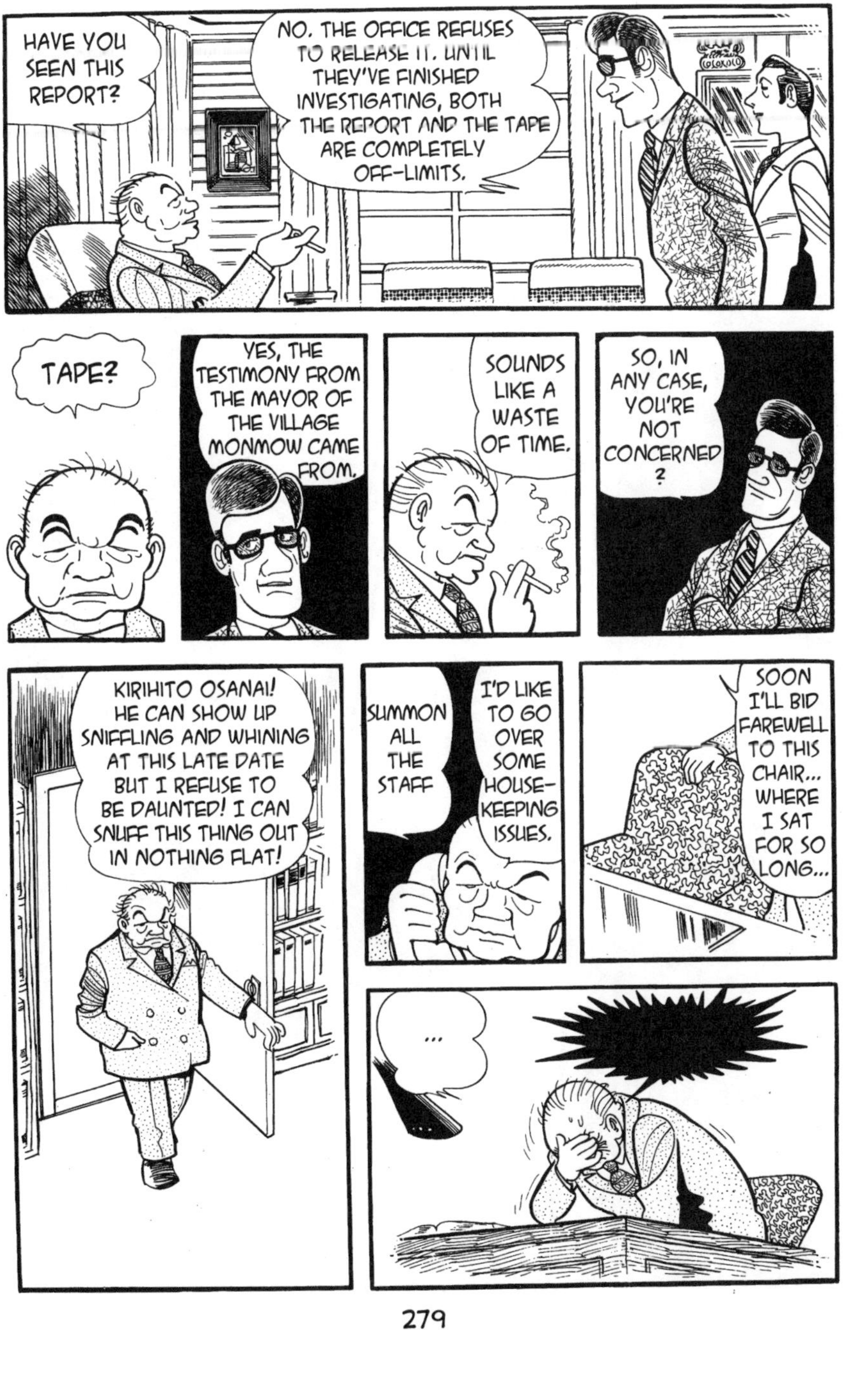
HAVE YOU SEEN THIS REPORT?
NO. THE OFFICE REFUSES TO RELEASE IT. UNTIL THEY'VE FINISHED INVESTIGATING, BOTH THE REPORT AND THE TAPE ARE COMPLETELY OFF-LIMITS.
TAPE?
YES, THE TESTIMONY FROM THE MAYOR OF THE VILLAGE MONMOW CAME FROM.
SOUNDS LIKE A WASTE OF TIME.
SO, IN ANY CASE, YOU'RE NOT CONCERNED?
KIRIHITO OSANAI! HE CAN SHOW UP SNIFFLING AND WHINING AT THIS LATE DATE BUT I REFUSE TO BE DAUNTED! I CAN SNUFF THIS THING OUT IN NOTHING FLAT!
SUMMON ALL THE STAFF
I'D LIKE TO GO OVER SOME HOUSE-KEEPING ISSUES.
SOON I'LL BID FAREWELL TO THIS CHAIR... WHERE I SAT FOR SO LONG...
...

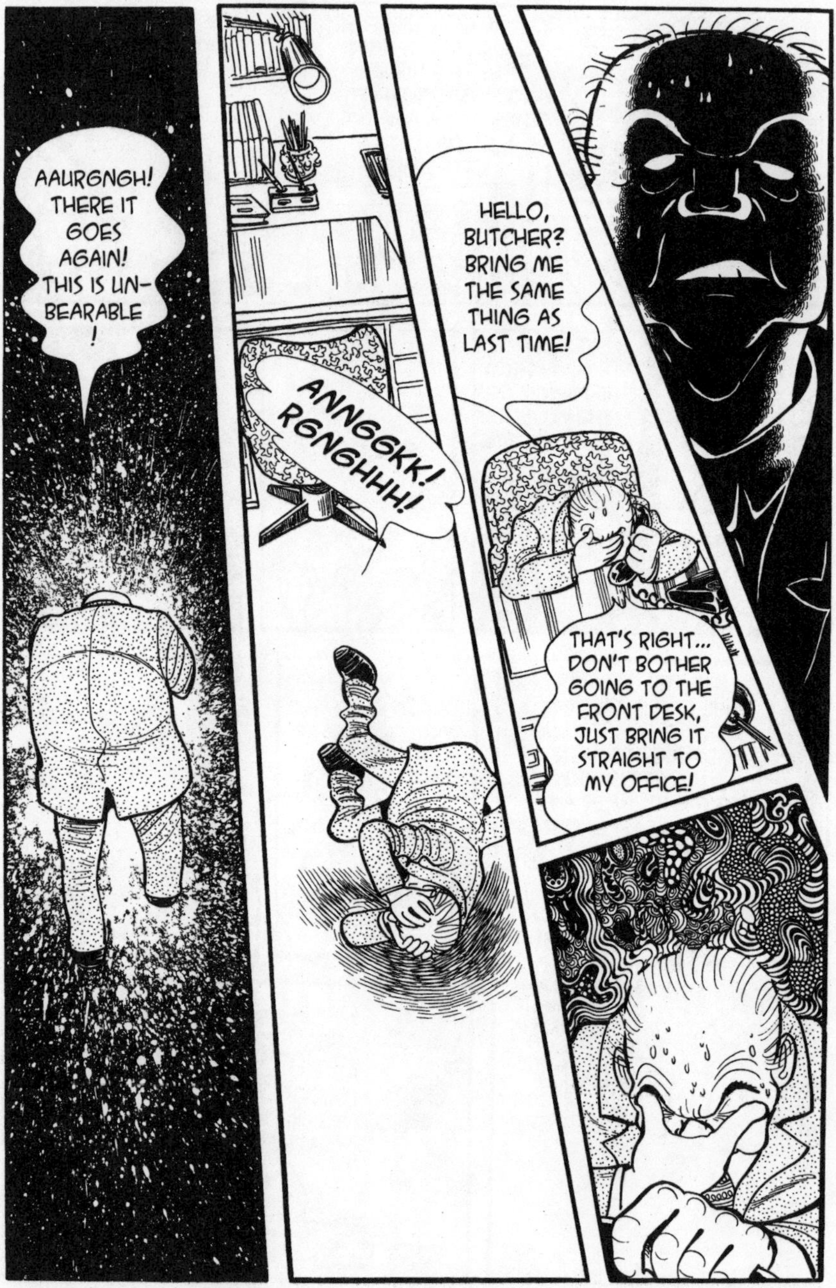
AAURGNGH! THERE IT GOES AGAIN! THIS IS UN-BEARABLE!
ANNGGKK! RGNGHHH!
HELLO, BUTCHER? BRING ME THE SAME THING AS LAST TIME!
THAT'S RIGHT... DON'T BOTHER GOING TO THE FRONT DESK, JUST BRING IT STRAIGHT TO MY OFFICE!

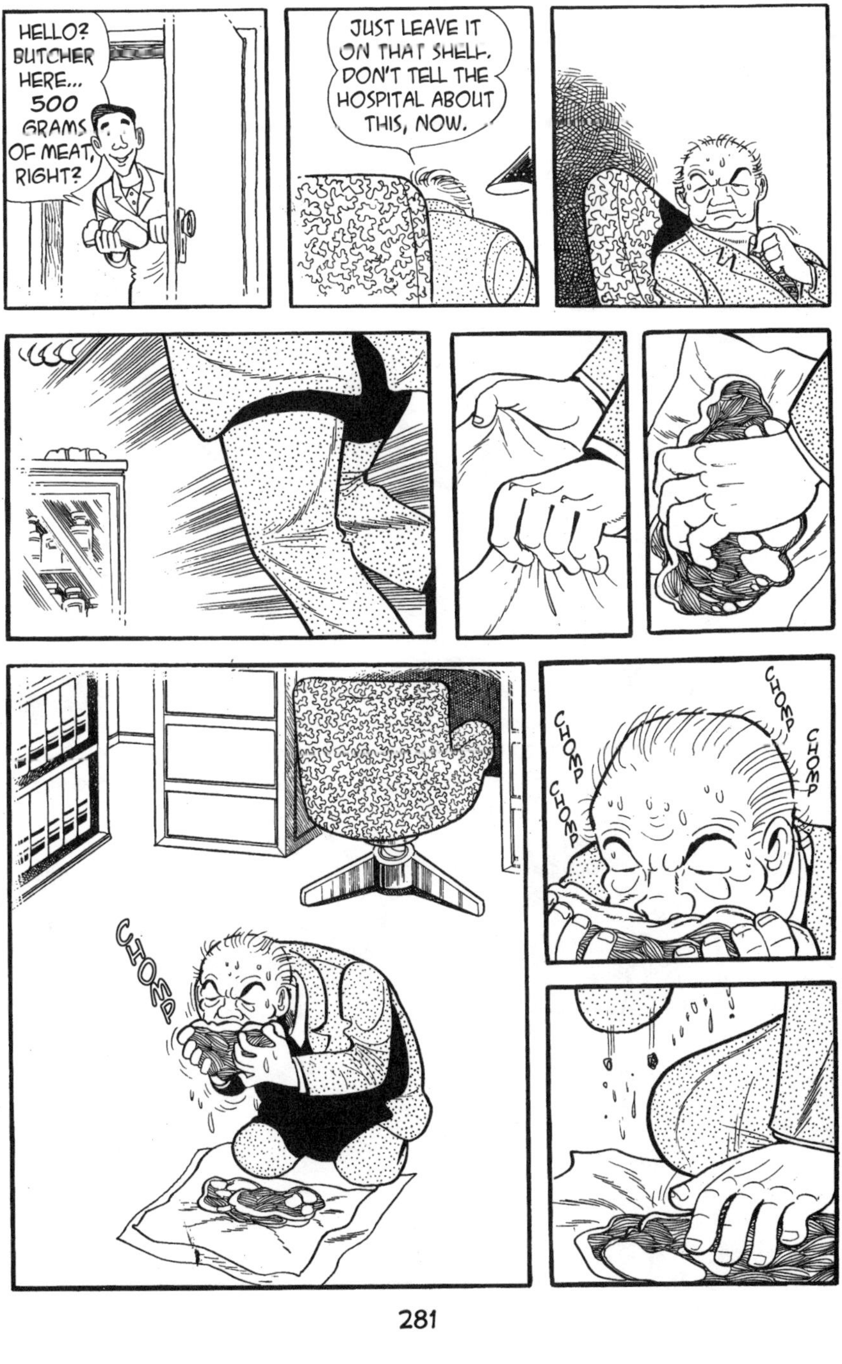
HELLO? BUTCHER HERE... 500 GRAMS OF MEAT, RIGHT?
JUST LEAVE IT ON THAT SHELF. DON'T TELL THE HOSPITAL ABOUT THIS, NOW.
CHOMP
CHOMP
CHOMP
CHOMP
CHOMP

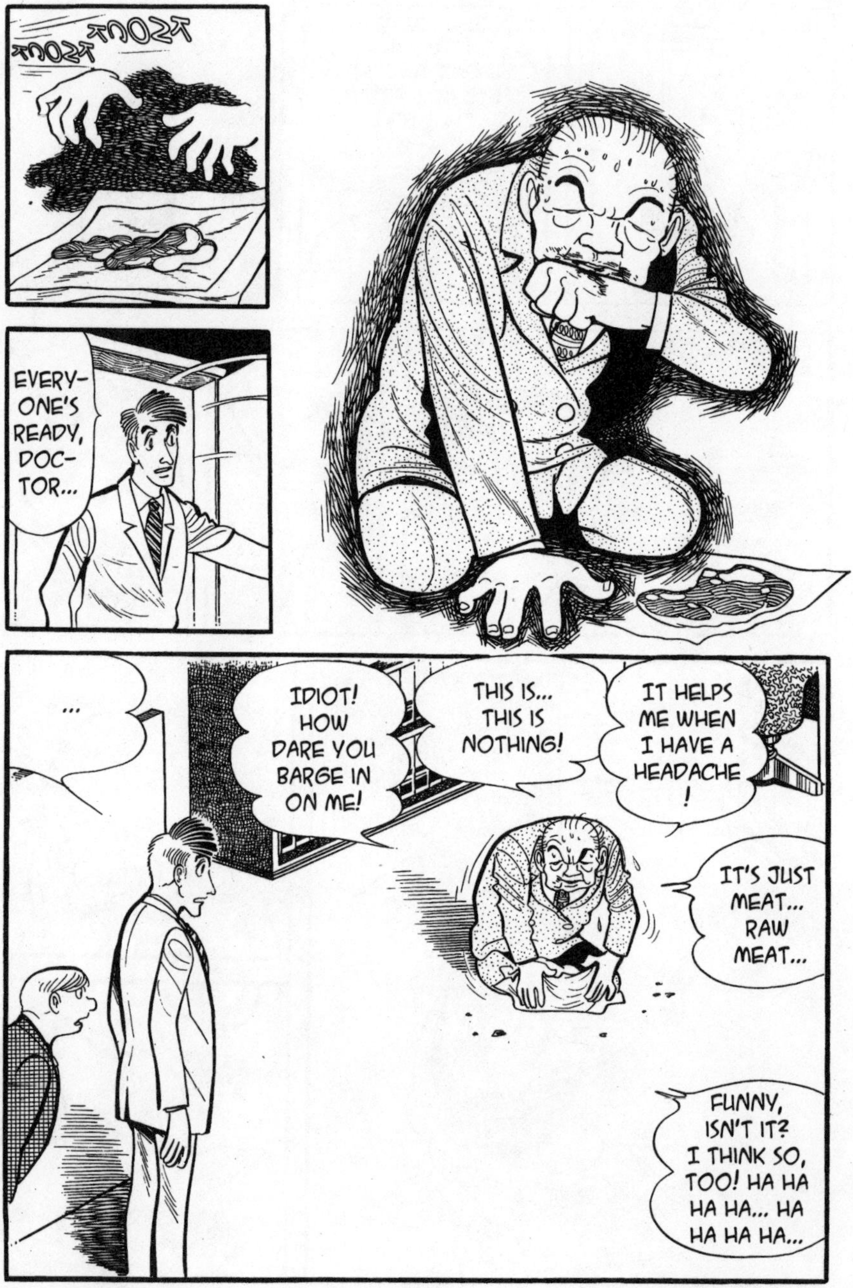
EVERYONE'S READY, DOCTOR...
...
IDIOT! HOW DARE YOU BARGE IN ON ME!
THIS IS... THIS IS NOTHING!
IT HELPS ME WHEN I HAVE A HEADACHE!
IT'S JUST MEAT... RAW MEAT...
FUNNY, ISN'T IT? I THINK SO, TOO! HA HA HA HA... HA HA HA HA...

CHAPTER 19

CATASTROPHE

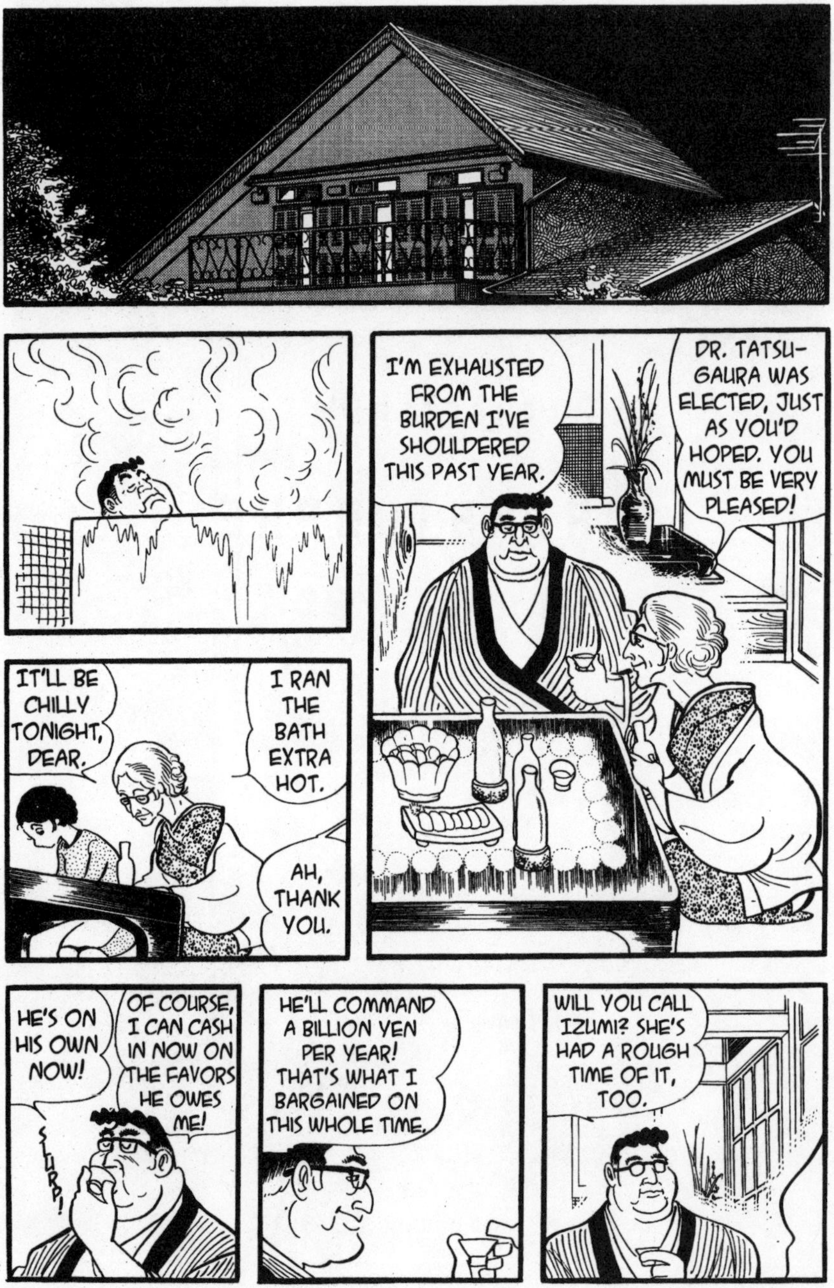
IT'LL BE CHILLY TONIGHT, DEAR.
I RAN THE BATH EXTRA HOT.
AH, THANK YOU.
I'M EXHAUSTED FROM THE BURDEN I'VE SHOULDERED THIS PAST YEAR.
DR. TATSUGAURA WAS ELECTED, JUST AS YOU'D HOPED. YOU MUST BE VERY PLEASED!
HE'S ON HIS OWN NOW!
OF COURSE, I CAN CASH IN NOW ON THE FAVORS HE OWES ME!
SLURP!
HE'LL COMMAND A BILLION YEN PER YEAR! THAT'S WHAT I BARGAINED ON THIS WHOLE TIME.
WILL YOU CALL IZUMI? SHE'S HAD A ROUGH TIME OF IT, TOO.

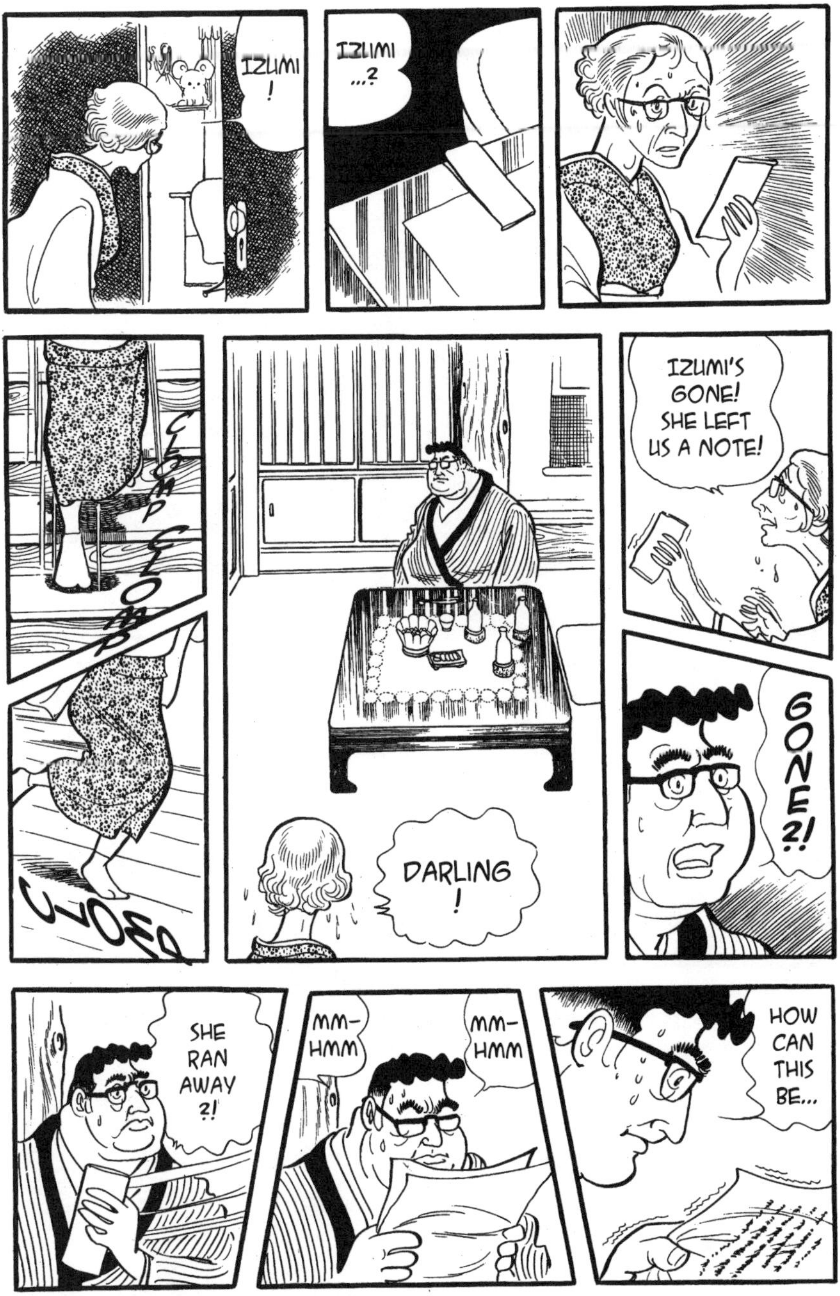
IZUMI !
IZUMI ...?
CLOMP CLOMP CLOMP
CLOMP
DARLING !
IZUMI'S GONE! SHE LEFT US A NOTE!
GONE?!
SHE RAN AWAY ?!
MM-HMM
MM-HMM
HOW CAN THIS BE...

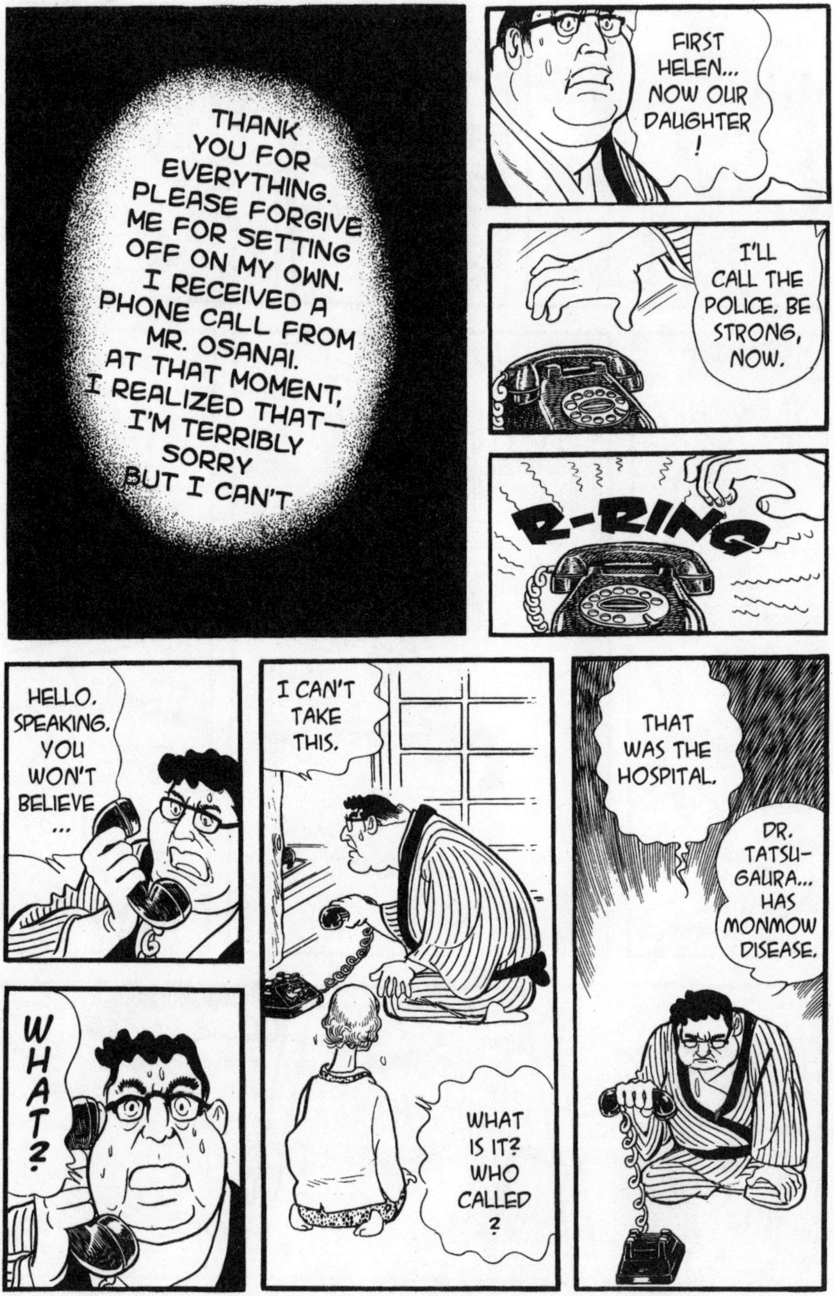
THANK YOU FOR EVERYTHING. PLEASE FORGIVE ME FOR SETTING OFF ON MY OWN. I RECEIVED A PHONE CALL FROM MR. OSANAI. AT THAT MOMENT, I REALIZED THAT— I'M TERRIBLY SORRY BUT I CAN'T
FIRST HELEN... NOW OUR DAUGHTER!
I'LL CALL THE POLICE. BE STRONG, NOW.
R-RING
HELLO. SPEAKING. YOU WON'T BELIEVE ...
WHAT?
I CAN'T TAKE THIS.
WHAT IS IT? WHO CALLED?
THAT WAS THE HOSPITAL.
DR. TATSU-GAURA... HAS MONMOW DISEASE.

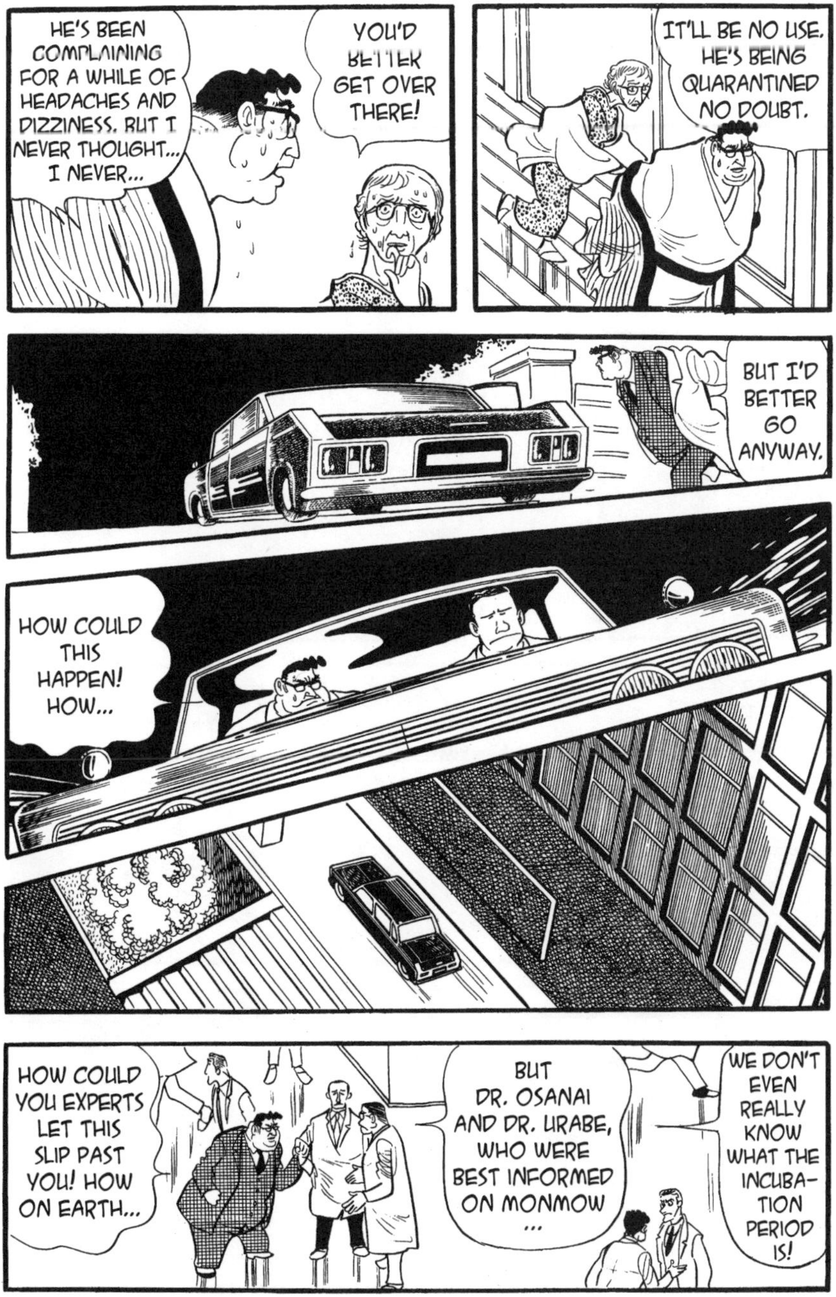
HE'S BEEN COMPLAINING FOR A WHILE OF HEADACHES AND DIZZINESS. BUT I NEVER THOUGHT... I NEVER...
YOU'D BETTER GET OVER THERE!
IT'LL BE NO USE. HE'S BEING QUARANTINED NO DOUBT.
BUT I'D BETTER GO ANYWAY.
HOW COULD THIS HAPPEN! HOW...
HOW COULD YOU EXPERTS LET THIS SLIP PAST YOU! HOW ON EARTH...
BUT DR. OSANAI AND DR. URABE, WHO WERE BEST INFORMED ON MONMOW ...
WE DON'T EVEN REALLY KNOW WHAT THE INCUBA- TION PERIOD IS!

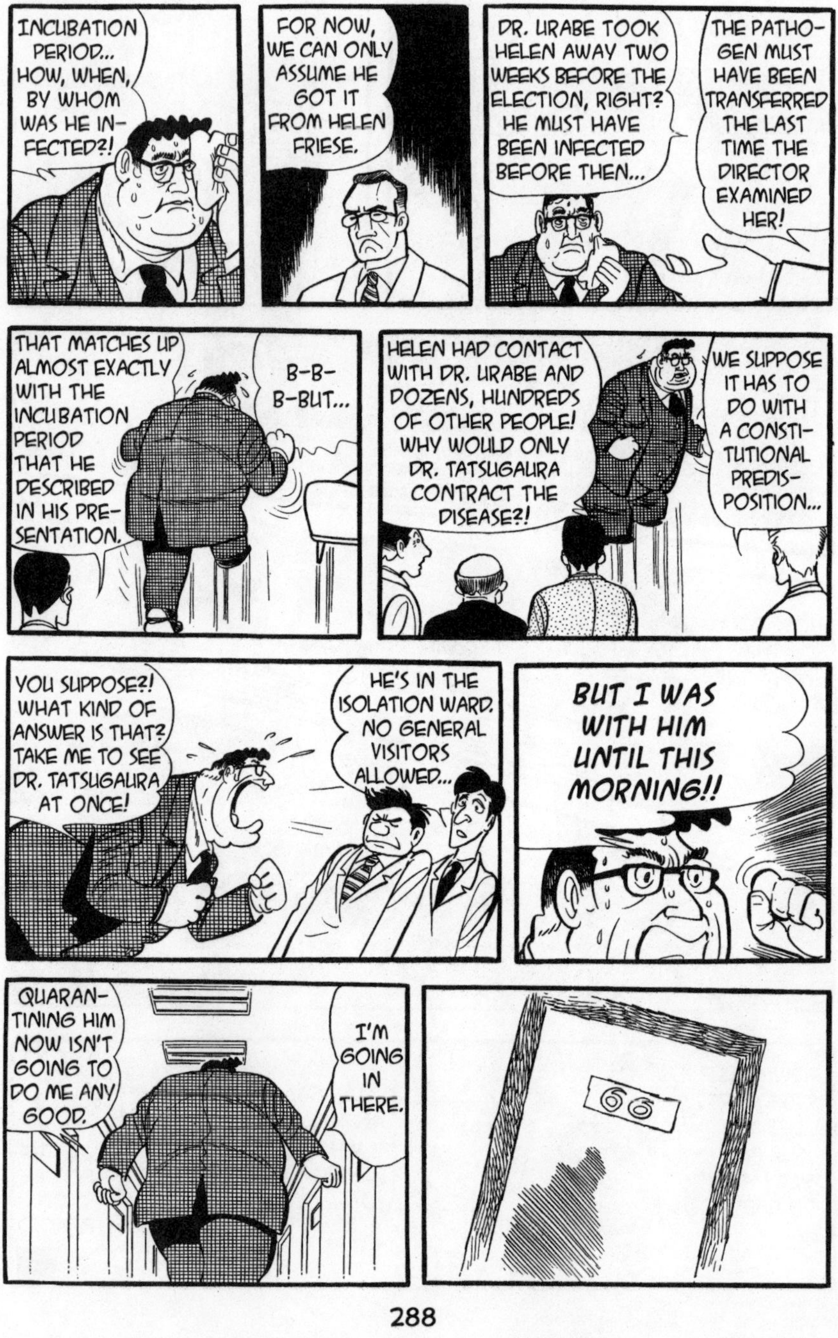
INCUBATION PERIOD... HOW, WHEN, BY WHOM WAS HE INFECTED?!
FOR NOW, WE CAN ONLY ASSUME HE GOT IT FROM HELEN FRIESE.
DR. URABE TOOK HELEN AWAY TWO WEEKS BEFORE THE ELECTION, RIGHT? HE MUST HAVE BEEN INFECTED BEFORE THEN...
THE PATHOGEN MUST HAVE BEEN TRANSFERRED THE LAST TIME THE DIRECTOR EXAMINED HER!
THAT MATCHES UP ALMOST EXACTLY WITH THE INCUBATION PERIOD THAT HE DESCRIBED IN HIS PRESENTATION.
B-B-B-BUT...
HELEN HAD CONTACT WITH DR. URABE AND DOZENS, HUNDREDS OF OTHER PEOPLE! WHY WOULD ONLY DR. TATSUGAURA CONTRACT THE DISEASE?!
WE SUPPOSE IT HAS TO DO WITH A CONSTITUTIONAL PREDISPOSITION...
YOU SUPPOSE?! WHAT KIND OF ANSWER IS THAT? TAKE ME TO SEE DR. TATSUGAURA AT ONCE!
HE'S IN THE ISOLATION WARD. NO GENERAL VISITORS ALLOWED...
BUT I WAS WITH HIM UNTIL THIS MORNING!!
QUARANTINING HIM NOW ISN'T GOING TO DO ME ANY GOOD.
I'M GOING IN THERE.
66

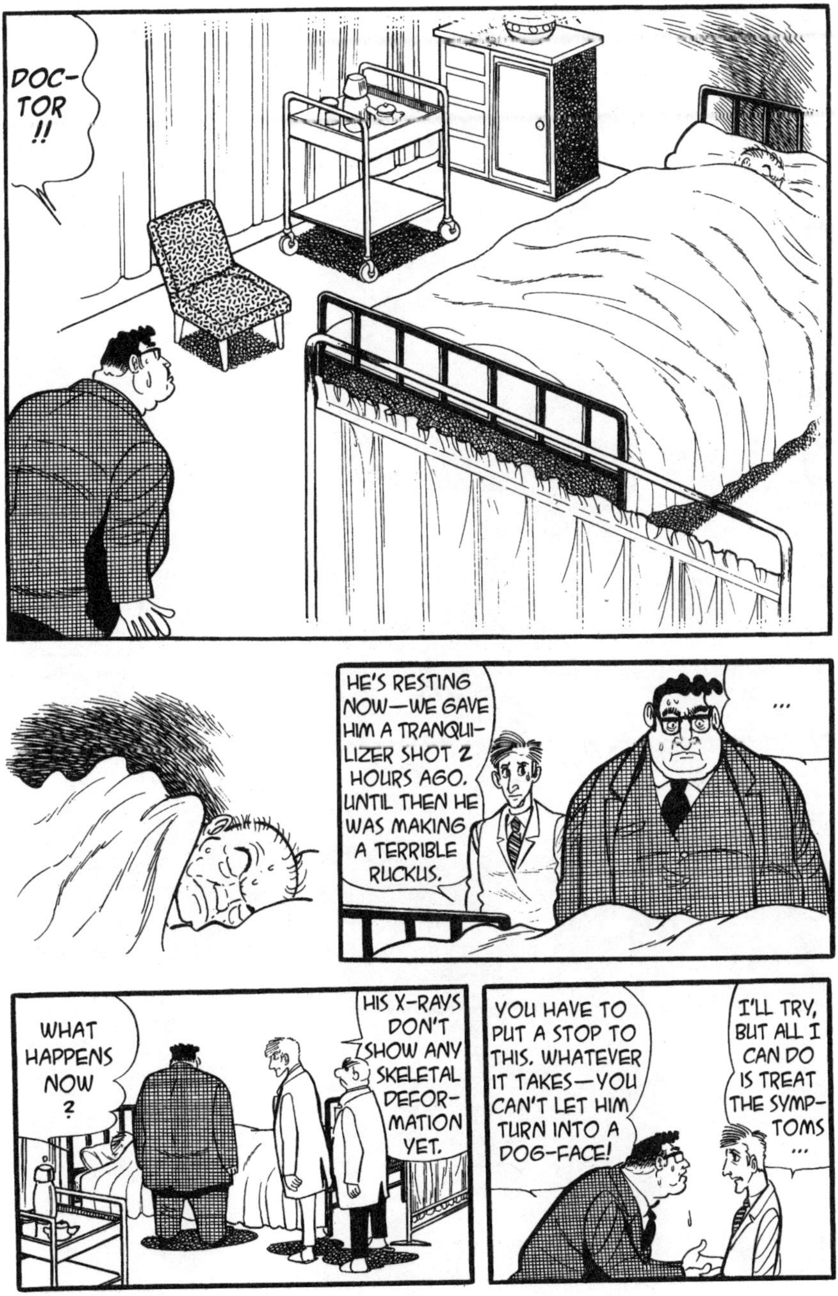
DOC-TOR !!
HE'S RESTING NOW—WE GAVE HIM A TRANQUILIZER SHOT 2 HOURS AGO. UNTIL THEN HE WAS MAKING A TERRIBLE RUCKUS.
...
WHAT HAPPENS NOW ?
HIS X-RAYS DON'T SHOW ANY SKELETAL DEFORMATION YET.
YOU HAVE TO PUT A STOP TO THIS. WHATEVER IT TAKES—YOU CAN'T LET HIM TURN INTO A DOG-FACE!
I'LL TRY, BUT ALL I CAN DO IS TREAT THE SYMPTOMS ...

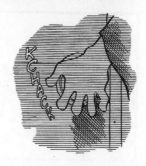

KCHACK

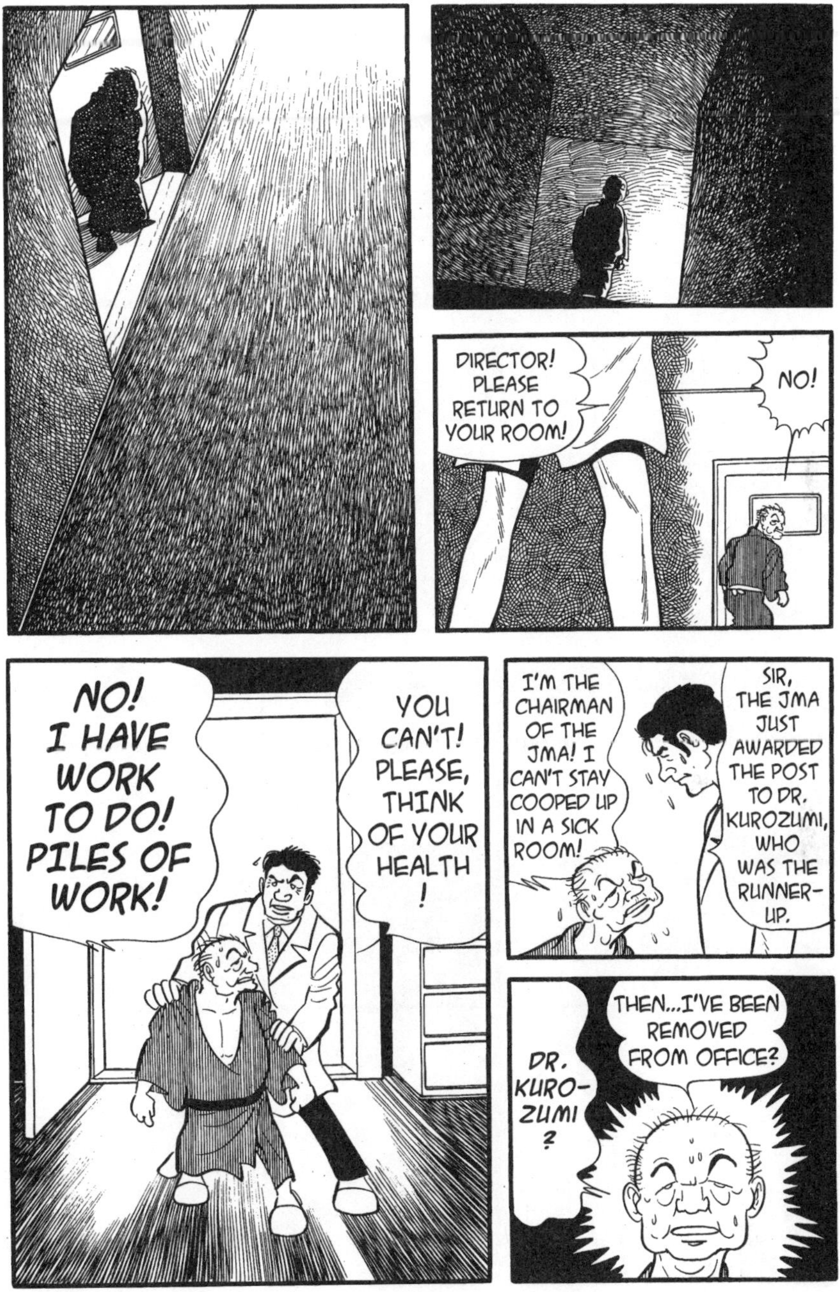
DIRECTOR! PLEASE RETURN TO YOUR ROOM!
NO!
NO! I HAVE WORK TO DO! PILES OF WORK!
YOU CAN'T! PLEASE, THINK OF YOUR HEALTH!
I'M THE CHAIRMAN OF THE JMA! I CAN'T STAY COOPED UP IN A SICK ROOM!
SIR, THE JMA JUST AWARDED THE POST TO DR. KUROZUMI, WHO WAS THE RUNNER-UP.
DR. KUROZUMI?
THEN...I'VE BEEN REMOVED FROM OFFICE?

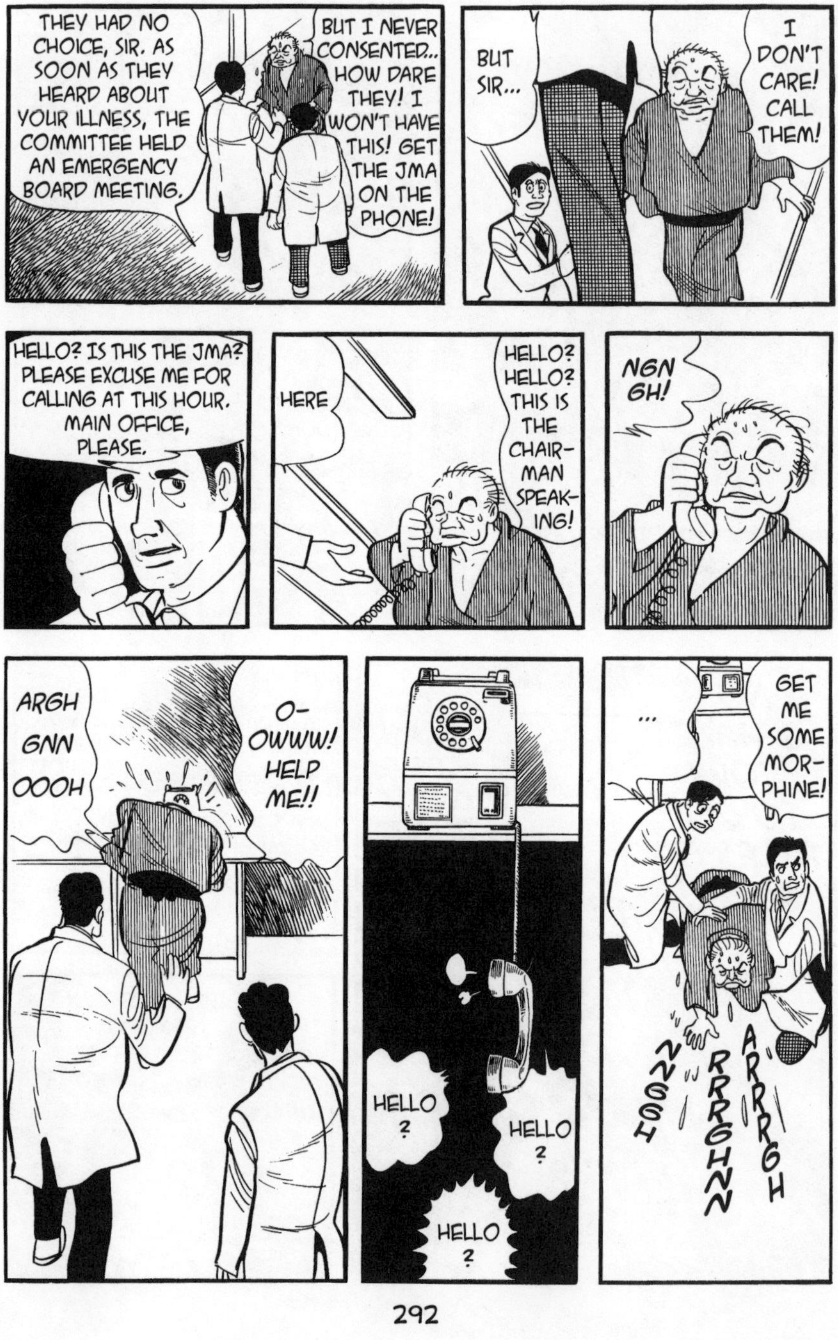
THEY HAD NO CHOICE, SIR. AS SOON AS THEY HEARD ABOUT YOUR ILLNESS, THE COMMITTEE HELD AN EMERGENCY BOARD MEETING.
BUT I NEVER CONSENTED... HOW DARE THEY! I WON'T HAVE THIS! GET THE JMA ON THE PHONE!
BUT SIR...
I DON'T CARE! CALL THEM!
HELLO? IS THIS THE JMA? PLEASE EXCUSE ME FOR CALLING AT THIS HOUR. MAIN OFFICE, PLEASE.
HERE
HELLO? HELLO? THIS IS THE CHAIR-MAN SPEAK-ING!
NGN GH!
ARGH GNN OOOH
O-OWWW! HELP ME!!
HELLO?
HELLO?
HELLO?
...
GET ME SOME MOR-PHINE!
NNGGH
RRRGHNN
ARRRRGH

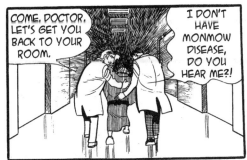

COME, DOCTOR, LET'S GET YOU BACK TO YOUR ROOM.

I DON'T HAVE MONMOW DISEASE, DO YOU HEAR ME?!

CAN I ASK YOU A FAVOR?

CAN YOU GET ME DR. OSANAI'S AND DR. URABE'S REPORTS ON MONMOW AND BRING THEM HERE?

I'D LIKE TO READ THEM NOW.

I UNDERSTAND. I'LL ASK THE JMA FOR COPIES.

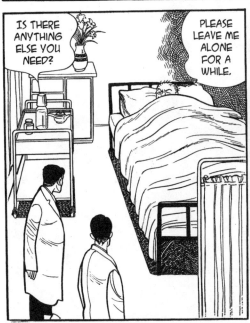

IS THERE ANYTHING ELSE YOU NEED?

PLEASE LEAVE ME ALONE FOR A WHILE.

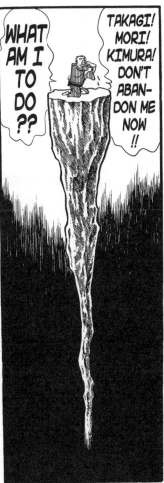

WHAT AM I TO DO??

TAKAGI! MORI! KIMURA! DON'T ABANDON ME NOW!!

293

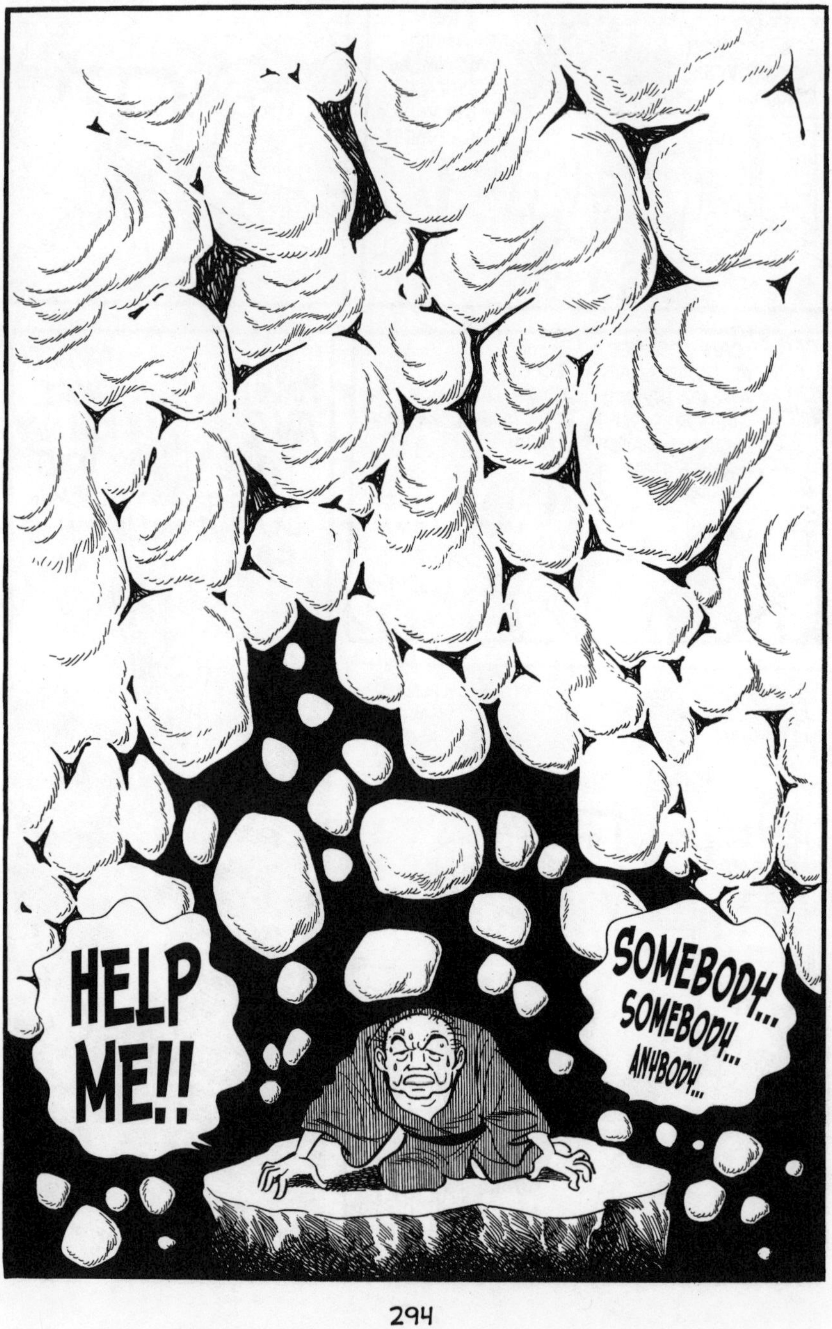
SOMEBODY... SOMEBODY... ANYBODY...
HELP ME!!

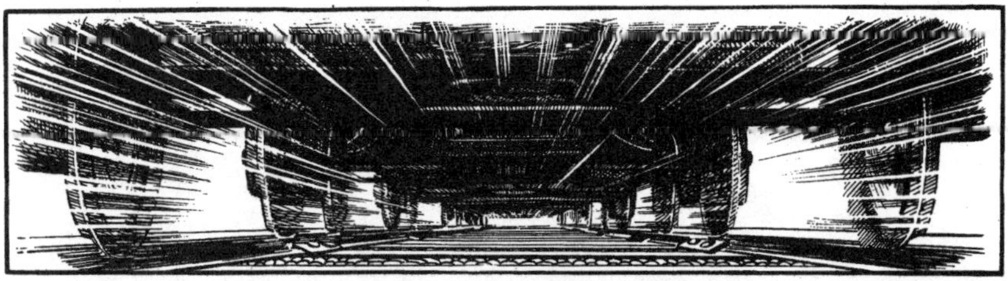

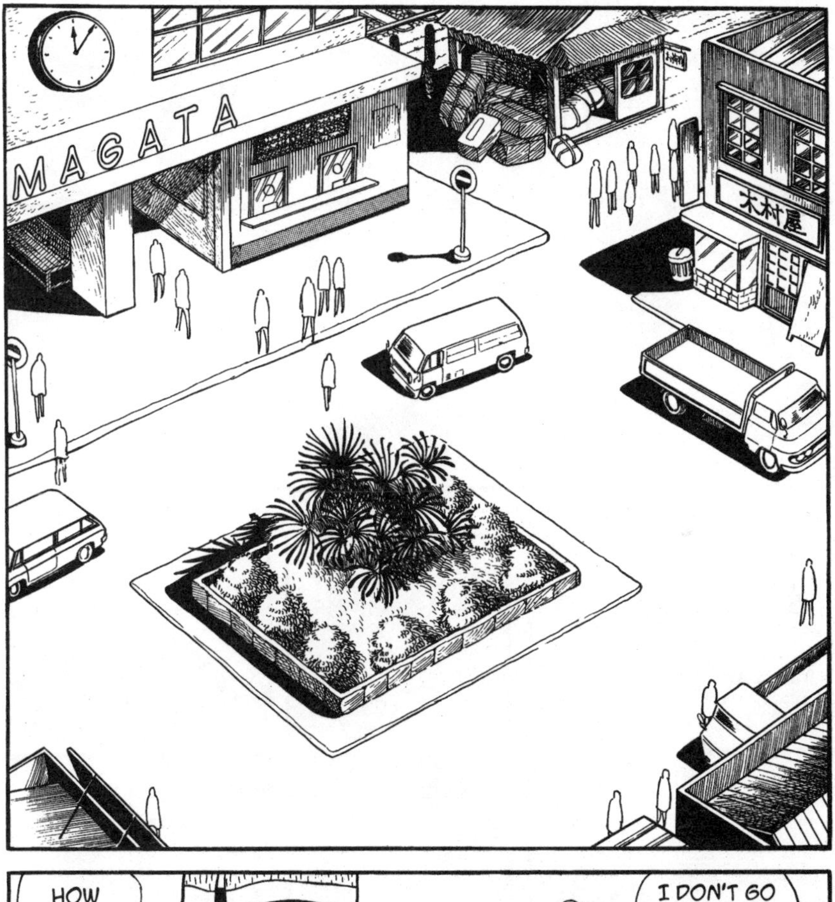
MAGATA
木村屋

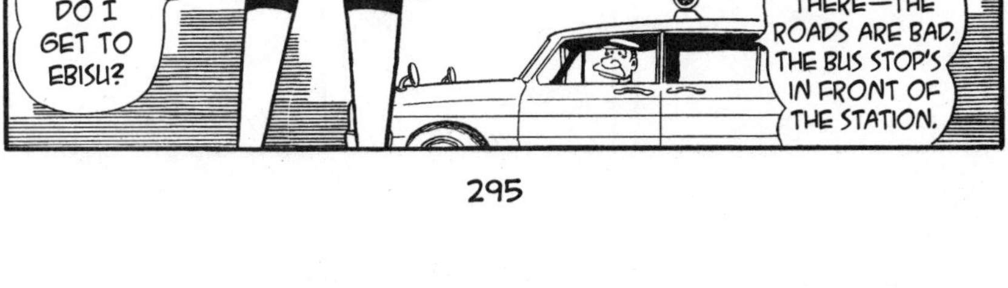
HOW DO I GET TO EBISU?
I DON'T GO THERE—THE ROADS ARE BAD. THE BUS STOP'S IN FRONT OF THE STATION.

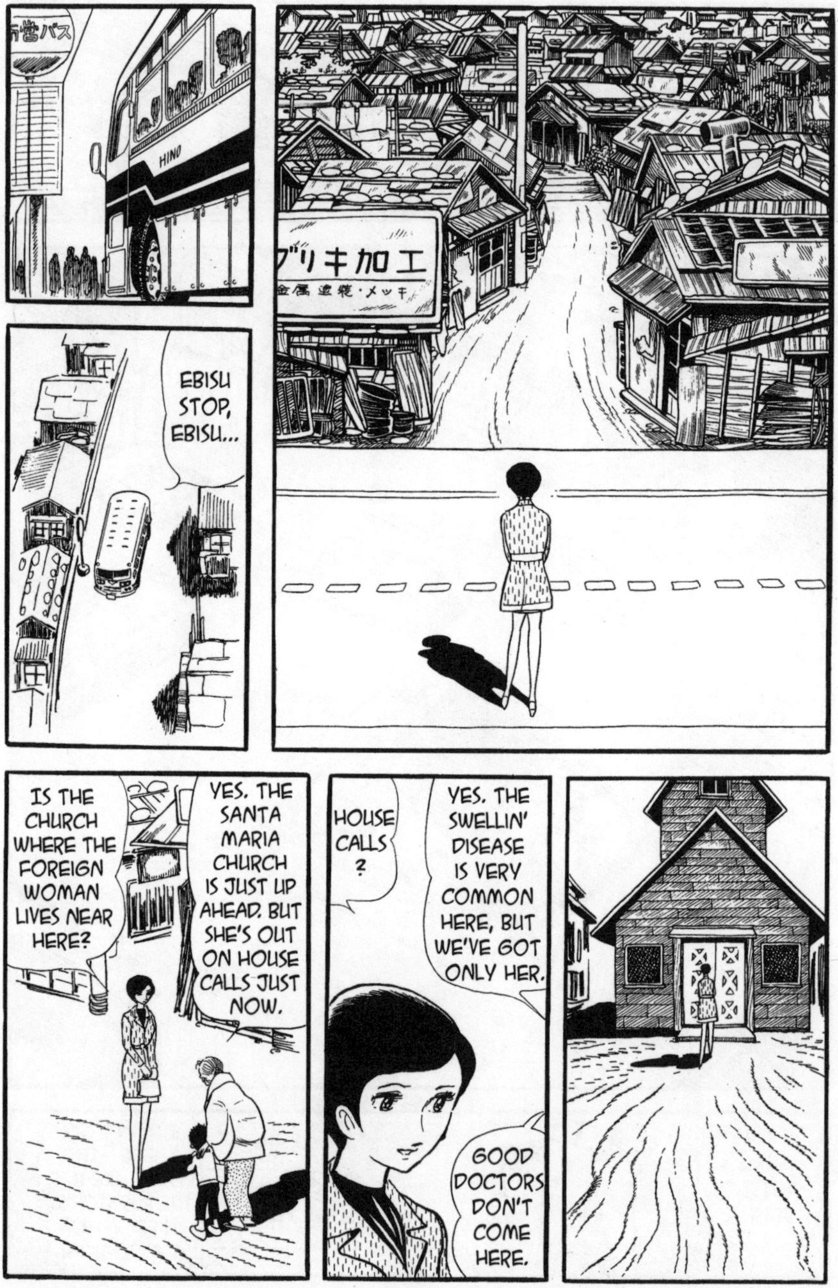
HINO
EBISU STOP, EBISU...
ブリキ加工
金属塗装・メッキ
IS THE CHURCH WHERE THE FOREIGN WOMAN LIVES NEAR HERE?
YES. THE SANTA MARIA CHURCH IS JUST UP AHEAD. BUT SHE'S OUT ON HOUSE CALLS JUST NOW.
HOUSE CALLS?
YES. THE SWELLIN' DISEASE IS VERY COMMON HERE, BUT WE'VE GOT ONLY HER.
GOOD DOCTORS DON'T COME HERE.

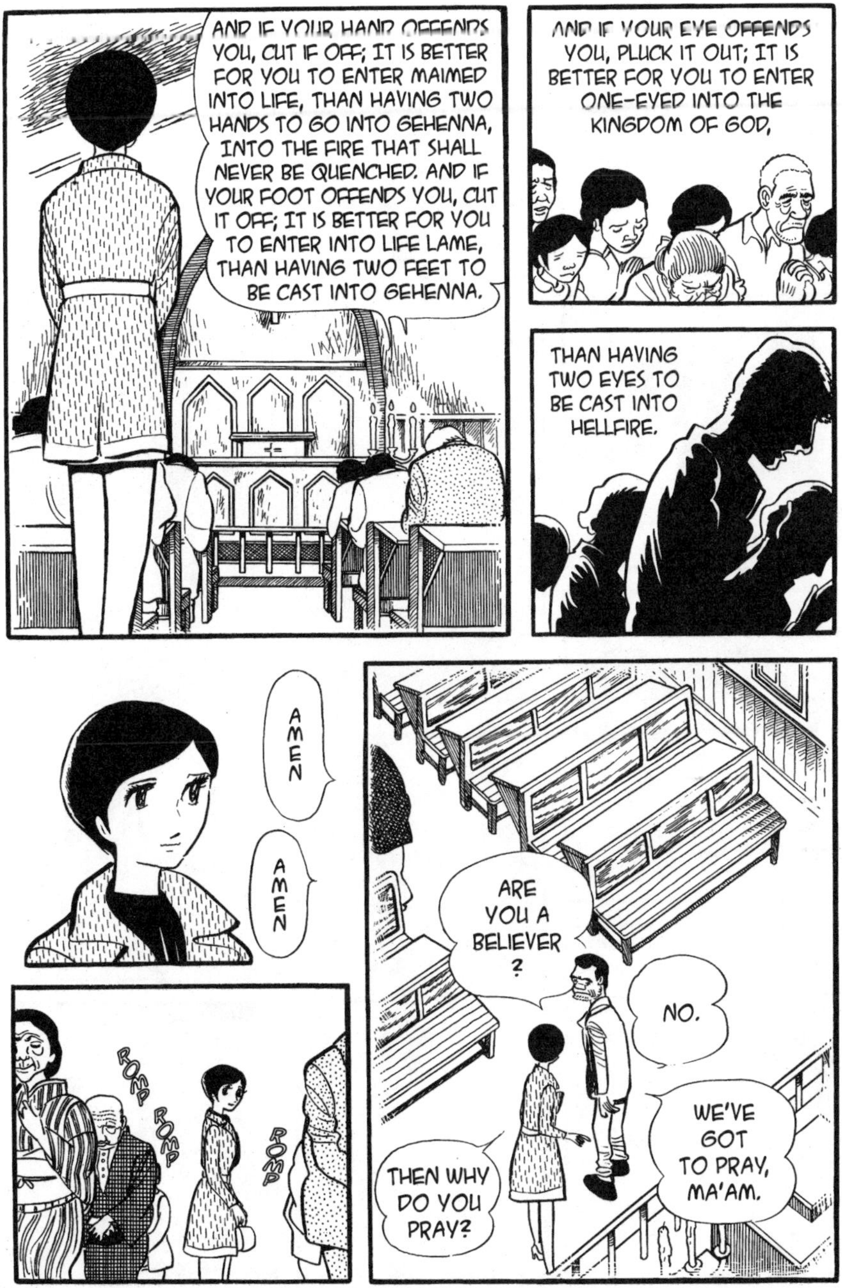
AND IF YOUR HAND OFFENDS YOU, CUT IF OFF; IT IS BETTER FOR YOU TO ENTER MAIMED INTO LIFE, THAN HAVING TWO HANDS TO GO INTO GEHENNA, INTO THE FIRE THAT SHALL NEVER BE QUENCHED. AND IF YOUR FOOT OFFENDS YOU, CUT IT OFF; IT IS BETTER FOR YOU TO ENTER INTO LIFE LAME, THAN HAVING TWO FEET TO BE CAST INTO GEHENNA.
AND IF YOUR EYE OFFENDS YOU, PLUCK IT OUT; IT IS BETTER FOR YOU TO ENTER ONE-EYED INTO THE KINGDOM OF GOD,
THAN HAVING TWO EYES TO BE CAST INTO HELLFIRE.
AMEN
AMEN
ROMP ROMP
ROMP
ARE YOU A BELIEVER?
NO.
THEN WHY DO YOU PRAY?
WE'VE GOT TO PRAY, MA'AM.

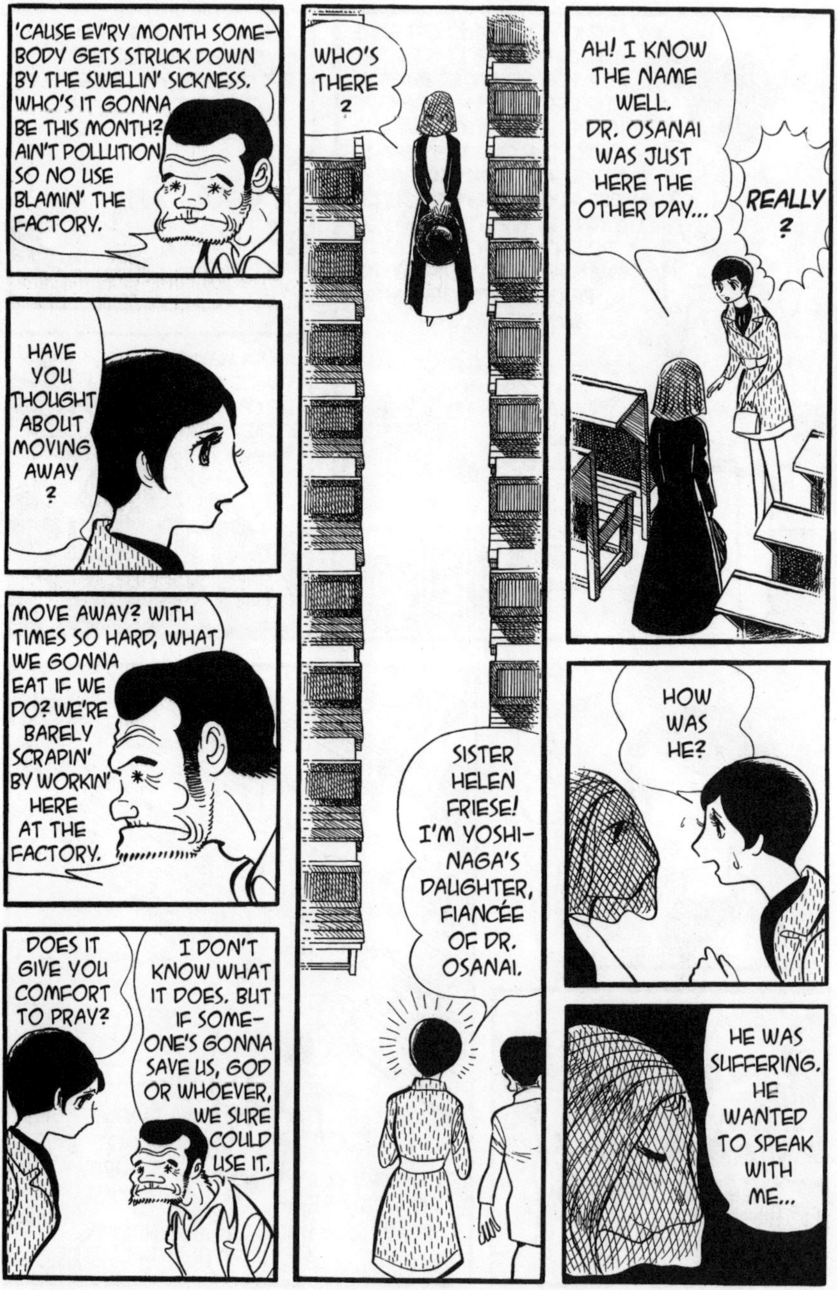
'CAUSE EV'RY MONTH SOMEBODY GETS STRUCK DOWN BY THE SWELLIN' SICKNESS. WHO'S IT GONNA BE THIS MONTH? AIN'T POLLUTION SO NO USE BLAMIN' THE FACTORY.
HAVE YOU THOUGHT ABOUT MOVING AWAY?
MOVE AWAY? WITH TIMES SO HARD, WHAT WE GONNA EAT IF WE DO? WE'RE BARELY SCRAPIN' BY WORKIN' HERE AT THE FACTORY.
DOES IT GIVE YOU COMFORT TO PRAY?
I DON'T KNOW WHAT IT DOES. BUT IF SOMEONE'S GONNA SAVE US, GOD OR WHOEVER, WE SURE COULD USE IT.
WHO'S THERE?
SISTER HELEN FRIESE! I'M YOSHINAGA'S DAUGHTER, FIANCÉE OF DR. OSANAI.
AH! I KNOW THE NAME WELL. DR. OSANAI WAS JUST HERE THE OTHER DAY...
REALLY?
HOW WAS HE?
HE WAS SUFFERING. HE WANTED TO SPEAK WITH ME...

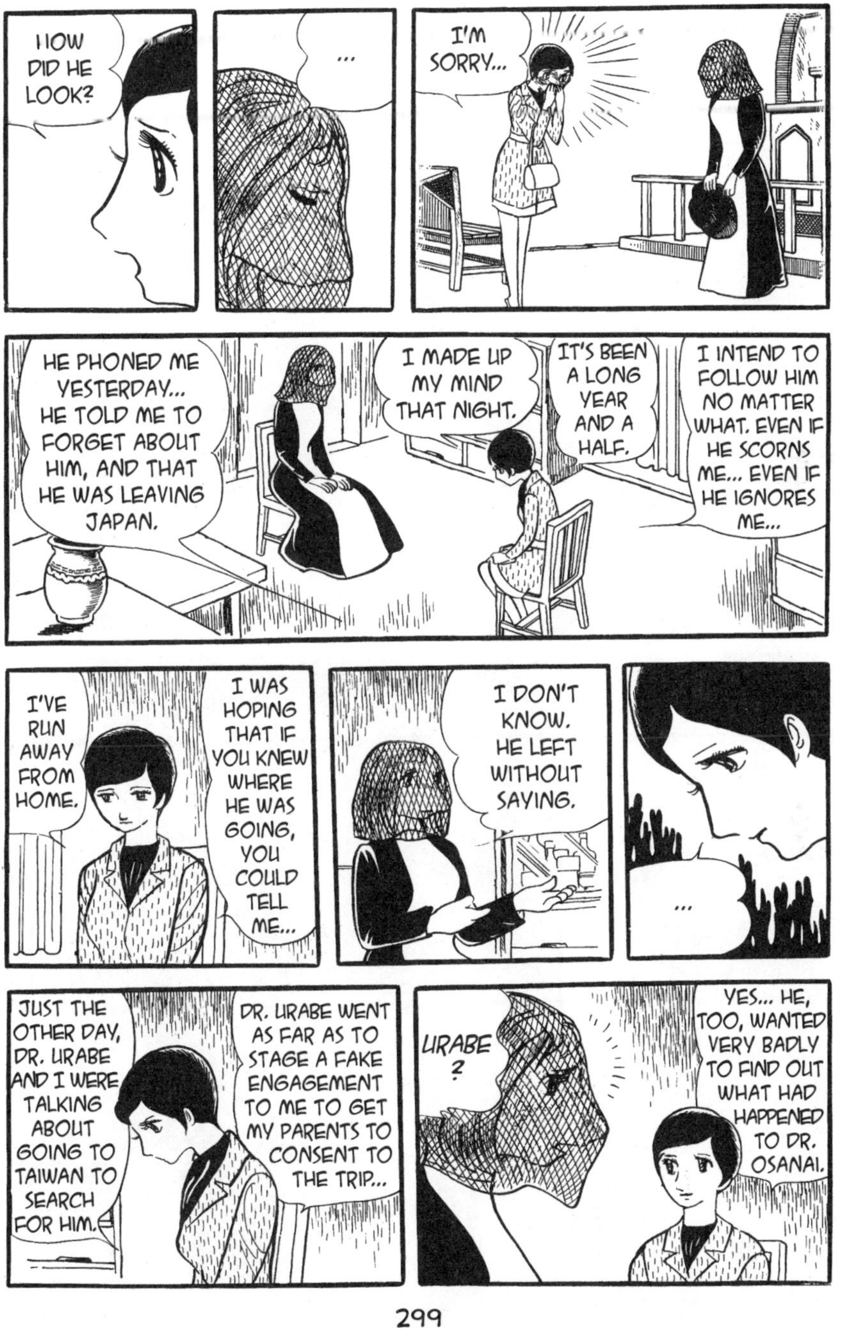
HOW DID HE LOOK?
...
I'M SORRY...
HE PHONED ME YESTERDAY... HE TOLD ME TO FORGET ABOUT HIM, AND THAT HE WAS LEAVING JAPAN.
I MADE UP MY MIND THAT NIGHT.
IT'S BEEN A LONG YEAR AND A HALF.
I INTEND TO FOLLOW HIM NO MATTER WHAT. EVEN IF HE SCORNS ME... EVEN IF HE IGNORES ME...
I'VE RUN AWAY FROM HOME.
I WAS HOPING THAT IF YOU KNEW WHERE HE WAS GOING, YOU COULD TELL ME...
I DON'T KNOW. HE LEFT WITHOUT SAYING.
...
JUST THE OTHER DAY, DR. URABE AND I WERE TALKING ABOUT GOING TO TAIWAN TO SEARCH FOR HIM.
DR. URABE WENT AS FAR AS TO STAGE A FAKE ENGAGEMENT TO ME TO GET MY PARENTS TO CONSENT TO THE TRIP...
URABE?
YES... HE, TOO, WANTED VERY BADLY TO FIND OUT WHAT HAD HAPPENED TO DR. OSANAI.

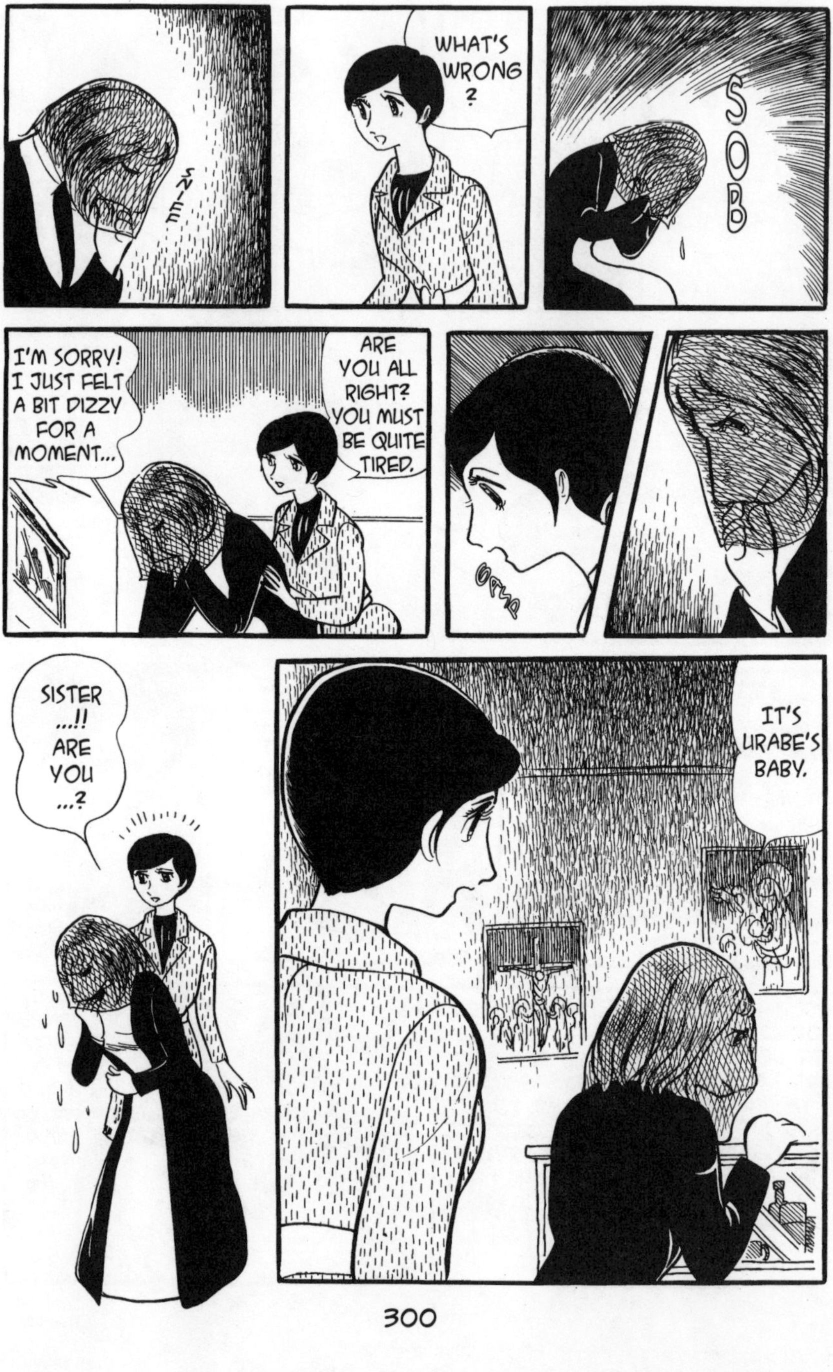
SNIFF
WHAT'S WRONG?
SOB
ARE YOU ALL RIGHT? YOU MUST BE QUITE TIRED.
I'M SORRY! I JUST FELT A BIT DIZZY FOR A MOMENT...
SISTER ...!! ARE YOU ...?
IT'S URABE'S BABY.

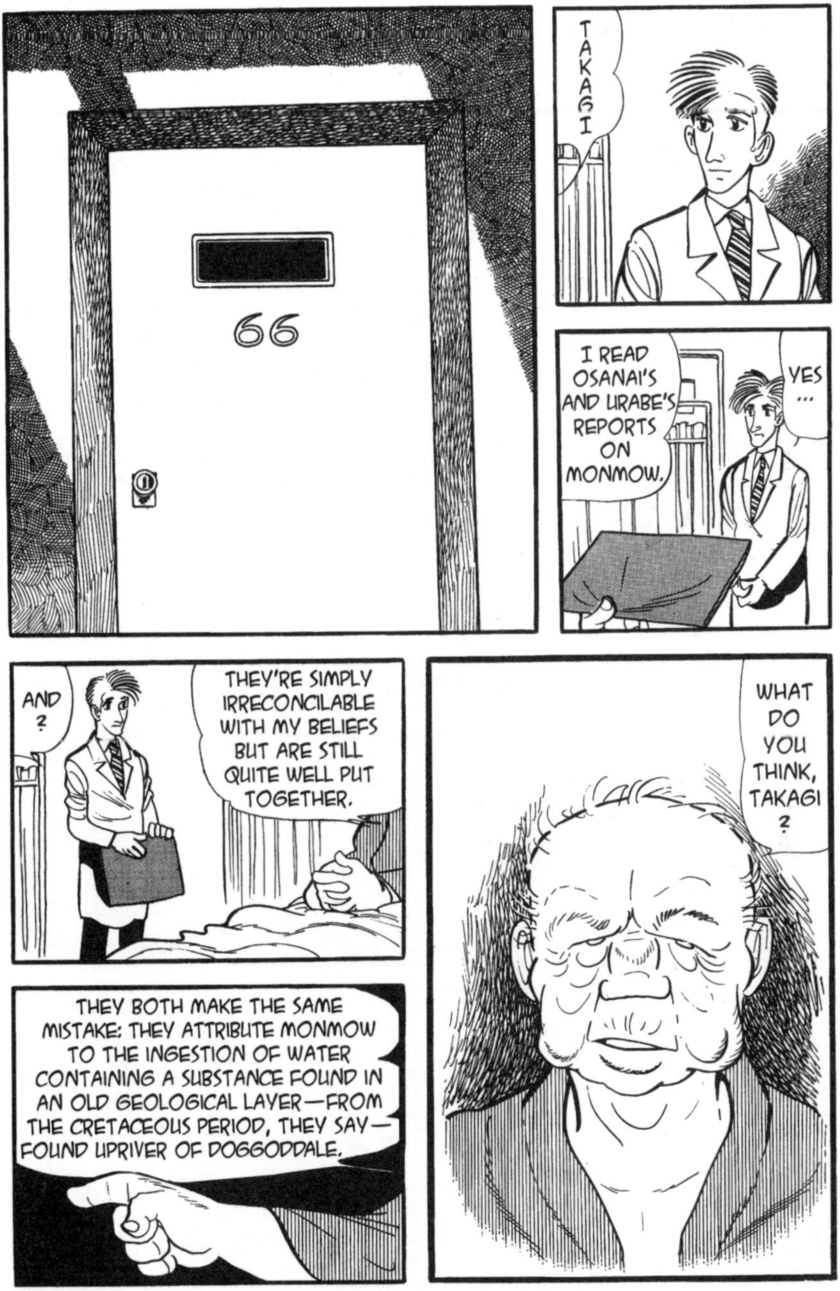
TAKAGI
YES ...
I READ OSANAI'S AND URABE'S REPORTS ON MONMOW.
66
WHAT DO YOU THINK, TAKAGI?
THEY'RE SIMPLY IRRECONCILABLE WITH MY BELIEFS BUT ARE STILL QUITE WELL PUT TOGETHER.
AND?
THEY BOTH MAKE THE SAME MISTAKE: THEY ATTRIBUTE MONMOW TO THE INGESTION OF WATER CONTAINING A SUBSTANCE FOUND IN AN OLD GEOLOGICAL LAYER—FROM THE CRETACEOUS PERIOD, THEY SAY—FOUND UPRIVER OF DOGGODDALE.

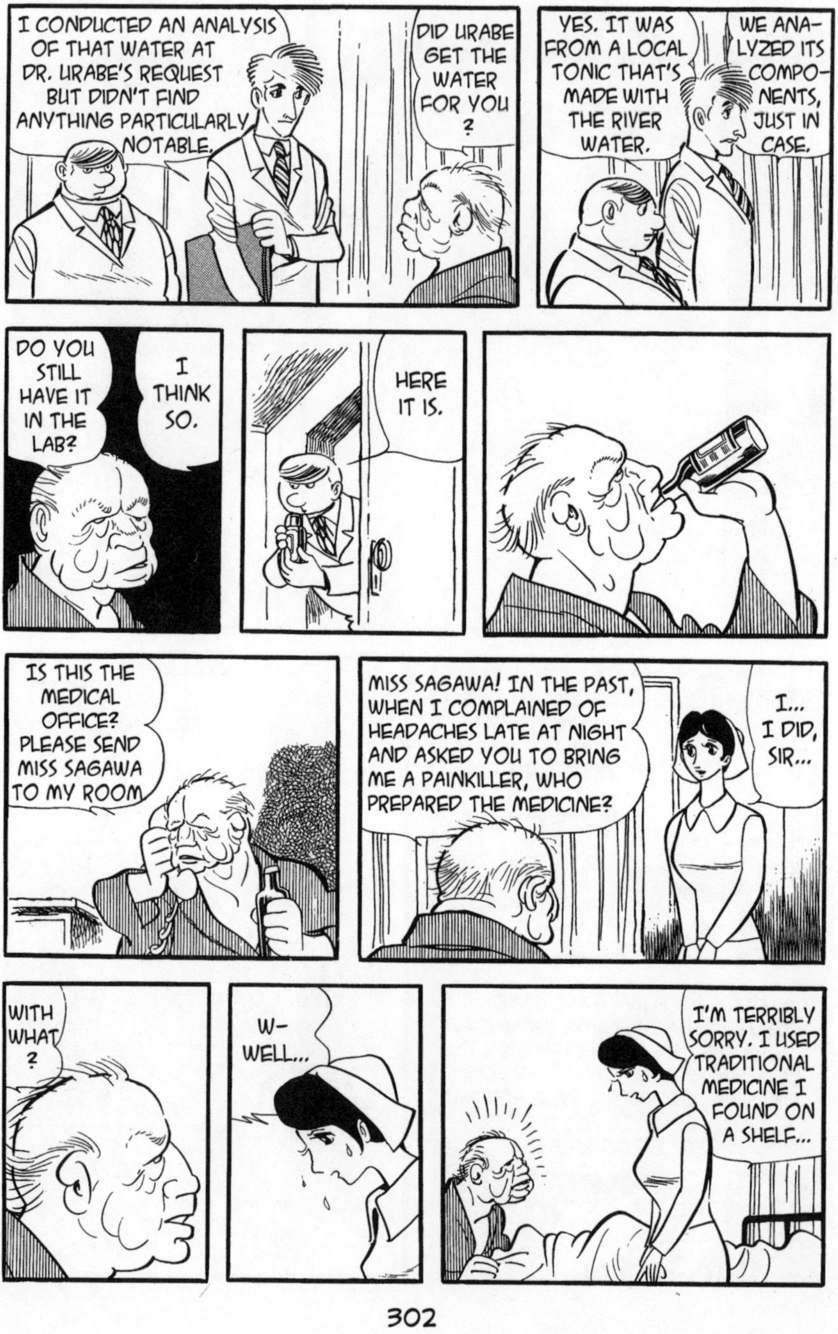
I CONDUCTED AN ANALYSIS OF THAT WATER AT DR. URABE'S REQUEST BUT DIDN'T FIND ANYTHING PARTICULARLY NOTABLE.
DID URABE GET THE WATER FOR YOU?
YES. IT WAS FROM A LOCAL TONIC THAT'S MADE WITH THE RIVER WATER.
WE ANALYZED ITS COMPONENTS, JUST IN CASE.
DO YOU STILL HAVE IT IN THE LAB?
I THINK SO.
HERE IT IS.
IS THIS THE MEDICAL OFFICE? PLEASE SEND MISS SAGAWA TO MY ROOM
MISS SAGAWA! IN THE PAST, WHEN I COMPLAINED OF HEADACHES LATE AT NIGHT AND ASKED YOU TO BRING ME A PAINKILLER, WHO PREPARED THE MEDICINE?
I... I DID, SIR...
WITH WHAT?
W-WELL...
I'M TERRIBLY SORRY. I USED TRADITIONAL MEDICINE I FOUND ON A SHELF...

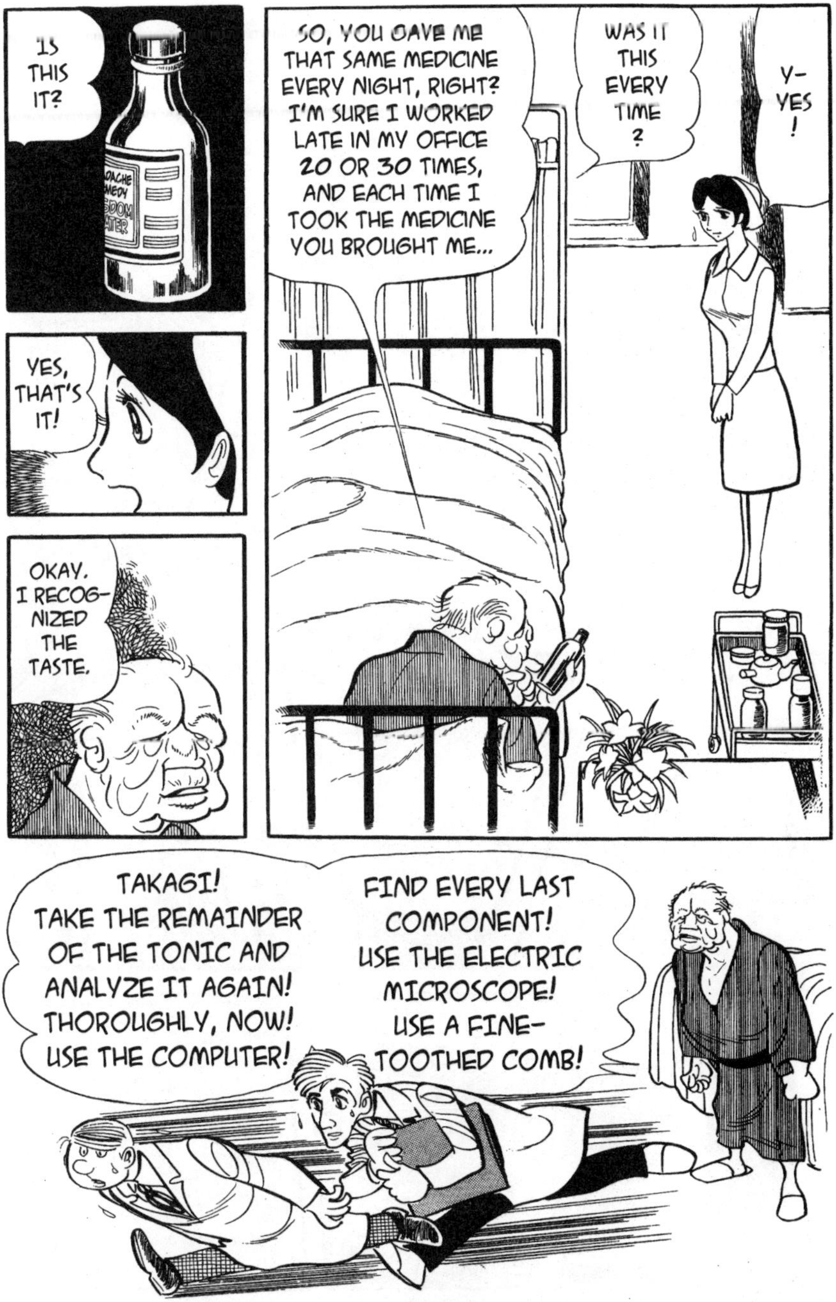
IS THIS IT?
YES, THAT'S IT!
OKAY. I RECOG-NIZED THE TASTE.
SO, YOU GAVE ME THAT SAME MEDICINE EVERY NIGHT, RIGHT? I'M SURE I WORKED LATE IN MY OFFICE 20 OR 30 TIMES, AND EACH TIME I TOOK THE MEDICINE YOU BROUGHT ME...
WAS IT THIS EVERY TIME?
Y-YES!
TAKAGI! TAKE THE REMAINDER OF THE TONIC AND ANALYZE IT AGAIN! THOROUGHLY, NOW! USE THE COMPUTER!
FIND EVERY LAST COMPONENT! USE THE ELECTRIC MICROSCOPE! USE A FINE-TOOTHED COMB!

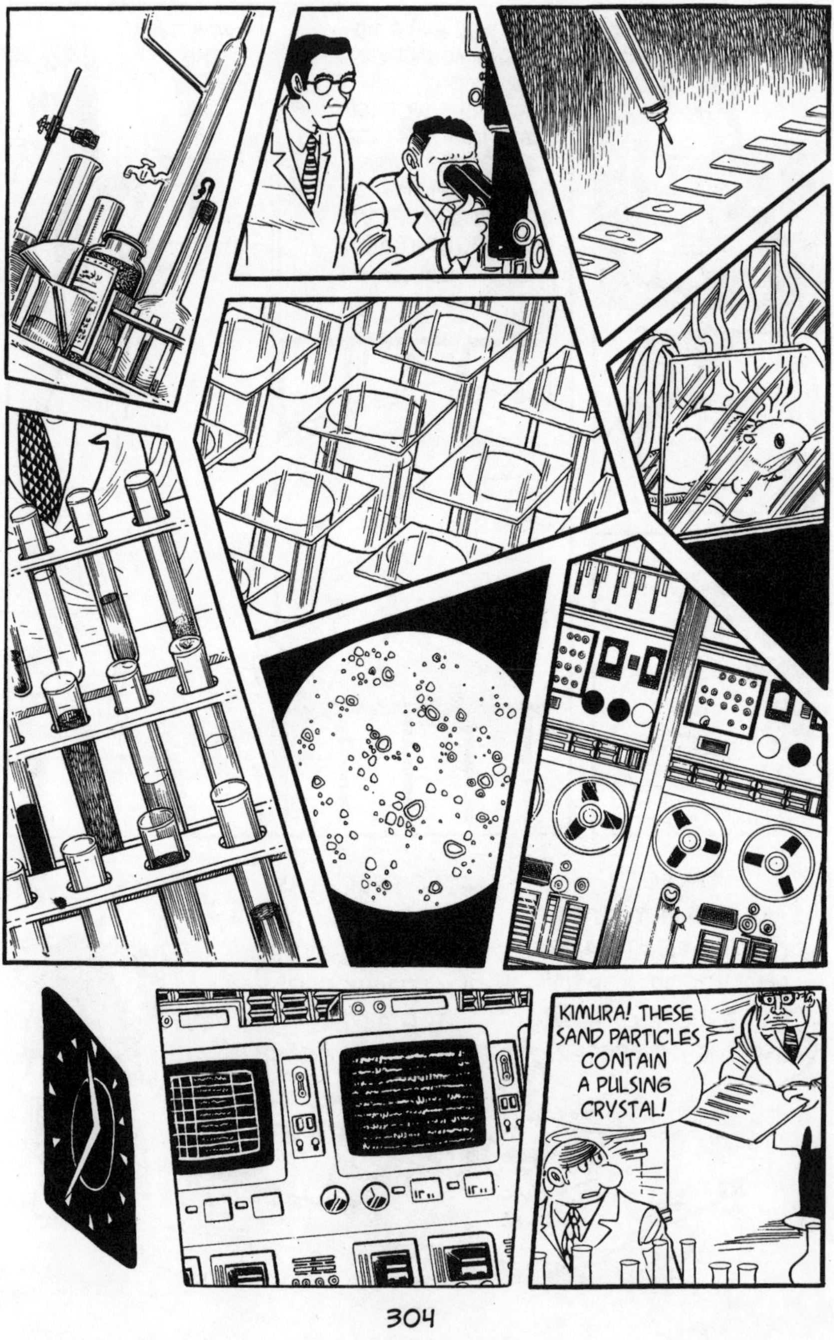
KIMURA! THESE SAND PARTICLES CONTAIN A PULSING CRYSTAL!

DON'T BE RIDIC-ULOUS!

I'VE NEVER HEARD OF CRYSTALS THAT VIBRATE!

LOOK! IT'S IN THE COMPUTER RESULTS. THERE'S A GRITSTONE THAT CONTAINS TRACE AMOUNTS OF SODIUM AND PHOSPHORUS. THESE ARE THE COMPO-NENTS OF THE DEPOSIT. WE ANALYZED THE CONTENT IN 15 OR 16 BOTTLES...

BUT IN JUST THIS ONE, WE WERE ABLE TO EXTRACT TRACES OF A SUBSTANCE THAT RESEMBLES GADOLINITE. THEY COLLIDE WITH EACH OTHER TO PRODUCE THE PULSE.

GADO-LINITE? WHAT'S THAT?

HERE, LOOK AT THE CRYS-TALS

THOSE BAR-SHAPED CRYSTALS.

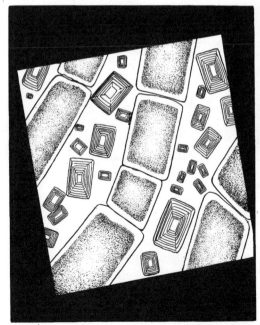

THEY CONTAIN THE ELEMENTS YTTRIUM AND SAMARIUM.

YTTRIUM AND SAMARIUM? SO WHAT DOES THAT MEAN?

SAMARIUM HARDLY EVER OCCURS IN NATURE. IT'S A MEMBER OF THE RARE EARTH GROUP.

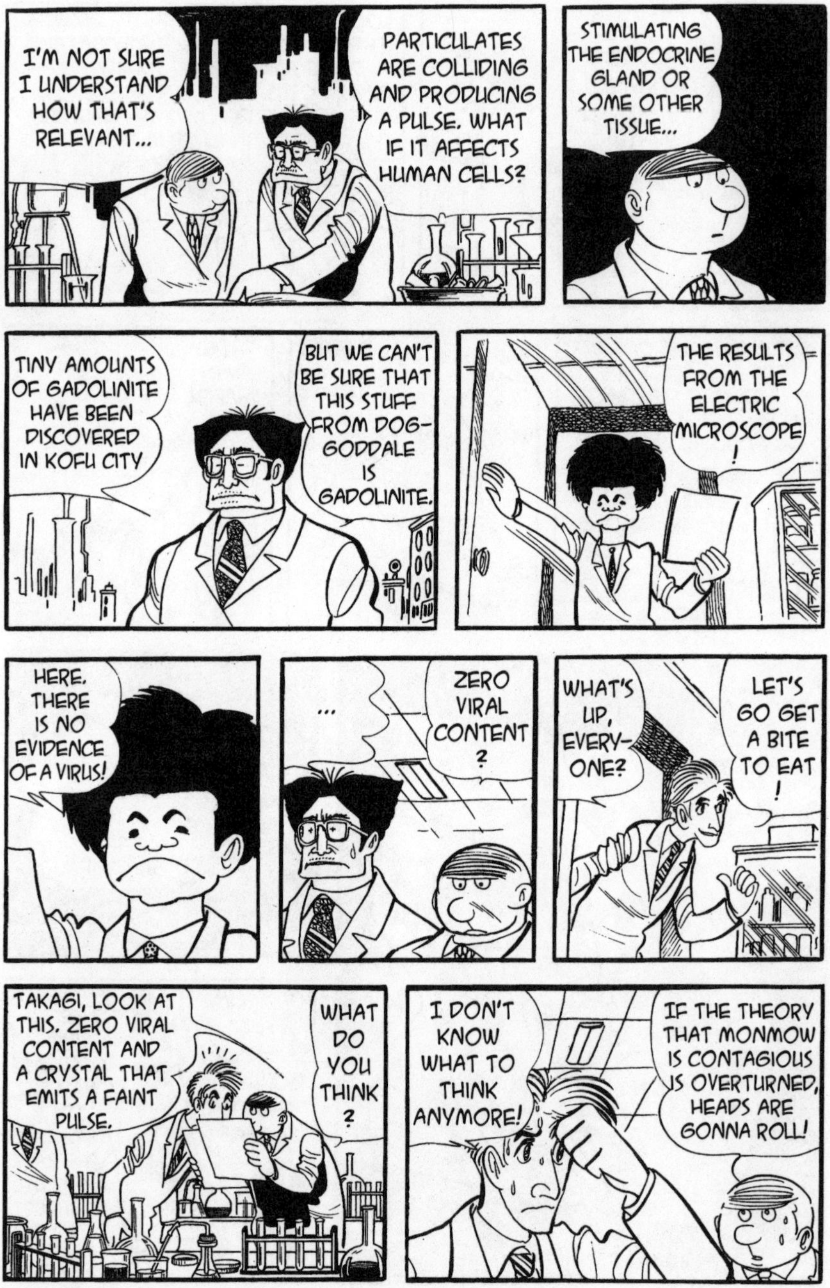
I'M NOT SURE I UNDERSTAND HOW THAT'S RELEVANT...
PARTICULATES ARE COLLIDING AND PRODUCING A PULSE. WHAT IF IT AFFECTS HUMAN CELLS?
STIMULATING THE ENDOCRINE GLAND OR SOME OTHER TISSUE...
TINY AMOUNTS OF GADOLINITE HAVE BEEN DISCOVERED IN KOFU CITY
BUT WE CAN'T BE SURE THAT THIS STUFF FROM DOG-GODDALE IS GADOLINITE.
THE RESULTS FROM THE ELECTRIC MICROSCOPE!
HERE. THERE IS NO EVIDENCE OF A VIRUS!
...
ZERO VIRAL CONTENT?
WHAT'S UP, EVERY-ONE?
LET'S GO GET A BITE TO EAT!
TAKAGI, LOOK AT THIS. ZERO VIRAL CONTENT AND A CRYSTAL THAT EMITS A FAINT PULSE.
WHAT DO YOU THINK?
I DON'T KNOW WHAT TO THINK ANYMORE!
IF THE THEORY THAT MONMOW IS CONTAGIOUS IS OVERTURNED, HEADS ARE GONNA ROLL!

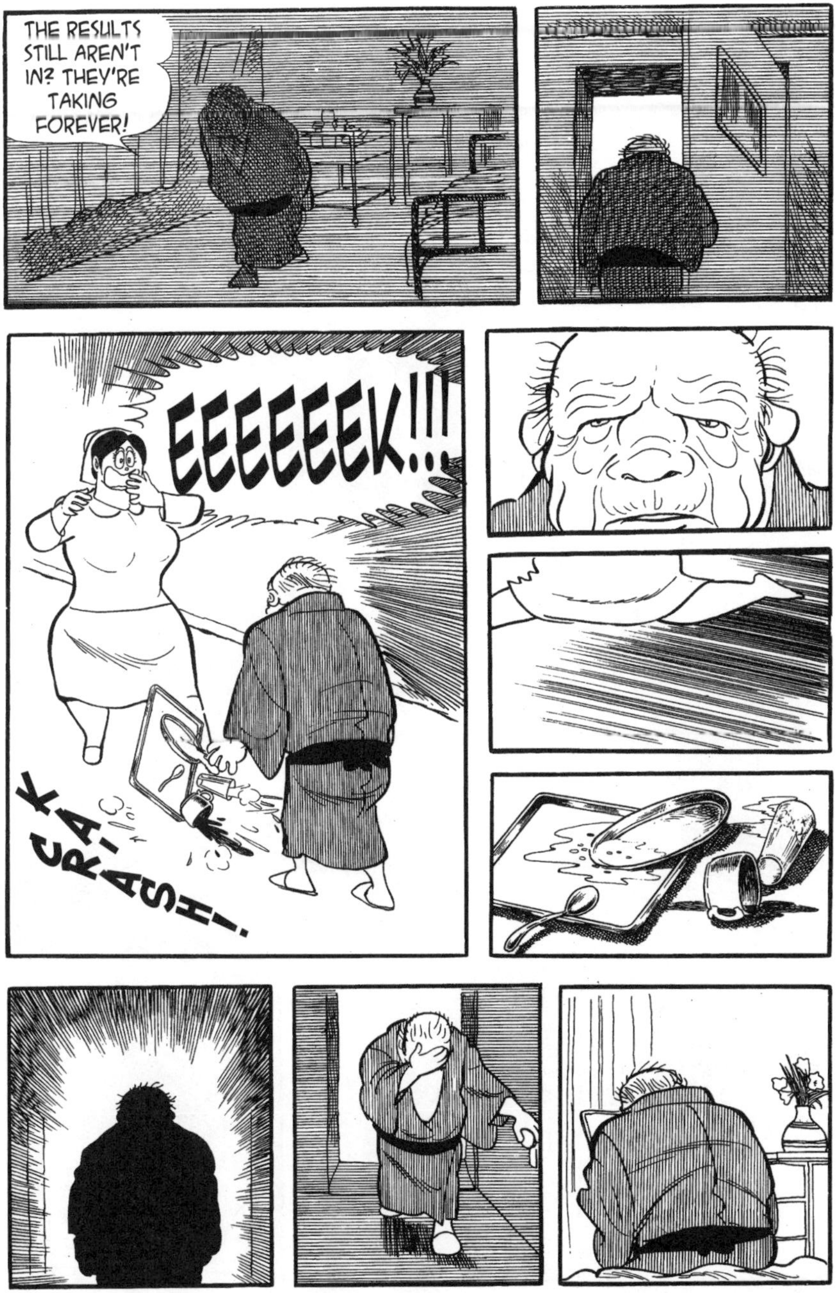
THE RESULTS STILL AREN'T IN? THEY'RE TAKING FOREVER!
EEEEEEK!!!
KA-CRASH!

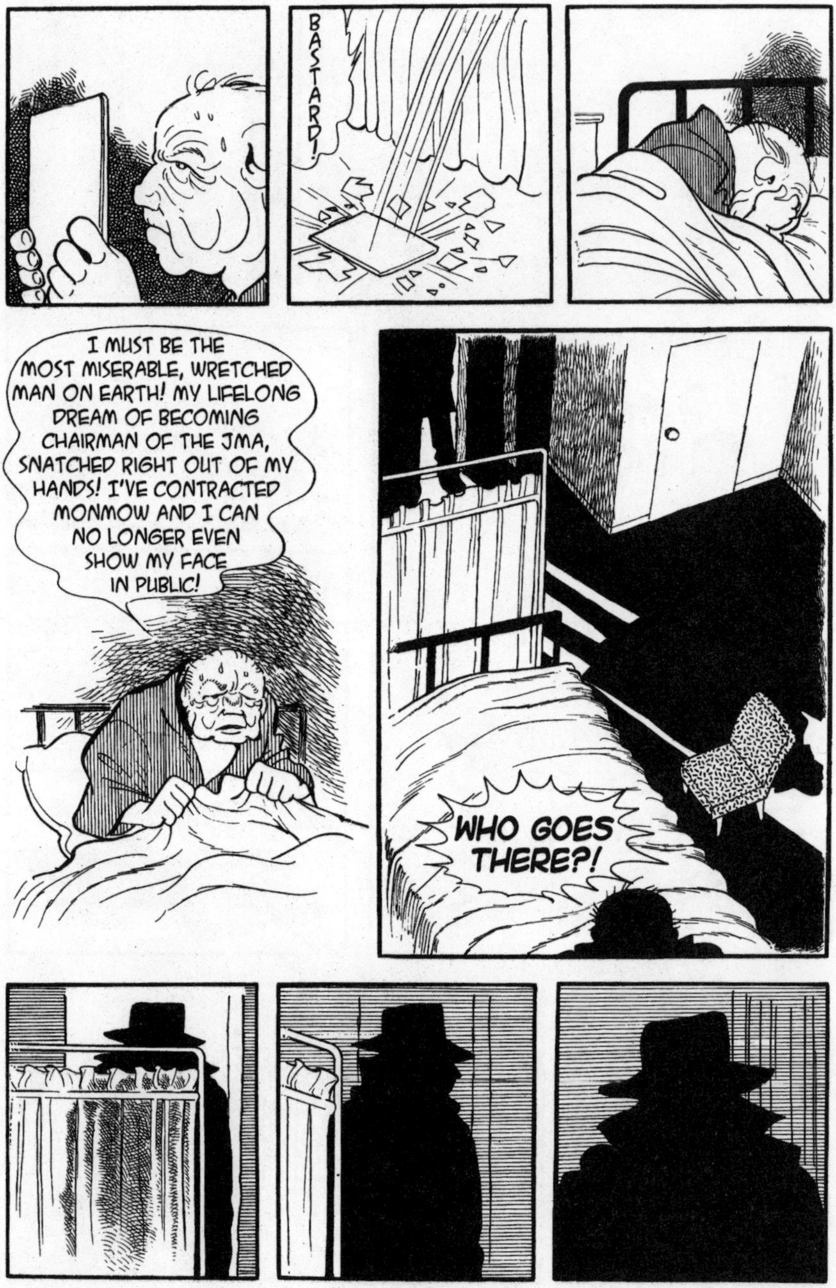
BASTARD!
I MUST BE THE MOST MISERABLE, WRETCHED MAN ON EARTH! MY LIFELONG DREAM OF BECOMING CHAIRMAN OF THE JMA, SNATCHED RIGHT OUT OF MY HANDS! I'VE CONTRACTED MONMOW AND I CAN NO LONGER EVEN SHOW MY FACE IN PUBLIC!
WHO GOES THERE?!

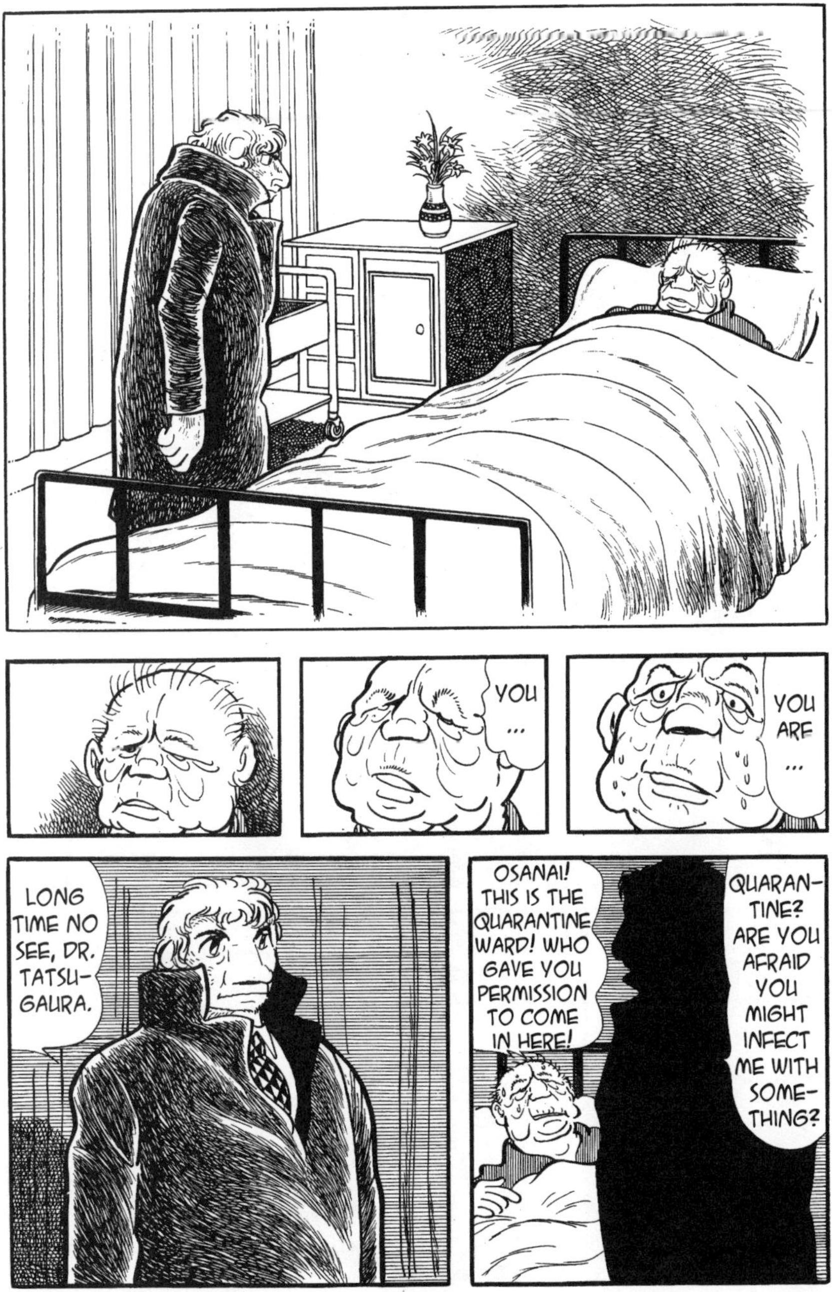
YOU ...
YOU ARE ...
LONG TIME NO SEE, DR. TATSUGAURA.
OSANAI! THIS IS THE QUARANTINE WARD! WHO GAVE YOU PERMISSION TO COME IN HERE!
QUARANTINE? ARE YOU AFRAID YOU MIGHT INFECT ME WITH SOMETHING?

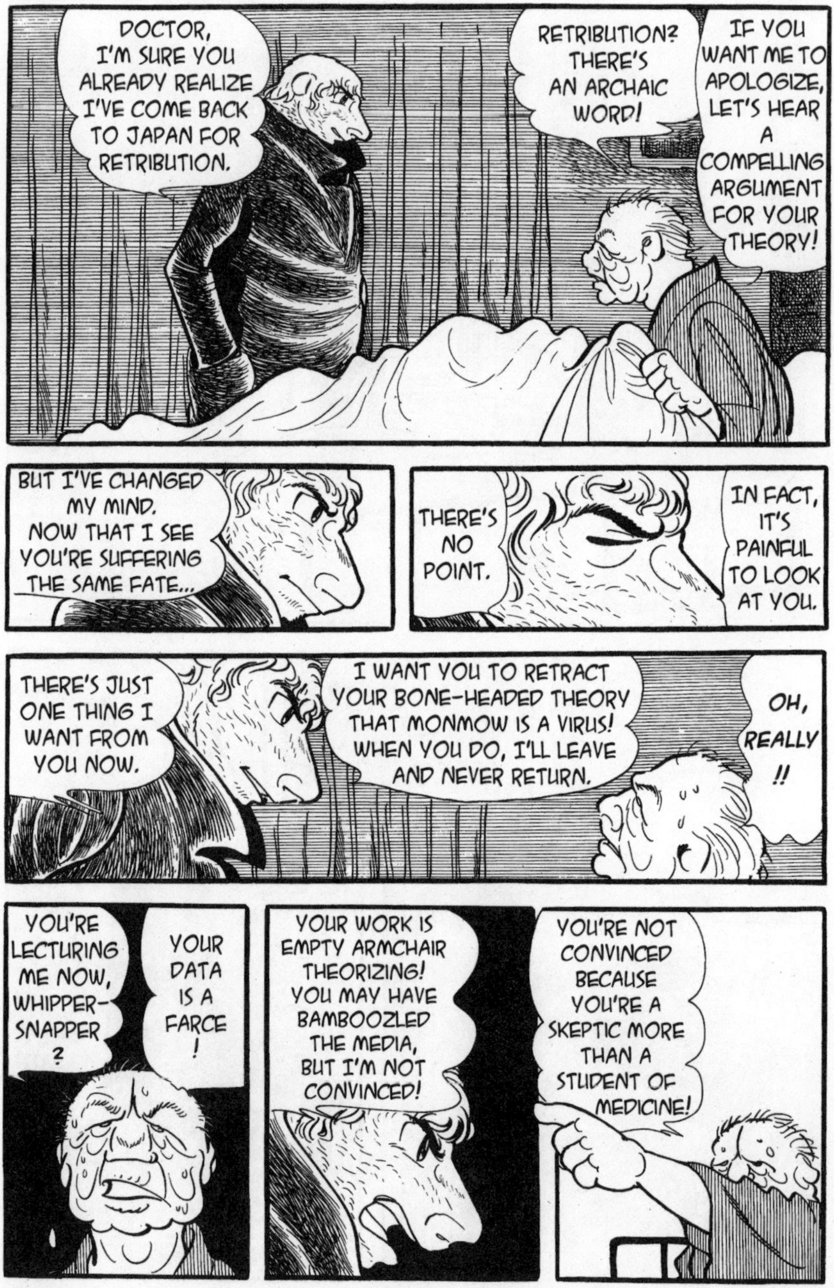
DOCTOR, I'M SURE YOU ALREADY REALIZE I'VE COME BACK TO JAPAN FOR RETRIBUTION.
RETRIBUTION? THERE'S AN ARCHAIC WORD!
IF YOU WANT ME TO APOLOGIZE, LET'S HEAR A COMPELLING ARGUMENT FOR YOUR THEORY!
BUT I'VE CHANGED MY MIND. NOW THAT I SEE YOU'RE SUFFERING THE SAME FATE...
THERE'S NO POINT.
IN FACT, IT'S PAINFUL TO LOOK AT YOU.
THERE'S JUST ONE THING I WANT FROM YOU NOW.
I WANT YOU TO RETRACT YOUR BONE-HEADED THEORY THAT MONMOW IS A VIRUS! WHEN YOU DO, I'LL LEAVE AND NEVER RETURN.
OH, REALLY!!
YOU'RE LECTURING ME NOW, WHIPPER-SNAPPER?
YOUR DATA IS A FARCE!
YOUR WORK IS EMPTY ARMCHAIR THEORIZING! YOU MAY HAVE BAMBOOZLED THE MEDIA, BUT I'M NOT CONVINCED!
YOU'RE NOT CONVINCED BECAUSE YOU'RE A SKEPTIC MORE THAN A STUDENT OF MEDICINE!

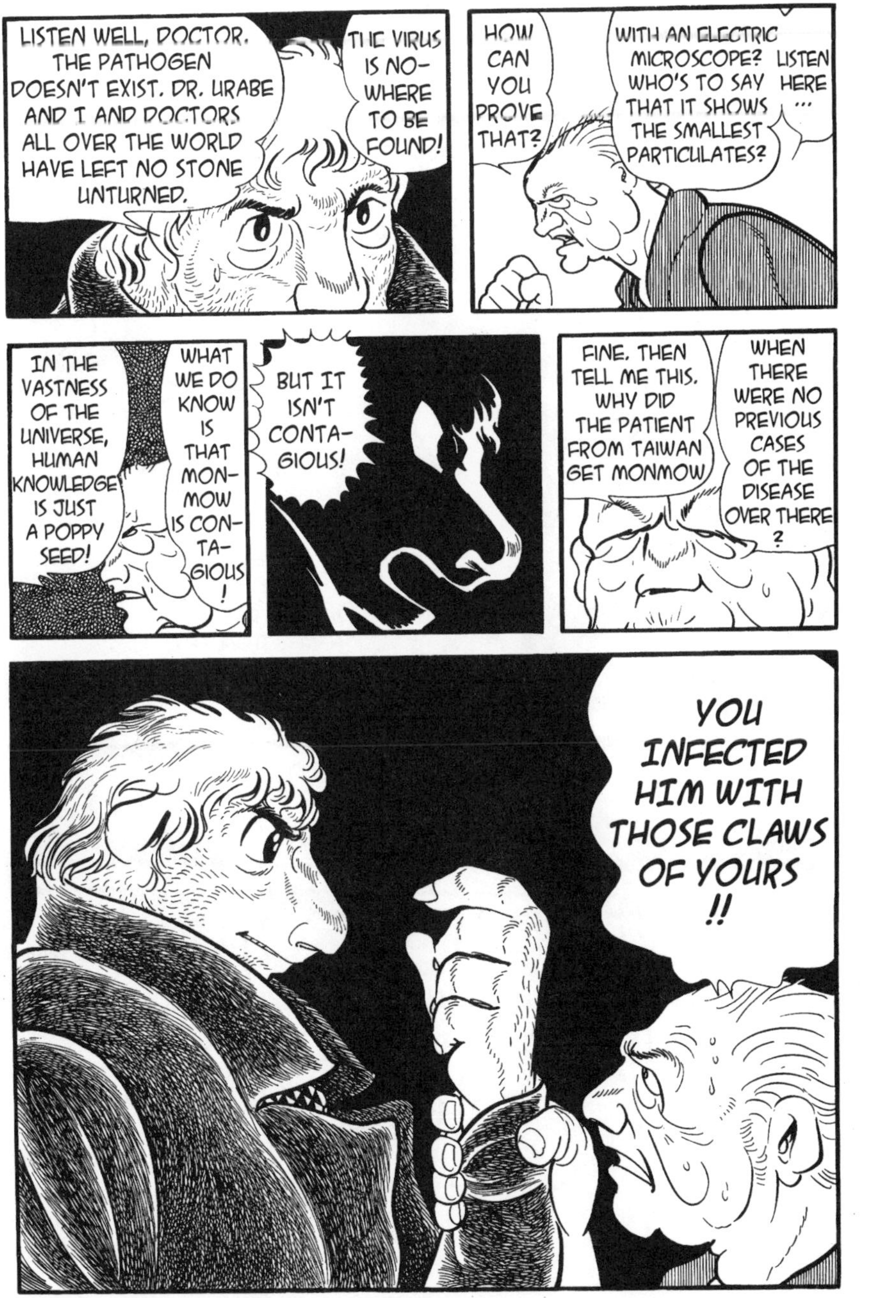
LISTEN WELL, DOCTOR. THE PATHOGEN DOESN'T EXIST. DR. URABE AND I AND DOCTORS ALL OVER THE WORLD HAVE LEFT NO STONE UNTURNED.
THE VIRUS IS NOWHERE TO BE FOUND!
HOW CAN YOU PROVE THAT?
WITH AN ELECTRIC MICROSCOPE? WHO'S TO SAY THAT IT SHOWS THE SMALLEST PARTICULATES?
LISTEN HERE ...
IN THE VASTNESS OF THE UNIVERSE, HUMAN KNOWLEDGE IS JUST A POPPY SEED!
WHAT WE DO KNOW IS THAT MONMOW IS CONTAGIOUS!
BUT IT ISN'T CONTAGIOUS!
FINE. THEN TELL ME THIS. WHY DID THE PATIENT FROM TAIWAN GET MONMOW
WHEN THERE WERE NO PREVIOUS CASES OF THE DISEASE OVER THERE?
YOU INFECTED HIM WITH THOSE CLAWS OF YOURS!!

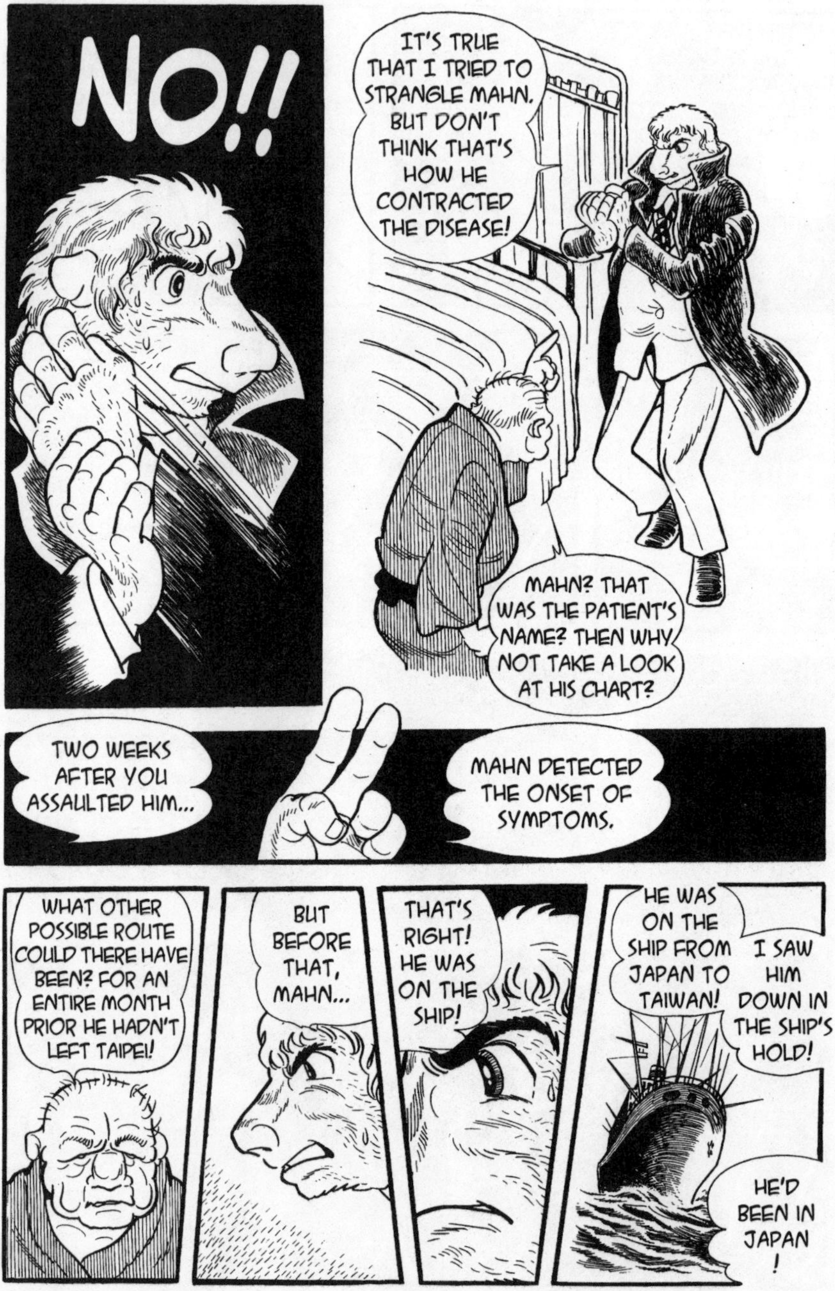
NO!!
IT'S TRUE THAT I TRIED TO STRANGLE MAHN. BUT DON'T THINK THAT'S HOW HE CONTRACTED THE DISEASE!
MAHN? THAT WAS THE PATIENT'S NAME? THEN WHY NOT TAKE A LOOK AT HIS CHART?
TWO WEEKS AFTER YOU ASSAULTED HIM...
MAHN DETECTED THE ONSET OF SYMPTOMS.
WHAT OTHER POSSIBLE ROUTE COULD THERE HAVE BEEN? FOR AN ENTIRE MONTH PRIOR HE HADN'T LEFT TAIPEI!
BUT BEFORE THAT, MAHN...
THAT'S RIGHT! HE WAS ON THE SHIP!
HE WAS ON THE SHIP FROM JAPAN TO TAIWAN!
I SAW HIM DOWN IN THE SHIP'S HOLD!
HE'D BEEN IN JAPAN!

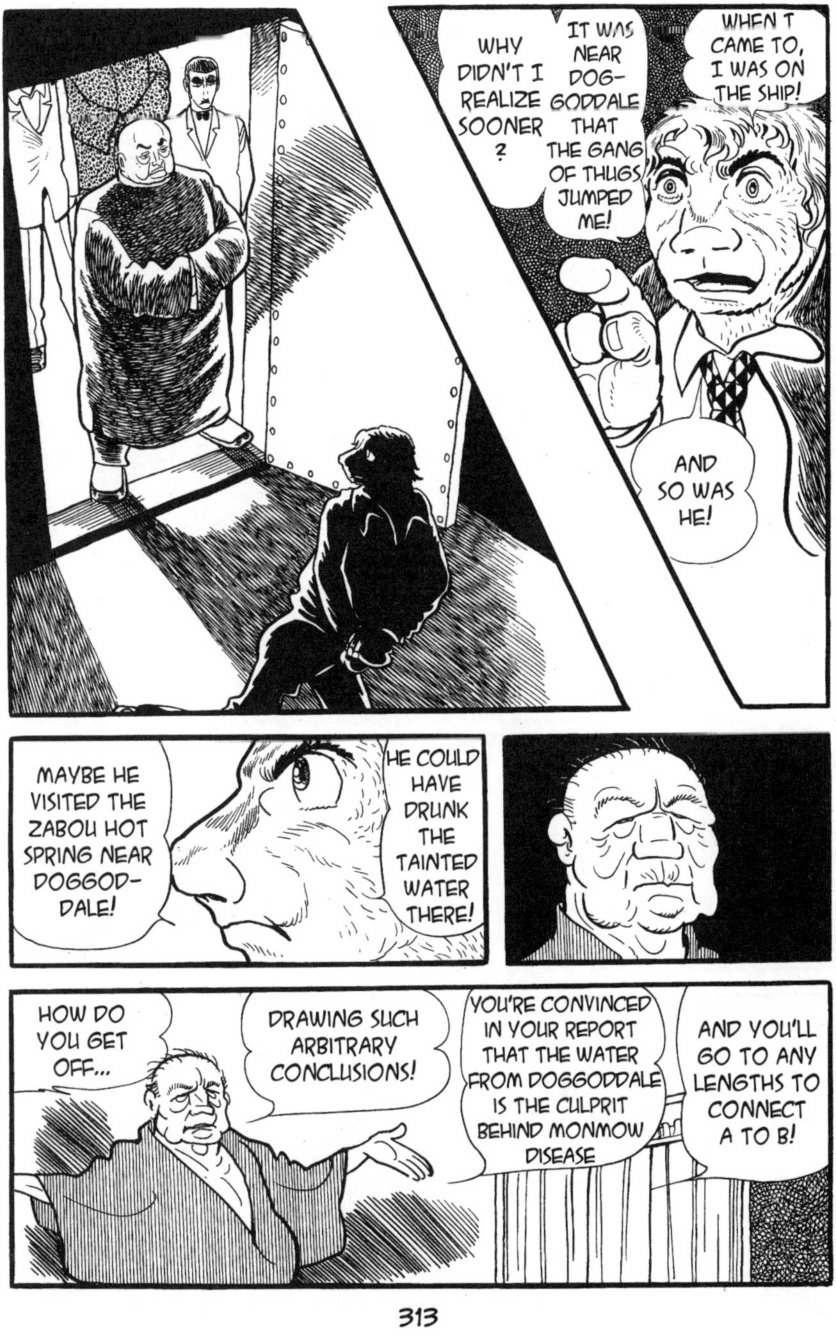
WHY DIDN'T I REALIZE SOONER ?
IT WAS NEAR DOG-GODDALE THAT THE GANG OF THUGS JUMPED ME!
WHEN I CAME TO, I WAS ON THE SHIP!
AND SO WAS HE!
MAYBE HE VISITED THE ZABOU HOT SPRING NEAR DOGGOD-DALE!
HE COULD HAVE DRUNK THE TAINTED WATER THERE!
HOW DO YOU GET OFF...
DRAWING SUCH ARBITRARY CONCLUSIONS!
YOU'RE CONVINCED IN YOUR REPORT THAT THE WATER FROM DOGGODDALE IS THE CULPRIT BEHIND MONMOW DISEASE
AND YOU'LL GO TO ANY LENGTHS TO CONNECT A TO B!

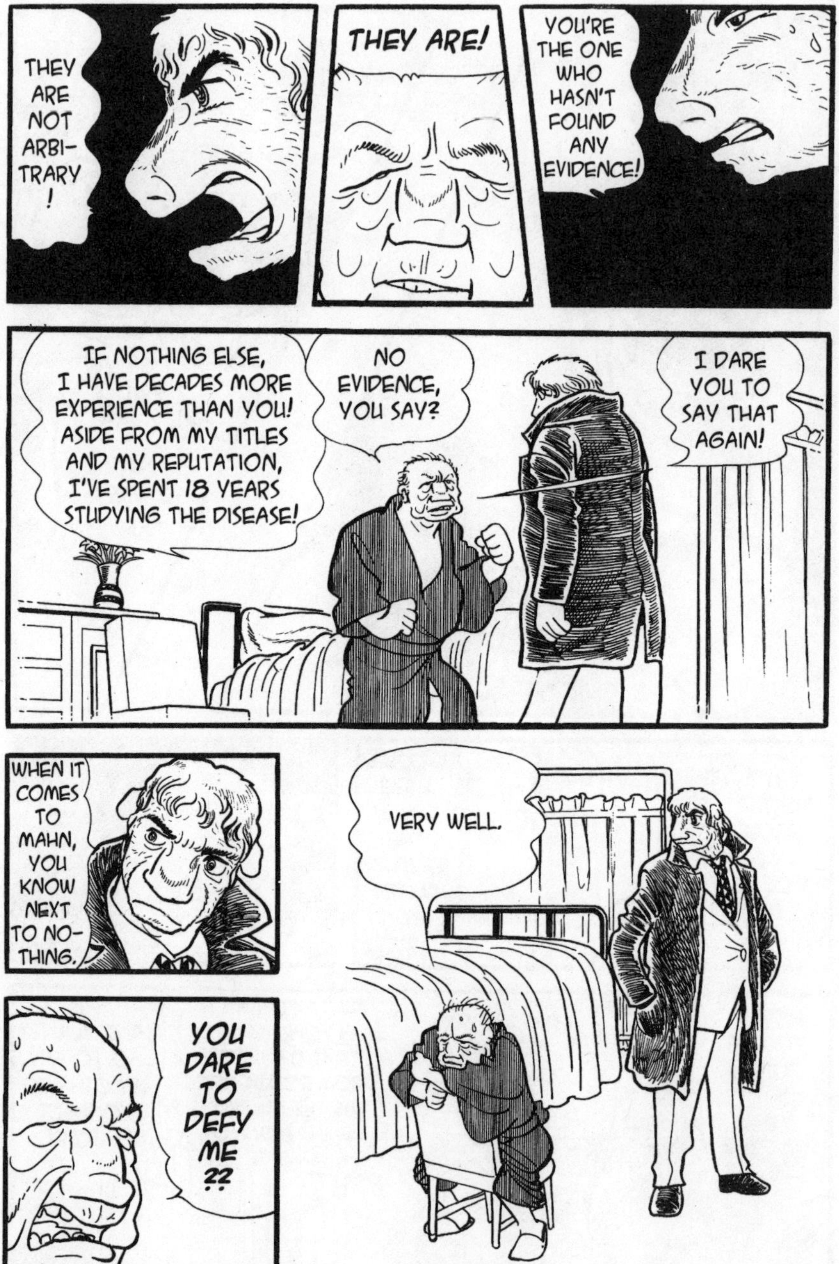

THEY ARE NOT ARBITRARY!
THEY ARE!
YOU'RE THE ONE WHO HASN'T FOUND ANY EVIDENCE!
IF NOTHING ELSE, I HAVE DECADES MORE EXPERIENCE THAN YOU! ASIDE FROM MY TITLES AND MY REPUTATION, I'VE SPENT 18 YEARS STUDYING THE DISEASE!
NO EVIDENCE, YOU SAY?
I DARE YOU TO SAY THAT AGAIN!
WHEN IT COMES TO MAHN, YOU KNOW NEXT TO NOTHING.
YOU DARE TO DEFY ME??
VERY WELL.

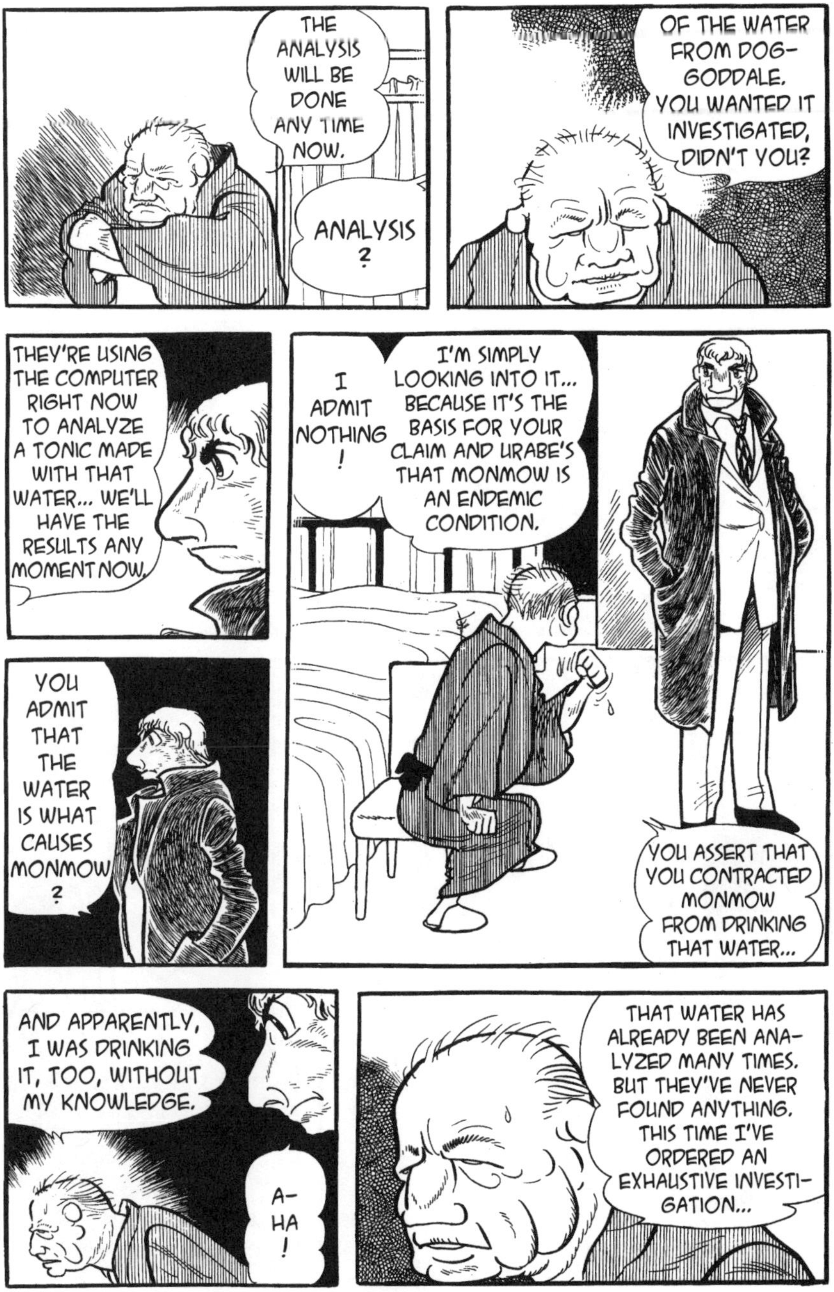
THE ANALYSIS WILL BE DONE ANY TIME NOW.
ANALYSIS?
OF THE WATER FROM DOG-GODDALE. YOU WANTED IT INVESTIGATED, DIDN'T YOU?
THEY'RE USING THE COMPUTER RIGHT NOW TO ANALYZE A TONIC MADE WITH THAT WATER... WE'LL HAVE THE RESULTS ANY MOMENT NOW.
YOU ADMIT THAT THE WATER IS WHAT CAUSES MONMOW?
I ADMIT NOTHING!
I'M SIMPLY LOOKING INTO IT... BECAUSE IT'S THE BASIS FOR YOUR CLAIM AND URABE'S THAT MONMOW IS AN ENDEMIC CONDITION.
YOU ASSERT THAT YOU CONTRACTED MONMOW FROM DRINKING THAT WATER...
AND APPARENTLY, I WAS DRINKING IT, TOO, WITHOUT MY KNOWLEDGE.
A-HA!
THAT WATER HAS ALREADY BEEN ANALYZED MANY TIMES. BUT THEY'VE NEVER FOUND ANYTHING. THIS TIME I'VE ORDERED AN EXHAUSTIVE INVESTIGATION...

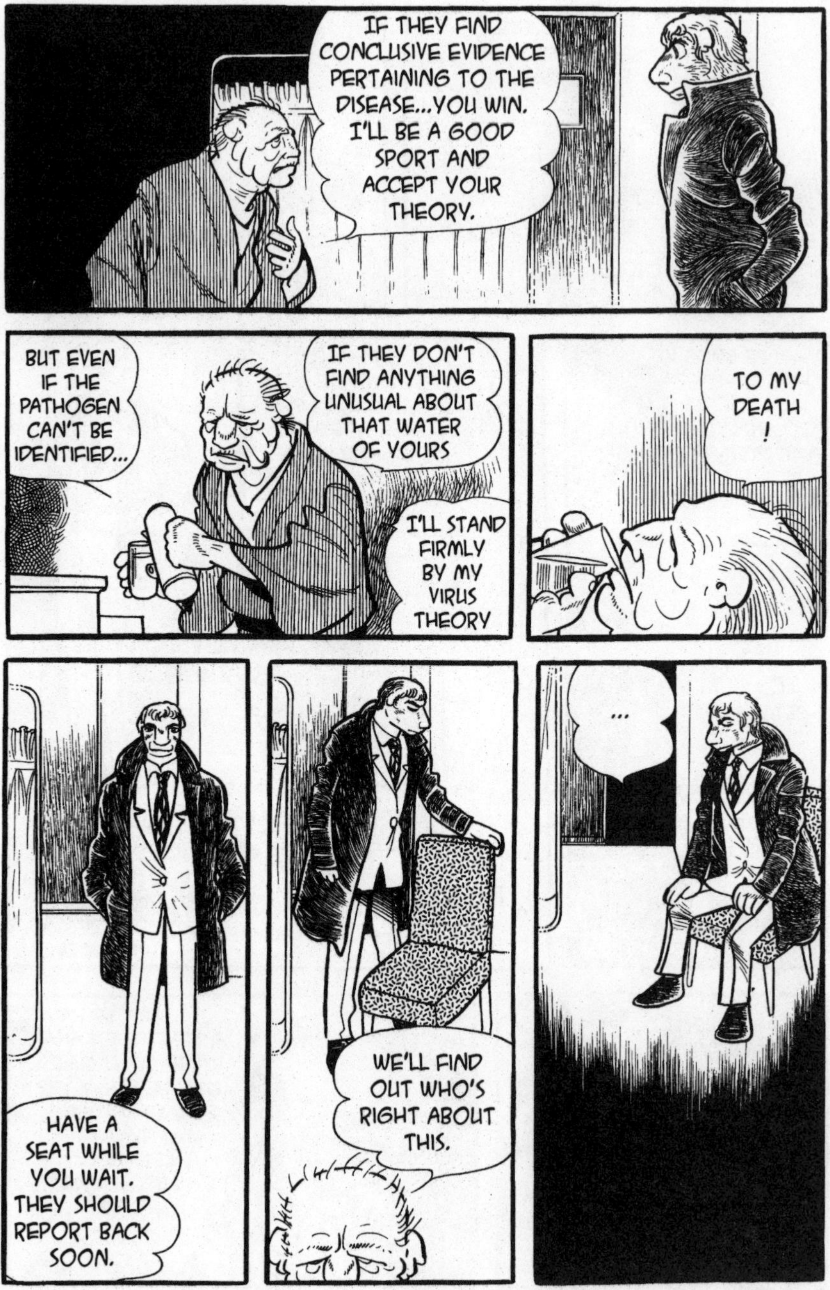
IF THEY FIND CONCLUSIVE EVIDENCE PERTAINING TO THE DISEASE...YOU WIN. I'LL BE A GOOD SPORT AND ACCEPT YOUR THEORY.
BUT EVEN IF THE PATHOGEN CAN'T BE IDENTIFIED...
IF THEY DON'T FIND ANYTHING UNUSUAL ABOUT THAT WATER OF YOURS
I'LL STAND FIRMLY BY MY VIRUS THEORY
TO MY DEATH!
HAVE A SEAT WHILE YOU WAIT. THEY SHOULD REPORT BACK SOON.
WE'LL FIND OUT WHO'S RIGHT ABOUT THIS.
...

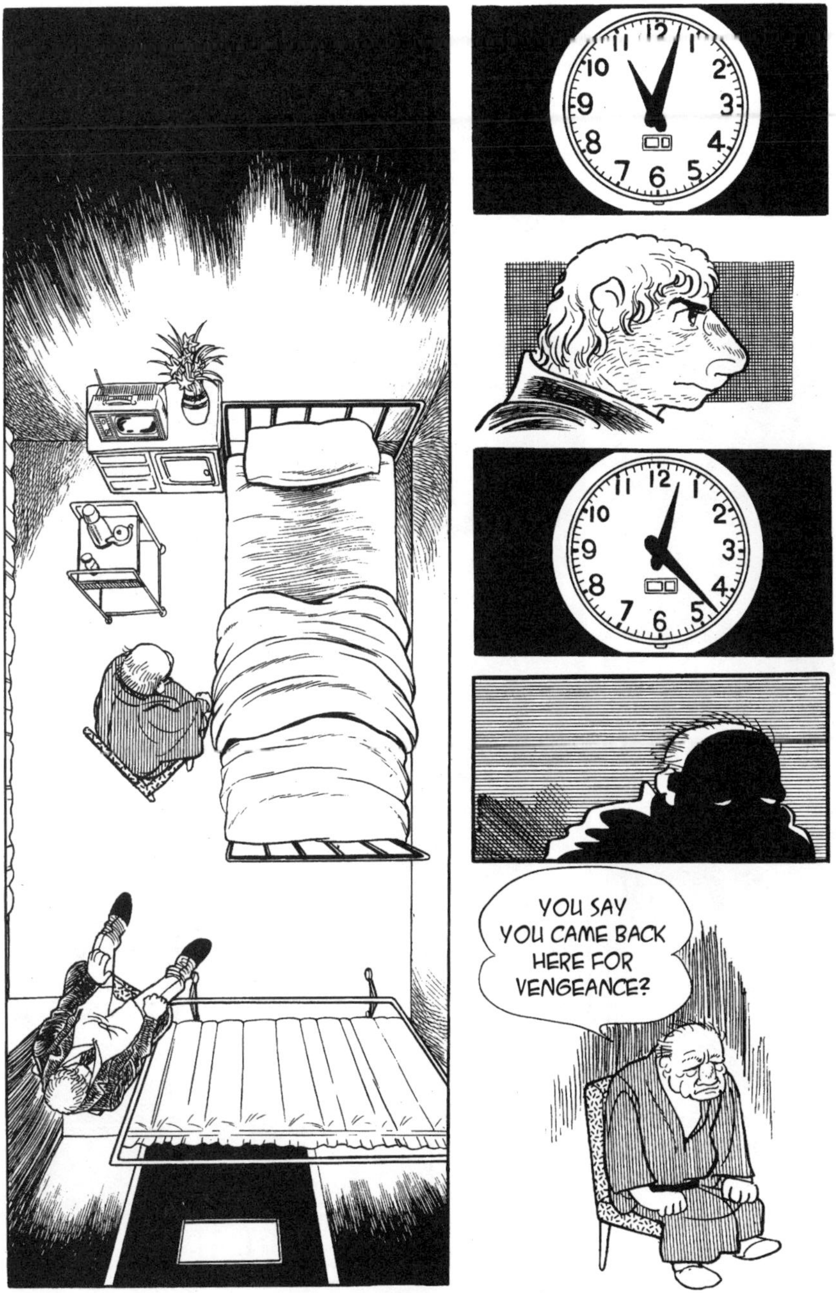
YOU SAY YOU CAME BACK HERE FOR VENGEANCE?

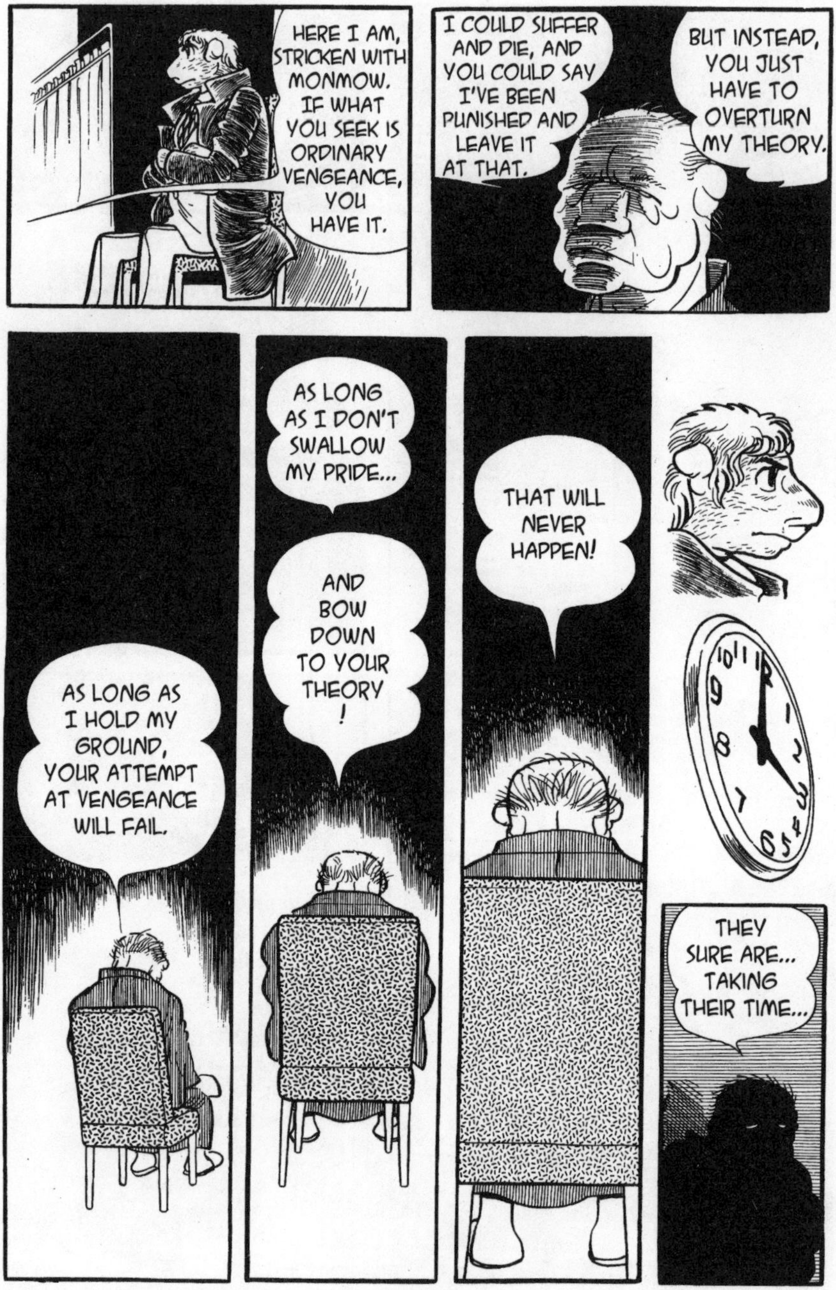

HERE I AM, STRICKEN WITH MONMOW. IF WHAT YOU SEEK IS ORDINARY VENGEANCE, YOU HAVE IT.
I COULD SUFFER AND DIE, AND YOU COULD SAY I'VE BEEN PUNISHED AND LEAVE IT AT THAT.
BUT INSTEAD, YOU JUST HAVE TO OVERTURN MY THEORY.
AS LONG AS I HOLD MY GROUND, YOUR ATTEMPT AT VENGEANCE WILL FAIL.
AS LONG AS I DON'T SWALLOW MY PRIDE...
AND BOW DOWN TO YOUR THEORY!
THAT WILL NEVER HAPPEN!
THEY SURE ARE... TAKING THEIR TIME...

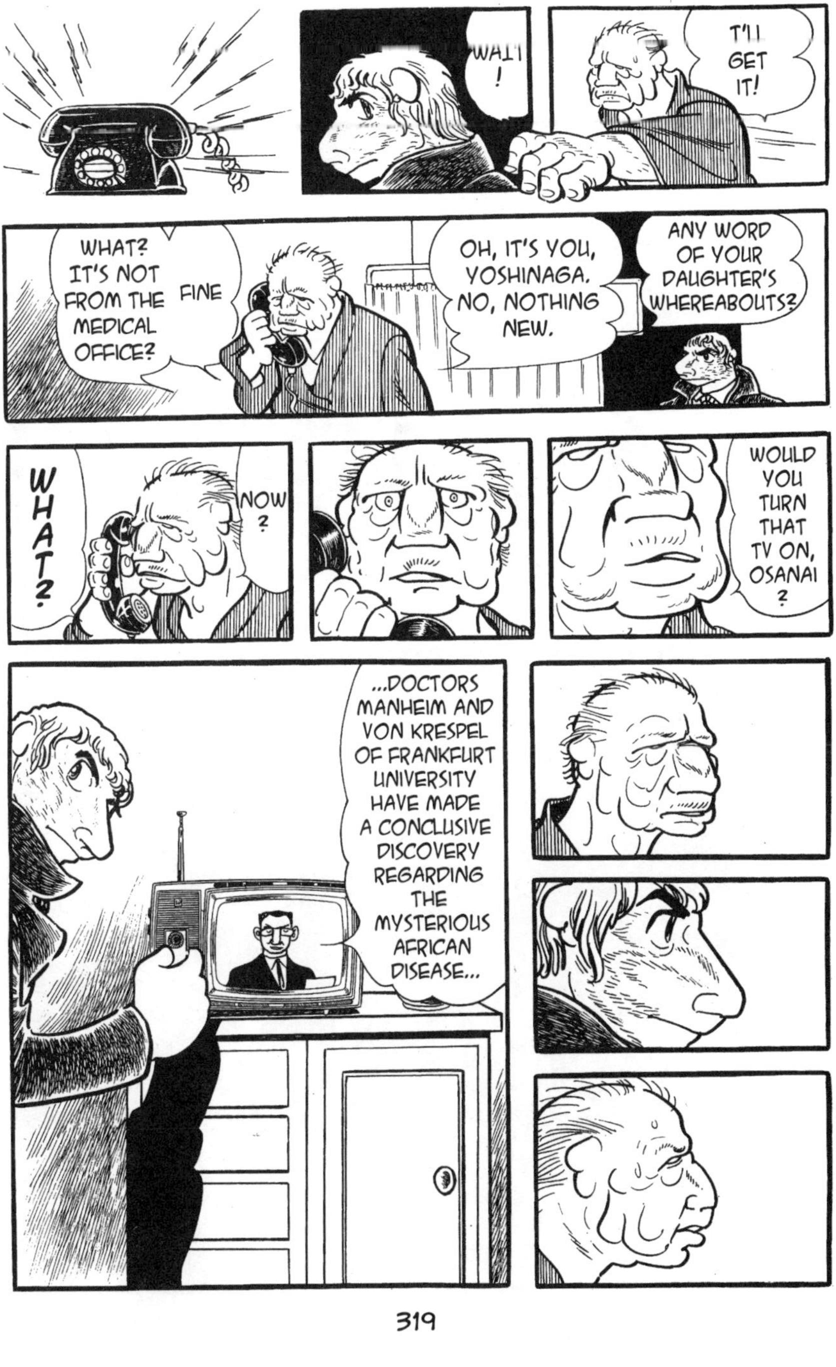
WAIT!
I'LL GET IT!
WHAT? IT'S NOT FROM THE MEDICAL OFFICE?
FINE
OH, IT'S YOU, YOSHINAGA. NO, NOTHING NEW.
ANY WORD OF YOUR DAUGHTER'S WHEREABOUTS?
WHAT?
NOW?
WOULD YOU TURN THAT TV ON, OSANAI?
...DOCTORS MANHEIM AND VON KRESPEL OF FRANKFURT UNIVERSITY HAVE MADE A CONCLUSIVE DISCOVERY REGARDING THE MYSTERIOUS AFRICAN DISEASE...

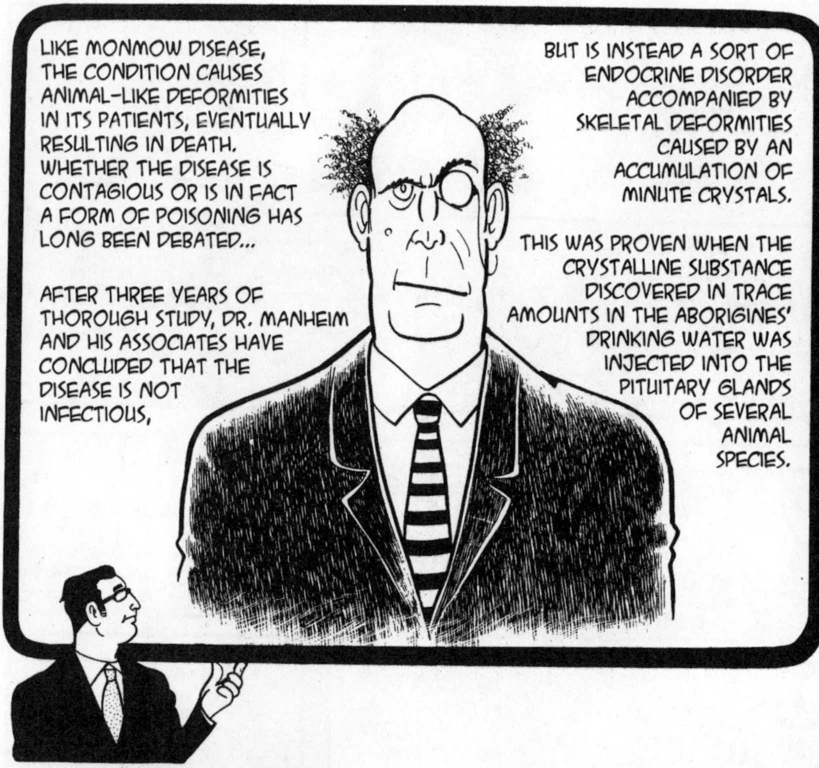
LIKE MONMOW DISEASE, THE CONDITION CAUSES ANIMAL-LIKE DEFORMITIES IN ITS PATIENTS, EVENTUALLY RESULTING IN DEATH. WHETHER THE DISEASE IS CONTAGIOUS OR IS IN FACT A FORM OF POISONING HAS LONG BEEN DEBATED...
AFTER THREE YEARS OF THOROUGH STUDY, DR. MANHEIM AND HIS ASSOCIATES HAVE CONCLUDED THAT THE DISEASE IS NOT INFECTIOUS,
BUT IS INSTEAD A SORT OF ENDOCRINE DISORDER ACCOMPANIED BY SKELETAL DEFORMITIES CAUSED BY AN ACCUMULATION OF MINUTE CRYSTALS.
THIS WAS PROVEN WHEN THE CRYSTALLINE SUBSTANCE DISCOVERED IN TRACE AMOUNTS IN THE ABORIGINES' DRINKING WATER WAS INJECTED INTO THE PITUITARY GLANDS OF SEVERAL ANIMAL SPECIES.
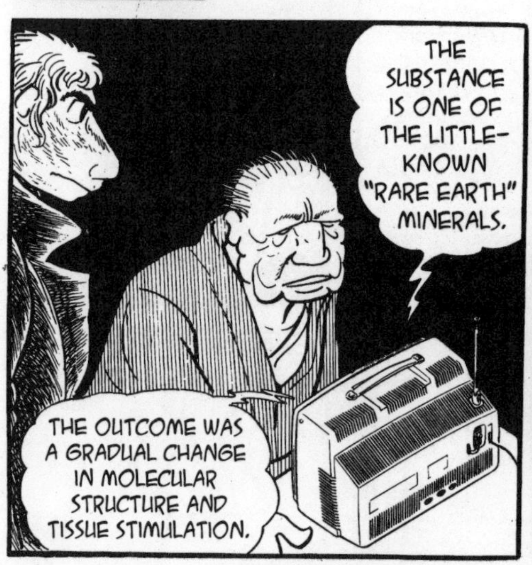
THE OUTCOME WAS A GRADUAL CHANGE IN MOLECULAR STRUCTURE AND TISSUE STIMULATION.
THE SUBSTANCE IS ONE OF THE LITTLE-KNOWN "RARE EARTH" MINERALS.
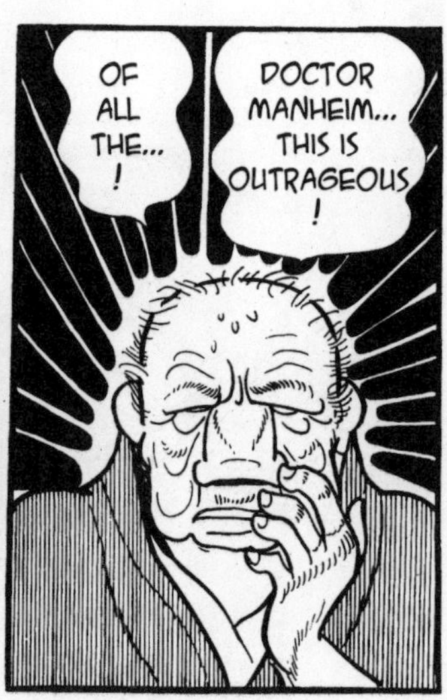
DOCTOR MANHEIM... THIS IS OUTRAGEOUS!
OF ALL THE...!

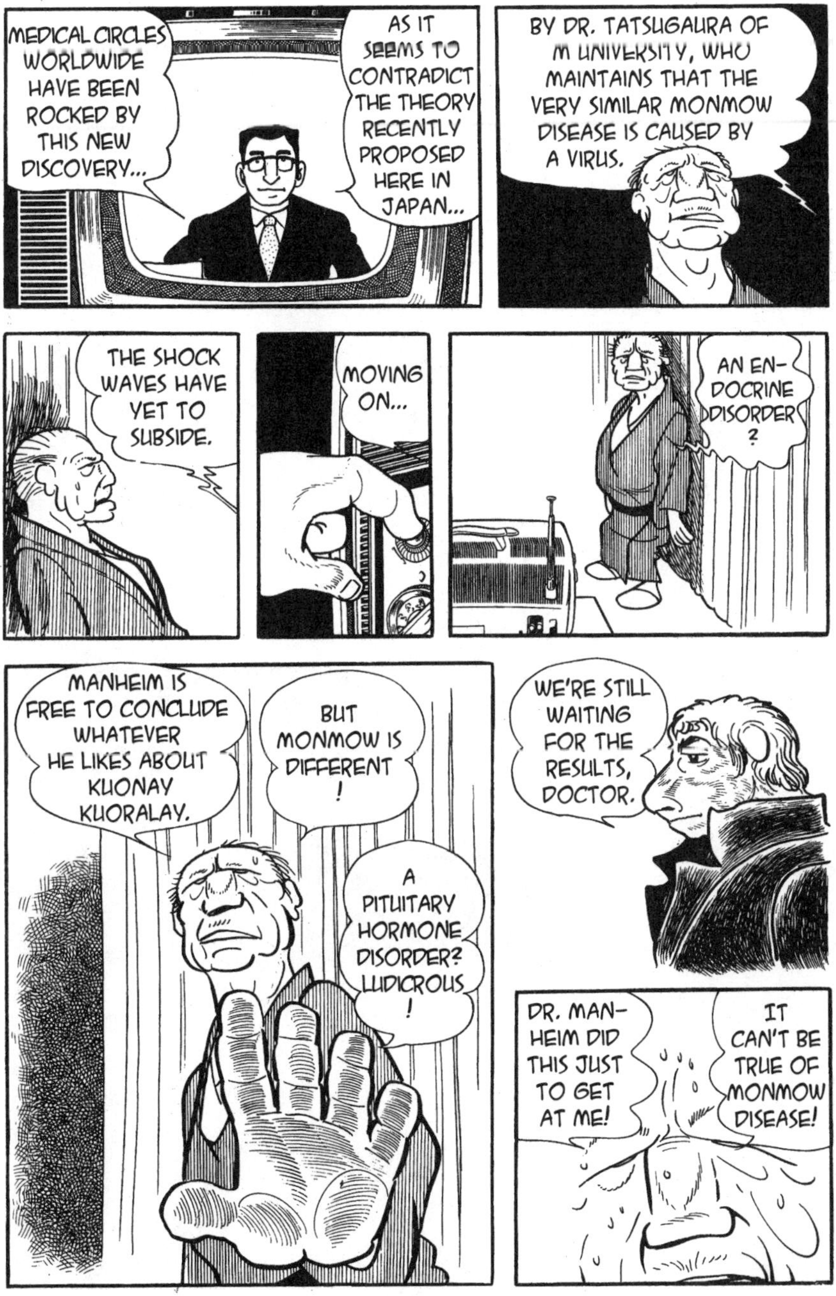
MEDICAL CIRCLES WORLDWIDE HAVE BEEN ROCKED BY THIS NEW DISCOVERY...
AS IT SEEMS TO CONTRADICT THE THEORY RECENTLY PROPOSED HERE IN JAPAN...
BY DR. TATSUGAURA OF M UNIVERSITY, WHO MAINTAINS THAT THE VERY SIMILAR MONMOW DISEASE IS CAUSED BY A VIRUS.
THE SHOCK WAVES HAVE YET TO SUBSIDE.
MOVING ON...
AN ENDOCRINE DISORDER?
MANHEIM IS FREE TO CONCLUDE WHATEVER HE LIKES ABOUT KUONAY KUORALAY.
BUT MONMOW IS DIFFERENT!
A PITUITARY HORMONE DISORDER? LUDICROUS!
WE'RE STILL WAITING FOR THE RESULTS, DOCTOR.
DR. MANHEIM DID THIS JUST TO GET AT ME!
IT CAN'T BE TRUE OF MONMOW DISEASE!

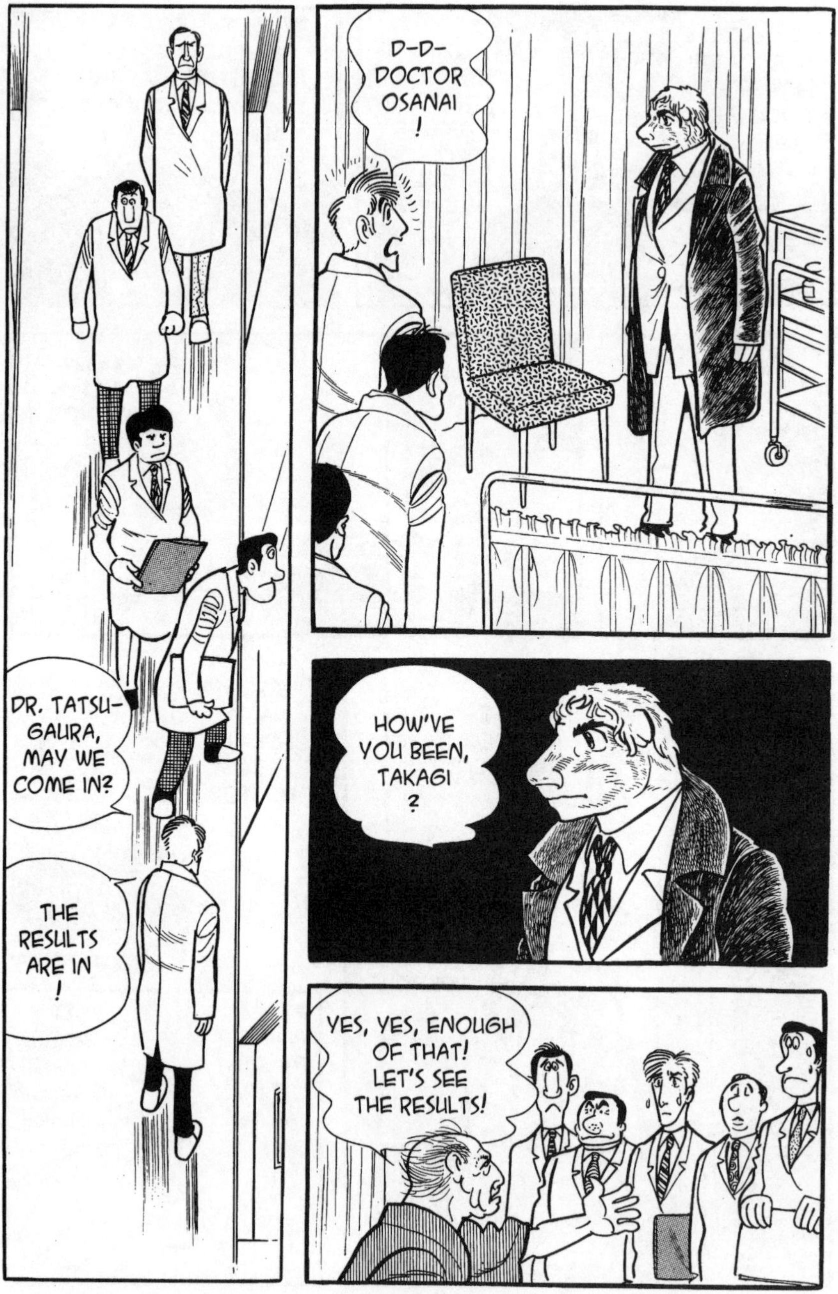
D-D-DOCTOR OSANAI!
HOW'VE YOU BEEN, TAKAGI?
YES, YES, ENOUGH OF THAT! LET'S SEE THE RESULTS!
DR. TATSU-GAURA, MAY WE COME IN?
THE RESULTS ARE IN!

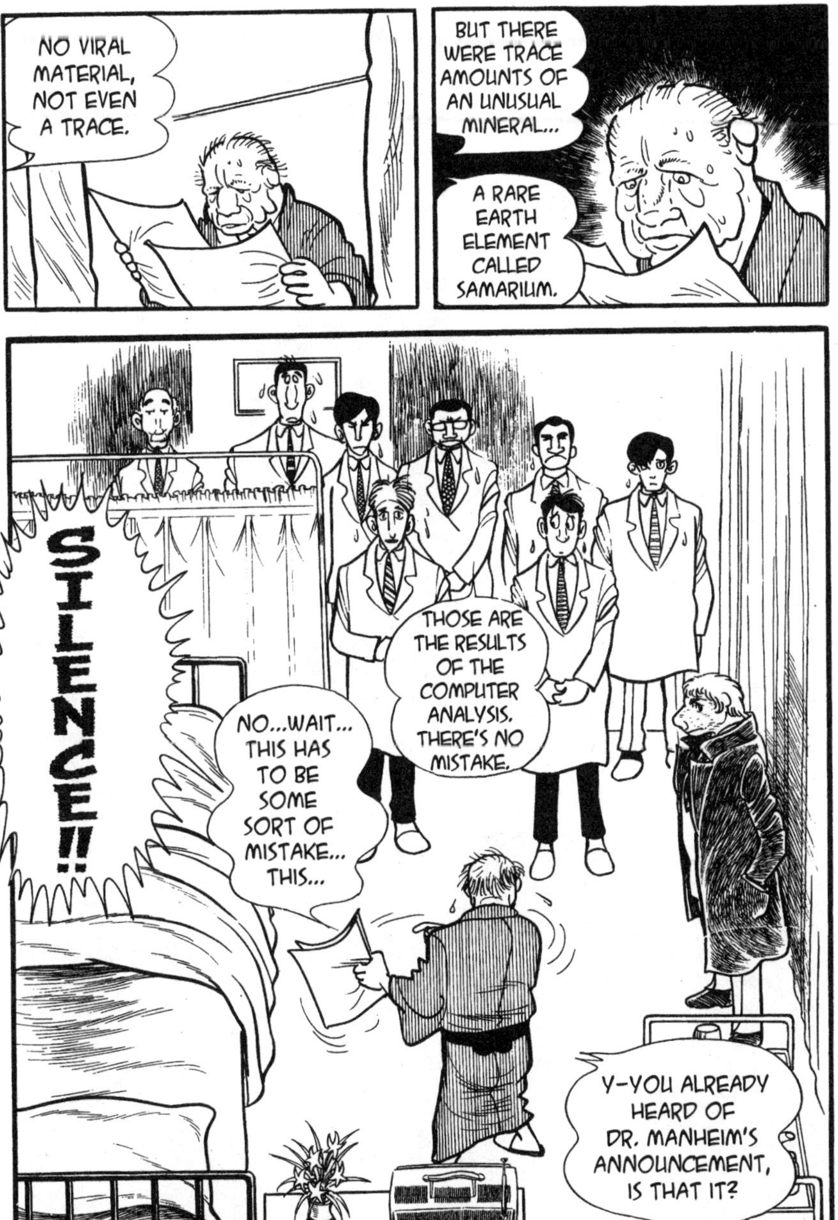
NO VIRAL MATERIAL, NOT EVEN A TRACE.
BUT THERE WERE TRACE AMOUNTS OF AN UNUSUAL MINERAL...
A RARE EARTH ELEMENT CALLED SAMARIUM.
SILENCE!!
NO...WAIT... THIS HAS TO BE SOME SORT OF MISTAKE... THIS...
THOSE ARE THE RESULTS OF THE COMPUTER ANALYSIS. THERE'S NO MISTAKE.
Y-YOU ALREADY HEARD OF DR. MANHEIM'S ANNOUNCEMENT, IS THAT IT?

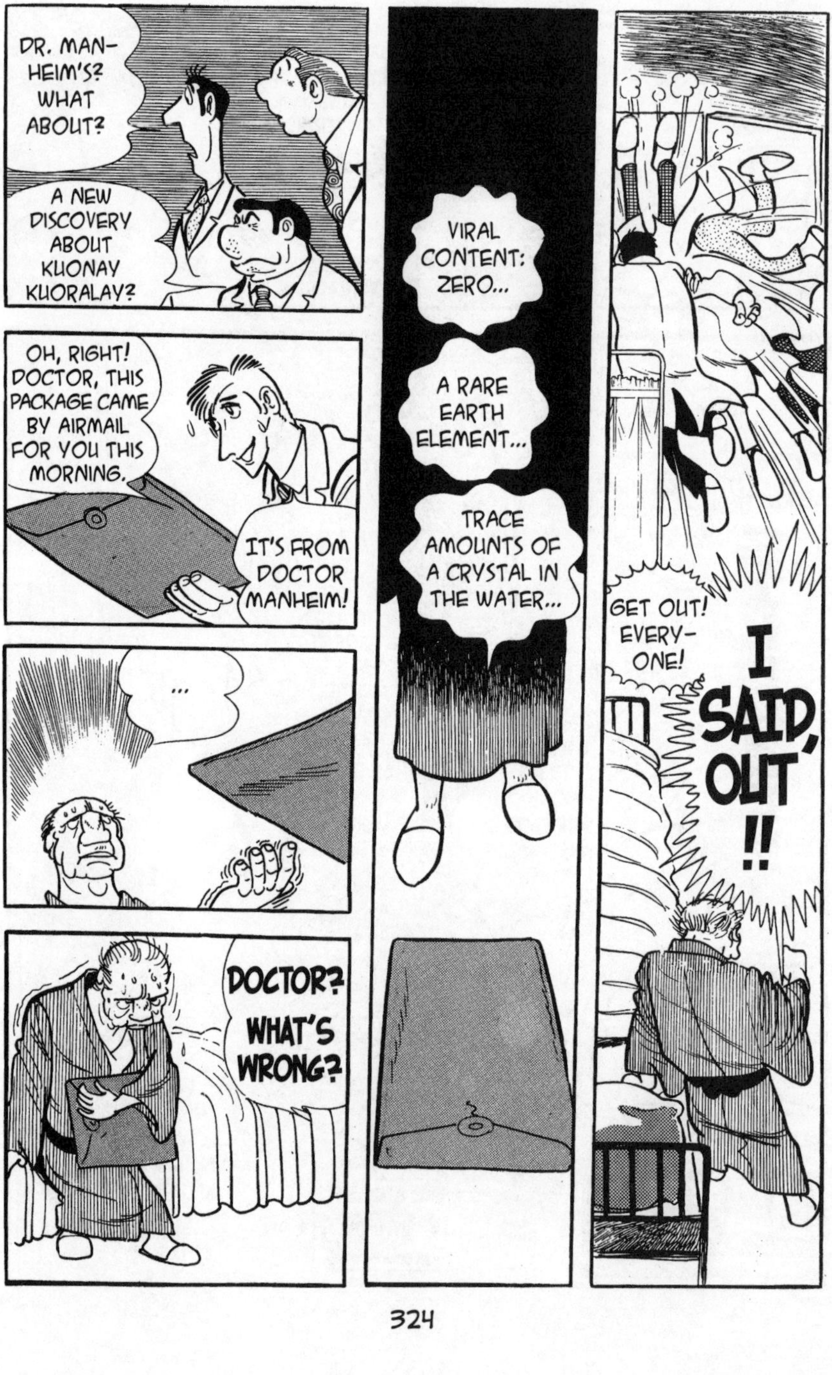
DR. MAN-HEIM'S? WHAT ABOUT?
A NEW DISCOVERY ABOUT KUONAY KUORALAY?
OH, RIGHT! DOCTOR, THIS PACKAGE CAME BY AIRMAIL FOR YOU THIS MORNING.
IT'S FROM DOCTOR MANHEIM!
...
DOCTOR? WHAT'S WRONG?
VIRAL CONTENT: ZERO...
A RARE EARTH ELEMENT...
TRACE AMOUNTS OF A CRYSTAL IN THE WATER...
GET OUT! EVERY-ONE!
I SAID, OUT!!

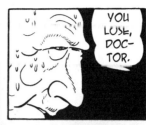

YOU LOSE, DOC- TOR.

NO!

I'M RIGHT! I WILL NOT GIVE IN!

I'LL NEVER... EVER CHANGE MY MIND!

I'LL FIND A NEW PATHOGEN... I'LL SHOW YOU!

IF IT'S THE LAST THING I DO...

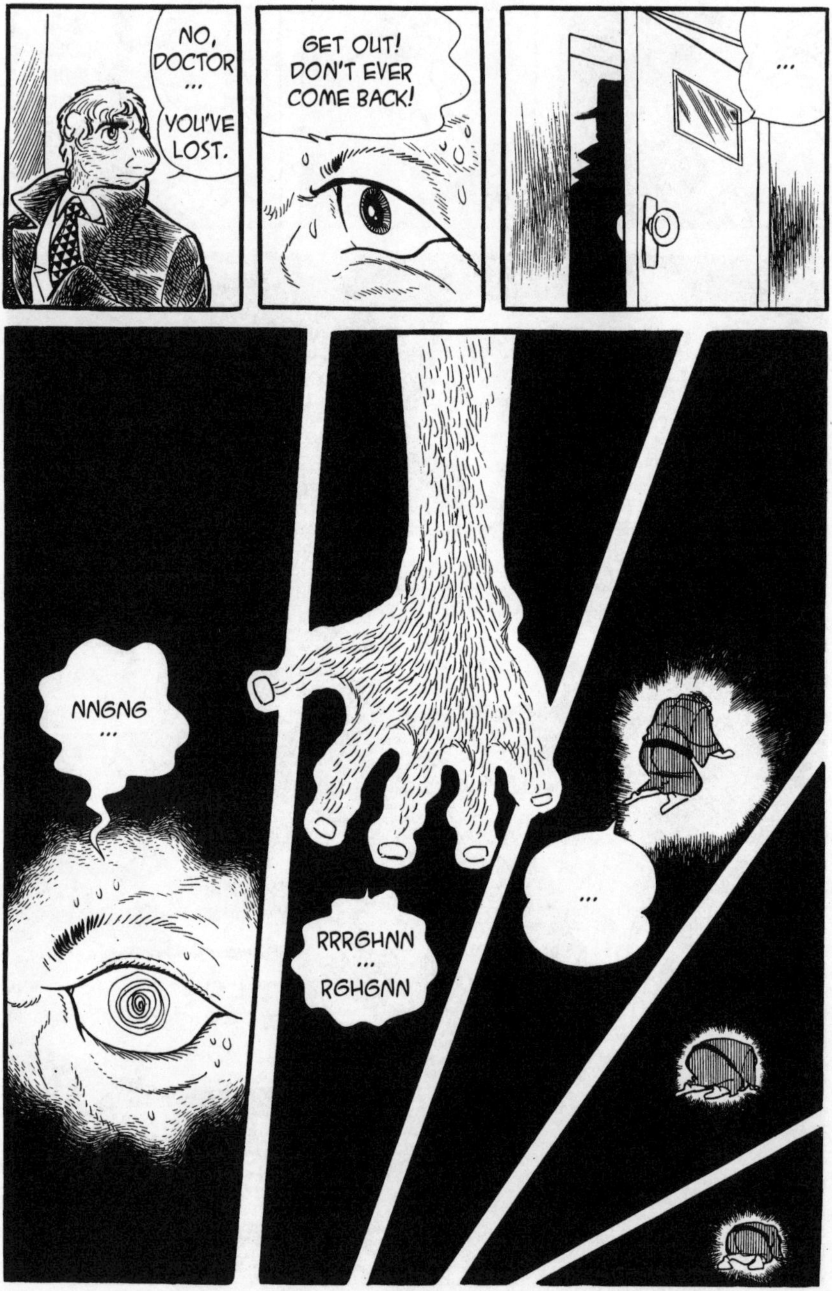
NO, DOCTOR ... YOU'VE LOST.
GET OUT! DON'T EVER COME BACK!
...
NNGNG ...
RRRGHNN ... RGHGNN
...

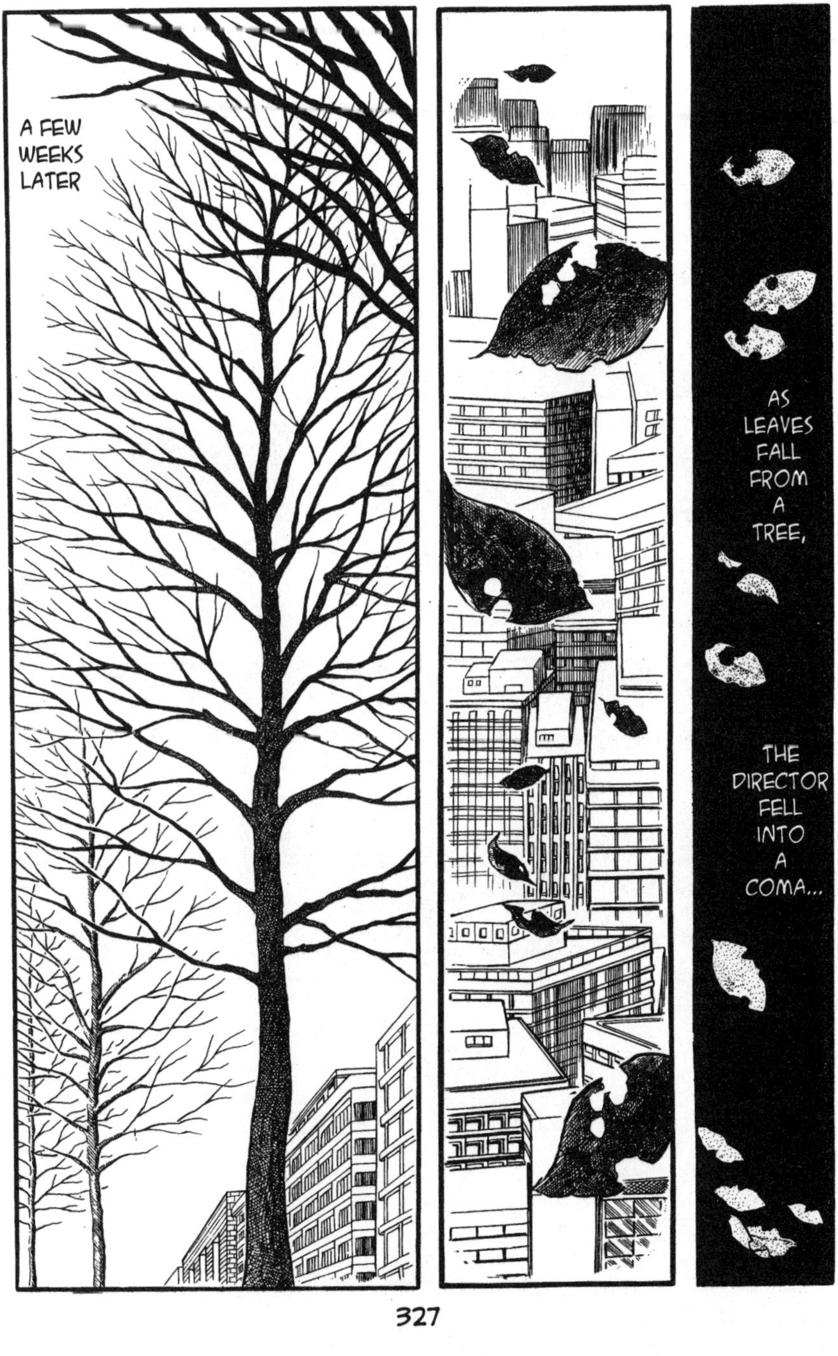
A FEW WEEKS LATER
AS LEAVES FALL FROM A TREE,
THE DIRECTOR FELL INTO A COMA...

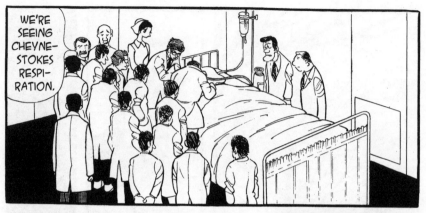

WE'RE SEEING CHEYNE-STOKES RESPIRATION.

HE'S REGAINED CONSCIOUSNESS!

DOCTOR!

GET BACK TO YOUR POSTS. DON'T NEGLECT YOUR WORK.

DOCTOR!

MR. YOSHINAGA... SORRY I CAUSED YOU WORRY...

IS OSANAI STILL AROUND?

IF YOU SEE HIM, TELL HIM THIS FOR ME...

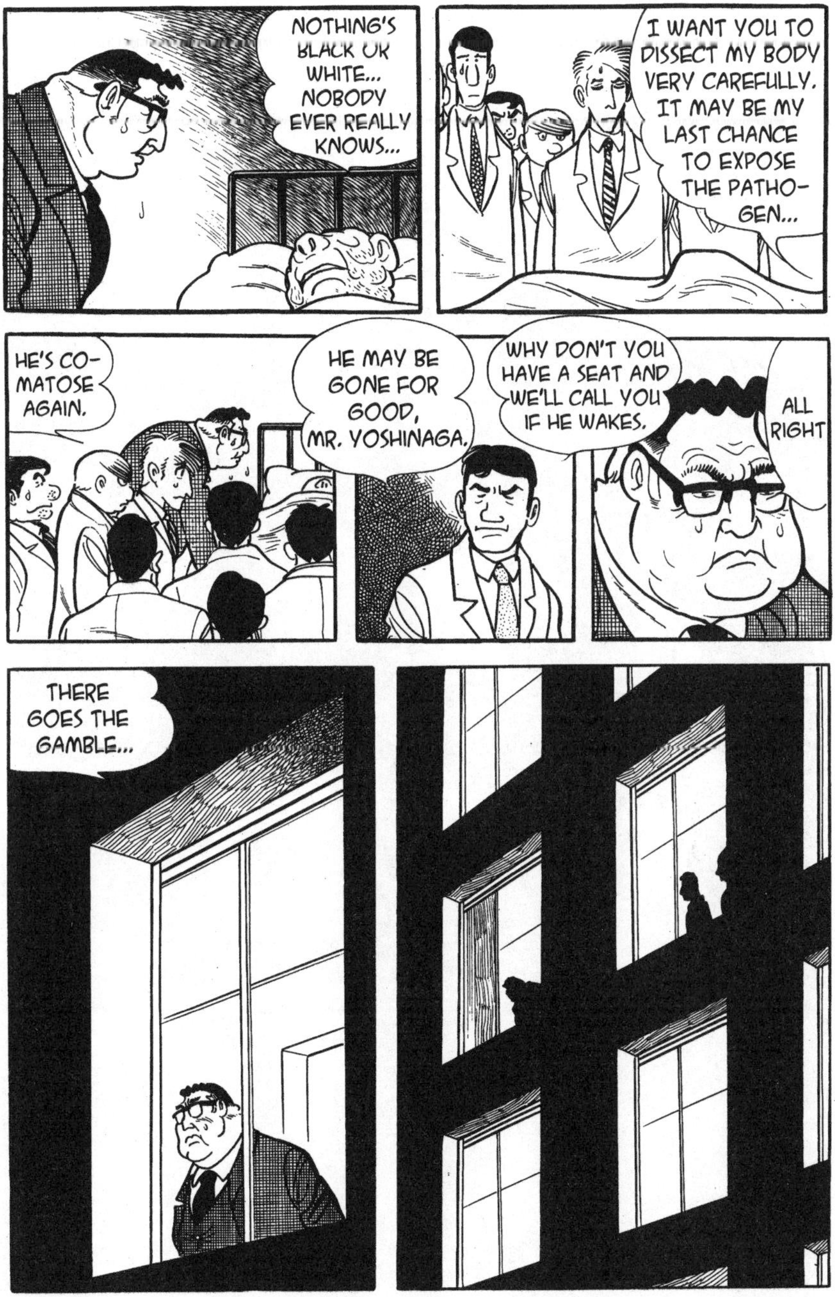
NOTHING'S BLACK OR WHITE... NOBODY EVER REALLY KNOWS...
I WANT YOU TO DISSECT MY BODY VERY CAREFULLY. IT MAY BE MY LAST CHANCE TO EXPOSE THE PATHO-GEN...
HE'S CO-MATOSE AGAIN.
HE MAY BE GONE FOR GOOD, MR. YOSHINAGA.
WHY DON'T YOU HAVE A SEAT AND WE'LL CALL YOU IF HE WAKES.
ALL RIGHT
THERE GOES THE GAMBLE...

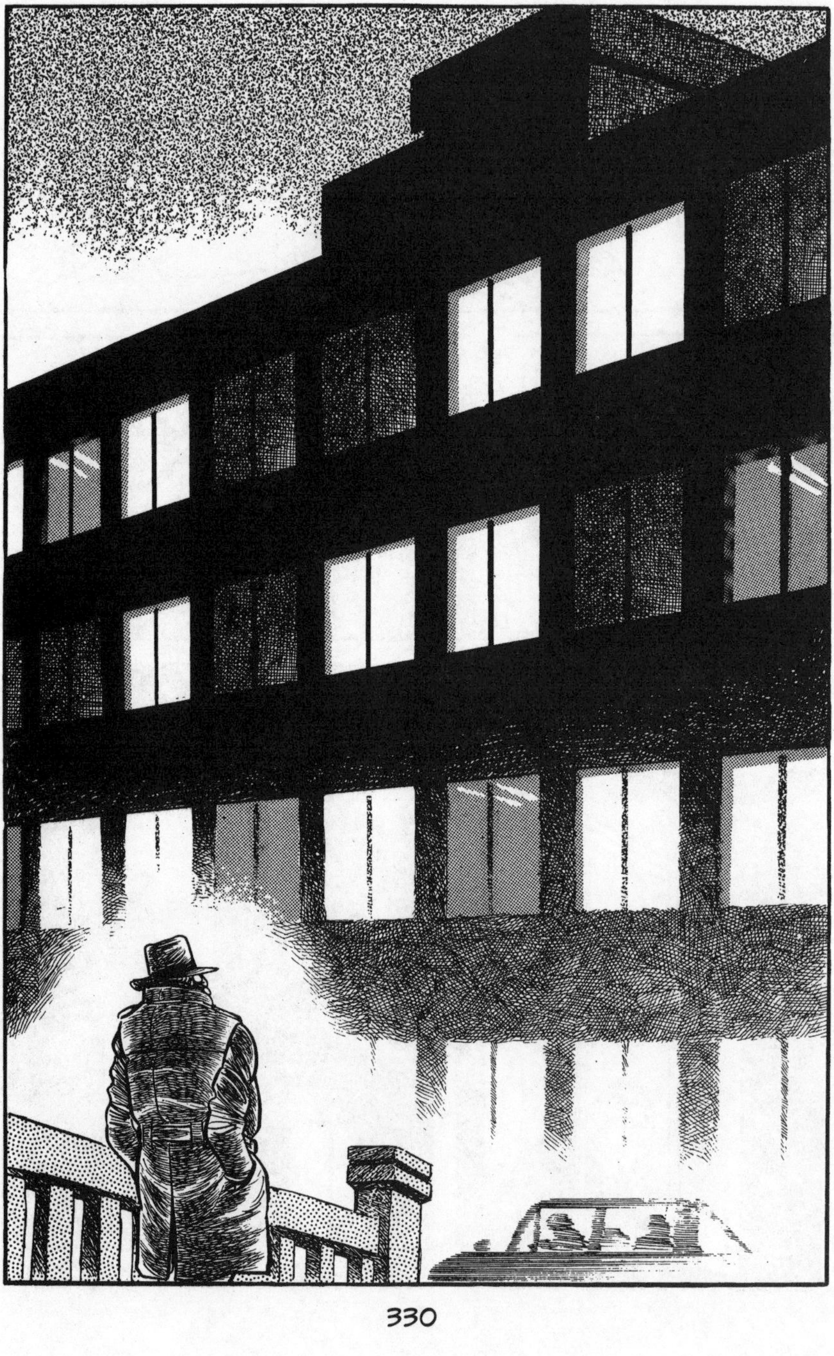

CHAPTER 20

PROGNOSIS

TAZU...

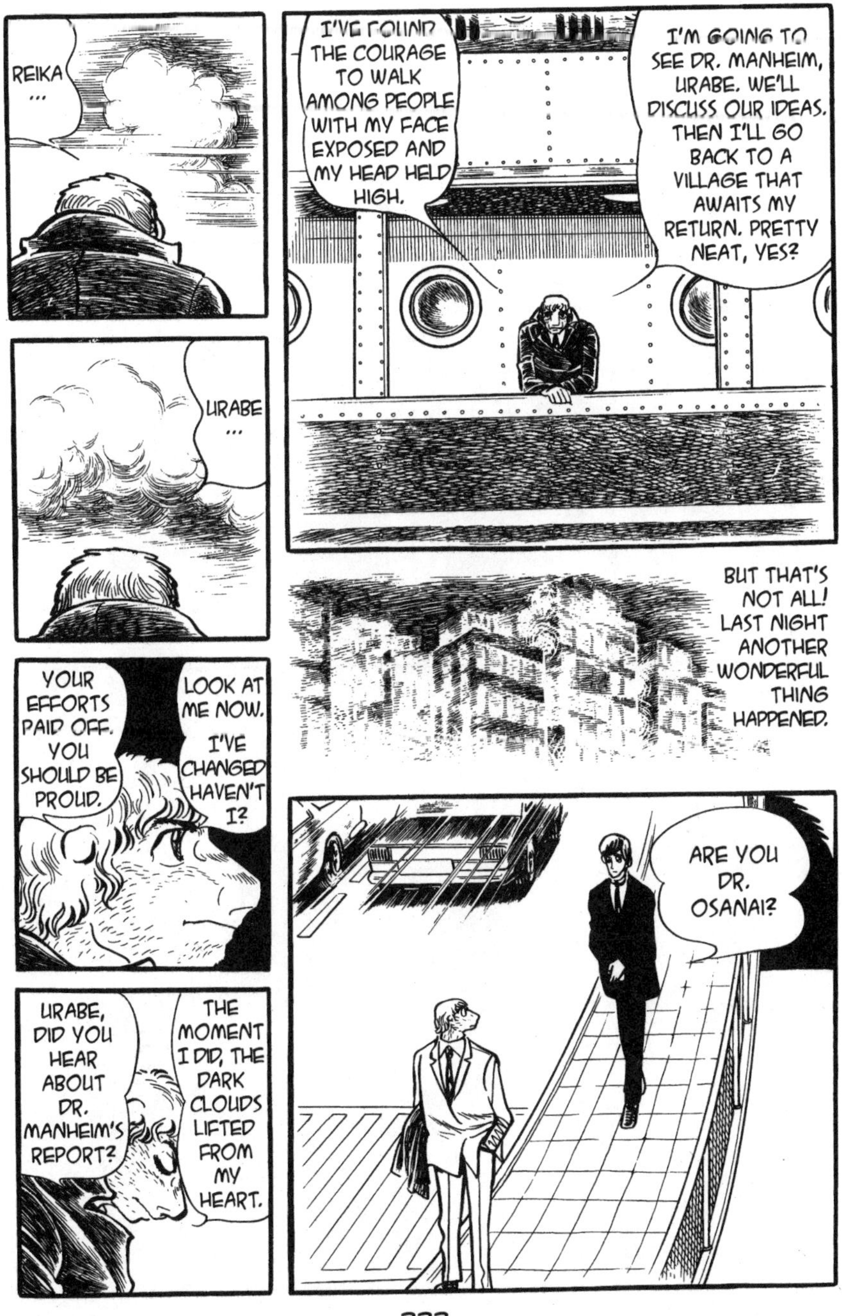

REIKA ...
URABE ...
YOUR EFFORTS PAID OFF. YOU SHOULD BE PROUD.
LOOK AT ME NOW.
I'VE CHANGED HAVEN'T I?
URABE, DID YOU HEAR ABOUT DR. MANHEIM'S REPORT?
THE MOMENT I DID, THE DARK CLOUDS LIFTED FROM MY HEART.
I'VE FOUND THE COURAGE TO WALK AMONG PEOPLE WITH MY FACE EXPOSED AND MY HEAD HELD HIGH.
I'M GOING TO SEE DR. MANHEIM, URABE. WE'LL DISCUSS OUR IDEAS. THEN I'LL GO BACK TO A VILLAGE THAT AWAITS MY RETURN. PRETTY NEAT, YES?
BUT THAT'S NOT ALL! LAST NIGHT ANOTHER WONDERFUL THING HAPPENED.
ARE YOU DR. OSANAI?

MY NAME IS SEKIBORI. I'M VERY PLEASED TO MEET YOU.

I INQUIRED AFTER YOU AT M UNIVERSITY... DR. TAKAGI INFORMED ME THAT YOU'D BE LEAVING JAPAN TOMORROW...

EVERYONE'S GATHERED. THEY WANT VERY MUCH TO MEET YOU...

EVERYONE...?

COULD YOU SPARE US A BRIEF VISIT? WE'D BE TERRIBLY GRATEFUL...

CERTAINLY.

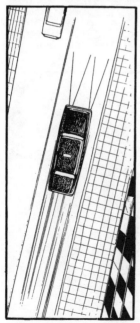

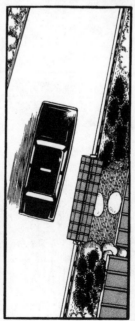

THIS WAY

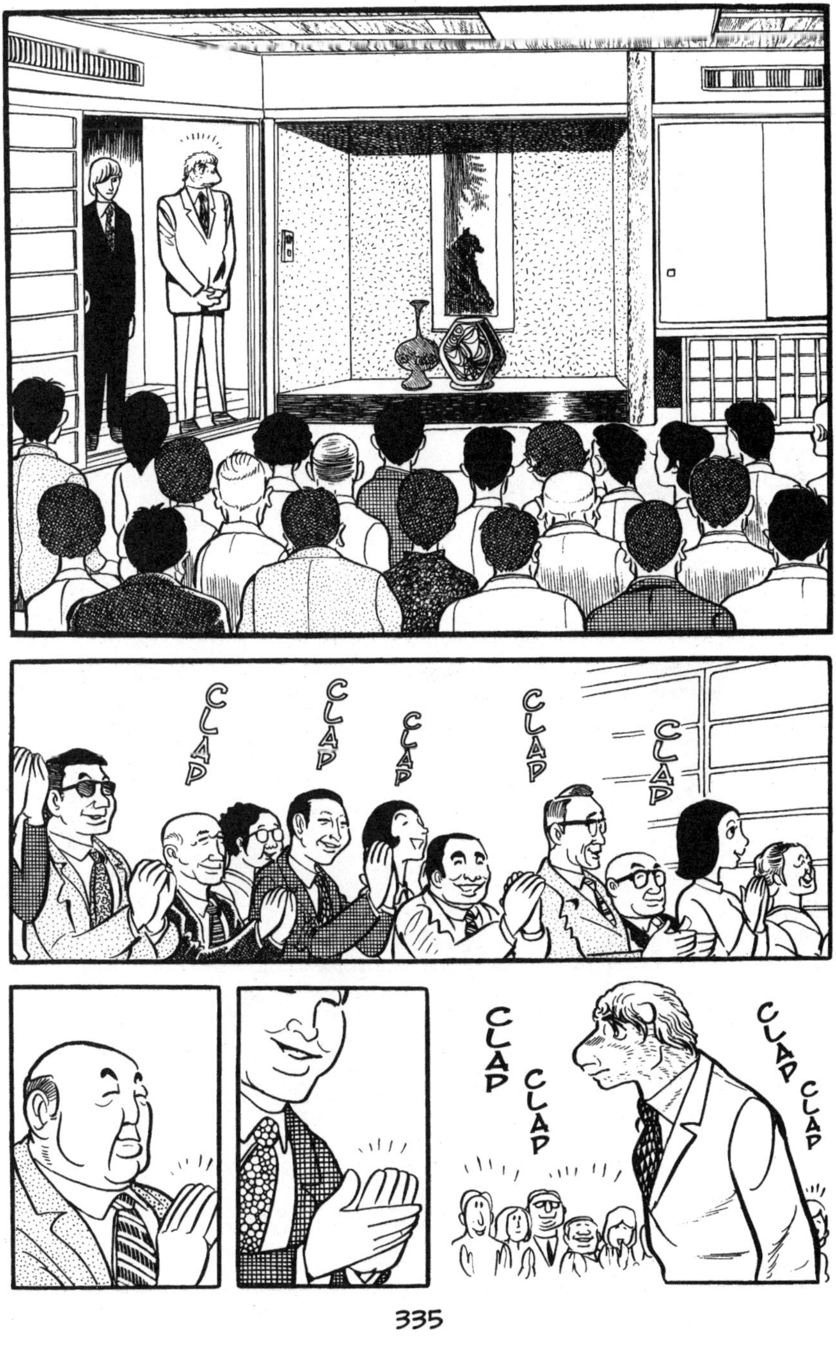
CLAP
CLAP
CLAP
CLAP
CLAP
CLAP
CLAP
CLAP
CLAP

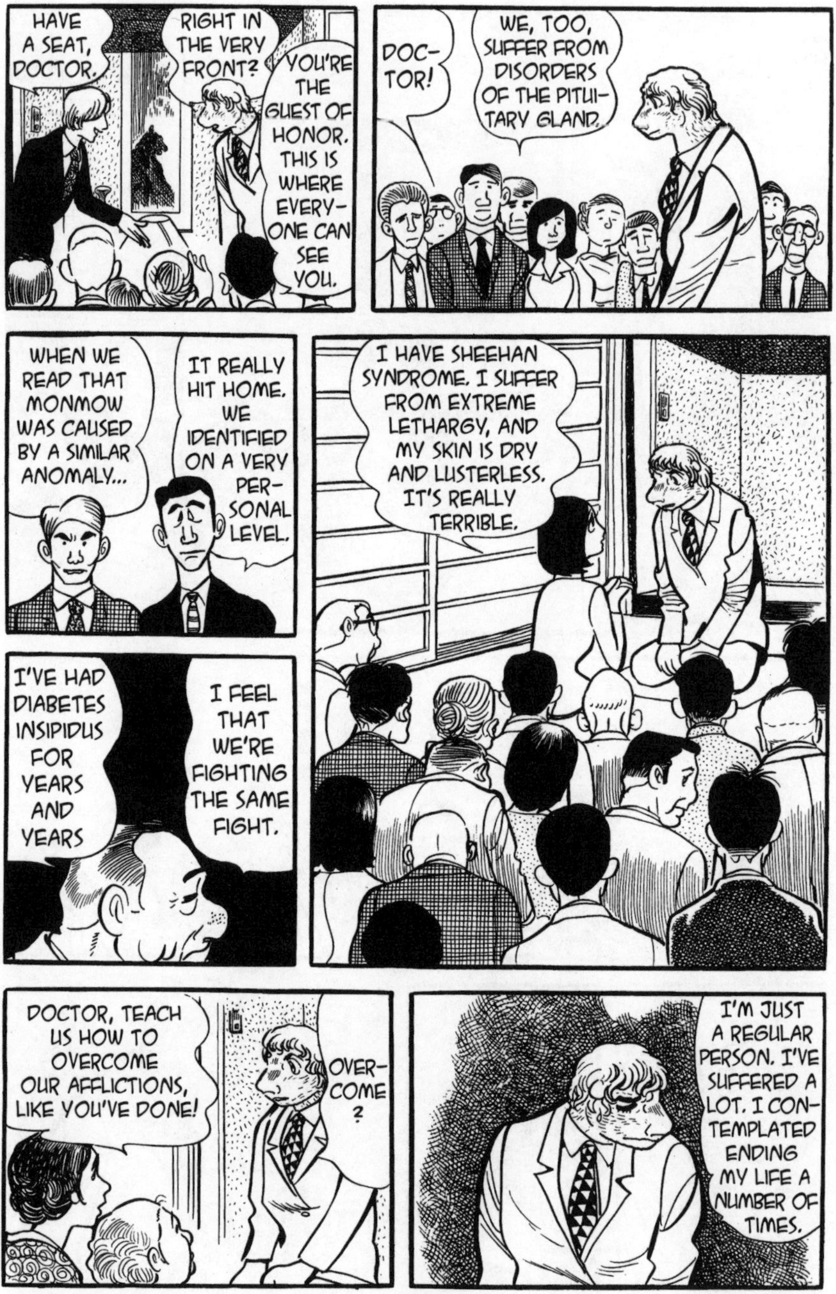
HAVE A SEAT, DOCTOR.
RIGHT IN THE VERY FRONT?
YOU'RE THE GUEST OF HONOR. THIS IS WHERE EVERYONE CAN SEE YOU.
DOCTOR!
WE, TOO, SUFFER FROM DISORDERS OF THE PITUITARY GLAND.
WHEN WE READ THAT MONMOW WAS CAUSED BY A SIMILAR ANOMALY...
IT REALLY HIT HOME. WE IDENTIFIED ON A VERY PERSONAL LEVEL.
I'VE HAD DIABETES INSIPIDUS FOR YEARS AND YEARS
I FEEL THAT WE'RE FIGHTING THE SAME FIGHT.
I HAVE SHEEHAN SYNDROME. I SUFFER FROM EXTREME LETHARGY, AND MY SKIN IS DRY AND LUSTERLESS. IT'S REALLY TERRIBLE.
DOCTOR, TEACH US HOW TO OVERCOME OUR AFFLICTIONS, LIKE YOU'VE DONE!
OVERCOME?
I'M JUST A REGULAR PERSON. I'VE SUFFERED A LOT. I CONTEMPLATED ENDING MY LIFE A NUMBER OF TIMES.

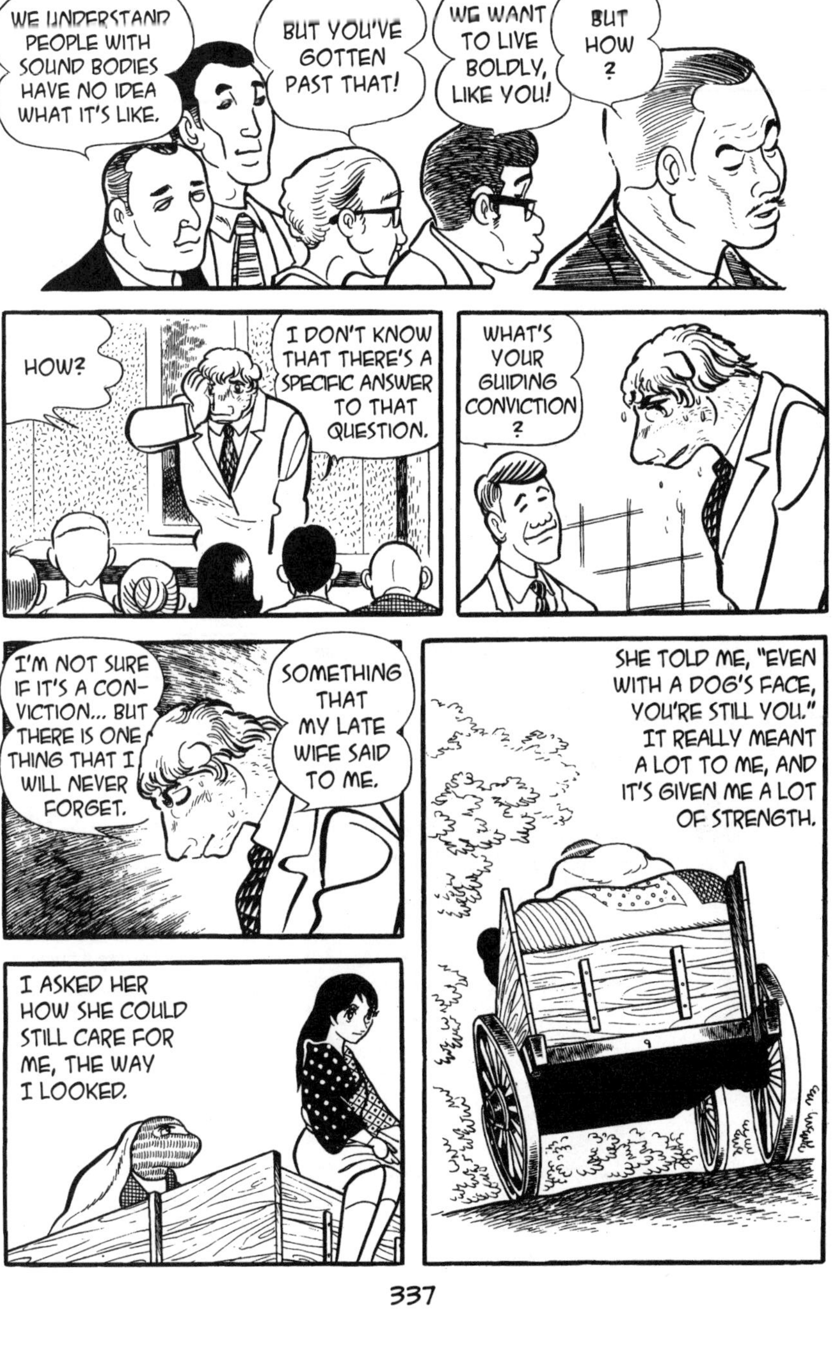
WE UNDERSTAND PEOPLE WITH SOUND BODIES HAVE NO IDEA WHAT IT'S LIKE.
BUT YOU'VE GOTTEN PAST THAT!
WE WANT TO LIVE BOLDLY, LIKE YOU!
BUT HOW?
HOW?
I DON'T KNOW THAT THERE'S A SPECIFIC ANSWER TO THAT QUESTION.
WHAT'S YOUR GUIDING CONVICTION?
I'M NOT SURE IF IT'S A CONVICTION... BUT THERE IS ONE THING THAT I WILL NEVER FORGET.
SOMETHING THAT MY LATE WIFE SAID TO ME.
I ASKED HER HOW SHE COULD STILL CARE FOR ME, THE WAY I LOOKED.
SHE TOLD ME, "EVEN WITH A DOG'S FACE, YOU'RE STILL YOU." IT REALLY MEANT A LOT TO ME, AND IT'S GIVEN ME A LOT OF STRENGTH.

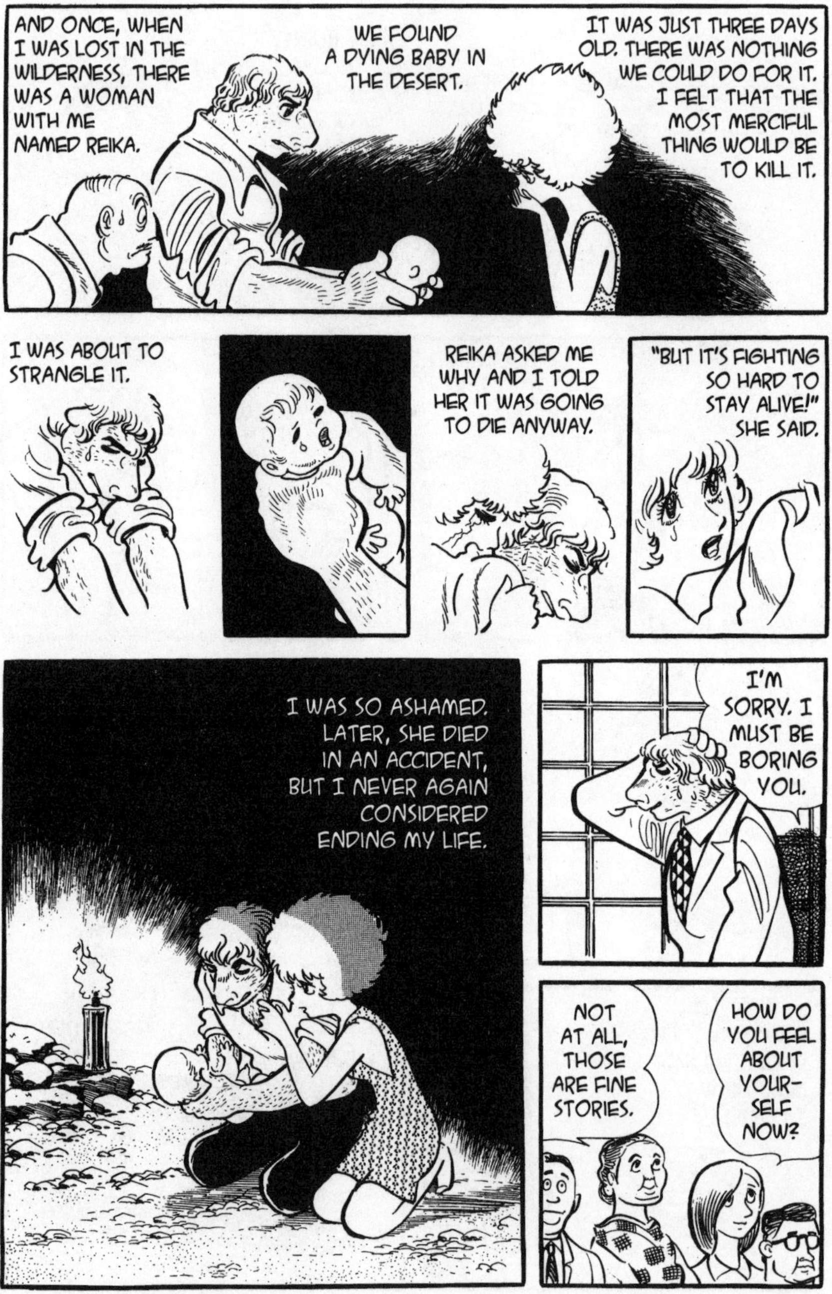
AND ONCE, WHEN I WAS LOST IN THE WILDERNESS, THERE WAS A WOMAN WITH ME NAMED REIKA.
WE FOUND A DYING BABY IN THE DESERT.
IT WAS JUST THREE DAYS OLD. THERE WAS NOTHING WE COULD DO FOR IT. I FELT THAT THE MOST MERCIFUL THING WOULD BE TO KILL IT.
I WAS ABOUT TO STRANGLE IT.
REIKA ASKED ME WHY AND I TOLD HER IT WAS GOING TO DIE ANYWAY.
"BUT IT'S FIGHTING SO HARD TO STAY ALIVE!" SHE SAID.
I WAS SO ASHAMED. LATER, SHE DIED IN AN ACCIDENT, BUT I NEVER AGAIN CONSIDERED ENDING MY LIFE.
I'M SORRY. I MUST BE BORING YOU.
NOT AT ALL, THOSE ARE FINE STORIES.
HOW DO YOU FEEL ABOUT YOUR-SELF NOW?

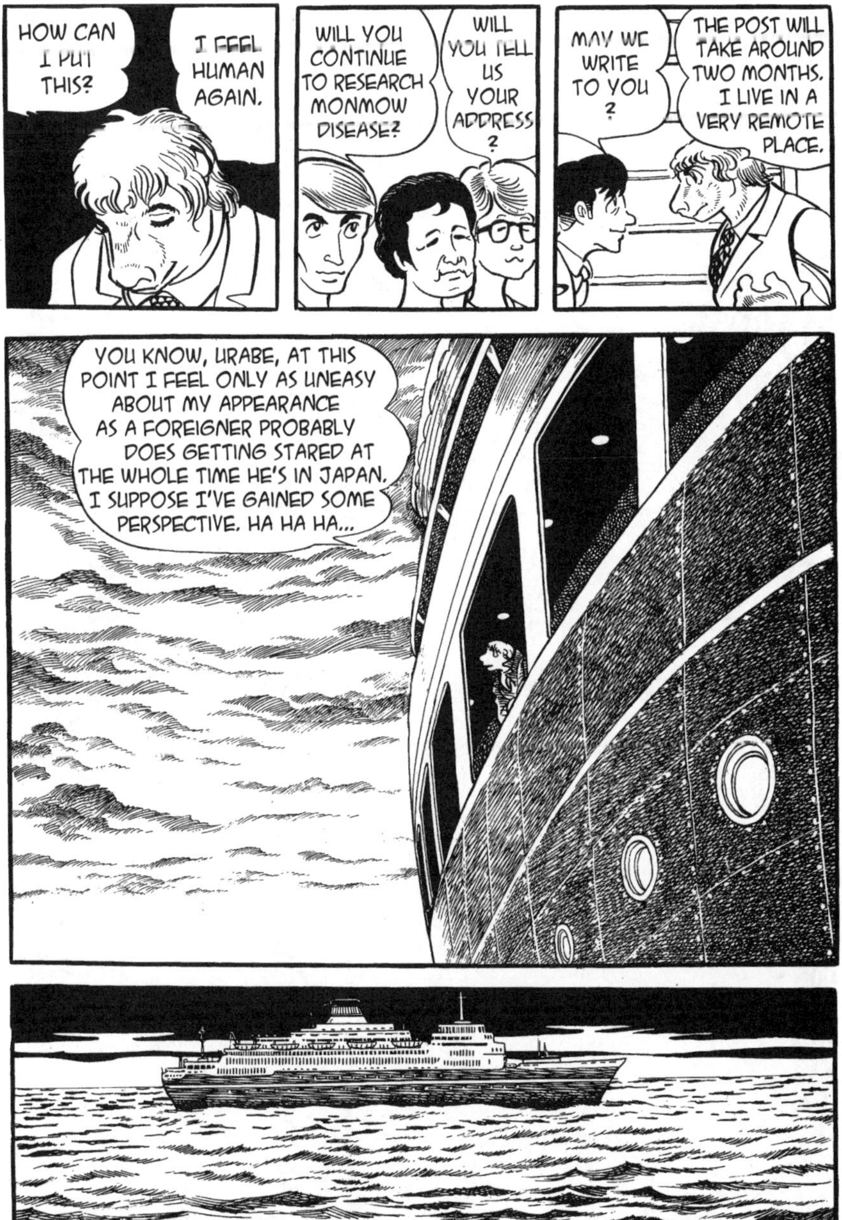
HOW CAN I PUT THIS?
I FEEL HUMAN AGAIN.
WILL YOU CONTINUE TO RESEARCH MONMOW DISEASE?
WILL YOU TELL US YOUR ADDRESS?
MAY WE WRITE TO YOU?
THE POST WILL TAKE AROUND TWO MONTHS. I LIVE IN A VERY REMOTE PLACE.
YOU KNOW, URABE, AT THIS POINT I FEEL ONLY AS UNEASY ABOUT MY APPEARANCE AS A FOREIGNER PROBABLY DOES GETTING STARED AT THE WHOLE TIME HE'S IN JAPAN. I SUPPOSE I'VE GAINED SOME PERSPECTIVE. HA HA HA...

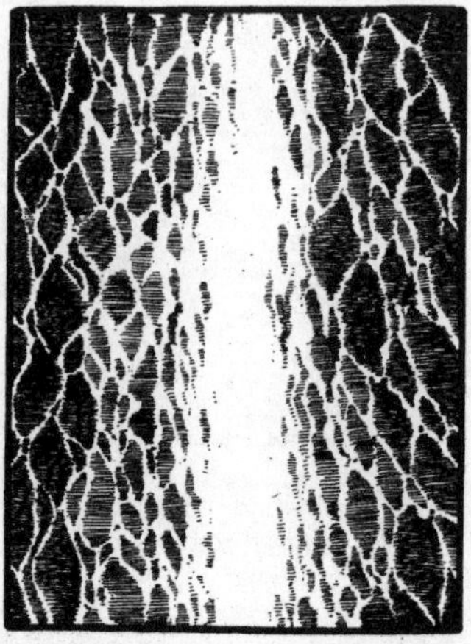
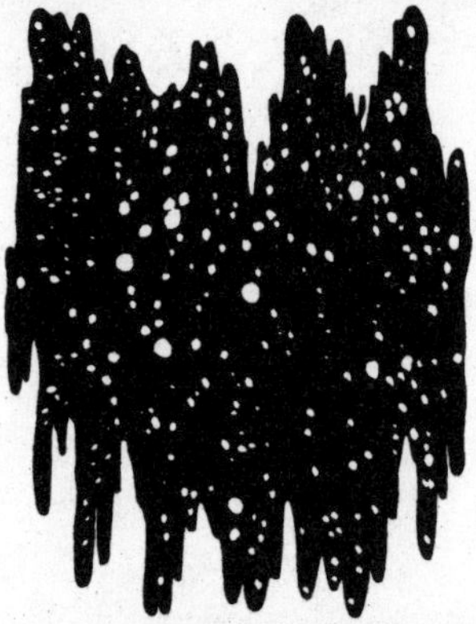
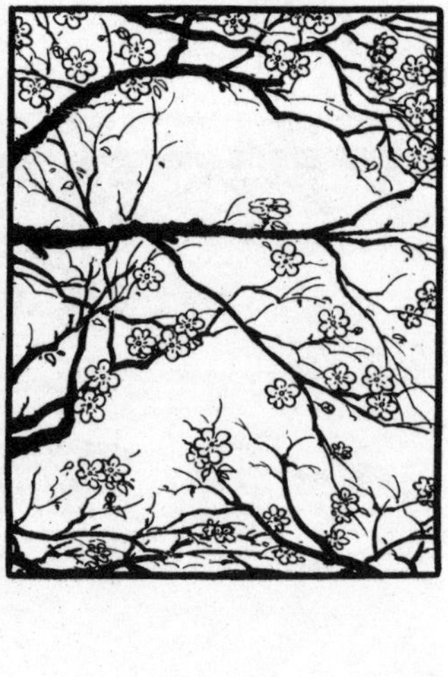
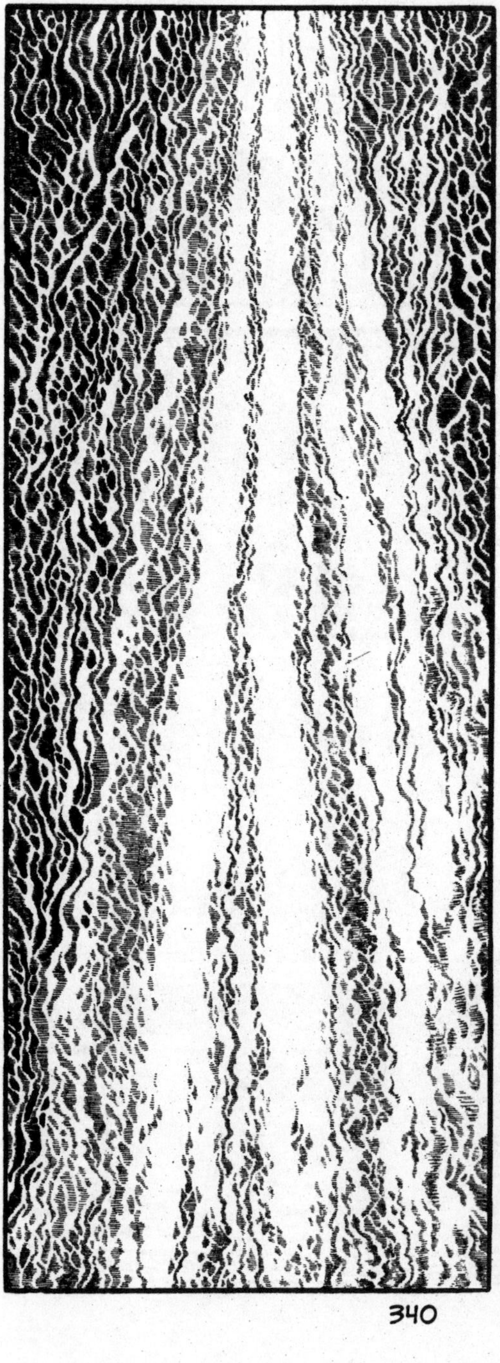

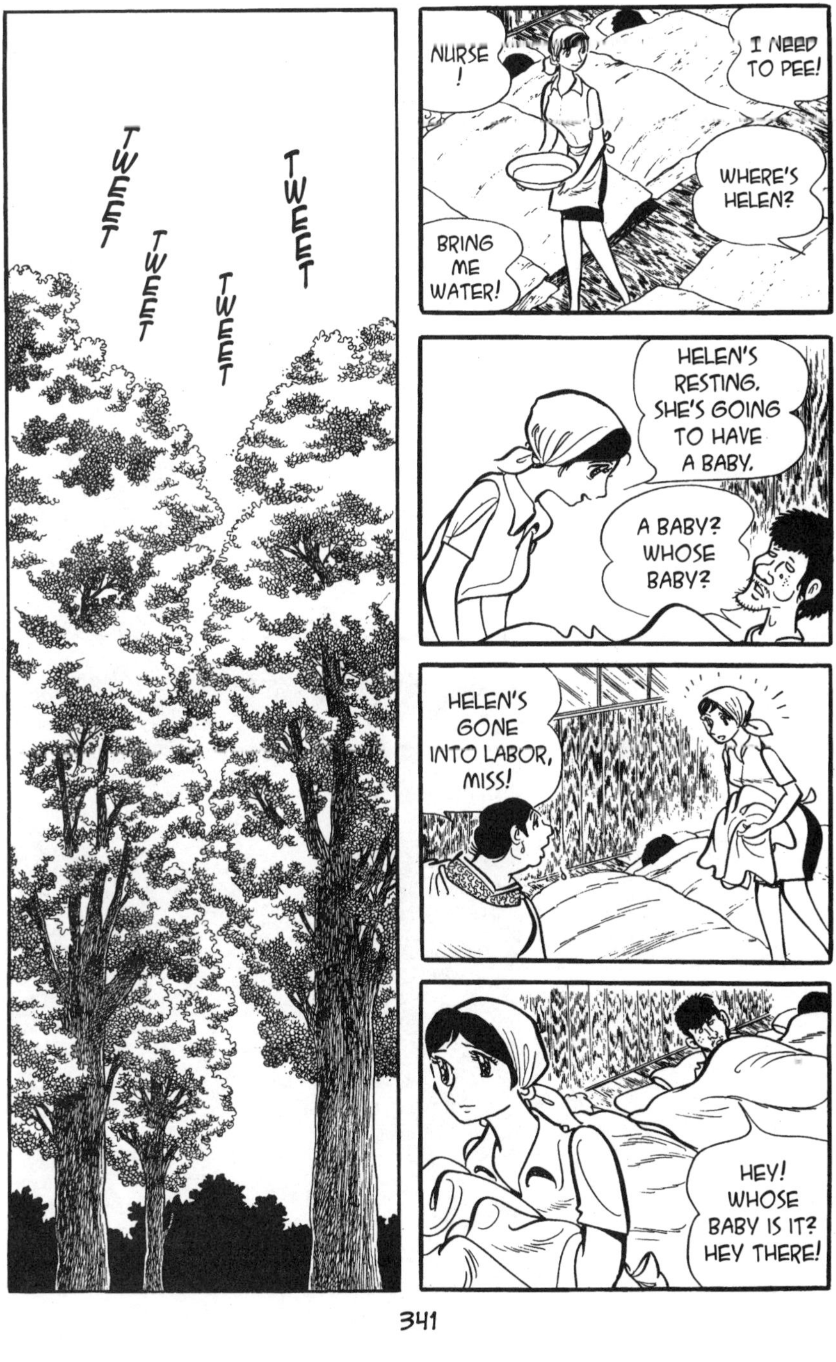
I NEED TO PEE!
NURSE!
WHERE'S HELEN?
BRING ME WATER!
HELEN'S RESTING. SHE'S GOING TO HAVE A BABY.
A BABY? WHOSE BABY?
HELEN'S GONE INTO LABOR, MISS!
HEY! WHOSE BABY IS IT? HEY THERE!
TWEET
TWEET
TWEET
TWEET

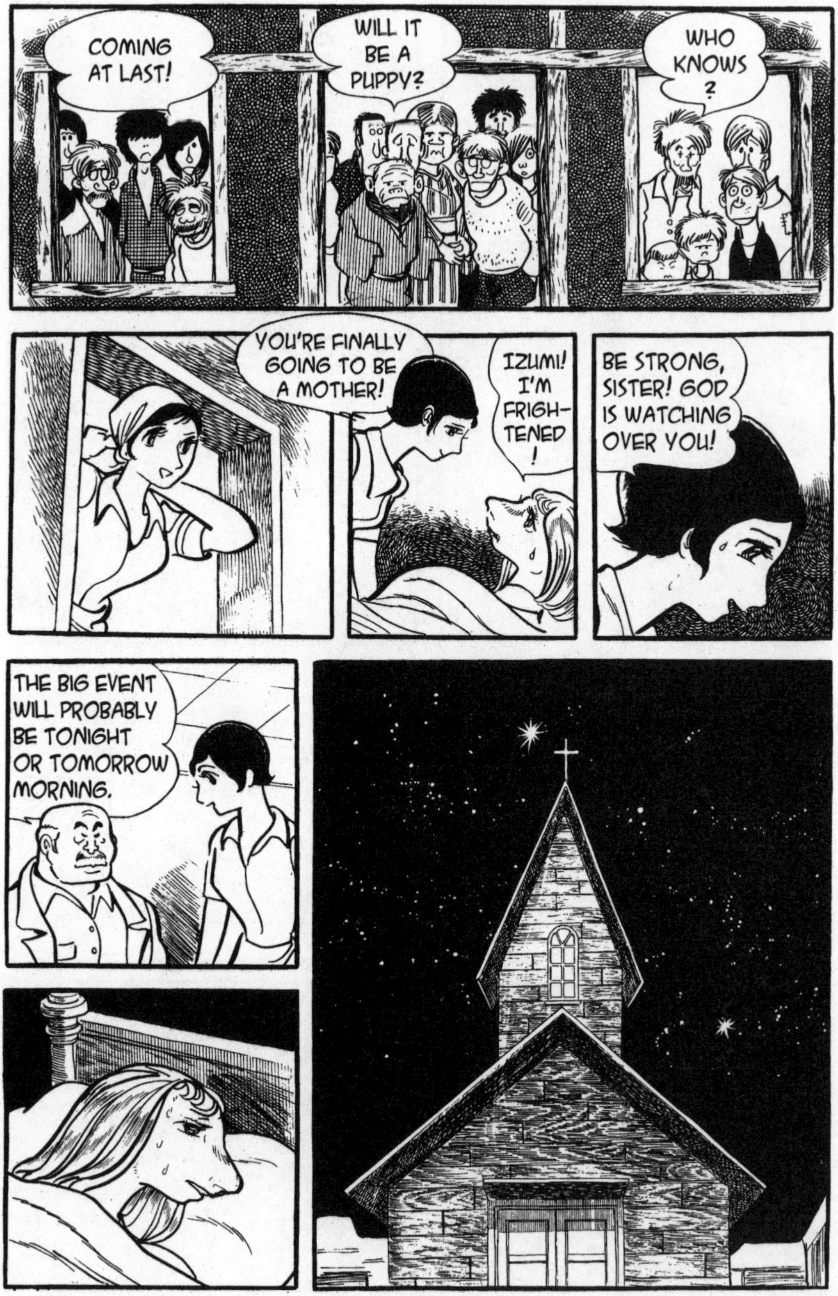
COMING AT LAST!
WILL IT BE A PUPPY?
WHO KNOWS?
YOU'RE FINALLY GOING TO BE A MOTHER!
IZUMI! I'M FRIGHTENED!
BE STRONG, SISTER! GOD IS WATCHING OVER YOU!
THE BIG EVENT WILL PROBABLY BE TONIGHT OR TOMORROW MORNING.

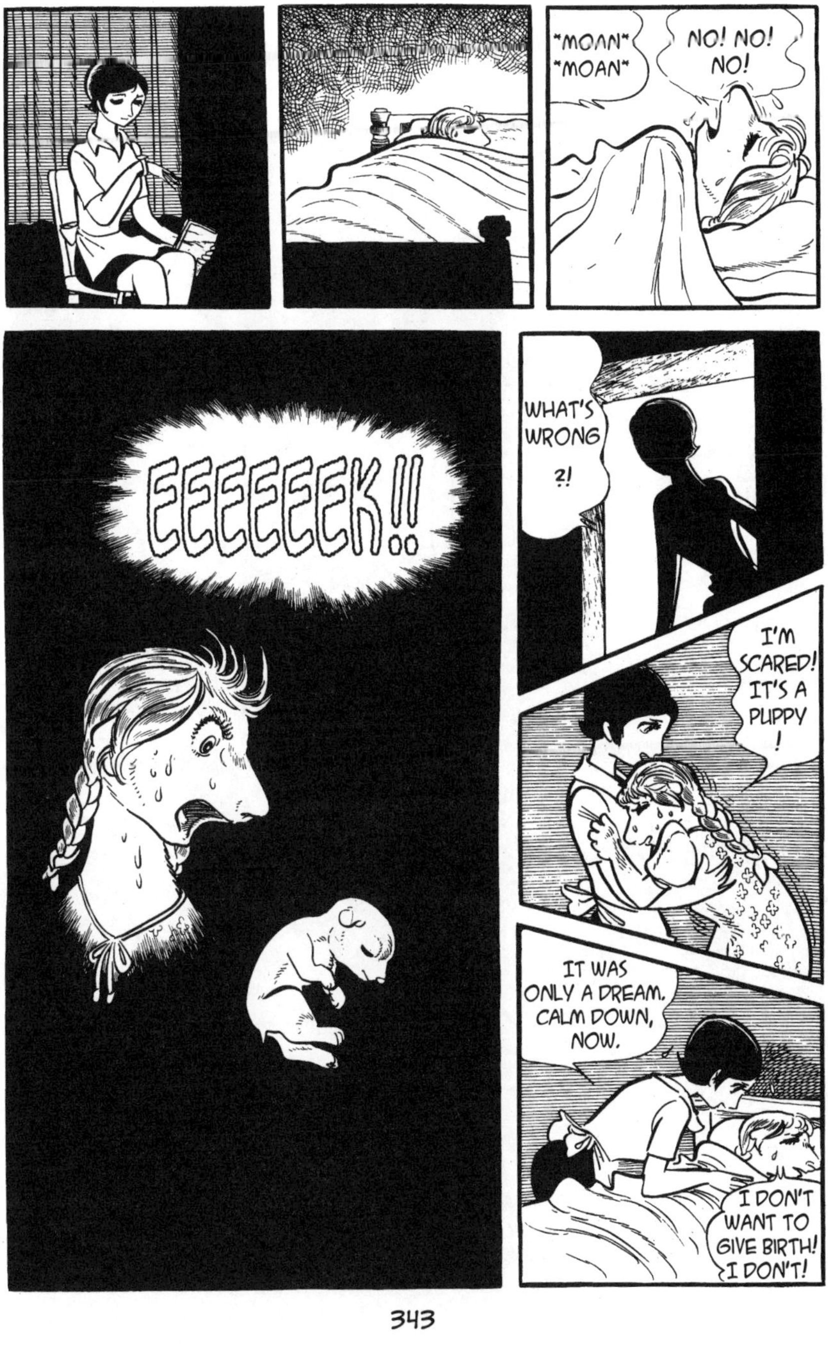
MOAN *MOAN*
NO! NO! NO!
EEEEEEEK!!
WHAT'S WRONG ?!
I'M SCARED! IT'S A PUPPY!
IT WAS ONLY A DREAM. CALM DOWN, NOW.
I DON'T WANT TO GIVE BIRTH! I DON'T!

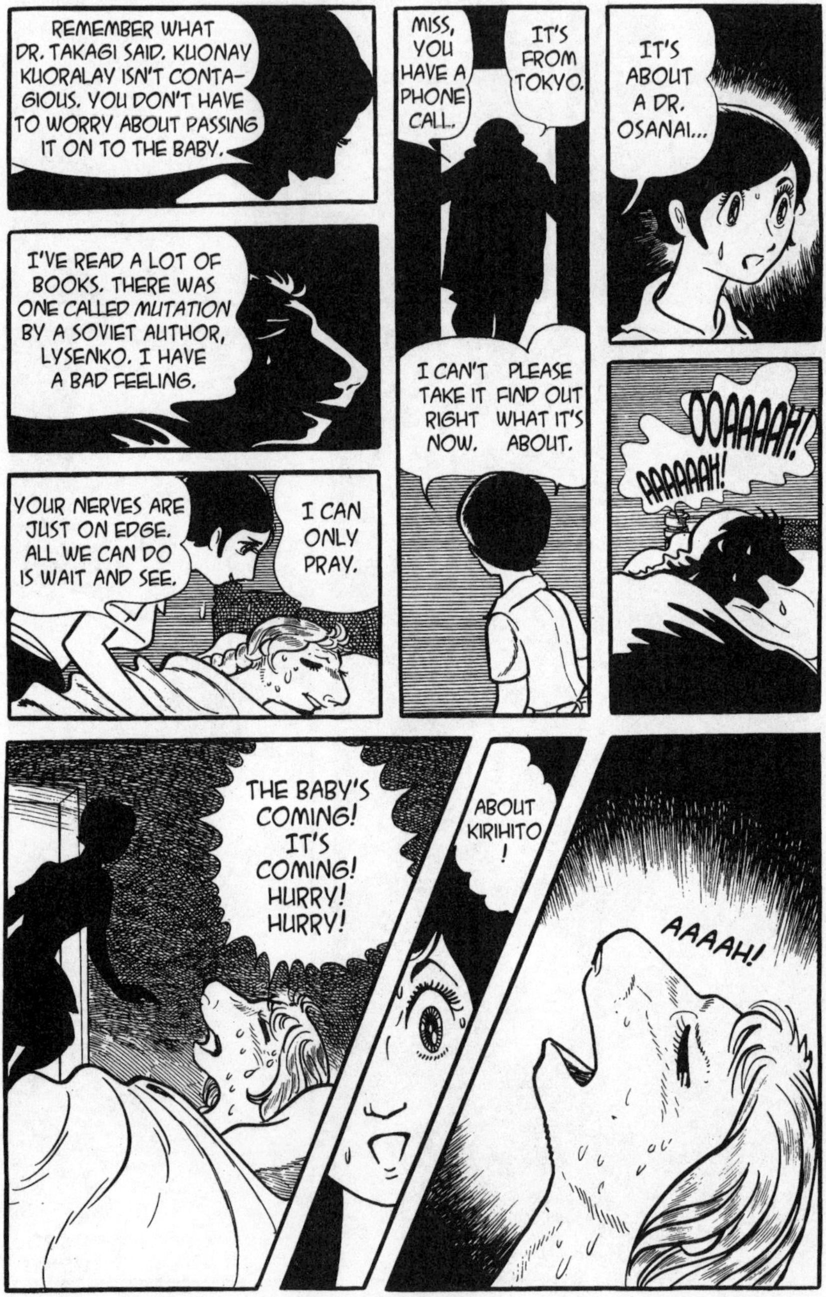
REMEMBER WHAT DR. TAKAGI SAID. KUONAY KUORALAY ISN'T CONTAGIOUS. YOU DON'T HAVE TO WORRY ABOUT PASSING IT ON TO THE BABY.
I'VE READ A LOT OF BOOKS. THERE WAS ONE CALLED *MUTATION* BY A SOVIET AUTHOR, LYSENKO. I HAVE A BAD FEELING.
YOUR NERVES ARE JUST ON EDGE. ALL WE CAN DO IS WAIT AND SEE.
I CAN ONLY PRAY.
MISS, YOU HAVE A PHONE CALL.
IT'S FROM TOKYO.
I CAN'T TAKE IT RIGHT NOW.
PLEASE FIND OUT WHAT IT'S ABOUT.
IT'S ABOUT A DR. OSANAI...
OOAAAAH!
AAAAAAH!
THE BABY'S COMING! IT'S COMING! HURRY! HURRY!
ABOUT KIRIHITO!
AAAAH!

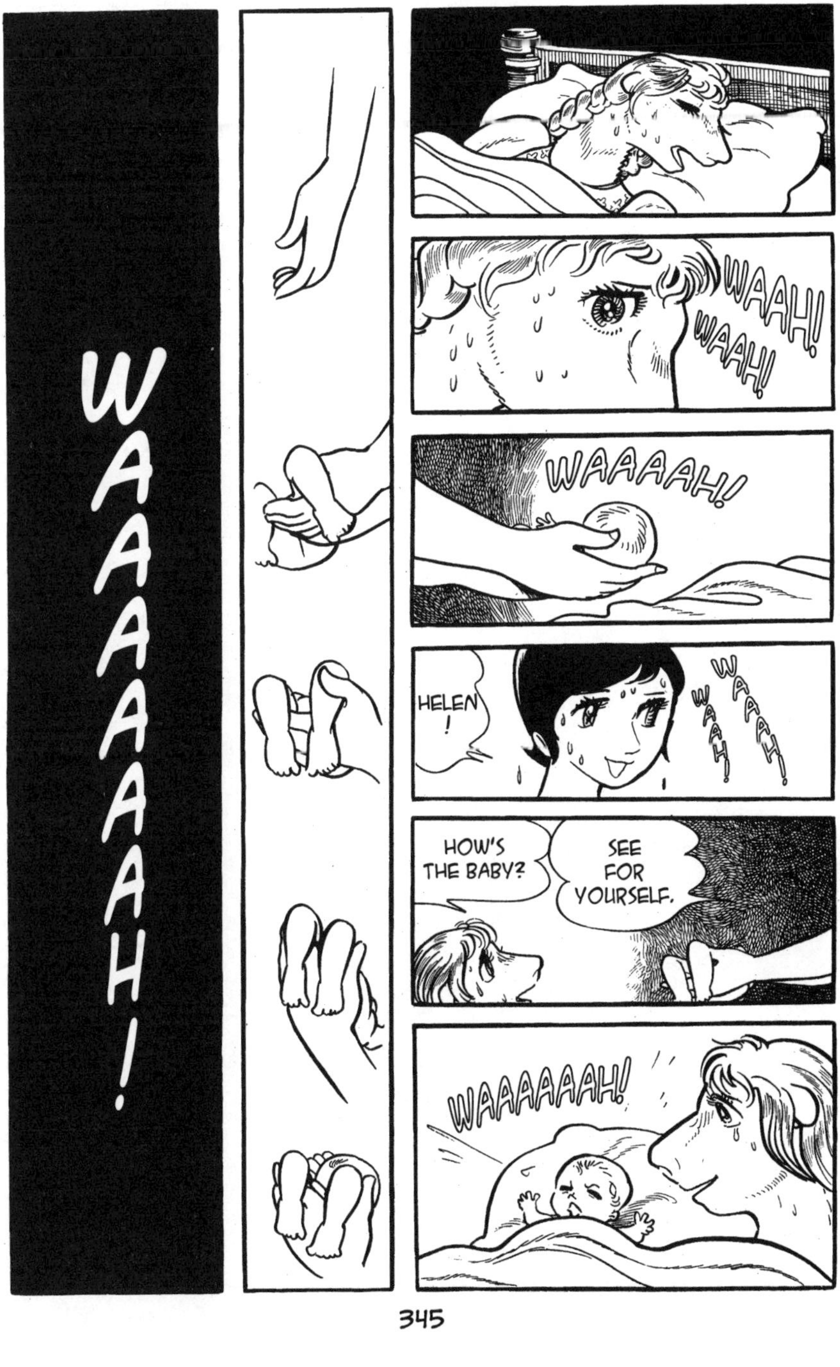
WAAH!
WAAH!
WAAAAAH!
HELEN!
WAAAH!
WAAH!
HOW'S THE BABY?
SEE FOR YOURSELF.
WAAAAAAH!
WAAAAAAH!

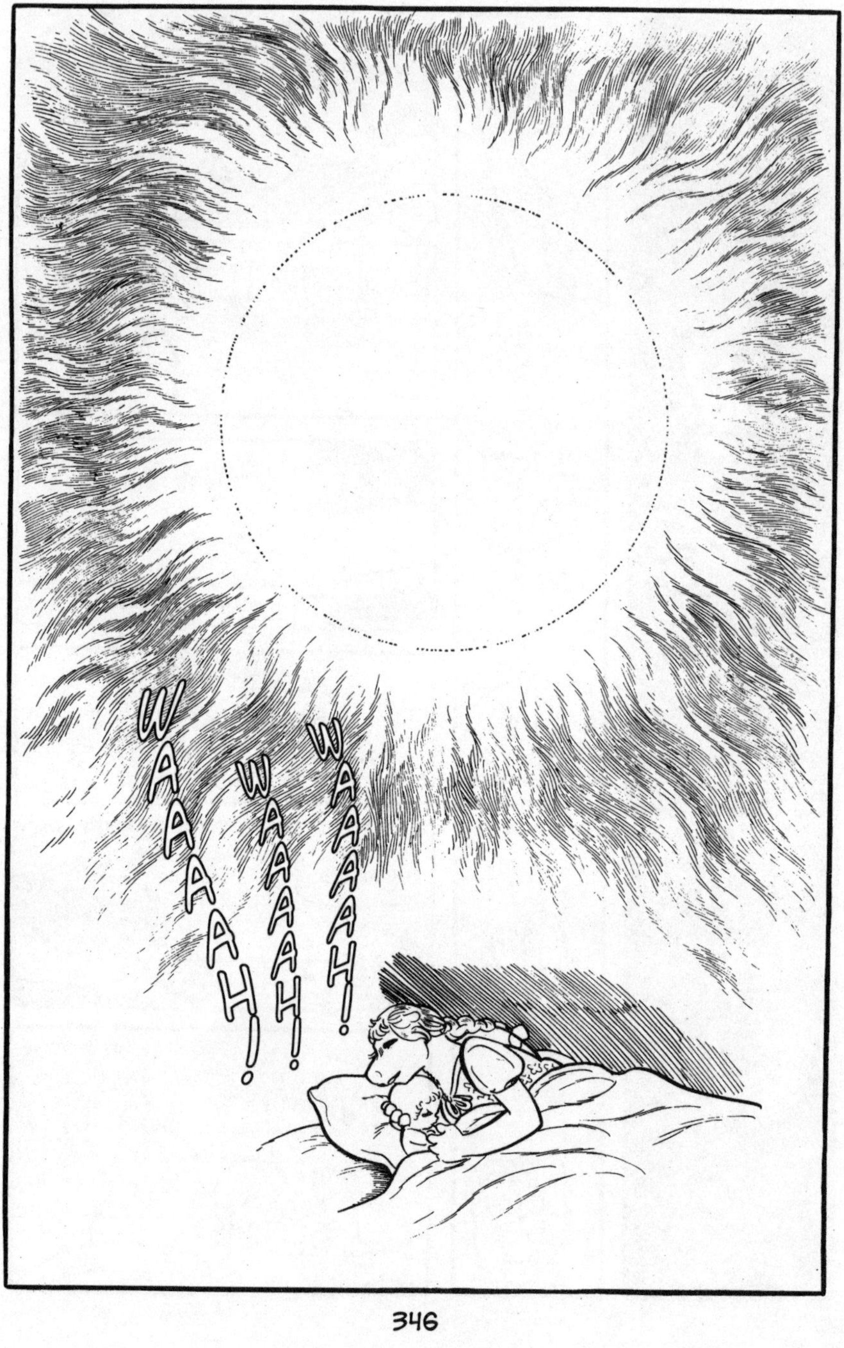
WAAAAAH!
WAAAAAAH!
WAAAAAAH!

IZUMI!

DARLING! IT'S IZUMI!

WHAT? IS SHE BACK?

I'M SO GLAD YOU CHANGED YOUR MIND!

I'LL NEVER SCOLD YOU AGAIN. I WON'T SAY A THING.

I'LL BE LEAVING AGAIN, MOTHER.

WHAT'S THIS?

SOMEONE WAS KIND ENOUGH TO CALL ME...

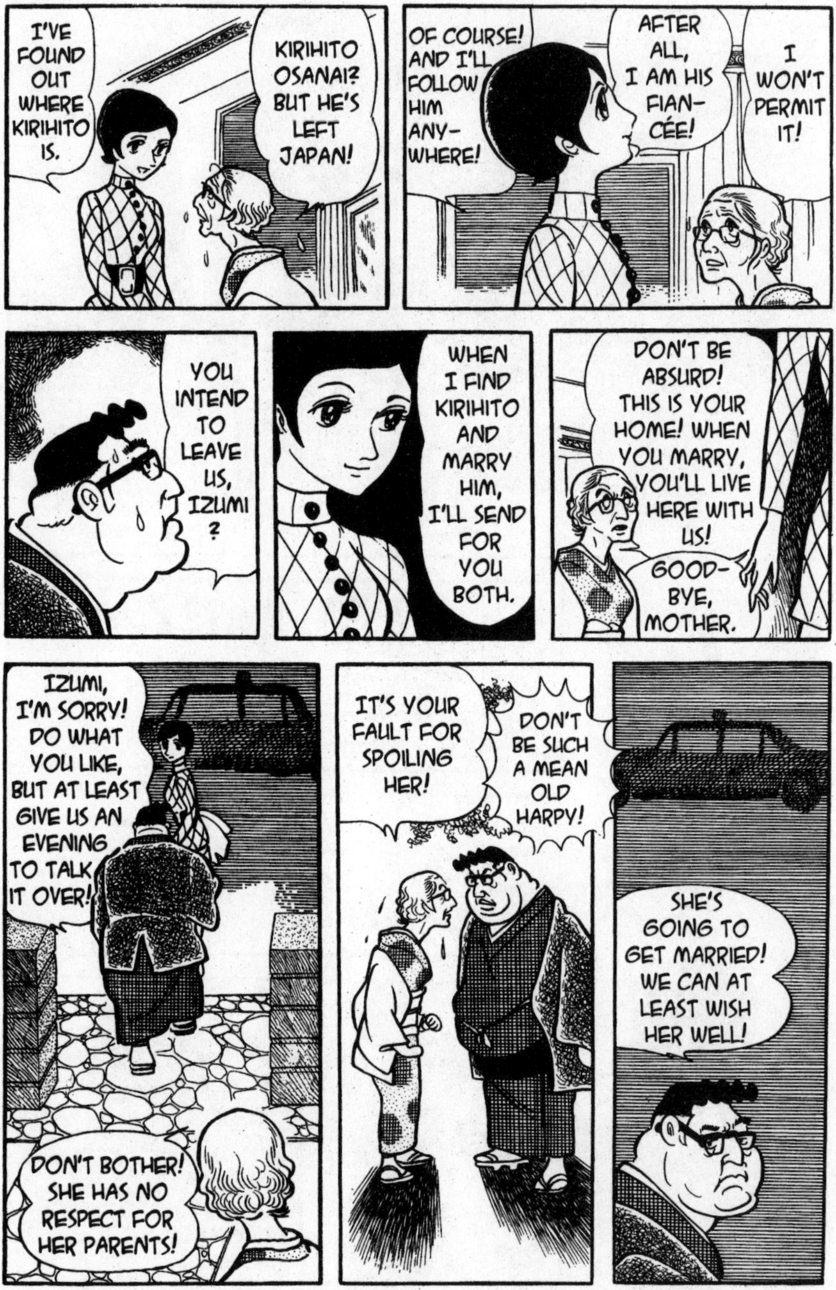
I'VE FOUND OUT WHERE KIRIHITO IS.
KIRIHITO OSANAI? BUT HE'S LEFT JAPAN!
OF COURSE! AND I'LL FOLLOW HIM ANY-WHERE!
AFTER ALL, I AM HIS FIAN-CÉE!
I WON'T PERMIT IT!
YOU INTEND TO LEAVE US, IZUMI?
WHEN I FIND KIRIHITO AND MARRY HIM, I'LL SEND FOR YOU BOTH.
DON'T BE ABSURD! THIS IS YOUR HOME! WHEN YOU MARRY, YOU'LL LIVE HERE WITH US!
GOOD-BYE, MOTHER.
IZUMI, I'M SORRY! DO WHAT YOU LIKE, BUT AT LEAST GIVE US AN EVENING TO TALK IT OVER!
DON'T BOTHER! SHE HAS NO RESPECT FOR HER PARENTS!
IT'S YOUR FAULT FOR SPOILING HER!
DON'T BE SUCH A MEAN OLD HARPY!
SHE'S GOING TO GET MARRIED! WE CAN AT LEAST WISH HER WELL!

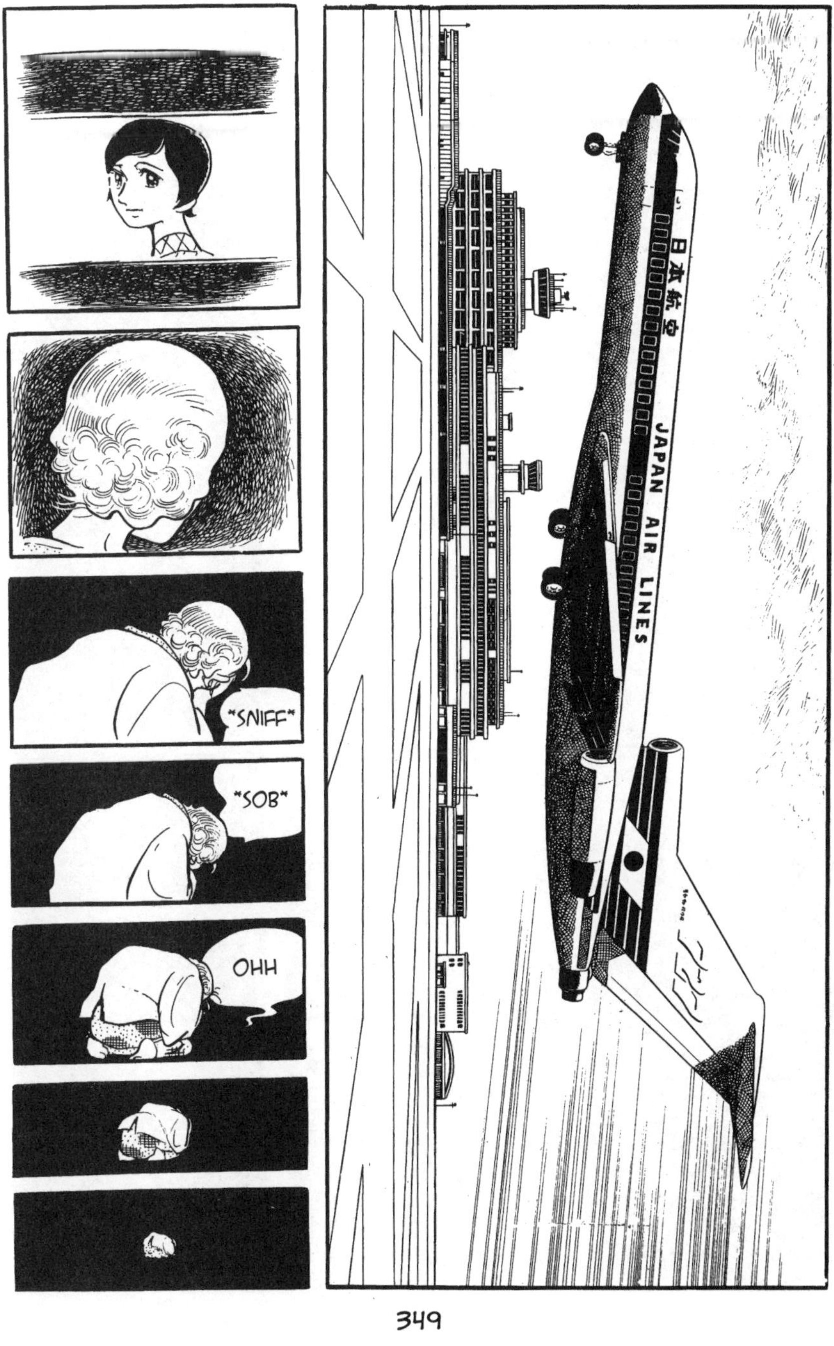
日本航空
JAPAN AIR LINES
SNIFF
SOB
OHH

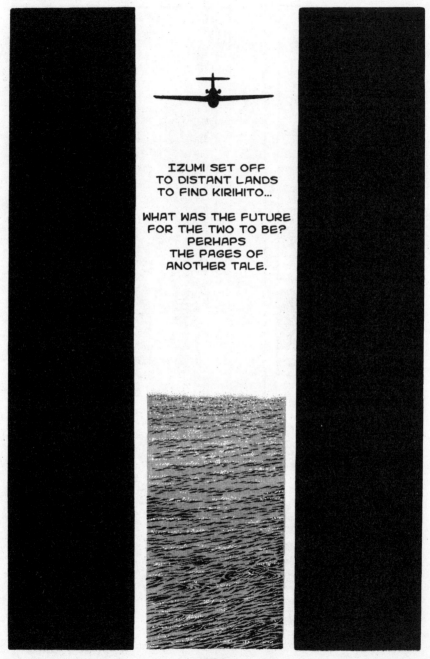

IZUMI SET OFF
TO DISTANT LANDS
TO FIND KIRIHITO...

WHAT WAS THE FUTURE
FOR THE TWO TO BE?
PERHAPS
THE PAGES OF
ANOTHER TALE.

THE END

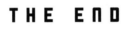

ABOUT THE AUTHOR

Osamu Tezuka (1928-1989) is the godfather of Japanese manga comics. He originally intended to become a doctor and earned his degree before turning to what was still then considered a frivolous medium. With his sweeping vision, deftly intertwined plots, and indefatigable commitment to human dignity, Tezuka elevated manga to an art form.